Handbook of Cognitive-Behavioral Th

Handbook of Cognitive-Behavioral Therapies

Edited by
KEITH S. DOBSON
University of British Columbia

THE GUILFORD PRESS
New York   *London*

© 1988 The Guilford Press
A Division of Guilford Publications, Inc.
72 Spring Street, New York, NY 10012

Chapter 9 © Michael J. Mahoney

Printed in the United States of America

Last digit is print number: 9 8 7 6 5 4

Library of Congress Cataloging in Publication Data

Handbook of cognitive-behavioral therapies.

    Includes bibliographies and index.
    1. Cognitive therapy—Handbooks, manuals, etc.
2. Behavior therapy—Handbooks, manuals, etc.
I. Dobson, Keith S. [DNLM: 1. Behavior Therapy—
handbooks. 2. Cognition—handbooks. WM 34 H236]
RC489.C63H36 1988   616.89′142   87-27
ISBN 0-89862-704-4   ISBN 0-89862-524-6 (pbk)

ACKNOWLEDGMENTS

There are many people who deserve acknowledgment for their part in the eventual completion of this book. Several people have been responsible for the genesis and maintenance of my interest in cognitive-behavioral models of human functioning and therapy. Certainly the most important person to shape my interests was Brian Shaw, to whom I am most grateful. Others who have helped me refine my ideas include Jeff Young, Mike Vallis, Mike Mahoney, Steve Hollon, and Myles Genest.

While the original impetus for this volume came from a graduate seminar course I taught, several people have helped to bring the original idea to completion. These include Seymour Weingarten, who encouraged the development of this text. Secretarial assistance was provided by Liz McCririck. Most important, emotional support and encouragement were always forthcoming from my wife, Debbie, my son, Chris, and my daughter, Beth. My family is the source of much of my energy, and they have certainly shaped much of my personal and professional life for the better.

CONTRIBUTORS

AARON T. BECK, MD, Center for Cognitive Therapy, Philadelphia, Pennsylvania

LORY BLOCK, MA, Department of Psychology, University of British Columbia, Vancouver, British Columbia, Canada

LAUREN BRASWELL, PhD, North Memorial Medical Center, Robinsdale, Minnesota

ROBERT J. DERUBEIS, PhD, Department of Psychology, University of Pennsylvania, Philadelphia, Pennsylvania

KEITH S. DOBSON, PhD, Department of Psychology, University of British Columbia, Vancouver, British Columbia, Canada

WINDY DRYDEN, PhD, Department of Psychology, Goldsmith's College, University of London, London, England

THOMAS J. D'ZURILLA, PhD, Department of Psychology, State University of New York, Stony Brook, Stony Brook, New York

ALBERT ELLIS, PhD, Institute for Rational-Emotive Therapy, New York, New York

VITTORIO F. GUIDANO, MD, Center for Cognitive Psychotherapy, Rome, Italy

PHILIP C. KENDALL, PhD, Department of Psychology, Temple University, Philadelphia, Pennsylvania

MICHAEL J. MAHONEY, PhD, Department of Education, University of California at Santa Barbara, Santa Barbara, California

LYNN P. REHM, PhD, Department of Psychology, University of Houston, Houston, Texas

PAUL ROKKE, PhD, Department of Psychology, North Dakota State University, Fargo, North Dakota

ZINDEL V. SEGAL, PhD, Clarke Institute of Psychiatry, Toronto, Ontario, Canada

BRIAN F. SHAW, PhD, Department of Psychology, Toronto General Hospital, Toronto, Ontario, Canada

PREFACE

In the fall of 1983, I was faced with the prospect of teaching a graduate seminar in the general area of cognitive-behavioral therapy. I wanted a text that provided some of the basic theoretical and philosophical bases of the cognitive mediation model of human functioning, one that would proceed to present the theoretical underpinnings of the major cognitive-behavioral models as well as descriptions of the clinical assessment and intervention techniques that were predicated upon these theoretical models. No such text existed. While Kendall and Hollon's (1979) *Cognitive-Behavioral Interventions: Theory, Research and Procedures* was the best publication that provided a comprehensive review of models and methods in the area, I had some difficulties with using this book. To my mind, it was somewhat redundant, overly restrictive in their coverage of the topic, and somewhat out of date. I put together a series of articles, chapters and books as the readings for the course.

It struck me that a succinct, comprehensive handbook of the field of cognitive-behavioral therapies was needed. Cognitive-behavioral therapies were being developed in increasingly broad areas of application, and the treatment success of these therapies was generally quite sound. Also, innovative therapy models such as that proposed by Guidano and Liotti (*Cognitive Processes and Emotional Disorders*, 1983) needed to be considered in light of the field at large. On this basis, I undertook to organize this volume.

One of the primary questions that first occupied me, and still receives revisitation from time to time, was related to the definition of "cognitive-behavioral." What are the cardinal aspects of a "cognitive-behavioral" therapy? When is a treatment model no longer "behavioral" but "cognitive-behavioral"? Is a purely "cognitive" treatment also "cognitive-behavioral"? These questions help to frame the general coverage of this book. For the purposes of this book, "cognitive-behavioral" therapies are those that assume that patterns of cognition shape the emotional and behavioral consequences of that cognition. Therapy approaches that do not assume cognitive mediation, or see the concept of cognition as unnecessary—primarily those based on classical and operant conditioning—are not considered here as "cognitive-behavioral." Similarly, therapies that focus exclusively on intrapsychic processes or insight, but that do not explicitly reference psychotherapy outcome by behavioral change are not "cognitive-behavioral."

Generally, then, cognitive-behavioral therapies focus on relatively discrete behavioral problems, and these therapies attempt to induce psychotherapeutic gain through changes in the cognition-behavior complex.

This extremely broad definition of the scope of this text encompasses many therapy models and interventions. This volume reviews the major cognitive-behavioral treatments, but is not exhaustive of the field. Many intervention techniques can be developed within the cognitive-behavioral model (see Rian McMullin's recent compendium of such methods in his *Handbook of Cognitive Therapy Techniques*, 1986), and when the application of these techniques are systematized, they form a powerful set of tools for engendering change in maladaptive thinking and behavior.

One way to categorize the treatment models that are covered within this book is to consider them as either process-oriented or structural. Process-oriented therapies identify causal mechanisms within the process that eventuate in the client's problem and then directly intervene in that process. For example, problem-solving therapies assume that some people with interpersonal problems have difficulties in perceiving the interpersonal "problem," and then generating and executing an effective response to that problem. These treatments focus on the training of the *process* of how to solve problems. Stress-inoculation training and self-control therapies also share a process orientation to therapeutic change.

Structural cognitive-behavioral therapies are distinguished from process-oriented models by virtue of their additional assumption that cognitive processes are influenced by temporally stable cognitive structures. These structures are incorporated in the individual's cognitive-perceptual-emotional system and are activated in certain circumstances, leading to dysfunctional cognitive processes and behavioral consequences. Ellis's notion of irrational beliefs is an example of these cognitive structures that lead to negative behavioral and emotional consequences. Other structural models include Beck's Cognitive Therapy and Guidano and Liotti's treatment approach. The treatment models of these approaches, as can be seen in the relevant chapters of this book, suggest that the modification of cognitive processes is not sufficient for complete therapy success. According to these models in order to be considered fully treated, clients must also achieve some degree of the "insight" and awareness of their habitual patterns of cognition that reflect underlying dysfunctional cognitive structures.

One of the interesting questions for the future will be the extent to which process-oriented and structural cognitive-behavioral therapies achieve acceptance and can demonstrate clinical utility. There appear to be some logical limitations of each of these approaches to intervention, and future research will help to define the nature of these limitations. In the interim, it is clear that considerable work is being done, particularly in the development of structural models of dysfunction and structural cognitive-behavioral therapies. It is an exciting time to be involved in cognitive-behavioral research.

One disturbing aspect of this book, at least for me, is the manner in which the treatment models discussed in this text deal with the topic of emotion. The mediational model assumes emotional responses follow cognitive appraisal, which is a theoretically and empirically defensible position. What is much less completely described in cognitive-behavioral terms, however, is the reciprocal relationship between emotion and cognitive processes. Research from mood-dependent memory and other areas has demonstrated that mood does influence cognition, and yet most cognitive-behavioral models do not adequately deal with this issue. Greenberg and Safran's *Emotion in Psychotherapy* (1987) acutely points out the limitations of models that fail to account for the role of emotion in dysfunction and treatment. It is to be hoped that future theorists will work to help overcome this limitation of current cognitive-behavioral therapies.

Much has occurred in the near-decade between the publication of Kendall and Hollon's *Cognitive-Behavioral Interventions* and the publication of this book. I hope that this volume captures much of the development of the area and can be considered, at least for a while, a current comprehensive review of the field of cognitive-behavioral therapies. If it is an adequate review, I will be pleased. Even more, if the book spurs further throught and research in the area I will be more than pleased. There are many issues that require consideration and research. The next decade will likely bring a great deal of attention to this field, and will bring, it is hoped, a greater understanding of the mechanisms of human distress and dysfunction, as well as treatment methods to help people achieve more satisfying and complete lives.

Keith Dobson, Ph.D.
Vancouver, British Columbia

CONTENTS

Handbook of Cognitive-Behavioral Therapies

PART I

INTRODUCTION

1

HISTORICAL AND PHILOSOPHICAL BASES OF THE COGNITIVE-BEHAVIORAL THERAPIES

KEITH S. DOBSON
LORY BLOCK

One of the difficulties that has persisted through the development of cognitive-behavioral therapies has been the definition of their scope. While the earliest of the cognitive-behavioral therapies emerged in the early 1960s (Ellis, 1962), it wasn't until the 1970s that the first major texts on "cognitive-behavior modification" appeared (Hollon & Kendall, 1978; Mahoney, 1974; Meichenbaum, 1977). The intervening period was one of considerable interest in cognition and in the application of cognitive theory to behavior change. Mahoney (1977), for example, noted that while psychology had generally undergone a "cognitive revolution," the same theoretical focus was being brought to bear upon clinical psychology. In creating a cognitive revolution in clinical psychology, different theorists and practitioners brought their own interests and perspectives to the problems at hand. As a result, a large number of models for cognitive and behavior change have been advanced, and a veritable armamentarium of clinical techniques have been added to the clinician's repertory.

In this chapter a review of the major developments in the history of cognitive-behavioral therapies will be undertaken, with a focus on the period from the early 1960s to the mid 1970s. Included in this review will be a number of specific topics. After briefly defining the current scope of cognitive-behavioral therapies and the essential nature of the model for cognitive-behavior therapy (CBT), we shall review the historical bases of CBT. Six major reasons for the development of cognitive-behavioral therapies will be proposed and discussed. The chapter will then summarize the major philosophical underpinnings of the various forms of cognitive-behavioral therapies, with a view to both the principles that all of these therapies share and those that vary from approach to approach. The last section of the chapter will present a formal chronology of the major cognitive-behavior therapy approaches. This section will also describe unique contemporary approaches within the overall field of CBT in terms of the historical developments for each approach and the behavior change principles each approach encourages.

DEFINING COGNITIVE-BEHAVIOR THERAPY (CBT)

At their core, cognitive-behavioral therapies share three fundamental propositions:

1. Cognitive activity affects behavior
2. Cognitive activity may be monitored and altered
3. Desired behavior change may be affected through cognitive change

Although using a slightly different title, Kazdin (1978) has argued a similar implicit set of propositions in his definition of cognitive-behavior modification: "The term 'cognitive-behavior modification' encompasses treatments that attempt to change overt behavior by altering thoughts, interpretations, assumptions, and strategies of responding" (p. 337). Cognitive-behavior modification and cognitive-behavior therapy can thus be seen as nearly identical in their basic assumptions, and highly similar in treatment methods. Perhaps the one area where the two labels identify divergent therapies is with respect to treatment outcomes. While cognitive-behavior modification seeks overt behavior change as an end result (Kazdin, 1978; Mahoney, 1974); it appears that some forms of CBT focus their treatment effects on cognitions per se, in the belief that behavior change will follow. Ellis' (1962; 1979b; Dryden & Ellis, Chapter 6, this volume) efforts on belief change, for example, constitute a type of therapy that Kazdin's (1978) definition would not incorporate as a form of cognitive-behavioral modification. The term "cognitive-behavior therapy," therefore, is a broader term than "cognitive-behavior modification," subsuming cognitive-behavior modification within it.

The first of the three fundamental propositions of CBT, that cognitive activity affects behavior, is a restatement of the basic mediational model. Although early theorists supporting cognitive-behavioral approaches had to document the theoretical and empirical legitimacy of this proposition (e.g., Mahoney, 1974), there is now overwhelming evidence that cognitive appraisals of events can affect the response to those events (e.g., Houston & Holmes, 1974; Lazarus & Folkman, 1984; Lazarus, Opton, Nomikos, & Rankin, 1965; Neufeld, 1976) and that there is clinical value in modifying the content of these appraisals (e.g., Beck, Rush, Shaw, & Emery, 1979; Meichenbaum, 1969). While debate certainly continues about the degree and exact nature of the appraisals an individual makes in different contexts (c.f.

Greenberg & Safran, 1984; Zajonc, 1980), the fact of mediation is no longer strongly contested.

The second cognitive-behavior therapy proposition states that cognitive activity may be monitored and altered. Implicit in this statement are a number of corollaries. For example, it is assumed that we may gain access to cognitive activity. As such, cognitions must be knowable and assessable. There is, however, reason to believe that access to cognitions is not perfect, and that people may report cognitive activities on the basis of their likelihood of occurrence, rather than actual occurence (Nisbett & Wilson, 1977). Most researchers in the area of cognitive assessment, however, continue to attempt to document reliable and valid, cognitive assessment strategies, usually with behavior as the source of validational data (Merluzzi, Glass, & Genest, 1981; Segal & Shaw, Chapter 2, this volume). This area continues to be one where further research efforts are required.

A second corollary stemming from the second CBT proposition is that assessment of cognitive activity is a prelude to the alteration of cognitive activity. This view, however, must be considered speculative. Although it makes conceptual sense that once we may measure a construct we may then begin to manipulate it, one does not *necessarily* follow from the other. For example, because we may measure gamma radiation from the sun does not mean we may alter it. In the arena of human change the measurement of cognition may not necessarily assist change efforts. As has been written elsewhere (Mischel, 1981; Shaw & Dobson, 1981), most current cognitive assessment strategies emphasize the content of cognitions and the assessment of cognitive results, rather than the cognitive process. Our understanding of change, on the other hand, will most likely be advanced by examining the process of cognition, as well as the interdependence between cognitive, behavioral, and affective systems. This form of cognitive monitoring is only at a very rudimentary stage of development.

The third CBT proposition is a direct result of the adoption of the mediational model. It states that desired behavior change may be effected through cognitive change. Thus, while cognitive-behavioral theorists do not argue that overt reinforcement contingencies cannot alter behavior, they are likely to emphasize that there are alternative methods for behavior change, one in particular being cognitive change. This emphasis on cognitive mechanisms to create behavioral effects is what differentiates the cognitive-behavioral therapist from his or her behavioral counterpart.

Due to the statement that cognitive change may influence behavior, much of the efforts of cognitive-behavioral researchers has been to attempt to document a mediational influence. In one of the earliest demonstrations of this type, Nomikos, Opton, Averill, and Lazarus (1968) demonstrated that the same loud noise created different degrees of physiological disturbance, based upon the subjects' expectancy for the noise. In a similar vein, Bandura (1977) has employed the construct of self-efficacy to document that a subject's perceived ability to approach a fearful object is a strong predictor of actual behavior. Many studies have documented the role of cognitive appraisal processes in a variety of laboratory and clinical settings.

Although the inference of cognitive activity has been generally accepted, it is still extremely difficult to document the further assumption that changes in cognition mediate behavior change. In order to do so, the assessment of cognitive change must occur independent of behavior. For example, if a phobic person approaches within 10 feet of a feared object, is treated through a standard type of systematic desensitization (including graduated approach), and is then able to predict and demonstrate a closer approach to the feared object, making the inference that cognitive mediation of the behavior change is difficult at best and unnecessary at worst. On the other hand, if the same phobic person is treated with some form of cognitive intervention (e.g., imagined approach of the feared object), and then demonstrates the same behavior change, then cognitive mediation of that behavior change is much more plausible. Moreover, if that same phobic person demonstrates changes in his or her behavior towards objects previously feared but not specifically treated, then the cognitive mediation of that behavior change is essential, in that there must be some cognitive "matching" between the treated object and the other object of generalization.

WHAT CONSTITUTES COGNITIVE-BEHAVIORAL THERAPY?

A number of current approaches to therapy fall within the scope of cognitive-behavior therapy as it is defined above. These approaches all share a theoretical perspective that assumes that internal covert processes called thinking or cognition occur, and that cognitive events may mediate behavior change. Furthermore, these approaches all assume that behavioral change does not have to involve elaborate cognitive mechanisms. In some forms of therapy the interventions may have very little to do with cognitive appraisals and evaluations, but may be heavily dependent upon client action and behavior change. In fact, many of the cognitive-behavioral theorists explicitly state that because of the mediational hypothesis, not only is cognition able to alter behavior, but it must alter behavior, so that behavior change may thus be used as an indirect index of cognitive change. The actual outcomes of cognitive-behavior therapy will vary from client to client, of course, but in general the two main indices used for change are cognition and behavior. To some extent emotional and physiological changes are also used as change indices, particularly where emotional or physiological disturbance is a major manifestation of the presenting problem in therapy (e.g., anxiety disorders, psychophysiological disorders).

There are three major classes of cognitive-behavioral therapies, each with a slightly different class of change goals (Mahoney & Arnkoff, 1978). The three classes of therapies are Coping-Skills Therapies, Problem-Solving Therapies, and Cognitive Restructuring Methods. Since a later section of this chapter will detail the specific therapies that fall within these categories of cognitive-behavioral therapies, this topic will not be reviewed here. What is important to note, however, is that the different classes of therapy orient themselves towards different degrees of cognitive versus behavioral change. For example, Coping-Skills therapies are of primary use in dealing with problems in which a person is largely reacting to events outside of him- or herself, the focus of therapy therefore being on the ways in which the person may exacerbate the influence of negative events (e.g., engaging in anxiety-provoking thoughts and images), or the actions that the person may take to lessen the impact of the negative events. The primary markers of success within this form of therapy, therefore, are reductions in the consequences of negative events (e.g., less demonstrated anxiety) and behavioral signs of better coping abilities. In the case of cognitive restructuring techniques, however, the desired change is more a result of disturbance created from within the person him- or herself. An excellent example here is the instance of depressed persons who may by their negativistic thinking make events worse than they otherwise are, thereby creating much of their own unhappiness (Beck, 1976; DeRubeis & Beck, Chapter 7 this volume). In these instances a much more appropriate index of change is the client's verbal report that their thinking is less dysfunctional, and this self-report would secondarily be assessed against the client's behavior and mood.

Although cognitive-behavior therapy targets both cognition and behavior as primary change areas, there are certain types of desired change that would clearly fall outside of the realm of cognitive-behavior therapy. For example, a therapist who focuses on head banging in an autistic child, and adopts a classical conditioning approach to the treatment of this problem is not employing a cognitive-behavioral therapy. In fact, any therapeutic regimen that adopts a stimulus–response model is not a cognitive-behavioral therapy. Only in instances where cognitive mediation can be demonstrated, and where cognitive mediation is an important component of the treatment plan can the label "cognitive-behavioral" be applied.

Just as strictly behavioral therapies are not cognitive-behavioral, strictly cognitive therapies are also not cognitive-behavioral. For example, a therapeutic model that states that memories of a long-past traumatic event cause current disturbance and that consequently targets those memories for change is not a cognitive-behavioral therapy. It should be noted that this example carries the provision that no association between the current disturbance and past trauma is possible. In a case where a past trauma has occurred, but a recent event is highly similar to that past event and the client is experiencing distress as a function of both the past trauma and the current event, then cognitive mediation is much more likely and the therapy may be cognitive-behavioral in nature.

Finally, therapies that base their theories in the expression of excessive emotions, as may be seen in cathartic models of therapy (Janov, 1970) are not cognitive-behavioral. Thus, although these therapies may posit that the emotions derived from extreme or negative mediational processes, the lack of a clear mediational model of change places them outside the field of cognitive-behavior therapy.

HISTORICAL BASES OF COGNITIVE-BEHAVIORAL THERAPY

As students of modern psychological history know, cognitive-behavioral therapies grew out of traditional behavior therapy, which in turn was an innovation from radical behavioral approaches to human problems. The major distinction between cognitive-behavioral and behavioral therapies, as previously stated, is the incorporation of the mediational perspective into the cognitive-behavioral approaches to problems. This incorporation phenomenon occurred at different times with different cognitive-behavioral approaches, but occurred mainly in the end of the 1960s and early part of the 1970s (Kazdin, 1978). There were a number of specific factors that conspired at this time to make the development of cognitive-behavior theory possible, and cognitive-behavior therapy a logical necessity. These factors included the following contingents.

1. Although the behavioral perspective had been a dominant force for some time in psychological approaches to disturbance, it was becoming apparent by the end of the 1960s that a nonmediational approach was not expansive enough to account for all of human behavior (Breger & McGaugh, 1965; Mahoney, 1974). Bandura's (1965, 1971) accounts of vicarious learning defied traditional behavioral explanation, as did the work on delay of gratification by Mischel (Mischel, Ebbesen, & Zeiss, 1972). Similarly, children were learning grammatical rules well out of the ability of most parents and educators to discriminatively reinforce (Vygotsky, 1962) and behavioral models of language learning were under serious attack. Yet another sign of dissatisfaction with behavioral models was the attempt to expand these models to incorporate "covert" behaviors (i.e., thought) (Homme, 1965). Although this approach met with some limited optimism, criticisms from behavioral quarters made it apparent that extensions of this sort were not consistent with the behavioral emphasis on overt phenomena.

2. Just as there was growing dissatisfaction with the strict S–R nonmediational model of behavior, there continued to be a rejection of the strongest alternative perspective, the psychodynamic model of personality and therapy. Early writings in the area of cognitive-behavior therapy (e.g., Beck,

1967, pp. 7–9; Ellis, 1973; 1979a, p. 2) included statements that summarily rejected psychoanalytic emphases on unconscious processes, historical material, and the need for long-term therapy that relied heavily on the development of insight regarding the transference—countertransference relationship. Beyond philosophical disagreements with some of the basic tenets of psychodynamic models, reviews of the experimental literature suggested that the efficacy of traditional psychotherapy was not particularly impressive (Eysenck, 1969; Luborsky, Singer & Luborsky, 1975; Rachman & Wilson, 1971, 1980). Perhaps the boldest evaluative comment about the demonstrated efficacy of psychodynamic therapies comes from Rachman and Wilson (1980), where they state "there still is no acceptable evidence to support the view that psychoanalysis is an effective treatment" (pp. 76).

3. A third factor that facilitated the development of cognitive-behavior therapy was the fact that the targets of interventions, by their very nature, sometimes made interventions of a noncognitive nature irrelevant. For example, it is not surprising that behavioral treatments for compulsive behavior were established even while obsessive thinking was not targeted for change. Behavior therapy, as was appropriate, was applied to disorders that were primarily demarcated by their behavioral correlates. Also, where disorders were multifaceted, behavioral therapists targeted the behavioral symptoms for change (e.g., Ferster, 1974). This focus on behavior provided a significant increase in therapeutic potential over past efforts, but was not fully satisfying to therapists who recognized that entire problems or major components of problems were going untreated. The development of cognitive-behavioral treatment interventions helped to fill a void in the clinician's treatment techniques.

4. Within cognitive psychology (Neisser, 1967; Paivio, 1971) a number of mediational concepts were being developed, researched and established. Perhaps one of the most important developments in this sense were the information processing models of cognition that were elaborated. These models were explicitly mediational and were receiving considerable support from cognition laboratories. One of the developments that was perhaps natural was the development of information-processing models of clinical constructs (e.g., Hamilton, 1979, 1980; Neufeld & Mothersill, 1980).

Even beyond general cognitive models being developed, a number of researchers in the 1960s and 1970s conducted basic research into the cognitive mediation of clinically relevant constructs. Lazarus and associates, for example, conducted a number of studies during this time period in which they documented data showing that anxiety processes involve cognitive mediation (Lazarus, 1966; Lazarus & Alfert, 1964; Lazarus & Averill, 1972; Monat, Averill, & Lazarus, 1972; Nomikos, Opton, Averill, & Lazarus, 1968). This line of research clearly established that the anxiety process had significant cognitive components, and that models of the etiology of anxiety required attention to this component of functioning. Taken together, the two research areas of general cognitive psychology and what may be termed "applied cognitive psychology" challenged behavioral theorists to account for the data being accumulated. In essence, the challenge amounted to a need for behavioral models to redefine their limits and incorporate cognitive phenomena into the models of behavioral mechanisms. Perhaps one of the earliest signs of this attempt at incorporation can be seen in the self-regulation and self-control literature, which developed during the early part of the 1970s (Cautela, 1969; Goldfried & Merbaum, 1973; Mahoney & Thoreson, 1974; Rachlin, 1974; Stuart, 1972). All of these various attempts to delineate self-control perspectives on behavioral modification shared the idea that the individual has some capacity to monitor his or her behavior, to set internally generated goals for behavior, and to orchestrate both environmental and personal variables to achieve some form of regulation in the behavior of interest. In order to develop these self-control models, several cognitive processes had to be hypothesized, including attempts to define self-control strategies largely in terms of internal "cybernetic" components of functioning (e.g., Jeffrey & Berger, 1982). Clearly, the early attempts to retain strictly behavioral models of behavior change were not successful, so that behavior theorists and therapists have adapted behavior change principles to incorporate concepts of self-control theory.

5. Another component of the change in behavior therapy to the incorporation of cognitive-behavioral principles was the development and identification of a number of theorists and therapists who clearly identified themselves as being cognitive-behavioral in orientation. Some of the people to begin this process explicitly were Beck (1967, 1970), Cautela (1967, 1969), Ellis (1962, 1970), Mahoney (1974), Mahoney & Thoreson, (1974), and Meichenbaum (1973, 1977). The establishment of several key proponents of a cognitive-behavioral perspective clearly had the effect of creating a *zeitgeist* that drew the attention of others in the field. In addition, the creation of a journal specifically tailored to the emerging cognitive-behavioral field helped to further this trend. Thus, the establishment in 1977 of *Cognitive Therapy and Research*, with Michael Mahoney as editor, provided a forum "to stimulate and communicate research and theory on the role of cognitive processes in human adaptation and adjustment" (from the cover of the journal). The existence of a regular publication in the area of cognitive-behavior theory and modification allowed researchers and therapists to present provocative ideas and research findings to a wide audience.

6. A final but not unimportant historical factor that has contributed to the continued interest in the cognitive-behavioral perspective has been the publication of research studies that have found treatment outcomes for cognitive-behavioral treatments equally or more effective than strictly behavioral approaches. In a critical review of cognitive-behavior modification, Ledgewidge (1978) reviewed 13 studies that contrasted cognitive-behavioral versus behavioral therapies and found no demonstrated superior-

ity for either, although he noted that the studies he reviewed were based upon analogue populations, and that clinical trials were required for a more summative judgment. His largely critical review prompted a reply that largely dismissed Legewidge's criticisms as "premature" (Mahoney & Kazdin, 1979). Since this early controversy about the efficacy of cognitive-behavioral therapies, there have been a number of reviews that clearly demonstrate that cognitive-behavioral therapies have a clinical impact (Berman, Miller, & Massman, 1985; Dush, Hirt, & Schroeder, 1983; Miller & Berman, 1983; Shapiro & Shapiro, 1982). It is important to note, however, that meta-analyses of therapeutic effectiveness question the extent to which cognitive-behavioral treatments are superior to strictly behavioral treatments (Berman *et al.*, 1985; Miller & Berman, 1983). The results of such meta-analyses notwithstanding, there are several research studies that have documented clear advantages for cognitive-behavioral therapies over other more traditional modalities of treatment. Perhaps the most striking and well-cited of these findings has been in the area of the treatment of depression, where a number of research studies have shown that cognitive-behavioral therapies have had better therapy outcome than pharmacotherapy (Blackburn, Bishop, Glen, Whalley, & Christie, 1981; McLean & Hakstain, 1979; Rush, Beck, Kovacs, & Hollon, 1977; Simons, Garfield, & Murphy, 1984). Even though there have been a number of criticisms of the methodology of these studies (most notably, the rigidity of the drug regimen), such research findings have done much to stimulate continued research into cognitive-behavioral interventions. The most ambitious of these investigations, conducted by the National Institute of Mental Health (Elkin, Parloff, Hadley, & Autry, 1985) will soon begin to publish its results on the relative effectiveness of a cognitive-behavioral therapy (Beck *et al.*, 1979) versus a short-term dynamically based therapy (Klerman, Weissman, Rounsaville, & Chevron, 1984) and pharmacotherapy. As the data base is further enlarged, more definitive statements will be possible about the effectiveness of these types of therapy. What will hopefully emerge from continued research will be specific conclusions about not only the overall efficacy of cognitive-behavioral therapies, but also specific statements about the relative efficacy of different types of cognitive-behavioral therapies with specific types of clinical problems.

It becomes apparent from the above review that a number of compelling reasons have existed and continue to exist for the development of cognitive-behavioral models of dysfunction and therapy. These reasons include dissatisfaction with previous models of therapy, clinical problems that emphasize the need for a cognitive-behavioral perspective, the research conducted into cognitive aspects of human functioning, the *zeitgeist* phenomenon that has lead to an identified group of cognitive-behavioral theorists and therapists, and the growing body of research that supports the clinical efficacy of cognitive-behavioral interventions. With this general trend in mind, this chapter now returns to provide more in-depth summaries of the historical developments behind the large number of specific cognitive-behavioral therapies that have evolved over the past 25 years.

CONTEMPORARY COGNITIVE-BEHAVIORAL THERAPIES: A CHRONOLOGY

Cognitive-behavioral therapies represent the hybrid of behavioral strategies and cognitive processes with the goal of achieving behavioral and cognitive change. The relations among these various approaches remain unclear. However, a brief overview of the major therapeutic procedures subsumed under the heading of cognitive-behavior modification reveals a diverse amalgam of principles and procedures.

The diversification in the development and implementation of the cognitive-behavioral approach may be explained, in part, by the differing theoretical orientations of those who generated intervention strategies based on this perspective. For example, Ellis and Beck, authors of rational-emotive therapy and cognitive therapy respectively, came from psychoanalytic backgrounds. In contrast, Goldfried, Meichenbaum, and Mahoney were trained originally in the principles of behavior modification.

Mahoney and Arnkoff (1978) have organized the contemporary cognitive-behavioral therapies into three major divisions: (1) cognitive restructuring, (2) coping-skills therapies, and (3) problem-solving therapies. Table 1.1 presents an historical outline of the contemporary therapies included

Table 1.1. A Chronology of Cognitive–Behavioral Therapies

Year of first publication	Therapy title	Author(s)	Type of therapy
1962	Rational–Emotive Therapy	Ellis	CR
1963	Cognitive Thearpy	Beck	CR
1971	Self-Instructional Training	Meichenbaum	CR
1971	Anxiety-Management Training	Suinn & Richardson	CS
1971	Problem-Solving Therapy	D'Zurilla & Goldfried	PS
1971	Problem-Solving Therapy	Spivack & Shure	PS
1973	Stress Inoculation Training	Meichenbaum	CS
1974	Systematic Rational Restructuring	Goldfried	CS
1974	Personal Science	Mahoney	PS
1975	Rational Behavior Therapy	Maultsby	CR
1977	Self-control Therapy	Rehm	PS
1983	Structural Psychotherapy	Guidano & Liotti	CR

Legend for types of therapy: CR = Cognitive Restructuring; CS = Coping Skills Therapies; PS = Problem-Solving Therapies within this classification. Therapies included under the heading of cognitive restructuring assume that emotional distress is the consequence of maladaptive thoughts. Thus, the goal of these clinical interventions is to establish more adaptive thought patterns. By comparison, coping skills therapies represent a more heterogeneous collection of techniques that as a whole focus on the development of a repertoire of skills designed to assist the client in coping with a variety of stressful situations. The problem-solving therapies may be characterized as a combination of cognitive restructuring techniques and coping-skills training procedures. This final class of intervention techniques emphasizes the development of general strategies for dealing with a broad range of personal problems and stress the importance of an active collaboration between client and therapist in the planning of the treatment program.

In the sections that follow, the evolution of the major therapies associated with the cognitive-behavioral tradition will be described. This review is not intended to be exhaustive and therefore will exclude a number of therapies that have not stimulated a significant amount of research or clinical application.

RATIONAL–EMOTIVE THERAPY

Rational–emotive therapy (RET) is regarded by many as one of the premiere examples of the cognitive-behavioral approach. The basic theory and practice of RET was formulated by Albert Ellis almost 30 years ago. Following extensive training and experience in psychoanalysis, Ellis began to question the efficacy and efficiency of the classical analytic method. He observed that patients tended to remain in therapy for considerable periods of time and frequently resisted psychoanalytic techniques such as free association and dream analysis. Moreover, Ellis questioned whether the personal insight that was assumed to lead to therapeutic change according to psychoanalytic theory resulted in durable changes in behavior.

Still, however, I was not satisfied with the results I was getting. For, again, a great many patients improved considerably in a fairly short length of time, and felt much better after getting certain seemingly crucial insights. But few of them were really cured, in the sense of being minimally assailed with anxiety or hostility. And, as before, patient after patient would say to me: "Yes, I see exactly what bothers me now and why I am bothered by it; but I nevertheless still am bothered. Now what can I do about that?" (Ellis, 1962, p. 9)

Discouraged by the limitations of the analytic method, Ellis began to experiment with more active and directive treatment techniques. Through a process of clinical trial and error, he gradually formulated a theory of emotional disturbance and a set of treatment methods that emphasized a practical approach to dealing with life problems. While advocates of analytic theory considered Ellis's methods heretical, the advent of behavior therapy in the 1960s and the growing acceptance of the role of cognitions in understanding human behavior eventually fostered the acceptance of RET as a potentially valid alternative to the more traditional models of psychotherapy.

At the core of RET is the assumption that human thinking and emotion are significantly interrelated. According to Ellis's *ABC* model, neurotic symptoms or consequences (*C*) are determined by a person's belief systems (*B*) regarding particular activating experiences or events (*A*). The goal of therapy is to identify and challenge the irrational beliefs that are the root of emotional disturbance. RET assumes that individuals possess innate and acquired tendencies to think and behave irrationally. Thus, in order to maintain a state of emotional health, individuals must constantly monitor and challenge their basic belief systems.

Ellis (1970) identified 12 basic irrational beliefs that take the general form of unrealistic or absolutistic expectations. RET assumes that by substituting unrealistic, overgeneralized demands with realistic desires, preferences, or wishes, major changes in emotions and behaviors can occur. However, since individuals tend to forcefully preserve their irrational thought patterns, significant and durable changes require forceful methods of intervention.

RET employs a multidimensional approach that incorporates cognitive, emotive, and behavioral techniques. Nevertheless, the major therapeutic tool remains a "logico-empirical method of scientific questioning, challenging, and debating" (Ellis, 1979a, p. 20) designed to assist individuals in surrendering irrational beliefs. In addition to disputation, RET therapists may selectively employ a broad variety of techniques including self-monitoring of thoughts, bibliotherapy, role playing, modeling, rational–emotive imagery, shame-attacking exercises, relaxation methods, operant conditioning, and skill training (Ellis, 1979b). The theory and practice of RET have not undergone any major reformulations since their introduction. Thus, Ellis' original conceptualization of rational–emotive therapy as outlined in this book, *Reason and Emotion in Psychotherapy* (1962), remains a primary reference for this approach.

One of the major differences between RET and other cognitive-behavioral approaches lies in its philosophical emphasis. Ellis's (1980) distinctly philosophical outlook is reflected in what he identifies as the major goals of RET: self-interest, social interest, self-direction, tolerance of self and others, flexibility, acceptance of uncertainty, commitment to vital interests, self-acceptance, scientific thinking, and a nonutopian perspective on life. RET assumes that individuals who adopt this type of rational philosophy will experience a minimum of emotional disturbance.

RET has generated a large body of literature. Unfortunately, the majority of articles published have been authored by enthused advocates of Ellis' theory and methods as opposed to researchers concerned with collecting objective data concerning their validity and utility (Mahoney, 1979). Recent publications suggest, however, that RET is beginning to receive the objective empirical scrutiny that has been notably absent in the past (Kendall & Bemis, 1983).

RATIONAL BEHAVIOR THERAPY

In 1975, Maxie Maultsby presented a paper at the First National Conference of Rational Emotive and Behavioral Therapists outlining the development of rational behavior therapy (RBT). While he received his early training in family medicine and psychiatry, Maultsby (1984) acknowledges the contributions of several sources in the formulation of RBT including neuropsychology, classical and operant learning theories, psychosomatic research, and RET. However, as even the name suggests, Maultsby's RBT was primarily influenced by his association with Albert Ellis and, in essence, represents a restatement of the theory and methods of RET.

Despite a unique attempt to couch his theory of emotional disturbance in terms in neuropsychophysiology and learning theory, Maultsby (1984) adheres closely to the *ABC* model outlined earlier by Ellis (1962). RBT assumes that repeated pairings of a perception (*A*) with evaluative thoughts (*B*) lead to rational or irrational emotive and behavioral reactions (*C*). Maultsby suggests that self-talk, which originates in the left hemisphere of the brain, triggers corresponding right hemisphere emotional equivalents. Thus, in order to maintain a state of psychological health, individuals must practice rational self-talk that will, in turn, cause the right brain to convert left brain language into appropriate emotional and behavioral reactions. Stated another way, "human beings are disturbed not by things, but by the views they take of them" (Ellis, 1962, p. 54).

The similarity between RBT and RET extends beyond theory into the domain of treatment techniques. Both therapies stress the importance of monitoring one's thoughts in order to become aware of the ABC's of emotional disturbance. Maultsby (1984) refers to this technique as rational self-analysis (RSA). In addition, Maultsby advocates the use of rational-emotive imagery, behavioral practice, and relaxation methods in order to minimize emotional distress and achieve a state of healthy emotional and behavioral self-control. Once again, these methods are also employed by RET therapists to achieve similar goals.

While Maultsby (1984) does not identify a set of basic irrational beliefs, he characterizes a number of "self-defeating cognitive habits" that bear a remarkable resemblance to Ellis's (1970) notion of absolutistic thinking. The obvious philosophical overtones of RET are not as apparent in Maultsby's approach. Nevertheless, the five rules for rational behavior that he proposes will lead to optimal health have a distinctly philosophical flavor:

"Rational behavior is based on obvious fact." "Rational behavior best helps you protect your life and health." ". . . best helps you achieve . . . goals," ". . . best helps you avoid. . . ." and ". . . best helps you feel. . . ." (Maultsby, 1984, p. 16). Finally, perhaps the most notable similarity between Maultsby's and Ellis's approaches is the confidence with which they are both presented:

> RBT is an ideal cognitive behavior therapy because it has each of the six characteristics that identify all ideal psychotherapies. RBT is (1) comprehensive, (2) short-term, (3) cross-cultural; (4) drug-free, (5) it produces long-term results, and (6) the . . . self-help techniques used in RBT . . . offer . . . people effective, yet economical and preventive mass mental-health programs (Maultsby, 1984, p. 10).

> On most of these counts some amount of clinical and experimental evidence now exists that RET works as well or better than other commonly used therapeutic procedures (Ellis, 1979b, p. 98).

Despite Maultsby's (1984) claims, RBT has remained a relatively obscure cognitive-behavioral approach. Recent reviews of cognitive-behavioral interventions have not included RBT (Kendall & Bemis, 1983; Kendall & Kriss, 1983) and there is a notable lack of attention to this approach in the empirical literature. Thus, it appears that among researchers interested in a theory and therapy based on rational thinking, RBT will continue to play a secondary role to Ellis's (1962) rational–emotive therapy.

COGNITIVE THERAPY

Aaron Beck, the author of cognitive therapy, was originally trained in psychoanalytic theory. Like Ellis, albeit independently, Beck began to question psychoanalytic formulations of the neuroses, in particular with respect to the concept of depression. Conscious of the long-term nature of analytic treatment and the frequently negative reactions of patients to analytic methods, Beck initiated a critical investigation of psychoanalytic theory (Beck, 1976). Thus, the late 1950s marked the beginning of a period of systematic clinical observation and research that ultimately led to the evolution of Beck's cognitive therapy of depression.

In 1963, Beck observed that cognitive factors associated with depression were largely ignored in favor of the psychoanalytic bias towards motivational–affective conceptualizations. However, on the basis of an investigation into the thematic content of cognitions in psychiatric patients, Beck was able to distinguish consistent difference in the ideational content associated with common neurotic disorders including depression. He also found that patients exhibited systematic distortions in their thinking patterns. Consequently, Beck generated a typology of cognitive distortions to describe these systematic errors, which included the now well-known concepts of arbitrary inference, selective abstraction, overgeneralization, magnification, and minimization. Beck also observed that these cognitions were automatic, involuntary, and highly plausible to the patient.

The findings of a 5-year research project at the University of Pennsylvania culminated in the publication in 1967 of a book entitled *Depression: Causes and Treatment*. In this volume, Beck outlined his cognitive model and therapy of depression and other neuroses. Nine years later, he published a second volume, *Cognitive Therapy and the Emotional Disorders*, which presented in more detail the specific cognitive distortions associated with each of the neuroses and described the principles of cognitive therapy, with special reference to depression (Beck, 1976). In 1979, Beck co-authored a comprehensive treatment manual for depression that presented cognitive techniques that had been refined over the course of 20 years of clinical work and empirical inquiry (Beck *et al.*, 1979).

Despite Beck's early emphasis on thought disorders in depression, his cognitive model represents a comprehensive formulation of psychopathology in general. According to this model, emotional disorders are the results of distorted thinking or unrealistic cognitive appraisals of life events. Therefore, it is assumed that the way in which an individual structures reality determines his or her affective state. Furthermore, the cognitive model proposes that a reciprocal relation exists between affect and cognition such that one tends to reinforce the other, resulting in an escalation of emotional and cognitive impairment (Beck, 1971).

Schemata, defined as cognitive structures that organize and process incoming information, are proposed to represent the thought patterns acquired early in an individual's development. Logical errors in thinking acquired during the developmental period become the substance of schemata that predispose individuals to experience emotional problems. Whereas the schemata of the well-adjusted individual allows for the realistic appraisal of life events, those of the maladjusted individual result in the distortion of reality and facilitate psychological disorder.

The depressive schema is characterized by Beck in terms of a negative cognitive triad. Accordingly, depressed individuals view themselves, their world, and their futures in a negative manner (Hollon & Beck, 1979). The more severe the depression, the more this schema dominates the cognitive processes. Schemata associated with other emotional disorders are distinguished by the content of their cognitions (Beck, 1976). To date, theoretical analyses and empirical investigation concerning the schemata of psychological disorders other then depression are limited.

Cognitive therapy involves the application of empirical procedures to the cognitive, behavioral, and affective processes of the client and represents a logical extension of Beck's cognitive model. The goal of therapy is to replace the client's presumed distorted appraisals of life events with more realistic cognitive appraisals. Treatment involves designing specific learning experiences in order to teach clients: (1) to monitor automatic thoughts, (2) to recognize the relations between cognition, affect, and behavior, (3) to test the validity of automatic thoughts, (4) to substitute more realistic cognitions for these distorted thoughts, and (5) to learn to indentify and alter the underlying assumptions or beliefs that predispose individuals to engage in faulty thinking patterns (Kendall & Bemis, 1983).

Unlike RET, Beck's cognitive theory of psychopathology and cognitive techniques have been subjected to a substantial degree of empirical scrutiny. However, most of this research has focused on depressed samples. While the cognitive theory and treatment of depression is considered by many to be a viable alternative to behavioral and biochemical interventions (Hollon & Beck, 1979), the issue of the generalizability of Beck's model and therapy with respect to other psychiatric disorders requires further research (Beck & Emery, 1985). Nonetheless, the contributions of Beck and his associates have made a significant impact on researchers and clinicians alike, and will in all probability continue to stimulate research for many years to come.

SELF-INSTRUCTIONAL TRAINING

Donald Meichenbaum's clinical interests developed during a period when the technology of behavior therapy was flourishing and the then radical ideas of Ellis (1962), Beck (1963), and other advocates of cognitive treatment approaches were beginning to attract the attention of a new generation of clinicians. Amidst this climate, Meihenbaum (1969) carried out a doctoral research program that investigated the effects of an operant treatment procedure for hospitalized schizophrenic patients trained to emit "healthy talk." By chance, he observed that patients who engaged in spontaneous self-instruction to "talk healthy" were less distracted and demonstrated superior task performance on a variety of measures. This serendipitous finding became the impetus for a long-term research program focusing on the role of cognitive factors in behavior modification (Meichenbaum, 1973, 1977).

The direction of Meichenbaum's research was influenced heavily by two Soviet psychologists, Luira (1961) and Vygotsky (1962), who studied the developmental relation between language, thought, and behavior. They suggested that the development of voluntary control over one's behavior involves a gradual progression from external regulation by significant others (e.g., parental instructions) to self-regulation as a result of the internalization of verbal commands. Consequently, the relation between verbal self-instruction and behavior became the major focus of Meichenbaum's research. He proposed that covert behaviors operate according to the same principles as do overt behaviors and that covert behaviors are thus subject to modification using the same behavioral strategies employed to modify overt behaviors (Meichenbaum, 1973).

Meichenbaum's early attempts to explore the validity of this proposal involved the development of a self-instructional training (SIT) program designed to treat the mediational deficiencies of impulsive children (Meichenbaum & Goodman, 1971). The goals of the treatment program were fourfold: (1) to train impulsive children to generate verbal self-commands and respond to them appropriately; (2) to strengthen the mediational properties of children's inner speech in order to bring their behavior under their own verbal control; (3) to overcome any comprehension, production, or mediational deficiencies; and (4) to encourage children to self-reinforce their behavior appropriately (p. 116). The specific procedures employed were designed to replicate the developmental sequence outlined by Luria (1961) and Vygotsky (1962): (1) a model performed a task talking aloud while a child observed; (2) the child performed the same task while the model gave verbal instructions; (3) the child performed the task while instructing him- or herself aloud; (4) the child performed the task while whispering the instructions; and (5) the child performed the task covertly. The self-instructions employed in the program included: (1) questions about the nature and demands of the task, (2) answers to these questions in the form of cognitive rehearsal, (3) self-instructions in the form of self-guidance while performing the task, and (4) self-reinforcement (p. 117). Meichenbaum and Goodman found that their self-instructional training program significantly improved the task performance of impulsive children across a number of measures relative to attentional and control groups.

Encouraged by the results of their initial studies, Meichenbaum and his associates sought to expand and refine SIT. Additional investigations over the course of the next 10 years were designed to examine the ability of SIT to generalize in the treatment of a variety of psychological disorders including schizophrenia, speech anxiety, test anxiety, and phobias (Mahoney, 1974).

The behavioral background of Meichenbaum is evident in the procedural emphasis that SIT places on graduated tasks, cognitive modeling, directed mediational training, and self-reinforcement. However, the goal of this approach is not significantly different from that of Ellis (1962) or Beck (1963), whose approaches developed out of a markedly different orientation to clinical work. SIT provides a basic treatment paradigm that may be modified to suit the special requirements of a particular clinical population. In general, clients are trained in six global skills related to self-instruction: (1) problem definition, (2) problem approach, (3) attention focusing, (4) coping statements, (5) error-correcting options, and (6) self-reinforcement (Kendall & Bemis, 1983). The flexibility of SIT is perhaps one of its most attractive features and not surprisingly, a large literature has accumulated on the utility of SIT for a variety of psychological disorders

(Mahoney, 1974). The commitment of Meichenbaum and his associates to the empirical method is admirable and will likely continue to add breadth to the clinician's store of potential intervention strategies in the future.

SYSTEMATIC RATIONAL RESTRUCTURING

Marvin Goldfried was among the growing number of clinicians in the early 1970s who challenged the adequacy of learning theory and advocated the incorporation of cognitive processes into conceptualizations of human behavior. Like many other behaviorally oriented researchers during this period, he supported the shift in emphasis from discrete situation-specific responses and problem-specific procedures to a focus on coping skills that could be applied across response modalities, situations, and problems (Mahoney, 1974). In 1971, Goldfried proposed that systematic desensitization be conceputalized in terms of a general mediational model in contrast to Wolpe's (1958) counterconditioning model. Goldfried interpreted systematic desensitization as a means of teaching clients a general self-relaxation skill. In attempting to transform desensitization into a more comprehensive coping skills training program, emphasis was placed on four components: (1) the description of the therapeutic rationale in terms of skills training, (2) the use of relaxation as a generalized or multipurpose coping strategy, (3) the use of multiple-theme hierarchies, and (4) training in "relaxing away" scene-induced anxiety as opposed to the traditional method of terminating the imaginal scene at the first indication of subjective distress (Goldfried, 1973).

Goldfried's coping skills orientation eventually led to the development of a technique called systematic rationale restructuring (SRR; Goldfried, Decenteceo, & Weinberg, 1974). This approach represents an integration of Ellis's (1962) rational–emotive therapy within a social learning framework. Thus, SRR assumes that maladaptive cognitions elicit maladaptive emotional and behavioral reactions. However, whereas Ellis emphasizes the irrationality of higher-order beliefs or assumptions, Goldfried places greater emphasis on the functionality of conscious self-statements (Kendal & Bemis, 1983). Borrowing from the work of Dollard and Miller (1950) on the development of symbolic thinking processes, Goldfried (Goldfried & Sobocinski, 1975) suggested that early social learning experiences teach individuals to label situations in different ways. Emotional reactions may be understood as responses to the way individuals label situations as opposed to responses to situations. The extent to which individuals inappropriately distinguish situational cues as personally threatening will determine their subsequent maladaptive emotional and behavioral responses. Goldfried assumes that individuals can acquire more effective coping repertoires by learning to modify the maladaptive cognitive sets that are engaged automatically when faced with anxiety-provoking situations. Thus, the goal of SRR is to train clients to perceive situational cues more accurately.

In addition to modifying the confrontational nature of rational–emotive techniques, Goldfried (1979) sought to systematize Ellis's therapeutic procedures and to facilitate empirical investigations concerning their efficacy. Thus, the implementation of SRR is divided into five discrete stages: (1) exposure to anxiety-provoking situations using imaginal presentation or role-playing, (2) self-evaluation of subjective anxiety level, (3) monitoring anxiety-provoking cognitions, (4) rational reevaluation of these maladaptive cognitions, and (5) observing one's subjective anxiety level following the rational reevaluation. Techniques utilized in therapy include relaxation methods, behavioral rehearsal, *in vivo* assignments, modeling, and bibliotherapy (Goldfried & Davison, 1976). As a coping-skills approach, the ultimate goal of SRR is to provide clients with the personal resources to cope independently with future life stresses.

Systematic rational restructuring was introduced during a period when a variety of coping-skills training approaches were being designed and tested by behavioral researchers. Some of these multicomponent treatment packages have received more research attention than others and many are similar in terms of their underlying rationale and therapeutic strategies. Unfortunately, SRR has not been investigated as extensively as other coping-skills training programs. Nevertheless, it represents one of the first attempts to make operational a self-control treatment model designed to enhance treatment generalization through the use of training in the general coping skills that we believed applicable in a variety of stress-provoking situations.

ANXIETY-MANAGEMENT TRAINING

Suinn and Richardson's (1971) anxiety-management training (AMT) program was introduced around the same time that Goldfried (1971) proposed a reconceptualization of systematic desensitization. In their original article, Suinn and Richardson discussed three shortcomings of desensitization procedures: (1) the time-consuming nature of constructing anxiety hierarchies for each problem presented by clients undergoing treatment, (2) the relatively long duration of treatment, and (3) the absence of generalized coping strategies to prepare clients to deal effectively with future problems. These suggested limitations of conventional systematic desensitization techniques led to the development of a nonspecific approach for anxiety control that was designed to provide clients with a short-term coping-skill training program applicable to a wide range of problem areas.

The theory underlying AMT assumes that anxiety is an acquired drive that has stimulus generalization properties. Autonomic responses associated with anxiety act as cues that facilitate and maintain avoidance behavior. Clients can be conditioned to respond to these discriminative cues with responses that eliminate the anxiety through the process of reciprocal inhibition. Thus, the goal of AMT is to teach clients to use relaxation and competency skills in order to control their feelings of anxiety.

AMT emphasizes the elimination of anxiety without specific attention to the particular anxiety-provoking stimulus. In the first stage of treatment, clients receive training in deep muscle relaxation. Following this, clients are instructed to visualize anxiety-arousing scenes and then practice their relaxation skills and/or imagine responding to stimuli in a competent fashion (Suinn, 1972). A variety of anxiety-arousing scenes that may be unrelated to clients' specific problems are incorporated into the treatment program.

Empirical data regarding AMT are almost nonexistent. Only one experimental study has examined the efficacy of this coping strategy (Richardson & Suinn, 1973). Unfortunately, a matched control group was not included in the design, making the data difficult to interpret. Given the notable lack of research, anxiety management training has remained a rather obscure cognitive-behavioral technique.

STRESS INOCULATION TRAINING

Like many of his contemporaries in the 1970s, Meichenbaum developed an interest in the multicomponent coping-skills approach as a potentially effective therapeutic strategy. Following a review of the stress literature, Meichenbaum, Turk, and Burstein (1975) suggested several guidelines for the development of a coping-skills treatment program which were later incorporated into Meichenbaum's 1977 volume:

1. Coping devices are complex and need to be flexible. . . . [A]ny coping-skills training approach should be flexible enough to incorporate a variety of cognitive and behavioral strategies that can be differentially employed.
2. [It is necessary] for any training technique to be sensitive to individual differences, cultural differences, and situational differences.
3. Skills training should encourage the utilization of available information and the incorporation of potentially threatening events into cognitive plans. To be effective, information should stimulate mental rehearsal . . . which may "short circuit" the experience of stress or reduce its after-effects.
4. Actual exposure during training to less threatening events has a beneficial effect (Meichenbaum, 1977, pp. 148–149).

In particular, Meichenbaum emphasized the systematic acquisition of coping skills, highlighting the importance of learning to cope with small, manageable amounts of stress as a means of facilitating treatment maintenance and generalization. This emphasis is consistent with the immunization model outlined by Orne (1965):

One way of enabling an individual to become resistant to stress is to allow him to have appropriate prior experience with the stimulus involved. The biological notion of immunization provides such a model. If an individual is given the opportunity to deal with a stimulus that is mildly stressful and he is able to do so successfully (mastering it in a psychological sense) he will tend to be able to tolerate a similar stimulus of somewhat greater intensity in the future . . . It would seem that one can markedly affect an individual's tolerance of stress by manipulating his beliefs about his performance in the situation . . . and his feeling that he can control his own behavior (pp. 315-316).

Stress inoculation training is the behavioral analogue of Orne's immunization model and incorporates the guidelines that Meichenbaum and his associates gleaned from their review of the stress literature. The rationale underlying this approach assumes that clients who learn ways of coping with mild levels of stress are "inoculated" against uncontrollable levels of stress.

Meichenbaum and Cameron (1973) made operational the theory of stress inoculation training in terms of three stages. The first stage is an educational one, designed to provide the client with a conceptual understanding of the nature of stressful reactions (didactic training). The second stage involves the presentation of a number of behavioral and cognitive coping skills including relaxation exercises, coping self-statements, and self-reinforcement. In the final stage of application training, the client is exposed to a variety of stressors in order to practice his or her newly acquired coping skills (behavioral rehearsal).

Since the introduction of stress-inoculation training in 1973, researchers have employed this approach in the treatment of a variety of disorders including anxiety, anger, and pain (Meichenbaum & Jaremko, 1983, Meichenbaum & Turk, 1976). However, as Jaremko (1979) has observed, investigations into stress-inoculation training have introduced a considerable degree of procedural variation. In this regard, Jaremko has proposed a revised procedural model that is intended to add greater uniformity to the current research as well as increase the "usability" of this approach as a therapeutic procedure. As in the case with other multicomponent treatment programs, there remains a need for further empirical investigations to demonstrate the utility of the individual treatment components employed in stress inoculation training. Moreover, the validity of the underlying rationale requires additional research. Nonetheless, stress-inoculation training is regarded by many as a promising therapeutic approach for the development of generalized coping skills.

PROBLEM-SOLVING THERAPY

In 1971, D'Zurilla and Goldfried published an article that proposed the application of problem-solving theory and research in behavior modification. With the goal of facilitating "generalized" behavior change, D'Zurilla and Goldfried conceptualized problem-solving therapy as a form of self-control training, emphasizing the importance of training the client to function as his or her own therapist. The rationale underlying this approach is summarized by its authors as follows:

ineffectiveness in coping with problematic situations, along with its personal and social consequences, is often a necessary and sufficient condition for an emotional or behavior disorder requiring psychological treatment; . . . general effectiveness may be most efficiently facilitated by training individuals in general procedures or skills which would allow them to deal independently with the critical problematic situations that confront them in day-to-day living (p. 109).

According to D'Zurilla and Goldfried, problem-solving refers to an overt or cognitive process that makes available a variety of effective response alternatives for coping with a problem situation and increases the likelihood of selecting the most effective response available (p. 108). Drawing upon a large body of research regarding the fundamental operations involved in effective problem solving, D'Zurilla and Goldfried identified five overlapping stages as representative of the problem-solving process: (1) general orientation or "set," (2) problem definition and formulation, (3) generation of alternatives, (4) decision making, and (5) verification. Training in problem solving involves teaching clients these basic skills and guiding their application in actual problem situations.

Spivack and Shure (1974) initiated the systematic investigation into the efficacy of a problem-solving treatment approach. The interpersonal cognitive problem-solving (ICPS) model proposed by these researchers involves essentially the same skills outlined by D'Zurilla and Goldfried (1971). According to Spivack, Platt, and Shure (1976), effective interpersonal problem solving involves: (1) the ability to recognize the range of possible problem situations in the social environment, (2) the ability to generate multiple, alternative solutions to interpersonal problems, (3) the ability to plan a series of steps necessary to achieve a given goal, (4) the ability to foresee the short-term and long-term consequences of a given alternative, and (5) the ability to identify the motivational elements related to one's actions and those of others. ICPS training has been most commonly used with preschoolers and emotionally disturbed children. In general, ICPS training programs include discussion and structured activities involving hypothetical and actual interpersonal problem situations designed to teach problem-solving skills. Despite numerous methodological problems, the work of Spivack and his colleagues has resulted in the development of a growing interest in the potential of problem-solving therapies.

D'Zurilla and Nezu (1982) have reviewed the recent applications of D'Zurilla and Goldfried's (1971) original model of problem solving in adult clinical populations. Like Spivack and Shure (1974), they conclude that the available data support the existence of a relation between problem-solving skills and psychopathology. However, the evidence regarding the importance of the individual problem-solving components is less clear. Nonetheless, the broadening of clinical intervention objectives as recommended by D'Zurilla and Goldfried has stimulated the development of a number of problem-solving therapies (D'Zurilla, Chapter 3, this volume; Mahoney & Arnkoff, 1978). It is likely that the flexibility and pragmatism of these approaches will continue to attract the attention of clinicians in search of comprehensive treatment programs.

PERSONAL SCIENCE

Following a comprehensive review of traditional learning theory and its associated therapies, Mahoney (1974) concluded that the emergence of mediational models and broad-spectrum clinical intervention strategies represented a positive shift toward meeting the therapeutic objectives of generalization and maintenance. Like D'Zurilla and Goldfried (1971), Mahoney recommended the application of empirical skills of problem solving to personal problems. The personal science paradigm developed by Mahoney views emotional distress as the consequence of life crises and/or shortcomings in the development or utilization of coping skills. As a treatment model, this approach is aimed at teaching clients the skills employed by researchers in approaching and resolving problem situations. Therapy is conceptualized as an apprenticeship process designed to teach clients to approach their problems as personal scientists. At the core of the personal science paradigm is a strong emphasis on the importance of an active, coping self-theory. Thus, the client plays an active and collaborative role in therapy and is viewed as a "responsible agent of self-control" (Mahoney, 1977, p. 352).

The personal science approach to treatment consists of seven basic components that follow in an orderly sequence and are represented by the mnemonic SCIENCE. According to Mahoney (1977), these components constitute the fundamental problem-solving skills:

S   Specify general problem area
C   Collect data
I   Identify patterns or sources
E   Examine options
N   Narrow and experiment
C   Compare data
E   Extend, revise, and replace

The purpose of this seven-step process is to organize a set of learning experiences that will maximize opportunities for the client to develop coping skills that are relevant to the immediate problem situation as well as to future problems. In order to teach the client this empirical approach to problem solving, the therapist may incorporate a variety of clinical techniques including stimulus control, motivational incentives, task gradation, observational learning, and active practice. The final stages of therapy are designed to gradually shift increasing amounts of responsibility and control to the client so that generalization and maintenance of treatment gains are facilitated.

Despite the intuitive appeal of Mahoney's personal science paradigm, empirical data regarding the utility of this approach is nonexistent. It appears that other problem-solving therapies such as Spivack and Shure's (1974) interpersonal cognitive problem-solving approach have generated considerably more research interest. Thus, the status of the personal science paradigm remains unknown and appears headed for obscurity unless empirical data demonstrating its validity are forthcoming.

SELF-CONTROL THERAPY

The trend toward developing treatment models that promoted a philosophy of self-control influenced Rehm's (1977) development of a self-control model of depression. The work of Rehm was guided, to a great extent, by the general model of self-regulation proposed by Kanfer (1970, 1971) that explains the persistence of certain behaviors in the absence of reinforcement in terms of a closed loop feedback system of adaptive self-control. Kanfer suggested that three interconnected processes are involved in self-regulation: self-monitoring, self-evaluation, and self-reinforcement. Rehm adapted this model in order to explain the multivariate nature of depressive symptomatology. Thus, symptoms of depression are conceptualized as the reflection or consequence of one or some combination of six deficits in self-control behavior. In the self-monitoring phase, potential deficits include the selective monitoring of negative events and the selective monitoring of immediate versus delayed consequences of behavior. Self-evaluative deficits consist of stringent self-evaluative criteria and inaccurate attributions of responsibility. In the third phase, self-reinforcement, deficits involving insufficient self-reward and excessive self-punishment may be observed in depressed individuals. According to Rehm (1981), the varied symptom profile in clinical depression is a function of different subsets of these deficits. Furthermore, these deficits may exist in varying degrees across individuals and can be observed prior to depressive episodes. The occurrence of a depressive episode is postulated to be a joint function of the degree of stress experienced and the self-control skills available for coping with the stressful situation.

Fuchs and Rehm (1977) developed the original treatment package based on Rehm's (1977) model of depression. Self-control therapy involves the sequential application of Kanfer's (1970, 1971) three self-regulatory processes as adapted by Rehm. "The assumption is that each may be conceptualized as a therapy module and that self-evaluation builds on self-monitoring, and that self-reinforcement builds on self-evaluation" (O'Hara & Rehm, 1983, p. 69). Each of the six self-control deficits is described over the course of treatment with an emphasis on how a particular deficit is causally related to depression and what can be done to remedy the deficit. A variety of clinical strategies are employed to teach clients self-control skills including therapist-directed group discussion, overt and covert reinforcement, behavioral assignments, self-monitoring, and modeling.

The appeal of Rehm's (1977) self-control model lies in its integration of a range of cognitive and behavioral variables on which other models of depression focus exclusively. In addition, Rehm's framework provides a logical analysis of the manner in which each of the various symptoms of depression are associated with a particular aspect of self-control. From a broader perspective, this self-control model appears to have potential as a general model of psychopathology. Unfortunately, the ability of Rehm's theoretical approach to generalize to other clinical disorders has not been researched. However, efforts to develop a comprehensive self-control therapy would seem a worthwhile endeavor.

STRUCTURAL PSYCHOTHERAPY

In a recent book entitled *Cognitive Processes and Emotional Disorders*, Guidano and Liotti (1983) introduced a structural approach to psychotherapy. This comprehensive volume represents the culmination of 10 years of clinical research and experience that began with the observation of a significant discrepancy between the demonstrated efficacy of behavioral techniques and the limited explanatory potential of learning theory. Following an extensive study of numerous literatures, including behavior therapy, social learning theory, evolutionary epistemology, cognitive psychology, psychodynamic theory, and cognitive therapy, Guidano and Liotti concluded that in order to understand the full complexity of emotional disorder and subsequently to develop an adequate model of psychotherapy, an appreciation of the development and the active role of an individual's knowledge of self and the world is critical. "only a consideration of the structure within which the single elements of an individual's knowledge are placed allows us to understand how these elements rule and coordinate that individual's emotions and actions" (p. 34).

Guidano and Liotti's structural model of cognitive dysfunction borrows heavily from Bowlby's (1977) attachment theory. They suggest that relationships with significant others (i.e., parents) determine the development of a child's self-image and provide continuous confirmation and reinforcement of this self-image. The definition of self is assumed to coordinate and integrate cognitive growth and emotional differentiation. If the self-concept is distorted or rigid, the individual is unable to assimilate life experiences effectively. This, in turn, leads to maladjustment and subsequent emotional distress, the final product being cognitive dysfunction. Different abnormal patterns of attachment are assumed to correspond to different clinical syndromes.

Problem behaviors are believed to be the consequence of an individual's cognitive organization (i.e., the causal theories, basic assumptions, and tacit rules of inference that determine thought content). The patient is perceived as struggling to maintain a particular dysfunctional cognitive organization in the face of a continuously challenging environment. Thus, the ultimate goal of psychotherapy is to modify these cognitive structures. In order for therapy to be effective, Guidano and Liotti propose that the therapist begin by identifying and modifying superficial cognitive structures that will lead in turn to the identification and modification of deeper cognitive structures (i.e., the implicit causal theories held by the patient). This therapeutic strategy bears close resemblance to Beck's (Beck *et al.*, 1979) cognitive therapy that begins with the assessment of the patient's automatic thoughts and subsequently leads to the specification of basic assumptions underlying these thoughts.

In discussing psychotherapy as a strategic process, Guidano and Liotti refer to the analogy between the empirical problem-solving approach of the scientist and that of the patient. "Therapists should enable patients to disengage themselves from certain engrained beliefs and judgments, and to consider them as hypotheses and theories, subject to disproof, confirmation, and logical challenge" (p. 144). This analogy is similar to that drawn by Mahoney (1977) in his personal science approach. A variety of behavioral experiments and cognitive techniques compose the therapeutic armory from which the therapist selects a range of suitable tactics for a particular patient. They include such techniques as imaginal flooding, systematic desensitization, assertiveness training, coping-skills training, problem-solving procedures, and rational restructuring. The final stage of the therapeutic process is conceptualized in terms of a "personal revolution" (Mahoney, 1980) during which the patient, having rejected his or her old view of self and the world, is in a state of transformation and is establishing a new, more adaptive belief system.

Those who are familiar with the work of Beck *et al.*, (1979), Ellis (1962), Mahoney (1977), and other advocates of the congitive-behavioral perspective will recognize the many parallels between their writings and the structural approach of Guidano and Liotti. *Cognitive Processes and Emotional Disorders* represents the first English presentation of Guidano and Liotti's work, thus the jury is still out with regard to the utility of their structural model. The task of testing out the validity of structural psychotherapy and its underlying theory will be as comprehensive as the authors' presentation of it, however, the challenge will likely be a profitable one.

SIMILARITY AND DIVERSITY IN
THE COGNITIVE-BEHAVIORAL THERAPIES

As the above chronology of cognitive-behavioral models of psychopathology and therapy suggest, there are a large number of approaches that can be identified as cognitive-behavioral in nature. At the very basis these approaches all share the three fundamental assumptions discussed earlier in this chapter related to the mediational position. Briefly stated, the mediational position is that cognitive activity mediates the responses the individual has to his or her environment, and to some extent dictates the degree of adjustment or maladjustment of the individual. As a direct result of the mediational assumption, the cognitive-behavioral therapies share a belief that therapeutic change can be effected through an alteration of idiosyncratic, dysfunctional modes of thinking. Additionally, due to the behavioral heritage, many of the cognitive-behavioral methods draw upon behavioral principles and techniques in the conduct of therapy, and many of the cognitive-behavioral models rely to some extent upon behavioral assessment of change to document therapeutic progress.

Beyond the above central assumptions regarding the mediated nature of therapeutic change, there are a number of commonalities that occur between limited sets of cognitive-behavioral therapies. Kendall and Kriss (1983), for example, have suggested that five dimensions can be employed to characterize cognitive-behavioral therapies: the theoretical orientation of the therapeutic approach and the theoretical target of change, various aspects of the client–therapist relationship, the cognitive target for change, the type of evidence used for cognitive assessment, and the degree of emphasis on self-control on the part of the client. The scheme that they have proposed is a useful one for the identification of both similarities and differences between the various cognitive-behavioral therapies. Notwithstanding the coverage of the topic by Kendall and Kriss (1983), it also appears that other commonalities between the approaches that are not theoretically central can be identified. For example, one commonality among the various cognitive-behavioral therapies is their time-limited nature. In clear distinction from longer term psychoanalytic therapy, cognitive-behavioral therapies attempt to effect change rapidly, and often with specific pre-set lengths of therapeutic contact. Related to the time-limited nature of cognitive-behavior therapy is the fact that cognitive-behavior therapy is usually also limited in the target of change. There are numerous examples of the applications of cognitive-behavior therapy (see for example, Miller & Berman, 1983). The point, however, is that almost all of the applications of this general therapeutic approach are to specific problems. While this commonality is in no way a criticism of the various cognitive-behavioral therapies, the problem-focused nature of cognitive-behavioral interventions does in part explain the time limitations that are commonly set in these approaches to therapy. Indeed, the utilization of these therapies for specific disorders and problems is a direct heritage from the behavior therapy emphasis on the collection of outcome data, and the focus on the remediation of specific, predefined problems. Thus, rather than being a limitation of cognitive-behavioral therapies, the application of these therapies to specific problems serves as a further demonstration of the continuing desire for the complete documentation of therapeutic effects. Also, the focus on specific problems allows for the experimental determination of the therapeutic limits of these various approaches, and potentially to the future ability of therapists to select the most efficacious therapy for the patient problem they are asked to assist.

A third commonality between the various cognitive-behavioral approaches is the belief that the client is the architect of their own misfortune, and that they therefore have control over their thought and action. This assumption is clearly reflected in the type of patient problems that have been identified for cognitive-behavioral interventions. The most frequently cited appropriate problems include the "neurotic" conditions (e.g., anxiety, depression, and anger problems), self-control problems (e.g., overeating, behavioral management difficulties, child dysfunction), and general problem-solving abilities. These types of problems all make the assumption of patient control tenable. One must question, of course, whether this assumption therefore makes unlikely the development of cognitive-behavioral interventions in situations where the assumption of patient control is untenable. For example, does the fact that schizophrenic patients do not have the type of cognitive and behavioral control that can be assumed in other patients mean that these interventions are not appropriate for schizophrenic populations? Further research is required to test the limits of use for a number of these therapies.

Related to the assumption of patient control is another element shared by a number of the cognitive-behavioral therapies. This commonality has to do with the fact that many of the cognitive-behavioral therapies are by nature either explicitly or implicitly educative. Many of the therapeutic approaches include the explication of the therapeutic model to the patient, and many also involve the explication of the rationale for any interventions that are undertaken. This type of educative interaction between the therapist and patient is one facet that the various cognitive-behavioral therapies share, and which again set them apart from other schools of therapy. Compare traditional psychoanalytic therapy, in which the therapist offers interpretations to the client (Blanck, 1976; Kohut, 1971), or strategic family therapy, in which the therapist may even dictate that the client do the opposite of what the therapeutic goal is in a "paradoxical" intervention (Haley, 1976 Minuchin & Fishman, 1981). Directly related to the educative process often seen in cognitive-behavioral therapies is the implicit goal that many cognitive-behavioral therapists set, which is that the patient will not only overcome the referral problem during the course of therapy, but that they will also learn something about the process of therapy. In the event that the patient suffers a recurrence of their problem they will therefore have some therapeutic skills to deal with the problem themselves. In some of the cognitive-behavioral therapies the desire to have patients learn about the process of therapy is taken to its logical conclusion, so that time is spent in therapy reviewing the therapeutic concepts and skills that the patient has learned over the course of therapy, and that they may later employ in a maintenance or preventive manner (Beck *et al.*, 1979; DeRubeis & Beck, Chapter 7, this volume; D'Zurilla & Goldfried, 1971; Mahoney, 1977).

Up to this point in this review, it may appear that cognitive-behavioral therapies have so many commonalities that distinctions between them are more illusory than real. In fact, however, Kendall and Kriss (1983) have provided an excellent framework for the identification of differences between the specific approaches. Further, even the brief overview of the various cognitive-behavioral therapies provided in this chapter demonstrates a very real diversity of models and techniques that have been developed by cognitive-behavioral therapists. It is thus no more appropriate to state that there is really one cognitive-behavioral approach than it is to state that there is one monolithic psychoanalytic therapy. As the chapters in this volume demonstrate, there are many different facets of the cognition-behavioral processes that may be attended to, identified, and altered within the overarching definition of the cognitive-behavioral approach. The diversity of the cognitive-behavioral therapies, while undeniably present, do argue for further definitional and technical discussion between the proponents of the various approaches. There are at least two areas where further theory and research are required to help to further differentiate the different therapies that are labeled as "cognitive-behavioral." These areas are the targets of therapeutic change and the modality specificity of intervention techniques.

Although cognitive-behavioral therapies share the mediational approach and therefore all target "cognitions" for change, the variety of different specific labels and descriptions of cognitions seen in the cognitive-behavioral literature is truly overwhelming. A partial list of the various terms that have applied to cognitive constructs and processes includes: cognitions, thoughts, beliefs, attitudes, ideas, assumptions, rules for living, self-statements, cognitive distortions, expectancies, notions, ideas, stream of consciousness, ideation, private meanings, illusions, self-efficacy predictions, cognitive prototypes and schemas. Adding further to the confusion is that a number of the above constructs have been developed in a purely clinical context (e.g., self-efficacy predictions) and therefore have relatively clear definitions, but many others are terms also employed in other areas of psychology. Where terms are shared across disciplines of psychology the application may not be identical, and semantic confusion may be the end result. The use of the schema notion, for example, is fraught with potential difficulty, since the concept was first developed within cognitive psychology (Neisser, 1967), later applied to social cognition (Markus, 1977), and now has been applied to clinical problems (Dobson, 1986; Goldfried & Robins, 1983; Turk & Speers, 1983). Even a quick reading of the various applications of the term reveals that while the essence of the schema concept is intact throughout its various uses, there are several idiosyncratic applications suggested by various authors. Thus, while the elaboration of various specific cognitive processes and constructs is useful, it is important for theorists to define constructs precisely, and for others in the field to subscribe to these definitions. This increase in precision would help to clarify the terrain of cognitive-behavioral theory, and also may assist the efforts of researchers whose interest is cognitive assessment (Meichenbaum & Cameron, 1981). In this latter regard, it is clear that cognitive assessment is severely hampered by a lack of clear definitions of cognitive phenomena (e.g., Genest & Turk, 1981; Glass & Merluzzi, 1981; Shaw & Dobson, 1981), and it is equally clear that further efforts in the area of cognitive assessment are required to be able to fully document the nature and process of change during cognitive-behavioral therapy (Kendall & Bemis, 1983; Segal & Shaw, Chapter 2, this volume; Sutton-Simon, 1981).

A second major area where the further delineation of different approaches to cognitive-behavior therapy may be possible is with respect to modality-specific techniques. Cognitive-behavioral therapists have been extremely innovative in the development of techniques, and have thereby added to the clinical armamentareum in numerous ways. In doing so, however, it is not always clear what manner of technique is being developed (i.e., whether it is a generic and nonspecific technique, or is a modality-specific method). While it may be reasonably argued that such distinctions are not important at a practical level, it is important from a theoretical perspective to know what limits different theorists place upon their models of therapy. Process research that actually records and analyzes therapeutic interventions espoused by various therapeutic models, while often suggested (DeRubeis, Hollon, Evans, & Bemis, 1982; Kendall & Bemis, 1983; Mahoney & Arnkoff, 1978), has not yet become well-advanced. This type of research has the potential of adding greatly to our knowledge of the extent to which different descriptions of therapies translate themselves in different clinical practice. Finally, another area of research that may be profitably expanded is that which investigates the applications of various modes of cognitive-behavioral therapy to different presenting problems. By contrasting different approaches in the context of different problems, it may become possible to start to suggest preferred treatment methods for specific patient problems. This matching of problems to therapies would not only represent a practical advantage over current clinical practice, but would also enable a better understanding of the mechanisms of change within each type of intervention, and within different types of patient problems.

Clearly, the field of cognitive-behavior therapy has developed dramatically since its inception in the 1960s and 1970s. There are now a number of identifiable models that are of a cognitive-behavioral nature, and the demonstrated efficacy of these methods is as good as the behavioral forebears (Berman, Miller, & Massman, 1985; Miller & Berman, 1983), if not more so (Shapiro & Shapiro, 1982). The continuing emphasis on the development of an adequate data base has enabled cognitive-behavioral theorists and therapists to make steady progress in research and practice, and can be expected to lead to continued improvements in the future. Some of the most pressing areas that require further conceptualization and research include the definition of cognitive phenomena (both at construct and process levels), and the procedural overlap among the variety of cognitive-behavioral therapies that currently exist. The next decade is likely to see considerable advances in the field.

ACKNOWLEDGMENT

Thanks are extended to D. Dobson for reviewing an earlier draft of this chapter and to E. McCririck for assistance in manuscript preparation.

REFERENCES

Bandura, A. (1965). Vicarious processes: A case of no-trial learning. In L. Berkowitz (Ed.), *Advances in experimental social psychology* (Vol. 2). New York: Academic Press.

Bandura, A. (1971). Vicarious and self-reinforcement processes. In R. Glaser (Ed.), *The nature of reinforcement*. New York: Academic Press.

Bandura, A. (1977). Self-efficacy: Toward a unifying theory of behavioral change. *Psychological Review, 84,* 191–215.

Beck, A. T. (1963). Thinking and depression. I. Idiosyncratic content and cognitive distortions. *Archives of General Psychiatry, 9,* 36–46.

Beck, A. T. (1967). *Depression: Causes and treatment.* Philadelphia: University of Pennsylvania Press.

Beck, A. T. (1970). Cognitive therapy: Nature and relation to behavior therapy. *Behavior Therapy, 1,* 184–200.

Beck, A. T. (1971). Cognition, affect, and psychopathology. *Archives of General Psychiatry, 24,* 495–500.

Beck, A. T. (1976). *Cognitive therapy and the emotional disorders.* New York: International Universities Press.

Beck, A. T., & Emery, G. (1985). *Anxiety disorders and phobias: A cognitive perspective.* New York: Basic Books.

Beck, A. T., Rush, A. J., Shaw, B. F., & Emery, G. (1979). *Cognitive therapy of depression.* New York: Guilford.

Berman, J. S., Miller, R. C., & Massman, P. J. (1985). Cognitive therapy versus systematic desensitization: Is one treatment superior? *Psychological Bulletin, 97,* 451–461.

Blackburn, I., Bishop, S., Glen, I., Whalley, L., & Christie, J. (1981). The efficacy of cognitive therapy in depression: A treatment trial using cognitive therapy and pharmacotherapy, each alone and in combination. *British Journal of Psychiatry, 139*, 181–189.

Blanck, G. (1976). Psychoanalytic technique. In B. J. Wolman (Ed.), *The therapist's handbook*. New York: Van Nostrand Reinhold.

Bowlby, J. (1977). The making and breaking of affectional bonds: I. Etiology and psychopathology in the light of attachment theory. *British Journal of Psychiatry, 130*, 201–210.

Breger, L., & McGaugh, J. L. (1965). Critique and reformulation of "learning-theory" approaches to psychotherapy and neurosis. *Psychological Bulletin, 63*, 338–358.

Cautela, J. R. (1967). Covert sensitization. *Psychological Reports, 20*, 459–468.

Cautela, J. R. (1969). Behavior therapy and self-control: Techniques and implications. In C. M. Franks (Ed.), *Behavior therapy: Appraisal and status*. New York: McGraw-Hill.

DeRubeis, R., Hollon, S. D., Evans, M., & Bemis, K. (1982). Can psychotherapies be discriminated? A systematic investigation of cognitive therapy and interpersonal therapy. *Journal of Consulting and Clinical Psychology, 50*, 744–756.

Dobson, K. S. (1986). The self-schema in depression. In L. M. Hartman & K. R. Blankstein (Eds.), *Perception of self in emotional disorders and psychotherapy*. New York: Plenum.

Dollard, J., & Miller, N. E. (1950). *Personality and psychotherapy*. New York: McGraw-Hill.

Dush, D. M., Hirt, M. L., & Schroeder, H. (1983). Self-statement modification with adults: A meta-analysis. *Psychological Bulletin, 94*, 408–422.

D'Zurilla, T. J., & Goldfried, M. R. (1971). Problem-solving and behavior modification. *Journal of Abnormal Psychology, 78*, 107–126.

D'Zurilla, T. J., & Nezu, A. (1982). social problem solving in adults. In A. C. Kendall (Ed.), *Advances in cognitive-behavioral research and therapy* (Vol. 1). New York: Academic Press.

Elkin, I., Parloff, M. B., Hadley, S. W., & Autry, J. H. (1985). NIMH Treatment of Depression Collaborative Research Program: Background and research plan. *Archives of General Psychiatry, 42*, 305–316.

Ellis, A. (1962). *Reason and emotion in psychotherapy*. New York: Stuart.

Ellis, A. (1970). *The essence of rational psychotherapy: A comprehensive approach to treatment*. New York: Institute for Rational Living.

Ellis, A. (1973). *Humanistic psychotherapy*. New York: McGraw-Hill.

Ellis, A. (1979a). The basic clinical theory of rational emotive therapy. In A. Ellis & M. M. Whitelay (Eds.), *Theoretical and empirical foundations of rational-emotive therapy*. Monterey, CA: Brooks/Cole.

Ellis, A. (1979b). The practice of rational emotive therapy. In A. Ellis & J. M. Whiteley (Eds.), *Theoretical and empirical foundations of rational-emotive therapy*. Monterey, CA: Brooks/Cole.

Ellis, A. (1980). Rational–emotive therapy and cognitive-behavior therapy: Similarities and differences. *Cognitive Research and Therapy, 4*, 325–340.

Eysenck, H. (1969). *The effects of psychotherapy*. New York: Science House.

Ferster, C. G. (1974). Behavior approaches to depression. In R. J. Friedman & M. M. Katz (Ed.), *The psychology of depression: Contemporary theory and research*. New York: Wiley.

Fuchs, C. Z., & Rehm, L. P. (1977). A self-control behavior therapy program for depression. *Journal of Consulting and Clinical Psychology, 45*, 206–215.

Genest, M., & Turk, D. C. (1981). Think aloud approaches to cognitive assessment. In T. Merluzzi, C. R. Glass, & M. Genest (Eds.), *Cognitive assessment*. New York: Guilford.

Glass, C., & Merluzzi, T. (1981). Cognitive assessment of social-evaluative anxiety. In T. Merluzzi, C. R. Glass, & M. Genest (Eds.), *Cognitive assessment*. New York: Guilford.

Goldfried, M. R. (1971). Systematic desensitization as training in self-control. *Journal of Consulting and Clinical Psychology, 37*, 228–234.

Goldfried, M. R. (1973). Reduction of generalized anxiety through a variant of systematic desensitization. In M. R. Goldfreid, & M. Merbaum (Eds.), *Behavior change through self-control.* New York: Holt, Rinehart & Winston.

Goldfried, M. R. (1979). Anxiety reduction through cognitive-behavioral intervention. In P. C. Kendall & S. D. Hollon (Eds.), *Cognitive-behavioral interventions: Theory, research, and procedures.* New York: Academic Press.

Goldfried, M. R., & Davison, G. C. (1976). *Clinical behavior therapy.* New York: Holt, Rinehart & Winston.

Goldfried, M. R., Decenteceo, E. T., & Weinberg, L. (1974). Systematic rational restructuring as a self-control technique. *Behavior Therapy, 5,* 247–254.

Goldfried, M. R., & Merbaum, M. (Eds.). (1973). *Behavior change through self-control.* New York: Holt, Rinehart & Winston.

Goldfried, M. R., & Robins, C. (1983). Self-schema, cognitive bias, and the processing of therapeutic experiences. In P. C. Kendall (Ed.), *Advances in cognitive-behavioral research and therapy* (Vol. 2). New York: Academic Press.

Goldfried, M. R., & Sobocinski, D. (1975). Effect of irrational beliefs on emotional arousal. *Journal of Consulting and Clinical Psychology, 43,* 504–510.

Greenberg, L., & Safran, J. (1984). Integrating affect and cognition: A perspective on the process of therapeutic change. *Cognitive Therapy and Research, 8,* 559–578.

Guidano, V. F., & Liotti, G. (1983). *Cognitive pocesses and emotional disorders: A structural approach to psychotherapy.* New York: Guilford.

Haley, J. (1976). *Problem solving therapy.* San Francisco: Jossey-Bass.

Hamilton, V. (1979). An information processing approach to neurotic anxiety and the schizophrenias. In V. Hamilton & D. M. Warburton (Eds.), *Human stress and cognition: An information processing approach.* Chichester: Wiley.

Hamilton, V. (1980). An information processing analysis of environmental stress and life crises. In I. G. Sarason & C. D. Spielberger (Eds.), *Stress and anxiety* (Vol. 7). Washington, DC: Hemisphere.

Hollon, S. D., & Beck, A. T. (1979). Cognitive therapy of depression. In P. C. Kendall & S. D. Hollon (Eds.), *Cognitive-behavioral interventions.* New York: Academic Press.

Hollon, S. D., & Kendall, P. C. (1978). Cognitive self-statements in depression: Development of an Automatic Thoughts Questionnaire. *Cognitive Therapy and Research, 4,* 383–395.

Homme, L. E. (1965). Perspectives in psychology: XXIV. Control of coverants, the operants of the mind. *Psychological Reports, 15,* 501–511.

Houston, B. K., & Holmes, D. S. (1974). Effect of avoidant thinking and reappraisal for coping with threat involving temporal uncertainty. *Journal of Personality and Social Psychology, 30,* 382–388.

Janov, A. (1970). *The primal scream.* New York: Dell.

Jaremko, M. E. (1979). A component analysis of stress inoculation: Review and prospectus. *Cognitive Therapy and Research, 3,* 35–48.

Jeffrey, D. B., & Berger, L. H. (1982). A self-environmental systems model and its implications for behavior change. In K. R. Blankstein & J. Polivy (Eds.), *Self-control and self-modification of emotional behavior.* New York: Plenum.

Kanfer, F. H. (1970). Self-regulation: Research issues and speculations. In C. Neuringer & L. L. Michael (Eds.), *Behavior modification in clinical psychology.* New York: Appleton-Century-Crofts.

Kanfer, F. H. (1971). The maintenance of behavior by self-generated stimuli and reinforcement. In A. Jacobs & L. B. Sachs (Eds.), *The psychology of private events: Perspectives on covert response systems.* New York: Academic Press.

Kazdin, A. E. (1978). *History of behavior modification: Experimental foundations of contemporary research.* Baltimore, MD: University Park Press.

Kendall, P. C., & Bemis, K. M. (1983). Thought and action in psychotherapy: The cognitive-behavioral approaches. In M. Hersen, A. E. Kazdin, & A. S. Bellack (Eds.), *The clinical psychology handbook*. New York: Pergamon.

Kendall, P. C., & Kriss, M. R. (1983). Cognitive-behavioral interventions. In C. E. Walker (Ed.), *The handbook of clinical psychology: Theory, research, and practice*. Illinois: Dow Jones-Irwin.

Klerman, G. L., Weissman, M. M., Rounsaville, B., & Chevron, E. (1984). *Interpersonal psychotherapy of depression*. New York: Basic Books.

Kohut, H. (1971). *The analysis of the self*. New York: International Universities Press.

Lazarus, R. S. (1966). *Psychological stress and the coping process*. New York: McGraw-Hill.

Lazarus, R. S., & Alfert, E. (1964). Short-circuiting of threat by experimentally altering cognitive appraisal. *Journal of Abnormal and Social Psychology, 69*, 195–205.

Lazarus, R. S., & Averill, J. R. (1972). Emotion and cognition: With special reference to anxiety. In C. D. Spielberger (Ed.), *Anxiety: Current trends in theory and research* (Vol. 2). New York: Academic Press.

Lazarus, R. S., & Folkman, C. (1984). *Stress, appraisal and coping*. New York: Springer.

Lazarus, R. S., Opton, E. M., Jr., Nomikos, M. S., & Rankin, N. O. (1965). The principle of short-circuitry of threat: Further evidence. *Journal of Personality, 33*, 622–635.

Ledgewidge, B. (1978). Cognitive behavior modification: A step in the wrong direction? *Psychological Bulletin, 85*, 353–375.

Luborsky, L., Singer, G., & Luborsky, L. (1975). Comparative studies of psychotherapies. Is it true that everyone has one and that all must have prizes? *Archives of General Psychiatry, 32*, 995–1008.

Luria, A. R. (1961). *The role of speech in the regulation of normal and abnormal behavior*. New York: Liveright.

Mahoney, M. J. (1974). *Cognition and behavior modification*. Cambridge, MA: Ballinger.

Mahoney, M. J. (1977). Personal science: A cognitive learning therapy. In A. Ellis & R. Grieger (Eds.), *Handbook of rational psychotherapy*. New York: Springer.

Mahoney, M. (1979). A critical analysis of rational–emotive theory and therapy. In A. Ellis & J. M. Whiteley (Eds.), *Theoretical and empirical foundations of rational–emotive therapy*. Monterey, CA: Brooks/Cole.

Mahoney, M. J. (1980). Psychotherapy and the structure of personal revolution. In M. H. Mahoney (Eds.), *Psychotherapy process*. New York: Plenum.

Mahoney, M. J., & Arnkoff, D. B. (1978). Cognitive and self-control therapies. In S. L. Garfield & A. E. Bergin (Eds.), *Handbook of psychotherapy and behavior change: An empirical analysis*. New York: Wiley.

Mahoney, M. J., & Kazdin, A. E. (1979). Cognitive-behavior modification: Misconceptions and premature evacuation. *Psychological Bulletin, 86*, 1044–1049.

Mahoney, M. J., & Thoresen, C. E. (1974). *Self-control: Power to the person*. Monterey, CA: Brooks/Cole.

Markus, H. (1977). Self-schemata and processing information about the self. *Journal of Personality and Social Psychology, 35*, 63–78.

Maultsby, M. C. (1975, June). *The evolution of rational behavior therapy*. Paper presented at the First National Conference of Rational Emotive and Behavior Therapists, Chicago.

Maultsby, M. C. (1984). *Rational behavior therapy*. Englewood Cliffs, NJ: Prentice Hall.

McLean, P., & Hakstain, A. R. (1979). Clinical depression: Comparative efficacy of outpatient treatments. Journal of Consulting and Clinical Psychology, 47, 818–836.

Meichenbaum, D. (1969). The effects of instructions and reinforcement on thinking and language behaviors of schizophrenics. *Behaviour Research and Therapy, 7*, 101–114.

Meichenbaum, D. H. (1973). Cognitive factors in behavior modification: Modifying what clients say to themselves. In C. M. Franks & G. T. Wilson (Eds.), *Annual review of behavior therapy, theory, and practice*. New York: Brunner/Mazel.

Meichenbaum, D. H. (1977). *Cognitive behavior modification*. New York: Plenum.

Meichenbaum, D. H., & Cameron, R. (1973). Training schizophrenics to talk to themselves. *Behavior Therapy, 4*, 515-535.

Meichenbaum, D. H., & Cameron, R. (1981). Issues in cognitive assessment: An overview. In T. Merluzzi, C. R. Glass, & M. Genest (Eds.), *Cognitive assessment.* New York: Guilford.

Meichenbaum, D. H., & Goodman, J. (1971). Training impulsive children to talk to themselves. *Journal of Abnormal Psychology, 77* 127-132.

Meichenbaum, D., & Jaremko, M. (Eds.). (1983). *Stress management and prevention: A cognitive-behavioral perspective.* New York: Plenum.

Meichenbaum, D., Turk, D., & Burstein, S. (1975). The nature of coping with stress. In I. G. Sarason & C. D. Spielberger (Eds.), *Stress and anxiety: Vol. II.* New York: Wiley.

Meichenbaum, D., & Turk, D. (1976). The cognitive-behavioral management of anxiety, anger, and pain. In P. O. Davidson (Eds.), *The behavioral management of anxiety, depression, and pain.* New York: Brunner/Mazel.

Merluzzi, T., Glass, C., & Genest, M. (1981). *Cognitive assessment.* New York: Guilford.

Miller, R. C., & Berman, J. S. (1983). The efficacy of cognitive behavior therapists: A quantitative review of the research evidence. *Psychological Bulletin, 94*, 39-53.

Minuchin, S., & Fishman, H. C. (1981). *Family therapy techniques.* Cambridge, MA: Harvard University Press.

Mischel, W. (1981). A cognitive-social learning approach to assessment. In T. Merluzzi, C. Glass, & M. Genest (Eds.), *Cognitive assessment.* New York: Guilford.

Mischel, W., Ebbesen, E. B., & Zeiss, A. (1972). Cognitive and attentional mechanisms in delay of gratification. *Journal of Personality and Social Psychology, 21*, 204-218.

Monat, A., Averill, J. R., & Lazarus, R. S. (1972). Anticipating stress and coping reactions under various conditions of uncertainty. *Journal of Personality and Social Psychology, 24*, 237-253.

Neisser, U. (1967). *Cognitive psychology.* New York: Appleton-Century-Crofts.

Neufeld, R. W. J. (1976). Evidence of stress as a function of experimentally altered appraisal of stimulus aversiveness and coping efficacy. *Journal of Personality and Social Psychology, 33*, 632-646.

Neufeld, R. W. J., & Mothersill, K. J. (1980). Stress as an irritant of psychopathology. In I. G. Sarason & C. D. Spielberger (Eds.), *Stress and anxiety* (Vol. 7). Washington, DC: Hemisphere.

Nisbett, R. E., & Wilson, T. D. (1977). Telling more than we can know: Verbal reports on mental processes. *Psychological Review, 84*, 231-259.

Nomikos, M. S., Opton, E. M., Jr., Averill, J. R., & Lazarus, R. S. (1968). Surprise versus suspense in the production of stress reaction. *Journal of Personaligy and Social Psychology, 8*, 204-208.

O'Hara, M. W., & Rehm, L. P. (1983). *Self-control group therapy of depression.* New York: Plenum.

Orne, M. (1965). Psychological factors maximizing resistance to stress with special reference to hypnosis. In S. Klausner (Ed.), *The quest for self-control.* New York: Free Press.

Paivio, A. (1971). *Imagery and verbal processes.* New York: Holt, Rinehart, & Winston.

Rachlin, H. (1974). Self-control. *Behaviorism, 2*, 94-107.

Rachman, S. J., & Wilson, G. T. (1971). *The effects of psychological therapy.* Oxford, Pergamon.

Rachman, S. J., & Wilson, G. T. (1980). *The effects of psychological therapy, Second edition.* Oxford: Pergamon.

Rehm, L. (1977). A self-control model of depression. *Behavior Therapy, 8*, 787-804.

Rehm, L. (1981). A self-control therapy program for treatment of depression. In J. F. Clarkin & H. I. Glazer (Eds.), *Depression: Behavioral and directive intervention strategies.* New York: Garland STPM Press.

Richardson, F. C., & Suinn, R. M. (1973). A comparison of traditional systematic desensitization, accelerated massed desensitization, and anxiety management training in the treatment of mathematics anxiety. *Behavior Therapy, 4*, 212–218.

Rush, A. J., Beck, A. T., Kovacs, M., & Hollon, S. D. (1977). Comparative efficacy of cognitive therapy and pharmacotherapy in the treatment of depressed outpatients. *Cognitive Therapy and Research, 1*, 17–37.

Shapiro, D. A., & Shapiro, D. (1982). Meta-analysis of comparative therapy outcome studies: A replication and refinement. *Psychological Bulletin, 92*, 581–604.

Shaw, B. F., & Dobson, K. S. (1981). Cognitive assessment of depression. In T. Merluzzi, C. Glass, & M. Genest (Eds.), *Cognitive assessment.* New York: Guilford.

Simons, A. D., Garfield, S. L., & Murphy, G. E. (1984). The process of change in cognitive therapy and pharmacotherapy of depression: Changes in mood and cognition. *Archives of General Psychiatry, 41*, 45–51.

Spivack, G., Platt, J. J., & Shure, M. B. (1976). *The problem-solving approach to adjustment.* San Francisco: Jossey-Bass.

Spivack, G., & Shure, M. B. (1974). *Social adjustment of young children.* San Francisco: Jossey-Bass.

Stuart, R. B. (1972). Situational versus self-control. In R. D. Rubin, H. Fensterheim, J. D. Henderson, & L. P. Ullmann (Eds), *Advances in behavior therapy.* New York: Academic Press.

Suinn, R. M. (1972). Removing emotional obstacles to learning and performance by visuomotor behavior rehearsal. *Behavior Therapy, 3*, 308–310.

Suinn, R. M., & Richardson, F. (1971). Anxiety management training: A nonspecific behavior therapy program for anxiety control. *Behavior Therapy, 2*, 498–510.

Sutton-Simon, K. (1981). Assessing belief systems: Concepts and strategies. In P. C. Kendall & S. D. Hollon (Eds.), *Assessment strategies for cognitive-behavioral interventions.* New York: Academic Press.

Turk, D. C., & Speers, M. A. (1983). Cognitive schemata and cognitive processes in cognitive-behavioral interventions: Going beyond the information given. In P. C. Kendall (Ed.), *Advances in cognitive-behavioral research and therapy* (Vol. 2). New York: Academic Press.

Vygotsky, L. S. (1962). *Thought and language.* Cambridge, MA: M.I.T. Press.

Wolpe, J. (1958). *Psychotherapy by reciprocal inhibition.* Stanford, CA: Stanford University Press.

Zajonc, R. (1980). Feeling and thinking: Preferences need no inferences. *American Psychologist, 35*, 151–175.

2

COGNITIVE ASSESSMENT: ISSUES AND METHODS

ZINDEL V. SEGAL
BRIAN F. SHAW

There are a thousand thoughts lying within a man that he does not know till he takes up the pen to write.
—Henry Esmond *by William Makepeace Thackery*

While Thackery's advice may have been intended for the earnest young authors of his day, his observation rings equally true to those involved in the present day enterprise of cognitive assessment. As those involved in this field will recognize, however, the complexities associated with the assessment of cognitive processes only start to surface once the thoughts have been written down or collected. This chapter will address a number of conceptual and methodological issues relevant to the practice of cognitive assessment. An attempt will be made to answer questions regarding what is actually being measured by cognitive assessment, what are the potential threats to the accurate and reliable report of cognitive events, and what type of cognitive content we are most interested in knowing about. Finally, with this last question in mind, a resource list of currently available instruments to assess anxiety and depressive disorders will be presented and evaluated.

DEFINITIONAL ISSUES AND LEVEL OF ANALYSIS

Implicit in the thinking behind this chapter is a view of human cognitive functioning derived from an information processing perspective. Within this model, humans are portrayed as actively seeking, selecting, and utilizing information (both internal and external) in the process of constructing the mind's view of reality (Gardner, 1985; Merluzzi, Rudy, & Glass, 1981; Neisser, 1976). Such activity is an essential feature of the cognitive system and is thought to produce varied contents at different levels of operation (Anderson, 1985). While the passage of information through the system is conceived of as both a synthetic and reciprocal process (Neisser, 1976), most of the attention in the literature seems directed at three distinct levels of analysis. Cognitive structures, processes, and products have been identified by Hollon and Kriss (1984) and others (Arnkoff & Glass, 1982; Ingram, 1984; Turk & Salovey, 1985) as representing the principles or framework through which knowledge about the world is organized, how this framework guides ongoing processing, and what the most accessible products of this processing are.

An illustrative case of the interface of this typology and clinical theory can be found by examining the cognitive model of depression (Beck, Rush, Shaw, & Emery, 1979). This model specifies the operation of cognitive factors at a number of different levels that are then used to explain various features of the disorder. For example, consider the construct of cognitive structures. Beck (1967) has postulated the existence of maladaptive self-schemata that serve as mnemonic representations of the depressed person's negative view of self. One source of information used to assess the self-schema derives from attempts to map out relatively enduring dysfunctional attitudes regarding the contingencies for self-worth that are assumed to reflect schematic content. Another level of assessment directs attention to the putative characteristic style of information processing in depression. The observation that depressed patients selectively attend to negative information may be seen as a function of the individual's self-schema that facilitates the efficient processing of schema-congruent (negative) information (Kuiper, Olinger, MacDonald, & Shaw, 1985). Beck (1967) refers to the various biases of information processing as cognitive distortions (e.g., selective abstraction, arbitrary inference). Cognitive products are considered as the end results or output of the information processing stream (Hollon & Kriss, 1985) and are thought to correspond to the "automatic thoughts" or negative self-statements that are largely accessible to the individual and are often the focus of assessment on self-statement inventories (e.g., Automatic Thoughts Questionnaire; Hollon & Kendall, 1980).

Two points from the preceding example are worthy of more comment. First, as the level of analysis moves from cognitive factors that are more accessible to those that are less readily accessible, (e.g., self-schema), our reliance on inference increases. Hollon & Bemis (1981) explain this by invoking the linguistic based concepts of "surface" and "deep" structure representations. According to this view, the assessment of surface structure content is more observable and corresponds to the propositional type of content most questionnaires and inventories attempt to measure. Deep structure is not as uniformly propositional and hence not as easily captured by the majority of paper and pencil cognitive assessment formats. As a result, deeper structure content is more often endorsed than produced spontaneously, with the endorsement itself reflecting an inferred relationship between the material and its deep structure representation. Second, by specifying the level of cognition we are most interested in, our efforts can be maximized by choosing the assessment format most compatible with that level of analysis (Hollon & Bemis, 1981; Meichenbaum & Cameron, 1981).

PROCESS AND METHODS OF COGNITIVE ASSESSMENT

Cognitive assessment can be organized in terms of seven categories: the assessment of imagery, attributions, beliefs, self-efficacy expectations, cognitive style, self-statements, and *in vivo* thought-sampling (Kendall & Korgeski, 1979). These approaches cut across all three cognitive domains—the structures, processes, and products outlined earlier.

Choosing a particular method of cognitive assessment is best conceived of as a theory guided process (Segal & Shaw, 1986). The type of cognition to be studied and its relationship to performance reflect a specification of the cognitive conceptualization of the disorder utilized by the clinician. Similarly, the existence of a number of different instruments that perform similar functions has led some authors to suggest that what is needed is a framework of cognitive assessment procedures that will facilitate the matching of assessment needs with available methods (Kendall & Hollon, 1981). One such approach has been presented by Glass and Arnkoff (1982). They organize the methods of cognitive assessment according to two dimensions: temporality and degree of structure. The temporal classification examines when the assessment was administered relative to the occurrence of the thoughts one is interested in studying. The resulting scheme yields a continuum of assessment procedures ranging from concurrent evaluations to retrospective evaluations. Figure 2.1 indicates the placement of some of the more common measures on this continuum and provides a brief description of each. Recordings of spontaneous speech have been employed in a number of studies purportedly assessing subject's actual self-talk. These recordings can be taken unobtrusively or following specific instructions. They represent verbal behavior that can then be transcribed and coded into categories (Kendall & Hollon, 1981). This format is one of the most concurrent methods for assessing private speech, yet the investigator is limited to the subject's verbalizations and can never be fully certain that silences are synonymous with the lack of cognitive processing. The free association method as it is used in psychoanalysis also meets the concurrence criterion since patients are asked to verbalize their thoughts as they experience them throughout the therapy session (Bowers & Meichenbaum, 1984).

Think aloud procedures require subjects to provide a continuous monologue of their thoughts during the performance of a specific task. The exact wording of the think aloud instructions may well influence the content of the protocol (Ericsson & Simon, 1984) yet most instructions capture the spirit of this request by Duncker (1926) to his subjects:

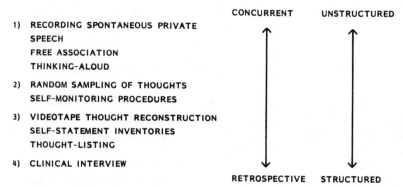

Figure 2.1. Contuiuum of temporal and structural dimensions of cognitive assessment (adapted from Glass & Arnkoff, 1982).

I am not primarily interested in your final solution, still less in your reaction time, but in your thinking behavior, in all your attempts, in whatever comes to your mind, no matter whether it is a good or less good idea or a question. Be bold. I do not count your wrong attempts, therefore speak them all out.

At the next level on the continuum we find methods such as random sampling of thoughts and techniques for self-monitoring. The former procedure attempts to provide an unbiased estimate of cognitive frequencies by requesting subjects to record their current thoughts when cued (either in person or by a portable mechanical device) at random intervals. This procedure enables data to be gathered over relatively long periods of time in the subject's own milieu, at intervals that are not contingent on the occurrence of any particular environmental events (Hurlburt, 1979). Newton and Barbaree (in press), for example, utilized *in vivo* random sampling to assess pain related thoughts in a population of chronic headache sufferers. They report a significant shift in appraisal processes and coping strategies following a cognitive-behavioral treatment program for headaches.

With self-monitoring procedures the individual is asked to record the occurrence of specific thoughts in a particular stimulus situation or at a particular time. Their utility lies in the fact that they maximize the probability of gathering clinically relevant information concerning important but possibly infrequent situations. In headache research for example, the experience of pain is a salient event that serves as an internal signal to begin self-monitoring; therefore, cognitive samples are collected during this period (Newton & Barbaree, in press). However, a number of problems reflecting concerns regarding reactivity, social desirability and evaluation apprehension (Nelson, 1977) inherent in self-monitoring procedures in general do exist.

Videotape thought reconstruction allows a subject to reconstruct his or her train of thought by viewing a videotape of an actual or roleplayed problematic situation. Subjects may be asked to think aloud while watching themselves, or alternatively, to record the occurrence of specific cognitive events (Genest & Turk, 1981). With respect to temporality, these procedures are classified as more retrospective than techniques discussed earlier since their aim is to facilitate the subject's "re-living" and reporting of a prior experience, as opposed to reporting on the original experience while it is occurring. A methodology related to videotape thought reconstruction is thought listing, where the subject is asked to report what thoughts he or she experienced while being in a particular stimulus situation. This procedure is more constrained than think aloud methods since the assessment takes place once the subject is out of the situation. The method can be likened to videotape thought reconstruction without the videotape. Cacioppo and Petty (1981) distinguish between listings that examine (1) thoughts elicited by the stimulus situation, (2) general thoughts about the situation or problems, and (3) all thoughts that occurred while subjects anticipated and/or attended to the stimulus. Thoughts can then be coded and scored on a number of dimensions that are of interest to the investigator. Segal and Marshall (1985), using such a procedure in a study of incarcerated sex offenders found that negative self-evaluative thoughts bore a stronger relation to poor heterosexual social skill than did task-referent thoughts, regardless of valence.

Endorsement methods such as self-report inventories or questionnaires contain a predetermined set of thoughts that subjects are asked to rate with respect to whether or not they had experienced the specific thought in the assessment situation, as well as its frequency of occurrence (Kendall & Hollon, 1981). Such instruments have been developed to assess cognitive contents particular to a number of domains such as depression (Hollon & Kendall, 1980), assertion (Schwartz & Gottman, 1976), social anxiety (Glass, Merluzzi, Biever, & Larson, 1982), chronic headaches (Newton & Barbaree, in press) and pedophilia (Abel, Becker, Cunningham-Ratner, Rouleau, & Kaplan, 1984). Finally, the clinical interview can be used as a retrospective cognitive assessment tool, in which case the therapist will ask the client to recall a recently upsetting situation and then recount what he or she was thinking and feeling at the time (Glass & Arnkoff, 1982).

Cognitive assessment procedures may also be organized on the basis of structure, wherein the extent to which the assessment imposes its own limits or format on the individual determines its placement on this continuum (see Figure 2.1). Structured assessments offer the benefits of economy, ease of scoring and administration, as well as a greater potential for standardization across studies (Meichenbaum & Cameron, 1981). The trade-off, however, is against a potentially richer data source and the investigator's ability to uncover unexpected information about unpredicted relationships (Genest & Turk, 1981). Deciding on the degree of structure in an assessment often requires the specification of the extent to which the individual's ongoing cognitive activity can be "punctuated" while still providing an accurate picture of its flow. This concern is introduced by Glass & Arnkoff (1982), who point out that as structure is added, the demand characteristics of the assessment also increases.

While think aloud procedures have an appeal due to their provision of the unaltered flow of subjects' thoughts, the instructions given to subjects to "think aloud" are consequential (Cacioppo & Petty, 1981) and can result in the reporting of varying contents. The rationale for videotape thought reconstruction is that providing subjects with a record of their performance will yield a richer description of what the person was thinking at the time, due to the enhancement of memory functions (Genest & Turk, 1981). Yet it is also possible that subjects are reporting what they guess they could have been thinking in the situation, rather than reporting on the basis of a visual and auditory aided re-experience of the event (Meichenbaum, 1977; Nisbett & Wilson, 1977).

It has long been the consensus within the field that a convergent operations approach is optimal (Webb, Campbell, Schwartz, & Sechrest, 1966). Such an approach minimizes the drawbacks of relying on any one format alone and, if dissimilar measures produce similar findings, construct validity increases (Kendall, 1984; Meichenbaum & Cameron, 1981). As our discussion is now moving into the area of psychometrics, we will turn our focus to questions of threats to the validity of the assessment process.

THREATS TO THE VALIDITY OF COGNITIVE ASSESSMENT

The proliferation of research aimed at explicating cognitive factors in various populations has led to the development of numerous new assessment tools for this express purpose. Thus, it is very important not to lose sight of the fact that methodology is no substitute for validity. At a theoretical level, cognitive assessment endeavours to demonstrate that the self-report of cognitive experience generated by the subject is the result of a patterned and consistent model, albeit idiosyncratic, of information processing. This systematic approach is in contrast to the same self-report generated by an essentially random, individual process that tells us nothing about the way in which an individual's cognitive experience is patterned, much less about the utility of our assessment.

Ericsson and Simon (1984) suggest three criteria that verbal reports should meet if they are to be validly used to infer underlying cognitive processes. The relevance criterion specifies that verbalizations should be relevant to the given task or performance. To be considered pertinent, verbalizations should be logically consistent with those that have just preceded them, and the memory criterion states that some of the information attended to during the situation will be remembered. The authors then go on to illustrate how these criteria can be used as validity checks on verbal protocols:

First, if a verbalization describes a situation that the subject can perceive directly, its correspondence with the stimulus can be checked. Second, its relevance to the task and to plausible steps toward a solution (as determined by task analysis) can be assessed. Third, its consistency with just previously verbalized information presumed to be in STM (short term memory) can be checked. Finally, whenever there is reason to believe that verbalized information will be committed to memory, its presence in memory can be tested by subsequent demands for recall or recognition. (p. 172)

Assumptions regarding the temporal and situational stability of cognitive contents impact on the validity of the assessment process by portraying these contents according to models that do not capture their inherent variability (Kendall, 1982). Arguing against the notion of cognitive intransience (the belief that people think the same things in the same situations at all times), Hollon and Bemis (1981) point out that the burden of proof falls on the assessor to demonstrate that this stability of thinking is, in fact, real. By way of illustration, let us take the case of self-efficacy versus attribution assessment. The assessment of self-efficacy expectations dictates that the rating of the particular behavioral item be taken just prior to performance (Bandura, 1977), in this way providing the investigator with an index of self-efficacy specific to the assessment session. Measuring attributions involves asking individuals to provide their explanations for the causes of events in their lives usually at a point farther removed in time from the actual event. While in the case of self-efficacy ratings we have access to the individual's beliefs at the time of performance, applying this same model to measuring attributions would require that "a retrospectively recalled attribution of job loss to bad luck was indeed the attribution made *at the time* the job was actually lost" (Hollon & Bemis, 1981, p. 150; emphasis added). This type of verification is rarely sought.

Situational instability is another reason why the assumption of cognitive intransience seems to be ill founded. Perhaps the best illustration of this phenomenon can be seen in the differences between thoughts elicited by imagining a stressful situation in the therapist's office as opposed to the thoughts elicited by the situation *in vivo* (Hollon & Bemis, 1981; Kendall, 1982). Data from a study by Last, Barlow, and O'Brien (1985) makes this point forcefully. In an attempt to assess the congruence between three cognitive measures of anxiety these authors compared an *in vivo* think aloud procedure performed with subjects in a shopping mall to a thought-listing procedure that was administered after the *in vivo* assessment. Their final measure was an imaginal cognitive assessment task. Last *et al.*, (1985) found little congruence between the *in vivo*, think-aloud procedure and the thought-listing protocol that was taken when subjects were no longer in the situation they dreaded. Their conclusion that there was little evidence of a direct one-to-one correspondence between these two measures underlines the need to take situationally induced variance into account when deciding at what point in time and where the assessment process will take place.

Questions regarding the construct validity of cognitive assessment focus not on the prediction of a criterion or the match between the content of a test and a specific domain, but rather on the ability of the test itself to measure the cognitive processes of interest (Ghiselli, Campbell & Zedeck, 1981). This issue particularly applies to questionnaire or self-report formats that supply the subject with a particular content. He or she is then asked to provide ratings on dimensions such as presence or absence, frequency, or degree of belief in the cognitions. The best example of this format is the self-statement inventory, which as Kendall (1984) points out is one of the most popular formats for assessing self-talk. The question of content validity should not be confused with concerns regarding construct validity, for while we can establish that the self-statements of which the inventory is composed are a representative sample of what people in general think in the assessment situation, we are less clear on what actual meaning an endorsement of one of these statements carries for the individual. Furthermore, meaning checks or inquiries are rarely conducted in conjunction with the administration of self-statement inventories (Arnkoff & Glass, 1982; Kendall, 1982), leaving us with the assumption that self-statements have the same personal meanings for all individuals involved. One step towards remediation can be found in the "degree of belief" ratings that some inventories require in addition to the usual frequency tallies (e.g., Automatic Thoughts Questionnaire, Hollon & Kendall, 1980).

Glass and Arnkoff (1982) provide a cogent critique of the assumption of an isomorphic relationship between cognition and its representation on self-statement inventories. They list four possibilities that reflect different processes underlying item endorsement. One possibility is that subjects who report having a thought "very frequently" may be indicating the impact or the importance of the thought to them, and not necessarily its frequency. This concern is problematic for most self-statement inventories, since scores usually reflect a simple tally of items endorsed. The second possibility is that a translation process is occurring on the part of the subjects, whereby the idiosyncratic or fragmented thoughts the subject experiences in the situation are translated into grammatically correct sentences as they appear on the inventory. Alternatively, a decision to endorse a thought may reflect the view that the thought matches one's view of oneself, rather than the actual experience of that specific thought. For example, a woman who sees herself as poorly skilled at solving math problems may endorse an item such as "I'm no good at math so why even try" for an exam anxiety question-naire, because it corresponds to her self-image rather than because she necessarily had the thought.

A final possibility is that endorsement may reflect the translation of affective experiences into a language-based format. While a subject who is in a highly aroused state may or may not be aware of any ongoing cognitive activity, self-statement inventories may provide the opportunity for convert-ing this experience into a linguistic representation of the event. In this sense, the subject may endorse a thought such as "I'm really getting worked up about this" without necessarily having experienced it at the time (Glass & Arnkoff, 1982).

The preceding sections were meant to raise some of the issues that are current concerns in the field of cognitive assessment. While no definitive answers to these questions are as yet forthcoming, there does seem to be agreement that more methodological studies are needed to examine how best to conduct cognitive assessment (Kendall, 1984; Meichenbaum & Ca-meron, 1981). In addition, the integration of cognition with affect is an area that will hopefully receive more research interest in the near future (Green-berg & Safran, 1984; Segal & Shaw, 1986). Having raised these points, we move now to an examination of the various methods of assessing cognition within the respective domains of anxiety and depression.

COGNITIVE ASSESSMENT OF ANXIETY

That the phenomenology of anxiety is predominantly cognitive has not been overlooked by a number of theorists who posit a significant role for maladaptive cognitions in the development and maintenance of anxiety disorders (Beck & Emery, 1985; Ellis, 1962). Cognitive assessment is, there-fore, especially suited to this domain, yet cannot be considered as a sufficient description until it is integrated with the other response modes (behavioral, physiological) characteristic of anxiety (Nelson, Hayes, Felton, & Jarrett, 1985; Nietzel & Bernstein, 1981). In fact, the synchrony or lack thereof between the various response modes is an issue in its own right, but one which is elaborated more fully elsewhere (e.g., Mavissakalian & Barlow, 1981; Rachman & Hodgson, 1974).

The cognitive assessment of anxiety disorders is a relatively recent development and so it is encouraging to note that the range of measures in this area covers both micro (e.g. self-efficacy) and macro (e.g. articulated thoughts during simulated interaction) levels of analysis. While most of the instruments reflect applications of self-report methodology to a particular cognitive target (e.g., self-statements), others are more closely linked to a model of dysfunction, and assess theory specific contents (e.g. based on the cognitive model of anxiety, assessing the degree of threat or perceived danger). The following section describes and critically evaluates a number of these measures with the intent being to provide the reader with enough information to allow him or her to decide on the utility of using these instruments in his or her assessment context.

Questionnaires that purport to measure some of the general cognitive features of anxiety have been used for some time. While the routine use of a standard test battery offers the advantage of comparability to previously published research using these measures, their relative lack of specificity and cumbersome format (e.g. true-false endorsements) often requires the administration of other measures to tap more differentiated cognitive content. The Fear of Negative Evaluation (FNE) Scale (Watson & Friend, 1969) is a 30-item, true-false questionnaire designed to measure the degree of apprehension about receiving social disapproval by others in social situations, whereas the Social Avoidance and Distress (SAD) Scale (Watson & Friend, 1969) uses a similar format with 28 items, to measure the experience of distress and discomfort in social situations. Both scales show good internal consistency with KR-20 reliabilities for the FNE and SAD being .94 for both measures. Test–retest reliabilities are reported as .78 and .68 for the FNE and SAD over a 1-month interval. As a way of broadening the subject's range of response on these scales, some authors have suggested adopting a 5-point response format ranging from "never" to "always" as an alternative to the true-false version of these scales (Bellack, 1979; Glass et al., 1982).

Another general cognitive assessment measure that has been used with anxiety populations is the Irrational Beliefs Test (IBT: Jones, 1969). This 100-item self-report inventory asks subjects to indicate the degree to which they endorse certain beliefs. Items such as "I want everyone to like me" or "I can't stand to make changes" are rated on a 5-point scale. The measure itself shows adequate concurrent validity and internal consistency. A recent factor analysis of the IBT yielded 10 factors that closely match specific beliefs characteristic of those addressed in rational–emotive therapy (Lohr & Bonge, 1982). Scores from the three measures previously described have also been used to categorize subjects into extreme groups (e.g., high vs. low irrational types, high vs. low socially anxious types), thereby utilizing the scales as independent variables in a particular research design. Yet, the implied homogeneity of groups chosen on the basis of having scored in the same upper quartile of a self-report inventory can be questioned (Arkowitz, 1977; Bellack, 1979). Perhaps application of these measures for purposes of classification should be limited to initial screenings.

Another concern about the IBT expressed by Smith and colleagues (Smith, 1982; Smith & Zurawski, 1983) is that the IBT actually measures anxiety and general distress (e.g., neuroticism) rather than irrational beliefs per se. Their work was conducted with a student sample and requires replication with a clinical population. Furthermore, the IBT may not be specific to anxiety disorders as it has also been correlated with depression (Cash, 1984; Nelson, 1977). A more differentiated assessment of cognitive content is provided by self-statement inventories that sample content specific to particular problem areas, and are constructed to reflect the typical types of thoughts that subjects in the situation of interest may experience. Heterosexual social anxiety is the focus of the Social Interaction Self-Statement Test (SISST: Glass et al., 1982), in which subjects are asked to rate 15 positive and 15 negative thoughts (1 = hardly ever had the thought to 5 = very often had the thought) after participating in a live heterosexual social interaction. Split-half reliability of the SISST, based on odd versus even items, is .73 for the positive and .86 for the negative scale. Concurrent validity, as evidence by correlations with other measures of social anxiety, is stronger for the negative self-statements than for the positive ones (negative scale with SAD = .74, with FNE = .58; positive scale with SAD = −.57, with FNE = −.32) using a written stimulus presentation format (Zweig & Brown, 1985). This pattern of functional asymmetry between positive and negative thoughts has been replicated using the SISST with other populations (Segal & Marshall, 1985) and has been suggested as a feature of the relationship between self-statements and affect in general (Safran, 1983). Given that a recent review of cognitive interventions for social anxiety reported that few studies actually assessed cognitive variables (Glass & Merluzzi, 1981), and that those that did often relied on a single measure, the SISST may help to bolster cognitive assessment efforts in this area.

The role of self-statements in assertiveness is relevant to this discussion since high anxiety levels are one of the explanatory constructs that have been proposed to account for nonassertive behavior (Galassi & Galassi, 1979). Schwartz and Gottman (1976) developed the Assertive Self-Statement Test (ASST), which asks subjects to rate on a 5-point scale the frequency of occurrence of 16 positive and 16 negative assertive responses. The self-statements represent thoughts that are believed to facilitate or inhibit the refusal of an unreasonable request and as such represent a more detailed elaboration of cognitive content associated with a specific behavioral performance. Fiedler and Beach (1978) have adopted a different perspective, in that their interest lies in measuring the types of consequences subjects believe are associated with refusal behavior, rather than just positive or negative self-statements. Their Subjective Probability of Consequences Inventory (SPCI) lists positive and negative consequences that could result from complying with or refusing an unreasonable request. The SPCI was constructed by choosing items based on clinical experts' consensual validation of representative consequences. Bruch, Haase, and Purcell (1984) report that both the ASST and SPCI show adequate internal reliability and that the factor structure of the ASST is more complex than was initially assumed, whereas the factor structure of the SPCI corresponds more closely to the dimensions originally outlined by Fiedler and Beach (1978).

Cognitive assessment of agoraphobia is the focus of a self-statement inventory developed by Chambless, Caputo, Bright, and Gallagher (1984).

This measure consists of thoughts concerning negative consequences of experiencing anxiety, and its 14 items were generated through interviews with agoraphobic clients as well as during imaginal and *in vivo* exposure sessions. Each item on their Agoraphobic Cognitions Questionnaire (ACQ) is rated on a 5-point scale ranging from (1) "thought never occurs" to (5) "thought always occurs," and clients are asked to judge the frequency of thoughts when they are in an anxious state. Reliability data show good test–retest stability ($r = .86$) but low internal consistency (Cronbach alpha $= .48$). Validity analyses have shown this scale to be sensitive to treatment-induced changes as well as being able to discriminate the scores of an agoraphobic and normal control sample. Together with its companion scale, the Body Sensations Questionnaire (BSQ: Chambless *et al.*, 1984), which measures physical sensations associated with autonomic arousal, the ACQ represents the first step towards a comprehensive cognitive assessment for agoraphobia. By considering both cognitions and sensations, assessment efforts will be more finely tuned to cognitive conceptualizations of agoraphobia (Goldstein & Chambless, 1978), which stress the fact that catastrophic thinking about anxiety in agoraphobic clients is often precipitated by arousal-mediated internal cues.

Moving away from self-statement inventories, we find a number of alternative structured measures of thought that have been employed in the cognitive assessment of anxiety. Some of these instruments are simply scales that have been devised to measure constructs suggested by the cognitive model of anxiety (Beck & Emery, 1985), whereas others have been generated in different domains.

Consistent with the cognitive model of anxiety, a number of authors have assessed the constructs of perceived danger or the overestimation of personal risk as the salient cognitive processes in anxiety. Butler and Mathews (1983) asked subjects to fill out separate questionnaires requiring interpretations of ambiguous scenarios, rating 20 threatening items in terms of their subjective cost to the subject (e.g., "how bad would it be for you"), and rating a number of positive and negative items in terms of their subjective probability of occurrence. Anxious subjects interpreted the ambiguous material as more threatening and rated the subjective cost of the threatening events as higher than did a control group of nonanxious subjects. Anxious subjects also tended to think that negative events were more likely to happen to them than to someone else. While it is difficult to attribute a high degree of specificity to these findings, since a control group of depressed patients scored similarly on two of these scales, the anxiety group was characterized by inflated estimations of threat and personal risk. Williams (1985) describes a measure of perceived danger, defined as a subject's perception of the probability of a negative event occurring given a specific performance. This measure is quantified as a likelihood or probability rating from 0% ("believe it is not possible") to 100% ("believe it is certain"). He reports that perceived danger ratings did not correlate with behavioral test performance before treatment ($r = .07$), but did correlate significantly after treatment ($r = .56$). Two additional measurement areas are anticipated anxiety, which refers to the degree of anxiety subjects think they would experience if they were to perform a specific task, and perceived self-efficacy, which addresses subjects' beliefs that they can perform a specific task and their confidence in those beliefs (Bandura, 1977). The strength of self-efficacy assessment lies in its operational specification of the behaviors to be measured. Subjects are provided with a series of specific behaviors and asked to rate whether they believe they can perform these behaviors, as well as how confident they are of their judgment, on a scale ranging from 10 to 100. Anticipated anxiety is rated using a 0–10 scale for each specific behavioral task described. In comparing these two indices, Williams (1985) points out that self-efficacy tends to be more accurate in predicting behavior, whereas anticipated anxiety ratings are superior in predicting performance-related anxiety. Given that the correlations between anticipated anxiety and behavior range from .40 to .80 across different studies, Williams (1985) goes on to suggest that perhaps self-efficacy is the major cognitive mediator of phobic avoidance behavior, whereas anticipated anxiety serves the same function for phobic anxiety.

Less structured formats for the cognitive assessment of anxiety have ranged from attempts to sample thinking during *in vivo* (Last *et al.*, 1985) or simulated (Davison, Robins, & Johnston, 1983) anxiety-arousing situations, to the random sampling of thoughts experienced by anxious individuals (Hurlbert & Sipprelle, 1978). Thought-listing has been used in a number of studies where the aim has been to record subjects' thoughts immediately following *in vivo* performance. Last *et al.* (1985), for example, had agoraphobics report what was going through their minds during an exposure session conducted at a shopping mall, while Segal and Marshall (1985) asked rapists to recall what their thoughts were in conjunction with an interaction they just had with an attractive female.

Thought-sampling was employed by Williams and Rappoport (1983) in their research comparing cognitive- and exposure-based treatments for agoraphobia. Subjects were provided with a beeper that would activate periodically, thus cueing the individual to record whatever he or she was thinking about on a tape recorder. The assessments had high ecological validity, as they were taken during behavioral tests of driving capability. A related approach was used by Sewitch and Kirsch (1984), who provided subjects with small booklets in which subjects were instructed to try and recall what thoughts or feelings they were experiencing each time they felt anxious or uptight within a specified 24-hour interval.

The popularity and appeal, due to high face validity, of the two general methodologies described above should not lead to complacency regarding the type of data produced by each approach. In a direct comparison of thought-listing with thinking aloud for the assessment of math anxiety, Blackwell, Galassi, Galassi, and Watson (1985) conclude that different procedures may reveal different cognitive contents. On the basis of using these two methods to assess thinking associated with solving a set of math problems, the authors point out that "think aloud and thought-listing are not equivalent either in the data they produce or in the effects they have on subjects" (p. 409). It seems that the former approach yields relatively more cognitions related to problem solving, whereas the latter format is superior for accessing evaluative processes and other non-problem-solving thought. Findings such as these serve to illustrate the problems of comparability and reactive potential associated with different cognitive assessment measures and point to the need for further research addressing the effects of such method variance.

While the majority of material covered in this section has described efforts at measuring these cognitive aspects of anxiety within the individual's awareness, attempts have also been made to assess the "deep" structure representations of anxious individuals; processes that are inferred from behavior (Landau, 1980; Rudy, Merluzzi, & Henahan, 1982). Rather than focus on the actual cognitive content that subjects are able to report in the assessment situation, these studies aim at a level of analysis that describes the operation of certain cognitive processes or structures, thought to play a key role in the experience of anxiety (Goldfried & Robins, 1983; Segal & Hood, 1985). Multidimensional scaling has been used by a number of investigators in an attempt to map the semantic structure of social anxiety (Goldfried, Padawer, & Robins, 1984; Rudy & Merluzzi, 1984). Similarity ratings on a given dimension for a set of objects serve as the input, in this approach, and yield proximity scores. The output produced is a spatial representation that reflects the data structure, so that the more dissimilar subjects' ratings are, the farther apart they will be represented on a spatial map. In this way, similarity ratings as represented by geometric distance are thought to reflect psychological space, and offer a view of the "deep" structure of a chosen data base (Merluzzi & Rudy, 1982).

Goldfried *et al.* (1984) used multidimensional scaling with a sample of socially anxious college males and found that they weighted the dimension of "chance of being evaluated" the highest with respect to the likelihood of generating anxiety, while giving lower weights to dimensions of "intimacy" and "academic relevance." Nonanxious males, on the other hand, weighted "intimacy" twice as heavily as "chance of being evaluated," suggesting a possible difference in the saliencies that stand out for these two groups when confronted by an opportunity for heterosexual interaction. Huber and Altmaier (1983) report using a different methodology to investigate the self-statement system of snake phobics. Phobic and nonphobic controls were asked to record their thoughts associated with an avoidance task and these were subsequently rated on a number of dimensions by two trained graduate students. Results indicated that while phobics and non-phobics did not differ in the content of their self-statement systems, the organization of these systems was different for each group. The degree of threat, as a content variable, was equal among the two groups whereas the salience of threat at either end of the dimension (snake will bite vs. snake will not bite) was stronger in the phobics' self-statements.

Finally, Mathews and his colleagues (Butler & Mathews, 1983; MacLeod, Mathews, & Tata, 1986; Mathews & MacLeod, 1985) propose that activation of schemata biased towards the processing of information related to personal danger is characteristic of anxiety states. Mathews and MacLeod (1985), for example, used the Stroop Color-Naming task and found that anxious subjects took longer than controls in color-naming words with a threatening (disease, coffin) as opposed to a neutral (welcome, holiday) content. Studies utilizing other measures derived from cognitive science, such as the degree of visual capture associated with a particular stimulus (MacLeod et al., 1986), have reported findings in a similar direction— namely that anxious subjects are more vigilant for or distracted by threat-related stimuli than are normal controls. The authors interpret these results as supporting the existence of cognitive "danger" schemata, which when activated bias information processing at a preattentive level. Whether this bias is perceptual or attentional in nature, it is thought to play an important role in the maintenance of the disorder, since it has an impact on the interpretations that individuals make at a later point in the information-processing stream.

Before leaving this section and moving on to the cognitive assessment of depression, it is important to consider a number of issues that interface with both domains. While cognitive assessment efforts in anxiety are a more recent development than those in depression, it is equally accurate to characterize both endeavours as still in their infancy. As a result, more work is needed to refine and evaluate the measures that exist in these already method-rich areas (Meichenbaum & Cameron, 1981; Segal & Shaw, 1986). Scoring criteria for thought-listing or think-aloud protocols are a good example of an area where the injection of some degree of regularity in the dimensions or attributes scored would aid comparability among investigations. Similarly, the increasing attention being paid to cognitive structures or "deeper" levels of processing would benefit from a focus on resolving some of the definitional issues surrounding the operation of these constructs. When descriptions of processing along schematic (Segal, Hood, Shaw, & Higgins, 1986), semantic–structural (Goldfried, Padawer, & Robins, 1984) or superordinal (Huber & Altmaier, 1983) construct lines, for example, have their maximal meaning solely for the investigators involved and few others in the field, then terminological clarification at both a conceptual and operational level becomes a necessity (Segal & Hood, 1985).

Readers should also bear in mind the close relationship between anxiety and depression symptoms. Up to 90% of patients report both symptoms of anxiety and depression (Brier, Charney, & Heninger, 1984; Dobson, 1985; Fawcett & Kravitz, 1983; Hamilton, 1981; Swinson & Kirby, 1987). Most researchers have set out to differentiate the various syndromes of anxiety and depression using diagnostic systems or symptom inventories. Dobson (Dobson, 1985; Shaw & Dobson, 1981), using an interactive model of life events and traits tired to differentiate the disorders using a self-report measure to evaluate the subjects' self-descriptive responses to various stressful situations. Investigators have only recently made attempts to document the relative contribution of anxiety-related and depression-related cognitions within an individual diagnosed as suffering from an anxiety and/or depressive disorder. Considerable work is needed to clarify the value of cognition and cognitive processes for the differentiation of these disorders. Acknowledging that their resolution will no doubt be a gradual process, we now move on to consider the cognitive assessment of depression.

COGNITIVE ASSESSMENT OF DEPRESSION

Most of the cognitive assessment measures of depression are paper and pencil instruments designed to capture either the content of the patients' thinking or their underlying attitudes or beliefs. Other significant efforts have addressed the manner in which depressed patients process information, particularly of self-referent descriptions or feedback from task performances (Shaw & Dobson, 1981). Few investigators have concerned themselves with thought-listing or think-aloud procedures although the recall (reconstruction) of automatic thoughts or self-statements in specific situations is widely employed in the clinical interview format (Beck *et al.*, 1979.

Our review of depression measures will capitalize on previous reviews of this subject matter (Hammen & Krantz, 1985; Rush, 1983; Shaw & Dobson, 1981) and provide a selective reporting. Our choice of measures is meant to illustrate categories of cognitive assessment with particular reference to the clinical utility and the psychometric evaluations of the measure. The majority of our efforts in this section will be spent on a review of self-report measures of the cognitive changes that accompany depression. Later we shall go on to discuss neomentalistic strategies (Paivio, 1975), particularly those addressing the self-schema construct to assess cognitive change. Along with a review of the various measures the reader can consult Tables 2.1, 2.2, and 2.3 for the scores of depressed patients on selected cognitive assessment instruments.

The Dysfunctional Attitude Scale (DAS) was designed by Weissman and Beck (Weissman, 1979; Weissman & Beck, 1978) to identify the relatively stable set of attitudes associated with depressive disorders. It is now clear that these attitudes are relevant to several psychopathological conditions although the actual DAS score may differentiate various groups (Dobson & Shaw, 1986; Hollon, Kendall, & Lumry, 1986). As dysfunctional attitudes are thought to reflect prepotent self-schemata, the DAS has been proposed as one measure of cognitive vulnerability to major depressive disorder (cf. Olinger, Kuiper, & Shaw, 1987; Olinger, Shaw, & Kuiper, 1987). The DAS is a self-report inventory available in three forms. The original 100-item inventory (DAS-T) is only occasionally employed in research studies. From the DAS-T, two 40-item parallel forms (DAS-A and DAS-B) have been derived, with the former being the most commonly used. Patients indicate the degree to which they agree or disagree with the stated attitudes on a 7-point scale. The scores range from 100 to 700, while on the DAS-A and DAS-B the range is from 40 to 280.

The DAS items are typically stated as contingencies concerning approval from others, prerequisites for happiness or perfectionistic standards; for example, "It is difficult to be happy unless one is good looking, intelligent, rich and creative"; "People will probably think less of me if I make a mistake"; and "If someone disagrees with me, it probably indicates he or she does not like me."

Weissman (1979) developed the DAS on a sample of college students and more recently, Oliver and Baumgart (1985) evaluated all three forms in a sample of adult hospital workers and their spouses. A psychometric study with a nonselected normative sample remains to be completed. The DAS has been widely researched on depressed and psychiatric control patients. In the Oliver and Baumgart (1985) study the mean score on the DAS-T was 296 ($SD = 75$), while according to Weissman (1979) the mean total score for students using either the DAS-A or the DAS-B was 117.7 ($SD = 26.8$). Depressed patients typically receive scores of 150 ($SD = 40$). Both short forms of the DAS have good internal consistency and stability over time, with coefficient alphas ranging from .89 to .92 and a test–retest correlation of .84 over an 8-week period (Weissman, 1979). Oliver and Baumgart (1985) reported alpha coefficients of .90, .85, and .81 for the DAS-T, DAS-A, and DAS-B respectively. Their 6-week test–retest reliability for the DAST was .73 ($N = 43$).

One area of controversy in the research concerns the stability of DAS scores in samples of depressed patients. Some investigators report a relatively stable pattern of DAS scores, while others find a marked change in scores. The concurrent validity of the DAS has been tested in several studies but there have been few evaluations of construct validity. It is expected that the DAS would have moderate correlations with measures of depressive severity and with measures of negative automatic thoughts, or cognitive distortions. For example, in three studies (Dobson & Shaw, 1986; Hamilton & Abramson, 1983; O'Hara, Rehm, & Campbell, 1982) the DAS correlations with the Beck Depression Inventory (BDI) were in the moderate range (i.e., 40-.65). Riskind, Beck, and Smucker (1983) found that the DAS remained significantly correlated with the Hopelessness Scale ($r = .22$) and a self-concept test ($r = -.15$), with the effects of depression severity partialled out. The DAS correlates .52 with the Cognitive Bias Questionnaire and with the Automatic Thoughts Questionnaire, both of which are state-dependent measures of depressive cognitions (Hollon et al., 1986). While the DAS discriminates groups of depressed and psychiatric control patients, it is not specifically associated with a major depressive disorder. Patients with generalized anxiety disorder, anxorexia nervosa, panic disorder or dysthymia may manifest abnormal DAS scores (Dobson & Shaw, 1986). In addition, it is notable that approximately 15% of depressed patients do not have abnormally high (i.e., at least one standard deviation above the mean) scores (Hamilton & Abramson, 1983).

The DAS has been employed to evaluate attitudes hypothesized to change as a function of cognitive therapy of other treatments of depression. Several studies have found the DAS to be a sensitive measure of clinical improvement. Keller (1983) found that DAS scores were useful to predict the outcome of a cognitive therapy treatment. Simons, Garfield, and Murphy (1984) reported that the DAS scores were lowered following *either* cognitive therapy or pharmacotherapy for depression. Silverman, Silverman, and Eardley (1984) also noted a significant reduction in the DAS scores following pharmacotherapy. The stability of the DAS scores of depressed patients following a remission of the depression is a matter of some controversy. Eaves and Rush (1984), Dobson and Shaw (1986), and Isaacs and Silver (1980) observed a reduction in DAS scores associated with a reduction in depressive symptoms, but found that remitted depressed patients continue to have abnormally high scores. Reda, Carpiniello, Secchiaroli, & Blanco (1985) used a shortened form of the DAS (NB a 37-item version that was neither Form A nor Form B) to evaluate depressed inpatients. Sixty patients were tested originally, and 30 of these were retested at a 1-year followup. Patients were treated with drugs (typically, amitriptyline and, when indicated, a benzodiazepine), but *not* with psychotherapy. They found a parallel reduction in the Hamilton Rating Scale (the HRSD) and the DAS total scores in both the acute and the follow-up phases. At discharge from hospital when the depression had remitted, the DAS scores of the depressed group did not differ from a group of 60 normal controls. These investigators identified specific, persistent, dysfunctional assumptions that continued to be endorsed even at follow-up. These included: "I feel well only when I have complete control over the situation"; "Turning to someone else for advice or help is an admission of weakness"; and "I should be able to please everybody." The pattern reflected a cognitive style with the following elements: (1) a pessimistic view of life; (2) a need for complete control; (3) overvaluing the judgements of others; and (4) a view that personal problems should be solved rapidly and independently. In contrast, other investigators (Hamilton & Abramson, 1983; Silverman et al., 1984; Simons *et al.*, 1984) observed that the DAS scores returned to normal as the depression remitted. These disparate results may be accounted for in part by the definition of remission and the time of retesting. Many of the studies (e.g., Dobson & Shaw, 1986; Hamilton & Abramson, 1983; Eaves & Rush, 1984) tested patients shortly after the remission, when patients no longer met depression diagnostic criteria but still had some symptoms of the disorder (i.e., the depression had not been completely resolved). Nevertheless, it is clear that dysfunctional attitudes abate with a range of treatments; a change in DAS scores is by no means specific to cognitive therapy.

The DAS may also be useful in the prediction of future depressive symptomatology in remitted depressed patients (Rush, Weissenberger, & Eaves, 1986; Simons, Murphy, Levine & Wetzel, 1986). Furthermore, the DAS has been used in several studies as an independent variable, to identify subjects who are assumed to have a cognitive vulnerability to depression (Kuiper *et al.*, 1985; Kuiper & Olinger, 1986).

The DAS has been factor analyzed in a number of investigations. Originally, Weissman (1979) used factor analysis on the DAS-T to devise the two parallel short forms. Olinger *et al.* (1987), in a study of college students, reported two factors, one involving a concern for performance evaluation and another a need for approval. Oliver and Baumgart (1985) found four factors from both the DAS-A and DAS-B in their study of adult volunteers. Unfortunately, the two-factor structure from the DAS-A and the DAS-B differed with the exception of a need for approval factor. This factorial incongruence is a concern that led these authors to conclude that the shortened forms cannot replace the DAS-T. (See Table 2.1 for comparative data of reviewed and related studies.)

Several conceptual questions may be raised about the use of the DAS. First, are dysfunctional attitudes meaningful reflections of the self-schema? Some authors (Beck, 1967; Rush, 1983) equate the two constructs, while our position is that different aspects of the patient's cognitive organization are tapped by the self-schema and dysfunctional attitude constructs. Second, what are the most theoretically and clinically meaningful methods of scoring the DAS? Weissman (1979) used a total score from either of the 40-item short forms of the test to quantify the severity of dysfunctional attitudes endorsed by the individual. It is expected that most subjects will endorse some dysfunctional attitudes to various degrees. From a theoretical viewpoint, is it more meaningful to consider the total score on the DAS or some other metric, such as the proportion of attitudes that are held in an extreme (presumably rigid) fashion? Clinically, an individual with a few dysfunctional attitudes held in an extreme and inflexible degree may be more vulnerable and/or more difficult to treat. In addition we must remain uncertain about the scoring until we obtain more information on the relationship between dysfunctional attitudes and vulnerability to psychopathology. A third question about the DAS is how stable the total scores on

Table 2.1. Dysfunctional Attitude Scale

Study	Sample	Pre		Post		Pre- and Post-Period (Days)
		$\bar{x}$	SD	$\bar{x}$	SD	
Simons, Garfield, & Murphy (1984)	70 RDC Depressed Outpatients	158.9	29.0	119.8	—	112
Isaacs & Silver (1980)	38 RDC-Depressed Outpatients (12 were age 60 or older)	150.6	—	—	—	N/A
Rapp (1985)	100 RDC-Depressed Patients (74 Inpatients)	150.3	37.4	—	—	N/A
Hamilton & Abramson (1983)	20 RDC-Depressed Patients	148.5	46.8	116.6	27.7	17
Eaves & Rush (1984)	31 RDC-Depressed Female Outpatients (26 Outpatients)	162.8	43.8	132.4	38.3	74
Dobson & Shaw (1986)	35 RDC-Depressed Inpatients	146.8	41.3	136.8[a]	34.6	60
Silverman, Silverman, & Eardley (1984)	35 DSM-III-Depressed Outpatients	147.5	—	113.3	—	
Silverman, Silverman, & Eardley (1984)	63 DSM-III-Unipolar Depressed Patients	N/A		123.4	29.2	
Blackburn & Smyth (1985)	10 Remitted RDC-Depressed Patients	N/A				
Keller & Haase (1984)	19 DSM-III-MDD Patients	146.8	32.0	N/A		
Blackburn & Jones (in press)	72 RDC-Depressed Patients (62 Major, 10 Minor)	147.7	4.1[b]	—	—	
	29 Recovered Depressed Patients	—	—	127.7	5.4[b]	120

[a] n = 15 at post. [b] standard error.

the DAS are, as well as how stable the specific items of the test are. Theoretically, dysfunctional attitudes are assumed to be more stable than other measures of cognition, such as the frequency of negative automatic thoughts or the probability of negatively biased recall of information. During a major depressive episode it has been generally observed that most patients exhibit abnormally high scores on the DAS (i.e., greater than 140), yet it is still unclear whether these DAS scores remain abnormal once the episode has remitted.

The Cognitive Bias Questionnaire (CBQ: Hammen & Krantz, 1983; Krantz & Hammen, 1979) is a self-report measure consisting of six stories, three with primarily a social/interpersonal theme and three with primarily an achievement/competence theme. Each story is followed by four multiple-choice questions (one story has only three questions) designed to reflect the central character's feelings, thoughts, and expectations. Each question, in turn, has four response options, constructed along two dichotomous and crossed dimensions: (1) depressed versus nondepressed responses (note: depression refers to dysphoria, not the syndrome of depression), and (2) distorted versus nondistorted responses, in terms of logical inference. An example of a depressed/distorted response to a situation involving the first thoughts following an election loss is "feel bad and imagine I've lost by a landslide" (Krantz & Hammen, 1979, p. 613).

Researchers and clinicians focus on the depressed/distorted category, since it is this category that is the most relevant to Beck's (1967) cognitive theory of depression. In the original validation Krantz and Hammen (1979) studied two clinical samples, 29 unipolar depressed patients meeting the Research Diagnostic Criteria (RDC: Spitzer, Endicott, & Robins, 1978) for a major depressive episode, and 10 RDC depressed male inpatients. They reported means (standard deviations in parentheses) of 4.3 (3.5) and 7.0 (4.4) of depressed distortions respectively in the two samples. Norman, Miller, & Klee (1983) reported means of 3.3 (3.0) and 2.6 (1.9) from a group of 30 (24 females) primary depressed inpatients and a group of 30 (13 females) secondarily depressed inpatients.

In two student samples studied, Krantz and Hammen (1979) reported coefficients of internal consistency (alphas) to be .62 and .69. These modest alpha coefficients may reflect the heterogeneous nature of the cognitive distortion construct (Hammen & Krantz, 1985), which was based on the initial observations of depressed patients reported by Beck (1970). Distortions such as arbitrary inference, overgeneralization, and selective abstraction do describe quite different biases in information processing. Test–retest correlations across 4 to 8 weeks were acceptable ($r = .48$ and $r = .60$). To date, no tests of the reliability of the CBQ have been reported with a clinically depressed sample.

The construct validity of the CBQ was demonstrated in two clinical samples (Krantz & Hammen, 1979; Norman et al., 1983). The correlation between the CBQ depressed/distorted score and the Beck Depression Inventory were significant (e.g., $r = .46$ with the full scale, $r = .50$ with the adult factor, and $r = .47$ with the retardation factor of the BDI). The BDI–CBQ depressed/distortion score correlations in student samples have been consistent and significant (see Blaney, Behar, & Head, 1980; Frost & MacInnis, 1983).

It is by no means clear whether the CBQ changes are specific to depression, however. As Hammen and Krantz (1985) have stated, the concept of cognitive biases is a complex one and there has been little work on the discriminant validity of the CBQ. Krantz and Hammen (1979) noted differences between depressed and nondepressed psychiatric patients in the predicted direction, although Norman et al. (1983) could not differentiate primary from secondary depressed samples using the CBQ.

Another potentially significant problem for the CBQ is its lack of sensitivity (Rush, 1984), since the depressed/distorted response constitutes only 6 of the 23 responses available to subjects. Nevertheless, the CBQ is sensitive to changes in mood following induction procedures with students (Goodwin & Williams, 1982; Riskind & Rholes, 1984). Future studies are needed to evaluate the CBQ's sensitivity, specificity, and stability in clinical samples.

The Automatic Thoughts Questionnaire (ATQ: Hollon & Kendall, 1980) is a 30-item self-report test designed to assess the frequency and the intensity of negative automatic thoughts typically associated with depression (Beck, 1976). Clinically, this test may be useful to identify changes in the content of thinking, although it is not clear whether depressed patients can reliably estimate the frequency of their negative thinking in a week (Coyne & Gotlib, 1983). The items are face-valid and are rated on a 5-point scale from "not at all" (1) to "all the time" (5), based on the occurrence of such thoughts in the past week. Using a 5-point scale, ratings of the degree of belief in each thought are also included.

The ATQ does not control for either social desirability or acquiescence (Jackson, 1970). The test has consistently been shown to have strong internal consistency with Cronbach alpha in the 0.90's across different samples (Dobson & Breiter, 1983; Harrell & Ryan, 1983; Hollon & Kendall, 1980; Rapp, 1985).

The ATQ has reasonable test–retest reliability, providing that the person's severity of depression has not changed. It seems clear that the ATQ is a state-dependent measure that is significantly related to the severity of depression. Correlations with the BDI (Beck, Ward, Mendelson, Mock, & Erbaugh, 1961) and other measures of depression severity (i.e., Hamilton Rating Scale for Depression [HRSD], SCL-90 Depression) tend to be high. For example, Dobson and Shaw (1986) reported an ATQ–BDI correlation of .84 and an ATQ–HRSD correlation of .80.

The ATQ has strong construct validity with acceptable to high correlations with several other measures of cognitive content. One factor analytic study reported four factors: (1) personal maladjustment and desire for change, (2) negative self-concept and expectations, (3) low self-esteem, and (4) helplessness and giving up (Hollon & Kendall, 1980). These factors are all consistent with the cognitive theory of depression (Beck, 1967).

To interpret the ATQ results, one can use the following guidelines. The mean ATQ frequency in a combined sample of depressed patients (inpatients and outpatients) is approximately 104 with standard deviations in the range of 26. When the depression remits, scores in the range of 67 (standard deviation of 24) can be expected. With this range of scores the ATQ is clearly a sensitive cognitive measure of change in depression. Early studies (e.g., Dobson & Shaw, 1986; Hollon et al., 1986) reveal that the ATQ can discriminate depressed from other psychiatric groups, although more work on this issue is needed.

No concurrent validity data have been reported comparing other measures of automatic thoughts (e.g., using the Daily Record of Dysfunctional Thoughts in Beck et al., 1979) and the ATQ. Rush (1984) questioned the face validity of the specific items for depressed patients, given that the ATQ was developed with college students. This concern is somewhat lessened now that several clinical studies have produced results similar to the college student studies. (See Table 2.2 for studies examining the ATQ in clinical samples).

The Cognitive Response Test (CRT: Watkins & Rush, 1983) is a self-report sentence-completion type of measure that uses an unstructured format for subjects to report their automatic thoughts. Originally validated as a 50-item questionnaire, the form in use today has 36-items. The completed sentences are scored into one of four categories: rational responses, irrational–depressed, irrational–nondepressed, and unscorable. Example items include "Lately my work has become more and more demanding. I think _____" and "When I consider being married, my first thought is _____." The irrational–depressed scale is of most theoretical and practical interest. Interestingly, the CRT-36 scores are signficantly affected by the severity of depression but not neuroticism (Wilkinson & Blackburn, 1981), indicating a greater specificity for the CRT than other tests. On the negative side, the CRT accounted for a relatively small amount of the variance of the BDI (36%; a BDI–CRT correlation of .60) compared to other measures of cognitive bias. This scale differentiated a sample of depressed from nondepressed subjects in four studies (Dobson & Shaw, 1986; Simons et al., 1984; Watkins & Rush, 1983; Wilkinson & Blackburn, 1981). The CRT is scored by raters who are guided by a standardized scoring manual. The interrater reliabilities have been reported to range from .72 to .88. Rush (1984) pointed out that while the CRT avoids the "transparency problems" of fixed-choice tests, it

Table 2.2. Automatic Thoughts Questionnaire

Study	Sample	Pre		Post		Pre- and Post-Period (Days)
		$\bar{x}$	SD	$\bar{x}$	SD	
Simons, Garfield, & Murphy (1984)	70 RDC-Depressed Outpatients	108.5	21.9	62.3	—	
Eaves & Rush (1984)	31 RDC-Depressed Females	110.9	26.6	50.7	23.7	74
Dobson & Shaw (1986)	35 RDC-Depressed Inpatients	93.3	29.7	88.3[a]	23.7	60
Rapp (1985)	100 RDC-Depressed Patients (74 Inpatients and 26 Outpatients)	105.9	27.8	—	—	
Blackburn, Jones, & Lewin (1986)	72 Depressed Patients	82.5	3.9[b]	—	—	
	(64 Inpatients and 8 Outpatients)	42.4			5.1[b]	>120

[a]retest on 15 Ss only [b]standard error.

is more time-consuming to score. Clinically, it is expected that depressed patients will obtain scores around 10.2, with a standard deviation of 4.9. When the depression remits, scores range around 5.0, with a standard deviation of 3.2.

The Cognitive Style Test (CST: Wilkinson & Blackburn, 1981) is a self-report, fixed-response measure of cognitive style. The CST was rationally designed to reflect Beck's (1967) theory, as well as the reformulated learned helplessness theory (Abramson, Seligman, & Teasdale, 1978). The authors also based their thinking on the notion that there are multiple causal pathways to depression (Akiskal & McKinney, 1975). Subjects respond to 30 vignettes of everyday events designed to address Beck's (1967) cognitive triad (negative views of self, world, and future). Each part of the triad is represented by five pleasant and five unpleasant situations. For each situation subjects choose one of four responses that receive scores on a 0 to 3 scale. Numerical indices are derived for the degree of negative interpretation of pleasant events, of unpleasant events, and of the combination of the two events. Examples of responses reflecting a depressed cognitive style are:

1. A person you admire tells you that he or she likes people like you. Response: He or she is being sarcastic. (3)

2. You go out socially with some people you have just met, but the evening is not very enjoyable. Response: They didn't like me. (3)

Clearly, the first event is pleasant while the second is unpleasant. High scores on the CST reflecting a depressed cognitive response are obtained if the subject makes external attributions (or negative interpretations) for pleasant events and internal attributions (or positive interpretations) for unpleasant events. The test controls for acquiescence but not social desirability.

Test–retest reliability was established over an interval of 16 days in a small sample of normal subjects. Split-half reliability was 0.68. The CST scales regarding total, pleasant, and unpleasant events differentiated depressed subjects from normal and recovered depressed subjects. The CST total score mean was 54.9 ($SD = 10.3$) for the depressed group, while the normal and recovered depressed samples had means of 36.7 (6.4) and 32.0 (5.4) respectively. Notably, Wilkinson and Blackburn (1981) report that the CST is affected by both depression severity and the level of neuroticism. On the positive side, the CST has good concurrent validity (e.g., the correlations with the CRT-36 (irrational–depressed scale was .67). The CST–BDI correlation was 0.68, while the correlation between the CST and a measure of neuroticism (the Middlesex Hospital Questionnaire (MHQ: Crown & Crisp, 1970)) was .59.

The CST may prove to be a useful measure of cognitive bias relevant to several psychopathological disorders. It is unlikely to be specific to major depression. More work on the psychometric properties of the CST is needed.

Notably, Blackburn, Jones, and Lewin (1986) revised the CST to make it more suitable for a middle-aged target population by changing some of the stimulus situations and clarifying the response options. The resulting measure provides scores for five subscales: pleasant events, unpleasant events, events relating to the self, the world, and the future, as well as a total score. They demonstrate high internal consistency, and strong concurrent validity using the revised scale.

The Hopelessness Scale (HS: Beck, Weissman, Lester, & Trexler, 1974) is a 20-item, self-report test designed to measure the person's negative expectancies about future events. Theoretically, the measure taps the negative view of the future proposed by Beck (1967) as one of the central constructs of depression. Example items include "I might as well give up because I can't make things better for myself" and "The future seems dark to me."

Acquiescence is controlled for by keying patient responses in a true-false format (11 of the 20 items are keyed as true). HS scores are expected to fluctuate with subjects' changing negative expectations about coping with life stressors or attaining valued outcomes. The HS is a state-dependent measure like the ATQ and CBQ.

The item-total correlations of the HS range from .39 to .76. The internal consistency was high (coefficient alpha = .93). Mendonca, Holden, Mazmanian, and Dolan (1983) cautioned that the high degree of internal consistency was attributable to a negative desirability set. They pointed to the importance of separating hopelessness from the tendency to view one's condition unfavourably in a crisis situation. These investigators observed that crisis patients often obtained high hopelessness scores when in interview they were anxious and/or depressed but "not particularly hopeless." Furthermore, they found the HS to be more sensitive to a socially undesirable response set than to the degree of suicidal behavior. This work demonstrates an important caution in the use of the HS and may serve as a motive to develop other measures of hopelessness.

The HS correlates significantly with the BDI (r's range from .68 to .84) and with clinical ratings of hopelessness ($r = .60$ to .74) (Minkoff, Bergman, Beck, & Beck, 1973). The construct validity of the HS has been further demonstrated by significant relationships with the Cognitive Style Test ($r = .64$) and the Cognitive Response Test irrational–depressed subscale ($r = .57$). Wilkinson and Blackburn (1981) and Keller and Haase (1984) found the HS–DAS relationship to be significant ($n = 19$, $r = .66$).

The HS scores differentiate depressed from recovered depressed and normal subjects (Wilkinson & Blackburn, 1981). The HS is also a sensitive measure of treatment outcome with depressed patients treated by either pharmacotherapy or cognitive therapy (Rush, Beck, Kovacs, Weissenburger, & Hollon, 1982).

Perhaps, most importantly, hopelessness as measured by the HS has been shown to be a predictor of suicidal ideation (Beck, Steer, Kovacs, & Garrison, 1985). Early studies found that the intensity of suicidal intent was more highly correlated with hopelessness than depression (Minkoff et al., 1973). More recently, the Beck et al. (1985) study found that the HS score differentiated a group of suicidal ideators who eventually died by suicide from ideators who did not. A cutoff score of 9 on the HS separated the completer from the noncompleter group. The major problem with this finding from a practical perspective, however, is that there was a 88.4% false positive rate with this cutoff. Nevertheless, it seems reasonable to increase clinical concern and further assessment for suicidal ideation when patients have high HS scores. (See Table 2.3 for clinical samples using the Hopelessness Scale.)

The Attributional Style Questionnaire (ASQ: Peterson, et al., 1982) is designed to detect the negatively biased attributions found in depression. Subjects are presented with twelve hypothetical situations, six with good outcomes and six with bad outcomes. The themes of affiliation and achievement concern are also balanced across the situations.

The subject is asked to imagine him- or herself in each situation and then to describe the major cause of the event. The subject is then asked to rate whether the cause is due to (1) internal versus external reasons; (2) stable versus unstable factors, and (3) global versus specific factors. These dimensions reflect the reformulated learned helplessness theory (Abramson, et al., 1978). The affiliation and achievement subtypes are typically more difficult to separate consistently than the good and bad outcome grouping. Five-week, test–retest correlations are moderate, ranging from .67 to .70 for good outcomes and .64 to .67 for bad (Golin, Sweeny, & Schaeffer, 1981; Peterson et al., 1982). Examples of good outcome situations are "You do a project that is highly praised" and "Your spouse (boyfriend/girlfriend) has been treating you more lovingly." Examples of bad outcome situations are "You can't get all of the work done that others expect of you" and "You meet a friend who acts hostilely toward you."

The internal consistency of the ASQ is problematic, with alphas for good outcomes ranging from .44 to .58 and those for bad outcomes ranging from .46 to .69 (Peterson et al., 1982). If the internality, stability, and globality dimensions are combined to form a composite good or bad outcome score, the alphas are acceptable (.75 and .72, respectively). For the assessment of attributional biases, the differences between depressed and nondepressed subjects are only found with the bad outcomes (Seligman, Abramson, Semmel, & von Baeyer, 1979). Some investigators get around this problem by aggregating the two scales (see, e.g., Hamilton & Abramson, 1983). Hammen and Krantz (1985) have indicated that the relationship between ASQ scores and depressed mood, while significant, is quite modest (mean $r = .21$ with the bad outcomes composite score). Another

Table 2.3. Hopelessness Scale

Study	Sample	Pre		Post		Pre- and Post-Period (Days)
		$\bar{x}$	SD	$\bar{x}$	SD	
Hamilton & Abramson (1983)	20 RDC-Depressed Inpatients	10.2	7.4	4.1	4.9	17
Keller & Haase (1984)	19 DSM-III-MDD Volunteers	9.6	4.9	—	—	
Blackburn, Jones, & Lewin (1986)	72 RDC-Depressed Patients (64 Inpatients and 8 Outpatients)	11.4	0.6[a]	6.0	1.1[a]	

[a] standard error.

66

problem with the ASQ is that subjects present a different pattern of attributions on the ASQ compared to their causal explanations for stressful life events or for laboratory tasks (Miller, Klee, & Norman, 1982).

Like the DAS, the ASQ may identify a subset of depressed patients who are vulnerable to future episodes. Some investigators observed that the ASQ behaves in a state-like manner, while others noted a more trait-like style. Zimmerman, Coryell, and Corenthal (1984) compared ASQ scores in major depressed patients who either did or did not meet criteria for melancholia. The ASQ did not differentiate between these subtypes. Hamilton and Abramson (1983) and Dobson and Shaw (1986) observed that the ASQ was basically a state-dependent measure of depression, while Eaves and Rush (1984) reported a stability of ASQ scores between periods of the episode and periods of remission. They noted that the ASQ decreased somewhat as the depression remitted but still remained abnormally high.

Adding to this controversy is the recent study by Winters and Neale (1985). They tested 16 remitted unipolar depressed outpatients on the pragmatic inference task, a measure of attributional bias. This measure was proposed as less sensitive than the ASQ to a self-presentation bias. The task differs from the ASQ in that (1) both success and failure are embedded in each story, (2) subjects are required to answer questions about facts and inferences not related to causality, and (3) the task is presented as a nonspecific memory task (Winters & Neale, 1985, p. 284). Their important finding was that the remitted depressed patients were found to retain "depressive-like cognitions." Winters and Neale argued that the Hamilton and Abramson (1983) findings are subject to a self-presentation bias (presumably a positive bias) before discharge. More research is needed to clarify the stability of any attributional biases following a depressive episode.

There are several other cognitive assessment measures relevant to the study of depression. Since these measures were judged to lack important reliability or validity data or were viewed as preliminary for other reasons, we shall describe them only in passing. The Cognitions Questionnaire (Fennell & Campbell, 1984) was designed to assess a cognitive style that would reflect a cognitive vulnerability to depression. Like the ASQ, eight scenarios were developed, with subjects' responses following each description. These responses tape the emotional impact, attribution of causality, generalization across time, generalization across situations, and perceived uncontrollability. Unfortunately, while the scale is sensitive to the depressed state, no evidence of an enduring vulnerability based on this measure has been shown. Munoz (1977) in collaboration with Lewinsohn designed three questionnaires to detect negative cognitions. These scales (the Subjective Probability Questionnaire, the Personal Beliefs Inventory and the Cognitive Events Schedule) are dependent upon depressed mood but are neither antecedents of nor sequels to depression (Lewinsohn, Steinmetz, Larson, & Franklin, 1981).

The Self-Control Schedule (SCS: Rosenbaum, 1980) is a 36-item questionnaire designed to evaluate the use of cognitions to control emotional responses (e.g., depression, anger, anxiety, pain), the use of problem-solving strategies, the ability to delay gratification, and the sense of self-efficacy. Sample items tapping these various dimensions include "When I plan to work, I remove all the things that are not relevant to my work" and "I often find it difficult to overcome my feelings of nervousness and tension without any outside help." The SCS was not developed as a specific measure of cognition in depression but rather was meant to assess the broad construct of self-control or learned resourcefulness. As it turns out, however, the SCS has been useful in some studies of depression. The internal reliability of the SCS is acceptable, ranging from .78 to .88. Test–retest reliability over a 4-week period was good ($r = .86$). As noted by Hammen and Krantz (1985), little information exists on the validity of the SCS for the measurement of self-control processes in depression. In fact, Rude (1983) reported nonsignificant correlations with two measures of depression severity (SCS–BDI correlation was $-.08$ and the SCS–Dempsey-30 correlation was $-.28$).

The most intriguing finding with the SCS to date was presented by Simons, Lustman, Wetzel, and Murphy (1985). These investigators treated 35 unipolar depressed patients with either cognitive therapy or pharmacotherapy. The SCS was the single best predictor variable in treatment outcome (percent change in Beck Depression Inventory scores). The higher the SCS score, the better the response to cognitive therapy but the worse the response to medication. Subjects who had low scores on the SCS responded better to medication than to cognitive treatment.

The Crandell Cognitions Inventory (CCI: Crandell & Chambless, 1981) is a 34-item scale developed to assess the frequency of negative cognitions in depression. In this respect it is simlar to the ATQ, perhaps one of the reasons accounting for its limited use.

The Cognitive Error Questionnaire (CEQ: Lefebvre, 1981) is another instrument that has received little attention. Patterned after the CBQ (Krantz & Hammen, 1979) the CEQ consists of 24 short vignettes. Subjects indicate their likely responses in the situations and raters evaluate these responses for cognitive distortions. While the CEQ differentiates depressed from control subjects, the raters could not distinguish the various cognitive distortions specified by Beck et al. (1979).

The Self-Verbalization Questionnaire (Missel & Sommer, 1983) is a 38-item measure describing 19 everyday situations. Each situation has either a positive or negative outcome and patient responses (positive, negative, or externally attributed) are scored. Depressed patients exhibit a bias of more negative than positive self-verbalizations.

Thus far we have reported on a variety of self-report measures of cognitive assessment in depression. We now turn to assessments of depression based on models of memory and social cognition. There is a substantial literature on the cognitive functioning of depressed patients. Much of this literature concerns deficits in memory functioning and/or attentional processes (see Shaw & Dobson, 1981; Miller, 1975). In this chapter we concern ourselves with information processing as it reflects on the cognitive theories of depression. This literature includes studies on self-schema and personal constructs.

Beck (1967; Beck *et al.*, 1979) proposed that a negative self-schema becomes prepotent in depression, thereby biasing information processing in two ways. The depressed patients' views of their current experiences, their future, and their recall of past events are thoughts that are affected by the dominance of a negative self-schema. The schema construct refers to cognitive structures of organized prior knowledge, abstracted from experience with specific instances (see Fiske & Linville, 1980). Schemas guide the processing of new information by directing attention to schema-congruent material. In addition, they affect the retrieval of stored information by increasing the accessibility of schema-related memories. Beck's original notion was that the development of depression involved the activation of a primitive cognitive organization of the self. These negative self-schemata were elicited by life event stressors. The main theme of the person's experience was a sense of loss from the personal domain, the areas of his or her life that were the most meaningful. This stress diathesis model puts a negative self-schema in a central position for the development and maintenance of major depression.

The vulnerability of the depression-prone individual is the result of these enduring negative concepts. Though schemata may be latent at a given time, they are activated by particular kinds of experiences and consequently, may lead to a full-blown depression (Beck & Rush, 1978, p. 238).

The measurement of self-schema remains an enduring challenge for the field. There continues to be some conceptual confusion about which cognitive variables reflect self-schema. Mostly, however, the problems have been in the measurement of the construct. Beck (1967) viewed dysfunctional attitudes—as measured, for example, by the DAS—as reflecting the negative self-schema. Depression-prone persons were seen as judging their self-worth in terms of their acceptability by others (an approval-seeking style), by achievements, or by other external events. They were seen as rigid and extreme in the way that they endorsed various dysfunctional attitudes. As a result, when the approval-seeking or achievement contingencies were not met, these individuals experienced a significant loss attributable to their own unworthiness. Clinically, these attitudes were reflected by the theme that others wouldn't respect or care for the person if they knew what the depressed person was really like. Thus, one method consistent with cognitive theory to determine negative self-schema was indirectly via his or her dysfunctional attitudes.

An alternate method of detecting negative self-schema has emerged from investigators of social cognition, a field that applies methods of cognitive psychology, particularly information-processing paradigms, to evaluate socially-relevant phenomena (see, e.g., Kuiper & Higgins, 1985). Information processing paradigms typically involve testing the patient's memory for self-descriptive adjectives. In addition, several studies employ reaction time to determine the efficiency with which patients recognize or recall this information.

Our review here will not attempt to cover all of the different methodologies addressing self-schema in depression. Instead, we will selectively attend to some of the most widely researched paradigms and present examples of newer methodologies pursuing similar objectives.

The first experimental work on the self-schema of depressed patients was completed by Davis (Davis 1979a, 1979b; Davis & Unruh, 1981). He employed the incidental recall paradigm proposed by Rogers, Kuiper, and Kirker (1977), which in turn was based on the depth-of-processing model of Craik and Lockhart (1972). Essentially, this paradigm requires subjects to rate adjectives according to questions tapping structural, phonemic, schematic, or self-referent dimensions. For example, the self-referent task is to rate whether a personally relevant adjective (e.g., sincere, loyal) describes the subject. The prediction was that self-referent adjectives in the Rogers *et al.* (1977) study would be processed at a deeper level and that this would be evidenced by superior recall for this material.

Davis (1979b) tested depressed patients and concluded that "a self-schema is not an active agent in the encoding of personal information in depression" (p. 107). He based this conclusion on data that showed that depressed subjects recalled significantly fewer self-referent adjectives than controls. Other investigators have criticized this conclusion because of the disproportionate number of positively valenced adjectives in the list (Derry & Kuiper, 1981; Ingram, Smith, & Brehm, 1983). Davis and Unruh (1981) pursued this line of research, using the same set of adjectives to evaluate the subjective organization of depressed patients. Again, the conclusion was that the self-schema of patients who had been depressed for less than 1 year was "not a strong organizer of personal information" (p. 126).

In contrast, Roth and Rehm (1980), using a different but comparable memory paradigm, tested depressed male inpatients and nondepressed controls. They employed equal numbers of positive and negative adjectives and found that the two groups did not differ in either their recognition or their recall. The major problem with this study is that the time of exposure to each adjective was not controlled (Bradley & Matthews, 1983).

Derry and Kuiper (1981) have extended this early work by employing the depth of processing paradigm with both depressed and nondepressed content adjectives. They found that depressed patients exhibited enhanced recall for negative self-referent adjectives, despite having endorsed equal numbers of negative and positive adjectives as self-referent. In addition, the depressed subjects were as efficient as normal controls and nondepressed psychiatric controls in processing the self-referent information. This bias was viewed as supporting Beck's (1967) cognitive model, while demonstrating the existence of a negative self-schema. Research in this area continued with attempts to detect a similar processing bias in nondepressed subjects identified as vulnerable according to the DAS. (Kuiper et al., 1985). It does not appear, however, that this methodology is sensitive enough to detect a cognitively vulnerable individual. Recent evidence using this paradigm revealed that the ratio balance between positive to negative self-referent words during the episode changes once the depression remits (Dobson & Shaw, 1986). Furthermore, the possibilities for the replication of Derry and Kuiper's (1981) recall findings are drawn into question.

Bradley and Matthews (1983) designed an experiment similar to Derry and Kuiper (1981). "Recall and processing time for self and other referent adjectives was studied in clinically depressed patients and in matched controls" (p. 175). As in other studies, they found that depressed patients rate more negative adjectives as being self-descriptive. This finding may bias the results, since "yes"-rated words are likely to be recalled more easily. To control for this possibility, a covariance analysis removed the influence of decision frequency. Results indicated that depressed subjects recalled more negative than positive words when this material was presented as self-referent. Notably, if the information was presented with a general focus or in relation to other people, the bias was not observed. The negative bias in recall was not influenced by more severe or more prolonged depression in this study. This finding is somewhat discrepant with other studies of Kuiper and his colleagues (e.g., Kuiper & Derry, 1982), who found mildly depressed subjects to exhibit less of a negative bias in their recall pattern.

There are other methods of assessing self-schema in depression. One intriguing development is the use of the Stroop (1938) color-naming task as adapted by Warren (1972). In this procedure, subjects are presented with a list of three semantically related words (e.g.: cow, horse, chicken). They are then asked to name the ink color of a fourth word (the target word), which varies in its semantic relatedness to the list (e.g.: pig, crow, table). When the target word is closely related in meaning to the list words, subjects exhibit longer latencies in color naming. The explanation of this effect is that response competition occurs when a meaning structure is accessed. Several investigators are using this procedure to explore accessibility effects in depression (Gotlib & McCann, 1984) and the structural basis of self-schemata (Segal et al., 1986).

Another method used to assess self-schema is known as the behavioral example recall procedure (e.g., Hammen, Marks, Mayol, & de Mayo, 1985; Markus, 1977). The assumption of this method is that "schema consistent information will be relatively accessible in memory compared with schema noncongruent information and can be used to index the strength of a schema for that information" (Hammen *et al.*, 1985, p. 310). Subjects are asked to list specific examples of events that actually occurred within the past month. They follow instructions to provide examples of times when they felt bad about themselves, good about themselves, helpless, and critical (or guilty). Raters then evaluate each example for consistent themes such as the schema subtypes of dependent or achievement-oriented individuals.

Up to this point we have discussed efforts to assess self-schema in depression in some detail. There are, of course, other methods to assess cognition in depression but as with the self-report measures we shall only describe these briefly. Depressed subjects have consistently been shown to manifest an increased probability of recalling sad memories compared to happy ones (Fogarty & Hemsley, 1983). This method of assessment requires subjects to recall past real-life experiences associated with 20 stimulus words (e.g., ice, wood, letter, house). None of the stimulus words are self-referent. Subjects indicate whether or not they can recall a specific event (associated with the word but not a word association), and if so, are asked to describe the event in enough words to be used as a prime later on. Depressed patients recall a greater percentage of unhappy compared with happy memories (Lishman, 1972; Lloyd & Lishman, 1975), yet this measure like so many others is likely state-dependent, returning to "normal" when the depression remits (Fogarty & Hemsley, 1983).

The final method of cognitive assessment for depression that we shall review is the Role Construct Repertory Test (Kelly, 1955). Again, this test will not be reviewed in detail; the interested reader may refer to recent work by Neimeyer (1985). Basically, the technique is designed to assess the organization of cognitive structure along various dimensions used by the subject rather than imposed by the experimenter. Prior to computer-aided scoring, the method was difficult to utilize because of the time for administration and analysis. Space & Cromwell (1980) tested depressed, psychiatric control, and normal subjects with the repertory grid test. Depressed patients had more mixed (positive & negative) self-descriptions than other patients, and tended to view themselves as different from others.

In summary, research on depression has resulted in a range of measures addressing the content, process, and "deep structure" of cognition. It remains to be seen whether cognitive variables are important markers of a vulnerability to depression. The clinician has many ways to assess cognitive changes during a depressive episode. Depending on his or her particular theoretical concerns, measures of cognition may be taken prior to, during, and following treatment. Most measures discussed in this chapter will be useful indicators of improvement. On the other hand, it is not easy to determine the cognitive changes that are uniquely influenced by cognitive-behavioral treatments. At present it seems that any treatment (or, for that matter, time alone) that serves to alter the state of depression will also result in substantial cognitive changes.

Cognitive therapists (e.g., Beck *et al.*, 1979) have proposed that altering the cognitive dysfunction associated with affective and/or anxiety disorders provides a powerful means of treating these disorders. The evidence to date supports this proposal. It is not clear, however, whether cognitive therapies alter the likelihood of future episodes by reducing the individual's vulnerability to the disorder. It would be a significant breakthrough in our field if it could be shown (1) that there are enduring cognitive characteristics that differentiate those who have had the disorder from those who have not, (2) that cognitive-behavioural therapies have a specific (if not unique) impact on these characteristics, and (3) that changing the vulnerable characteristics of depressed cognition influences the probability of future episodes. For now, it will suffice to say that the cognitive assessment of depressive and anxiety disorders has developed to the point that clinicians are relatively well served.

ACKNOWLEDGMENTS

The authors would like to acknowledge Anne Simons, John Rush, Ivy Blackburn, Kevin Keller, Stephen Rapp, Nick Kuiper, and Joan Olinger for providing current data on a number of measures described in this chapter. We would also like to thank Jane Burnie, Doreen Vella, and Debi Wilson for their assistance in the preparation of this manuscript. Dr. Segal is a Medical Research Council of Canada Fellow. This work was supported in part by grants from the Laidlaw Foundation and the Canadian Psychiatric Research Foundation.

REFERENCES

Abel, G. G., Becker, J. V., Cunningham-Ratner, J., Rouleau, J. L., & Kaplan, M. (1984). The treatment of child molesters. *Treatment Manual*, Emory University, Atlanta.

Abramson, L. Y., Seligman, M. E. P., & Teasdale, J. D. (1978). Learned helplessness in humans: Critique and reformulation. *Journal of Abnormal Psychology, 87*, 102–109.

Akiskal, H. S., & McKinney, W. T. (1975). Overview of recent research in depression. *Archives of General Psychiatry, 32*, 285–305.

Anderson, J. R. (1985). *Cognitive psychology and its implications* (2nd ed.). New York: W. H. Freeman.

Arkowitz, H. (1977). Measurement and modification of minimal dating behavior. In M. Hersen, R. M. Eislen, & P. M. Miller (Eds.), *Progress in behavior modification* (Vol. 5). New York: Academic Press.

Arnkoff, D. B., & Glass, C. R. (1982). Clinical cognitive constructs: Examination, evaluation, and elaboration. *Advances in Cognitive Behavioral Research and Therapy*, Vol. 1. New York: Academic.

Bandura, A. (1977). Self-efficacy: Toward a unifying theory of behavioral change. *Psychological Review, 84*, 191–215.

Beck, A. T. (1967). *Depression: Clinical, experimental and therapeutic aspects*. New York: Harper & Row.

Beck, A. T. (1976). *Cognitive therapy and the emotional disorders.* New York: International Universities Press.

Beck, A. T., & Emery, G. (1985). *Anxiety disorders and phobias.* New York: Basic Books.

Beck, A. T., & Rush, A. J. (1978). Cognitive approaches to depression and suicide. In G. Serban (Ed.), *Cognitive defects in development of mental illness.* New York: Brunner/Mazel.

Beck, A. T., Rush, A. J., Shaw, B. F., & Emery, G. (1979). *Cognitive therapy of depression.* New York: Guilford.

Beck, A. T., Steer, R. A., Kovacs, M., & Garrison, B. S. (1985). Hopelessness and eventual suicide: A 10-year prospective study of patients hospitalized with suicidal ideation. *American Journal of Psychiatry, 142,* 559-563.

Beck, A. T., Ward, C. H., Mendelson, M., Mock, J., & Erbaugh, J. (1961). An inventory for measuring depression. *Archives of General Psychiatry, 4,* 561-571.

Beck, A. T., Weissman, A., Lester, D., & Trexler, L. (1974). The measurement of pessimism: The Hopelessness Scale. *Journal of Consulting and Clinical Psychology, 42,* 861-865.

Bellack, A. S. (1979). Behavioral assessment of social skills. In A. S. Bellack & M. Hersen (Eds.), *Research and practice in social skills.* New York: Plenum.

Blackburn, I. M., Jones, S. & Lewin, R. J. P. (1986). Cognitive style in depression. *British Journal of Clinical Psychology, 25,* 241-252.

Blackburn, I. M., & Smythe, P. (1985). A test of cognitive vulnerability in individuals prone to depression. *British Journal of Clinical Psychology, 24,* 61-62.

Blackwell, R. T., Galassi, J. P., Galassi, M. D., & Watson, T. E. (1985). Are cognitive assessment methods equal? A comparison of think aloud and thought listing. *Cognitive Therapy and Research, 9,* 399-413.

Blaney, P. H., Behar, V., & Head, R. (1980). Two measures of depressive cognitions: Their association with depression and with each other. *Journal of Abnormal Psychology, 89,* 678-682.

Bowers, K. S., & Meichenbaum, D. (1984). *The unconscious reconsidered.* New York: Wiley.

Bradley, B., & Matthews, A. (1983). Negative self-schemata in clinical depression. *British Journal of Clinical Psychology, 22,* 173-181.

Breir, A., Charney, D. S., & Heninger, G. R. (1984). Major depression in patients with agoraphobia and panic disorder. *Archives of General Psychiatry, 41,* 1129-1135.

Bruch, M. A., Haase, R. F., & Purcell, M. J. (1984). Content dimensions of self-statements in assertive situations: A factor analysis of two measures. *Cognitive Therapy and Research, 8,* 173-186.

Butler, G., & Mathews, A. (1983). Cognitive processes in anxiety. *Advances in Behavior Research Therapy, 5,* 51-62.

Cacioppo, J. T., & Petty, R. E. (1981). Social psychological procedures for cognitive response assessment: The thought-listing technique. In T. V. Merluzzi, C. R. Glass, & M. Genest (Eds.), *Cognitive assessment.* New York: Guilford Press.

Cash, T. F. (1984). The Irrational Beliefs Test: Its relationship with cognitive-behavioral traits and depression. *Journal of Clinical Psychology, 40,* 1399-1405.

Chambless, D. L., Caputo, G. C., Bright, P., & Gallagher, R. (1984). Assessment of fear in agoraphobics: The body sensations questionnaire and the agoraphobic cognition questionnaire. *Journal of Consulting and Clinical Psychology, 52,* 1090-1097.

Coyne, J. C., & Gotlib, I. H. 1983). The role of cognition in depression: A critical appraisal. *Psychological Bulletin, 94,* 472-505.

Craik, F. M., & Lockhart, R. S. (1972). Levels of processing: A framework for memory research. *Journal of Verbal Learning and Verbal Behaviour, 11,* 671-684.

Crandell, C. J., & Chambless, D. L. (1981, November). *A validation of an inventory for measuring depressive thoughts.* Toronto: Paper presented at the Annual Meeting of the Association for Advancement of Behavior Therapy.

Crown, S., & Crisp, A. H. (1970). *Manual of the Middlesex Hospital Questionnaire (MHQ)*. Barnstaple, Devon: Psychological Test Publication.

Davis, H. (1979a). Self-reference and the encoding of personal information in depression. *Cognitive Therapy and Research, 3,* 97-110.

Davis, H. (1979b). The self-schema and subjective organization of personal information in depression. *Cognitive Therapy and Research, 3,* 415-425.

Davis, H., & Unruh, W. R. (1981). The development of the self-schema in adult depression. *Journal of Abnormal Psychology, 90,* 125-133.

Davison, G. C., Robins, C., & Johnston, M. K. (1983). Articulated thoughts during simulated situations: A paradigm for studying cognition in emotion and behavior. *Cognitive Therapy and Research, 7,* 17-40.

Derry, P. A., & Kuiper, N. A. (1981). Schematic processing and self-reference in clinical depression. *Journal of Abnormal Psychology, 90,* 286-297.

Dobson, K. S. (1985). The relationship between anxiety and depression. *Clinical Psychology Review, 5,* 307-324.

Dobson, K. S., & Breiter, H. J. (1983). Cognitive assessment of depression: Reliability and validity of three measures. *Journal of Abnormal Psychology, 92,* 107-109.

Dobson, K. S., & Shaw, B. F. (1986). Cognitive assessment with major depressive disorders. *Cognitive Therapy and Research, 10,* 13-29.

Duncker, K. (1926). A qualitative (experimental and theoretical) study of productive thinking (solving of comprehensible problems). *Pedagogical Seminary, 33,* 642-708.

Eaves, G., & Rush, A. J. (1984). Cognitive patterns in symptomatic and remitted major depression. *Journal of Abnormal Psychology, 93,* 31-40.

Ellis, A. (1962). *Reason and emotion in psychotherapy.* New York: Lyle Stuart.

Ericsson, K. A., & Simon, H. A. (1984). *Protocol analysis.* Cambridge, MA: MIT Press.

Fawcett, J., & Kravitz, H. M. (1983). Anxiety syndromes and their relationship to depressive illness. *Journal of Clinical Psychiatry, 44,* 8-11.

Fennell, M. J. V., & Campbell, E. A. (1984). The Cognitions Questionnaire: Specific thinking errors in depression. *British Journal of Clinical Psychology, 23,* 81-92.

Fiedler, R., & Beach, L. R. (1978). On the decision to be assertive. *Journal of Consulting and Clinical Psychology, 46,* 537-546.

Fiske, S., & Linville, P. (1980). What does the schema concept buy us? *Personality and Social Psychology Bulletin, 6,* 543-557.

Fogarty, S. J., & Hemsley, D. R. (1983). Depression and the accessibility of memories. A longitudinal study. *British Journal of Psychiatry, 142,* 232-237.

Frost, R. D., & MacInnis, D. J. (1983). The Cognitive Bias Questionnaire: Further evidence. *Journal of Personality Assessment, 47,* 173-177.

Galassi, J. P., & Galassi, M. D. (1979). Modification of heterosocial skills deficits. In A. S. Bellack & M. Hersen (Eds.). *Research and Practice in Social Skills.* New York: Plenum.

Gardner, H. (1985). *The mind's new science: A history of the cognitive revolution.* New York: Basic Books.

Genest, M., & Turk, D. C. (1981). Think-aloud approaches to cognitive assessment. In T. V. Merluzzi, C. R. Glass, & M. Genest (Eds.), *Cognitive assessment.* New York: Guilford.

Ghiselli, E. E., Campbell, J. P., & Zedeck, S. (1981). *Measurement theory for the behavioral sciences.* San Francisco: Freeman.

Glass, C. R., & Arnkoff, D. B. (1982). Think cognitively: Selected issues in cognitive assessment and therapy. In P. C. Kendall (Eds.). *Advances in cognitive-behavioral research and therapy, (Vol. 1).* New York: Academic.

Glass, C. R., & Merluzzi, T. V. (1981). Cognitive assessment of social evaluative anxiety. In T. V. Merluzzi, G. R. Glass, & M. Genest (Eds.), *Cognitive Assessment.* New York: Guilford.

Glass, C. R., Merluzzi, T. V., Biever, J. L., & Larsen, K. H. (1982). Cognitive assessment of social anxiety: Development and validation of a self-statement questionnaire. *Cognitive Therapy and Research, 6*, 37-55.

Goldfried, M. R., & Robins, C. (1983). Self-schema, cognitive bias, and the processing of therapeutic experiences. In P. C. Kendall (Ed.), *Advances in cognitive-behavioral research and therapy*. New York: Academic.

Goldfried, M. R., Padawer, W., & Robins, C. (1984). Social anxiety and the semantic structure of heterosocial interactions. *Journal of Abnormal Psychology, 93*, 86-97.

Goldstein, A. J., & Chambless, D. L. (1978). A reanalysis of agoraphobia. *Behavior Therapy, 9*, 47-59.

Golin, S., Sweeny, P. D., & Schaeffer, D. E. (1981). The causality of causal attributions in depression: A cross-lagged panel correlation analysis. *Journal of Abnormal Psychology, 90*, 14-22.

Goodwin, A. M., & Williams, J. M. G. (1982). Mood induction research: Its implication for clinical depression. *Behaviour Research and Therapy, 20*, 373-382.

Gotlib, I. H., & McCann, C. D. (1984). Construct accessibility and depression: An examination of cognitive and affective factors. *Journal of Personality and Social Psychology, 47*, 427-439.

Greenberg, L. S., & Safran, J. D. (1984). Integrating affect and cognition: A perspective on the process of therapeutic change. *Cognitive Therapy and Research, 8*, 559-578.

Hamilton, M. (1981). Depression and anxiety: A clinical viewpoint. In M. Hamilton & J. B. Bakker (Eds.). *Psychiatry in the 80's: Ideas, Research, Practice*. Exerpta Medica.

Hamilton, E. W., & Abramson, L. Y. (1983). Cognitive patterns and major depressive disorder: A longitudinal study in a hospital setting. *Journal of Abnormal Psychology, 92*, 173-184.

Hammen, C. L., & Krantz, S. E. (1983). Effects of success and failure on depressive cognitions. *Journal of Abnormal Psychology, 85*, 577-586.

Hammen, C. L., & Krantz, S. E. (1985). Measures of psychological processes in depression. In E. E. Beckham & W. R. Leber (Eds.). *Handbook of Depression: Treatment, Assessment and Research*. Homewood, IL: Dorsey Press.

Hammen, C., Marks, T., Mayol, A., & de Mayo, R. (1985). Depressive self-schemas, life stress and vulnerability to depression. *Journal of Abnormal Psychology, 94*, 308-319.

Harrell, T. H., & Ryan, N. B. (1983). Cognitive–behavioral assessment of depression: Clinical validation of the Automatic Thoughts Questionnaire. *Journal of Consulting and Clinical Psychology, 51*, 721-725.

Hollon, S. D., & Bemis, K. M. (1981). Self-report and the assessment of cognitive functions. In M. Hersen & A. S. Bellack (Eds.), *Behavioral assessment: A practical handbook*. New York: Pergamon.

Hollon, S. D., & Kendall, P. C. (1980). Cognitive self-statements in depression: Development of an automatic thoughts questionnaire. *Cognitive Therapy and Research, 4*, 383-396.

Hollon, S. D., Kendall, P. C., & Lumry, A. (1986). Specificity of depressotypic cognitions in clinical depression. *Journal of Abnormal Psychology, 95*, 52-59.

Hollon, S. D., & Kriss, M. R. (1984). Cognitive factors in clinical research and practice. *Clinical Psychology Review, 4*, 35-76.

Huber, J. W., & Altmaier, E. M. (1983). An investigation of the self-statements of phobic and nonphobic individuals. *Cognitive Therapy and Research, 7*, 355-362.

Hurlburt, R. T. (1979). Random sampling of cognitions and behavior. *Journal of Research in Personality, 13*, 103-111.

Hurlburt, R. T., & Spirelle, C. N. (1978). Random sampling of cognitions in alleviating anxiety attacks. *Cognitive Therapy and Research, 2*, 165-169.

Ingram, R. E. (1984). Toward an information processing analysis of depression. *Cognitive Therapy and Research, 5*, 443-478.

Ingram, R. E., Smith, T. W., & Brehm, S. S. (1983). Depression and information processing: Self-schemata and the encoding of self-referent information. *Journal of Personality and Social Psychology, 45*, 412–420.

Isaacs, K., & Silver, R. J. (1980, November). *Cognitive structure in depression.* Toronto: Paper presented at the annual meeting of the Association for Advancement of Behavior Therapy.

Jackson, D. N. (1970). A sequential system for personality scale development. In C. D. Spielberger (Ed.), *Current topics in clinical and community psychology.* New York: Academic.

Jones, R. G. (1969). A factored measure of Ellis's irrational belief system. (Doctoral dissertation, Texas Technological College, 1968). *Dissertation Abstracts International, 29*, 4379B–4380B.

Keller, K. E. (1983). Dysfunctional attitudes and cognitive therapy for depression. *Cognitive Therapy and Research, 7*, 437–444.

Keller, E. K., & Hasse, R. F. (1984). The relationship of dysfunctional attitudes to depression and hopelessness in a depressed community sample. *British Journal of Cognitive Psychotherapy, 2*, 61–66.

Kelly, G. A. (1955). *The psychology of personal constructs.* New York: Norton.

Kendall, P. C. (1982). Behavioral assessment and methodology. In C. M. Franks, G. T. Wilson, P. C. Kendall, & K. D. Brownell (Eds.). *Annual review of behavior therapy* (Vol. 8). New York: Guilford.

Kendall, P. C. (1984). Behavioral assessment and methodology. In C. M. Franks, G. T. Wilson, K. D. Brownell, & P. C. Kendall (Eds.), *Annual review of behavior therapy* (Vol. 9). New York: Guilford.

Kendall, P. C., & Hollon, S. D. (1981). Assessing self-referent speech: Methods in the measurement of self-statements. In P. C. Kendall & S. D. Hollon (Eds.), *Assessment strategies for cognitive-behavioral interventions.* New York: Academic.

Kendall, P. C., & Korgeski, G. P. (1979). Assessment and cognitive-behavioral interventions. *Cognitive Therapy and Research, 3*, 1–21.

Krantz, S., & Hammen, C. L. (1979). Assessment of cognitive bias in depression. *Journal of Abnormal Psychology, 88*, 611–619.

Kuiper, N. A., & Derry, P. A. (1982). Depressed and nondepressed content self-reference in mild depressives. *Journal of Personality, 50*, 67–79.

Kuiper, N. A., & Higgins, E. T. (1985). Social cognition and depression: A general integrative perspective. *Social Cognition, 3*, 1–15.

Kuiper, N. A., & Olinger, L. J. (1986). Dysfunctional attitudes and a self-worth contingency model of depression. In P. C. Kendall (Ed.), *Advances in cognitive-behavioral research and therapy, Vol. 5.* New York: Academic.

Kuiper, N. A., Olinger, L. J., MacDonald, M. R., & Shaw, B. F. (1985). Self-schema processing of depressed and nondepressed content: The effects of vulnerability to depression. *Social Cognition, 3*, 77–93.

Landau, R. J. (1980). The role of semantic schemata in phobic word interpretation. *Cognitive Therapy and Research, 4*, 427–434.

Last, C. G., Barlow, D. H., & O'Brien, G. T. (1985). Assessing cognitive aspects of anxiety: Stability over time and agreement between several methods. *Behavior Modification, 9*, 72–93.

Lefebvre, M. (1981). Cognitive distortion and cognitive errors in depressed psychiatric and low back pain patients. *Journal of Consulting and Clinical Psychology, 49*, 517–525.

Lewinsohn, P. M., Steinmetz, J. L., Larson, D. W., & Franklin, J. (1981). Depression-related cognitions: Antecedent or consequence? *Journal of Abnormal Psychology, 90*, 213–219.

Lishman, W. A. (1972). Selective factors in memory: Part 2: Affective disorders. *Psychological Medicine, 2*, 121–138.

Lloyd, G. G., & Lishman, W. A. (1975). Effect of depression on the speed of recall of pleasant and unpleasant experiences. *Psychological Medicine, 5,* 173–180.

Lohr, J. M., & Bonge, D. (1982). The factorial validity of the Irrational Beliefs Test: A psychometric investigation. *Cognitive Therapy and Research, 6,* 225–230.

MacLeod, C., Mathews, A., & Tata, P. (1986). Attentional bias in emotional disorders. *Journal of Abnormal Psychology, 95,* 15–20.

Markus, H. (1977). Self-schema and processing information about the self. *Journal of Personality and Social Psychology, 35,* 63–78.

Mathews, S. A., & MacLeod, C. (1985). Selective processing of threat cues to anxiety states. *Behaviour Research and Therapy, 23,* 563–569.

Mavissakalian, M., & Barlow, D. H. (1981). Phobia: An overview. In M. Mavissakalian & D. H. Barlow (Eds.), *Phobia: Psychological and pharmacological treatment.* New York: Guilford.

Meichenbaum, D. (1977). *Cognitive-behavior modification: An integrative approach.* New York: Plenum.

Meichenbaum, D., & Cameron, R. (1981). Issues in cognitive assessment: An overview. In T. V. Merluzzi, C. R. Glass, & M. Genest (Eds.), *Cognitive assessment.* New York: Guilford.

Mendonca, J. D., Holden, R. D., Mazmanian, D., & Dolan, J. (1983). The influence of response style on the Beck Hopelessness Scale. *Canadian Journal of Behavioral Science, 15,* 237–247.

Merluzzi, T. V., & Rudy, T. E. (1982, August). *Cognitive assessment of social anxiety: A "surface" and "deep" structure analysis in social anxiety: Social, personality, and clinical perspectives.* Paper presented at the American Psychological Association, Washington, DC.

Merluzzi, T. V., Rudy, T. E., & Glass, C. R. (1981). The information-processing paradigm: Implications for clinical science. In T. V. Merluzzi, C. R. Glass, & M. Genest (Eds.), *Cognitive Assessment.* New York: Guilford.

Miller, W. R. (1975). Psychological deficit in depression. *Psychological Bulletin, 2,* 238–260.

Miller, I. W., Klee, S. H., & Norman, H. W. (1982). Depressed and nondepressed inpatients' cognitions of hypothetical events, experimental tasks and stressful life events. *Journal of Abnormal Psychology, 91,* 78–81.

Minkoff, K., Bergman, E., Beck, A. T., & Beck, R. (1973). Hopelessness, depression, and attempted suicide. *American Journal of Psychiatry, 130,* 455–459.

Missel, P., & Sommer, G. (1983). Depression and self-verbalization. *Cognitive Therapy and Research, 7,* 141–148.

Munoz, R. F. (1977). Cognitive approach to the assessment and treatment of depression. Unpublished doctoral dissertation, University of Oregon.

Neimeyer, R. A. (1985). Personal constructs in clinical practice. In P. C. Kendall (Ed.), *Advances in cognitive-behavioral research and therapy, Vol. 4.* New York: Academic.

Neisser, V. (1976). *Cognition and reality: Principles and implications of cognitive psychology.* San Francisco: Freeman.

Nelson, R. D. (1977). Methodological issues in assessment and self-monitoring. In J. D. Cone & R. P. Hawkins (Eds.), *Behavioral assessment: New directions in clinical psychology.* New York: Brunner/Mazel.

Nelson, R. D., Hayes, S. C., Felton, J. L., & Jarrett, R. B. (1985). A comparison of data produced by different behavioral assessment techniques with implications for models of social-skills inadequacy. *Behaviour Research and Therapy, 23,* 1–11.

Newton, C. R., & Barbaree, H. E. (in press). Cognitive changes accompanying headache treatment: The use of a thought-sampling procedure. *Cognitive Therapy and Research.*

Nietzel, M. T., & Bernstein, D. A. (1981). Assessment of anxiety and fear. In M. Hersen & A. S. Bellack (Eds.), *Behavioral assessment: A practical handbook.* New York: Pergamon.

Nisbett, R. E., & Wilson, T. D. (1977). Telling more than we can know: Verbal reports on mental processes. *Psychological Review, 84*, 231-259.

Norman, W. H., Miller, I. W., & Klee, S. H. (1983). Assessment of cognitive distortion in a clinically depressed population. *Cognitive Therapy and Research, 7*, 133-140.

O'Hara, M. W., Rehm, L. P., & Campbell, S. B. (1982). Predicting depressive symptomatology: Cognitive behavioral models and post-partum depression. *Journal of Abnormal Psychology, 91*, 457-461.

Olinger, L. J., Kuiper, N. A., & Shaw, B. F. (1987). Dysfunctional attitudes and stressful life events: An interactive model of depression. *Cognitive Therapy and Research, 11*, 25-40.

Olinger, L. J., Shaw, B. F., & Kuiper, N. A. (1987). Nonassertiveness and vulnerability to depression: A cognitive perspective. *Canadian Journal of Behavioural Science, 19*, 40-49.

Oliver, J. M., & Baumgart, E. P. (1985). The Dysfunctional Attitude Scale: Psychometric properties and relation to depression in an unselected adult population. *Cognitive Therapy and Research, 9*, 161-168.

Paivio, A. (1975). Neomentalism. *Canadian Journal of Psychology, 29*, 263-291.

Peterson, C., Semmel, A., von Baeyer, C., Abramson, L., Metalsky, G., & Seligman, M. E. P. (1982). The Attributional Style Questionnaire. *Cognitive Therapy and Research, 6*, 287-299.

Rachman, S., & Hodgson, R. (1974). 1. Synchrony and desynchrony in fear and avoidance. *Behaviour Research and Therapy, 12*, 311-318.

Rapp, S. R. (1985, November). *Cognitive and behavioral patterns among depressive subtypes.* Paper presented at the Association for Advancement of Behavior Therapy. Houston, TX.

Reda, M. A., Carpiniello, B., Secchiaroli, L., & Blanco, S. (1985). Thinking, depression, and antidepressants: Modified and unmodified depressive beliefs during treatment with amitriptyline. *Cognitive Therapy and Research, 9*, 135-144.

Riskind, J. H., Beck, A. T., & Smucker, M. R. (1983, December). *Psychometric properties of the Dysfunctional Attitude Scale in a clinical population.* Paper presented at the meeting of the World Congress of Behavior Therapy, Washington, D.C.

Riskind, J. H., & Rholes, W. S. (1984). Cognitive accessibility and the capacity of cognitions to predict future depression: A theoretical note. *Cognitive Therapy and Research, 8*, 1-12.

Rogers, T. B., Kuiper, N. A., & Kirker, W. S. (1977). Self-reference and the encoding of personal information. *Journal of Personality and Social Psychology, 35*, 677-688.

Rosenbaum, M. (1980). A schedule for assessing self-control behaviors: Preliminary findings. *Behavior Therapy, 11*, 109-121.

Roth, D., & Rehm, L. P. (1980). Relationships among self-monitoring processes, memory and depression. *Cognitive Therapy and Research, 4*, 149-157.

Rude, S. S. (1983). *An investigation of differential response to two treatments of depression.* Unpublished doctoral dissertation, Stanford University.

Rudy, T. E., & Merluzzi, T. V. (1984). Recovering social-cognitive schemata: Descriptions and applications of multidimensional scaling for clinical research. In P. C. Kendall (Ed.), *Advances in cognitive-behavioral research and therapy.* Orlando, FL: Academic.

Rudy, T. E., Merluzzi, T. V., & Henahan, P. T. (1982). Construal of complex assertive situations: A multidimensional analysis. *Journal of Consulting and Clinical Psychology, 50*, 125-137.

Rush, A. J. (1983). Cognitive therapy for depression. In M. Zales (Ed.), *Affective and schizophrenic disorders: New approaches to diagnosis.* New York: Brunner/Mazel.

Rush, A. J. (1984, March). *Measurement of the cognitive aspects of depression.* Paper presented at the NIMH Workshop on Measurement of Depression. Honolulu, HI.

Rush, A. J., Beck, A. T., Kovacs, M., Weissenburger, J., & Hollon, S. D. (1982). Comparison of the effects of cognitive therapy and pharmacotherapy on hopelessness and self-concept. *American Journal of Psychiatry, 139*, 862-866.

Rush, A. J., Weissenberger, J., & Eaves, G. (1986). Do thinking patterns predict depressive symptoms? *Cognitive Therapy and Research, 10,* 225-236.

Safran, J. D. (1983). The functional asymmetry of negative and positive self-statements. *The British Journal of Clinical Psychology, 21,* 223-224.

Schwartz, R., & Gottman, J. (1976). Toward a task analysis of assertive behavior. *Journal of Consulting and Clinical Psychology, 44,* 910-920.

Segal, Z. V., & Hood, J. (1985, June). *Measures of self-schema in depression: A construct in search of a structure.* Paper presented at the Society for Psychotherapy Research Meeting, Evanston, IL.

Segal, Z. V., Hood, J. E., Shaw, B. F., & Higgins, E. T. (1986). *A structural analysis of the self-schema construct in major depression.* Manuscript submitted for publication.

Segal, Z. V., & Marshall, W. L. (1985). Heterosexual social skills in a population of rapists and child molesters. *Journal of Consulting and Clinical Psychology, 53,* 55-63.

Segal, Z. V., & Shaw, B. F. (1986). Cognition in depression: A reappraisal of Coyne and Gotlib's critique. *Cognitive Therapy and Research, 10,* 671-694.

Seligman, M. E. P., Abramson, L., Semmel, A., & von Baeyer, C. (1979). Depressive attributional style. *Journal of Abnormal Psychology, 88,* 242-248.

Sewitch, T. S., & Kirsch, I. (1984). The cognitive content of anxiety: Naturalistic evidence for the predominance of threat-related thoughts. *Cognitive Therapy and Research, 8,* 49-58.

Shaw, B. F., & Dobson, K. S. (1981). Cognitive assessment of depression. In T. V. Merluzzi, C. R. Glass, & M. Genest (Eds.), *Cognitive assessment.* New York: Guilford.

Simons, A. D., Garfield, S. L., & Murphy, G. E. (1984). The process of change in cognitive therapy and pharmacotherapy for depression: Changes in mood and cognition. *Archives of General Psychiatry, 41,* 45-51.

Simons, A. D., Lustman, P. J., Wetzel, R. D., & Murphy, G. E. (1985). Predicting response to cognitive therapy of depression: The role of learned resourcefulness. *Cognitive Therapy and Research, 9,* 79-90.

Simons, A. D., Murphy, G. E., Levine, J. L., & Wetzel, R. D. (1986). Cognitive therapy and pharmacotherapy for depression. *Archives of General Psychiatry, 43,* 43-48.

Silverman, J. S., Silverman, J. A., & Eardley, D. A. (1984). Do maladaptive attitudes cause depression? *Archives of General Psychiatry, 41,* 28-30.

Smith, T. W. (1982). Irrational beliefs in the cause and treatment of emotional distress: A critical review of the Rational-Emotive model. *Clinical Psychology Review, 2,* 505-522.

Smith, T. W., & Zurawski, R. M. (1983). Assessment of irrational beliefs: The question of discriminant validity. *Journal of Clinical Psychology, 39,* 976-979.

Space, L. G., & Cromwell, R. L. (1980). Personal constructs among depressed patients. *The Journal of Nervous and Mental Disease, 168,* 150-518.

Spitzer, R. L., Endicott, J., & Robins, E. (1978). *Research Diagnostic Criteria (RDC) for a selected group of functional disorders.* New York: Biometrics Research.

Stroop, J. R. (1938). Factors affecting speed in serial verbal reactions. *Psychological Monographs, 50,* No. 225.

Swinson, R., & Kirby, M. (1987). The differentiation of anxiety and depressive syndromes. In B. F. Shaw, Z. V. Segal, T. M. Vallis, & F. E. Cashman (Eds.), *Anxiety disorders: Psychological and biological perspectives.* New York: Plenum.

Turk, D. C., & Salovey, P. (1985). Cognitive structures, cognitive processes, and cognitive-behavior modification: 1. Client issues. *Cognitive Therapy and Research, 9,* 1-17.

Warren, R. E. (1972). Stimulus encoding and memory. *Journal of Experimental Psychology, 94,* 90-100.

Watkins, J., & Rush, A. J. (1983). The cognitive response test. *Cognitive Therapy and Research, 7,* 425-436.

Watson, D., & Friend, R. (1969). Measurement of social-evaluative anxiety. *Journal of Consulting and Clinical Psychology, 33,* 448-457.

Webb, E. J., Campbell, D. T., Schwartz, R. D., & Sechrest, L. (1966). *Unobtrusive measures: Non-reactive research in the social sciences.* Chicago: Rand McNally.

Weissman, A. N. (1979). *The Dysfunctional Attitude Scale: A validation study.* Unpublished dissertation. University of Pennsylvania.

Weissman, A. N., & Beck, A. T. (1978). *Development and validation of the Dysfunctional Attitude Scale: A preliminary investigation.* Paper presented at the Annual Meeting of the American Educational Research Association. Toronto, Canada.

Wilkinson, I. M., & Blackburn, I. M. (1981). Cognitive style in depressed and recovered depressed patients. *British Journal of Clinical Psychology, 20,* 283-292.

Williams, S. L. (1985). On the nature and measurement of agoraphobia. In M. Hersen, R. M. Eisler, & P. M. Miller (Eds.), *Progress in behavior modification.* New York: Academic.

Williams, S. L., & Rappoport, A. (1983). Cognitive treatment in the natural environment for agoraphobics. *Behavior Therapy, 14,* 299-313.

Winters, K. C., & Neale, J. M. (1985). Mania and low self-esteem. *Journal of Abnormal Psychology, 94,* 282-290.

Zimmerman, M., Coryell, W., & Corenthal, C. (1984). Attribution style, the Dexamethasone Suppression Test and the diagnosis of melancholia in depressed inpatients. *Journal of Abnormal Psychology, 93,* 373-377.

Zweig, D. R., & Brown, S. D. (1985). Psychometric evaluation of a written stimulus presentation format for the Social Interaction Self-Statement Test. *Cognitive Therapy and Research, 9,* 285-296.

PART II

THE THERAPIES

3

PROBLEM-SOLVING THERAPIES

THOMAS J. D'ZURILLA

Problem-solving therapy, or the clinical application of problem-solving training (PST)[1], had its beginnings in the late 1960s and early 1970s as part of the growing trend in clinical psychology and psychiatry toward the development of clinical intervention and prevention strategies that focus on the facilitation of social competence (Gladwin, 1967). Within the field of behavior modification during the same period of time, the development of PST received impetus from the emergence of the cognitive-behavioral approach, which focuses on cognitive mediation in an attempt to facilitate self-control and thus produce more durable and generalized behavior changes (Kendall & Hollon, 1979).

At a symposium on the role of cognitive factors in behavior modification at the 1968 APA convention, D'Zurilla and Goldfried argued that social-skills training programs should include training in problem-solving skills in order to produce more generalized improvements in social competence. This viewpoint was later expanded in an article published in 1971 under the title "Problem Solving and Behavior Modification." In 1976, Spivack, Platt, and Shure published their influential book *The Problem-Solving Approach to Adjustment,* which presented evidence on the relationship between problem-solving ability and psychopathology, and described several early studies on PST with both children and adults. At about this point in time, Mahoney (1974) described the promise of problem solving for behavior modification as follows:

The potential relevance of problem solving to both clients and therapists needs little elaboration. In terms of adaptive versatility and the ability to cope with an ever-changing array of life problems, these cognitive skills may offer an invaluable personal paradigm for survival. Their potential contribution to therapeutic efficacy and independent self-improvement will hopefully become an issue of priority in future empirical scrutiny (p. 212).

Since the early 1970s, there has been a rapid increase in the number of PST programs reported in the clinical and counseling psychology literature

1. In this chapter, the abbreviation "PST" will refer to either "problem-solving therapy" or "problem-solving training."

(see also Durlak, 1983; D'Zurilla, 1986a; D'Zurilla & Nezu, 1982; Pellegrini & Urbain, 1985; Spivack & Shure, 1974; Spivack *et al.*, 1976; Urbain & Kendall, 1980). Focusing on children as well as adults, these programs have employed PST as either a treatment method (used alone or in conjunction with other treatment techniques), a treatment maintenance strategy, or a prevention strategy. These applications have occurred within a variety of clinical settings, including individual therapy and counseling, group therapy, marital therapy, and family therapy. In addition, there have been a number of applications in nonclinical settings such as workshops, academic courses, and seminars. Target populations have ranged from institutionalized psychiatric patients to individuals with relatively minor maladjustments (e.g., weight-control problems, study problems) to normal individuals and groups interested in maximizing their problem-solving effectiveness and preventing future problems. Problems focused on in training have ranged from an individual's personal problems to marital and family conflicts to broader community problems.

The present chapter will focus on the use of PST with adults. Following a discussion of the theoretical and empirical foundations of PST, assessment methods will be discussed and then a problem-solving approach to social competence enhancement will be described. This approach may serve as a model for PST as either a treatment method, a treatment maintenance strategy, or a prevention program, with goals of increasing general social competence and reducing stress. A case study that illustrates the application of PST as part of a broader treatment program for a disorder involving generalized anxiety will be presented. This will be followed by a discussion of some of the variations in PST programs for different target populations and different program goals. The chapter will conclude with a discussion of the empirical status of PST.

THEORETICAL AND EMPIRICAL FOUNDATIONS

DEFINITIONS

A discussion of the problem-solving approach to clinical intervention must begin with a definition of the terms "problem-solving," "problem," and "solution." In the real-life social context, *problem solving* may be defined as a cognitive-affective-behavioral process through which an individual (or group) attempts to identify, discover, or invent effective or adaptive means of coping with problems encountered in everyday living (D'Zurilla, 1986a; D'Zurilla & Goldfried, 1971; D'Zurilla & Nezu, 1982). In the clinical and counseling psychology literature, problem solving in the real-life social setting has been referred to frequently as *social problem solving* (D'Zurilla & Nezu, 1982; Krasnor & Rubin, 1981). However, the terms *interpersonal prob-*

lem solving (Shure, 1981), *interpersonal cognitive problem solving* (Spivack et al., 1976), *personal problem solving* (Heppner & Petersen, 1982) and *applied problem solving* (Heppner, Neal, & Larson, 1984) have also been used.

Social problem solving is at the same time a social-learning process, a self-management technique, and a general coping strategy. Since problem solving results in a change in performance capability, it qualifies as a learning process (Gagné, 1966). Since problem solving can be applied by an individual independently (i.e., with little or no external direction or control) to a wide variety of problems in living, it is a useful self-management technique and a versatile coping strategy that has important implications for treatment maintenance, generalization, and prevention (D'Zurilla & Goldfried, 1971; Mahoney, 1974).

A *problem* is defined here as a life situation that demands a response for effective functioning, but for which no effective response is immediately available to the individual (or group) confronted with the situation (D'Zurilla & Goldfried, 1971). In such a situation, the individual perceives a discrepancy between "what is" (i.e., present conditions) and "what should be" (i.e., conditions that are demanded or desired), but the means for reducing this discrepancy are not immediately apparent or available due to some obstacle or obstacles (e.g., ambiguity, uncertainty, unfamiliarity, conflict, etc.). The "demands" in the situation may originate in the environment (e.g., task demands), or within the person (e.g., a personal goal or commitment). They are best described as perceived demands, rather than objective demands, since an individual is likely to be influenced more by his perception of the demands in the situation when identifying problems than by the objective demands themselves. As it is defined here, a problem should not be viewed as a characteristic of the environment alone, nor as a characteristic of the person alone. Instead, it is best described as a person–environment encounter or "transaction" (Lazarus, 1981), which involves a reciprocal relationship between environmental variables and person variables that is constantly changing over time. Thus, a problem can be expected to increase or decrease in difficulty or significance over time, depending on changes in the environment (e.g., objective demand characteristics), the person (e.g., appraisal of task demands, response availability), or both.

Problems are likely to be stressful if they are at all difficult and significant for well-being because such problems are likely to involve conflict, uncertainty, threat, and/or perceived uncontrollability (Epstein, 1982; Hamberger & Lohr, 1984; Janis, 1982; Phillips, 1978). If problems can be viewed as stressors, then social problem solving is an activity that often takes place under stressful conditions (Janis, 1982; Janis & Mann, 1977). The role of stress and other emotional variables in problem solving has been a neglected topic in most laboratory-based theories of rational problem solving and decision making (Kleinmuntz, 1966; Newell & Simon, 1972). An adequate theory of social problem solving must account for the effects of these variables on problem-solving performance, and PST programs must include methods for controlling disruptive emotions in order to facilitate problem-solving effectiveness (D'Zurilla, 1986a).

A *solution* is a coping response or response pattern that is effective in altering the problematic situation and/or one's own personal reactions to it so that it is no longer perceived as a problem, while at the same time maximizing other positive consequences (benefits) and minimizing negative consequences (costs) (D'Zurilla & Goldfried, 1971). The relevant benefits and costs include both immediate and long-term personal/social consequences. The "effectiveness" of any particular solution may vary for different individuals or different environments, depending on the norms, values, and goals of the problem solver or significant others who are responsible for judging the problem solver's performance.

It is important for theory, research, and practice to distinguish between the concepts "problem solving," "solution implementation," and "social competence" (D'Zurilla & Goldfried, 1971; D'Zurilla & Nezu, 1982). As defined above, problem solving refers to the process by which an individual or group discovers a solution to a problem. *Solution implementation*, on the other hand, refers only to the performance of the solution response, which is a function not only of problem solving, but also of other factors related to the individual's learning history, such as performance-skill deficits, emotional inhibitions, and motivational (reinforcement) deficits. *Social competence* is the broadest concept of the three, referring to a wide range of social skills, behavioral competencies, and coping behaviors that enable an individual to deal effectively with the demands of everyday living (Goldfried & D'Zurilla, 1969; McFall, 1982; Wrubel, Benner, & Lazarus, 1981). Effective problem-solving performance is only one component of social competence, albeit a very significant one (Sarason, 1981).

It is also important to clarify the relationship between PST and social-skills training (SST). It should now be clear that PST and SST are both interventions designed to enhance social competence. In the past, SST programs have focused almost exclusively on social performance skills (Bellack & Hersen, 1979). However, the concept of social skills has been broadened in recent years to include cognitive skills (Kagan, 1984; McFall, 1982). A number of investigators in the area of SST now consider problem solving to be an important cognitive skill that should be incorporated into SST programs (Kagan, 1984; Goldstein, 1973; McFall, 1982; Sarason, 1981; Sprafkin, Gershaw, & Goldstein, 1980).

THE SOCIAL PROBLEM-SOLVING PROCESS

The variables involved in the social problem-solving process include cognitions, affective responses, and behavioral activities. These variables can be described at three different levels, each reflecting increased specificity of effects on problem-solving performance. These three levels of problem-solving variables will be referred to here as (1) problem-orientation cognitions, (2) specific problem-solving skills, and (3) basic problem-solving abilities. Each level affects problem-solving performance in a different way.

Problem-Orientation Cognitions

At the most general level are the problem-orientation cognitions. These variables tend to have generalized or nonspecific effects on problem-solving performance. They do not include the specific skills or abilities that are required to solve a particular problem successfully. Rather, they may be described as higher order "metacognitive" variables (Butler & Meichenbaum, 1981; Meichenbaum & Asarnow, 1979) that define an individual's general orientation to problems in living (i.e., the way a person attends to and thinks about problems, independent of any particular problematic situation). This general problem orientation reflects the person's beliefs, values, and commitments concerning real-life problems and problem solving as a means of coping with them, as well as his or her past reinforcement history related to independent problem solving (i.e., successes and failures). Important problem-orientation variables include problem perception, causal attributions, problem appraisals, beliefs about personal control, and values concerning the commitment of time and effort to problem solving.

The different problem-orientation cognitions do not operate separately from one another; they are constantly interacting and influencing each other. Depending on the nature of particular problem-orientation variables, they may facilitate or inhibit problem-solving performance, influencing the initiation and generalization of problem-solving activities, the amount of time and effort expended, and persistence in the face of obstacles such as emotional distress. A facilitative set of problem-orientation cognitions contributes to a positive coping style, which may be described as a generalized problem-solving style. An inhibitive set of problem-orientation cognitions, on the other hand, reflects a negative coping style, such as "defensive avoidance," "helplessness," or "dependency" (Janis, 1982; Janis & Mann, 1977).

Specific Problem-Solving Skills

At an intermediate level of specificity are the specific problem-solving skills, each of which has a definite purpose or function in the problem-solving process. This set of skills can be described as a sequence of specific goal-directed tasks that must be performed in order to solve a particular problem successfully. They include the tasks of defining and formulating the problem, generating a list of alternative solutions, making a decision, and assessing the solution outcome (D'Zurilla & Goldfried, 1971). In behavioral terms, this series of problem-solving tasks can be conceived of as a behavioral chain, where the successful completion of each task reinforces performance on that task, and the satisfactory solution to the problem reinforces the entire problem-solving sequence.

Basic Problem-Solving Abilities

At the most specific level are the basic problem-solving abilities that underlie and affect the ability to learn and implement the problem-solving operations at the general and intermediate levels. Relatively little is known about these basic abilities at the present time. They are, however, likely to include the cognitive abilities described by Spivack et al., (1976) as being important for social problem solving: sensitivity to problems (ability to recognize that a problem exists), alternative thinking (ability to generate alternative solutions, means–ends thinking (ability to conceptualize relevant means to a goal), consequential thinking (ability to anticipate consequences), and perspective taking (ability to perceive a situation from another person's perspective).

The above cognitive abilities and other basic abilities that may underlie the social problem-solving process are all likely to be included in J. P. Guilford's (1967, 1968) Structure-of-Intellect model. This model has three dimensions: (1) contents (major kinds of information), (2) products (how information is structured or organized), and (3) operations (intellectual processes). There are five kinds of informational content (visual, auditory, symbolic, semantic, and behavioral), six kinds of products (units, classes, relations, systems, transformations, and implications), and five kinds of operations (memory, cognition, convergent production, divergent production, and evaluation). Each cell in the model represents a specific ability. The abilities that are measured by traditional IQ tests are included in the intellectual operations of memory (storage and retrieval of information), cognition (knowing and understanding), convergent production (focused search for one correct answer or conclusion), and evaluation (comparing and judging information). The operation of divergent production (broad search for alternative ideas or solutions) is not included in traditional IQ tests, nor is it correlated with traditional IQ measures. However, according to Guilford, divergent production abilities are major determinants of creativity. They include abilities such as fluency (ability to produce a large number of ideas), flexibility (ability to produce a variety of kinds of ideas), and originality (ability to produce unusual or novel ideas).

Guilford (1967, 1977) sees much overlap between creative abilities and problem-solving abilities. In his Structure-of-Intellect Problem-Solving model, all five intellectual operations are represented, but divergent production is emphasized. Within the informational content dimension, the abilities associated with the categories labeled semantic (verbal, meaningful information) and behavioral (personal/social information) are considered most relevant for social problem solving. The operation of memory is important because it involves the storage and retrieval of information as needed during the problem-solving process. The operation of cognition focuses on two important problem-solving events: awareness that a problem exists (cognition of implications) and comprehension of the nature of the problem (cognition of relations and systems). Convergent production and divergent production both contribute to the generation of solutions, with the latter being most important because of the emphasis on fluency, flexibility, and originality. In addition, the abilities associated with the product category of transformations (ability to modify and improve information or ideas) are considered important for the generation of appropriate and useful solution alternatives. Finally, the operation of evaluation is necessary for comparing and judging solutions and assessing solution outcome.

Research is needed to determine what basic abilities account most for individual differences in social problem-solving performance. The Guilford model and many of the tests that have been developed to measure the abilities that make up the model could contribute much to this research (Guilford, 1967, 1977; Parnes & Noller, 1973). Research is also needed to clarify the relationship between social problem-solving ability and general intelligence. Several studies have found low correlations between social problem-solving measures and general intelligence as measured by traditional IQ tests and academic aptitude tests (Heppner & Petersen, 1982; Spivack et al., 1976). Low correlations have also been found between measures of Guilford's divergent production operation and IQ tests (Guilford, 1977). However, according to Guilford, an interesting kind of relationship exists between divergent production ability and IQ. Individuals with low IQs have only low scores on divergent production tests. However, individuals with higher IQs show more variability in divergent production scores. Thus it appears that IQ puts an upper limit on divergent production performance, but high IQ does not ensure high divergent production ability. If divergent production ability is important for social problem solving, as Guilford suggests, then there may be a similar relationship between social problem solving and IQ. Such a relationship would be consistent with the observation that mentally retarded individuals are generally deficient in both general intelligence and adaptive social functioning, while individuals with higher IQs show greater variability in social competence.

A PRESCRIPTIVE MODEL OF SOCIAL PROBLEM SOLVING

Based on a review of the most relevant problem-solving theory and research from the fields of experimental psychology, education, and industry, D'Zurilla and Goldfried (1971) proposed a prescriptive or normative model of social problem solving to serve as a guide for the development of PST programs. A prescriptive problem-solving model attempts to specify how individuals should solve problems in order to maximize their effectiveness, as compared to a descriptive model, which describes how individuals typically go about solving problems. The D'Zurilla and Goldfried model, as revised by D'Zurilla and Nezu (1982) and D'Zurilla (1986a) has five components or stages that include skills and abilities at all three levels. These five components are: (1) problem orientation, (2) problem definition and formulation, (3) generation of alternative solutions, (4) decision making, and (5) solution implementation and verification. Individually, each component has a definite purpose or function in the problem-solving process. Together, the five components, when applied effectively to a particular problem, are expected to maximize the probability of discovering the most effective solution.

Problem orientation consists of a set of facilitative problem-orientation cognitions that may be described as a generalized problem-solving cognitive set. As noted earlier, this cognitive set is expected to have a generalized, facilitative effect on problem-solving performance throughout the problem-solving process. Specifically, the function of these problem-orientation variables is to (1) increase sensitivity to problems and set the occasion for problem-solving activity, (2) focus attention on positive problem-solving behaviors and away from unproductive worries or "self-preoccupying thoughts" (Sarason, 1980), (3) maximize effort and persistence in the face of obstacles and emotional stress, and (4) minimize disruptive emotional distress, while attempting to maximize positive, facilitative emotional states.

The major problem-orientation variables are (1) problem perception, (2) problem attribution, (3) problem appraisal, (4) personal control, and (5) time/effort commitment. Problem perception refers to the likelihood that the individual will attend to and monitor his or her transactions with the environment in such a way as to recognize problems accurately and label them appropriately. Problem attribution refers to the person's causal attributions concerning problems in living. A positive or facilitative problem attribution involves the readiness to attribute the cause of problems to changeable, relatively benign environmental and personal factors, instead of attributing the cause primarily to some stable internal defect or abnormality (Abramson, Seligman, & Teasdale, 1978; Beck, 1967; Ellis, 1977). Problem appraisal refers to the individual's evaluation of the significance of a problem for his or her personal/social well-being (Lazarus & Folkman, 1984). A positive problem appraisal is to view a problem as a "challenge" (i.e., opportunity for personal growth or mastery) instead of viewing it only as a "threat" (i.e., potential for harm or loss). Personal control has two components: (1) the likelihood that the individual will perceive a problem as soluble or controllable, and (2) the likelihood that the individual will believe that he or she is capable of solving a problem through his or her own efforts (Bandura, 1977). Time/effort commitment also has two components:

(1) the likelihood that the individual will estimate accurately the time it will take to solve a particular problem successfully, and (2) the likelihood that he or she will be willing to devote the necessary time and effort to problem solving (Baumgardner, Heppner, & Arkin, 1984).

The second component of the model, problem definition and formulation, is an assessment process that involves (1) gathering relevant, factual information about the problem, (2) clarifying the nature of the problem, (3) setting a realistic problem-solving goal, and (4) reappraising the significance of the problem for personal/social well-being. The emphasis in this stage is on skills and abilities related to social information processing (McFall, 1982), problem conceptualization, goal setting, rational thinking (Beck, 1967; Ellis, 1977), and cognitive appraisal (Lazarus & Folkman, 1984). The purpose of the model's third component, generation of alternative solutions, is to make available as many solution alternatives as possible in order to maximize the likelihood that the "best" (most preferred) solution will be among them. This task focuses on Guilford's (1967) operation of divergent production. Based on the creative abilities of fluency, originality, and flexibility, the generation-of-alternatives procedure emphasizes three major principles: (1) the quantity principle (the more solution alternatives that are produced, the more good ideas will be made available), (2) the deferment-of-judgment principle (more good solution ideas will be generated if a person suspends critical evaluation of ideas until later on in the problem-solving process), and (3) the variety principle (the greater the range or variety of solution ideas, the more good ideas will be discovered).

The function of the fourth component of the problem-solving model, decision making, is to evaluate the available solution alternatives and to select the best one(s) for implementation in the problematic situation. The decision-making procedure is based on expected utility theory (Beach & Mitchell, 1978; Edwards, 1961) and prospect theory (Kahnemann & Tversky, 1979; Tversky & Kahnemann, 1981). In expected utility theory, choice behavior is based on a rational benefit/cost analysis. Prospect theory takes into account the effects of perceptual and subjective factors on choice behavior. Studies have found that an individual's solution preferences are significantly influenced by the way problems are formulated and the way solution alternatives and outcomes are conceived or "framed" (Tversky & Kahnemann, 1981).

The purpose of the final component of the model, solution implementation and verification, is to assess the solution outcome and verify the "effectiveness" of the chosen solution strategy in the real-life problematic situation. Up to this point in the problem-solving process, the problem has been solved symbolically, but the effectiveness of the solution in coping with the real-life problem has not yet been established empirically. The only way to accomplish this is to implement the solution strategy and evaluate the outcome as objectively as possible. The conceptual framework for this task is based on control theory or cybernetics (Carver & Scheier, 1982; Miller, Galanter, & Pribram, 1960) and the cognitive-behavioral conception of self-control (Bandura, 1971; Kanfer, 1970). Four steps are involved: (1) performance of the solution behavior, (2) self-monitoring of the solution behavior and/or its outcome, (3) self-evaluation, involving a comparison between the actual outcome and the expected outcome, and either (4) self-reinforcement or (5) "troubleshooting" and recycling (i.e., returning to the problem-solving process), depending on the degree of satisfaction with the outcome.[2]

The order in which the five components of the model are presented above represents a logical and practical sequence for training and systematic, efficient application. Problem solving should begin with a positive problem orientation since such a cognitive set is likely to facilitate general problem-solving performance (Butler & Meichenbaum, 1981; Heppner & Petersen, 1982; Heppner, Hibel, Neal, Weinstein, & Rabinowitz, 1982). In addition, a problem should be clarified and formulated carefully before beginning the tasks of generating alternative solutions and decision making, since a clear definition of the problem is likely to influence performance on these tasks (Nezu & D'Zurilla, 1981a, 1981b; Tversky & Kahnemann, 1981). Finally, it is necessary to generate solution alternatives before the decision-making task can be started, and to choose a solution before the final stage of solution implementation and verification can be carried out to complete the problem-solving process. The order in which the model's components are presented does *not* mean that problem solving should always proceed in a one-directional sequence beginning with step one and ending with step five. Effective problem solving is likely to involve movement back and forth from one task to another before the process is finally terminated (see D'Zurilla, 1986a). The problem solver completes the process only when a satisfactory solution is found, or when it is determined that the problem is insoluble and must be accepted and coped with as it is.

Several experimental studies have investigated the effects of individual model components or principles on problem-solving performance. Such studies are important in order to establish what components or principles contribute significantly to problem-solving effectiveness. Most of these studies have been described previously by D'Zurilla (1986a), D'Zurilla and Goldfried (1971), and D'Zurilla and Nezu (1982). Results supporting the efficacy of a positive problem orientation have been reported by Cormier, Otani, and Cormier (1986). Strong support for the efficacy of training in problem definition and formulation has been found in studies by Cormier *et al.* (1986) and by Nezu and D'Zurilla (1981a, 1981b). Support for principles involved in the generation-of-alternative-solutions task has been found

---

2. For a more thorough discussion of the principles, procedures, and empirical findings related to each component of the problem-solving model, the reader is referred to D'Zurilla (1986a), D'Zurilla and Goldfried (1971), and D'Zurilla and Nezu (1982).

in studies by Bayless (1967), Brilhart and Jochem (1964), D'Zurilla and Nezu (1980), Meadow, Parnes and Reese (1959), Nezu and D'Zurilla (1981b), Nezu and Ronan (in press), Parloff and Handlon (1964), Parnes and Meadow (1959), and Weisskopf-Joelson and Eliseo (1961). The model's decision-making method has received strong support in studies by Nezu and D'Zurilla (1979, 1981a) and Nezu and Ronan (in press).

No experimental studies have specifically investigated the solution-implementation-and-verification component of the model. However, the general evidence supporting the use of behavioral self-monitoring in any behavior modification program can be used as support for the efficacy of this component (Barlow, Haynes, & Nelson, 1984; Bellack & Hersen, 1977). Without an objective evaluation of outcome, it would not be possible to establish clearly the success of any behavior modification procedure.

ROLE OF EMOTIONS IN SOCIAL PROBLEM SOLVING

Unlike human problem solving in a laboratory setting, emotional factors play an important role in problem solving within the real-life social setting. There are three possible sources of emotional arousal in social problem solving: (1) the objective problematic situation, (2) the problem-orientation cognitions (e.g., problem appraisal, problem attribution, etc.), and (3) the specific problem-solving tasks (e.g., problem definition and formulation, decision making, etc.). These emotions may include unconditioned and conditioned emotional responses (Staats, 1975), emotions associated with the perceptual characteristics (i.e., meaning, significance) of problem-solving variables such as problem appraisals and problem formulations (Lazarus, 1982; Lazarus, Kanner, & Folkman, 1980), and emotions produced by reinforcement and punishment occurring as consequences of problem-solving task performance (Mowrer, 1960a, 1960b).

Emotional responses may facilitate or inhibit problem-solving performance, depending on such variables as the intensity and duration of emotional arousal (i.e., autonomic nervous system activity) and the subjective quality of the emotional response (pleasure vs. pain). For example, a high level of autonomic arousal may cause negative affect and a narrowing of attention to task-irrelevant cues, which may disrupt problem-solving thinking and reduce performance efficiency at any point in the problem-solving process (D'Zurilla, 1986a; Mandler, 1982). Emotional variables may also significantly affect problem recognition, the setting of problem-solving goals, the evaluation of solution alternatives, and the assessment of solution outcome.[3]

---

3. For a more comprehensive discussion of the effects of emotional variables on social problem-solving performance, the reader is referred to D'Zurilla (1986a), Janis (1982), and Janis and Mann (1977).

Awareness and control of emotional responses is important for efficient and effective problem-solving performance. When excessive emotional distress appears to be a significant factor affecting problem-solving performance, the PST program should include training in various facilitative coping skills (D'Zurilla, 1986a). Important techniques might include cognitive restructuring (e.g., reappraisal of threat, correcting misconceptions: see Dryden & Ellis, Chapter 6, this volume; Goldfried, Decenteceo, & Weinberg, 1974), self instruction (e.g., coping self-directions, positive self-talk: Janis, 1983; Meichenbaum & Cameron, 1983), and relaxation/desensitization techniques (Bernstein & Borkovec, 1973; Woolfolk & Lehrer, 1984). Cognitive restructuring techniques, especially the reappraisal of threat, may help to reduce anxiety resulting from irrational beliefs and exaggerated threatening appraisals. Self-instruction may help the problem solver focus attention on task-relevant cues and on beliefs and expectations that are likely to facilitate problem-solving performance. Finally, relaxation and self-desensitization techniques, including the use of "relaxation breaks" during difficult or extended problem solving, may help the problem solver to maintain an optimal level of arousal for effective problem solving.

SOCIAL PROBLEM-SOLVING AND ADJUSTMENT

The problem-solving approach to clinical intervention and prevention is based on four assumptions or hypotheses:

1. Social problem solving is positively related to social competence and inversely related to psychopathology or maladaptive behavior.

2. Training in problem-solving skills will increase social competence and help to reduce maladaptive behavior in certain patients who are in need of therapy (i.e., patients with deficits in problem-solving ability and/or performance).

3. Training in problem-solving skills will increase social competence and help to prevent the recurrence of maladaptive behavior in certain patients following other forms of therapy (i.e., patients with deficits in problem-solving ability and/or performance).

4. Training in problem-solving skills will increase social competence and help to prevent the development of new maladaptive behavior in certain "vulnerable" or "at risk" populations (i.e., people who are experiencing an increase in the number and/or complexity of stressful problems with which they must cope, such as recently divorced people, adolescents, new parents, etc.).

About 30 years ago, Jahoda (1953, 1958) argued that problem-solving ability is an important criterion to consider in defining positive mental health, suggesting that deficiencies in problem-solving ability might be associated with maladjustment or psychopathology. This hypothesis has been elaborated on in recent years (D'Zurilla, 1986a; Mechanic, 1970, 1974; Phillips, 1978; Spivack *et al.*, 1976), and has received support in a number of experimental and correlational studies (see also Nezu, in press; Nezu & D'Zurilla, in press).

Experimental Studies

According to Phillips's (1978) "functional definition of psychopathology," maladaptive behavior occurs when an organism lacks the immediate capability to solve a problem or reach a goal, and its repeated efforts to do so are ineffective or unsuccessful. Phillips's problem-solving deficit view of psychopathology is based on a number of experimental studies in which laboratory animals were placed in aversive problematic situations where the availability of a solution was impossible or highly unlikely (e.g., Maier, 1949; Masserman, 1943; Seligman, 1975; Seligman & Maier, 1967; Solomon, 1964). In such situations, the animals showed a variety of "neurotic" or maladaptive behaviors, including perplexity, loss of control, rigidity, stereotyped behavior, and "bizarre" or unusual behavior.

Similar studies have been done with humans in which subjects are placed in problematic situations where the ability of the subject to predict or control an aversive or rewarding outcome is manipulated. Under conditions of unpredictability or uncontrollability, the subjects have shown a variety of negative stress effects and maladaptive behaviors, including "learned helplessness" (Hiroto & Seligman, 1975), anxiety or discomfort (Corah & Boffa, 1970; Geer, Davison, & Gatchel, 1970), obsessive-compulsive behavior (Marquart & Arnold, 1952; Jones, 1954), and high blood pressure (Hokanson, DeGood, Forrest, & Brittain, 1971). When predictability, control, or the perception of control (whether veridical or nonveridical) is introduced into the situation, stress effects are generally reduced (Badia, Suter, & Lewis, 1967; Corah & Boffa, 1970; Geer *et al.*, 1970).

One must use caution in generalizing from the results of the above laboratory-analogue studies to real-life problem-solving situations. It is possible that the differences in relevant variables between the laboratory setting and the real-life social setting may be too great to permit any meaningful conclusions regarding the determinants of psychopathology. However, these studies do help to strengthen the hypothesis that problem-solving deficits might be related to psychological stress and maladaptive behavior.

Correlational Studies

The relationship between social problem solving and either positive adjustment or psychopathology has also been investigated in a number of correlational studies. Heppner and his associates and others have reported a number of studies that have focused on Heppner and Petersen's (1982)

Problem-Solving Inventory (PSI). The PSI has been described as a measure of self-appraisal of problem-solving ability (Heppner *et al.*, 1984) and as a measure of problem-solving style (Sherry, Keitel, & Tracey, 1984). Focusing primarily on college student subjects, a number of studies have found significant differences between self-appraised effective problem solvers and self-appraised ineffective problem solvers on a variety of measures of social competence, positive adjustment, maladjustment, and psychopathology.

Specifically, the results show that self-appraised effective problem solvers are more motivated to solve problems, have higher expectations of success, are less impulsive and avoidant, more systematic and persistent, and have a clearer understanding of problems (Heppner *et al.*, 1982). They have a more positive self-concept, a greater need to understand their experiential world, less dysfunctional thoughts, and less irrational beliefs (Heppner, Reeder, & Larson, 1983). In addition, these individuals are more interpersonally assertive and less anxious (Neal & Heppner, 1982). They also tend to employ more rational decision-making strategies (Phillips, Pazienza, & Ferrin, 1984) and are less intuitive and less dependent in their decision making (Neal & Heppner, 1982). In the area of vocational planning and decision making, these individuals are more confident about their career decision-making ability and occupational potential, and they tend to utilize career planning resources more often (Heppner & Krieshok, 1983; Larson & Heppner, 1985).

Self-appraised ineffective problem solvers, on the other hand, report more current life problems (Heppner *et al.*, 1982; Nezu, 1985); more health and physical symptoms (Sherry *et al.*, 1984; Neal & Heppner, 1982; Nezu, 1985); more depression (Heppner, Baumgardner, & Jackson, 1985; Heppner, Kampa, & Brunning, 1984; Nezu, 1985; Nezu & Ronan, 1985; Nezu, Kalmar, Ronan, & Clavijo, 1986); more anxiety (Nezu, 1986b); more psychological distress as measured by the SCL-90 (Heppner *et al.*, 1984); and more psychological maladjustment as measured by the MMPI (Heppner & Anderson, 1985).

The relationship between social problem-solving abilities and maladjustment or psychopathology has also been investigated in a series of studies conducted by Spivack, Platt, Shure and their associates at the Hahnemann Community Mental Health/Mental Retardation Center in Philadelphia (see Spivack *et al.*, 1976). Most of the Hahnemann group's studies have focused on a self-report measure that they have called Means–Ends Problem Solving (MEPS) (Platt & Spivack, 1975). The MEPS involves the written or verbal presentation of a series of story stems that depict situations in which a need is aroused in a protagonist at the onset of the story, and is satisfied by him or her at the conclusion. The means by which the protagonist achieves the goal is left out. The subject is required to complete the story by filling in those events that might have enabled the protagonist to achieve his or her goal of satisfying the need. Using the MEPS as their dependent measure, the

Hahnemann investigators compared the performance of various disturbed and maladjusted groups of subjects to that of "normal" matched controls. They found deficits in MEPS performance in such groups as adolescent psychiatric patients (Platt, Spivack, Altman, Altman, & Peizer, 1974), heroin addicts (Platt, Scura, & Hannon, 1973), and adult psychiatric patients (Platt & Spivack, 1972, 1973).

Several investigators outside of the Hahnemann group have done similar studies using the MEPS with noninstitutionalized subjects that generally support the findings reported above. Appel and Kaestner (1979) found significant differences in MEPS performance between a group of narcotic drug abusers judged to be in "poor" standing in an outpatient rehabilitation program and a group judged to be in "good" standing. Gotlib and Asarnow (1979) found highly significant differences on several MEPS measures between depressed and nondepressed college students. In the same study, these investigators also found significant correlations between MEPS measures and scores on the Beck Depression Inventory (BDI) (Beck, 1967), which provides another test of the relationship between MEPS performance and depression.

Two studies focusing on depression have used specific problem-solving performance tasks to measure problem-solving ability. Nezu and Ronan (in press) found deficits in depressed as compared to nondepressed subjects on a generation-of-alternatives task and a decision-making task. The nondepressed subjects generated better quality solutions and chose more effective solution alternatives than the depressed subjects. The mean BDI scores of the depressed subjects in this study were similar to that of the depressed group in the Gotlib and Asarnow study. In another study using conceptual problems, Dobson and Dobson (1981) found results that implicate both a problem-solving deficit and a conservative problem-solving style in depression.

A major problem in interpreting the results of all of the above correlational studies is that no conclusions can be made regarding cause–effect relationships. It is possible that problem-solving deficits cause or contribute to maladaptive behavior, but it is also possible that some factors associated with psychopathology—such as apathy, high levels of anxiety, distractibility, or the effects of psychiatric medication—may cause the deficiencies in problem-solving performance. Another likely possibility is that a reciprocal cause–effect relationship exists where problem solving and psychopathology influence each other (Mitchell & Madigan, 1984).

In conclusion, there is considerable support for the first assumption underlying the problem-solving approach to clinical intervention and prevention, namely that social problem solving is positively related to social competence and inversely related to maladjustment or psychopathology. Regardless of the nature of this relationship, PST has potential utility as a treatment approach, a maintenance strategy, or a prevention method (assumptions two, three, and four, discussed under "Social Problem-Solving and Adjustment"). If problem-solving deficits cause psychopathology, or if a reciprocal relationship exists, the potential value of PST is obvious. If psychopathology causes or is associated with problem-solving deficits, then PST may still be useful as part of a treatment package to help improve coping performance and minimize the negative effects of psychopathology on personal/social functioning. In addition to these treatment effects, an improvement in social competence through the use of PST might also help to ensure the maintenance and generalization of treatment gains as well as the prevention of future psychological problems. Empirical evidence supporting the efficacy of PST as a treatment, maintenance, and prevention method will be presented later in this chapter.

CLINICAL APPLICATIONS

ASSESSMENT

During the assessment phase of PST, it is important to determine not only whether a problem-solving deficiency exists, but also whether the deficiency is general or specific (e.g., a decision-making deficit), so that the most appropriate and efficient training program can be planned and the most appropriate measures can be selected to evaluate treatment progress and outcome. It is also important for both training and research to distinguish between measures of problem-solving *ability* and measures of problem-solving *performance* (D'Zurilla, 1986a; D'Zurilla & Nezu, in press).

Problem-Solving Ability Versus Performance

The assessment of problem-solving ability focuses on the problem-solving process (i.e., the discovery process). Assessment techniques measure the extent of an individual's knowledge or possession of the important problem-solving process variables, including problem-orientation cognitions, specific problem-solving skills, and basic problem-solving abilities. Measures of problem-solving ability are important for identifying specific skill deficits and planning an appropriate training program, as well as assessing training progress and outcome.

While problem-solving ability refers to the possession of component problem-solving skills and abilities, problem-solving performance refers to the appropriate application of these skills to solve a particular problem. The assessment of problem-solving performance focuses, therefore, on the product or outcome of the problem-solving process (i.e., the chosen solution). A measure of social problem-solving performance can be viewed as a measure of social competence or coping effectiveness. Measures of problem-solving performance are particularly important for assessing treatment progress and outcome. Improvements in problem-solving ability do not have practical significance without concomitant improvements in problem-solving performance. The distinction between problem-solving ability and problem-solving performance is also important for research on the relationship between social problem solving and adaptational outcomes because it helps to avoid a confounding between measures of the problem-solving *process* (i.e., problem-solving skills) and problem-solving *outcome* (i.e., judged effectiveness of the reported solution or solution implementation).

There are two general approaches to the assessment of problem-solving ability and performance: (1) self-report or verbal assessment and (2) observational assessment. Verbal assessment employs such methods as questionnaires, inventories, interviews, and verbal problem-solving tests (using real or hypothetical problems). Observational assessment involves the direct observation of an individual's performance in problematic situations either in the natural environment or in simulated problematic situations in an experimental or clinical setting (e.g., role playing).

Verbal Assessment

Several investigators have developed questionnaires and structured interviews to assess social problem-solving abilities. One of the most popular questionnaires is Heppner and Petersen's (1982) Problem-Solving Inventory (PSI). Referred to as a measure of self-appraisal of problem-solving ability, the PSI uses 35 Likert-type items to assess problem-orientation cognitions and several specific problem-solving skills. Heppner *et al.* (1982) also used a 1-hour structured interview to assess how subjects solved real-life problems. Following the interview, the interviewers rated the subjects on several cognitive and behavioral variables related to problem solving.

Another verbal method for assessing problem-solving ability is one that requires subjects to demonstrate their skills or abilities by performing specific tasks designed to test these skills or abilities. For example, the popular Means–Ends Problem-Solving (MEPS) method (Platt & Spivack, 1975) attempts to assess means–ends ability by asking subjects to conceptualize the possible means by which a person might achieve a specific goal in a particular life situation. Other specific problem-solving tests include measures of the generation of alternative solutions, decision making (D'Zurilla & Nezu, 1980; Nezu & D'Zurilla, 1981a, 1981b; Nezu & Ronan, in press), consequential thinking, perspective taking (Spivack *et al.*, 1976), and various basic abilities that make up Guilford's *Structure of Intellect Problem-Solving* model (Guilford, 1967, 1977; Parnes & Noller, 1973). The major advantage of these specific problem-solving tests over questionnaires and inventories for assessing problem-solving skills and abilities is that they assess not only the subject's knowledge of the content of the problem-solving process, but also the ability to apply this knowledge effectively to specific problematic tasks. They are thus likely to have greater external validity.

The verbal approach to assessing problem-solving performance (i.e., the product of problem solving) requires subjects to solve particular test problems (either the subject's real problems or hypothetical problems) and report their solutions. Specific measures may use a pencil-and-paper format, a structured interview, or a dyadic or group discussion format (in the case of interpersonal or group problem solving). This approach can also be used to assess problem-solving ability at the same time by incorporating the "think aloud" method, which requires subjects to verbalize (or provide a written description of) their problem-solving thoughts as they solve the problem (Meichenbaum, Henshaw, & Himel, 1982).

Goldfried and D'Zurilla (1969) have provided a set of guidelines for the construction of verbal problem-solving performance tests for particular subject populations or environments (e.g., college freshmen). These guidelines include the following steps: (1) situational analysis (identifying significant problematic situations), (2) response enumeration (determining a range of possible responses or solutions for each situation), (3) response evaluation (judging the solutions), (4) development of a measuring instrument format (e.g., pencil-and-paper, structured interview, free response, multiple-choice), and (5) evaluation of the measure (i.e., reliability and validity studies). Depending on the nature of the measuring instrument format, a variety of different measures can be derived from this method, including solution effectiveness, solution productivity (number of solutions), and coping style (e.g., approach, avoidance, dependency). Two problem-solving measures that are based specifically on this approach are the Adolescent Problem Inventory (API) (Freedman, Rosenthal, Donahoe, Schlundt, & McFall, 1978), used to assess social competence in delinquent adolescents, and the Family Problem Questionnaire (Claerhout, Elder, & Janes, 1982), used to assess the problem-solving performance of rural battered women.

Verbal measures of social problem-solving ability and performance are subject to the same reliability and validity problems as any other self-report measures (see Bellack & Hersen, 1977). The major problem with current verbal problem-solving measures is the limited evidence in support of the ecological validity of these instruments (Butler & Meichenbaum, 1981; Kendall & Fischler, 1984). While it is possible that these measures can be improved methodologically (see Bellack & Hersen, 1977), it is likely that the relationship between these measures and real-life problem-solving performance is limited somewhat by several other factors that may influence problem-solving performance in the natural environment, such as instrumental skills deficits, emotional inhibitions, deviant social values, and motivational (reinforcement) deficits. Therefore, it is probably best to view current verbal measures of problem solving as an indication of a person's problem-solving potential, which alone may not necessarily predict that person's real-life problem-solving performance with a high degree of accuracy.

Observational Assessment

The second approach to problem-solving assessment is the observational assessment of overt problem-solving performance in the natural environment or in simulated problem-solving situations in the experimental or clinical setting. This approach has limited utility for directly assessing problem-solving ability, or the process of problem solving, since overt behavioral activities do not play as great a role in the problem-solving process as do cognitive activities. The observational approach is more useful for assessing problem-solving performance, or the product of the problem-solving process. The major advantage of this approach is its potential for a high degree of external validity.

The major problem with the use of observational methods alone to assess problem-solving performance is that it may not always be possible to determine whether a person's response to a problematic situation in the natural environment is in fact the product of an antecedent problem-solving process, or whether it is a coping response prompted directly by cues in the situation, resulting from some other social-learning process, such as instrumental learning, modeling, or direct verbal instruction. In the former case, the observed behavior is problem-solving performance. In the latter case, it is not, although it may still be an effective coping response.

One solution to the above problem is to use a self-observational approach, which combines the advantages of self-report and observational assessment. To use this approach, subjects can be asked to keep careful records on a daily basis of significant problem-solving situations as they occur in the natural environment. One example of this approach is the Problem-Solving Self-Monitoring (PSSM) method (D'Zurilla, 1986a), which uses the following A-B-C-D-E format:

A: *Problem Information.* The subject describes all the relevant facts about the problematic situation (Who was involved? What happened? Where and when did it happen? Why was the problem important? What was your goal?).

B: *Emotions.* The subject describes all the feelings and emotions that were experienced when the problem occurred. The subject also rates the intensity of emotional distress on a 9-point rating scale.

C: *Alternative Solutions Considered.* The subject describes all the possible "solutions," or ways of coping with the problematic situation, that were considered before deciding on a particular course of action.

D: *Solution Choice.* The subject identifies the solution or coping method that he or she chose to implement and describes the reasons for the choice.

E: *Solution Implementation and Outcome.* The subject describes what happened when he or she implemented the solution, including the specific steps that were involved in its implementation, the obstacles that may have been encountered, and the consequences or results. The subject also rates the degree of his or her satisfaction with the overall outcome of the solution on a 10-point scale from "extremely unsatisfactory" to "extremely satisfactory."

Since it would be impracticable to self-record all problematic situations that occur in everyday living, the subject may be asked to record the two or three most stressful or significant problems that occurred during the previous week. This method can be used to assess (1) deficiencies in problem-solving ability and performance, (2) progress during training, and (3) outcome of PST, including a follow-up evaluation. However, to obtain complete and accurate data, careful training and feedback is required.

PROBLEM-SOLVING TRAINING (PST)

Based on a thorough assessment of a particular client's clinical problems, a decision will be made as to whether PST may be a useful intervention strategy and, if so, how it may be used most effectively. The most appropriate case for PST is one in which maladaptive behavior or negative stress effects, such as anxiety, depression, or psychophysiological symptoms (e.g., pain), are associated with deficits in problem-solving ability and/or performance. Then, depending on the nature and severity of the maladaptive behavior and negative stress effects, PST might be used as the sole treatment, as part of a broader treatment program, or as a treatment maintenance/ prevention strategy.

The goal of PST is to help the client identify and resolve current life problems that are antecedents of maladaptive responses, while at the same time teaching the client general skills that will enable him or her to deal more effectively and independently with future problems. In addition to solving these antecedent problems, PST might also contribute to a therapy program by focusing directly on maladaptive responses, such as anxiety, depression, pain, overeating, or problem drinking, and viewing them as "problems-to-be-solved." For example, a problem formulation for depression may be: "My girl friend has just informed me that she is ending our relationship because she no longer loves me. I am feeling extremely depressed and inadequate. What can I do to make myself feel better?" For tension-induced pain, a problem statement may be: "I am sitting at my desk trying to complete a difficult report that is due tomorrow but I cannot concentrate because I have a terrible headache. I have already taken aspirin but it has not worked. What can I do to relieve my headache pain?" An example of a problem statement for overeating is: "I am sitting at home alone watching T.V. and I have a strong urge to go out and buy some ice cream, but I know that I have already reached my calorie limit for the day. What can I do to keep myself from giving in to the urge to go out and get some ice cream?"

While it is often useful to treat maladaptive responses as problems-to-be-solved, the emphasis in PST should always be on the identification and resolution of the current antecedent problems that are causally related to these responses, since this strategy is more likely to produce durable and generalized reductions in maladaptive behavior. However, in cases where antecedent problematic situations are difficult to identify, define, and/or change, a problem-solving strategy that focuses on changing maladaptive responses to the problem (e.g., emotional distress) may be the only effective or adaptive coping strategy (see D'Zurilla, 1986a; Lazarus & Folkman, 1984).

When PST is used with other treatment methods, it should not be applied apart from these other methods as a separate, distinct treatment procedure. Instead, it is the viewpoint here that therapy is best conducted within an overall PST framework, where the other treatment methods are applied at the appropriate points in training, as needed, either to facilitate problem-solving performance or to deal directly with some serious problematic situation or maladaptive response. For example, cognitive-restructuring techniques might be needed to correct cognitive distortions when focusing on the identification and assessment of current life problems. Anxiety-reduction techniques may be required when anxiety is disrupting problem-solving thinking or when fear or anxiety is seriously inhibiting adaptive instrumental performance. Social-skills training and self-control techniques may also be necessary to facilitate instrumental coping performance.

Although deficits in problem-solving ability and/or performance are used to identify the most appropriate cases for PST, the problem-solving approach to clinical intervention is concerned with higher-level functioning, not merely the correction of skill deficits below the "normal" or average level. Thus, it can be argued that *most* clients are likely to benefit from conducting therapy within a general PST framework, even though they may not show significant deficiencies in problem-solving skills.

In addition to its application within a broader, open-ended therapy structure, PST may also be applied as a time-limited, competence-enhancement or stress-management training "package," which is designed to be carried out in approximately 15 2-hour weekly sessions (see D'Zurilla, 1986a, 1986b). This training program may be used as a treatment, maintenance, or prevention strategy. It may be adapted to an individual (one-to-one) setting, a small group setting with six to eight group members, or a larger group setting, such as a course or workshop structure. The advantages of individual training are privacy, more individual attention, and greater flexibility to tailor the program to a particular individual's needs. The advantages of a group program are the motivating effects of group discussion, the sharing of ideas and experiences, modeling, social support, and the efficient use of trained therapists or instructors.

Training employs direct verbal instruction (e.g., information giving) and the Socratic (dialogic) method of instruction, which emphasizes the use of questions and discussions that guide and encourage clients to formulate their own conclusions, deductions, and elaborations. Such instruction is consistent with the PST goals of facilitating independent productive thinking. In addition to these methods, other important training procedures include coaching, modeling, rehearsal, performance feedback, positive reinforcement, and shaping. Coaching primarily involves verbal prompting, such as leading questions, suggestions, and directions. Modeling includes written and verbal problem-solving examples and demonstrations, using hypothetical problems and real problems presented by the clients (or trainees) and the therapist (or instructor). Rehearsal involves problem-solving practice exercises and homework assignments. Performance feedback is provided by the therapist and through self-monitoring and self-evaluation, using the Problem-Solving Self-Monitoring (PSSM) method described earlier. Positive reinforcement includes the therapist's praise and approval and the natural reinforcement of successful verbal problem solving in session, as well as successful problem-solving performance in the real-life setting. Shaping involves specific training in the problem-solving process in progressive steps, with each new step being contingent on successful performance in the previous step. These steps are presented below.

Initial Structuring

The objectives of this initial phase of the process involve discussing program goals, beginning training in problem perception (recognition and labeling of problems), and providing training in the use of the PSSM method.

The goals of the program are to enhance general coping effectiveness (one form of social competence) and to reduce or control stress through training in problem-solving skills.[4] Following a discussion of these goals,

4. For a discussion of the theoretical and empirical rationale for using PST as a stress-management approach, see D'Zurilla (1986a, 1986b) and Meichenbaum *et al.* (1982).

Table 3.1. Overview of Problem-Solving Model

I. *Problem Orientation* (PO)
   A. Problem Perception
   B. Problem Attribution
   C. Problem Appraisal
   D. Personal Control
   E. Time/Effort Commitment

II. *Problem Definition and Formulation* (PDF)
   A. Gathering Relevant, Factual Information
   B. Understanding the Problem
   C. Setting a Realistic Problem-Solving Goal
   D. Reappraising the Problem

III. *Generation of Alternative Solutions* (GAS)
   A. Quantity Principle
   B. Deferment-of-Judgment Principle
   C. Variety Principle

IV. *Decision Making* (DM)
   A. Anticipating Solution Outcomes
   B. Evaluating (Judging and Comparing) Solution Outcomes
   C. Preparing a Solution Plan

V. *Solution Implementation and Verification* (SIV)
   A. Carrying out the Solution Plan
   B. Self-Monitoring
   C. Self-Evaluation
   D. Self-Reinforcement
   E. Troubleshooting and Recycling

an overview of the problem-solving process is then presented and discussed (see Table 3.1). Training in problem perception (one component of problem orientation) is begun by asking the client(s) to generate common real-life problems, beginning with community and societal problems, and later asking for individual problems (i.e., personal and interpersonal problems). After spending several minutes generating common problems, the PSSM method is explained and the client(s) is given the opportunity to practice using this method with one or two of the problems that have been generated.

The initial structuring phase of the program takes one or two sessions. It ends with a homework assignment to (1) list problems that occur in day-to-day activities, whether relatively minor or serious, and (2) record the one or two most stressful or significant problems using the PSSM method. These assignments are continued on a regular basis throughout the training program. They provide the major real-life problem-solving tasks to be used for both training and assessment. As training progresses, it is expected that improvements in problem-solving knowledge and skills will be reflected in the PSSM records. For the next ten sessions, approximately, training focuses on the five components of the problem-solving process. Each session begins with a statement of the training objectives for the session, followed by the presentation and discussion of the relevant information for that session, interspersed with examples, demonstrations, and problem-solving exercises, using both hypothetical and real problems. Space limitations prevent a description here of all the specific skills, instructions, exercises, and examples that are included in the training program. For this information, the reader is referred to D'Zurilla (1986a). In addition, another rich source for information related to training methods and materials is Parnes, Noller, and Biondi (1977) and Noller, Parnes, and Biondi (1976).

Problem Orientation

The objectives of this next stage are to (1) increase sensitivity to problems and set the occasion for problem-solving activity, (2) focus attention on positive solving expectations and activities and away from unproductive worries and "self-preoccupying thoughts" (Sarason, 1980), (3) maximize effort and persistence when obstacles and emotional distress are encountered, and (4) minimize emotional distress while maximizing positive emotional states.

Training in problem perception is continued during this phase of the program by teaching the client(s) to use his or her feelings and ineffective behavior as cues for problem recognition. In addition, the use of problem checklists are recommended as an aid in problem-recognition training (e.g., Mooney & Gordon, 1950; see also D'Zurilla, 1986a). The remaining components of a facilitative problem orientation (problem attribution, problem appraisal, etc.) are taught by presenting and discussing a model of a negative or maladaptive coping style (e.g., avoidance, helplessness, dependency), followed by the presentation and discussion of a positive, problem-solving coping style.

MALADAPTIVE COPING STYLE

1. The individual blames him- or herself for the problem and thinks that it means that there is something wrong with him or her (e.g., he or she is abnormal, incompetent, stupid, bad, or unlucky).

2. The individual perceives the problem as a significant threat to his or her well-being (physical, emotional, social, economic). He or she minimizes the benefits of solving the problem and exaggerates the harm or losses that may result from failure to solve the problem successfully.

3. The individual has little real hope of coping with the problem effectively, either because the problem is regarded by the individual as insoluble, or because the problem does not seem capable of being solved

successfully through his or her own efforts. As a result, he or she avoids the problem or tries to get someone else to solve it.

4. The individual believes that a competent person should be able to solve the problem quickly, without much effort. He or she believes that the failure to do so indicates inadequacy or incompetence. In addition, he or she does not place a high value on independent, effortful, problem-solving activity, preferring to have someone else solve the problem.

PROBLEM-SOLVING COPING STYLE

1. The individual perceives the problem as a normal, ordinary, inevitable event in life. He or she realizes that the problem is not an indication of inadequacy. He or she sees the problem as being caused by environmental circumstances and/or relatively benign personal factors (e.g., lack of experience), rather than by severe and stable personal defects or abnormalities. The individual believes that when a problem is a result of his or her own ineffective behavior or personal deficit, this usually means only that he or she is human and is not perfect, that the important thing is to learn from one's mistakes and problems and to try to improve oneself.

2. Instead of appraising the problem primarily as a threat-to-be-avoided, the individual sees the problem as a "challenge" or opportunity for personal growth or self-improvement (e.g., learning something new, changing one's life for the better, feeling better about oneself). The individual does *not* view failure as a catastrophe, but instead, views it as a corrective learning experience. He or she believes in the general philosophy that it is better to take on a problem or a challenge and fail, than to not try to solve the problem at all.

3. The individual believes that there is a solution to the problem and that he or she is capable of finding this solution independently and implementing it successfully. He or she understands that the more one believes that one can cope with problems successfully, the better one will be able to cope with them.

4. The individual realizes that solving the problem is likely to take time and effort. He or she resists the temptation to respond to the problem on the basis of the first impulse or idea to come to mind. He or she understands that the first impulses and ideas are not usually the best because they tend to be influenced more by feelings than by reasoning. He or she values independent, effortful, well-planned problem solving, and is prepared to be persistent and to not give up too easily if the solution is not quickly discovered. He or she realizes that even the best problem solvers need time to think in order to solve difficult problems effectively. However, he or she also understands that if one has tried the very best to solve the problem and still cannot succeed, then he or she must either accept the problem and try to see it from a different perspective, or go get help with it.

The Use and Control of Emotions During Problem Solving

The objectives of this phase are to discuss the effects of emotions on problem solving, and to provide training in facilitative coping methods.

At this point in the program, a session is devoted to a discussion of the important role of emotions in real-life problem solving and of the methods to control these emotions so that they do not disrupt problem-solving thinking and performance (see "Role of Emotions in Social Problem Solving" this chapter; see also D'Zurilla, 1986a). This phase of the program includes instruction and training, as necessary, in facilitative coping, which is aimed at controlling and overcoming cognitive–emotional obstacles to effective and efficient problem-solving performance. This instruction identifies and describes cognition-oriented coping and emotion-oriented coping. Cognition-oriented coping includes cognitive restructuring (e.g., correcting exaggerated threatening appraisals, correcting distorted or irrational beliefs and expectations, correcting unrealistic goals and performance standards) and self-instruction (e.g., positive self-talk, coping self-statements). Emotion-oriented coping includes a variety of relaxation and self-desensitization methods, such as progressive muscle relaxation, meditation, autogenic methods, and anxiety-management training (Woolfolk & Lehrer, 1984).

Self-help books on stress and anxiety management should be required reading as a homework assignment at this point in the program in order to provide further instruction and home-based practice in the above facilitative coping skills (e.g., McKay, Davis, & Robbins-Eshelman, 1982). Further training may also be provided in later sessions, if needed. However, it is the viewpoint here that most clients already have a variety of resources available to them for coping with anxiety and tension in everyday living (e.g., music, hobbies, exercise, social support, etc.) and may not require extensive training in specialized relaxation techniques. What they need most is training in how and when to use the resources they already have to help them cope with stress and solve problems more effectively. At the conclusion of this session, the client(s) is instructed to try to become more aware of the sources of disruptive emotions during problem-solving activities, and to begin using facilitative coping methods to control these emotions.

Problem Definition and Formulation

This phase has the following objectives: (1) to gather as much relevant, factual information about the problem as possible, (2) to clarify the nature of the problem, (3) to set a realistic problem-solving goal, and (4) to reappraise the significance of the problem for personal/social well-being.

In this phase of the program, the client(s) is taught how to gather objective information about the problem and avoid cognitive distortions when "processing" (interpreting, appraising) this information. The client(s) is taught to conceptualize a problem as an imbalance or discrepancy between "what is" (i.e., present conditions) and "what should be" (i.e., conditions that are demanded or desired), and to identify the obstacle or obstacles preventing the availability of an effective response for reducing this discrepancy. In the instructions for setting problem-solving goals, two important rules are emphasized: (1) state the goals in specific, concrete terms, and (2) avoid stating goals that are unrealistic or unattainable. Once the problem has been clearly defined, it may no longer be as threatening as it appeared to be when it was still vague and poorly defined. Therefore, the client(s) is instructed to reappraise the problem at this point. This is done by considering the benefits and costs of solving the problem versus not solving the problem.

In addition to the above instructions, the client(s) is also trained to consider alternative problem formulations. In some cases, the problem focused on initially may not be the "real" problem (i.e., the basic, primary, or most important problem). The basic problem in some cases may be an earlier problem in a current cause–effect problem chain, where problem A is causing problem B, which in turn is causing problem C. Another possibility is that the more important problem may be a broader or more complex problem of which the specific problem focused on initially is only a part. Once this broader, more complex problem is identified, it can then be dealt with as a whole, or it may be solved more effectively by breaking it down into more manageable subproblems and working on each of them one at a time.

When dealing with highly stressful problems, an important distinction is made between *problem-focused* formulations and *emotion-focused* formulations, which is similar to Lazarus and Folkman's (1984) distinction between problem-focused coping and emotion-focused coping. Problem-focused formulations emphasize problem-solving goals that are aimed at changing the problematic situation for the better (i.e., meeting the demands in the situation or reducing or changing the demands to make them more manageable). Emotion-focused formulations, on the other hand, emphasize goals that are aimed at changing one's own personal reactions to the situation in order to reduce stress (e.g., changing the "meaning" or appraisal of the situation, enhancing personal growth, reducing autonomic arousal). If the problematic situation is appraised as *changeable*, then problem-focused formulations should be emphasized. However, if the situation is appraised as *un*changeable, then the only realistic or adaptive problem formulation would be an emotion-focused one. In cases where the problematic situation is appraised initially as changeable, but later after unsuccessful problem-solving attempts it is reappraised as *un*changeable, then the problem should be reformulated to include emotion-focused goals. In many problematic situations, particularly those that are highly emotionally stressful, it may be most adaptive to include both problem-focused goals and emotion-focused goals in the problem formulation (D'Zurilla, 1986b).

At this phase in the program, some clients may show frequent cognitive distortions, misconceptions, or irrational beliefs when attempting to define and formulate problems. In such cases further cognitive restructuring is required to correct these tendencies. Training for these clients should place more emphasis on this method and/or refer the client(s) to Ellis and Harper's (1975) *A New Guide to Rational Living* or any of the rational thinking self-help books focusing on specific problem areas (e.g., sexual problems, anger problems). These books are available from the Institute for Rational–Emotive Therapy in New York City.

Generation of Alternative Solutions

The objective in this phase of the program involves making available as many alternative solutions (coping options) as possible, in such a way as to maximize the likelihood that the "best" solution will be among them.

The first solutions to come to mind when trying to solve a problem are not always the best solutions. Therefore, in order to maximize problem-solving effectiveness it is important for the client(s) to learn to generate alternative solutions. The kinds of alternative solutions generated during this phase of problem solving are limited only by two criteria: relevancy and specificity. In order to maximize problem-solving efficiency and effectiveness, the problem solver should generate solutions that are relevant to the problem-solving goal(s) and that are stated in specific, concrete terms. The latter criterion is particularly important for an accurate evaluation of solution alternatives during the decision-making phase of problem solving. With these two criteria in mind, the client(s) is instructed to generate alternative solutions following three basic principles that are designed to maximize creativity and solution production: (1) the quantity principle, (2) the deferment-of-judgment principle, and (3) the variety principle.

The quantity principle states that the more alternative solutions that are produced, the more quality ideas will be made available. To apply this principle, the client is instructed to think of as many alternative solutions as possible without limiting his or her production of ideas to conventional solutions, ordinary solutions, or solutions that have worked well in the past. The client(s) is encouraged to be persistent, to not give up the search for ideas too soon. If he or she "blocks" and cannot think of any more ideas, he or she is instructed to take a break and return to the task later.

According to the deferment-of-judgment principle, more quality solution ideas will be produced when the problem solver suspends judgment or critical evaluation of the ideas until later on in the problem-solving process (i.e., during decision making). To apply this principle, the client(s) is instructed to let his or her imagination run loose and try to think of as many new and original ideas as possible without filtering them through any evaluative screens such as appropriateness, conventionality, practicality, feasibility, or utility. The only requirement is that the solution ideas should be relevant to the problem-solving goal.

The variety principle states that the greater the range or variety of solution alternatives generated, the more quality ideas will be made available. When generating specific solution alternatives, the problem solver may fall into a set pattern, producing ideas that reflect only one strategy or general approach to the problem. This limiting pattern may occur even when the quantity principle and the deferment-of-judgment principle are being followed. To apply the variety principle, the client(s) is instructed to look over his or her list of solution alternatives, after using the other two principles, and to identify all the different strategies that are represented. If any of the strategies have very few alternative solutions, the client(s) is instructed to try to generate more solutions for that particular strategy. In addition, he or she is instructed to think of new strategies that are not yet represented by the list of available solutions, and then to generate additional solutions for those new strategies.

In applying the above principles, two aids that the problem solver can use to increase the quantity and variety of solution alternatives are combinations and modifications. To create combinations, the problem solver is instructed to look over his or her list of solution alternatives and determine what ideas can be combined to produce new solution ideas. To produce modifications or "transformations" (Guilford, 1977), the problem solver considers how different solution ideas can be changed or elaborated on in order to improve the idea or create a new one.

Decision Making

This phase has as its objective evaluating (judging and comparing) the available solution alternatives and selecting the best solution for implementation in the actual problematic situation. In the present model, the best solution is the one that is expected to be most effective in achieving the problem-solving goal (i.e., resolving the problem) while maximizing significant benefits and minimizing significant costs (personal and social, immediate and longterm).

As a first step in decision making, the client(s) is instructed to conduct a rough screening of the list of available solution alternatives and eliminate any that are clearly inferior because there are unacceptable risks associated with their implementation and/or they are not feasible due to a lack of ability or resources to implement them. Next, the client(s) is instructed to anticipate solution outcomes for each alternative. A solution outcome refers to the total expected benefits (positive consequences) and costs (negative consequences) of a particular solution, including long-term as well as immediate consequences, and social as well as personal consequences. Since the preference for solutions will vary depending on how the solution outcomes are conceived, the client(s) is asked to consider as many different consequences as possible when formulating solution outcomes.

After anticipating outcomes for all the available solutions, the client(s) is instructed to judge each solution by considering four criteria: (1) problem resolution, (2) emotional well-being, (3) amount of time and effort required, and (4) overall personal/social well-being (i.e., total benefit/cost ratio). The solutions may be evaluated informally by considering the four criteria and making an overall judgment of each alternative as satisfactory or unsatisfactory. They may be evaluated more formally by using a rating scale to measure the degree of solution quality, which allows the client(s) to make finer discriminations between alternatives.

After evaluating the available solution alternatives, the client(s) is instructed to ask three questions: (1) Is the problem solvable? (2) Do I need more information before I can select and implement a solution? (3) What solution or solution combination should I choose to implement it? If the problem is appraised as unsolvable and/or the answer to the second question is positive, the client(s) is instructed to return to the problem definition and formulation task to seek more information and/or to reformulate the problem in a way that might make it solvable (e.g., goals that emphasize acceptance, emotional control, or personal growth). However, if the problem is appraised as solvable and the answer to the second question is negative, the client(s) is instructed to focus on the third question and formulate a solution plan, which may involve a single, simple solution or a combination of solutions. The choice of a solution plan should be consistent with the general goal of attempting to resolve the problem satisfactorily, while maximizing emotional well-being and overall personal/social well-being and minimizing time and effort.

Solution Implementation and Verification

The objective at this point in the process is to assess the solution outcome and verify the effectiveness or utility of the chosen solution in the actual problematic situation.

The problem has been solved symbolically in the preceding phases, but the effectiveness of the solution in the real-life problematic situation has not yet been verified. The only way to accomplish this verification is to implement the solution plan and evaluate the solution outcome objectively. There are four components to this process: (1) solution implementation, (2) self-monitoring, (3) self-evaluation, and (4) self-reinforcement.

Solution implementation involves the performance of the activities or procedures that make up the solution plan. Possible obstacles at this point include a lack of performance skills or abilities, emotional inhibitions, and motivational (reinforcement) deficits. To deal with these obstacles the client can either choose an alternative solution plan or try to overcome the obstacles by acquiring necessary performance skills, using the facilitative coping methods described earlier, and/or using self-control techniques such as behavioral contracting. Self-monitoring involves the self-observation of solution performance and/or its products. At this point, the client(s) should be instructed in the use of different behavioral measurement methods (e.g., frequency counts, time sampling methods, ratings) as they are necessary.

Self-evaluation refers to the judgment of a solution outcome using the same outcome criteria and rating methods that were used during decision making to judge the anticipated solution outcomes (i.e., problem resolution, emotional well-being, time and effort expended, and total benefit/cost ratio). If the match between the actual solution outcome and the outcome anticipated during the decision-making task is satisfactory, then the client(s) is instructed to go to the final step in solution implementation and verification, namely, self-reinforcement. At this point, the client(s) terminates the problem-solving process and rewards him- or herself (e.g., self-praise, tangible rewards) for successful problem-solving performance. However, if the discrepancy between the actual solution outcome and the anticipated outcome is unsatisfactory, the client must "troubleshoot" and "recycle" (i.e., return to the problem-solving process to determine where corrections must be made in order to find a more effective solution). If the client cannot succeed after several attempts, he or she is encouraged to recognize the futility of further independent problem-solving efforts, and either reformulate the problem as one that must be accepted, or seek help with the problem from someone who may be more knowledgeable about that particular type of problem.

At this point in the program, training in each of the specific problem-solving tasks (e.g., problem definition and formulation, generation of alternative solutions, etc.) has been completed. Although a part of each session focuses on didactic instruction in a specific problem-solving task or skill, approximately one half of every session is devoted to guided problem solving, where the therapist guides the client(s) through all of the problem-solving tasks while solving a current real-life problem. During this process, the therapist gradually provides less direct guidance as more problem-solving tasks are learned. For example, during an early session focusing on problem-orientation variables, the therapist would provide much guidance and direction in all four specific problem-solving tasks. Later, however, during a session focusing on solution implementation and verification, the therapist would be much less directive in the application of problem definition and formulation, the generation of alternative solutions, and decision making. This is because training would have already been provided in these tasks and the client(s) should now be able to perform them independently.

Maintenance and Generalization

The last few sessions of the program are spent "putting it all together" and focusing on the client(s) real problems, with the therapist providing feedback and a minimum of direction. In addition, the therapist attempts to facilitate the maintenance and generalization of effective problem-solving performance by (1) continuing to provide positive reinforcement and corrective feedback; (2) reviewing positive problem-orientation cognitions and strengthening them by recognizing the clients' progress in learning to cope more effectively with everyday problems (based on PSSM records); (3) directing the clients' attention to the wide range of real-life problems for which the problem-solving approach is applicable, including different kinds of personal problems, interpersonal problems, family and group problems, and broader community problems; and (4) anticipating obstacles and future problems and preparing solution strategies for coping with them. Following these sessions, formal training can be terminated if the client(s) has achieved an acceptable level of problem-solving effectiveness based on the PSSM records and other assessment methods which are being used. Follow-up sessions should be scheduled at increasing intervals for purposes of assessment and maintenance. If an acceptable level of problem-solving effectiveness has not been achieved at this point, training should be continued on an appropriate schedule, focusing on the client's (or clients') real problems, until the client(s) is able to solve problems effectively on his or her own.

Cautions

There are several important cautions regarding the practice of PST that can have a significant effect on its outcome. The first one concerns the danger of failing to recognize when other intervention methods are necessary or more appropriate for a particular case. It was argued earlier that most, if not all, clients are likely to benefit from conducting therapy within an overall PST framework, in which a concerted effort is made to teach clients general skills that will enable them to assess and cope more independently and effectively with their own problems. However, within this overall framework, the amount of emphasis on training in problem-solving skills will necessarily vary across clients and therapy sessions, depending on the needs of the particular client. The therapist must possess the clinical skills to recognize when it is important to deviate from PST procedures in order to apply some other intervention strategy or technique that may be necessary for the effective management of a particular case. At some point in therapy, it may be necessary for the therapist to deal directly with an immediate serious problem or severe maladaptive behavior that cannot be handled adequately by the client through independent problem solving alone. For example, a highly anxious client may require immediate relaxation training or desensitization before PST can be applied effectively; a phobic client may require a series of *in vivo* exposure sessions in order to facilitate therapeutic progress; and a depressed client may require intensive cognitive restructuring, social skills training, or social support in order to deal effectively with a severe depressive episode.

A second caution involves the danger of viewing PST primarily as a "rational" or "intellectual" form of therapy, rather than as an active coping process involving an interaction between cognitive, behavioral, and emotional variables. The danger here is that the important role of behavioral and emotional factors in social problem solving may be neglected. Important behavioral variables include actively seeking information about the problem, actively experimenting with options, and actively self-monitoring to evaluate the solution outcome. In order to facilitate problem-solving effectiveness, emotional factors must be taken into account when setting goals, evaluating solution alternatives, and evaluating solution outcomes. In addition, it is often necessary to take steps to control intense emotional arousal in order to facilitate problem-solving efficiency. If these behavioral and emotional variables are ignored in PST, then problem solving may become a mere intellectual exercise, which may result in the failure to achieve any real therapeutic effects, that is, improvement in coping actively with real-life problems and stresses.

A third caution concerns the danger of failing to recognize that a positive therapeutic relationship is important for the success of any psychological treatment—and PST is no exception. Some clients enter therapy with little faith in the particular treatment, or in any psychological treatment. Some clients lack the commitment to change for various reasons. Some are actually afraid to change or try out new behaviors. Because of these factors, clients may show resistance to therapy requirements in a number of different ways (see Goldfried, 1982). A positive therapeutic relationship characterized by such factors as warmth, empathy, genuineness, and support will help to overcome these resistance problems. If the variables associated with a positive therapeutic relationship are neglected, then therapeutic success will be limited.

CASE ILLUSTRATION

The following case study illustrates the application of PST as part of a broader therapy program for a case in which the major presenting complaints are a high level of generalized anxiety, depression, and poor self-esteem.

Mrs. S was a 36-year-old housewife and part-time junior high school art teacher at the time she entered therapy. She was married for 8 years to a bank vice-president and had one child—a 6-year-old son. During the first session,

Mrs. S described herself as extremely tense, uptight, impatient, indecisive, and fearful. She reported worrying about "everything" (e.g., chemicals in food, people who might try to take advantage of her, the family's health). She even worried about worrying too much, afraid that worrying might eventually make her physically ill. In addition to generalized anxiety, Mrs. S reported feeling very depressed, bored, and dissatisfied with her life. Her self-confidence and self-esteem were very poor. She perceived herself as inadequate, incompetent, and lacking in control over her life and her emotions. She reported that her self-esteem had been deteriorating steadily since she left her full-time job about 6 years ago as an art teacher in an elementary school. Mrs. S had stopped working soon after she became pregnant with her son. She started working again after he started school but she could only find a job working 45 minutes each day as an art teacher in a junior high school. In addition to the reduced working time each week, Mrs. S was not satisfied with the job because she had much more difficulty managing the behavior of the junior high school students in her class than she had had managing the elementary school students in her previous job.

In addition to gathering information about the dimensions of Mrs. S's emotional and self-esteem problems and their development over time, the pretreatment assessment phase of therapy focused also on the identification of current antecedent life problems and stresses, consequences of maladaptive behaviors, assessment of problem solving and other coping skills, and initial structuring for therapy. The latter included an explanation and discussion of the rationale and course of problem-solving therapy, with the major objectives being to develop a problem-solving cognitive set and to strengthen expectations of benefit. Problem-solving skills were assessed using the Problem-Solving Inventory (PSI) and the Problem Solving Self-Monitoring (PSSM) method. In addition to these assessment methods, self-ratings were used to assess anxiety state, mood, and self-esteem throughout the course of therapy.

Mrs. S was seen in therapy for 28 sessions. The major specific problems and stresses identified and focused on during therapy fell into five problem areas: (1) her mother's illness, (2) the family's health and well-being, (3) work and other personal achievements, (4) social relationships, and (5) her marriage. In addition to the problems in the above areas, a major problem that occurred during therapy was related to the husband's expected transfer to a new job in another state within the next 3 months.

About 4 months before entering therapy, Mrs. S was informed that her mother had cancer. At the time she started therapy, the prognosis was still uncertain. About 2 months after learning about her mother's cancer, Mrs. S's son caught a bad cold that developed into pneumonia. Both of these illnesses created considerable stress and anxiety for Mrs. S, which reduced her ability to deal effectively with these problems. Shortly after beginning therapy, more anxiety was produced when Mrs. S was informed by her son's school teacher that he had a reading problem that was interfering seriously with his school performance. This problem was also handled poorly by Mrs. S.

With regard to work and personal achievements, Mrs. S was not involved in any meaningful work or constructive activity that could give her a sense of mastery or competence. In her brief period that she spent each day as an art teacher, she did not believe that she was managing the class effectively. Mrs. S was also unhappy because she had no close friends. Since she engaged in few activities outside of the home, she rarely had opportunities to meet people. On a few occasions when she did meet someone new, the person failed to show an interest in her as a friend later.

At first, Mrs. S described her husband as a wonderful person for being so patient and understanding about her anxiety problems. Later, however, she complained that he was against her going for therapy because he felt that she should not discuss her personal problems with a stranger. Moreover, she complained that her husband never praised her or gave her recognition for anything. Instead, he frequently criticized her and put her down. They spent very little time together because he commuted a long distance to work each day and, as a result, would arrive home sometime between 7:30 P.M. and 11:00 P.M., eat dinner, and go right to bed. On weekends, he frequently spent hours doing paper work related to his job. When she complained about the lack of time together, he told her that there was nothing he could do about it and that she was wrong to complain. With regard to the husband's expected job transfer, Mrs. S was fearful because she did not know anything about the area and she was concerned that they would not be able to find a satisfactory residence in so short a period of time.

The problem-solving and coping skills assessment revealed significant deficits in problem-solving oriented coping. Deficits were found in both problem orientation and specific problem-solving skills. Mrs. S tended to appraise a problem as a threat-to-be-avoided instead of as a "challenge" or problem-to-be-solved, which caused fear and anxiety. She also tended to appraise the threat to her well-being (or a loved one's well-being) as being more serious or significant than it actually was on the basis of minimal information, which exacerbated the anxiety. She blamed herself for the problem, ignoring the important role of other factors, and tended to conclude, inappropriately, that there was nothing she could do to change the problem or reduce its stressfulness. This contributed to a feeling of helplessness and a sense of losing control. For example, when the teacher told Mrs. S about her son's reading problem, her immediate response was: "I failed him. If I didn't have so many problems, he wouldn't have problems." She then cried and apologized profusely to the teacher for her son's reading problem, instead of gathering information about the problem and considering alternatives for dealing rationally and effectively with it. When a woman from the neighborhood whom Mrs. S met and had lunch with one day seemed to ignore her the next day, she blamed herself, thinking that she had said or done something wrong. She felt rejected and upset and did nothing further to clarify the problem and find a way to solve it.

The anxiety generated by the negative problem-orientation cognitions, together with the failure to gather sufficient information to clarify, understand, and reappraise a problem accurately, tended to result in misconceptions and distortions that created pseudo-problems. These pseudo-problems, reflecting Mrs. S's fears and anxieties, were more threatening than the real problems. For example, Mrs. S incorrectly believed that the women whom she had met in the neighborhood did not like her. When her son showed signs of developing a cold, she was certain he had developed pneumonia again. When her husband informed her that he was going to be transferred to a new job within 3 months, she believed, without attempting to clarify the problem, that it would be impossible to find a satisfactory home in so short a period of time.

In addition to the above deficits in problem-solving performance, it was determined during training that Mrs. S also had deficits in facilitative coping skills, which are important for overcoming cognitive and emotional obstacles to effective problem solving. Moreover, when it was necessary to implement her problem solutions, it was learned that she had deficits in some of the instrumental skills that were required to implement certain problem solutions effectively (i.e., assertiveness skills and communication skills). During the course of therapy, it also became increasingly clear that it was going to be necessary for the husband to become involved in conjoint communication/problem-solving training at some point because he often responded negatively to her assertive problem solutions and to other attempts to communicate and resolve the conflicts between them. However, he was very resistant to this idea.

A major goal of therapy was to help Mrs. S develop a more effective problem-solving coping style. Instead of viewing a stressful problem primarily as a threat and worrying about it, she gradually learned to approach the problem as a challenge or problem-to-be-solved. This prompted her to gather relevant information and to state the problem in problem-solving terms. Some of the problem statements that were developed and focused on in therapy are the following:

1. What can I do to minimize my distress about my mother's cancer?

2. What can I do to help my mother adjust to having cancer? [An alternative statement of the problem of how to deal with the mother's cancer.]

3. My son is showing symptoms of a cold. What can I do to prevent a more serious illness from developing?

4. What can I do to ensure a safe, healthy diet for my family?

5. What can I do to find a satisfying, productive full-time job?

6. What can I do to give myself a greater sense of personal achievement and accomplishment? [A broader statement of problem #5.]

7. How can I reduce disruptive behavior in my classroom?

8. What can I do to overcome feelings of boredom when I am home alone?

9. How can I meet more people?

10. How can I communicate with people in a way which will ensure that they will enjoy my company and want to be my friends?

11. How can I get my husband to praise me more often and recognize the good things that I do to please him?

12. What can I do to get my husband to stop criticizing me and putting me down so often?

13. What can my husband and I do to make available more time to spend together?

14. How can my husband and I improve the quality of the time we spend together?

15. How can I persuade my husband to participate with me in marital counseling?

Instead of simply providing solutions to the above problems and teaching Mrs. S how to implement them effectively (i.e., the behavioral approach), the therapist attempted to teach her how to generate alternative solutions, evaluate these solutions, select the "best" solution, implement this solution, and evaluate the outcome. When Mrs. S was not able to generate any more solution alternatives using the principles she was taught, the therapist sometimes suggested additional alternatives so as to maximize her effectiveness and build her response repertoire for future, similar problems. When certain solutions required instrumental skills that Mrs. S did not have (e.g., assertiveness skills), training was provided in these skills using skill-training methods such as coaching, modeling, behavior rehearsal, performance feedback, and positive reinforcement.

In addition to the above training in goal-oriented coping skills (i.e., discovering and implementing problem solutions), training was provided in facilitative coping skills when cognitive and emotional obstacles to effective problem solving occurred (e.g., exaggerated appraisals of threat, irrational assumptions, intense emotional arousal). Mrs. S required training in both cognition-oriented facilitative coping (e.g., cognitive reappraisal) and emotion-oriented facilitative coping (e.g., relaxation). For example, Mrs. S was taught to test the validity of threatening beliefs and assumptions instead of accepting them automatically. A problem-solving approach was used for this purpose. When the woman in the neighborhood had ignored Mrs. S, she had assumed that she had said or done something wrong and that, as a result, the woman disliked her and did not want to be her friend. Instead of accepting this threatening assumption, Mrs. S was taught to generate as many alternative explanations for the woman's behavior as possible (e.g., she was in a bad mood, she was preoccupied and did not see Mrs. S, she has poor eyesight and did not recognize Mrs. S). She was then asked to generate or seek as many facts as possible for and against each explanation and to decide which one was most likely to be valid. To deal with excessive emotional arousal, Mrs. S was trained in progressive muscle relaxation and meditation. In addition, a desensitization procedure was used that involved verbal problem solving in the session (including imaginal solution implementation), while at the same time applying relaxation skills (e.g., muscle relaxation, slow and deep breathing) to reduce anxiety.

During the first 4 weeks of therapy, which focused primarily on assessment, Mrs. S's self-ratings consistently showed a high level of anxiety and low mood and self-esteem. As she developed more effective problem-solving oriented coping skills during the next 12 weeks of therapy, her anxiety level reduced to a moderate range and her mood and self-esteem began to improve. At about the 16th week of therapy, however, Mrs. S's anxiety level suddenly increased again and her mood and self-esteem deteriorated. These negative changes occurred when Mrs. S's husband informed her about the expected job transfer within the next 3 months. Her immediate response was: "We don't know anything about that area. How are we going to find a place to live in 3 months? What if we don't like it there?" Mrs. S experienced considerable anxiety because she appraised the problem as a significant threat to the well-being of the entire family and was inclined to believe that it could not be satisfactorily solved without gathering sufficient information to clarify and understand the real nature of the problem. When she was encouraged to view the situation as a "problem-to-be-solved" and to use her problem-solving skills, she was able to clarify that she was concerned mainly about the health and safety of the neighborhood in which they would live and about the quality of the schools. This clarification led to relevant information gathering strategies during the next few weeks that resulted eventually in the purchase of a home in a satisfactory area within the 3-month period.

As Mrs. S made progress in coping with the job transfer problem, her ratings showed a decrease in anxiety level once again and better mood and self-esteem. The ratings continued to show good improvement for the next several weeks of therapy, after which treatment was terminated because the family moved. At that point, Mrs. S felt more capable of solving her own current problems, except for some of the marital problems (e.g., the lack of positive feedback, the lack of time together). Therefore it was recommended that the couple seek marital counseling in their new location. In a follow-up telephone conversation 3 months later, Mrs. S indicated that her husband was still refusing to become involved in marital therapy. As a result, her dissatisfaction with the marriage remained, but she was coping well with her other problems and continuing to feel less anxious, less depressed, and much better about herself.

VARIATIONS IN PST PROGRAMS

PST programs have varied in terms of (1) target population, (2) program goals, (3) setting, (4) amount of training in other coping skills within the overall PST framework, (5) instructional methods used, and (6) overall program structure (see D'Zurilla, 1986a; D'Zurilla & Nezu, 1982; Spivack *et al.*, 1976). The target populations have included hospitalized psychiatric patients, substance abusers, cigarette smokers, hypertensives, people with stress and anxiety problems, people with weight-control problems, depressed individuals, people with marital and family problems, academic underachievers, elderly persons with problems related to aging, other vulnerable or at risk populations (i.e., people experiencing many difficult life problems and stresses, especially those with problem-solving skill deficits), and community problem-solving groups (e.g., a community policy-making committee). PST has been conducted in both individual and group settings (mostly group), and in both clinical and community settings (e.g., the home, the classroom). Program goals have included treatment goals (i.e., reduction of stress and maladaptive behavior), maintenance goals (i.e., prevention of relapse), prevention goals (i.e., control and prevention of stress and maladaptive behavior in vulnerable or at risk groups), and positive competence-enhancement goals (i.e., achieving a higher level of functioning).

Training in other coping skills within an overall PST framework has included training in specific self-control skills (e.g., stimulus control, behavioral contracting), cognitive-restructuring skills, anxiety-management skills, and instrumental performance skills. Instructional methods in PST programs have included verbal instruction, group discussion, self-instruction, problem-solving demonstrations and examples (modeling), problem-solving exercises and homework assignments (rehearsal), role playing, covert rehearsal, performance feedback, positive reinforcement, and shaping. These procedures have included the use of workbooks, forms, videotapes and audiocassettes. The overall program structure has differed on such variables as number of sessions, duration of sessions, time devoted to different problem-solving skills, time devoted to training in other coping skills, and emphasis on different instructional methods.

At the present time there is a lack of data relevant to the question of what variations in PST result in the most effective or efficient training. One example of an alternative PST program is Mahoney's (1977, 1980) "personal science." Cast within a scientific or experimental framework, this self-help approach adopts a broad cognitive-behavioral perspective with an emphasis on personal problem solving and a variety of other coping skills. Therapy is viewed as an apprenticeship in cognitive-behavioral assessment and self-management-oriented intervention. The therapist acts as a consultant or coach whose primary responsibility is to teach the client how to assess his or her own clinical problems, plan an appropriate self-management intervention program, and implement it effectively. The role of the client is one of active collaboration and participation in the behavior change process. Other variations in PST programs include Coché's group therapy program for psychiatric patients (Coché, 1985), Black's weight-control program (Black, 1987; Black & Scherba, 1983; Black & Threlfall, 1986), Jacobson's marital therapy program (Jacobson & Margolin, 1979), Robin's parent–adolescent program (Robin, 1979), Heppner's prevention-oriented program for college students with problem-solving deficits (Heppner, Baumgardner, Larson, & Petty, 1983), and Parnes's creative problem-solving program (Parnes *et al.*, 1977), which focuses on positive competence enhancement in a normal college student population. Although Parnes's program does not focus on a clinical or at risk population, it is an excellent, comprehensive training program that has important implications for primary prevention and community psychology.

THE EMPIRICAL STATUS OF PST

D'Zurilla (1986a) and D'Zurilla and Nezu (1982) have reviewed a number of PST outcome studies focusing on a variety of different adult populations and clinical problems. Encouraging, beneficial treatment effects have been reported in studies focusing on psychiatric patients with severe social-skills deficits (Bedell, Archer, & Marlow, 1980; Coché & Douglas, 1977; Coché & Flick, 1975; Edelstein, Couture, Cray, Dickins, & Lusebrink, 1980), alcoholism (Chaney, O'Leary, & Marlatt, 1978; Intagliatia, 1978), depression (Hussian & Lawrence, 1981; Nezu, 1986a), stress and anxiety (Ewart, Burnett, & Taylor, 1983; Ewart, Taylor, Kraemer, & Agras, 1984; Moon & Eisler, 1983; Petty, Moeller, & Campbell, 1976; Tableman, Marciniak, Johnson, & Rodgers, 1982; Toseland, 1977), and agoraphobia (Jannoun, Munby, Catalan, & Gelder, 1980).

In addition to the above studies, favorable results have also been reported in outcome studies focusing on adolescent adjustment problems (Christoff *et al.*, 1985; Sarason & Sarason, 1981), weight-control problems (Black, 1987; Black & Scherba, 1983; Black & Threlfall, 1986; Straw & Terre, 1984), cigarette smoking (Karol & Richards, 1978), academic underachievement (Richards & Perri, 1978), vocational indecision (Mendonca & Siess, 1976), and marital and family problems (Foster, Prinz, & O'Leary, 1983; Jacobson, 1977a, 1977b, 1978, 1984; Jacobson & Follette, 1985; Robin, 1981; Robin, Kent, O'Leary, Foster, & Prinz, 1977).

In addition to the studies that focus on various maladjusted groups, several outcome studies have focused on normal individuals and groups interested in maximizing their general problem-solving effectiveness and achieving a higher level of functioning (Briscoe, Hoffman, & Bailey, 1975; Dixon, Heppner, Petersen, & Ronning, 1979; Heppner et al., 1983; Parnes & Noller, 1973; Schinke, Blythe, & Gilchrist, 1981). These studies have produced promising results that have important implications for prevention and community psychology.

The Nezu (1986a) study on unipolar depression and the Black (1987) study on weight control are particularly noteworthy because they provide strong support for both the theory and practice of PST. The Nezu study is a well-controlled, well-executed outcome study in which 26 clinically depressed community-residing subjects were randomly assigned to one of three conditions: (1) problem-solving therapy (PST), (2) problem-focused therapy (PFT), or (3) waiting-list control (WLC). Both therapy conditions were conducted in a group setting over eight weekly sessions lasting 1½-2 hours. PST involved training in the problem-solving skills described by D'Zurilla and Nezu (1982). PFT involved discussions of the subjects' current life problems with a problem-solving goal, but provided no systematic training in problem-solving skills.

Dependent measures were obtained at pretreatment, posttreatment, and a 6-month follow-up assessment. These measures included the Beck Depression Inventory (BDI), the Depression Scale of the Minnesota Multiphasic Personality Inventory (MMPI-D), the Problem-Solving Inventory (PSI), and the Internal–External Locus of Control Scale (I-E).

Both traditional statistical analyses and an analysis of the clinical significance of the results indicated substantial reductions in depression in the PST group, as measured by both the BDI and the MMPI-D, which were maintained over the 6-month follow-up period. Moreover, the improvement in depression in the PST condition was significantly greater than in the PFT and WLC conditions. The superiority of PST was maintained at the 6-month follow-up evaluation. The results for the PSI and the I-E scale showed that the PST subjects increased significantly more than the other two groups in self-appraisal of problem-solving effectiveness, and also changed significantly in locus of control orientation from external to internal. These improvements were also maintained at the 6-months follow-up. These results provide support for the basic assumption that PST produces its effects by increasing problem-solving ability and strengthening personal control expectations.

The Black (1987) study evaluated the efficacy of a weight-control program that consisted of a "minimal intervention" followed by a PST program that focused on weight- and exercise-related life problems. The subjects for this study were seven moderately obese women (27% to 54% overweight). The minimal intervention consisted of verbal instructions regarding nutrition, physical activity, and gradual weight loss, and self-monitoring of weight and calories consumed and expended. The PST program involved 20 2-hour sessions over a 10-week period, which focused on the problem-solving skills described by D'Zurilla and Goldfried (1971). If subjects were having difficulty solving problems and implementing solutions, training was provided in facilitative coping techniques such as covert modeling, self-reinforcement, attention diversion, relaxation, and behavioral contracting. In addition to weight-loss measures, the dependent measures included a measure of the frequency of weight- and exercise-related problems, a verbal problem-solving performance test that employed hypothetical problematic situations, and a "think aloud" procedure that permitted the assessment of specific problem-solving cognitions. After the formal treatment period, 3- and 6-month follow-up meetings were held.

The major findings were (1) that weight loss increased dramatically during the PST program compared to the minimal intervention program, (2) that weight loss was variable during minimal intervention but very homogeneous during PST, and (3) that weight loss continued after treatment, with six subjects losing weight at the 3-month follow-up and three subjects continuing to lose weight at the 12-month follow-up. Clinically significant weight losses occurred for five subjects. The study found a strong relationship between weight loss and both problem-solving ability and the number of weight-related problems during the PST period. Greater weight losses were associated with higher problem-solving ability and less frequent problems. The average weight loss of 25 pounds in this study is one of the best reported in the behavioral weight loss literature to date.

Taken together, the outcome studies on PST have produced very positive and encouraging results. Although the evidence from some of the studies is limited and inconclusive because of methodological problems (e.g., inadequate controls), the consistency with which positive treatment effects have been found with programs involving PST argues strongly for the efficacy of this approach for a variety of clinical problems. The evidence indicates that PST contributes not only to immediate treatment effects, but to the maintenance of treatment gains as well. The results have been particularly impressive in studies focusing on stress, depression, and weight-control problems. Moreover, the results of studies involving prevention-oriented programs in nonclinical community settings suggest that PST also helps to minimize stress effects and enhance personal/social competence in a positive manner. These results are particularly important for various vulnerable or at risk populations in the community (e.g., the elderly, individuals on public assistance, adolescents with problem-solving deficits). Finally, the results of one study even suggest that the effectiveness of community policy-making committees can be enhanced significantly through PST (Briscoe et al., 1975), which has important implications for the field of community psychology.

There are several areas that should be emphasized in future research on PST. In the area of treatment, PST seems to be a particularly appropriate treatment for stress-related disorders such as generalized anxiety, psychophysiological disorders (e.g., tension headaches), and depression because of the possible critical role of perceived uncontrollability in the etiology and/or maintenance of these disorders (Abramson et al., 1978; Hamberger & Lohr, 1984). More outcome studies that focus on these disorders are needed. With regard to the maintenance of treatment effects, the impressive results reported in studies on weight control and cigarette smoking suggest that PST might be useful as a maintenance strategy in the treatment of other disorders as well. This possibility should be explored in future outcome studies.

A popular and promising direction in the mental health field today is primary and secondary prevention, using programs that focus on positive competence enhancement (Felner, Jason, Moritsugu, & Farber, 1983; Wine & Smye, 1981). Studies focusing on PST-oriented prevention programs have produced very promising results, but most of them have been uncontrolled case studies. More well-controlled studies are needed in this area.

In order to facilitate research in the above areas, more comprehensive, reliable, and valid assessment measures of social problem-solving ability and performance are badly needed. Finally, continued research is needed on the social problem-solving model itself. As more is learned about the specific abilities required for effective social problem solving, the model can be modified and improved, which will in turn lead to refinements and improvements in PST programs.

REFERENCES

Abramson, L. Y., Seligman, M. E. P., & Teasdale, J. D. (1978). Learned helplessness in humans: Critique and reformulation. *Journal of Abnormal Psychology, 87*, 49–74.

Appel, P. W., & Kaestner, E. (1979). Interpersonal and emotional problem solving among narcotic drug abusers. *Journal of Consulting and Clinical Psychology, 47*, 1125–1127.

Badia, P., Suter, S., & Lewis, P. (1967). Preferences for warned shock: Information and/or preparation. *Psychological Reports, 20*, 271–274.

Bandura, A. (1971). Vicarious and self-reinforcement process. In R. Glasner (Ed.), *The nature of reinforcement*. New York: Academic Press.

Bandura, A. (1977). Self-efficacy: Toward a unifying theory of behavioral change. *Psychological Review, 84*, 191–215.

Barlow, D. H., Haynes, S. C., & Nelson, R. O. (1984). *The scientists practitioner: Research and accountability in clinical and educational settings*. New York: Pergamon.

Baumgardner, P., Heppner, P. P., & Arkin, R. M. (1984, August). *The role of causal attribution in personal problem solving*. Paper presented at the 92nd annual convention of the American Psychology Association, Toronto.

Bayless, O. L. (1967). An alternative pattern for problem-solving discussion. *Journal of Communication, 17*, 188–197.

Beach, L. R., & Mitchell, T. R. (1978). A contingency model for the selection of decision strategies. *Academy of Management Review, 3,* 439–449.

Beck, A. T. (1967). *Depression.* New York: Hoeber.

Bedell, J. R., Archer, R. P., & Marlow, H. A., Jr. (1980). A description and evaluation of a problem solving skills training program. In D. Upper & S. M. Ross (Eds.), *Behavioral group therapy: An annual review.* Champaign, IL: Research Press.

Bellack, A. S., & Hersen, M. (1977). Self-report inventories in behavioral assessment. In J. D. Cone & R. P. Hawkins (Eds.), *Behavioral assessment: New directions in clinical psychology.* New York: Brunner/Mazel.

Bellack, A. S., & Hersen, M. (Eds.). (1979). *Research and practice in social skills training.* New York: Plenum.

Bernstein, D. A., & Borkovec, T. D. (1973). *Progressive relaxation training: A manual for the helping professions.* Champaign, IL: Research Press.

Black, D. R. (1987). A minimal intervention program and a problem-solving program for weight control. *Cognitive Therapy and Research, 11,* 107–120.

Black, D. R., & Scherba, D. S. (1983). Contracting to problem solve versus contracting to practice behavioral weight loss skills. *Behavior Therapy, 14,* 100–109.

Black, D. R., & Threlfall, W. E. (1986). A stepped approach to weight control: A minimal intervention and a problem-solving program. *Behavior Therapy, 17,* 144–157.

Brilhart, J. K., & Jochem, L. M. (1964). Effects of different patterns on outcome of problem-solving discussion. *Journal of Applied Psychology, 48,* 175–179.

Briscoe, R. V., Hoffman, D. B., & Bailey, J. S. (1975). Behavioral community psychology: Training a community board to problem solve. *Journal of Applied Behavioral Analysis, 8,* 157–168.

Butler, L., & Meichenbaum, D. (1981). The assessment of interpersonal problem-solving skills. In P. C. Kendall & S. D. Hollon (Eds.), *Assessment strategies for cognitive-behavioral interventions.* New York: Academic Press.

Carver, C. G., & Scheier, M. F. (1982). Control therapy: A useful conceptual framework for personality-social, clinical, and health psychology. *Psychological Bulletin, 92,* 111–135.

Chaney, E. F., O'Leary, M. R., & Marlatt, G. A. (1978). Skill training with alcoholics. *Journal of Consulting and Clinical Psychology, 46,* 1092–1104.

Christoff, K. A., Scott, W. O. N., Kelley, M. L., Schlundt, D., Baer, G., & Kelly, J. A. (1985). Social skills and social problem-solving training for shy young adolescents. *Behavior Therapy, 16,* 468–477.

Claerhout, S., Elder, J., & Janes, C. (1982). Problem-solving skills of rural battered women. *American Journal of Community Psychology, 10,* 605–612.

Coché, E. (1985). Problem-solving training: A cognitive group therapy modality. In A. Freeman & V. Greenwood (Eds.), *Cognitive therapy: Applications in psychiatric and medical settings.* New York: Human Sciences Press.

Coché, E., & Douglas, A. A. (1977). Therapeutic effects of problem-solving training and play-reading groups. *Journal of Clinical Psychology, 33,* 820–827.

Coché, E., & Flick, A. (1975). Problem solving training groups for hospitalized psychiatric patients. *Journal of Psychology, 91,* 19–29.

Corah, N. C., & Boffa, J. (1970). Perceived control, self-observation, and response to aversive stimulation. *Journal of Personality and Social Psychology, 16,* 1–4.

Cormier, W. H., Otani, A., & Cormier, S. (1986). The effects of problem-solving training on two problem-solving tasks. *Cognitive Therapy and Research, 10,* 95–108.

Dixon, D. N., Heppner, P. P., Petersen, C. H., & Ronning, R. R. (1979). Problem-solving workshop training. *Journal of Counseling Psychology, 26,* 133–139.

Dobson, D. J., & Dobson, K. S. (1981). Problem-solving strategies in depressed and nondepressed college students. *Cognitive Therapy and Research, 5,* 237–249.

Durlak, J. A. (1983). Social problem-solving as a primary prevention strategy. In R. D. Felner, L. A. Jason, J. N. Noritsugu, & S. S. Farber (Eds.), *Preventive psychology: Theory, research and practice.* New York: Pergamon.

D'Zurilla, T. J. (1986a). *Problem-solving therapy: A social competence approach to clinical intervention.* New York: Springer.

D'Zurilla, T. J. (1986b, November). *A problem-solving approach to stress management and prevention.* Paper presented at the annual convention of the Association for Advancement of Behavior Therapy, Chicago.

D'Zurilla, T. J., & Goldfried, M. R. (1971). Problem solving and behavior modification. *Journal of Abnormal Psychology, 78,* 107-126.

D'Zurilla, T. J., & Nezu, A. (1980). A study of the generation-of-alternatives process in social problem solving. *Cognitive Therapy and Research, 4,* 67-72.

D'Zurilla, T. J., & Nezu, A. (1982). Social problem solving in adults. In P. C. Kendall (Eds.), *Advances in cognitive-behavioral research and therapy* (Vol. 1). New York: Academic Press.

D'Zurilla, T. J., & Nezu, A. M. (in press). The Heppner and Krauskopf Approach: A model of personal problem solving or social skills? *The Counseling Psychologist.*

Edelstein, B. A., Couture, E. T., Cray, M., Dickens, P., & Lusebrink, N. (1980). Group training of problem-solving with chronic psychiatric patients. In D. Upper & S. Ross (Eds.), *Behavioral group therapy: An annual review* (Vol. 2). Champaign, IL: Research Press.

Edwards, W. (1961). Behavioral decision theory. *Annual Review of Psychology, 12,* 473-498.

Ellis, A. (1977). The basic clinical theory of rational–emotive therapy. In A. Ellis & R. Grieger (Eds.), *Handbook of rational–emotive therapy.* New York: Springer.

Ellis, A., & Harper, R. A. (1975). *A new guide to rational living.* Englewood Cliffs, NJ: Prentice-Hall.

Epstein, S. (1982). Conflict and stress. In L. Goldberger & S. Breznitz (Eds.), *Handbook of stress: Theoretical and clinical aspects.* New York: Free Press.

Ewart, C. K., Burnett, K. F., Taylor, C. B. (1983). Communication behaviors that affect blood pressure: An A-B-A-B analysis of marital interaction. *Behavior Modification, 7,* 331-344.

Ewart, C. K., Taylor, C. B., Kraemer, H. C., & Agras, W. S. (1984). Reducing blood pressure reactivity during interpersonal conflict: Effects of marital communication training. *Behavior Therapy, 15,* 473-484.

Felner, R. D., Jason, L. A., Moritsugu, J. N., & Farber, S. S. (1983). *Prevention psychology: Theory, research and practice.* New York: Pergamon.

Foster, S. L., Prinz, R. J., & O'Leary, K. D. (1983). Impact of problem-solving communication training and generalization procedures on family conflict. *Child and Family Behavior Therapy, 5,* 1-23.

Freedman, B. I., Rosenthal, L., Donahoe, C. P., Schlundt, D. G., & McFall, R. M. (1978). A social-behavioral analysis of skill deficits in delinquent and nondelinquent adolescent boys. *Journal of Consulting and Clinical Psychology, 46,* 1448-1462.

Gagné, R. M. (1966). Human problem solving: Internal and external events. In B. Kleinmuntz (Ed.), *Problem solving: Research, method and theory.* New York: Wiley.

Geer, J. H., Davison, G. C., & Gatchel, R. I. (1970). Reduction of stress in humans through nonveridical perceived control of aversive stimulation. *Journal of Personality and Social Psychology, 30,* 30-43.

Gladwin, T. (1967). Social competence and clinical practice. *Psychiatry: Journal for the Study of Interpersonal Processes, 3,* 30-43.

Goldfried, M. R. (1980). Psychotherapy as coping skills training. In M. J. Mahoney (Ed.), *Psychotherapy process: Current issues and future directions.* New York: Plenum.

Goldfried, M. R. (1982). Resistance and clinical behavior therapy. In P. L. Wachtel (Ed.), *Resistance: Psychodynamic and behavioral approaches.* New York: Plenum.

Goldfried, M. R., Decenteceo, E. T., & Weinberg, L. (1974). Systematic rational restructuring as a self-control technique. *Behavior Therapy, 5*, 247–252.

Goldfried, M. R., & D'Zurilla, T. J. (1969). A behavior-analytic model for assessing competence. In C. D. Spielberger (Ed.), *Current topics in clinical and community psychology* (Vol. 1). New York: Academic Press.

Goldstein, A. P. (1973). *Structured learning therapy.* New York: Academic Press.

Gotlib, I. H., & Asarnow, R. F. (1979). Interpersonal and impersonal problem-solving skills in mildly and clinically depressed university students. *Journal of Consulting and Clinical Psychology, 47*, 86–95.

Guilford, J. P. (1967). *The nature of human intelligence.* New York: McGraw-Hill.

Guilford, J. P. (1968). *Intelligence, creativity, and their educational implications.* San Diego, CA: Knapp.

Guilford, J. P. (1977). *Way beyond the IQ: Guide to improving intelligence and creativity.* Great Neck, NY: Creative Synergetic Associates.

Hamberger, L. K., & Lohr, J. M. (1984). *Stress and stress management.* New York: Springer.

Heppner, P. P., & Anderson, W. P. (1985). The relationship between problem solving self-appraisal and psychological adjustment. *Cognitive Therapy and Research, 9*, 415–427.

Heppner, P. P., Baumgardner, A., & Jackson, J. (1985). Problem solving self-appraisal, depression, and attribution styles: Are they related? *Cognitive Therapy and Research, 9*, 105–113.

Heppner, P. P., Baumgardner, A. H., Larson, L. M., & Petty, R. E. (1983, August). *Problem-solving training for college students with problem-solving deficits.* Paper presented at the Annual Convention of the American Psychological Association, Anaheim, CA.

Heppner, P. P., Hibel, J. H., Neal, G. W., Weinstein, C. L., & Rabinowitz, F. E. (1982). Personal problem solving: A descriptive study of individual differences. *Journal of Counseling Psychology, 29*, 580–590.

Heppner, P. P., Kampa, M., & Brunning, L. (1984, August). *Problem solving appraisal as a mediator of stress.* Paper presented at the Annual Convention of the American Psychological Association, Toronto.

Heppner, P. P., & Krieshok, T. S. (1983). An applied investigation of problem-solving appraisal, vocational identity, and career service requests, utilization, and subsequent evaluations. *The Vocational Guidance Quarterly, 31*, 249–259.

Heppner, P. P., Neal, G. W., & Larson, L. M. (1984). Problem-solving training as prevention with college students. *Personnel and Guidance Journal, 62*, 514–519.

Heppner, P. P., & Petersen, C. H. (1982). The development and implications of a personal problem solving inventory. *Journal of Counseling Psychology, 29*, 66–75.

Heppner, P. P., Reeder, B. L., & Larson, L. M. (1983). Cognitive variables associated with personal problem-solving appraisal: Implications for counseling. *Journal of Counseling Psychology, 30*, 537–545.

Hiroto, D. S., & Seligman, M. E. P. (1975). Generality of learned helplessness in man. *Journal of Personality and Social Psychology, 31*, 311–327.

Hokanson, J. E., DeGood, D. E., Forrest, M. S., & Brittain, T. M. (1971). Availability of avoidance behaviors for modulating vascular-stress responses. *Journal of Personality and Social Psychology, 19*, 60–68.

Hussian, R. A., & Lawrence, P. S. (1981). Social reinforcement of activity and problem-solving training in the treatment of depressed institutionalized elderly patients. *Cognitive Therapy and Research, 5*, 57–69.

Intagliatia, J. C. (1978). Increasing the interpersonal problem solving skills of an alcoholic population. *Journal of Consulting and Clinical Psychology, 46*, 489–498.

Jacobson, N. S. (1977a). Problem solving and contingency contracting in the treatment of marital discord. *Journal of Consulting and Clinical Psychology, 45*, 92–100.

Jacobson, N. S. (1977b). Training couples to solve their marital problems: A behavioral approach to relationship discord. Part I: Problem-solving skills. *International Journal of Family Counseling, 5*, 22-31.

Jacobson, N. S. (1978). Specific and nonspecific factors in the effectiveness of a behavioral approach to the treatment of marital discord. *Journal of Consulting and Clinical Psychology, 46*, 442-452.

Jacobson, N. S. (1984). A component analysis of marital behavior therapy: The relative effectiveness of behavior change and communication/problem-solving training. *Journal of Consulting and Clinical Psychology, 52*, 295-305.

Jacobson, N. S., & Follette, W. C. (1985). Clinical significance of improvement resulting from two behavioral marital therapy components. *Behavior Therapy, 16*, 249-262.

Jacobson, N. S., & Margolin, G. (1979). *Marital therapy: Strategies based on social learning and behavior exchange principles.* New York: Brunner/Mazel.

Jahoda, M. (1953). The meaning of psychological health. *Social Casework, 34*, 349-354.

Jahoda, M. (1958). *Current concepts of positive mental health.* New York: Basic Books.

Janis, I. L. (1982). Decision making under stress. In L. Goldberger & S. Breznitz (Eds.), *Handbook of stress: Theoretical and clinical aspects.* New York: Free Press.

Janis, I. L. (1983). Stress inoculation in health care: Theory and research. In D. Meichenbaum & M. E. Jaremko (Eds.), *Stress reduction and prevention.* New York: Plenum.

Janis, I. L., & Mann, L. (1977). *Decision making: A psychological analysis of conflict, choice, and commitment.* New York: Free Press.

Jannoun, L., Munby, M., Catalan, J., & Gelder, M. (1980). A home-based treatment program for agoraphobia: Replication and controlled evaluation. *Behavior Therapy, 11*, 294-305.

Jones, L. C. T. (1954). Frustration and stereotyped behavior in human subjects. *Quarterly Journal of Experimental Psychology, 6*, 12-20.

Kagan, C. (1984). Social problem solving and social skills training. *British Journal of Clinical Psychology, 23*, 161-173.

Kahnemann, D., & Tversky, A. (1979). Prospect theory: An analysis of decisions under risk. *Econometrica, 47*, 263-291.

Kanfer, F. H. (1970). Self-regulation: Research, issues, and speculations. In C. Neuringer & J. L. Michael (Eds.), *Behavior modification in clinical psychology.* New York: Appleton-Century-Crofts.

Karol, R. L., & Richards, C. S. (1978, November). *Making treatment effects last: An investigation of maintenance strategies for smoking reduction.* Paper presented at the Annual Convention of the Association for Advancement of Behavior Therapy, Chicago.

Kendall, P. C., & Fischler, G. L. (1984). Behavioral and adjustment correlates of problem solving: Validational analyses of interpersonal cognitive problem solving measures. *Child Development, 55*, 879-892.

Kendall, P. C., & Hollon, S. D. (Eds.). (1979). *Cognitive-behavioral interventions: Theory, research, and procedures.* New York: Academic Press.

Kleinmuntz, B. (Ed.). (1966). *Problem solving: Research, method, and theory.* New York: Wiley.

Krasnor, L. R., & Rubin, K. H. (1981). The assessment of social problem-solving skills in young children. In T. Merluzzi, C. Glass, & M. Genest (Eds.), *Cognitive assessment.* New York: Guilford.

Larson, L. M., & Heppner, P. P. (1985). The relationship of problem-solving appraisal to career decision and indecision. *Journal of Vocational Behavior, 26*, 55-65.

Lazarus, R. S. (1981). The stress and coping paradigm. In C. Eisdorfer, D. Cohen, A. Kleinman, & P. Maxim (Eds.), *Theoretical bases for psychopathology.* New York: Spectrum.

Lazarus, R. S. (1982). Thoughts on the relations between emotion and cognition. *American Psychologist, 37*, 1019-1024.

Lazarus, R. S., & Folkman, S. (1984). *Stress, appraisal, and coping.* New York: Springer.

Lazarus, R. S., Kanner, A., & Folkman, S. (1980). Emotions: A cognitive phenomenological analysis. In R. Plutchik & H. Kellerman (Eds.), *Theories of emotion.* New York: Academic Press.

Mahoney, M. J. (1974). *Cognition and behavior modification.* Cambridge, MA: Ballinger.

Mahoney, M. J. (1977). Personal science: A cognitive learning therapy. In A. Ellis & R. Grieger (Eds.), *Handbook of rational-emotive therapy.* New York: Springer.

Mahoney, M. J. (1980). A strategy for generating self-help. In G. L. Martin & J. G. Osborne (Eds.), *Helping in the community: Behavioral applications.* New York: Plenum.

Maier, N. R. F. (1949). *Frustration: A study of behavior without a goal.* New York: McGraw-Hill.

Mandler, G. (1982). Stress and thought processes. In L. Goldberger & S. Breznitz (Eds.), *Handbook of stress: Theoretical and clinical aspects.* New York: Free Press.

Marquart, D. I., & Arnold, L. P. (1952). A study in the frustration of human adults. *Journal of General Psychology, 47,* 43-63.

Masserman, J. H. (1943). *Behavior and neurosis.* Chicago: University of Chicago Press.

McFall, R. M. (1982). A review and reformulation of the concept of social skills. *Behavioral Assessment, 4,* 1-33.

McKay, M., Davis, M., & Robbins-Eshelman, E. (1982). *The relaxation and stress reduction workbook* (2nd Ed.). Oakland, CA: New Harbinger Publications.

Meadow, A., Parnes, S. J., & Reese, H. (1959). Influence of instructions and problems sequence on a creative problem-solving test. *Journal of Applied Psychology, 43,* 413-416.

Mechanic, D. (1970). Some problems in developing a social psychology of adaptation to stress. In J. E. McGrath (Ed.), *Social and psychological factors in stress.* New York: Holt, Rinehart & Winston.

Mechanic, D. (1974). Social structure and personal adaptation: Some neglected dimensions. In G. Coelho, C. M. Hamburg, & J. E. Adams (Eds.), *Coping and adaptation.* New York: Basic Books.

Meichenbaum, D., & Asarnow, J. (1979). Cognitive-behavioral modification and metacognitive development: Implications for the classroom. In P. C. Kendall & S. D. Hollon (Eds.), *Cognitive-behavioral interventions: Theory, research, and procedures.* New York: Academic Press.

Meichenbaum, D., & Cameron, R. (1983). Stress inoculation training: Toward a general paradigm for training in coping skills. In D. Meichenbaum & M. E. Jaremko (Eds.), *Stress reduction and prevention.* New York: Plenum.

Meichenbaum, D., Henshaw, D., & Himel, N. (1982). Coping with stress as a problem-solving process. In W. Krohne & L. Luax (Eds.), *Achievement stress and anxiety.* New York: Hemisphere.

Mendonca, J. D., & Siess, T. F. (1976). Counseling for indecisiveness: Problem solving and anxiety management training. *Journal of Counseling Psychology, 23,* 330-347.

Miller, G. A., Galanter, E., & Pribram, K. H. (1960). *Plans and the structure of behavior.* New York: Holt, Rinehart, & Winston.

Mitchell, J. E., & Madigan, R. J. (1984). The effects of induced elation and depression on interpersonal problem solving. *Cognitive Therapy and Research, 8,* 277-285.

Moon, J. R., & Eisler, R. M. (1983). Anger control: An experimental comparison of three behavioral treatments. *Behavior Therapy, 14,* 493-505.

Mooney, R. L., & Gordon, L. V. (1950). *Manual: The Mooney problem checklist.* New York: Psychological Corporation.

Mowrer, O. H. (1960a). *Learning theory and behavior.* New York: Wiley.

Mowrer, O. H. (1960b). *Learning theory and the symbolic processes.* New York: Wiley.

Neal, G. W., & Heppner, P. P. (1982, March). *Personality correlates of effective personal problem solving.* Paper presented at the Annual Meeting of the American Personnel and Guidance Association, Detroit.

Newell, A., & Simon, H. A. (1972). *Human problem solving*. Englewood Cliffs, NJ: Prentice-Hall.

Nezu, A. M. (1985). Differences in psychological distress between effective and ineffective problem solvers. *Journal of Counseling Psychology, 32*, 135-138.

Nezu, A. M. (1986a). Efficacy of a social problem solving therapy approach for unipolar depression. *Journal of Consulting and Clinical Psychology, 54*, 196-202.

Nezu, A. M. (1986b). Negative life stress and anxiety: Problem solving as a moderator variable. *Psychological Reports, 58*, 279-283.

Nezu, A. M. (in press). A problem-solving formulation of depression: A literature review and proposal of a pluralistic model. *Clinical Psychology Review*.

Nezu, A., & D'Zurilla, T. J. (1979). An experimental evaluation of the decision-making process in social problem solving. *Cognitive Therapy and Research, 3*, 269-277.

Nezu, A., & D'Zurilla, T. J. (1981a). Effects of problem definition and formulation on decision making in the social problem-solving process. *Behavior Therapy, 12*, 100-106.

Nezu, A., & D'Zurilla, T. J. (1981b). Effects of problem definition and formulation on the generation of alternatives in the social problem-solving process. *Cognitive Therapy and Research, 5*, 265-271.

Nezu, A. M., & D'Zurilla, T. J. (in press). Social problem solving and negative affective states. In P. C. Kendall & D. Watson (Eds.), *Anxiety and depression: Distinctive and overlapping features*. New York: Academic.

Nezu, A. M., Kalmar, K., Ronan, G. F., & Clavijo, A. (1986). Attributional correlates of depression: An interactional model including problem solving. *Behavior Therapy, 17*, 50-56.

Nezu, A. M., & Ronan, G. F. (1985). Life stress, current problems, problem solving, and depressive symptomatology: An integrative model. *Journal of Consulting and Clinical Psychology, 53*, 693-697.

Nezu, A. M., & Ronan, G. F. (in press). Social problem solving and depression: Deficits in generating alternatives and decision making. *Southern Psychologist*.

Noller, R. B., Parnes, S. J., & Biondi, A. M. (1976). *Creative actionbook: Revised edition of creative behavior workbook*. New York: Charles Scribner's Sons.

Osborn, A. (1963). *Applied imagination: Principles and procedures of creative problem solving* (3rd ed.). New York: Scribner's.

Parloff, M. B., & Handlon, J. H. (1964). The influence of criticalness on creative problem-solving in dyads. *Psychiatry, 27*, 17-27.

Parnes, S. J., & Meadow, A. (1959). Effects of "brainstorming" instructions on creative problem solving by trained and untrained subjects. *Journal of Educational Psychology, 50*, 171-176.

Parnes, S. J., & Noller, R. B. (1973). *Toward supersanity: Channeled freedom*. New York: D. O. K. Publishers.

Parnes, S. J., Noller, R. B., & Biondi, A. M. (1977). *Guide to creative action: Revised edition of creative behavior guidebook*. New York: Charles Scribner's Sons.

Pellegrini, D. S., & Urbain, E. S. (1985). An evaluation of interpersonal cognitive problem solving training with children. *Journal of Child Psychology and Psychiatry, 26*, 17-41.

Petty, B. J., Moeller, T. P., & Campbell, R. Z. (1976). Support groups for elderly persons in the community. *Gerontologist, 16*, 522-528.

Phillips, E. L. (1978). *The social skills basis of psychopathology: Alternatives to abnormal psychology and psychiatry*. New York: Grune & Stratton.

Phillips, S. D., Pazienza, N. J., & Ferrin, H. H. (1984). Decision making styles and problem solving appraisal. *Journal of Counseling Psychology, 31*, 497-502.

Platt, J. J., Scura, W. C., & Hannon, J. R. (1973). Problem solving thinking of youthful incarcerated heroin addicts. *Journal of Community Psychology, 1*, 278-281.

Platt, J. J., & Spivack, G. (1972). Problem solving thinking of psychiatric patients. *Journal of Consulting and Clinical Psychology, 39*, 148–151.

Platt, J. J., & Spivack, G. (1973). Studies in problem-solving thinking of psychiatric patients: Patient-control differences and factorial structure of problem-solving thinking. *Proceedings, 81st Annual Convention of the American Psychological Association, 8*, 461–462.

Platt, J. J., & Spivack, G. (1975). *Manual for the means–ends problem solving procedure (MEPS): A measure of interpersonal cognitive problem-solving skill.* Philadelphia: Hahnemann Community Mental Health/Mental Retardation Center.

Platt, J. J., Spivack, G., Altman, N., Altman, D., & Peizer, S. B. (1974). Adolescent problem solving thinking. *Journal of Consulting and Clinical Psychology, 42*, 787–793.

Richards, C. S., & Perri, M. G. (1978). Do self-control treatments last? An evaluation of behavioral problem solving and faded counselor contact as treatment maintenance strategies. *Journal of Counseling Psychology, 25*, 376–383.

Robin, A. L. (1979). Problem-solving communication training: A behavioral approach to the treatment of parent–adolescent conflict. *The American Journal of Family Therapy, 7*, 69–82.

Robin, A. L. (1981). A controlled evaluation of problem-solving communication training with parent–adolescent conflict. *Behavior Therapy, 12*, 593–609.

Robin, A. L., Kent, R. N., O'Leary, K. D., Foster, S., & Prinz, R. J. (1977). An approach to teaching parents and adolescents problem-solving communication skills: A preliminary report. *Behavior Therapy, 8*, 639–643.

Sarason, I. G. (1980). Life stress, self-preoccupation, and social supports. In I. G. Sarason & C. D. Spielberger (Eds.), *Stress and anxiety* (Vol. 7). New York: Hemisphere.

Sarason, B. R. (1981). The dimensions of social competence: Contributions from a variety of research areas. In J. D. Wine & M. D. Smye (Eds.), *Social competence.* New York: Guilford.

Sarason, I. G., & Sarason, B. R. (1981). Teaching cognitive and social skills to high school students. *Journal of Consulting and Clinical Psychology, 49*, 908–918.

Schinke, S. P., Blythe, B. J., & Gilchrist, L. D. (1981). Cognitive-behavioral prevention of adolescent pregnancy. *Journal of Counseling Psychology, 28*, 451–454.

Seligman, M. E. P. (1975). *Helplessness.* San Francisco: Freeman.

Seligman, M. E. P., & Maier, S. F. (1967). Failure to escape traumatic shock. *Journal of Experimental Psychology, 74*, 1–9.

Sherry, P., Keitel, M., & Tracey, T. J. (1984, August). *The relationship between person–environment fit, coping, and strain.* Toronto: Paper presented at the 92nd Annual Convention of the American Psychological Association.

Shure, M. B. (1981). Social competence as a problem-solving skill. In J. D. Wine & M. D. Smye (Eds.), *Social competence.* New York: Guilford.

Solomon, R. I. (1964). Punishment. *American Psychology, 19*, 239–253.

Spivack, G., Platt, J. J., & Shure, M. B. (1976). *The problem-solving approach to adjustment.* San Francisco: Jossey-Bass.

Spivack, G., & Shure, M. B. (1974). *Social adjustment of young children.* San Francisco: Jossey-Bass.

Sprafkin, R., Gershaw, N. J., & Goldstein, A. P. (1980). Structured-learning therapy: Overview and applications to adolescents and adults. In D. P. Rathjen & J. P. Foreyt (Eds.), *Social competence: Interventions for children and adults.* New York: Pergamon.

Staats, A. W. (1975). *Social behaviorism.* Homewood, IL: Dorsey Press.

Straw, M. K., & Terre, L. (1984). An evaluation of individualized behavioral obesity treatment and maintenance strategies. *Behavior Therapy, 14*, 255–266.

Tableman, B., Marciniak, D., Johnson, D., & Rodgers, R. (1982). Stress management for women on public assistance. *American Journal of Community Psychology, 10*, 357–367.

Toseland, R. (1977). A problem-solving group workshop for older persons. *Social Work, 22*, 325-326.

Tversky, A., & Kahneman, D. (1981). The framing of decisions and the psychology of choice. *Science, 211*, 453-458.

Urbain, E. S., & Kendall, P. C. (1980). Review of social-cognitive problem-solving interventions with children. *Psychological Bulletin, 88*, 109-143.

Weisskopf-Joelson, E., & Eliseo, A. (1961). An experimental study of the effectiveness of brainstorming. *Journal of Applied Psychology, 45*, 45-49.

Wine, J. D., & Smye, M. D. (Eds.). (1981). *Social competence.* New York: Guilford.

Woolfolk, R. L., & Lehrer, P. M. (Eds.). (1984). *Principles and practice of stress management.* New York: Guilford.

Wrubel, J., Benner, P., & Lazarus, R. S. (1981). Social competence from the perspective of stress and coping. In J. D. Wine & M. D. Smye (Eds.), *Social competence.* New York: Guilford.

4

SELF-MANAGEMENT THERAPIES

LYNN P. REHM
PAUL ROKKE

Self-management approaches to psychological treatment encompass a variety of techniques, strategies and models. The term self-management has developed a somewhat differentiated use from the similar terms in behavioral psychology of self-regulation and self-control. Self-regulation tends to be used as a more generic term referring to a variety of processes and techniques involving the voluntary control of psychological, behavioral, and physiological processes. Self-regulation is used to describe biofeedback procedures, for example, as well as cognitive-behavioral procedures. The terms self-control and self-management have been used more consistently to refer to tactics and procedures of control over cognitive and behavioral processes. The term self-control seems to be losing favor in the literature because of its connotations of will power and containment of the expression of emotions. Self-management is a semantically less loaded term. Within cognitive-behavioral theory and practice, the term self-management is applied in different ways as well. First, it refers to certain natural processes by which individuals direct and control their own behavior. The observable consequences of these processes may be assessed; for example, the ability to delay gratification or tolerate pain. Many therapy strategies and theories of self-management attempt to model these natural processes. Second, the term self-management refers to specific methods within cognitive-behavioral approaches to therapy. Often the term is used to refer to methods that are adjuncts to in-office therapy procedures. They are intended to extend the newly acquired behaviors to home and daily life. These generalization strategies depend upon the person being able to administer a program that may involve practicing new behaviors or manipulating antecedents and consequences of behaviors. Third, self-management can refer to specific theoretical models of processes by which people direct and control their behavior. Models may be abstractions of natural processes or may involve translations of learning principles into operations performed by an individual to control his or her own behavior. These models offer procedures and processes by which individuals acquire generalized skills for behavioral adaptation and change. This chapter will focus on models of self-management and their application as therapy methods or techniques.

Although specific definitions of self-management may vary with the individual models, the models themselves share certain common assumptions and features. To begin with, there is an underlying metaphor within these models that assumes that individuals can behave essentially as if they were two persons—a controlled person, who is acting in an environment and responding to a variety of internal and external cues and consequences, and secondly a controlling person who is capable of manipulating internal and external cues and consequences for the purposes of obtaining some long range goals. Again, this assumes that such processes normally and naturally operate within every individual and that thinking in terms of such processes is, therefore, useful for purposes of intervention and treatment. Intervention is seen as intervention on the controlling processes. Self-management therapies involve teaching new controlling processes derived from psychological concepts or behavior modification principles. Self-management therapy procedures can be typically characterized not as applying learning principles to individuals but as teaching the principles to those individuals so that they can apply them to themselves. The processes that psychology has found to be effective for one organism to influence another organism may be adapted for people to influence themselves. It is assumed that these controlling processes are learned in the same way that any other behavior is learned. Therapy thus involves procedures for teaching controlling strategies to the individual.

Self-management models stress the notion of the person in the person by situation interaction. The therapeutic skills represent individual differences that are relatively consistent across time and place. They are generalized skills that the person may apply as the strategy to similar situations. Generalized application to actual life situations is the central focus of self-management therapy procedures. Such therapies attempt to sample situations from real life, bring them into the therapy office for practice, and then send the individual out to apply the strategies in real life.

Self-management therapy procedures focus on methods for the individual to obtain long-term goals. Models and techniques have typically focused on problems of self-control behavior directed towards delayed reinforcers in conflict with immediate reinforcers. Traditional self-control or self-management problems include persistence, that is, maintaining behavior toward a delayed positive reinforcement despite immediate punishments (e.g., jogging), or resistance to temptation, (e.g., sticking to a diet). Individuals engage in these processes when they perceive that current behavior produces adverse consequences in the long run (e.g., their eating habits, their smoking, etc.). Self-management processes may be engaged when the new or changed environment is encountered to which the person may need to adapt. In the latter instance problem-solving procedures may be required. In any of the above situations, the goal is to obtain important distant rewards or reinforcers or to optimize reinforcement in the long run. Optimal long-term reinforcement requires effort, persistence, and resistance to temptation. In order to model this behavior, most self-management theories assume some sort of internal, unobservable processes. They assume that in one form or another individuals make inferences or abstractions about external contingencies and consequences and that response strategies are based on these internal representations. These models fall within the social-learning or cognitive-behavioral models in clinical psychology. The nature of these assumptions, however, vary among self-management theories. Some theoretical models of self-management avoid such internal constructs. For example, within a radical behavioral paradigm, Skinner (1957) suggested a number of strategies whereby individuals manipulate their environment in order to influence their own future behavior and obtain future rewards. This chapter will focus on three prominent models within the cognitive-behavioral literature. These are (1) Albert Bandura's self-efficacy model (1977a, 1977b), (2) Donald Meichenbaum's self-instruction strategies (e.g., Meichenbaum & Cameron, 1973), and (3) Frederick Kanfer's self-control model (1970; Kanfer and Karoly, 1972a, b). Other models that might have been included in the chapter include Carver and Scheier's (1982) information processing model, Eric Klinger's (1982) model of cognitive plans and concerns, or Richard Lazarus's (1974) work on coping strategies under stress.

MODELS OF SELF-MANAGEMENT

BANDURA

Bandura (1969, 1977a, b) has written extensively about social-cognitive factors that influence human learning and behavior change. A construct that has been given a primary role in his conceptual scheme is that of self-efficacy. The following discussion will focus on defining self-efficacy, on the role self-efficacy may play in behavioral performance, and on the implications this concept may have for self-management approaches to therapy.

Bandura (1977a) distinguishes between efficacy expectancies and outcome expectancies. An outcome expectancy can be defined as a person's judgment about whether the performance of a given behavior will produce a particular outcome. Efficacy expectancies, on the other hand, refer to the individual's estimate about whether he or she can successfully execute that behavior.

Bandura (1980) suggests that perceived self-efficacy is a major determinant in whether or not a behavior is initiated, in the amount of effort expended, and in how long a person will persist in the face of adverse circumstances. For example, people participate frequently in activities in which they feel competent and avoid those in which they feel less competent. Of course, a person can feel very competent at performing a particular behavior and still not perform it because there is no incentive for doing so. It also follows that those people who are more confident in their abilities will persist longer in the face of obstacles and adverse conditions than those who are not confident. An individual is more willing and more likely to expend effort on a task that he or she is sure of being able to do than he or she would on a task in which he or she is unsure of being able to do. Performance and persistence are dependent on the interaction of the strength of the person's evaluation of his or her abilities and the relative value of the anticipated outcome goal.

According to Bandura (1977a), efficacy expectations can be formed through information derived from four primary sources. Listed in order of their hypothesized power in influencing efficacy expectations, these sources are: (1) actual performance accomplishments, (2) vicarious experience, (3) verbal persuasion, and (4) physiological states. Note that these sources were also listed in order of the relative amounts of behavior and situation-specific information available from them.

Direct experience with the behavior and situation of interest is the most important source of information on which self-efficacy expectations can be based. Repeated successes in a particular situation may raise efficacy expectations, while failures may serve to lower them. How success or failure experiences influence efficacy, however, depends on the attributions of causation that the individual makes for the outcome (Weiner *et al.*, 1971). Whether an individual makes internal or external and stable or unstable attributions about the cause of the outcome will determine how efficacy expectations are influenced.

The observation of another person performing the behavior of interest can also influence an individual's efficacy expectations. This occurs primarily through a process of social comparisons. The degree of influence that observation will have on efficacy expectancies depends in part on the perceived personal relevance of the information obtained. Efficacy expectancies will be tempered by a number of factors, including the model's characteristics, the similarity of these characteristics to those of the observer, and the nature of the behavior by situation interaction, (i.e. whether the model exhibits mastery of the behavior or some initial failures followed by persistence and subsequent success).

Verbal persuasion is a valuable tool in changing a person's efficacy expectations largely because of its relative convenience in terms of availability and ease of implementation. Initial expectations may be raised in varying degrees depending on whether the content of the persuasive message is consistent with the individual's prior experience and depending on how well it matches with their understanding and beliefs about the causal relationships between the particular behaviors and outcomes involved. The effects of verbal persuasion, however, may be weak and temporary because they are not founded on experience and may be quickly dismissed in the face of experiential disconfirmation.

The final source of information relevant to judgments of personal efficacy is related to the perception of physiological arousal. This source is frequently relied on at the moment in which situational demands are placed on a person. Physiological arousal may interfere with performance and also signal vulnerability, thus serving as a negative influence on judgments of efficacy. The presence of physiological states that are associated with perceptions of relaxation and calm may be associated with feelings of confidence and expected success.

Several studies have been conducted by Bandura and his colleagues to validate the construct of self-efficacy. A strong association has been demonstrated between an individual's level of perceived self-efficacy and his or her subsequent level of performance accomplishments, regardless of the method used for enhancing self-efficacy (Bandura, 1982). Bandura also argues that self-efficacy theory explains the rate of change during the course of treatment (Bandura & Adams, 1977).

Bandura (1977a) argues that effective psychological treatments, of any form, are successful in part because they alter a person's expectations of personal efficacy. Self-management approaches to therapy that focus specifically on instigating the development of skills that can be implemented on one's own may be especially well suited to enhancing self-efficacy. While the causal role of perceived self-efficacy has yet to be demonstrated, the concept has many implications for clinical practice. Treatments that can maximally influence self-efficacy provide graduated success experiences in performance-based procedures, consider and utilize self-attributional processes and self-evaluative information, encourage individuals to develop their own abilities, and allow the individual personal choice and responsibility for the management of their behavior. Procedures that can maximally influence perceived self-efficacy will maximize treatment effectiveness.

MEICHENBAUM

Self-instructional training was an outgrowth of some particular ideas in the developmental literature (Meichenbaum, 1977). Luria (1961, cited in Meichenbaum, 1977), among others, suggested that self-control over the initiation and inhibition of voluntary motor behaviors in children developed through predictable stages. Control over a child's behavior, initially directed by parental speech, is gradually shifted to the child's own overt speech, and finally becomes internalized as the child's covert speech (thoughts, internal dialogue) assumes a self-directive role. Meichenbaum (1977) proposed a form of treatment that made this process explicit.

Self-instructional training is a form of self-management that focuses on the importance of a person's self-instructions. An explicit assumption is that an individual's self-instructions mediate behavior and behavior change. In many cases maladaptive self-statements may contribute to a person's problems. The learning and application of more adaptive self-instructions is the goal of self-instructional training. Since cognitive strategies are not situation bound and can be "carried with" the individual, it might be expected that training in the systematic use of self-instructional techniques could enhance treatment effectiveness and generalization.

Self-instructions can be taught to play two primary roles in governing desired behaviors. In the acquisition of new skills, self-instructions can serve as useful cues for the recall of appropriate behavior sequences or for redirecting and correcting behavior errors. In the correction of maladaptive behavior, self-instructions can serve to interrupt automatic behavioral or cognitive chains and to prompt the use of more adaptive responses. Self-instructional skills will most likely not be effective in the absence of requisite behavioral skills, but may be very useful in the learning of new skills and in enhancing the performance of adaptive responses.

Meichenbaum (1977) describes three phases of self-instructional training that outline his general approach to therapy. The first phase consists primarily of information gathering that would allow an accurate conceptualization of the problem. This process should involve a cooperative venture between the client and the therapist, each contributing their experience and expertise in such a way that the therapist can best understand the nature of the presenting problem and the client can feel that he or she has had direct input into the therapeutic process and has been understood.

In addition to generally assessing the nature, extent, and duration of the presenting problem, the therapist will begin to assess the role of maladaptive cognitions. Cognitive processes occurring in problem situations may be quite automatic and initially difficult for the client to identify clearly. Assessment strategies may be useful not only for evaluating the role of maladaptive cognitions, but for beginning to teach the client to pay attention to his or her covert language activity during problem situations. Common strategies for assessment include in-session imaginal techniques and extra-session self-monitoring assignments. One can have the client imagine a problem situation and describe his or her probable internal dialogue to the therapist. Discussion of the quality of these statements and their relationship to affect and behavior is a useful assessment and instructional procedure. Likewise self-monitoring, whether done in more formal written records or simply by having the client begin to listen to him- or herself with a "third ear" can be very useful. Homework assignments contribute to the gathering of information, as well as to the ability to make meaningful situational analyses and to understand the role cognitions play in maintaining the problem. Conducting initial sessions in this manner allows the client and therapist to develop a common conceptualization of the problem and sets the stage for the presentation of a treatment rationale that will be credible and acceptable to the client. This process should lead to the formulation of an initial treatment plan.

The second phase has been described as a process of "trying on" the conceptualization of the problem. Discussion of the rationale and treatment plan in the context of ongoing observation of the problem, allows the client the opportunity to test the logic of the rationale and to see if it "fits." The rationale of self-instructional training focuses on helping the client develop skills that would allow him or her to change the problem behavior or cope in problem situations, and especially on learning more adaptive self-statements and then substituting them for those that are currently contributing to the problem.

While the first two stages of therapy were primarily concerned with preparing the client for change, the third stage is directed toward promoting change. This occurs through active attempts to change the client's self-statements in order to modify behavior. Several authors have discussed a variety of techniques for modifying self-statements (e.g., Coleman & Beck, 1981; Ellis, 1962).

Meichenbaum and Goodman (1971) outlined their procedures for training impulsive children in self-instructional techniques. This involved a five-step process. First an adult model performed a task while talking to himself out loud. The important self-statements were thus modeled for the child. The child then performed the same task under direction of the therapist's instructions, (i.e., using the same or similar statements that the therapist had made to himself). The child then performed the task while instructing himself aloud. The overt nature of the self-instructions was gradually faded so that the child repeated the task while whispering the instructions to himself, and finally while guiding his performance solely by private (covert) speech. Meichenbaum and Goodman (1971) found that self-instructional procedures, in comparison to placebo and assessment control conditions, resulted in significantly improved performance for impulsive children on the Porteus Maze, on the Performance IQ on the WISC, and on a measure of cognitive impulsivity.

These procedures can and have been adapted for use with adults with a variety of problems (e.g., schizophrenia: Meichenbaum & Cameron, 1973; anger, anxiety, pain: Meichenbaum & Turk, 1976). Generally, the important features of self-instructional training include education about the particular problem and the modeling and rehearsal of relevant behavioral and cognitive skills. These may include problem-solving strategies, focusing attention, response guidance, self-evaluative, and self-reinforcement skills, all of which can serve to enhance coping and self-correcting skills. There should be opportunities for the client to develop self-instructional strategies that best fit their needs and desires and for them to rehearse these strategies under imaginal or *in vivo* conditions with input, modeling, and feedback from the therapist. Many cognitive-behavioral therapies can be expanded and perhaps enhanced by the inclusion of self-instructional strategies. Strategies such as relaxation training, systematic desensitization, and assertion training could all include a self-instructional component.

KANFER

Fredrick Kanfer (1970; Kanfer & Karoly, 1972a, 1972b) has proposed a feedback-loop model of self-management and has elaborated on the components of this process. He views self-control as a series of processes in which an individual engages in order to alter the probability of a response in the relative absence of immediate external supports. This process is engaged when the person perceives that ongoing behavior is not producing the desired consequences. For example, a person may perceive a problem in his or her eating behavior upon finding that last summer's clothes now fit too tightly, or a problem in his or her smoking behavior upon discovering that a pack of cigarettes that had been bought just a few hours earlier is empty. The same processes may be engaged if during a conversation at a party, an individual perceives that the other person seems irritated or disinterested. In each of these instances, the person would begin to employ a three-stage feedback-loop involving self-monitoring, self-evaluation, and self-reinforcement processes.

In the self-monitoring stage of the loop, the person observes his or her own behavior. This may involve the observation of the behavior itself or the behavior along with its antecedents and consequences, and the interrelationships among these elements. Self-monitoring may also involve attending to internal events, such as thoughts and emotions, which may also be monitored. Self-monitoring implies a conscious attention to some specific category of behavior. It may be accomplished in many ways. It may be done in a very informal, unsystematic fashion; for instance, one may have a general impression that a particular meal was consistent with long-range weight goals or not. On the other hand, self-monitoring can be very systematic, for example, recording calorie counts for each item consumed. Monitoring behavior involves awareness of and attention to certain classes of events, an ability to make accurate discriminations among them, and an awareness of the importance of relationships among events. Self-monitoring skills may be acquired in a variety of ways and this acquisition may be an important aspect of childhood social development. Individual differences in the use, skill, and effectiveness of self-monitoring exist among persons. One may speak of individuals developing certain self-monitoring styles or of behavior problems involving specific self-monitoring deficits. Certain styles of self-monitoring may be considered maladaptive.

The second stage in Kanfer's model is self-evaluation. Self-evaluation refers to a comparison between one's performance and a criterion or standard. The index of performance is derived from self-monitoring. The index may, therefore, be a relatively informal abstraction or a systematic measurement of the behavior. Criteria or standards may be derived from a variety of sources. Many generalized standards are internalized in the course of development and come in the form of internalized rules (e.g., "I should always do the best I can"). They may derive from experiences relative to other people, (e.g., "I should be in the top 5% of anything I do academically"), or from external sources of expertise (e.g., "For my sex and height, I should eat no more than 2000 calories per day"). Criteria may vary on many dimensions. They may be relatively specific and differentiated or general and undifferentiated. They may or may not be realistic or appropriate. Standard setting may be another potential form of maladaptive self-control.

On the basis of the comparison to a standard, the individual makes a judgment that their behavior did or did not meet the standard. This judgment is evaluative and involves a determination of whether a behavior was good or bad, a success or a failure. Such evaluative judgments may involve, therefore, an affective component depending upon the importance of the behavior involved. Negative affect about oneself and low self-esteem may derive from repeated judgments that one has not met internalized standards in the self-evaluation process.

The third stage in the self-control loop is self-reinforcement. It is the assumption of this model that individuals control their own behavior through the administration of contingent rewards and punishments just as one person might control the behavior of another. Self-reinforcement supplements external reinforcement in controlling behavior. Self-reinforcements may be covert or overt. People may reward themselves covertly with self-congratulation or an internal sense of accomplishment or pride, (patting oneself on the back). The same people may overtly reward the same behavior by allowing themselves a pleasurable experience (e.g., going to a movie contingent on a week of following a diet). Self-reinforcement is the mechanism whereby individuals strengthen and maintain behavior in the face of contradictory external reinforcement. Persistence and resistance to temptation are accomplished by self-administered reinforcement for attaining the behavior and self-punishment for lapses or giving in to temptations. Self-reinforcement functions to maintain consistency in behavior and to bridge situations in which desirable external reinforcers are delayed and immediate reinforcers for alternative behavior are readily available. Self-reward and self-punishment habits and skills may vary from one individual to another. Individuals may use reward more consistently or more effectively than others. Self-reward skills may vary independently of self-punishment skills.

In general, the self-control feedback loop could be used to describe the behavior by which people exert control over and modify their own behavior. Self-monitoring, self-evaluation, and self-reinforcement processes would be involved in developing a jogging program, in losing weight, or in quitting smoking. These processes may be involved in changing the topic of a conversation to maintain a positive relationship with another person at a party. The model assumes that these are processes that people engage in naturally but also implies that the processes can be made explicit and externalized for therapeutic purposes. Individuals can be taught specific new self-monitoring, self-evaluation, and self-reinforcement skills and procedures.

Two other concepts deserve comment for a full explication of Kanfer's model. Kanfer and his colleagues have also focused on the importance of *commitment* to engaging in self-correcting behavior. After perceiving the desirability of change, the client must make a commitment to continue engaging in the self-control process to accomplish such a change. This is an important issue, since in many instances, the self-modification program may involve considerable effort, and both positive and negative consequences accrue from making the change as well as from continuing the behavior as usual. Commitment may be made easier by discomfort, by fear of social disapproval over inaction, by the presence of others making similar commitments, or by the encouragement and support of relevant others. Commitment may be more difficult if the goal is difficult and distant, or if the behavior is not publicly observable and not supported by others in the environment (cf. Kanfer, 1977). Attention to issues involved in making commitments is very important for therapy procedures using self-management concepts.

The second important concept to add to the self-control model is that of attribution of causality. The various stages of the self-control process imply that the person believes that the behavior involved is under personal control. If the behavior or consequence is partly or entirely under the control of another person then efforts at self-control are futile. Rehm (1977) suggested that attributional processes are particularly important in the self-evaluation stage of the model. Attributions of causality must be internal before a behavior can be judged as good or bad, or as a success or a failure. A person may perceive him- or herself as being accurate and successful at a child's task but not evaluate this performance as commendable in any way because doing well is attributed to the easy nature of the task. Similarly a person may perceive him- or herself as failing at a task outside his or her own area of expertise and not condemn him- or herself for it. Attribution theory, developed by Weiner and his colleagues (e.g., Weiner *et al.*, 1971), is generally applicable to these considerations. They suggest that attributions of causality in real life can generally be classified according to two primary dimensions: (1) internal versus external, and (2) stable versus unstable over time. Kanfer and Hagerman (1981) have developed an elaborated form of the self-control model in which attributional processes are involved at each of the three major stages. This new model has yet to be as applied as extensively as the former model.

APPLICATIONS

TREATMENT OF ANXIETY

Several authors have suggested that perceived inefficacy may be related to fearful behavior, cognitions, and affect. Sarason (1975), for example, equated anxiety with a type of self-preoccupation that can be characterized by a heightened concern over one's inadequacies. Thus, if one were presented with a situation that demanded a decision or some type of active response, doubts about one's ability to cope with the situation would be associated with increased anxiety and would interfere with the individual's ability to attend to and carry out the task at hand. Beck (1967) proposed that the central mechanism of depression includes negative self-evaluations and expectancies. Others also postulate that self-doubt and the misattribution of cause away from the self are central mechanisms in problems of adjustment (e.g., Abramson, Seligman, & Teasdale, 1978; Lazarus, 1981).

Bandura focuses on the importance of an individual's perceived inability to cope with a potentially aversive situation as a primary mechanism in the development of anxiety and fear. To the extent that a particular therapy instills a sense of controllability or predictability, that is, to the extent that the individual comes to believe that he or she is able to prevent, change, avoid, or generally cope with the aversive situation, anxiety and fear will be reduced. From this point of view, low self-efficacy expectations are identified as the primary problem and improvements in self-efficacy during therapy are seen as the critical mechanisms of change. It is hypothesized that treatments that are effective in enhancing perceptions of self-efficacy should therefore be more effective in changing behavior.

Research conducted by Bandura and his colleagues has not focused on developing a treatment approach consistent with self-efficacy theory. Rather, they have utilized a variety of current behavioral and cognitive treatments in efforts to validate the concept of self-efficacy and to demonstrate its causal role in therapeutic change. Many of these treatments have utilized skills approaches that include *in vivo* and covert modeling, shaping, rehearsal, and feedback. A strong association has, in fact, been demonstrated between an individual's level of perceived self-efficacy and his or her subsequent level of performance accomplishments, regardless of the method used for enhancing self-efficacy (Bandura, 1982). Performance-based treatment strategies have been hypothesized to serve as the major source of efficacy information. These strategies have been demonstrated to increase levels of perceived self-efficacy (Bandura, 1982), were effective in the treatment of agoraphobia (Bandura, Adams, Hardy, & Howells, 1980), and were more effective than vicarious modes of therapy for snake phobia (Bandura, Adams, & Beyer, 1977).

Stress inoculation training is a variant of self-instructional training that consists of a multicomponent coping skills package that has particular applicability to anxiety. This approach has been successfullly tested with anxious and phobic subjects (Meichenbaum, 1972; Meichenbaum & Turk, 1976). Meichenbaum (1977) has described this approach as a behavioral analogue to the immunization model in medicine. When a person is inoculated, he or she is given an opportunity to deal with a low dose of the stress-related stimulus in a controlled environment. The experience of learning to cope with small and manageable units of the problematic stimuli will help the person develop skills to cope with larger concerns in other settings. There are three operational phases to stress inoculation training: education, rehearsal, and application. Each of these phases will be discussed in turn.

The first phase of stress inoculation training is educational in nature. The presentation of one or two current theoretical approaches to stress reactions can serve to provide the client with a conceptual framework for understanding his or her own responses. It is important that the theories used are credible, are easily adapted to the client's own experiences, and lead logically to the implementation of the particular coping strategies that will be recommended. While the scientific merit of any theory used is ultimately important, the face validity and practical usefulness of the theory may carry more weight in the decision to employ it in therapeutic settings than its current empirical status.

Meichenbaum and Turk (1976) suggested the use of Schachter's (1966) theory of emotion with anxious or phobic clients. Following Schacter's theory, they explain to the client that fear reactions appear to involve two major components, heightened physiological arousal and cognitive events (images and self-statements), which may enhance and in fact create more anxiety. From this perspective then, treatment can be focused on reducing physiological arousal and substituting more positive self-statements for the habitual anxiety producing self-statements. Various forms of relaxation training and cognitive coping techniques can be employed to enable the client to address these two components of anxiety related responses.

The second component of stress inoculation training is the rehearsal phase. During this period of treatment a variety of coping techniques are presented and discussed with the client. These may include active behavioral responses as well as cognitive coping strategies. Clients may learn as much as they can about the phobic object or an upcoming stressful event in order to be able to realistically assess the risks involved and to provide for more realistic expectations. They can explore escape and response alternatives to expected decision points in the stressful experience and can develop relaxation skills. Cognitive strategies may include changing negative self-statements to more positive and adaptive ones and using imaginal strategies to influence attentional and affective aspects of the setting (e.g., imagining a pleasant scene, or imagining successfully completing a sequence of coping behaviors). Having a "menu" of options for the clients to choose from will allow them to try out and pick those strategies that they are most comfortable with and that they feel they can use most effectively. This may also enhance their sense of control in the situation and contribute to the credibility of the treatment. Three or four different coping strategies can be generated and developed for use by the client. The client can rehearse these strategies in imagination and in role playing situations with the therapist, always with the goal of refining them and becoming more proficient in their use.

Phase three consists of the application of the coping strategies in a series of graduated stressful situations. It is generally recommended that the client begin with situations that are mildly stressful with the application of the strategies to the final target being held off until the client has successfully used the strategies in other situations and is well prepared to handle it. The therapist can expose the client to a variety of stressors in the office, including imaginal and *in vivo* stressors, in order to give the client practice in a controlled yet still stressful situation. It is suggested that clients begin to test out their skills in other mildly stressful situations as they go through their daily routines.

Throughout treatment a self-instructional approach is used so that clients learn to observe their responses and to use appropriate self-statements to guide them through the coping strategies. This includes preparing for a stressor by reminding oneself of the strategy to be used and the behaviors involved in carrying out the strategy, confronting the stressful situation and encouraging oneself to meet the challenge, engaging in the coping strategies themselves, and finally rewarding oneself for a successful performance by either covertly commenting on the good performance or by providing for some other positive consequence. The particular self-statements that a client uses can be tailored to their particular needs and situation. A number of statements, however, should be generated as examples, to encourage variety and differences among situations and to demonstrate the problem-solving, coping, and self-regulatory nature of covert dialogues.

TREATMENT OF PAIN

Self-efficacy notions can also be applied to situations involving pain tolerance. In this context, the idea that self-efficacy is a prime determinant in how long an individual will persist in the face of aversive experiences and in how much effort they will expend to cope with those experiences is equally applicable. Unfortunately, measures employed by Bandura in studies of fear cannot be directly applied to the study of pain tolerance and very few studies have looked at the relationship between self-efficacy and pain tolerance. Glasgow, Klepac, Dowling, and Rokke (1982) attempted to develop a self-efficacy measure that would be appropriate to cold pressor tolerance. They asked subjects how certain they were that they could tolerate cold water for various lengths of time. Two studies yielded congruence rates of 79% and 86% between self-efficacy ratings and actual tolerance times, though changes in self-efficacy, as a result of training in cognitive coping strategies, were not correlated with improvements in tolerance. There is a need for the development and comparison of alternate strategies for assessing self-efficacy in this area. It may be especially valuable to consider the relationship of self-efficacy concepts to other approaches to the study of expectancies (e.g., placebo and demand characteristics) and to more clearly delineate the constructs involved (e.g., Kirsch, 1985).

Self-instructional strategies and the stress inoculation program have also been applied to pain-related problems (e.g., Genest & Turk, 1979; Horan, Hackett, Buchanan, Stone, & Demchik-Stone, 1977; Klepac, Hauge, Dowling, & McDonald, 1981). As a further example of this form of self-management therapy, each of the three phases of stress inoculation will be presented as they are applied to coping with pain. Though the predictability of events associated with stressful medical and dental procedures make the stress inoculation package and its emphasis on preparatory practice especially useful for situations involving acute pain, it can also be applied to problems associated with chronic pain.

One conceptualization of pain that appears to fit well in the educational phase of stress inoculation is Melzack and Wall's (1965) gate control theory of pain. The gate control theory postulates that pain is a complex phenomenon that consists not only of the physiological and sensory-discriminative aspects that are often so readily apparent, but also includes motivational-affective and cognitive-evaluative components. While Melzack and Wall (1965) present a physiological basis for this theory, it is more important that the client simply understands that there is a scientific basis for these hypothesized components of pain than it is for him or her to know the physiological details. It should be emphasized that sensory, affective, and motivational components are recognized as being important aspects of the pain experience.

Commonly observed experiences can serve as useful analogies to this model and may help the client to come to accept the notion that influencing psychological parameters can affect his or her experience of pain. The physiological component can be illustrated easily by the expected reaction from accidentally putting one's hand on a hot stove top. There is an immediate reflexive motor reaction that removes the hand from the stove, which is followed by sensations described as pain. Often in these situations, not only does one have the intense noxious physical stimulus that is perceived as pain inducing, but there are also some automatic, self-protective, physiological responses, including increased muscle tension. This can be related to chronic or acute pain situations in which habitual muscle tension may serve to exacerbate the perception of anxiety and pain.

Situations analogous to the motivational and affective components may include the following: a football player or boxer who is injured during competition, but because he or she is in a particular motivational state continues in the competition without experiencing undue pain; a person who has a pounding headache goes to answer the telephone and doesn't realize that he or she has a headache again until several minutes later when he or she hangs up and his or her attention is no longer distracted by the conversation; personal experiences demonstrating that on days when one is "down," "tired," or "irritable," the pain is worse than when one is feeling good and ambitious.

Finally, the cognitive-evaluative component of this pain theory can be illustrated to the client by pointing out that it is a natural tendency for people to evaluate their behaviors and their experiences. Usually the kind of evaluation one makes, (i.e., good or bad) is based on one's prior experiences in similar situations. Thus one's experience of pain may be influenced by one's evaluation of the pain. For example, an evaluation like, "This headache is terrible, it's the worst one I've ever had," may not only indicate the severity of the pain, but may heighten the concern of the individual and thus exacerbate the headache. In contrast, if a person were able to say "Well, this headache isn't too bad, I can remember much worse," he or she may be able to continue with the tasks at hand and positively influence the experience of pain by reducing the adverse affects of negative evaluations. This conceptualization leads very nicely to the introduction of cognitive-behavioral techniques that can serve to influence attentional, motivational, emotional, and physical aspects of pain.

Skills taught during the second phase of treatment are very similar to those used with anxiety. A variety of coping techniques are presented and the client may choose and practice those that he or she and the therapist agree may be most useful. The client may learn as much as he or she can about the stressor (e.g., upcoming surgery) in order to develop realistic expectations and a plan for dealing with predictable stressors. Relaxation skills and cognitive coping skills may also be developed. A variety of cognitive coping strategies can be used as diversions and as ways to address affective and evaluative components of the pain. These could include imagining a pleasant scene, imagining that one is a secret agent resisting torture, describing the painful stimulus in terms other than painful (e.g., while having a tooth drilled a person may describe the sensations as warm, cool, vibrating, or massaging), counting backwards by multiples of seven, examining art work in the room, and listening to music. Any cognitive activity that the client would like to do and that can hold his or her attention and positively influence his or her mood under adverse conditions may be tried as a potentially useful strategy for coping with pain. Three to four particular strategies should be clearly defined and developed with enough detail so that they can be efficiently rehearsed and implemented.

The final phase of stress inoculation involves applying the developed strategies to painful situations. Some investigators have utilized laboratory methods of inducing pain (e.g., cold pressor, arm shock, and electrical stimulation of tooth pulp) in order to help clients practice their skills under controlled conditions and thus help improve their pain tolerance (Horan *et al.*, 1977; Klepac *et al.*, 1981). It should be noted that both Horan *et al.* and Klepac *et al.* tested for generalization of treatment effects and found that improvements that were made on one training stimulus were not evidenced on a second stimulus that was not targeted during treatment. Efforts should be made during treatment to enhance the generalization and maintenance of effects to the desired target objectives.

TREATMENT OF DEPRESSION

Neither the Bandura self-efficacy model nor the Meichenbaum self-instruction model has been applied extensively to treatment of depression. The Bandura model is theoretically quite applicable to depressive phenomena. Depression may be characterized by a generalized low self-efficacy. The model is related to Seligman's learned helplessness model of depression (Abramson *et al.*, 1978; Seligman, 1975, 1981). In the revised helplessness model, a factor contributing to vulnerability to depression is a negative attributional style. Derived from attribution theory (Weiner *et al.*, 1971), it is hypothesized that persons prone to depression attribute the causes of negative events to internal, stable, and global factors and attribute the causes of positive events to external, unstable, and specific causes. This tendency would produce helpless attributions in that the person would feel constantly responsible for negative events and incapable of producing positive events. Bandura (1977a) agrees that causal attributional processes may be important in developing efficacy expectations. The Seligman model suggests that a depressive attributional style would interact with an aversive major life event to produce a generalized helpless belief and thus depression. Seligman (e.g., 1981) differentiates between personal helplessness, that is, a belief that one is individually incapable of producing certain responses, and universal helplessness, that is, the belief that desirable consequences are not under anyone's personal control. The latter would correspond to Bandura's differentiation between conceptions of efficacy and outcome expectations. Efficacy is personal, whereas outcome expectations refer to contingencies in the external world.

Seligman suggests that four general therapy strategies would be useful in modifying helplessness: (1) *environmental enrichment,* which would involve placing the person in an environment that would be relatively undemanding and that would provide a variety of success and efficacy experiences; (2) *personal control training,* in which the individual would be taught specific skills to give him or her greater control in certain pertinent domains; (3) *resignation training*, in which the individual would be helped to accept his or her helplessness in certain domains in ways that would either reduce the aversiveness of the helplessness or reduce the desirability of the unattainable goal; and (4) *attribution retraining*, in which the individual would be taught to attribute failures and successes in a more positive and realistic fashion.

Meichenbaum's self-instruction approach is also related to certain ideas about the nature of depression. Various experts have identified negative thoughts or negative self-statements typical of depression (e.g., Beck, 1976; Ellis, 1962). There is empirical evidence that depressed individuals are more likely to make covert negative self-statements (e.g., Missel & Sommer, 1983; Vestre, 1984). Vasta and Brockner (1979) had subjects actually monitor their positive and negative self-evaluative thoughts and found that the frequency of negative self-statements correlated with self-esteem. Craighead and Craighead (1980) argued that negative self-statements may be typical of a number of psychological disorders and that modifying such self-statements is an important target of psychotherapy. They further argue that methods from attitude research that would produce persuasive modification of self-statements should be applicable to psychotherapy. Meichenbaum's methodologies could be considered as effective teaching methods relative to modifying self-statements. Self-statement change has been the target of some cognitive behavioral therapy interventions for depression. Mahoney (1971) had a depressed patient practice positive self-evaluative thoughts by pairing them with frequent daily events. Zeiss, Lewinsohn, and Munoz (1979) and Rehm, Kaslow, and Rabin (1987) describe therapy programs specifically targeting changes in self-statements. Applications of Meichenbaum's specific techniques to depression would be consistent with these efforts and could be a fruitful line of future research.

Extensive work on the treatment of depression has derived from the Kanfer self-control model. Several authors have suggested the applicability of self-control concepts to depression (Bandura, 1971; Marston, 1968; Mathews, 1977) and self-control procedures have been applied in various case studies (e.g., Jackson, 1972). The most extensive work has derived from the self-control or self-management model of depression proposed by Rehm (1977). This model suggested that depression could be thought of as a set of one or more deficits in self-control behavior. Six deficits were postulated: (1) depressed individuals attend selectively to negative events in their environment to the exclusion of positive events; (2) depressed persons attend selectively to the immediate as opposed to the long-range outcomes of their behavior; (3) depressed individuals tend to set stringent self-evaluative standards for their behavior; (4) depressed individuals make negative attributions for their behavior such that they attribute positive outcomes to external factors and negative outcomes to internal factors; (5) as a result of the above, depressed individuals administer insufficient positive reinforcement to themselves; and (6) depressed individuals administer excessive self-punishment to themselves. The first two deficits deal with self-monitoring behavior, the second two with self-evaluation behavior (assuming that self-attribution acts as a modifier on self-evaluation), and the final two with self-reinforcement behavior. Fuchs and Rehm (1977) developed a psychotherapy program based on this model to modify these deficits. The program has been expanded and revised in a series of therapy outcome studies (cf. Rehm, 1984). The program is a highly structured group therapy, the format of which is defined in a detailed therapist manual. The program involves didactic presentations of self-management concepts, exercises that help participants to acquire and use the concepts, discussion of the applicability of the concepts to individual participants, and homework assignments with which participants practice nondepressive self-management skills between sessions.

The therapy program begins by presenting the general argument that mood is related to activity and self-statements about activities. It is suggested that depressed individuals tend to focus in a distorted fashion on negative activities and make resulting negative self-statements. A homework assignment is given in which participants are required to keep a daily log, self-monitoring positive activities and self-statements. Daily mood is also recorded and an exercise in the second session plots daily mood and a daily number of events to point out the association between the two.

An immediate versus delayed outcome exercise focuses participants on positive delayed outcomes of behavior and continuing self-monitoring homework assignments focus on monitoring activities with positive delayed outcomes.

In the self-evaluation phase of the therapy program, goal-setting worksheets are filled out by subjects, helping them to define goals in positive, realistic, attainable ways and to break these goals down into subgoal activities. The self-monitoring assignment continues with special emphasis on monitoring subgoal behaviors. Attributional concepts are taught in sessions focusing on positive and negative events. Subjects practice writing nondepressed attributions as positive self-statements for positive and negative events during the week.

In the self-reinforcement phase of the program, participants are taught principles of self-reinforcement and develop both overt and covert self-reinforcement strategies. Overt self-reinforcement involves the use of easy and accessible positive activities to be engaged in contingently following more difficult subgoal activities. Covert reinforcement involves using positive self-statements as contingent rewards following difficult positive activities or subgoal activities. As the program is currently used, basic concepts are taught in the first seven weekly sessions of a ten-session program. The final three sessions are used for continued practice and consolidation of the use of the principles involved.

The therapy program has been evaluated in six outcome studies by Rehm and his colleagues. The first two studies involved validation of the program in contrast to traditional control conditions. Using symptomatic community volunteer depressed women, Fuchs and Rehm (1977) compared self-management therapy to a nonspecific group therapy condition and a waiting list control condition. On standard self-report measures of depression, the self-management therapy condition improved significantly more than the nonspecific group therapy condition, which in turn improved significantly in relationship to that of the waiting list control therapy. Rehm, Fuchs, Roth, Kornblith, and Romano (1979) compared the self-management program to a social skills assertiveness training program. Self-management subjects showed greater improvement on target measures of self-management behavior, and social skills subjects showed greater improvement on target measures of assertiveness. Both groups improved significantly in depression but the self-management condition was significantly superior. The 1-year follow-up of subjects in these two studies (Romano and Rehm, 1979) found that both self-management and control (nonspecific and assertion) therapy subjects remained improved relative to pretest. Self-management subjects reported fewer and less intense episodes of depression during the year and fewer instances of having obtained additional therapy. This finding, which has been replicated in 1-year follow-up studies of the subsequent four studies in this series, suggests that individuals who have been through the self-management program have acquired skills that allow them to deal more effectively with episodes of depression and to do so without additional therapy intervention.

The second two studies in the series attempted to dismantle the major components of the self-management program. Rehm, Kornblith, O'Hara, Lamparski, Romano, and Volkin (1981) compared five therapy conditions involving: (1) the self-monitoring therapy component alone, (2) self-monitoring plus self-evaluation components, (3) self-monitoring plus self-reinforcement components, (4) self-monitoring plus self-evaluation plus self-reinforcement components (i.e., the full self-management program), and, (5) a waiting list control condition. All of the active treatments did better than the waiting list control, but no consistent significant differences were found on a variety of depression outcome measures. Kornblith, Rehm, O'Hara, and Lamparski (1983) compared conditions involving: (1) the full self-management program, (2) self-monitoring and self-evaluation components, (3) the self-management principles without the behavioral homework assignments, and, (4) a control treatment consisting of a problem-oriented dynamic group psychotherapy. No significant differences resulted between the therapy conditions, all of which reduced depression to a clinically significant degree. Interpretation of these results is problematic. It may be that the major effects of the full self-control program are incorporated within the self-monitoring phase of the program and that the later components simply elaborate on those effects. Session-by-session tracking of the improvement in depression suggested that the vast majority of improvement in the program occurs in the first few weeks such that it may be very difficult to detect the effects due to later program components. The explicitness of the program led many of the subjects in the condition where no explicit homework assignments were given to develop their own homework assignments. Finally program revisions resulted from these studies, including revised self-evaluation and self-reinforcement components.

The final two studies in the series concern the specific behavioral and cognitive targets of the self-control program. Separate self-management programs were devised targeting activity increase (behavioral target) versus targeting of self-statements (cognitive target), along with a combined target condition. Rehm, Lamparski, Romano, and O'Hara (1985) compared these three versions of the self-management program to a waiting list control and found that all three active therapy conditions improved to a greater extent than the waiting list control, with no differences among them. This validated the idea that each therapy was indeed an active and effective therapy strategy in and of itself. Rehm et al. (1987) compared the same three conditions against one another with larger numbers in each condition. A variety of pre- and post-therapy measures were designed to assess specific behavioral and cognitive deficits. Again, all three programs were effective in alleviating depression, with no significant differences between them. Interestingly, each program was effective regardless of the degree of cognitive or behavioral deficits at pretest and each program was equally effective in producing changes in cognitive and behavioral targets.

The self-management program has also been evaluated in other contexts using the self-management therapy manuals. Fleming and Thornton (1980) compared a cognitive therapy based on Shaw (1977) with the self-management program based on the Fuchs and Rehm manual, and a nondirective therapy control condition. All conditions improved significantly at posttest and follow-up with the greatest improvement on several measures in the self-management therapy condition. Roth, Bielski, Jones, Parker and Osborn (1982) compared the self-management therapy to self-management therapy plus a tricyclic antidepressant drug. While the drug condition responded faster during therapy, at posttest and 3-month follow-up there were no significant differences between the two conditions. Two small studies using the Fuchs and Rehm manual were reported by Rothblum, Green, and Collins (1979). Both studies compared two versions of the self-management therapy program, one emphasizing client responsibility for selecting behaviors for monitoring and goal setting, and the other stressing the therapist's role in goal setting. Results tended to favor the active role of the therapist, which is more consistent with the original therapy. Tressler and Tucker (1980) compared a version of the self-management program consisting of self-monitoring and self-evaluation with a version consisting of self-monitoring and self-reinforcement. At posttest and 12-week follow-up, the self-monitoring and self-reinforcement condition proved significantly superior. Other investigators have reported preliminary results with varied populations. Glanz and Dietz (1980) offered the program as part of a community outreach program from a community mental health center. A diverse group of currently depressed, previously depressed, and spouses or other relatives of depressed persons participated and showed gains on depression inventory scores. Kornblith and Greenwald (1982) gave a preliminary report on applying the self-management program with inpatients. Rogers, Kerns, Rehm, Hendler, and Harkness (1982) reported that the program had been effective in reducing depression among renal dialysis patients. In general, the program appears to be an effective treatment for depression, with applicability to a variety of depressed patients and relatively nonspecific therapeutic effects.

It should also be noted that various self-management strategies and techniques are also incorporated in other major cognitive and behavioral programs for depression. For example, Lewinsohn's activity increase program (Lewinsohn, Antonuccio, Steinmetz, & Teri, 1984) involves extensive self-monitoring of pleasant events, although the self-monitoring is used primarily as an assessment device. Self-reinforcement methods are sometimes used to motivate involvement in pleasant activities. Self-monitoring is also used in Beck's cognitive therapy (Beck, Rush, Shaw, & Emery, 1979). Here self-monitoring data are primarily used to challenge irrational and distorted interpretations of events. Future research will be needed to identify the relative contribution of more specific components of the therapy program and to match self-management therapy or its components to specific subtypes of depressed individuals.

ASSESSMENT TECHNIQUES

SELF-MONITORING

The assessment methodology most clearly associated with self-management approaches to treatment is self-monitoring. Here self-monitoring refers to a systematic recording of observations by the client of his or her own behavior. A full discussion of the forms and characteristics of self-monitoring is beyond the scope of this chapter, which will focus on practical applications to anxiety, depression, and pain research. In the typical use of self-monitoring, clients keep logs of events that occur in their lives between therapy sessions. Most often, the occurrence of each event in a class is recorded, but time sampling formats may also be employed.

Self-monitoring has the advantage of providing real-life data on the client's functioning with regard to a problem behavior on a day-to-day basis. Since the clients themselves collect the data, subjective events can also be "observed." The client may, for example, record incidences of emotional responses or of thoughts associated with experiences. Frequently the purpose of the self-monitoring is to observe the connection between external events and internal subjective responses.

Self-monitoring requires daily effort on the part of the client, and thus, compliance may be a problem. In practice assignments must be kept simple, concise, and clearly relevant to the problem. The reactivity of self-monitoring is another important consideration. Having people record their own behavior influences the occurrence of the behavior. Ordinarily undesirable behaviors are decreased by self-monitoring and desirable behaviors are increased. Reactivity is a problem for representative sampling when self-monitoring is used for assessment, but it may be usefully employed when self-monitoring is part of an intervention. Self-monitoring may be used for the purposes of problem assessment, evaluation of progress or outcome, keeping track of completion of homework assignments, or as an intervention per se.

A typical use of self-monitoring in self-management therapy for anxiety is to record situations in which anxiety arises. This may be part of problem assessment as a way of discovering common characteristics of anxiety situations or it could be an evaluation of progress with the expectation of decreased frequency across weeks of therapy. Many aspects of the anxiety response may be monitored. Ratings of intensity of subjective anxiety or of physiological concomitants would be additional ways to assess progress. Monitoring correlated thoughts, self-evaluation, or efficacy ratings may provide useful feedback for therapy planning.

In his depression therapy program Peter Lewinsohn (Lewinsohn et al., 1984) has participants monitor daily mood and daily pleasant events in order to identify mood-related events as targets for intervention. He and his colleagues have developed lists of events for use in selecting items for self-monitoring for different purposes. They include the Pleasant Events Schedule, the Unpleasant Events Schedule, and the Cognitive Events Schedule. The Rehm self-management therapy program uses a Positive Activities List to prompt participants with classes of activities that may have occurred but that they may have overlooked. Activities are recorded at or close to the time they occur and summary mood is recorded at the end of the day. In recent versions of the program positive self-evaluations (self-statements) are also recorded throughout the day. Data are used to teach principles about behavior and emotion and as progress feedback. The self-monitoring assignment is viewed both as assessment and as a form of intervention on natural styles of self-observation.

Beck (Beck et al., 1979) uses self-monitoring in various ways in his cognitive therapy approach to depression. Among these is the triple column technique. When the client becomes aware of an increase in dysphoria, he or she is to record a brief description on the situation in the first column. In the second, the client records the thought that presumably intervened between the situation and the emotional reaction. In the third column a more rational, positive interpretation of the situation is recorded. Finally, the client rates his or her degree of confidence in the statements in columns two and three (e.g., "the boss's brusqueness shows he doesn't like me" (60% confident), and "He's just in a hurry" (50% confident). These data are used to help the client practice disputing distorted interpretations of experiences in a realistic and convincing manner.

Self-monitoring in pain programs again usually involves situational assessments of the occurrence and/or intensity of pain. The patient may attempt various activities and record pain levels or may employ various pain reduction techniques and record subsequent levels of pain. As with interventions for anxiety and depression, the data provide assessments for directing interventions; they may be part of the interventions per se, and they provide progress feedback to the patient.

SELF-CONTROL QUESTIONNAIRE

The Self-Control Questionnaire (SCQ) was initially developed as a device to assess the teaching effectiveness of the self-control therapy program for depression (Fuchs & Rehm, 1977). Item content is derived from the deficits in self-control behavior that the model posits are contributory causes of depression. The SCQ was intended as an outcome measure to assess the effectiveness of the program in accomplishing the specific proximal purpose of acquisition of these concepts by participants, that is, the modification of these attitudes and beliefs. The SCQ consists of 40 statements of attitudes and beliefs about self-control behaviors and cognitions related to depression. Instructions require the examinee to indicate the degree to which each statement is characteristic of him or her on a 5-point scale from "A = Very characteristic of me, extremely descriptive" to "E = Very uncharacteristic of me, extremely undescriptive." Nineteen items are phrased to reflect positive, nondepressive attitudes and 21 to reflect negative, depressed attitudes. Sample items include, "Planning each step of what I have to do helps me to get things done well" and "It's no use trying to change most of the things that make me miserable."

Internal consistency alpha coefficients of .82 and .88 have been reported in the literature. Test–retest reliability over a 5-week period was reported to be .86 by O'Hara, Rehm, and Campbell (1982). In a sample of 101 clinically depressed community volunteers the scale correlated .42 with the Rosenbaum Self-Control Schedule (Rosenbaum, 1980a; see below), which is a measure of a broad range of self-control skills. In the same sample the SCQ correlated .16 with the Beck Depression Inventory. In a sample of normal women, O'Hara, Rehm, and Campbell (1982) found a correlation of .31 with the BDI. In a series of outcome studies of the self-management therapy program for depression, the SCQ has consistently shown significant improvement in scores from pre- to posttherapy (cf. Rehm, 1984). Posttest scores have differentiated self-management patients from patients in waiting list, traditional therapy, and assertion training conditions. Pretreatment scores have not predicted depression outcome in these studies. O'Hara *et al.* (1982) did find that the SCQ contributed significantly to the prediction of postpartum depression when included in a battery administered in the second trimester of pregnancy.

The scale was constructed for a specific purpose and it was written on a purely rational basis with little psychometric development. Although data currently available suggest that it fulfills its initial purpose satisfactorily, further psychometric evaluation is clearly desirable. In addition to its use as an outcome measure for a specific therapy program, the scale may have further utility as an assessment of vulnerability to depression.

LEARNED RESOURCEFULNESS SCALE

The Learned Resourcefulness Scale was originally titled the Self-Control Schedule (Rosenbaum, 1980a). The scale consists of 36 statements of self-control behaviors to which subjects respond on a 6-point Likert scale to indicate the degree to which each behavior is characteristic of them. Twelve items refer to the use of cognitions to control emotional and physiological sensations; eleven items refer to the use of problem-solving strategies; four items refer to perceived ability to delay gratification; and nine items refer to general self-efficacy expectations. Psychometric data from 6 samples indicated good internal consistency and test–retest reliability (Rosenbaum, 1980a).

Rosenbaum has demonstrated the validity of the scale by showing that it is related to successful self-control behavior in several settings. Individuals scoring high on the scale have been shown to tolerate pain better on a cold pressor test (Rosenbaum, 1980b), and have been shown to cope better with seasickness (Rosenbaum & Rolnick, 1983). The scale has been reconceptualized as measuring the opposite of learned helplessness and was thus renamed the Learned Resourcefulness Scale (Rosenbaum, 1983). Recent work was reported on the relationship of the scale to coping among epilepsy patients (Rosenbaum & Palmon, 1984). The scale can be seen as a rather broad measure of self-control behaviors potentially applicable to many situations.

THE FREQUENCY OF
SELF-REINFORCEMENT QUESTIONNAIRE

Heiby (1982) has developed a scale aimed at assessing a much more specific form of self-control behavior, namely self-reinforcement. The Frequency of

Self-Reinforcement Questionnaire consists of 30 true–false items and is intended to assess use of self-reinforcing statements and positive self-attitudes. Validity has been shown by ratings by another person and by self-monitored self-reinforcement records (Heiby, 1982). Depressed subjects score lower on the scale (Heiby, 1981) and low scorers are more likely to respond with depression to low levels of external reinforcement (Heiby, 1983). Training in self-reinforcement was found to increase later self-monitored self-reinforcement behavior (Heiby, Ozaki, & Campos, 1984). This scale has the potential to be a useful scale for assessing a specific component of self-control behavior in various contexts.

EFFICACY

The measurement of efficacy expectations, as defined by Bandura, requires behavior and situation-specific information. There is thus no single-measurement instrument available for assessing self-efficacy; different problem areas and situations require different instruments. Bandura has developed his own instruments for the investigation of self-efficacy in the context of fearful situations (e.g., Bandura et al., 1977; Bandura et al., 1980; Bandura, Reese, & Adams, 1982). Other investigators have extended the investigation of self-efficacy into areas such as weight reduction (Chambliss & Murray, 1979), assertiveness (Kazdin, 1979; Lee, 1984), and cigarette smoking (Condiotte & Lichtenstein, 1981; DiClemente, 1981; McIntyre, Lichtenstein, & Mermelstein, 1983). In each of these cases, the assessment of self-efficacy has occurred within the context of a structured research program investigating the role of the self-efficacy construct in behavior change. None of these programs has commented on the clinical utility of this construct or on the use of the particular assessment devices in clinical settings.

In general, efficacy expectations can be measured along three primary dimensions: level, strength, and generality. That is, tasks can vary on several dimensions that can usually be ordered in terms of some attribute, such as their level of difficulty, complexity, or stressfulness. The level of an individual's efficacy expectations would correspond to the task level that he or she expected to be able to perform. The individual's degree of conviction about his or her ability to perform this particular task corresponds to the strength dimension. Finally, efficacy expectations may vary in how broadly they are applied across situational and time parameters.

Bandura (1977a, 1982) proposed a strategy for measuring self-efficacy. Subjects are presented with a list of behavioral tasks that are arranged in a hierarchical fashion, such that easier, less complex tasks appear early in the list followed by more difficult ones. For each of these tasks subjects are asked to respond simply whether or not they think they can perform the behavior in question. Then for each task that they state they could perform, subjects are asked to rate the strength of their self-judged efficacy on a 100-point probability scale. This scale ranges from 0 (high uncertainty) to 100 (complete certainty that the behavior can be performed). The number of items checked "Can Do" represents the level of self-efficacy, whereas the average certainty rating across all items represents the strength of self-efficacy.

Many of the studies of this construct have also included behavioral measures with tasks that correspond directly to the items on the self-efficacy measure. This has enabled the investigators to evaluate the relationship between perceived efficacy and the actual level of performance. Bandura's (1980) "microanalytic" technique calls for calculating the congruence (i.e., percent of agreement) between efficacy judgments and the performance of specific tasks. Others (e.g., Kirsch, 1985) have argued that correlational analyses may best reveal the relationship between self-efficacy and behavior. Lee (1985), in noting that the utility of any analysis of self-efficacy will be enhanced to the degree that it is both "fine-grained and interpretable," suggests that agreement measures such as the chi square and the phi coefficient may also be good alternatives.

Several assumptions and problems with this assessment model should be noted. One primary assumption is that the individual has had enough prior experience with the particular behaviors or situations to adequately estimate their abilities. Other assumptions are that the instrument elicits responses indicative of maximal rather than typical levels of performance and that the items are arranged in hierarchical order. Bandura developed this approach to assessment in the context of simple phobias while trying to understand or predict approach behavior. Items relevant to specific behaviors occurring in specific situations could be readily identified and arranged in hierarchical fashion without too much difficulty. These methods, however, do not lend themselves well to situations in which the problem behaviors involved are very complex or are by nature not clearly hierarchical. Although the concept of self-efficacy may be potentially useful in areas such as depression, pain, and social skills, strategies for measuring self-efficacy expectancies in these circumstances have not been well developed. Moe and Zeiss (1982) attempted to offer some solutions to these problems in the study of social skills by proposing the use of more molar attributes associated with acceptable performance, rather than limiting assessment to molecular behavior. They used 12 attributes (e.g., warm, attractive, friendly, trusting) that could be rated in each of 12 different social situations. These were not viewed as being hierarchical, yet level or magnitude of self-efficacy could still be assessed by calculating the mean number of attributes checked for the different situations. As research on self-efficacy is conducted in relation to new problem areas, the reliability of measurement must be demonstrated and the clinical utility of the construct should be addressed.

SELF-INSTRUCTION

Self-instructional training provides the therapist with a general framework for approaching a variety of problems. As a general approach, there is not a single assessment device or strategy associated with self-instructional training. Any measures that are typically used for a given problem area, (e.g., anxiety, fear, pain) may be incorporated into self-instructional therapy. As an approach that pays particular attention to self-evaluative cognitions, however, several measures directed specifically to self-statements may be of use. Recently, several authors have attempted to develop self-report measures to assess cognitive events (i.e., self-statements) that may be useful in studying depressive phenomena. These include the Attribution Style Scale (cf. Seligman, Abramson, Semmel, & von Baeyer, 1979), the Automatic Thoughts Questionnaire (Hollon & Kendall, 1980), the Dysfunctional Attitudes Scale (Weissman & Beck, 1978), and the Hopelessness Scale (Beck, Weissman, Lester, & Traxler, 1974).

CONCLUDING REFLECTIONS

Self-management interventions and assessment methods have been applied to many populations and problems. This chapter has focused on applications to anxiety, depression, and pain. It should also be clear that there are a number of specific models and theories under the general heading of self-management. This chapter focused on those of Bandura, Kanfer, and Meichenbaum. The common threads among the techniques and models involve the assumption that therapeutic change can occur by teaching individuals general skills in managing their own behavior in problematic situations toward long-range goals. Generalization and maintenance of outcome is enhanced by giving responsibility to the client for carrying out the change strategy in real-life situations. Self-management approaches will continue to make their contributions to therapy, assessment, and conceptualization of psychopathology independently and in conjunction with other models and methods.

REFERENCES

Abramson, L. Y., Seligman, M. E. P., & Teasdale, J. D. (1978). Learned helplessness in humans: Critique and reformulation. *Journal of Abnormal Psychology, 87,* 49–74.

Bandura, A. (1969). *Principles of behavior modification.* New York: Holt, Rinehart, & Winston.

Bandura, A. (1971). Vicarious and self-reinforcement processes. In R. Glaser (Ed.), *The nature of reinforcement.* New York: Academic Press.

Bandura, A. (1977a). Self-efficacy: Toward a unifying theory of behavioral change. *Psychological Review, 84,* 191–215.

Bandura, A. (1977b). *Social learning theory*. Englewood Cliffs, NJ: Prentice-Hall.

Bandura, A. (1980). Gauging the relationship between self-efficacy judgment and action. *Cognitive Therapy and Research, 4*, 263–268.

Bandura, A. (1982). Self-efficacy mechanism in human agency. *American Psychologist, 37*, 122–147.

Bandura, A., & Adams, N. E. (1977). Analysis of self-efficacy theory of behavioral change. *Cognitive Therapy and Research, 1*, 287–308.

Bandura, A., Adams, N. E., & Beyer, J. (1977). Cognitive processes mediating behavioral change. *Journal of Personality and Social Psychology, 35*, 125–139.

Bandura, A., Adams, N. E., Hardy, A. B., & Howells, G. N. (1980). Tests of the generality of self-efficacy theory. *Cognitive Therapy and Research, 4*, 39–66.

Bandura, A., Reese, L., & Adams, N. E. (1982). Microanalysis of action and fear arousal as a function of differential levels of perceived self-efficacy. *Journal of Personality and Social Psychology, 43*, 5–21.

Beck, A. T. (1967). *Depression: Causes and treatment*. Philadelphia: University of Pennsylvania Press.

Beck, A. T. (1976). *Cognitive therapy and the emotional disorders*. New York: International Universities Press.

Beck, A. T., Rush, A. J., Shaw, B. F., & Emery, G. (1979). *Cognitive therapy of depression*. New York: Guilford.

Beck, A. T., Weissman, A., Lester, D., & Trexler, L. (1974). The measurement of pessimism: The Hopelessness Scale. *Journal of Consulting and Clinical Psychology, 42*, 861–865.

Carver, C. S., & Scheier, M. F. (1982). An information processing perspective on self-management. In P. Karoly & F. H. Kanfer (Eds.), *Self-management and behavior change: From theory to practice*. New York: Pergamon.

Chambliss, C. A., & Murray, E. J. (1979). Efficacy attribution, locus of control, and weight loss. *Cognitive Therapy and Research, 4*, 349–353.

Condiotte, M. M., & Lichtenstein, E. (1981). Self-efficacy and relapse in smoking cessation programs. *Journal of Consulting and Clinical Psychology, 49*, 648–658.

Coleman, R. E., & Beck, A. T. (1981). Cognitive therapy for depression. In J. F. Clarkin & H. I. Glazer (Eds.), *Depression: Behavioral and directive intervention strategies*. New York: Garland STPM Press.

Craighead, L. W., & Craighead, W. E. (1980). Implications of persuasive communication research for the modification of self-statements. *Cognitive Therapy and Research, 4*, 117–135.

DiClemente, C. C. (1981). Self-efficacy and smoking cessation maintenance. *Cognitive Therapy and Research, 5*, 175–187.

Ellis, A. (1962). *Reason and emotion in psychotherapy*. New York: Lyle Stuart.

Fleming, B. M., & Thornton, D. W. (1980). Coping skills training as a component in the short-term treatment of depression. *Journal of Consulting and Clinical Psychology, 48*, 652–655.

Fuchs, C. Z., & Rehm, L. P. (1977). A self-control behavior therapy program for depression. *Journal of Consulting and Clinical Psychology, 45*, 206–215.

Genest, M., & Turk, D. C. (1979). A proposed model for behavioral group therapy with pain patients. In D. Upper & S. M. Ross (Eds.), *Behavioral group therapy, 1979: An annual review*. Champaign, IL: Research Press.

Glanz, L. M., & Dietz, R. E. (1980, August). *Building individual competence: Coping with depression and fear*. Paper presented at the meeting of the American Psychological Association, Montreal.

Glasgow, R. E., Klepac, R. K., Dowling, J., & Rokke, P. D. (1982, November). *Measures of self-efficacy in pain tolerance*. Paper presented at the annual convention of the Association for Advancement of Behavior Therapy, Los Angeles.

Heiby, E. M. (1981). Depression and frequency of self-reinforcement. *Behavior Therapy, 12,* 549–555.

Heiby, E. M. (1982). A self-reinforcement questionnaire. *Behaviour Research and Therapy, 20,* 397–401.

Heiby, E. M. (1983). Toward the prediction of mood change. *Behavior Therapy, 14,* 110–115.

Heiby, E. M., Ozaki, M., & Campos, P. E. (1984). The effects of training in self-reinforcement and reward: Implications for depression. *Behavior Therapy, 15,* 544–549.

Hollon, S. D., & Kendall, P. C. (1980). Cognitive self-statements in depression: Development of an automatic thoughts questionnaire. *Cognitive Therapy and Research, 4,* 383–395.

Horan, J., Hackett, G., Buchanan, J., Stone, C., & Demchik-Stone, D. (1977). Coping with pain: A component analysis. *Cognitive Therapy and Research, 1,* 211–221.

Jackson, B. (1972). Treatment of depression by self-reinforcement. *Behavior Therapy, 3,* 298–307.

Kanfer, F. H. (1970). Self-regulation: Research, issues, and speculations. In C. Neuringer & J. L. Michael (Eds.), *Behavior modification in clinical psychology.* New York: Appleton-Century-Crofts.

Kanfer, F. H. (1977). Self-regulation and self-control. In H. Zeir (Ed.), *The psychology of the 20th century.* Zurich: Kindler Verlag.

Kanfer, F. H., & Hagerman, S. (1981). The role of self-regulation. In L. P. Rehm (Ed.), *Behavior therapy for depression: Present status and future directions.* New York: Academic Press.

Kanfer, F. H., & Karoly, P. (1972a). Self-control: A behavioristic excursion into the lion's den. *Behavior Therapy, 2,* 398–416.

Kanfer, F. H., & Karoly, P. (1972b). Self-regulation and its clinical application: Some additional conceptualizations. In R. C. Johnson, P. R. Dokecki, & O. H. Mowrer, *Socialization: Development of character and conscience,* New York: Holt, Rinehart, & Winston.

Kazdin, A. E. (1979). Imagery elaboration and self-efficacy in the covert modeling treatment of unassertive behavior. *Journal of Consulting and Clinical Psychology, 47,* 725–733.

Kirsch, I. (1985). Response expectancy as a determinant of experience and behavior. *American Psychologist, 40,* 1189–1202.

Klepac, R. K., Hauge, G., Dowling, J., & McDonald, M. (1981). Direct and generalized effects of three components of stress inoculation for increased pain tolerance. *Behavior Therapy, 12,* 417–424.

Klinger, E. (1982). On the self-management of mood, affect, and attention. In P. Karoly & F. H. Kanfer (Eds.), *Self-management and behavior change: From theory to practice.* New York: Pergamon.

Kornblith, S. J., & Greenwald, D. (1982, November). *Self-control therapy with depressed inpatients.* Paper presented at the meeting of the Association for Advancement of Behavior Therapy, Los Angeles.

Kornblith, S. J., Rehm, L. P., O'Hara, M. W., & Lamparski, D. M. (1983). The contribution of self-reinforcement training and behavioral assignments to the efficacy of self-control therapy for depression. *Cognitive Therapy and Research, 7,* 499–527.

Lazarus, A. A. (1981). *The practice of multimodal therapy: Systematic, comprehensive, and effective psychotherapy.* New York: McGraw-Hill.

Lazarus, R. S. (1974). Psychologist stress and coping in adaptation and illness. *International Journal of Psychiatry in Medicine, 5,* 321–333.

Lee, C. (1984). Accuracy of efficacy and outcome expectations in predicting performance in a simulated assertiveness task. *Cognitive Therapy and Research, 8,* 37–48.

Lee, C. (1985). Efficacy expectations as predictors of performance: Meaningful measures of microanalytic match. *Cognitive Therapy and Research, 9,* 367–370.

Lewinsohn, P. M., Antonuccio, D. O., Steinmetz, J. L., & Teri, L. (1984). *The coping with depression course.* Eugene, OR: Castalia Publishing Company.

Mahoney, M. J. (1971). The self-management of covert behavior: A case study. *Behavior Therapy, 2,* 575–578.

Marston, A. R. (1968). Dealing with low self-confidence. *Educational Research, 10,* 134–138.

Mathews, C. O. (1977). A review of behavioral theories of depression and a self-regulation model for depression. *Psychotherapy: Theory, Research and Practice, 14,* 79–86.

McIntyre, K. O., Lichtenstein, E., & Mermelstein, R. J. (1983). Self-efficacy and relapse in smoking cessation: A replication and extension. *Journal of Consulting and Clinical Psychology, 51,* 632–633.

Meichenbaum, D. (1972). Cognitive modification of test anxious college students. *Journal of Consulting and Clinical Psychology, 39,* 370–380.

Meichenbaum, D. (1977). *Cognitive-behavior modification: An integrative approach.* New York: Plenum.

Meichenbaum, D., & Cameron, R. (1973). Training schizophrenics to talk to themselves: A means of developing attentional controls. *Behavior Therapy, 4,* 515–534.

Meichenbaum, D. H., & Goodman, J. (1971). Training impulsive children to talk to themselves: A means of developing self-control. *Journal of Abnormal Psychology, 77,* 115–126.

Meichbenbaum, D., & Turk, D. (1976). The cognitive-behavioral management of anxiety, anger, and pain. In P. O. Davidson (Ed.), *The behavioral management of anxiety, depression and pain.* New York: Brunner/Mazel.

Melzack, R., & Wall, P. (1965). Pain mechanisms: A new theory. *Science, 150,* 971.

Missel, P., & Sommer, G. (1983). Depression and self-verbalization. *Cognitive Therapy and Research, 7,* 141–148.

Moe, K. O., & Zeiss, A. M. (1982). Measuring self-efficacy expectations for social skills: A methodological inquiry. *Cognitive Therapy and Research, 6,* 191–205.

O'Hara, M. W., Rehm, L. P., & Campbell, S. B. (1982). Predicting depressive symptomatology: Cognitive-behavioral models and post-partum depression. *Journal of Abnormal Psychology, 91,* 457–461.

Rehm, L. P. (1977). A self-control model of depression. *Behavior Therapy, 8,* 787–804.

Rehm, L. P. (1984). Self-management therapy for depression. *Advances in Behavior Research and Therapy, 6,* 83–98.

Rehm, L. P., Fuchs, C. Z., Roth, D. M., Kornblith, S. J., & Romano, J. M. (1979). A comparison of self-control and assertion skills treatments of depression. *Behavior Therapy, 10,* 429–442.

Rehm, L. P., Kaslow, N. J., & Rabin, A. S. (1987). Cognitive and behavioral targets in a self-control therapy program for depression. *Journal of Consulting and Clinical Psychology, 55,* 60–67.

Rehm, L. P., Kornblith, S. J., O'Hara, M. W., Lamparski, D. M., Romano, J. M., & Volkin, J. (1981). An evaluation of major components in a self-control behavior therapy program for depression. *Behavior Modification, 5,* 459–490.

Rehm, L. P., Lamparski, D., Romano, J. M., & O'Hara, M. W. (1985). *A comparison of behavioral, cognitive, and combined target versions of a self-control therapy program for depression.* Manuscript in preparation.

Rogers, P. A., Kerns, R., Rehm, L. P., Hendler, E. D., & Harkness, L. (1982, August). *Depression mitigation in hemo-dialysands: A function of self-control training.* Paper presented at the meeting of the American Psychological Association, Washington, DC.

Romano, J. M., & Rehm, L. P. (1979, April). Self-control treatment of depression: One-year follow-up. In A. T. Beck (chair), *Factors affecting the outcome and maintenance of cognitive therapy.* Symposium presented at the meeting of the Eastern Psychological Association, Philadelphia.

Rosenbaum, M. (1980a). A schedule for assessing self-control behaviors: Preliminary findings. *Behavior Therapy, 1,* 109–121.

Rosenbaum, M. (1980b). Individual differences in self-control behaviors and tolerance of painful stimulation. *Journal of Abnormal Psychology, 89,* 581–590.

Rosenbaum, M. (1983). Learned resourcefulness as a behavioral repertoire for the self-regulation of internal events: Issues and speculations. In M. Rosenbaum, C. M. Franks, & Y. Jaffe (Eds.), *Perspectives on behavior therapy in the eighties*. New York: Springer.

Rosenbaum, M., & Palmon, N. (1984). Helplessness and resourcefulness in coping with epilepsy. *Journal of Consulting and Clinical Psychology, 52*, 244–253.

Rosenbaum, M., & Rolnick, A. (1983). Self-control behaviors and coping with seasickness. *Cognitive Therapy and Research, 7*, 93–98.

Roth, D., Bielski, R., Jones, M., Parker, W., & Osborn, G. (1982). A comparison of self-control therapy and combined self-control therapy and antidepressant medication in the treatment of depression. *Behavior Therapy, 13*, 133–144.

Rothblum, E., Green, L., & Collins, R. L. (1979, April). *A comparison of self-control and therapist control in the treatment of depression*. Paper presented at the meeting of the Eastern Psychological Association, Philadelphia.

Sarason, I. G. (1975). Anxiety and self-preoccupation. In I. G. Sarason & C. D. Spielberger (Eds.), *Stress and anxiety*, (Vol. 2). Washington, DC: Hemisphere.

Schachter, S. (1966). The interaction of cognitive and physiological determinants of emotional state. In C. Speilberger (Ed.), *Anxiety and behavior*. New York: Academic Press.

Seligman, M. E. P. (1975). *Helplessness: On depression, development, and death*. San Francisco: W. H. Freeman.

Seligman, M. E. P. (1981). A learned helplessness point of view. In L. P. Rehm (Ed.), *Behavior therapy for depression: Present status and future directions*. New York: Academic Press.

Seligman, M. E. P., Abramson, L. Y., Semmel, A., & von Baeyer, C. (1979). Depressive attributional style. *Journal of Abnormal Psychology, 88*, 242–247.

Shaw, B. F. (1977). Comparison of cognitive therapy and behavior therapy in the treatment of depression. *Journal of Consulting and Clinical Psychology, 45*, 543–551.

Tressler, D. P., & Tucker, R. D. (1980, November). *The comparative effects of self-evaluation and self-reinforcement training in the treatment of depression*. Paper presented at the meeting of Association for the Advancement of Behavior Therapy, New York.

Vasta, R., & Brockner, J. (1979). Self-esteem and self-evaluative covert statements. *Journal of Consulting and Clinical Psychology, 47*, 776–777.

Vestre, N. D. (1984). Irrational beliefs and self-reported depressed mood. *Journal of Abnormal Psychology, 93*, 239–241.

Weiner, B., Frieze, I., Kukla, A., Reed, L., Rest, S., & Rosenbaum, R. M. (1971). *Perceiving the causes of success and failure*. New York: General Learning Press.

Weissman, A. N., & Beck, A. T. (1978, November). *Development and validation of the dysfunctional attitude scale*. Paper presented at the meeting of Association for Advancement of Behavior Therapy, Chicago.

Zeiss, A. M., Lewinsohn, P. M., & Munoz, R. (1979). Nonspecific improvement effects in depression using interpersonal, cognitive, and pleasant events focused treatment. *Journal of Consulting and Clinical Psychology, 47*, 427–439.

5

COGNITIVE-BEHAVIORAL METHODS WITH CHILDREN

LAUREN BRASWELL
PHILIP C. KENDALL

Cognitive-behavioral therapy with children, as with adults, includes a variety of strategies and procedures. These methods follow from a number of different theoretical tenets, but as stated by Kendall (1985), the cognitive-behavioral methods share an "emphasis on (a) both the learning process and the influence of the contingencies and models in the environment while (b) underscoring the centrality of mediating/information-processing factors in both the development and remediation of childhood disorders" (p. 359). Cognitive-behavioral approaches emphasize the complex interaction among cognitive events, processes, products, and structures, affect, overt behavior, and environmental context and experiences as contributing to various facets of dysfunctional behavior. Similarly, the diverse approaches agree that learning has a pivotal role in the acquisition and maintenance of deviant and adaptive behavior, and like operant theories (but to a lesser degree) recognize the importance of environmental consequences—particularly those provided by the social environment—in these processes. Unlike operant theories, however, cognitive/social-learning theories postulate that most learning is a function of how the individual cognitively processes stimulus and consequence information (Foster, Kendall, & Guevremont, in press).

A fundamental premise underlying the cognitive-behavioral theories as applied to adults is that much of maladaptive behavior and negative emotion arises from *distorted* cognitively mediated representations of external events. Distorted processing and world views are causally linked to problems of depression, anger, anxiety, and other disturbances of thought and behavior (e.g., Beck, 1976; Beck, Rush, Shaw, & Emery, 1979; Ellis, 1970). In contrast with certain childhood disorders, such as attentional difficulties, impulsivity, hyperactivity, and some types of acting out, the child is considered to manifest a deficiency, that is, an absence of effective mediating strategies for controlling behavior. In such cases, the task of the cognitive-behavioral therapy is to train the child in the use of verbal mediation strategies for developing more reflective problem-solving behavior and self-control. With other more internalizing types of disorders, such as school phobia, childhood depression, and social withdrawal, the child's symptoms are believed to result, at least in part, from cognitive distortions (errors or misperceptions) in thinking similar to those described for anxious and depressed adults. With these children, intervention addresses the client's need to recognize and test the mistaken misperceptions, expectations, and/ or attributional preferences.

THEORETICAL PRÉCIS

The theoretical lines of influence that gave rise to cognitive-behavioral techniques used with adults, such as the development of behaviorists' interest in the phenomenon of self-control and the emergence of cognitive learning theories of psychotherapy, also contributed to the rise of cognitive-behavioral interventions with children (Kendall & Hollon, 1979). In addition, cognitive-behavioral interventions with children have benefited from the theoretical and empirical contributions of various areas in developmental psychology, such as studies of the development of self-control, social cognition, memory, metacognitive skills, and attributional processes.

The study of both the development of self-control and the factors interferring with self-control has contributed to the development of cognitive-behavioral intervention with children. The work of Luria (1961) and Vygotsky (1962), for instance, provided an initial theoretical formulation for understanding the emergence of verbal control or mediation of behavior. Failures or deviations from this developmental process are speculated to result in poor self-regulation in the child. This formulation ultimately became the basis for the development of self-instructional training procedures (Meichenbaum & Goodman, 1971).

The term social cognition (Shantz, 1975) refers to internal events or processes that are thought to mediate actions related to other people and their affairs. While Piaget (1926) began to address the child's development of social perspective taking over 60 years ago, developmentalists did not display intensive research interest in this area until the 1970s (Chandler, 1973; Hudson, 1978; Shantz, 1975). New theories have developed, such as the four level view of Selman (Selman, 1980; Selman & Byrne, 1974). According to this view, in the first stage the child lacks social perspective-taking abilities, and thus fails to consider the point of view of others. At the next level, the child can consider another's ideas and can recognize that these ideas may be different from his or her own, but has only a beginning awareness of the views of others. At the third level, the child continues to have difficulty considering different views at the same time but can, in sequence, consider his or her own view and then consider the perspective of the other. At the fourth and final level, the child is capable of simultaneously considering his or her own perspective as well as those of others. Accomplishing this requires some ability to step back from the social interaction and adopt what Selman (1984) calls "third-person" perspective. This theory provides one view of how the perspective-taking process emerges. Recognition of the developmental nature of this ability has resulted in theorizing about the extent to which anomalies in the development of perspective-taking account for certain types of behavioral disturbance.

Research on children's memory and metacognitive skills has influenced the development of cognitive-behavioral strategies (see discussions by Cohen & Schleser, 1984, and Reeve & Brown, 1985). An understanding of children's memory capacities and of the age at which children can begin to recognize their own need to employ specific strategies has provided treatment researchers with informational tools necessary for shaping age-appropriate interventions.

Children's expectations and attributional processes have also been an increasing focus of research (Braswell, Koehler, & Kendall, 1985). The findings of this body of literature suggest that children's attributions for specific events and their preferences for particular kinds of explanations (i.e., their attributional styles) have important therapeutic implications, both in their impact on the therapy process and outcome and in their potential to be the specific targets of intervention (Dweck, 1975; Andrews & Debus, 1978).

Some of these areas of theory and research will be discussed in greater detail as they relate to specific intervention methods, but the current brief account of these views highlights the extent to which advances in developmental theory and research have influenced the emergence of cognitive-behavioral methods with child populations.

The impact of developmental psychology upon the creation of cognitive-behavioral interventions with children belies the necessity of recognizing factors that distinguish intervention with children from intervention with adults. While there are many obvious differences between children and adults as targets for intervention, the factors having perhaps the greatest bearing on differences within cognitive-behavioral treatments include issues of the level of cognitive and affective development, referral status, and the role of the family and social context of children.

While attention to the cognitive and affective development of the client is important, even if one works only with adult clients, attention to these matters is crucial if children are the subjects of intervention. As alluded to above, an understanding of the subject's memory capacity is important to successful intervention, as well as an understanding of factors such as attentional capacity, verbal fluency and comprehension, and the capacity for conceptual reasoning. Many of the cognitive strategies that would be appropriate for use with adult clients may not be fully understood or managed by children. As children progress through adolescence they typically become cognitively and emotionally prepared for more adult-like interventions, but the problem of adequate cognitive and emotional preparation is a genuine issue for elementary school age and preschool children. For example, the successful application of Albert Ellis's rational–emotive therapy (Ellis, 1970) or Aaron Beck's cognitive therapy for depression (Beck, Rush, Shaw, & Emery, 1979) assumes that the client has the cognitive capacity to distinguish between rational and irrational, logical and illogical thinking, once this distinction has been discovered and identified by the therapist and client. While later in the chapter we shall discuss variations of cognitive therapy for working with depressed children, it would not be safe to assume that a randomly selected elementary-school-age child understands such distinctions. A child may be likely to perceive the confrontation of irrational thinking as a scolding, as well as finding it difficult to comprehend the intended outcome of philosophical change. Effective RET with children could involve preventive efforts, when children are taught rational expectations as a method of reducing subsequent psychological dysfunction.

Work with child versus adult clients also differs in terms of the typical method of referral for treatment. While a small number of adult clients are ordered into treatment by authorities such as the court system, the majority of adults receiving psychotherapy services make a personal choice to seek out this type of care. Children, however, do not typically call to initiate their own appointments for treatment, even if they are in great psychological pain. Rather, they receive treatment as a result of the concern of the adults around them, in most cases their parents or teachers. This difference in how one comes to therapy yields some interesting differences regarding what types of adults versus children are most typically seen for outpatient care. Adults tend to seek care for conditions that are causing pain to themselves, such as depression or anxiety problems. Children are most likely to be brought in for care when they display behaviors that are causing pain or irritation to the adults in their lives. Thus, children displaying difficulties with impulsivity, poor self-control, and/or various types of antisocial behavior are the ones most likely to be brought in for treatment. In recent years, the problems of depression and anxiety in children have received greater attention, and the general public is becoming more able to recognize symptoms of these difficulties. It is hoped that this change in public awareness will result in depressed and anxious children receiving the treatment that they need. At the current time, however, children presenting with externalizing problems continue to be more likely to be brought to the attention of mental health professionals. As a result, cognitive-behavioral interventions with children have tended to focus on meeting the treatment needs of externalizing rather than internalizing children. In a subsequent section discussing the applications of various cognitive-behavioral strategies, some examples of work with internalizing children will be presented, but these efforts are relatively few compared to the numerous studies focusing on the problems of poorly self-controlled, hyperactive, and/or aggressive children—those referred by others for treatment.

The child client is also much more embedded in the social context of his or her peers (Hartup, 1983), family, and school than is typically the case for adult clients (Craighead, Meyers, & Craighead, 1985). This state of affairs has implications both for the identification of the ongoing causes of the child's difficulties and for the preferred treatment. The recognition of the role of the parents and other powerful people in the child's life and the inclusion of these individuals in some aspect of the intervention process, whether it is in the actual context of the therapy or in a more educational role, becomes a crucial component to the successful treatment of the child client. Peers are potentially useful aids in child (Howard & Kendall, 1987) and adolescent (Kendall & Williams, 1986) treatments.

Recognition of these differences in the nature and context of the child client can lead to some interesting speculations regarding why some interventions are less successful or why their results fail to generalize maximally to the child's real-world environments. It is our belief that successful intervention requires careful attention to the cognitive and affective level of the development of the child client and recognition that he or she does not typically make a conscious choice to enter treatment. The child is there because some of his or her behavior is disturbing to adults, making the inclusion of parents, teachers, and others who play a significant role in the child's world for the achievement of a successful therapeutic outcome.

In the discussion that follows, we offer suggestions about evaluating a child's appropriateness for cognitive-behavioral intervention and then describe the procedures and components most common to cognitive-behavioral interventions with children. These descriptions will include attention to the theoretical and historical underpinnings of these key components. The methods of presenting or training these components will also be described, along with selected examples of clinical research applications. Special emphasis will be given to problem solving and self-instructional training interventions, since these are the most commonly evaluated types of cognitive-behavioral therapy with children. Finally, concerns relevant across the various treatment procedures, such as the lack of treatment generalization and the impact of subject variables, will be considered.

ASSESSMENT CONCERNS

As with adult clients, careful evaluation of the child client is crucial for discerning the child's true intervention needs. For example, children who are homogeneous with regard to their attentional deficits may vary tremendously in terms of their level of self-esteem and the quality of their peer relations. These factors may affect the type and content of the intervention enacted and the adjunctive treatments to be considered. The child is embedded in his or her familial context and expected to follow certain rules, and this fact further complicates the assessment process. The clinician must carefully weigh the extent to which the child's reported behavior represents a condition meriting treatment or reflects the parent's difficulty in coping with unpleasant but perhaps developmentally appropriate behavior on the part of the child. Given clarity on such questions, the clinician will be able to make a reasonable decision regarding whether treatment should focus on the child, the parents, or the entire family. The following comments are offered as brief guides to assessment, but the reader is referred to Kendall and Braswell (1982; 1985), Kendall, Pellegrini, and Urbain (1981), Harris (1985), and Roberts and Nelson (1984) for further details.

The intake interview is usually the primary source for gathering relevant information in implementing cognitive-behavioral interventions with children. When interviewing the parents, the clinician encourages them to translate terms such as "out of control" or "hyper" into specific behavioral examples. In accordance with a behavioral tradition, the interviewer works to clarify the current antecedents and consequences for these specific behaviors and the modes of intervention the parents have tried on their own. The cognitive-behaviorally oriented clinician views this data as providing information about the child *and* about the parents' problem-solving ability. Questions about what the parent thinks is responsible for creating the child's current symptoms can yield a preliminary picture of the parent's attributional processes and belief systems regarding the child. Obtaining a developmental history from the parents can be useful for detecting factors suggestive of gaps or lags in certain key areas of development and/or indications of the parent's role in the development of the current difficulties (e.g., unusually high expectations or difficulty allowing the child independent functioning).

The interview with the child can address his or her awareness and level of understanding of his or her current difficulties, and can solicit the child's explanation for the symptoms in order to begin to understand his or her attributional processes and world view. Asking the child what he or she thinks will be necessary to change the current circumstances, whether he or she feels capable of enacting these changes, and whether he or she thinks change will be noticed and appreciated by parents or teachers can provide important clues about the child's level of self-efficacy regarding behavior change, motivation for change, and level of interpersonal sophistication. Structured questionnaires, developed for specific programs, are recommended.

Behavior rating scales can be useful for presenting a global view of the child's behavior from the perspective of his or her parents and teachers. Broad spectrum rating scales such as the Child Behavior Checklist (CBCL: Achenbach, 1978; Achenbach & Edelbrock, 1978) or the Conners' Teacher and Parent Questionnaires (Conners, 1969) provide information about the extent to which the child displays a number of different types of behavior problems, while other scales, such as the Self-Control Rating Scales (SCRS: Kendall and Wilcox, 1979; Kendall, Zupan, & Braswell, 1981; Robin, Fischel, & Brown, 1984) can be more relevant for assessing specific targets for cognitive-behavioral intervention. The SCRS was developed to assess self-control in elementary school children as rated by their classroom teacher and/or parents (as in Kendall & Braswell, 1982). This 33-item measure is based on a cognitive-behavioral conceptualization of self-control, wherein self-controlled children are said to possess the cognitive skills necessary to generate and evaluate alternatives and the behavioral skills needed to inhibit unwanted behavior and engage in desired action.

Various task performance measures have been developed to assess children's level of impulsivity, attentional difficulties, perspective-taking, and problem-solving abilities. Measures such as the Porteus Maze Test (Porteus, 1955) and the Matching Familiar Figures Test (Kagan, 1966) allow the clinician to observe the child's potential to be impulsive on cognitive tasks. Cognitive impulsivity represents a potential problem in its own right and is associated with deficient cognitive processing in attentional difficulties and hyperactivity (Fuhrman & Kendall, 1986; Homatidis & Konstantareas, 1981). Selman's measure of interpersonal awareness (Selman, 1980) permits the assessment of the child's ability to recognize the thoughts and feelings of others and take the perspective of another. The Purdue Elementary Problem-Solving Inventory (PEPSI: Feldhusen, Houtz, & Ringenbach, 1972); and the Means–Ends Problem-Solving task (MEPS: Shure & Spivack, 1972) permit the assessment of the child's cognitive skills for solving interpersonal dilemmas. Dodge, McClaskey, and Feldman (1985) have developed a formalized role-play assessment to evaluate social competence. With this method, the experimenter initiates the role play and the child provides a verbal and behavioral response that is audiotaped for later coding. The role play situations were identified by teachers and clinicians as being problematic for children manifesting peer difficulties, and they include issues such as peer group entry, response to peer provocation, and response to failure. All of these measures have some problematic features, yet we prefer those that provide the clinician with an "in the office" opportunity to observe how the child negotiates a problem-solving situation. Beyond yielding a certain score, the evaluator can observe what if any problem-solving strategies the child possesses.

Self-report assessment of the child's expectancies, attributions, and self-talk can be quite valuable in preparation for a cognitive-behavioral intervention. Unfortunately, the assessment of these constructs in children is only beginning to receive the intense level of research attention associated with the adult literature. For example, while findings of research with adults are converging to suggest the existence of a depressotypic set of cognitive contents (self-talk) specific to depression (Dobson & Shaw, 1986; Hollon, Kendall, & Lumry, 1986; Ingram, Kendall, Smith, Donnelly, & Ronan, 1986), such a consensus has not yet developed in the child-related literature. Nonetheless, there is growing curiosity on the part of researchers and clinicians regarding the extent to which these variables have impacts on the child. For example, therapists and researchers have addressed the impact of expectancies upon behavior, particularly as defined by Bandura's concept of self-efficacy expectations (Bandura, 1977). According to this view, an individual's self-efficacy is the extent to which he or she feels capable of successfully executing the behaviors leading to desired outcomes. Changes in self-efficacy have been posited as the common underlying cognitive process that accounts for changes in behavior. Keyser and Barling (1981) have developed and replicated (Barling & Snipelisky, 1983) a 20-item self-report scale assessing children's academic self-efficacy beliefs. Brief assessments of self-efficacy expectations could be incorporated into traditional testing sessions by simply asking children how confident they are that they will be able to complete the task at hand, and then evaluating the fit between the child's expectations and the actual outcome of the task.

The concept of attributions is closely related to that of expectations, but attributions concern how we explain an event *after* it has occurred. The attributions children offer to explain their own task behavior can be quite interesting. For example, Asarnow and Callahan (1985) have developed a two-part interview assessment of social cognitive processes that includes attributional data. The first segment of the evaluation is referred to as the Knowledge of Interpersonal Problem-Solving Strategies Assessment, and involves presenting the child with four vignettes and asking what he or she thinks the child in the story should do. After the free response phase, the child is then asked to rate a series of prepared response alternatives. In the second part, labeled the Attributional Style Assessment, the child is again presented with four situations, but is now asked how he or she would feel and think in each situation. After the child has had an opportunity to respond freely, he or she is presented with possible self-statements and is asked to rate how likely it is that he or she may feel and think this way. This method has been demonstrated to distinguish elementary-school-aged boys of positive and negative peer status. The assessment of attributional biases in depressed children is not as advanced as the adult literature in this area; however, Haley, Fine, Varriage, Moretti, and Freeman (1985) have developed the Cognitive Bias Questionnaire for Children (CBQC). This method involves the presentation of 10 brief vignettes describing school, home, and social situations. Each vignette is followed by four response alternatives that reflect depressed-distorted, depressed-nondistorted, nondepressed-distorted or nondistorted-nondepressed interpretations/reactions to the situations. This measure has been able to discriminate successfully affective from nonaffective disordered children. A child's attributional style may also mediate treatment outcome. For example, children who attribute task success to their personal effort may be more likely to show improvement following cognitive-behavioral intervention than those who attribute their success to luck, fate, or other factors external to themselves (Braswell, Koehler, & Kendall, 1985).

A self-report assessment of test-anxious children's self-talk has been developed by Zatz and Chassin (1983, 1985). This scale consists of 40 yes–no items that begin with the stem "I thought _____." The items include both positive and negative self-statements and on- and off-task thoughts. The child endorses each item on a 4-point scale reflecting the frequency with which he or she experiences that thought during a test.

These various types of self-report measures can help the clinician understand what the child expects of him- or herself, how he or she explains personal success or failure, and the extent to which the child's cognitions are affecting his or her mood and performance. In the absence of well-established norms for many of these measures, clinicians should exercise caution in their interpretation of results, but these measures can be viewed as rich sources of idiographic data.

Behavioral observations at home and/or school, sociometric data, and archival data (grades, number of trips to the principal's office, number of skipped classes, etc.) provide information on the specific problems the child is experiencing and possibly on the conditions maintaining these problems. These forms of "objective" data can also be useful in detecting any positive and/or negative distortions on the part of the parent or child. For example, if there is concern that the parent tends to distort the intensity and frequency of the child's inappropriate school behavior, it would be valuable to know that the child has never been suspended or sent to the principal's office. Sociometric data could prove useful in helping the clinician confirm or disconfirm a child's belief that no one in the class likes him or her. Admittedly, behavioral observations, archival data, or sociometrics are often seen as difficult to obtain during the course of traditional clinical practice, but the effort can yield information that is quite valuable for both assessment and treatment.

The choice of assessment methods is ultimately guided by the nature of the clinician's questions. In evaluations prior to possible cognitive-behavioral intervention, the child clinician shares the questions of adult clinicians regarding the nature of the presenting problem and, as indicated previously, seeks to determine the child's developmental level across a range of cognitive and social-emotional variables. In addition, the child clinician must determine the extent to which cognitive deficiencies versus cognitive distortions contribute to the problem and the extent to which the child's family or school environment has contributed to the development of the problem. The clinician then considers how family and school personnel can be most effectively included in the treatment plan.

COMMON TREATMENT APPROACHES

PROBLEM-SOLVING TRAINING

The problem-solving component of treatment merits discussion before all others for two reasons. First it represents a specific type of training commonly seen in cognitive-behavioral interventions. For example, most applications of self-instructional training incorporate methods for systematically approaching and evaluating problem situations (see Kendall & Braswell, 1985; Kazdin, Esveldt-Dawson, French, & Unis, 1987). In addition, the adoption of a problem-solving approach to behavioral or interpersonal dilemmas is a general orientation or attitude that is common to interventions within this category. It is characteristic for the cognitive-behavioral therapist to approach the child's or family's difficulties as problems to be solved rather than the inevitable outcome of a specific disease process or family circumstance. This does not mean that the therapist ignores relevant biological, historical, or family systems data, but rather that he or she incorporates this data while collaborating with the child and parents/teachers to create a problem formulation. Various types of cognitive-behavioral interventions recommend that the therapist use this problem-solving orientation not only when addressing the specific issues of the client but also when confronting dilemmas that may occur during the course of the therapy. For example, the therapist would not only assist a family in problem solving that deals with how to cope with an attentionally disordered child's difficulty in complying with bedtime rules, he or she would also employ problem-solving with the family to handle issues such as their attendance at therapy sessions, their difficulties locating suggested training materials, or issues of emotional reactance that the family experiences as a result of being in therapy.

The study of human cognitive problem solving has a very long history (Davis, 1966; Duncan, 1959; Jahoda, 1953). The 1970s witnessed a number of attempts to formulate problem solving as a set of skills relevant for clinical endeavors (D'Zurilla & Goldfried, 1971; Mahoney, 1977). Spivack, Shure, Platt, and their associates hypothesized that effective interpersonal cognitive problem solving (ICPS) demands a number of subskills such as sensitivity to human problems, the ability to generate alternative solutions, the capacity to conceptualize the appropriate means to achieve a given solution, and a sensitivity to consequences and cause–effect relationships in human behavior (Shure & Spivack, 1978; Spivack, Platt, & Shure, 1976).

Spivack, Shure, and others have examined the nature of the relationship between these skills and overt social adjustment. (Spivack & Shure, 1974; Larcen, Spivack & Shure, 1972; Platt, Spivack, Altman, Altman, & Peizer, 1974; Platt & Spivack, 1972). Their work has been valuable in focusing research atttention on a problem solving view of adjustment, although other research groups have not confirmed the original conceptualizations of the relationship between interpersonal cognitive problem-solving skills and social behavior (see Krasnor & Rubin, 1983; Rickel & Burgio 1982; Rickel, Eishelman, & Loigman, 1983). In addition, Kendall and Fischler (1984) found only a negligible relationship between adjustment and the ICPS skills in a sample of 6- to 12-year-old children when IQ was carefully controlled (see also Kendall, 1986).

While the exact relationship between adjustment and the specific ICPS skills deficits proposed by Spivack, Shure, and their colleagues is unclear, other investigators have found support for the notion that children with adjustment problems differ from normal children in some of their social problem-solving processes. In a series of studies, Dodge and his colleagues (Dodge & Frame, 1982; Richard & Dodge, 1982) have observed that aggressive boys do display social cognitive biases and deficits that distinguish them from normal children. In comparing delinquents and nondelinquents at ages 10 to 11 and 14 to 15, Hains and Ryan (1983) found that while these two groups were similar on certain dimensions of social problem solving, the delinquents were less exhaustive or thorough in their consideration of different aspects of social problem solving. These findings led the authors to conclude that the acting-out behavior of these boys may be based, at least in part, on deficient or distorted inferences made from social situations. Their conclusions regarding delinquents are highly similar to those Dodge and his colleagues with school-aged acting-out children who have not yet been identified as delinquent.

Further research is needed to pinpoint clearly the problem-solving deficits associated with various types of childhood disorders, but the existing theoretical and empirical literature has provided a foundation for the development of problem-solving interventions. Most interventions of this type provide children with formal training in the application of problem-solving sequences, such as those proposed by D'Zurilla and Goldfried (1971), D'Zurilla (1986), Mahoney (1977), or Spivack and Shure (1974) with interpersonal problem situations. Problem-solving interventions, like other types of cognitive-behavioral therapies, vary in the extent to which the intervention focuses solely on the child or includes other members of the child's family. Programs also vary in the extent to which they include explicit behavioral contingencies as an aid to problem-solving training.

Problem-Solving Training with the Child

The turtle technique (Robin & Schneider, 1974; Robin, Schneider, & Dolnick, 1976; Schneider & Robin, 1976) is one of the earliest problem-solving approaches developed to help emotionally disturbed elementary-school-aged children inhibit aggressive or impulsive responding in social situations and generate alternate responses. This training is presented in four phases. First the children are taught the "turtle response" of pulling in one's limbs and lowering one's head to withdraw from a provoking situation. Next, the children are instructed in relaxation skills that they can utilize while "doing the turtle." Social problem-solving skills of generating alternative solutions and examining their consequences are then introduced. Finally, to encourage maintenance of the response, the problem children and their classmates are given social rewards for cueing and supporting a child who is "doing the turtle." The program was designed to require 15 minutes of instruction per day for 3 weeks. At the end of the 3-week period, sessions can be reduced to twice a week and then gradually faded. Following a successful but uncontrolled demonstration of treatment effectiveness by Robin and Schneider (1974), Robin *et al.* (1976) evaluated this procedure via a multiple baseline design and obtained significant decreases in aggressive behavior.

Problem-solving training was conducted by Sarason (1968) and Sarason and Ganzer (1973) with institutionalized delinquents. In his pilot work, Sarason (1968) found that a program emphasizing a problem-solving approach to problematic situations via modeling and role playing was effective in producing improved staff ratings of behavior. Sarason and Ganzer (1973) examined the effectiveness of this same program in a more extensive investigation. The modeling condition, as the authors labeled it, emphasized a practical approach to social problems. The subjects met in groups of four, with two models or tutors per group. The models demonstrated positive and negative approaches to certain problem situations and then asked the subjects to role play the same situations. These role plays were taped and played back for discussion. The discussion treatment condition covered the same content as the modeling group but no role play was involved. Those receiving the modeling treatment attained more favorable case outcomes, were more likely to evaluate their institutional experience as positive, displayed greater memory for the goals of the treatment, and demonstrated less recidivism than controls.

Building on this successful intervention with delinquents, Sarason and Sarason (1981) developed a problem-solving training package that was administered in a class format to high school students who were at risk for dropping out of school and becoming delinquents. Following treatment, an unobtrusive behavioral measure (behavior in a job interview) indicated the experimental subjects were able to present themselves in a more appropriate and effective manner than the controls. At 1-year follow-up, the experimental group tended to display fewer absences, lower rates of tardiness, and few referrals for disciplinary action.

Lochman and colleagues (Lochman, Burch, Curry, & Lampron, 1984; Lochman & Curry, 1986; Lochman, Nelson, & Sims, 1981) have conducted a series of studies evaluating the effects of an anger-coping training program with aggressive 9- to 11-year-old boys. This program involves 12 sessions of group training in interpersonal cognitive problem-solving skills. The effectiveness of the program in reducing aggressive behavior was initially established in the Lochman et al. (1981) study. Lochman et al. (1984) compared the effectiveness of the anger-coping program with and without a goal-setting component versus goal setting only. The goal-setting intervention involved having the boys establish weekly behavioral goals, which were then monitored daily by their classroom teacher. If the goals were met, the boys received contingent reinforcement. The results indicated both anger-coping groups achieved significant reductions in disruptive and aggressive off-task behaviors at the 4- to 6-week follow-up. Parent ratings suggested that there was some generalization of treatment effects to the home environment for both anger-coping groups and that the boys in these groups manifested an increase in home-related self-esteem. The addition of the goal setting tended to accentuate the treatment effects obtained in the classroom. Despite the evidence of change in behavioral observations of aggression, teacher and peer perceptions showed no significant change.

Lochman and Curry (1986) compared the effectiveness of an 18-session version of the anger coping program with a program including training in the anger-coping skills plus self-instructional training. Both conditions included the goal-setting component previously described. Both treatments were found to be effective in reducing passive off-task behaviors and reducing parent ratings of aggression. Both groups also yielded increases in self-esteem. In addition, the anger-coping groups displayed significant reductions in disruptive and aggressive off-task behavior. As in the previous study, there was a lack of change in teachers' ratings of aggression.

Problem-Solving Training with Families

Blechman and colleagues (Blechman, Olson, & Hellman, 1976; Blechman, Olson, Schornagel, Halsdorf, & Turner, 1976) examined the impact of a procedure called the Family Contract Game. This technique used a board game format to develop problem-solving and contingency-contracting skills in families experiencing significant parent–child conflict. Component problem-solving skills, such as identifying problems in behavioral terms, gathering relevant information, generating behavioral alternatives, choosing a specific alternative, and evaluating the outcome of the selected alternative, were taught within the game context. After a successful case study

(Blechman, Olson, Schornagel, *et al.*, 1976), Blechman, Olson, and Hellman (1976) implemented the Family Contract Game with six mother–child dyads. As in the case study, the use of the game procedure resulted in a significant increase in on-task behavior and decreased off-task behavior during problem discussion. This change was apparent in the first intervention session and remained fairly constant throughout treatment. Unlike the findings of the case study, these changes did not persist in the post-treatment problem discussions. Similar results were obtained by Robin, Kent, O'Leary, Foster, & Prinz (1977). Their problem-solving training produced highly significant increases in the use of problem-solving behaviors in the audiotaped discussions of both real and hypothetical conflicts, but ratings completed by the parents and adolescents failed to indicate improvement in home problem-solving and communication behaviors. These interventions appear capable of altering behavior but the altered patterns do not seem to generalize to real-world settings.

On the whole, the results of these studies indicate that problem-solving training can have an impact on the behavior of the child and his or her family, although generalization of in-treatment results remains a concern. Some research has raised a question regarding the most effective way to include the parents. For example, Kirmil-Gray, Duckham-Shoor, & Thoresen (1980) achieved positive results in the attempt to maintain appropriate behavior in severely hyperactive children undergoing complete withdrawal or significant reduction of their stimulant medication. There was, however, no indication that problem-solving training with the children added significantly to the effects achieved by providing the parents with behavior management training. Going a step further, Coyne, Meyers, and Clark (1985) examined the effects of conducting a behavioral weight-loss program for obese children in which one group of parents and children received training in behavioral weight-loss techniques, while children in another group received training in behavioral management and the parents received problem-solving training that would facilitate maintenance of the behavioral program. Children in the behavior management plus problem-solving condition lost significantly more weight during the 8-week treatment and maintained these changes at 3- and 6-month follow-up. Thus, the inclusion of parents, whether in treatment with the children or as recipients of training through separate parent groups, appears to result in improved outcome for the child.

The case of Sean provides a clinical example of problem-solving training involving both the child and parents. Sean, age 11, was referred for treatment by his parents due to concentration difficulties, restlesss behavior, and disobedience. He had previously been diagnosed as manifesting an attention deficit disorder with hyperactivity and was maintained on psychostimulant medication during the school year. In school he was able to achieve at an average to above average level and was considered to be only a moderate behavior problem, but his parents were very distressed over his persistent noncompliance in the home. After the initial assessment, the family was presented with treatment options and chose to enter a program that focused on the needs of attentionally disordered children and their families. This program emphasized training both the child and his or her parents in cognitive problem-solving methods via self-instructional training, role-play exercises, and reinforced practice.

Sean soon entered the first phase of the program, in which he received two individual sessions that introduced him to cognitive problem solving and to an explanation of how such an approach could be applied to academic and social problems. He quickly grasped the concept of using a series of problem-solving steps to cope with difficult situations.

The family then entered the second phase of the program, with Sean participating in a group of children with similar behavioral backgrounds while his parents met in a separate group with the parents of the other children. In the children's group, Sean received training in self-monitoring and problem recognition. In addition, he engaged in repeated practice in applying a problem-solving process with dilemmas that would arise in the group. The format of the group included ongoing behavioral contingencies that rewarded the members for identifying and coping with problems in their own behavior or the behavior of other group members. The children were also rewarded for relating examples of how they had attempted to use a problem-solving strategy with situations occurring outside of group. Sean was able to master the self-monitoring and problem recognition exercises with ease. He could demonstrate effective use of problem-solving strategies in the group context, but through the first six of the eight group sessions he could not identify examples of home use of the training strategies. In the parent group sessions, the adults were introduced to cognitive problem-solving strategies and were encouraged to cue and reward their child for using these strategies in the home. Sean's parents reported that he was, in fact, refusing to apply the problem-solving methods to his home behavior. The parents were extremely frustrated by his defiance and felt they were facing yet another power struggle with Sean.

Fortunately, between group sessions six and seven, all families met with the group leaders for individual family sessions. The goal of these sessions was to address any difficulties the families were experiencing in applying the methods and tailor the procedures to better meet their needs. During the session with Sean's family, the therapist encouraged the parents to use the problem-solving methods to deal with issues that affected the husband and wife but did not necessarily involve Sean. The parents then role played strategy use to deal with some of their work-related and household management concerns while Sean observed them. This seemed to spark his interest, for he then asked if the parents were the only ones who could identify family problems or if the children could too. The parents stated that they were receptive to Sean identifying formal problems but that then he would need to be willing to participate in the problem-solving process. The events of this session seemed to be quite significant for Sean, for in the remaining two groups he was able to bring in several examples of home applications and his parents reported that he had become much interested and cooperative regarding problem solving in the home. Obviously, Sean's resistance and subsequent change of heart appears to be related to some complexities of family interaction patterns. The therapist was able to work with these issues in the context of a problem-solving intervention and ultimately achieved a positive outcome, as self-reported by the child and parents.

These highlights from research and clinical applications of problem-solving training demonstrate that behavior change can be achieved through this method and the generalization to extra-therapy settings, while not universal, can be achieved. In addition to the further exploration of the impact of parent involvement, we would also encourage evaluation of added gains produced by peer involvement (Howard & Kendall, 1987; Kendall & Williams, 1986).

VERBAL SELF-INSTRUCTIONAL TRAINING

Self-instructions as an element of child cognitive-behavioral theory are the self-directed statements of an internal dialogue that an individual uses to guide him- or herself through a problem-solving process. Self-instructing occurs in an automatic manner and it may be most observable when an individual is attempting a new task. Self-instructional training programs with children are usually directed toward providing the child with a thinking strategy—not what to think, but how to think. The self-statements serve as guides for the child to follow through the process of problem solving.

As noted by Meichenbaum (1979) and Craighead (1982), two bodies of theoretical and empirical work have provided the background of current self-instructional training programs. The work of Soviet psychologists Luria (1959, 1961) and Vygotsky (1962) details the process through which verbal mediation of behavior is achieved. Vygotsky hypothesized that internalization of verbal commands is the key step in the child's establishment of verbal control over his or her behavior. Luria, a student of Vygotsky, elaborated a development theory of verbal control. Although this theory is not without its critics (Jarvis, 1968; Miller, Shelton & Falvell, 1970), it has proven quite valuable as a model for teaching children who display an apparent lack of verbal mediation of their behavior. It has also encouraged others to continue to explore the developmental significance of children's self-directed speech (Copeland, 1983; Zivin, 1979). The second body of research is represented by the work of Mischel and colleagues on the phenomenon of the delay of gratification. In his 1974 review, Mischel summarized data suggesting that self-generated strategies, such as self-instructions and self-praising statements helped children reduce the frustration they experienced during delay-of-gratification tasks. Patterson and Mischel also examined verbal self-control in a series of studies on verbal mediation strategies for use in resisting distraction (Mischel & Patterson, 1976; Patterson & Mischel, 1976). Their results indicated that preschoolers did not spontaneously produce instructions to help themselves cope with distracting stimuli, but that when these children were provided with a specific cognitive strategy they were able to work longer in the distracting environment. Similar strategies have been employed in studies of rule-following behavior (Monohan & O'Leary, 1971; O'Leary, 1968), with the data suggesting verbalization of simple self-statements can reduce rule breaking in some children.

In examining the myriad of experimental applications of self-instructional training, one can observe examples that conform more closely to the model of the Mischel and Patterson work in that the training provided is very brief and typically involves the experimenter simply instructing the child to say a particular sentence or think a particular thought in response to a well-defined problematic situation. The current authors have referred to this type of training as noninteractive, for the training involves the experimenter/clinician simply telling the child what to do or say. Studies that reflect more of the influence of Luria's stage theory are labeled interactive, for training involves a much greater degree of therapist–child exchange. Other investigators have labeled this interactive training based on the Luria model as the faded rehearsal method of self-instructional training, for the experimenter/clinician typically guides the child through a series of steps in using the self-instructions. The experimenter first models appropriate use of the self-instructions him- or herself and then has the child carry out a task while the clinician states the appropriate self-instructions. The child is then given practice in solving problems while verbalizing the self-instructions, and finally the child practices solving problems while making covert use of the self-instructing statements. Within recent years another mode of training has emerged. The directed discovery method, as developed by Schleser, Meyers, and Cohen (1981), involves the clinician leading the child to "discover" a specific set of self-guiding strategies through a Socratic dialogue. As indicated in our selective review of self-instructional training studies, this area of research is becoming increasingly well elaborated as experimenters attempt to create maximally effective treatment packages.

Self-Instructional Training with Behaviorally Disordered Children

Self-instructional training has frequently been applied with samples identified by teachers as being disruptive and/or impulsive in their classroom behavior. Meichenbaum and Goodman (1971) initiated the application of self-instructional training with children displaying a lack of self-control. Second graders who had been teacher-identified as hyperactive or lacking in self-control were randomly assigned to cognitive training, attention control, or assessment control conditions. The experimental and control groups received four 30-minute training sessions. Both groups used the same training tasks but only the experimental group received training in self-instructions. The results indicated that the self-instructional group improved significantly more than the two control groups on task performance measures of impulsivity. This pattern of relatively positive results was maintained at 4-week follow-up. However, the classroom measures revealed no significant group differences on behavioral observations or teacher ratings of classroom behavior. The design of this study has served as the model for many subsequent outcome studies.

Following this introduction of the self-instructional procedures, numerous studies have sought to attain the elusive goal of behavioral generalization. Kendall and colleagues have examined the efficacy of Meichenbaum and Goodman's self-instructional procedures when used in conjunction with various additional strategies such as explicit behavioral contingencies. After obtaining positive results on both task performance measures and behavior ratings in a preliminary case study (Kendall & Finch, 1976) and group outcome study (Kendall & Finch, 1978), Kendall and Wilcox (1980) examined the contribution of different types of self-instructional training with behavioral contingencies to the attainment of generalized change. Self-instructional training that focused on the specific training task (concrete labeling) was compared with training that was relevant to the task but was also general and could be applied to other situations (conceptual labeling). Training tasks included cognitive and interpersonal problems. Using 8- to 12-year-old teacher-referred subjects, they obtained results indicating that both concrete and conceptual self-instructional training produced increased self-control and decreased hyperactivity at posttest and 1-month follow-up, with the treatment effects stronger for the conceptual labeling group. Thus, generalization of treatment effects to the classroom was found. In addition, Kendall and Wilcox provided data on the self-control ratings of nonreferred children to give some guidelines or norms for assessing treatment impact. At both posttreatment and follow-up, the mean ratings of the conceptual treatment group fell just within one standard deviation of the mean for the nonreferred children. At 1-year follow-up (Kendall, 1981), teacher ratings showed differences favoring the conceptually trained children, but with the small number of children available, the differences did not reach statistical significance. It was observed that conceptually trained children showed significantly better recall of the material they had learned when compared with the concrete and control groups.

Kendall and Zupan (1981) examined the relative effectiveness of individual versus group training using subjects and procedures similar to those of Kendall and Wilcox (1980), but increasing the number of 1-hour treatment sessions to twelve. At posttreatment the group and individual treatment conditions demonstrated significant improvements on the self-control ratings. The changes in teacher's ratings of hyperactivity paralleled the self-control ratings, though the changes were significant for all three conditions. Both individual and group treatments produced changes in interpersonal perspective taking at follow-up; a nonspecific control condition did not. In terms of normative comparisons, the mean self-control and hyperactivity ratings of cognitive-behavioral treatment conditions at posttreatment were within one standard deviation of the normative mean. These improvements, resulting from lengthier treatments, were greater than those reported in Kendall and Wilcox (1980). At 1-year follow-up (Kendall, 1982) improvements were found for subjects across treatment conditions. Structured interviews indicated that individually treated children showed significantly better recall of the ideas they had learned and produced significantly more illustrations of use of the ideas than either group treatment or the nonspecific treatment conditions.

A component analysis of the Kendall treatment package was conducted by Kendall and Braswell (1982). A cognitive-behavioral treatment condition received self-instruction training via coping modeling and behavior contingencies, while the behavioral treatment condition involved only task modeling and contingencies. Following 12 individual treatment sessions, the cognitive-behavioral group showed significant improvement and maintenance of improvement on the ratings of self-control, while the behavioral and control groups did not. On the teacher ratings of hyperactivity, both the cognitive-behavioral and behavioral groups showed significant change at posttest and maintenance of change at follow-up. The two treatment groups also produced significant improvement and maintenance on the latency aspect of the impulsivity measure, while all three groups displayed significant improvement and maintenance on the error score. The cognitive-behavioral group produced more significant change on an achievement measure than did the behavioral group, and only the subjects in the cognitive-behavioral groups showed improvement on a self-concept measure. Classroom observations yielded a high degree of variability, but the cognitive-behavioral group displayed improvement in the categories of off-task verbal and physical behaviors. In terms of normative comparisons, subjects within the cognitive-behavioral group achieved self-control ratings within one standard deviation above the means of a nonreferred group when assessed at posttest. Parent ratings of behavior in the home environment did not reveal significant treatment effects. Thus treatment generalization to the classroom did occur, as indicated by the teacher ratings and classroom observations, but generalization to the home did not. At 1-year follow-up, significant group differences did not persist on any of the treatment outcome measures.

These studies suggest that when self-instructional training with disruptive/impulsive children is conducted with social as well as cognitive problem-solving tasks *and* when the training is accompanied by behavioral contingencies, it is possible to achieve some change on both cognitive and social/behavioral measures.

The experience of 9-year-old Jason is similar to many of the children participating in the studies of Kendall and his colleagues. Jason was referred to the intervention project by his 4th-grade teacher because he displayed an impulsive work style that resulted in numerous errors on homework and tests. He also displayed outbursts of aggression on the play ground that typically followed disputes with peers over appropriate game rules and procedures. Testing indicated Jason scored on the low average of general intellectual functioning, and that he was rated as functioning particularly poorly on subtests assessing verbal IQ. Jason's therapist initially began to train him in simple self-instructional statements while working on matching games and other psychoeducational tasks, but sensed that although Jason could "say the words," he was not grasping the concepts behind the self-instructional statements. Further information was obtained from Jason and his teacher to determine what types of games or activities were particular areas of competence for Jason. On the basis of this information, the therapist then began to teach Jason self-instructions for use in addressing dilemmas that arise in ice hockey games. Using a content area more familiar to him, Jason began to display a greater understanding of the meaning and purpose of the self-instructional steps. The therapist was then able to move on to the application of the self-instructional methods with academic materials and interpersonal problem situations. At the end of the intervention, ratings completed by Jason's teacher indicated improvement in self-control and a decrease in hyperactive behavior. She commented that she had observed Jason quietly talking himself through math problems during testing situations. Jason also displayed improvement on a measure of cognitive impulsivity.

While Kendall and others have been successful in achieving some behavior change with disruptive/impulsive teacher-referred children from regular schools, the results of self-instructional training with children meeting the full DSM-III criteria for attention deficit disorder with hyperactivity have been much more equivocal.

Elaborating on related cognitive-behavioral strategies Hinshaw, Henker, and Whalen (1984a) conducted a fascinating study assessing the effects of cognitive-behavioral training and methylphenidate hydrochloride (Ritalin) on the behavior of hyperactive boys in an anger-inducing situation. Hinshaw *et al.* recruited 24 hyperactives (8 to 13 years old) to participate in daily cognitive-behavioral training sessions during the course of a 5-week summer program. The children met in groups of four, with half of each group on medication and the other half receiving a placebo. All children were exposed to general cognitive-behavioral concepts such as self-instructions during the first 2 weeks. Then during the 3rd week the trainers introduced a behavioral provocation situation modeled on Goodwin and Mahoney's (1975) circle game, with each child serving a turn as the target of name calling by the others. The children were presented an array of different coping strategies and were encouraged to practice the strategies of their choice. Children in the control condition were instructed in the concept of perspective taking and received exposure to the general concepts of social problem solving but did not learn about their own anger cues or practice specific methods of coping. The behavioral provocation situation was then reintroduced. The results of pre–post comparisons of the children's behavior indicated that the treatment group scored significantly higher on a global rating of self-control and displayed significantly more purposeful coping strategies. Relative to the pretest, all children displayed less fidgeting, laughter, and verbal aggression and more neutral statements in response to provocation. The one significant effect for medication was observed in global ratings of the intensity of the children's behavior, with medicated children displaying less intensive behavior. These findings support the efficacy of the self-instructional, coping skills procedures as a means of changing the actual content of the child's behavior in a stressful situation.

Brown and colleagues (Brown, Borden, Wynne, Schleser, & Clingerman, 1986; Brown, Wynne, & Medenis, 1985) have also examined the individual and combined effects of stimulant drug therapy and cognitive training with 6- to 11-year-old hyperactive boys. The cognitive training involved individual twice-weekly 1-hour sessions for a total of 24 meetings. The therapists also worked with both the parents and teachers to help them apply the training strategies in extra-therapy environments. The training followed an elaborated version of Meichenbaum and Goodman's (1971) self-instructional training. Children received training in breaking tasks into component parts and using general problem-solving strategies with academic and social problem situations. No explicit behavioral contingencies accompanied the treatment. Treatment effects were assessed via tests of attention deployment and cognitive style, academic achievement, and behavioral ratings completed by parents and teachers. The results of Brown et al. (1985) indicated that those children receiving medication, whether with or without cognitive training, attained improvement on the measures of attention deployment and the behavior ratings. Those in the cognitive therapy only condition displayed improvement on measures of attention deployment. These findings of cognitive change in the absence of behavioral changes are similar to those obtained by Douglas, Parry, Marton, and Garson (1976).

Brown et al. (1986) also examined the efficacy of medication and cognitive methods similar to those used in Brown *et al.* (1985); however, in contrast to the earlier study, those in the medication conditions did not continue to receive medications during the posttest assessments. With this methodological change, it appeared that the effects of the medication treatment dissipated rapidly (within 1 week) and no main effects for medication, or cognitive training or the combined condition were obtained. Other investigators have also failed to obtain significant increments in behavioral change with cognitive therapy (Abikoff & Gittelman, 1985). It should be noted, however, that there are meaningful concerns regarding the Abikoff and Gittleman study such as the absence of contingent rewards and specific training for generalization (Kendall & Reber, 1987).

It appears that self-instructional training, when combined with related cognitive and behavioral procedures, is capable of producing some generalizable behavior change in children displaying subclinical levels of disturbance. Changes in subjects' response to provocation and performance on attentional measures have also been achieved with clinical samples of attentionally disordered, hyperactive children. Consistent, across-setting changes in overall behavior have not been observed with clinical samples.

Self-Instructional Training with Learning-Disabled Children

Self-instructional strategies have been used as means of treating educational difficulties. This application of cognitive-behavioral procedures has become increasingly popular in the past 5 years, as perspectives on learning-disabled children have changed. Current theories of learning disability in children emphasize difficulties in the self-regulation of planful behaviors as opposed to some type of inability to learn or execute certain strategies or some type of specific deficit. This view is supported by research suggesting the performance of disabled children who fail to produce spontaneously appropriate task strategies, can be improved by mild prompts or direct instruction in strategy usage (Hallahan & Reeve, 1980; Torgeson & Kail, 1980). Harris (1986) examined differences in the private speech of learning-disabled and normally achieving children. She found that while these groups had the same rate of private speech, the learning-disabled children had more task-irrelevant speech. Further research is needed to understand more about the nature of these self-regulation difficulties, but other investigators have used currently existing data to devise interventions. The earliest academically oriented self-instructional interventions successfully treated cognitive impulsivity using methods like those employed in the Meichenbaum and Goodman (1971) and Kendall and colleagues studies (see Nelson & Birkimer, 1978; Palkes, Stuart, & Kahana, 1968). Some treatments have focused on developing general learning strategies that can be applied with a variety of subject areas, while others have focused on interventions for specific academic contents, such as reading, math, and writing.

The work of Deshler, Alley, Warner, and Schumaker (1981) provides an example of an intervention that was designed to promote the acquisition and generalization of learning strategies that could be employed with a variety of academic content areas. Severely learning-disabled adolescents were trained individually via a series of steps that included an initial examination of the student's current learning habits, the instructor's description of the strategy to be learned, the instructor's modeling of the strategy, the student's verbalization of the strategy until mastery, the student's practice of implementing the strategy with specially selected materials, and finally practice of the strategy with classroom materials. In addition to the sequential approach for training strategy usage, these investigators included features designed to promote generalization, such as training with a variety of examples of usage and a variety of training formats, helping the students learn to cue others to provide reinforcement for the strategy use, providing the student with intermittent reinforcement once the student has mastered the strategy, and providing the student with explicit instructions to generalize their strategy usage (see also Hall, 1979; Zakraski, 1982).

Other investigators have examined the efficacy of self-instructional methods as a means of remediating deficits in specific academic content areas. Leon and Pepe (1983) compared the effectiveness of verbal self-instructional methods with traditional direct instruction for training math skills in learning-disabled and educable mentally handicapped children. The self-instructional methods produced superior results and induced greater generalization of the skills. Johnson (1983) obtained similar results with a sample of normally achieving first graders. In addition to comparing the efficacy of self-instruction and direct instruction methods, Johnson examined the impact of the specificity of the self-instructions. General problem-solving self-instructions plus specific task-oriented self-instructions proved to be the most effective, particularly for the less competent students in this sample.

Self-instruction interventions have been developed for addressing different types of written language skills. Both Robin, Armel, and O'Leary (1975) and Graham (1983) obtained results suggesting cognitive-behavioral techniques may not be appropriate for intervention with handwriting problems; however, Wong (1985) indicated that these studies may have failed because they did not address the issue of adequate preskills. She holds that if a child is still struggling to master basic letter knowledge, he or she may not have the linguistic skills necessary to implement a procedure such as self-instructional training. In support of this point, Kosiewicz, Hallahan, Lloyd, and Graves (1982) successfully improved the handwriting of a 9-year-old boy via self-instruction and self-correction procedures. Wong hypothesizes that the subject in this intervention did possess adequate letter knowledge and linguistic ability.

Written composition skills have also been the targets of cognitive-behavioral instructions. Scardamalia, Bareiter, and Steinbach (1984) trained novice writers in a thinking aloud process that involved self-questioning during the composition planning phase and the statement of strategy questions that helped the subject resolve conflicting ideas. The results indicated that this method yielded improvement in the writer's ability to reflect on ideas and improvement in the structure of the compositions. Using self-control strategies like those employed by Deshler *et al.* (1981) Harris and Graham (1985) were able to achieve improvement in the written composition skills of two learning-disabled 6th graders. Generalization from the skill-training setting to the children's work in their resource room was also accomplished, and was maintained through a 6-week follow-up period. An assessment at 14 weeks after the intervention did not yield continued evidence for skill maintenance. Interestingly, when the children were questioned, they could repeat the specific steps for writing good stories that they had learned during the training phase, despite the fact that they had ceased to apply the steps.

Echoing the concerns of Kendall and Wilcox (1980), other research teams have examined the merits of task-specific versus general self-instructional statements with academic problems. Schleser, Meyer, and Cohen (1981) compared the efficacy of task-specific versus general self-statements for training math skills with same-age children who varied in terms of level of cognitive development (Piaget's pre-operational versus concrete operational stages). The specific self-statement group showed the greatest posttest improvement on the task of training, while the general self-statements group manifested greater improvement on a generalization task. Cognitive level also affected performance; concrete operational children out-performed the preoperational group on both tasks. Thackwray, Meyers, Schleser, and Cohen (1985) obtained similar results, with those receiving specific self-instructions showing improvement on a test assessing training task materials, while those receiving general self-instructions did significantly better on tests in other academic content areas. The authors suggest that subjects in the general self-instructions condition were able to practice tailoring general problem-solving strategies to fit the demands of a specific task, in this case math problems, and such practice may have made it possible for them to successfully tailor these strategies for use with other subject areas. Unfortunately, despite test indications of change, teacher ratings of academic skills did not evidence improvement. Swanson (1985) did obtain successful generalization across settings and tasks using global strategies plus specific skill training for remediating academic deficits in conduct-disordered children. Swanson's intervention also included a token program that provided rewards for accuracy and appropriate conduct.

Self-instructional techniques have been employed to reduce anxiety that might interfere with adequate performance in mathematics. Working with 7th grade girls whose math achievements were below grade level and reading achievements were above grade level, Genshaft and Hirt (1980) compared the relative effectiveness of tutoring, tutoring plus self-instructions, and a no-treatment control condition. In this intervention the self-instructions focused on helping the student monitor her attention, make positive self-statements, and reduce arousal, rather than focusing on the details of the task. Results indicated that all three groups made improvements on a standardized math test, but the tutoring plus self-instructions group displayed the greatest improvement on the computational subtest and greater improvement in attitudes toward math.

Thus, self-instructional interventions appear to have demonstrated some potential for improving skills in reading, math, and written language, with treatments that include both task-specific self-instructions and general, problem-solving self-instructions being particularly likely to produce successful results. Self-instructional methods, often of a more concrete variety, are also beginning to be effectively used in the training of mentally retarded children (Whitman, Burgio, & Johnston, 1984) and of children experiencing fears and anxieties (Graziano & Mooney, 1980; Peterson & Shigetomi, 1981).

ATTRIBUTION RETRAINING

As indicated earlier in this chapter, a growing body of research in clinical, social, and developmental psychology suggests that children's attribution for specific events and their preferences for particular kinds of explanations (attributional styles) may have important therapeutic implications (Braswell, Koehler, & Kendall, 1985). Attributions have been of interest for their potential both to have an impact on therapy outcome and to be the actual targets of intervention.

Attributional retraining studies have a basis in the cognitive theories of motivation put forth by Bandura (1977) and Weiner (1979). These viewpoints emphasize how the child's causal explanations for why he or she is doing well or poorly have implications for his or her behavioral persistence, expectancies for future performance, and affective reactions to success and failure. Exploratory research has indicated that poor readers, learning-disabled students, and mentally retarded children all tend to make attributions that interfere with their optimal performance in achievement situations (Butkowsky & Willows, 1980; Pearl, 1985; Weisz, 1979). Even students of high ability have been found to make maladaptive attributions in some cases (Dweck & Reppucci, 1973).

Most efforts at attribution retraining attempt to create a training environment in which the child learns to take more individual credit for his or her achievements, thus encouraging the child's experience in positive control and/or self-efficacy. It is the goal of these interventions not only to increase the amount of behavioral persistence that these children display but also to foster the long-term maintenance of the beliefs and expectations that lead to these behavioral changes.

The seminal treatment research in the area of attribution retraining was conducted by Dweck (1975). Subjects for this original study were elementary-school-age children who were prone to expect failure and be debilitated by it. These children received 25 daily sessions, with each session consisting of 15 trials of solving math problems. In the attribution retraining condition, the children experienced some failure as they solved problems, and when this occurred they were told by the experimenter, "Failure means you should try harder." The attribution retraining condition was contrasted with a success-only condition, in which children solved math problems that were well within their ability and that would insure success. The results indicated that the attribution retraining condition was more successful in changing children's response to failure. Those in the treatment condition persisted longer in their attempts to solve problems. In addition, children receiving attribution retraining showed a change in their beliefs, with an increased tendency to attribute failure to a lack of effort rather than a lack of ability. Thus cognitive and behavioral changes were attained.

Further research has suggested that attribution retraining is most likely to be successful with students who are not applying the knowledge or skills they already possess or in conjunction with teaching new problem-solving strategies (Schunk, 1983). Pearl (1985) has emphasized that it is important to target for training those children who are truly making maladaptive attributions rather than assuming that poor academic performance is by definition the result of maladaptive thinking. Pearl notes that research also suggests the importance of linking attributional statements with specific behavioral efforts. When this is not done, one is less likely to achieve a positive outcome. For example, Short and Ryan (1984) had children make effort-oriented statements prior to reading a story passage rather than after having had difficulty with a specific passage. Their results indicated the attribution manipulation was largely ineffective.

Within this area of training, there currently seems to be a shift towards promoting the attribution of failure as the result of the use of ineffective strategies rather than as inevitably the result of a lack of effort (Clifford, 1984). Obviously, attribution focused interventions would be highly inappropriate when there is reason to believe the presenting problem or symptom is the result of an actual skills deficit (Fincham, 1983). In such cases the skills deficit must be remediated and then the child's attributional status can be reassessed. Another caution concerns the nature of internal versus external attributions. As Braswell, Koehler, and Kendall (1985) have stated, while the aim of encouraging a child's "internality" may be appropriate in some cases, an inappropriately internal attributional style can also be associated with maladaptive functioning (Dweck & Reppucci, 1973; Seligman et al., 1982). To give a clinical example, one would not want a child to attribute his parents' divorce to some behavior or lack of effort on the child's part. For the purposes of subsequent adjustment, attributions of causality must be reality-based and accurate. Different attributions are useful and appropriate for different situations at different points in time.

Attribution-retraining interventions have received much less research attention than problem-solving or self-instructional interventions. The demonstrated effects of attribution retraining have been rather specific and focused, but they suggest that interventions can have an impact on the child's emerging beliefs about the reasons for experiencing failure. By apparently changing these beliefs, behavioral persistence may be improved.

TREATMENT APPROACHES WITH INTERNALIZING DISORDER

The development and evaluation of cognitive-behavioral treatments for children experiencing anxiety, depression, and other types of internalizing symptomatology lags far behind the existing work with adults experiencing these disorders. Fortunately, research attention to this area is increasing in conjunction with our knowledge base regarding the manifestation of these disorders in childhood. The interventions that have been proposed thus far are developmentally tailored extensions of techniques used with adults and/ or combinations of the methods previously described in this chapter.

Emery, Bedrosian, and Garber (1983) argue that cognitive therapy techniques that have proved useful with depressed adults such as self-monitoring, activity scheduling, graded task assignments, and hypothesis testing of distorted beliefs can be effective with children. They also believe that children can be taught to generate alternate attributions regarding negative events or beliefs and can learn to "decatastrophize" about negative outcomes. These authors note the importance of including parents in the therapy process, particularly as aides when the child is attempting activity scheduling or hypothesis testing. Their contentions are buttressed by developmental research suggesting that latency-age children do have the capacity for such cognitive operations (Flavell, 1977). The authors presented case study data supporting the effectiveness of these procedures, but did not provide formal outcome data.

Stark, Kaslow, and Reynolds (1985) conducted one of the few group outcome studies that addresses the efficacy of cognitive-behavioral interventions with depressed children. Using 9- to 12-year-old subjects, these authors compared the efficacy of a self-control therapy and a behavior therapy based on Lewinsohn's (1974) model of depression. The self-control therapy was modeled after work by Fuchs and Rehm (1977) and involved teaching the children skills such as setting more realistic standards for performance, setting realistic subgoals, applying self-reinforcement, learning to self-punish less, and learning to examine one's attributions. Training in self-monitoring, with special attention to monitoring pleasant activities was also included. The behavioral therapy included training in self-monitoring, pleasant event scheduling, problem solving about social situations, and gaining an understanding about the relationship between feelings and social behavior. After 12 group sessions, both treatments produced statistically and clinically significant reductions in depressive symptomatology relative to a waiting-list control group. The positive results were most pronounced for the self-control therapy group, suggesting that the cognitive change strategies employed in this treatment were within the capacity of the target children.

The current authors have applied these concepts with individual cases of depressed children and adolescents. The case of 15-year-old Sharon provides an interesting example. When initially seen, she was extremely dysphoric, experienced recurrent suicidal ideation, and displayed a number of vegetative signs of depression. A psychiatric consultation was obtained and she was placed on antidepressant medication. In individual therapy she was introduced to a cognitive-behavioral approach to depression, and she completed self-monitoring and mood ratings on a regular basis. She was able to understand how her mood was affected by her thoughts and behavior and was able to engage in behavioral planning to increase the occurrence of pleasure and mastery-oriented events. Sharon manifested extremely high standards for evaluating her performance in a number of areas, and it became clear that her parents also ascribed to these standards, so that family therapy sessions were held to encourage Sharon and her parents to re-evaluate their standards.

Sharon had difficulty with the notion of changing her standards and noted that when she was not depressed she actually valued her perfectionism. At that point she resisted the therapy because she perceived it as trying to change something she valued in herself. With this in mind, we began to explore and identify those situations or domains in which her perfectionism worked for her and when and how it might work against her. She became increasingly comfortable with this perspective and decided she wanted to continue to set high standards regarding her performance in mathematical coursework (which was a clear area of strength), but she did not need to be so demanding of herself regarding art or physical education. Her parents were very willing to adjust their expectations for Sharon because of their great concern for her, but over time it became clear that the parents were quite demanding of themselves. Eventually Sharon was able to identify this familial pattern and became comfortable with the notion that she could choose different expectations for herself than her parents had adopted for themselves.

A cognitive-behavioral program for treating school phobia has been described in Kendall, Howard and Epps (in press). This program incorporates components of previous treatments that have demonstrated effectiveness, including *in vivo* exposure, modeling, social reinforcement, coping-skills training and parental involvement. In addition, the program addresses the cognitions of the child and parent and includes problem-solving training to cope with the new situations that arise from the child's return to school (e.g., peer relations difficulties, needing to elicit help from teachers, conflicts over homework). This treatment package offers a promising approach to returning the school-phobic child to school and improving the quality of his or her functioning at school. However, it awaits empirical confirmation of its efficacy.

These cognitive-behavioral approaches to the treatment of internalizing disorders represent the field's beginning attempts to address these serious problems in children. It is our hope that the pursuits in this area will build on knowledge gained by the earlier efforts with more externalizing types of children.

KEY METHODS OF TRAINING DELIVERY

While the cognitive-behavioral interventions we have described differ from each other in emphasis, they do share the goal of altering the child's thoughts and thinking processes in ways that lead to behavioral and emotional changes. These therapies also share some of the methods through which the content of the treatment is delivered or trained. The training methods of modeling, role play, and use of behavioral contingencies deserve special attention because they are so widely used in interventions with children.

MODELING

Virtually all effective cognitive-behavioral interventions with children involve some form of active modeling as a means of conveying the coping methods the therapist wishes to train. The therapeutic use of modeling involves the exposure of the client to an individual who actually demonstrates the behaviors to be learned by the client. Modeling as an intervention in its own right has been demonstrated as effective in achieving the elimination of behavioral deficits, the reduction of excessive fears, and the facilitation of social behavior (see Bandura, 1969, 1971; Rosenthal & Bandura, 1978). As a component in cognitive-behavioral interventions, modeling has been presented in a number of different forms, including filmed modeling, graduated modeling, symbolic modeling, and participant modeling.

The phenomenon of modeling has received significant research attention. Several factors or dimensions that influence the effectiveness of modeling have been delineated and some of these have particular implications for the therapeutic use of modeling. Having the model talk out loud, verbalizing his or her own thoughts, has been demonstrated to produce superior results relative to a model who does not verbalize (Meichenbaum, 1971). It appears that as the model speaks, he or she provides the observer with a demonstration of how to think him- or herself through a particular problem or situation. Talking out loud while performing an action also provides the learner with auditory as well a visual cues for acquiring the new behavior.

Another factor with therapeutic implications is the distinction between mastery and coping models. A *mastery model* demonstrates successful task performance without indications of anxiety or difficulty. In contrast, the *coping model* may demonstrate task performance that includes some mistakes. A coping model may also demonstrate some anxiety or feelings of discomfort while approaching and accomplishing the task and yet be able to fulfill the task requirements with persistent effort. Data from a number of different researchers suggest that the coping model produces superior behavioral results relative to the mastery model (Kazdin, 1974; Meichenbaum, 1971; Sarason, 1975). It is hypothesized that the superior effects of the coping model arise from the fact that this model appears to be more similar to the client, who is also likely to face difficulties when attempting to execute a new behavior. The coping model not only shows the client how to execute this behavior but also demonstrates how this can be accomplished despite cognitive, emotional, and/or behavioral difficulties.

In addition to the formal modeling that takes place during the process of teaching the child various problem-solving or self-instructional strategies, many intervention programs also emphasize the role of informal modeling. Through informal modeling the therapist is able to demonstrate how one copes with various dilemmas that may arise during the course of conducting the therapy. For example, in the cognitive-behavioral program developed by the current authors (Kendall & Braswell, 1985) therapists are encouraged to model problem solving when facing dilemmas such as locating the right room for conducting the therapy, obtaining the necessary materials, handling situations involving the loss or absence of materials, and handling details such as scheduling, which may require coordination with the child, parents, and school. Such examples provide natural demonstrations of the problem-solving process.

ROLE PLAYING

Role-playing methods are used in almost all cognitive–behavioral intervention programs that focus on social or classroom behaviors. Through role-playing exercises, the cognitive-behavioral therapist provides the client with performance-based learning experiences. In addition to serving as a vehicle for training, role-playing exercises also provide a method of ongoing assessment of the extent to which the client is able to produce the newly learned skills, at least in the context of the therapy setting. In this way, the therapist can continually monitor the type of feedback the client requires and detect any gaps or incomplete behavioral information that has been provided to the client. Role plays typically involve the therapist and child; however, there is an increasing tendency to design interventions so that children can participate in role-playing situations with age-appropriate peers (Bloomquist & Braswell, 1987; Hinshaw, Henker, & Whalen, 1984a; Sarason & Sarason, 1981).

Another variation of role-playing techniques includes the use of videotaped role playing, so that the participants can receive auditory and visual feedback about their performance (Chandler, 1973; Sarason & Ganzer, 1973). Sarason and Ganzer found that the effectiveness of the type of feedback may be mediated by certain subject variables. Hypothesizing that high testanxious delinquents would be upset by televised feedback of their roleplaying performance, these investigators compared the behavioral outcomes of high anxiety subjects who received audiotape feedback versus those receiving televised feedback. In support of their hypothesis, only 1 of 15 high anxious subjects in the televised modeling group received positive behavior ratings, while 14 of 19 test-anxious subjects in the nontelevised group received positive ratings.

Some investigators have made special attempts to make the role-playing situations particularly realistic in their potential for emotional arousal. Goodwin and Mahoney (1975) used a technique called the circle game to train hyperactive boys to control their responses to the verbal taunts of others. This procedure involved having the child play a game in which each one in turn was verbally assaulted by the other subjects. The children were then exposed to a model who appeared to remain calm and demonstrated the use of a series of self-statements to cope with the verbal taunts. Repeated exposure to this model was alternated with practice at "playing" the circle game. Posttreatment observations of the game indicated improvement in the children's ability to remain calm while exposed to the taunts of others and observations of the boys in the classroom indicated a decrease in disruptive behavior. As was stated previously, this method was also found to be an effective vehicle for training by Hinshaw, Whalen, and Henker (1984a) in their work with attention-deficit disordered children. Indeed, the nonsupportive data reported recently by Abikoff and Gittelman (1985) in which cognitive training did not enhance medication effects with hyperactive children has been criticized by Kendall and Reber (1986) for failing to bring the children's actual problem situations into role-play sessions.

BEHAVIORAL CONTINGENCIES

Interventions for children that are viewed as cognitive-behavioral vary to a surprising degree in the extent to which actual behavioral contingencies are used to reinforce the learning of new cognitive and behavioral skills (see reviews by Kendall & Braswell, 1985, and Urbain & Kendall, 1980).

The cognitive-behavioral package developed and evaluated by the authors (Kendall & Braswell, 1982; Kendall & Wilcox, 1980; Kendall & Zupan, 1981) provides an example of how multiple behavioral contingencies can be applied with cognitive techniques such as self-instructional and problem-solving training. The specific contingencies included in this treatment package were general social rewards and self-rewarding self-statements, response cost for errors, rewarded performance on homework assignments, and rewarded accurate self-evaluation.

Therapists are encouraged to use socially rewarding phrases liberally throughout each therapy session. These phrases are recommended not only to provide the child with immediate feedback about his or her behavior but also as a means of setting a positive tone in the therapy session. Such social rewards could take the form of phrases such as "Good," or "Nice job" or any number of phrases that represent appropriate social rewards with children. Braswell, Kendall, Braith, Carey, and Vye (1985) analyzed the verbal behavior of therapists in the context of this type of intervention and found that statements of encouragement such as "Keep up the good work," or "I see you're really working hard at this," were associated with more positive child outcomes than were simply confirming statements such as "That's correct," or "Right." The child is also encouraged to use positively self-rewarding statements. In this particular intervention package, the final step of the self-instructional sequence requires the child to make a self-rewarding statement in recognition of positive task performance. If the child makes an error he or she is encouraged to make a coping statement such as "The next time I'll go more slowly. That will help me do a better job." The coping statement is included because children are expected to encounter challenges and they need to be prepared with cognitive controls to avoid acting out when frustrated.

Mild punishment in the form of a response-cost contingency that operated throughout all sessions is also used in this treatment package. With this type of contingency the child receives a given number of reward tokens at the beginning of each session and is instructed regarding how tokens can be lost for the commission of certain specific behaviors. In the treatment packages that have been formally evaluated, there were three reasons a child could lose a token, including failure to use the self-instructions, going too fast on the assigned task, or getting the wrong answer on a task. Thus, the response-cost contingency serves not as a serious negative consequence but as a cue to inhibit action, to help the child slow him- or herself down and to use the self-instructions appropriately. When the therapist enacts a response cost, the reason for the loss is clearly and calmly stated so that the child knows exactly what he or she must do to improve performance on the next task. At the end of each session, the child is given an opportunity to cash in some or all of his or her remaining tokens for a prize. The child has the choice of buying a small prize and saving some tokens toward the purchase of a larger prize or of spending all the tokens at the end of each session. While this contingency operates effectively with the majority of children we have treated, we have encountered a small number of kids who have significant emotional reactions to the response-cost contingencies. The reader is referred to Kendall and Braswell (1985) for a discussion of how to manage these cases.

The Kendall program does include other opportunities for children to earn bonus tokens by completing "homework assignments." In this particular treatment package, homework assignments involve having the child think of a situation in which he or she might have been able to use the self instructions in an extra-therapy situation and then be able to describe this situation to the therapist.

Opportunities to earn bonus rewards through accurate self-evaluation are included. At the end of each session, the therapist shows the child a simple 5-point rating scale that reflects how the child performed during that session. The therapist tells the child that the therapist will pick a number that he or she thinks best described the child during that session. The child is then asked to pick a number. If his or her number equals or is within 1 point of the therapist's rating, the child earns a bonus token or chip. Hinshaw, Whalen, and Henker (1984b) trained self-evaluation skills in the context of a comprehensive behavioral training program with attention-deficit disordered children and found that children engaging in reinforced self-evaluation of their social behavior were able to display more appropriate behavior in a free play setting relative to children receiving more traditional external reinforcement for appropriate social behavior. Stimulant medication was also found to increase the accuracy of children's self-evaluations. Self-evaluation coupled with self-monitoring has yielded improvement with cognitive and academic performance of attention deficit disordered children (see Abikoff, 1985 for a review).

Other investigators have combined cognitive techniques with explicit behavioral contingencies. Lochman et al. (1984) included behavioral contingencies by adding a goal-setting component to their anger-coping training program. This procedure involved having the child establish weekly behavioral goals with the help of the group. These goals were then monitored by the child's classroom teacher and contingent reinforcement followed appropriate goal attainment. The authors believe that the addition of the goal setting tended to augment the treatment effects in the classroom. Positive results, including generalization across tasks and settings, were obtained by Swanson (1985) who combined self-instructional training for academic deficit with a token program that rewarded accuracy and appropriate behavior.

It seems unfortunate that many otherwise well-designed and intensive intervention programs have failed to incorporate explicit behavioral procedures (e.g., Abikoff & Gittleman, 1985) as a means of motivating the child to learn new cognitive strategies, rewarding rehearsal of these strategies and reducing off-task behavior that can significantly interfere with learning and rehearsal.

CONTINUING CONCERNS

SUBJECT VARIABLES

Given the demonstration of some positive treatment effects across these various forms of cognitive-behavioral intervention, it becomes relevant to examine individual difference factors that may moderate treatment gains. The variables of age, type of the disorder, sex, cognitive level, socioeconomic status (SES), ethnicity, and attributional style have all been suggested as possible influences on outcome (Copeland, 1982). In a similar vein, Abikoff (1985) has emphasized the need for a comprehensive skills analysis of the child in order to understand if he or she possesses the necessary preskills for the particular intervention to be applied. Unfortunately, even though the client uniformity myth (Kiesler, 1966) is well recognized, journal articles still omit potentially interesting information regarding the effects of subject variables. Thus our conclusions must be based on relatively small bodies of information and be related to findings from other areas of inquiry. Our discussion will focus on two subject variables that we believe have important implications for treatment outcome: developmental level and attributional/expectational style.

Developmental Level

Children are not a homogeneous group. Indeed, the "developmental uniformity myth" (Kendall, 1984) is an unfortunate belief, since children differ in meaningful ways in terms of cognitive and physical development, peer and family status, and the nature of the behaviors that define competence and skill across the ages.

Cognitive-behavioral interventions have been applied with children ranging in age from preschool to adolescence, although the majority of the reported studies are with elementary-school-aged children. Consideration of the child's level of development facilitates proper assessment and intervention.

With regard to evaluating the normality or abnormality of behavior, one must consider the symptoms against a background of developmental norms. As indicated in earlier discussions, problem-solving abilities and capacities for verbal mediation of behavior are all considered developmental phenomena. Egocentrism and/or impulsivity in a 3- or 4-year-old child are considered normal and would not merit intervention in the vast majority of cases. For example, considering the Lurian developmental model from which self-instructional training was derived, one might not expect language-based self-control to fully appear in "normal" children before the age of 6. The inconsistent results of cognitive-behavioral interventions with preschoolers may be the product of attempting to intervene before the child is developmentally ready for or in need of the skills to be trained. It may be the case, however, that when parents identify the child's normal developmental status as problematic, then the parents may be in need of an educational intervention that would inform them about the child's cognitive and emotional development and help them formulate more age-appropriate expectations. Cognitive-behavioral parent training, an idea whose time has come, would incorporate such material into behavioral programs.

The implications of developmental level for how one might best intervene are somewhat predictable. Copeland (1982) concluded that a broad age range of children do appear to benefit from self-instructional training, but specified that younger children may require more structured and specific training than do older children. Pressley (1979) also discussed the need for more concrete training with younger children. Bender (1976) found specific strategy training more effective than a general type of training with a sample of impulsive 1st graders, and Kendall and Wilcox (1980) found conceptual training more effective than concrete training among non-self-controlled 8- to 12-year-olds. But Schleser et al. (1981) and Thackwray et al. (1985) found specific plus general self-statements to be the most effective treatment for improving task performance and obtaining cross-task generalization in an elementary-school-aged sample. If development is conceptualized in terms of Piagetian stages, Schleser et al. (1981) found that concrete operational children outperformed preoperational children on both training task and generalization assessments.

Attributional/Expectational Styles

While we have addressed attributions as the target for intervention, the child's attributional style may also be an important mediator of treatment effects. Kopel and Arkowitz (1975) suggested that a child's feelings of personal control might influence his or her responsiveness to any type of self-control intervention. Studies examining a child's attributional style or generalized expectations, such as locus of control, speak to this issue. Beliefs and expectancies regarding personal control have been found to differ for a number of populations. For example, blacks tend to be more external in their locus of control relative to whites (Battle & Rotter, 1963; Ramey & Campbell, 1976) and hyperactive, attentionally disordered children have been observed to be more external than peers when matched for sex, age, mental age, and SES (Linn & Hodge, 1982).

In a study of the role of expectations and the differential effectiveness of external versus internal monitoring, Bugental, Whalen, and Henker (1977) provided treatment for hyperactive and impulsive boys, half of whom were receiving methylphenidate. Treatment was conducted twice a week for 8 weeks, with the experimenter tutors utilizing either self-instructional training or contingent social reinforcement. Both interventions were aimed at increasing the child's attention and correct performance on academic tasks. The results indicated that children whose attributional styles were congruent with their treatment (high personal control/self-control training or high external control/social contingency management) achieved better Porteus scores than those in noncongruent combinations. Also, self-instructional training was more effective with nonmedicated children, while external control was superior with the medicated subjects. As Bugental *et al.* state, "change strategies (behavioral management, educational programs, psychotherapy, medical intervention) have implicit attributional textures which interact with the attributional network of the individual to influence treatment impact" (p. 881). Unfortunately, neither intervention produced changes on a teacher rating scale.

The Bugental *et al.* (1977) results are consistent with the findings from the learning research of Baron and Ganz (1972). These researchers administered the Intellectual Achievement Responsibility (IAR) scale (Crandall, Katkovsky, & Crandall, 1965) to 5th-grade lower-class black males. Subjects scoring in an internal or external direction then executed a simple discrimination task under one of three feedback conditions. In the external condition the experimenter provided correctness feedback, in the internal condition the child checked his own choices, and in the combined condition the child received both types of feedback. The combined feedback proved to be equally effective for both internally and externally oriented children, while internals made more correct choices than externals in the internal feedback condition. Children scoring as externals showed greater performance improvement in the external feedback condition than did the internals. Baron, Cowan, Ganz, and McDonald (1974) replicated these findings with lower-class white children. Thus, a subject's pretreatment level of internality versus externality may facilitate his or her responsiveness to interventions that have matching assumptions regarding the individual's control over his or her behavior. Braswell (1984) obtained results consistent with this contention in an evaluation of the effects of self-instructional training in a racially and economically diverse sample of children. Those children who obtained improvement on the teacher ratings of classroom behavior tended to be more internal in locus of control at pretest and were more likely to provide effort-oriented attributions for their own change at posttest.

In addition to predicting treatment response, research also suggests that one's attributional style or generalized expectancies may change as a result of treatment. In a 6-month follow-up of the Bugental *et al.* (1977) intervention, Bugental, Collins, Collins, and Chaney (1978) found that the self-instructional training group as a whole had increased their perceptions of personal control (become more internal) relative to the social reinforcement group. Teacher ratings, however, indicated that the social reinforcement group showed more improved classroom behavior. In this case, increasing internality did not seem to be associated with greater behavioral change, at least from the perspective of the classroom teacher. Dweck's (1975) study on reattribution training also suggests that a child's perception of personal control can be altered via intervention. Both Bugental *et al.* (1978) and Dweck (1975) provide examples of children becoming more internal in their perceptions of control, but, as previously stated, an exclusive focus on making children more internal may be a less desirable goal than helping children develop an appropriately flexible attributional system in which one's perceived sense of personal control matches the reality of one's current situation.

GENERALIZATION AND ITS ABSENCE

One cannot review this literature without becoming keenly aware that while short-term or specific gains are achieved in many studies, there is an overall lack of generalization of treatment effects across behavioral domains and settings and a lack of maintenance of effects across time. These limitations may seem particularly disappointing in light of the original expectations that cognitive-behavioral methods would improve upon traditional interventions and produce lasting and far-reaching effects.

With over 10 years of research activity, researchers and readers have to accept the fact that boundless generalization of treatment effects seems to be and perhaps will continue to be something of a pipedream. As Foster *et al.* (in press) have noted, while cognitive strategies may be more efficient to teach due to their broad applicability, they may not generalize more readily than behavioral skills. As ever, generalization of both cognitive strategies and behavioral skills is not a magical process, but it is a trainable goal. But how is generalization best trained? A number of authors (Bransford, 1979; Cohen & Schleser, 1984; Kendall, 1977) have offered consistent suggestions. One common thought is to have training sessions resemble potential generalization targets as much as possible. This similarity could occur on a variety of dimensions. Considering the training tasks, it is no longer common wisdom to assume that one can train a child on psychoeducational tasks and obtain changes in performance on classroom academic tasks and class behavior. Overlap between training tasks and generalization targets is necessary for obtaining optimal gains. Training in applying the new skills to a variety of tasks provides the child with opportunities to learn how the strategies can be adapted to an as yet unexperienced situation. As Cohen and Schleser (1984) suggest, such training would involve analyzing task similarities and differences and considering how the differences may affect strategy application.

Overlap or similarity in the social context of the intervention may also enhance generalization. Thus, if the goal of the intervention is to obtain improved peer behavior, it would seem wisest to conduct at least a portion of the intervention in a peer group context (see also Howard & Kendall, 1987). If generalization to home or school is desired, then the intervention could be planned to include parents and teachers. The outcome studies we have reviewed indicated that the inclusion of peers, teachers, and/or parents in the treatment process certainly does not guarantee success, but it may heighten one's probability of making the intervention have an impact.

The provision of treatments of longer duration, allowing the child to reach an adequate level of skill mastery, would enhance treatment generalization. Implicit in this suggestion is the recognition that children acquire skills at varying rates and, therefore, treatment length should be flexible enough to allow for such variation. Clinical application, as opposed to research programs, have followed flexible timetables and there is presently a need for the evaluation of this approach.

Discussions about lengthening treatments may not be popular in light of the changing nature of health care delivery and funding, for the emphasis in many sectors is on providing brief treatment. It must be acknowledged, however, that the process of acquiring a more reflective thinking style or changing one's mode of attributing causality is a developmental process, not an event (Mahoney & Nezworski, 1985). In fact, some investigators emphasize that the goal is to change underlying cognitive structures rather than discrete cognitive events, and while these structures are viewed as malleable, they are not as readily changed as discrete thoughts or behaviors (see Foster et al., in press; Ingram & Hollon, 1986; Kendall & Ingram, 1987).

As stated previously and elsewhere (e.g., Kendall, 1985), we can not overemphasize our concern that cognitive-behavioral therapists undermine their own potential for impact when they fail to include ongoing behavioral contingencies in their training. We risk letting newly trained skills suffer an early extinction when we fail to establish rewards for skill use in the child's natural settings. The assumption that the child's new reflective thinking will immediately result in natural rewards is another example of magical thinking on the part of the experimenter/therapist. We have engaged in this type of thinking and the design of some of our treatment studies attests to this fact. Some researchers are attempting to rectify this difficulty. For example, Deshler et al. (1981) included a component in which the subjects—learning-disabled adolescents—were trained in how to cue others to provide them with reinforcement for their strategy use. Bloomquist and Braswell (1987) have developed an experimental training program for attention deficit disordered children and their parents that includes training the parents to observe and reinforce their children's fledgling attempts to engage in reflective problem solving in the home setting. Reports of more cognitive-behavioral training programs in which the child returns to an environment that shapes the use of the cognitive skills would be welcome additions to the literature.

REFERENCES

Abikoff, H. (1985). Efficacy of cognitive training interventions in hyperactive children: A critical review. *Clinical Psychology Review, 5,* 479-512.

Abikoff, H., & Gittelman, R. (1985). Hyperactive children treated with stimulants: Is cognitive training a useful adjunct? *Archives of General Psychiatry, 42,* 953-961.

Achenbach, T. M. (1978). The Child Behavior Profile: I. Boys aged 6-11. *Journal of Consulting and Clinical Psychology, 46,* 478-488.

Achenbach, T. M., & Edelbrock, C. S. (1978). The classification of childhood psychopathology: A review and analysis of empirical efforts. *Psychological Bulletin, 85,* 1275-1301.

Andrews, G. R., & Debus, R. L. (1978). Persistence and the causal perception of failure: Modifying cognitive attributions. *Journal of Educational Psychology, 70,* 154-166.

Asarnow, J. R., & Callahan, J. W. (1985). Boys with poor adjustment problems: Social cognitive processes. *Journal of Consulting and Clinical Psychology, 53,* 80-87.

Bandura, A. (1969). *Principles of behavior modification.* New York: Holt, Rinehart & Winston.

Bandura, A. (1971). Psychotherapy based upon modeling procedures. In A. Bergin & S. Garfield (Eds.), *Handbook of psychotherapy and behavior change.* New York: Wiley.

Bandura, A. (1977). Self-efficacy: Toward a unifying theory of behavior change. *Psychological Review, 84,* 191-215.

Barling, J., & Snipelisky, B. (1983). Assessing the determinants of childrens' academic self-efficacy beliefs: A replication. *Cognitive Therapy and Research, 7,* 371-376.

Baron, R. M., Cowan, G., Ganz, R. L., & McDonald, M. (1974). Interaction of locus of control and type of performance feedback: Considerations of external validity. *Journal of Personality and Social Psychology, 30,* 285-292.

Baron, R. M., & Ganz, R. L. (1972). Effects of locus of control and type of performance of lower-class black children. *Journal of Personality and Social Psychology, 21,* 124-130.

Battle, E. S., & Rotter, J. (1963). Children's feelings of personal control as related to social class and ethnic groups. *Journal of Personality, 31,* 482-490.

Beck, A. T. (1976). Cognitive therapy and the emotional disorders. New York: International Universities Press.

Beck, A. T., Rush, A. J., Shaw, B. F., & Emery, G. (1979). *Cognitive therapy of depression.* New York: Guilford.

Bender, N. (1976). Self-verbalization versus tutor verbalization in modifying impulsivity. *Journal of Educational Psychology, 68,* 347-354.

Blechman, E., Olson, D., & Hellman, I. (1976). Stimulus control over family problem-solving behavior: The family contract game. *Behavior Therapy, 7,* 686-692.

Blechman, E., Olson, D., Schornagel, C., Halsdorf, M., & Turner, A. (1976). The family contract game: Technique and case study. *Journal of Consulting and Clinical Psychology, 44,* 449-455.

Bloomquist, M. L., & Braswell, L. (1987). *A comprehensive child and family intervention program for attention deficit disorder.* Unpublished manuscript, North Memorial Medical Center, Minneapolis.

Bransford, J. D. (1979). *Human cognition: Learning, understanding and remembering.* Belmont, CA: Wadsworth Publishing.

Braswell, L. (1984). Cognitive-behavioral therapy with an inner-city sample of non-self-controlled children. Unpublished doctoral dissertation, University of Minnesota, Minneapolis.

Braswell, L., Kendall, P. C., Braith, J., Carey, M. P., & Vye, C. S. (1985). "Involvement" in cognitive-behavioral therapy with children: Process and its relationship to outcome. *Cognitive Therapy and Research, 9,* 611–630.

Braswell, L., Koehler, C., & Kendall, P. C. (1985). Attributions and outcomes in child psychotherapy. *Journal of Social and Clinical Psychology, 3,* 458–465.

Brown, R. T., Borden, K. A., Wynne, M. E., Schleser, R., & Clingerman, S. R. (1986). Methylphenidate and cognitive therapy with ADD children: A methodological reconsideration. *Journal of Abnormal Child Psychology, 14,* 481–497.

Brown, R. T., Wynne, M. E., & Medenis, R. (1985). Methylphenidate and cognitive therapy: A comparison of treatment approaches with hyperactive boys. *Journal of Abnormal Child Psychology, 13,* 69–87.

Bugental, D. B., Collins, S., Collins, L., & Chaney, L. A. (1978). Attributional and behavioral changes following two behavior management interventions with hyperactive boys: A follow-up study. *Child Development, 49,* 247–250.

Bugental, D. B., Whalen, C. K., & Henker, B. (1977). Causal attribution of hyperactive children and motivational assumptions of two behavior-change approaches: Evidence for an interactionist position. *Child Development, 48,* 874–884.

Butkowsky, I. S., & Willows, D. M. (1980). Cognitive-motivational characteristics of children varying in reading ability: Evidence for learned helplessness in poor readers. *Journal of Educational Psychology, 72,* 408–422.

Chandler, M. (1973). Egocentrism and anti-social behavior: The assessment and training of social perspective-taking skills. *Developmental Psychology, 9,* 326–332.

Clifford, M. M. (1984). Thoughts on a theory of constructive failure. *Educational Psychology, 19,* 108–120.

Cohen, R., & Schleser, R. (1984). Cognitive development and clinical interventions. In A. W. Meyers & W. E. Craighead (Eds.), *Cognitive behavior therapy with children.* New York: Plenum.

Conners, C. K. (1969). A teacher rating scale for use in drug studies with children. *American Journal of Psychiatry, 126,* 884–888.

Copeland, A. P. (1982). Individual differences factors in children's self-management: Toward individualized treatments. In P. Karoly & F. H. Kanfer (Eds.), *Self-management and behavior change: From theory to practice.* New York: Pergamon.

Copeland, A. P. (1983). Children's talking to themselves: Its developmental significance, function and therapeutic promise. In P. C. Kendall (Ed.), *Advances in cognitive-behavioral research and therapy* (Vol. 2). New York: Academic Press.

Coyne, T., Meyers, A., & Clark, L. (1985, November). *Behavioral treatment for obese children: Does parental problem solving solve the problem?* Paper presented at the meeting of the Association for Advancement of Behavior Therapy, Houston.

Craighead, W. E. (1982). A brief clinical history of cognitive-behavioral therapy with children. *School Psychology Review, 11,* 5–13.

Craighead, W. E., Meyers, A. W., & Craighead, L. W. (1985). A conceptual model for cognitive-behavior therapy with children. *Journal of Abnormal Child Psychology, 13,* 331–342.

Crandall, V. C., Katkovsky, W., & Crandall, V. G. (1965). Children's beliefs in their own control of reinforcement in intellectual academic achievement situations. *Child Development, 36,* 91–109.

Davis, G. (1966). Current status of research and theory in human problem-solving. *Psychological Bulletin, 66,* 36–54.

Deshler, D. D., Alley, G. R., Warner, M. M., & Schumaker, J. B. (1981). Instructional practices for promoting skill acquisition and generalization in severely learning disabled adolescents. *Learning Disability Quarterly, 6,* 231–234.

Dobson, K. S., & Shaw, B. F. (1986). Cognitive assessment with major depressive disorders. *Cognitive Therapy and Research, 10,* 13–29.

Dodge, K. A., & Frame, C. L. (1982). Social cognitive biases and deficits in aggressive boys. *Child Development, 53,* 620–635.

Dodge, K. A., McClaskey, C. L., & Feldman, E. (1985). Situational approach to the assessment of social competence in children. *Journal of Consulting and Clinical Psychology, 53,* 344–353.

Douglas, V. I., Parry, P., Marton, P., & Garson, C. (1976). Assessment of a cognitive training program for hyperactive children. *Journal of Abnormal Child Psychology, 4,* 389–410.

Duncan, C. P. (1959). Recent research on human problem-solving. *Psychology Bulletin, 56,* 397–429.

Dweck, D. S. (1975). The role of expectations and attributions in the alteration of learned helplessness. *Journal of Personality and Social Psychology, 31,* 674–685.

Dweck, C. S., & Reppucci, D. (1973). Learned helplessness and reinforcement responsibility in children. *Journal of Personality and Social Psychology, 25,* 109–116.

D'Zurilla, T. (1986). *Problem-solving therapy.* New York: Springer.

D'Zurilla, T. J., & Goldfried, M. R. (1971). Problem-solving and behavior modification. *Journal of Abnormal Psychology, 78,* 107–126.

Ellis, A. (1970). *The essence of rational psychotherapy: A comprehensive approach to treatment.* New York: Institute for Rational Living.

Emery, G., Bedrosian, R., & Garber, J. (1983). Cognitive therapy with depressed children and adolescents. In D. P. Cantwell & G. A. Carlson (Eds.). *Affective disorders in childhood and adolescence: An update.* New York: Spectrum Publications.

Feldhusen, J., Houtz, J., & Ringenbach, S. (1972). The Purdue Elementary Problem-Solving Inventory. *Psychological Reports, 31,* 891–901.

Fincham, F. D. (1983). Clinical applications of attribution theory: Problems and prospects. In M. Hewstone (Ed.), *Attribution theory: Social and functional extensions.* Oxford: Blackwells.

Flavell, J. (1977). *Cognitive development.* New Jersey: Prentice Hall.

Foster, S. L., Kendall, P. C., & Guevremont, D. (in press). Cognitive and social learning theory and therapy. In J. Matson (Ed.), *Handbook of treatment approaches in childhood psychopathology.* New York: Plenum.

Fuchs, C. Z., & Rehm, L. P. (1977). A self-control behavior therapy program for depression. *Journal of Consulting and Clinical Psychology, 45,* 206–215.

Fuhrman, M. J., & Kendall, P. C. (1986). Cognitive tempo and behavioral adjustment in children. *Cognitive Therapy and Research, 10,* 45–50.

Genshaft, J. L., & Hirt, M. (1980). The effectiveness of self-instructional training to enhance math achievement in women. *Cognitive Therapy and Research, 4,* 91–97.

Goodwin, S., & Mahoney, M. J. (1975). Modification of aggression through modeling: An experimental probe. *Journal of Behavior Therapy and Experimental Psychiatry, 6,* 200–202.

Graham, S. (1983). The effect of self-instructional procedures on LD students' handwriting performance. *Learning Disability Quarterly, 6,* 231–234.

Graziano, A. M., & Mooney, K. C. (1980). Family self-control instructions for children's nighttime fear reduction. *Journal of Consulting and Clinical Psychology, 48,* 206–213.

Hains, A. A., & Ryan, E. B. (1983). The development of social cognitive processes among juvenile delinquents and nondelinquents peers. *Child Development, 54,* 1536–1544.

Haley, G. M. T., Fine, S., Marriage, K., Moretti, M. M., & Freeman, R. J. (1985). Cognitive bias and depression in psychiatrically disturbed children and adolescents. *Journal of Consulting and Clinical Psychology, 53,* 535–537.

Hall, R. J. (1979). *An information processing approach to the study of learning disabilities.* Unpublished doctoral dissertation, University of California, Los Angeles.

Hallahan, D. P., & Reeve, R. E. (1980). Selective attention and distractibility. In B. K. Keogh (Ed.), *Advances in special education: Basic constructs and theoretical orientations* (Vol. 1). Greenwich, CT: JAI Press.

Harris, K. R. (1985). Conceptual, methodological, and clinical issues in cognitive-behavioral assessment. *Journal of Abnormal Child Psychology, 13,* 373–390.

Harris, K. R. (1986). The effects of cognitive-behavior modification on private speech and task performance during problem solving among learning disabled and normally achieving children. *Journal of Abnormal Child Psychology, 14,* 63–67.

Harris, K. R., & Graham, S. (1985). Improving learning disabled students' composition skills: Self-control strategy training. *Learning Disabilities Quarterly, 8,* 27–36.

Hartup, W. W. (1983). Peer relations. In E. M. Hetherington (Ed.), Mussen's *Handbook of Child Psychology* (Vol. 4). New York: Wiley.

Hinshaw, S. P., Henker, B., & Whalen, C. K. (1984a). Self-control in hyperactive boys in anger-inducing situations: Effects of cognitive-behavioral training and of methylphenidate. *Journal of Abnormal Child Psychology, 12,* 55–77.

Hinshaw, S. P., Henker, B., & Whalen, C. K. (1984b). Cognitive-behavioral and pharmacologic interventions for hyperactive boys: Comparative and combined effects. *Journal of Consulting and Clinical Psychology, 52,* 739–749.

Hollon, S. D., Kendall, P. C., & Lumry, A. (1986). Specificity of depressotypic cognition in clinical depression. *Journal of Abnormal Psychology, 95,* 52–59.

Homatidis, S., & Konstantareas, M. M. (1981). Assessment of hyperactivity: Isolating measures of high discriminant validity. *Journal of Consulting and Clinical Psychology, 49,* 533–541.

Howard, B., & Kendall, P. C. (1987). *Child interventions: Having no peers?* Manuscript submitted for publication: Temple University, Philadelphia.

Hudson, L. M. (1978). On the coherence of role-taking abilities: An alternative to correlational analysis. *Child Development, 49,* 223–227.

Ingram, R. E., & Hollon, S. D. (1986). Information processing and the treatment of depression. In R. E. Ingram (Ed.), *Information processing approaches to clinical psychology.* New York: Academic Press.

Ingram, R., Kendall, P. C., Smith, J., Donnelly, C., & Ronan, K. (in press). Cognitive specificity in emotional distress. *Journal of Personality and Social Psychology.*

Jahoda, M. (1953). The meaning of psychological health. *Social Casework, 34,* 349–354.

Jarvis, P. E. (1968). Verbal control of sensory-motor performance: A test of Luria's hypothesis. *Human Development, 11,* 172–183.

Johnson, M. B. (1983). *Self-instruction and children's math problem-solving: A study of training, maintenance, and generalization.* Unpublished doctoral dissertation, University of Notre Dame, South Bend.

Kagan, J. (1966). Reflection-impulsivity: The generality and dynamics of conceptual tempo. *Journal of Abnormal Psychology, 71,* 17–24.

Kazdin, A. E. (1974). Covert modeling, model similarity, and reduction of avoidance behavior. *Behavior Therapy, 5,* 325–340.

Kazdin, A. E., Esveldt-Dawson, K., French, N. H., & Unis, A. S. (1987). Problem-solving skills training and relationship therapy in the treatment of antisocial child behavior. *Journal of Consulting and Clinical Psychology, 55,* 76–85.

Kendall, P. C. (1977). On the efficacious use of verbal self-instructional procedures with children. *Cognitive Therapy and Research, 1,* 331–341.

Kendall, P. C. (1981). One year follow-up of concrete versus conceptual cognitive-behavioral self-control training. *Journal of Consulting and Clinical Psychology, 49,* 748–749.

Kendall, P. C. (1982). Individual versus group cognitive-behavioral self-control training: One year follow-up. *Behavior Therapy, 13,* 241–247.

Kendall, P. C. (1984). Social cognition and problem solving: A developmental and child-clinical interface. In B. Gholson & T. L. Rosenthal (Eds.), *Application of cognitive-developmental theory*. New York: Academic Press.

Kendall, P. C. (1985). Toward a cognitive-behavioral model of child psychopathology and a critique of related interventions. *Journal of Abnormal Child Psychology, 13*, 357–372.

Kendall, P. C. (1986). Comments on Rubin and Krasnor: Solutions and problems in research on problem solving. In M. Perlmutter (Ed.), *Cognitive perspectives on children's social and behavioral development: The Minnesota symposium on child psychology* (Vol. 18). Hillsdale, NJ: Erlbaum.

Kendall, P. C., & Braswell, L. (1982). Cognitive-behavioral self-control therapy for children: A components analysis. *Journal of Consulting and Clinical Psychology, 50*, 672–689.

Kendall, P. C., & Braswell, L. (1985). *Cognitive-behavioral therapy for impulsive children*. New York: Guilford.

Kendall, P. C., & Finch, A. J., Jr. (1976). A cognitive-behavioral treatment for impulsivity: A case study. *Journal of Consulting and Clinical Psychology, 44*, 852–857.

Kendall, P. C., & Finch, A. J., Jr. (1978). A cognitive-behavioral treatment for impulsivity: A group comparison study. *Journal of Consulting and Clinical Psychology, 46*, 110–118.

Kendall, P. C., & Fischler, G. L. (1984). Behavioral and adjustment correlates of problem-solving: Validational analyses of interpersonal cognitive problem-solving measures. *Child Development, 55*, 879–892.

Kendall, P. C., & Hollon, S. D. (Eds.). (1979). *Cognitive-behavioral interventions: Theory, research and procedures*. New York: Academic Press.

Kendall, P. C., Howard, B., & Epps, J. (in press). The anxious child: Cognitive–behavioral strategies. *Behavior Modification*.

Kendall, P. C., & Ingram, R. (1987). The future of cognitive assessment of anxiety: Let's get specific. In L. Michelson & M. Ascher (Eds.), *Anxiety and Stress Disorders: Cognitive-Behavioral Assessment and Treatment*. New York: Guilford Press.

Kendall, P. C., Pellegrini, D., & Urbain, E. S. (1981). Approaches to assessment for cognitive-behavioral interventions with children. In P. C. Kendall & S. D. Hollon (Eds.), *Assessment strategies for cognitive-behavioral interventions*. New York: Academic Press.

Kendall, P. C., & Reber, M. (1987). Cognitive training in treatment of hyperactive children. *Archives of General Psychiatry, 44*, 296.

Kendall, P. C., & Wilcox, L. E. (1979). Self-control in children: Development of a rating scale. *Journal of Consulting and Clinical Psychology, 47*, 1020–1029.

Kendall, P. C., & Wilcox, L. E. (1980). A cognitive-behavioral treatment for impulsivity: Concrete versus conceptual training in non-self-controlled problem children. *Journal of Consulting and Clinical Psychology, 48*, 80–91.

Kendall, P. C., & Williams, C. L. (1986). Adolescent therapy: Treating the "marginal man." *Behavior Therapy, 17*, 522–537.

Kendall, P. C., & Zupan, B. A. (1981). Individual versus group application of cognitive behavioral strategies for developing self-control in children. *Behavior Therapy, 12*, 344–359.

Kendall, P. C., Zupan, B. A., & Braswell, L. (1981). Self-control in children: Further analyses of the Self Control Rating Scale. *Behavior Therapy, 12*, 667–681.

Keyser, V., & Barling, J. (1981). Determinants of children's self-efficacy beliefs in an academic environment. *Cognitive Therapy and Research, 5*, 29–40.

Kiesler, D. J. (1966). Some myths of psychotherapy research and the search for a paradigm. *Psychological Bulletin, 65*, 110–136.

Kirmil-Gray, K., Dockham-Shoor, L., & Thoresen, G. R. (1980, November). *The effects of self-control instruction and behavior management training on the academic and social behavior of hyperactive children*. Paper presented at the meeting of the Association for Advancement of Behavior Therapy, New York.

Kopel, S., & Arkowitz, H. (1975). The role of attribution and self-perception in behavior change: Implications for behavior therapy. *Genetic Psychology Monographs, 92,* 175-212.

Kosiewicz, M. M., Hallahan, D. P., Lloyd, J. W., & Graves, A. W. (1982). Effects of self-instruction and self-correction procedures on handwriting performance. *Learning Disability Quarterly, 5,* 71-78.

Krasnor, L. R., & Rubin, K. H. (1983). Preschool social problem-solving: Attempts and outcomes in naturalistic interaction. *Child Development, 54,* 1545-1558.

Larcen, S., Spivack, G., & Shure, M. B. (1972, August). Problem-solving thinking and adjustment among dependent-neglected preadolescents. Paper presented at the meeting of the American Psychological Association, San Francisco.

Leon, J. A., & Pepe, H. J. (1983). Self-instructional training: Cognitive behavior modification for remediating arithmetic deficits. *Exceptional Children, 50,* 54-60.

Lewinsohn, P. M. (1974). A behavioral approach to depression. In R. M. Friedman & M. M. Katz (Eds.), *The psychology of depression: Contemporary theory and research.* New York: Wiley.

Linn, R. T., & Hodge, G. K. (1982). Locus of control in childhood hyperactivity. *Journal of Consulting and Clinical Psychology, 50,* 592-593.

Lochman, J. E., Burch, P. R., Curry, J. F., & Lampron, L. B. (1984). Treatment and generalization effects of cognitive-behavioral and goal-setting interventions with aggressive boys. *Journal of Consulting and Clinical Psychology, 52,* 915-916.

Lochman, J. E., & Curry, J. F. (1986). Effects of social problem-solving training and self-instruction training with aggressive boys. *Journal of Clinical Child Psychology, 15,* 159-164.

Lochman, J. E., Nelson, W. M. III, & Sims, J. P. (1981). A cognitive behavioral program for use with aggressive children. *Journal of Clinical Child Psychology, 10,* 146-148.

Luria, A. R. (1959). The directive function of speech in development and dissolution. *Word, 15,* 341-352.

Luria, A. R. (1961). *The role of speech in the regulation of normal and abnormal behaviors.* New York: Liveright.

Mahoney, M. J. (1977). Reflections in the cognitive-learning trend in psychotherapy. *American Psychologist, 32,* 5-18.

Mahoney, M. J., & Nezworski, M. T. (1985). Cognitive-behavioral approaches to children's problems. *Journal of Abnormal Child Psychology, 13,* 467-476.

Meichenbaum, D. (1971). Examination of model characteristics in reducing avoidance behavior. *Journal of Personality and Social Psychology, 17,* 298-307.

Meichenbaum, D. (1979). Teaching children self-control. In B. B. Lahay & A. E. Kazdin (Eds.) *Advances in Clinical Child Psychology,* (Vol. 2, pp. 1-33). New York: Plenum.

Meichenbaum, D., & Goodman, J. (1971). Training impulsive children to talk to themselves: A means of developing self-control. *Journal of Abnormal Psychology, 77,* 115-126.

Miller, S. A., Shelton, J., & Flavell, J. H. (1970). A test of Luria's hypothesis concerning the development of verbal self-regulation. *Child Development, 41,* 651-665.

Mischel, W. (1974). Processes in delay of gratification. In L. Berkowitz (Ed.), *Advances in Experimental Social Psychology* (Vol. 7). New York: Academic Press.

Mischel, W., & Patterson, C. J. (1976). Substantive and structural elements of effective plans for self-control. *Journal of Personality and Social Psychology, 34,* 942-950.

Monohan, J., & O'Leary, K. D. (1971). Effects of self-instruction in rule-breaking behavior. *Psychological Reports, 29,* 1051-1066.

Nelson, W., & Birkimer, J. C. (1978). Role of self-instruction and self-reinforcement in the modification of impulsivity. *Journal of Consulting and Clinical Psychology, 46,* 183.

O'Leary, K. D. (1968). The effects of self-instruction on immoral behavior. *Journal of Experimental Child Psychology, 6,* 297-301.

Palkes, H., Stewart, M., & Kahana, B. (1968). Porteus maze performance of hyperactive boys after training in self-directed verbal commands. *Child Development, 39,* 817-826.

Patterson, B. C., & Mischel, W. (1976). Effects of temptation-inhibiting and task-facilitating plans on self-control. *Journal of Personality and Social Psychology, 33,* 207-217.

Pearl, R. (1985). Cognitive-behavioral interventions for increasing motivation. *Journal of Abnormal Child Psychology, 13,* 443-454.

Peterson, L., & Shigetomi, C. (1981). The use of coping techniques to minimize anxiety in hospitalized children. *Behavior Therapy, 12,* 1-14.

Piaget, J. S. (1926). *The language and thought of the child.* New York: Harcourt-Brace.

Platt, J. J., & Spivack, G. (1972). Problem-solving thinking of psychiatric patients. *Journal of Consulting and Clinical Psychology, 39,* 148-151.

Platt, J. J., Spivack, G., Altman, N., Altman, D., & Peizer, S. B. (1974). Adolescent problem-solving thinking. *Journal of Consulting and Clinical Psychology, 42,* 787-793.

Porteus, S. D. (1955). *The maze test: Recent advances.* Palo Alto, CA: Pacific Books.

Pressley, M. (1979). Increasing children's self-control through cognitive interventions. *Review of Educational Research, 49,* 319-370.

Ramey, C. T., & Campbell, F. (1976). Parental attitudes and poverty. *Journal of Genetic Psychology, 120,* 3-6.

Reeve, R. A., & Brown, A. L. (1985). Meta-cognition reconsidered: Implications for intervention research. *Journal of Abnormal Child Psychology, 13,* 343-356.

Richard, B. A., & Dodge, K. A. (1982). School maladjustment and problem-solving in school-aged children. *Journal of Consulting and Clinical Psychology, 50,* 226-233.

Rickel, A. V., & Burgio, J. C. (1982). Assessing social competencies in lower-income preschool children. *American Journal of Community Psychology, 10,* 635-645.

Rickel, A. V., Eshelman, A. K., & Loigman, G. A. (1983). Social problem-solving training: A follow-up study of cognitive and behavioral effects. *Journal of Abnormal Child Psychology, 11,* 15-28.

Roberts, R. N., & Nelson, R. O. (1984). Assessment issues and strategies in cognitive-behavior therapy with children. In A. W. Meyers & W. E. Craighead (Eds.), *Cognitive behavior therapy with children* (pp. 99-128). New York: Plenum.

Robin, A. L., Armel, S., & O'Leary, K. D. (1975). The effects of self-instruction on writing deficiencies. *Behavior Therapy, 6,* 178-187.

Robin, A. L., Fischel, J. E., & Brown, K. E. (1984). *Validation of a measure of children's self-control.* Paper presented at the meeting of the Association for Advancement of Behavior Therapy, Toronto.

Robin, A. L., Kent, R., O'Leary, K. D., Foster, S., & Prinz, R. (1977). An approach to teaching parents and adolescents problem-solving communication skills: A preliminary report. *Behavior Therapy, 8,* 639-643.

Robin, A. L., & Schneider, M. (1974). *The turtle-technique: An approach to self-control in the classroom.* Unpublished manuscript, State University of New York, Stony Brook.

Robin, A. L., Schneider, M., & Dolnick, M. (1976). The turtle technique: An extended case study of self-control in the classroom. *Psychology in the Schools, 13,* 449-453.

Rosenthal, T., & Bandura, A. (1978). Psychological model: Theory and practice. In S. L. Garfield & A. E. Bergin (Eds.), *Handbook of psychotherapy and behavior change* (2nd ed.). New York: Wiley.

Sarason, I. G. (1968). Verbal learning modeling and juvenile delinquency. *American Psychologist, 23,* 254-266.

Sarason, I. G. (1975). Test anxiety and the self-disclosing model. *Journal of Consulting and Clinical Psychology, 43,* 148-153.

Sarason, I. G., & Ganzer, V. J. (1973). Modeling and group discussion in the rehabilitation of juvenile delinquents. *Journal of Counseling Psychology, 20,* 442-449.

Sarason, I. G., & Sarason, B. R. (1981). Teaching cognitive and social skills to high school students. *Journal of Consulting and Clinical Psychology, 49*, 908–918.

Scardamalia, M., Bereiter, C., & Steinbach, R. (1984). Teachability of reflective processes in written composition. *Cognitive Science, 8*, 173–190.

Schleser, R., Meyers, A., & Cohen, R. (1981). Generalization of self-instructions: Effects of general versus specific content, active rehearsal, and cognitive level. *Child Development, 52*, 335–340.

Schneider, M., & Robin, A. L. (1976). The turtle technique: A method for the self-control of impulsive behavior. In J. D. Krumboltz & C. E. Thoresen (Eds.), *Counseling Methods*. New York: Holt, Rinehart & Winston.

Schunk, P. H. (1983). Ability versus effort attributional feedback: Differential effects on self-efficacy and achievement. *Journal of Educational Psychology, 75*, 848–856.

Seligman, M. E. P., Peterson, C., Alloy, L., Abramson, L. Y., Kaslow, N. J., Tanenbaum, R. L., Kaysf, S., Semmel, A., Tolman, M., & von Baeyer, C. (1982). *Depressive symptoms, attributional style, and helplessness deficits in children.* Unpublished manuscript, University of Pennsylvania, Philadelphia.

Selman, R. L. (1980). *The growth of interpersonal understanding: Developmental and clinical analyses.* New York: Academic Press.

Selman, R. L., & Byrne, D. A. (1974). A structural developmental analysis of levels of role-taking in middle childhood. *Child Development, 45*, 803–806.

Shantz, C. V. (1975). The development of social cognition. In E. M. Hetherington (Ed.), *Review of child development and research* (Vol. 5). Chicago: University of Chicago Press.

Short, E. J., & Ryan, E. B. (1984). Metacognitive differences between skilled and less skilled readers: Remediating deficits through story grammar and attribution training. *Journal of Educational Psychology, 76*, 225–235.

Shure, M. B., & Spivack, G. (1972). Means–end thinking, adjustment and social class among elementary school-aged children. *Journal of Consulting and Clinical Psychology, 38*, 348–353.

Shure, M. B., & Spivack, G. (1978). *Problem-solving techniques in childrearing.* San Francisco: Jossey-Bass.

Spivack, G., Platt, J. J., & Shure, M. B. (1976). *The problem-solving approach to adjustment.* San Francisco: Jossey-Bass.

Spivack, G., & Shure, M. B. (1974). *Social adjustment of young children: A cognitive approach to solving real-life problems.* San Francisco: Jossey-Bass.

Stark, K. D., Kaslow, N. J., & Reynolds, W. M. (1985). *A comparison of the relative efficacy of self-control and behavior therapy for the reduction of depression in children.* Paper presented at the Fourth National Conference on the Clinical Application of Cognitive Behavior Therapy, Honolulu.

Swanson, H. L. (1985). Effects of cognitive-behavioral training on emotionally disturbed children's academic performance. *Cognitive Therapy and Research, 9*, 201–216.

Thackwray, D., Meyers, A., Schleser, R., & Cohen, R. (1985). Achieving generalization with general versus specific self-instructions: Effects on academically deficient children. *Cognitive Therapy and Research, 9*, 297–308.

Torgeson, J. K., & Kail, R. V. (1980). Memory process in exceptional children. In B. K. Keogh (Ed.) *Advances in special education: Basic constructs and theoretical orientations* (Vol. 1). Greenwich, CT: JAI Press.

Urbain, E. S., & Kendall, P. C. (1980). Review of social-cognitive problem-solving interventions with children. *Psychological Bulletin, 88*, 109–143.

Vygotsky, L. (1962). *Thought and language.* New York: Wiley.

Weiner, B. (1979). A theory of motivation of some classroom experiences. *Journal of Educational Psychology, 71*, 3–25.

Weisz, J. R. (1979). Perceived control and learned helplessness among mentally retarded and nonretarded children: A developmental analysis. *Developmental Psychology, 15*, 311–319.

Whitman, T., Burgio, L., & Johnston, M. B. (1984). Cognitive-behavioral intervention with mentally retarded children. In A. W. Meyers & W. E. Craighead (Eds.), *Cognitive behavior therapy with children* (pp. 193–227). New York: Plenum.

Wong, B. Y. L. (1985). Issues in cognitive-behavioral interventions in academic skill areas. *Journal of Abnormal Child Psychology, 13*, 425–442.

Zakraski, R. S. (1982). *Effects of context and training in the generalization of a cognitive strategy by normally achieving and learning disabled boys.* (Unpublished doctoral dissertation, University of Virginia, Richmond)

Zatz, S., & Chassin, L. (1983). Cognitions of test anxious children. *Journal of Consulting and Clinical Psychology, 51*, 526–534.

Zatz, S., & Chassin, L. (1985). Cognitions of test anxious children under naturalistic test-taking conditions. *Journal of Consulting and Clinical Psychology, 53*, 393–401.

Zivin, G. (1979). *The development of self-regulation through private speech.* New York: Wiley.

6

RATIONAL–EMOTIVE THERAPY

WINDY DRYDEN
ALBERT ELLIS

Rational–emotive therapy (RET) was founded by Albert Ellis in 1955. As such it has the longest history of any of the cognitive-behavioral therapies covered in the present handbook. Like many originators of new therapeutic systems of that time, Ellis had become increasingly disenchanted with the traditional psychoanalytic therapies as effective and efficient helping systems. Although this disillusionment was in part responsible for the creation of RET, a number of other influences can be detected in this regard. Ellis had had a long-standing interest in philosophy and was particularly influenced by the writings of Stoic philosophers such as Epictetus and Marcus Aurelius. In particular, the oft-quoted phrase of Epictetus, "People are disturbed not by things but by their view of things," crystallized Ellis's view that philosophical factors were more important than psychoanalytic and psychodynamic factors in accounting for psychological disturbance.

In addition to the influence of the Stoics, the impact of a number of other philosophers can be discovered in Ellis's ideas. For example, Ellis (1981a) has shown that he was influenced by Immanuel Kant's writings on both the power and the limitations of cognition and ideation, particularly those to be found in Kant's *Critique of Pure Reason*. From its inception Ellis has argued that RET is founded upon the tenets of logicoempirical methods of science, and in this respect has pointed to the writings of Popper (1959, 1963) and Reichenbach (1953) as having a distinct impact on his efforts to make these philosophical ideas core features of the therapeutic system of RET. Interestingly, George Kelly (1955), the founder of Personal Construct Therapy, was independently engaged in a very similar project at that same time.

RET is closely identified with the tenets of ethical humanism (Russell, 1930, 1965), particularly with respect to the idea that humans would do better to accept themselves and others as human and rid themselves of the notion that superhumans and subhumans exist. Further, RET has distinct existential roots; Ellis has said in this respect that he was particularly influenced by the ideas of Paul Tillich (1953) in the mid-1950s. Like other existentialists (e.g., Heidegger, 1949), RET theorists agree that humans are "at the centre of their universe (but not of *the* universe) and have the power of choice (but not of unlimited choice) with regard to their emotional realm" (Dryden & Ellis, 1986, p. 130). Ellis (1984a) has recently claimed that RET is doubly humanistic in its outlook in that it

a) attempts to help people maximize their individuality, freedom, self-interest, and self-control at the same time that it b) tries to help them live in an involved, committed, and selectively loving manner. It thereby strives to facilitate individual *and* social interest. (p. 23)

Although Ellis himself espouses atheistic values, a number of rational-emotive theorists and practitioners do subscribe to religious faiths (Hauck, 1972; Powell, 1976). RET is not against religion per se; rather, it opposes religiosity—a dogmatic and devout belief in faith by nature unfounded upon fact, which is deemed to lie at the heart of psychological disturbance (Ellis, 1983a). Indeed, RET shares with the philosophy of Christianity the view that we would do better to condemn the sin but forgive (or more accurately, accept) the sinner.

Finally, Ellis's ideas have been influenced by the work of the general semanticists (particularly Korzybski, 1933) who have argued that our psychological processes are to a great extent determined by our overgeneralizations and by the careless language we employ. Like Korzybski, Ellis holds that modification of the errors in our thinking and our language will have a marked effect on our emotions and actions.

While Ellis has claimed that the creation of RET owes more to the work of philosophers than to (pre-1955) psychologists, he was in fact influenced by the writings of a number of psychologists. Ellis was originally trained in psychoanalytic methods by a training analyst of the Karen Horney school; the influence of Horney's (1950) ideas on the "tyranny of the shoulds" is certainly apparent in the conceptual framework of RET. However, while Horney saw that this mode of thought had a profound impact on the development and maintenance of neurotic problems, she did not, as Ellis later did, emphasize the dogmatic and absolutistic nature of these cognitions. Furthermore, while Horney saw that these "shoulds" had a tyrannical effect on psychological disturbance, she did not take a vigorous and active stance in helping people to challenge and change them—an approach favored by RET therapists.

Ellis (1973) states that RET owes a unique debt to the ideas of Alfred Adler (1927), who held that a person's behavior springs from his or her ideas. Adler's concept of the important role played by feelings of inferiority in psychological disturbance predates Ellis's view that ego anxiety based on the concept of self-rating constitutes a fundamental human disturbance. As shown above, RET emphasizes the role of social interest in determining psychological health—a concept central to the philosophy of Adler (1964). Other Adlerian influences on RET are: the importance humans attribute to goals, purposes, values, and meanings; the emphasis on active–directive teaching; the employment of a cognitive–persuasive form of therapy; and the teaching method of holding live demonstrations of therapy sessions before an audience. However, RET differs from Adlerian therapy in that it gives more emphasis to the biological roots of human disturbance (Ellis, 1976a) and places less stress on the role of early childhood experience and birth-order factors in accounting for such disturbance. Furthermore, Adler did not discriminate among the various types of cognitions and did not mention the devout, absolutistic musts that are a central feature of the RET perspective on psychological disturbance. Finally, while Adler was some-what vague about advocating distinct therapeutic methods, and did not use behavioral technique, RET espouses many specific therapeutic techniques and methods and is notably both cognitive and behavioral (Dryden, 1984a).

When Ellis first gave presentations on what was at that time called 'Rational Psychotherapy' in the mid-1950s, he stressed the cognitive-philo-sophical aspects of the therapy to emphasize its differences with the psycho-analytic therapies. However, RET has always advocated the use of ac-tive-behavioral methods and, in this regard, Ellis has acknowledged the influence of some of the earliest pioneers of behavioral therapy (Dunlap, 1932; Jones, 1924; Watson & Rayner, 1920) on his ideas and therapeutic practice. Also, from its inception, RET has actively and systematically employed homework assignments to encourage clients to practice their newly acquired therapeutic insights in their own life situation. Ellis saw the importance of such assignments in his early work as a sex and marriage counselor (before creating RET), in overcoming his own early anxieties about approaching women and speaking in public, and from the pioneer-ing work of Herzberg (1945), who advocated the use of such assignments in his book *Active Psychotherapy*.

Students of the history of the development of psychotherapy will be interested to note that at the same time as Ellis was creating RET a number of other therapists, all working independently from each other, were devel-oping therapeutic systems that all had some cognitive-behavioral emphasis (Eric Berne, George Kelly, Abraham Low, E. Lakin Phillips, & Julian Rotter). Of these only RET is today recognized as a major form of CBT and as such is represented in the present handbook.

BASIC THEORY

In this section we shall begin by considering what image of the person is put forward by rational–emotive theory. We shall then outline the theory's perspective on (1) the nature of psychological health and disturbance; (2) the acquisition of psychological disturbance; and (3) how such disturbance is perpetuated. RET's theory of therapeutic change will then be examined, and we shall conclude this section by discussing how the RET theoretical model compares with those posited by other cognitive-behavioral therapies.

THE IMAGE OF THE PERSON

Rational–emotive theory conceives of the person as a complex, bio-social organism with a strong tendency to establish and pursue a wide variety of goals and purposes. While people differ enormously in *what* will bring them happiness, the fact that they do construct and pursue personally valued goals shows that they strive to bring a sense of meaning to their lives. Humans are thus seen as hedonistic in that their major goals appear to be to stay alive and to pursue happiness. In this respect they are further seen as having the related tasks of satisfying both their self-interests and their social interests. It is noted that humans normally do better at satisfying these twin interests by active rather than by passive pursuit.

The concept of *rationality* is central to an understanding of the rational–emotive image of the person. Here "rational" means that which aids and abets people achieving their basic goals and purposes. Although people are motivated by hedonistic concerns, they often experience a clash between short-range and long-range goals. RET theory holds that while people would do better to satisfy some of their short-range goals, if they are to achieve their basic goals and purposes, then they should adopt a philosophy of long-range hedonism. "Irrational," then, means that which hinders or obstructs people from achieving their basic (long-range) goals and purposes. It is thus apparent that rationality is not defined in any absolute sense in RET theory, since that which aids or hinders this goal achievement is defined dependent upon the individual in his or her own particular situation.

While RET theory does stress the role played by cognitive factors in human functioning, Ellis has from the beginnings of RET claimed that cognition, emotion, and behavior are not to be viewed as separate psychological processes but rather as processes that are highly interdependent and interactive. Thus, the statement "cognition leads to emotion" tends to accentuate a false picture of psychological separatism. In the famous *ABCs* of RET, *A* has traditionally stood for an *activating* event—or speaking strictly from a phenomenological point of view—the perception of the event; *B* for the way that perceived event is evaluated (i.e., a person's *beliefs*); and *C* for the emotional and behavioral *consequences* that stem from *B*. As stated, however, this model does not emphasize the interactive nature of the psychological processes contained within it (Ellis, 1985a). And yet, when humans adhere to a particular set of evaluative beliefs at *B*, this tends very much to influence the perceptions they make and the environments they seek out at *A*. While beliefs do affect emotion and behavior, it is equally true that the way we feel and act has a profound effect on our beliefs. Our emotional and behavioral reactions help to create environments and skew our perceptions of these environments, which in turn have a constraining effect on our emotional and behavioral repertoires (as in the "self-fulfilling prophecy" effect). Thus, it should be underscored that RET theory sees the person as having overlapping intrapsychic processes and as being in constant interaction with his or her social and material environment.

A model that emphasizes the interactive and interdependent nature of intrapsychic and interpersonal processes does not, however, have to take the position that all such processes have equal explanatory variance in accounting for human psychological disturbance. Indeed, RET has become renowned for the central role it has given to cognition in general and to evaluative beliefs in particular in its theory and practice. It is no accident, for example, that two of the major concepts in RET, rationality and beliefs, have been paired together. Rational–emotive therapists frequently talk about rational and irrational beliefs but far less frequently about rational and irrational emotions and behaviors.

When cognitive factors are considered from the vantage point of the rational–emotive view of the person, Ellis (1976a, 1979a) has stressed that humans have two major biological tendencies. First, they have a strong tendency to think irrationally. They appear, in particular, according to RET theory, to show great ease in converting their strong preferences into devout absolutistic demands. While Ellis (1984a) has acknowledged that there are social influences operating here, he has also noted that

even if everybody had had the most rational upbringing, virtually all humans would often irrationally escalate their individual and social preferences into absolutistic demands on (a) themselves, (b) other people, and (c) the universe around them. (p. 20)

Ellis (1976a, 1979a) has argued that the following constitutes evidence in favor of his hypothesis of the biological basis of human irrationality:

1. Virtually all humans, including bright and competent people, show evidence of major human irrationalities.

2. Virtually all the disturbance-creating irrationalities (absolutistic shoulds and musts) that are found in our society are also found in just about all social and cultural groups that have been studied historically and anthropologically.

3. Many of the irrational behaviors that we engage in, such as procrastination and lack of self-discipline, go counter to the teachings of parents, peers, and the mass media.

4. Humans—even bright and competent people—often adopt other irrationalities after giving up former ones.

5. People who vigorously oppose various kinds of irrational behaviors often fall prey to these very irrationalities. Atheists and agnostics exhibit zealous and absolutistic philosophies and highly religious individuals act immorally.

6. Insight into irrational thoughts and behaviors helps only partially to change them. For example, people can acknowledge that drinking alcohol in large quantities is harmful, yet this knowledge does not necessarily help them abstain from heavy drinking.

7. Humans often return to irrational habits and behavioral patterns even though they have often worked hard to overcome them.

8. People often find it easier to learn self-defeating than self-enhancing behaviors. Thus, people very easily overeat but have great trouble following a sensible diet.

9. Psychotherapists who should presumably be good role models of rationality often act irrationally in their personal and professional lives.

10. People frequently delude themselves into believing that certain bad experiences (e.g., divorce, stress, and other misfortunes) will not happen to them.

However, lest this evidence gives the impression that RET has a gloomy image of the person, it is important to state that RET theory stresses the existence of a second basic biological tendency. Here humans are seen as having both the ability to think about their thinking and the ability to exercise their power to choose to work towards changing their irrational thinking. Thus, people are by no means powerless slaves to their tendency towards irrational thinking; they can transcend (although not fully) its effects by deciding to actively and continually work towards changing this thinking by employing cognitive, emotive, and behavioral challenging or disputational methods. In the final analysis, then, the RET image of the person is quite an optimistic one.

The RET view is that the person is by nature fallible and most probably not perfectible. Humans "naturally" make errors and, as described above, often seem to defeat and obstruct themselves in the pursuit of their long-range goals. Therapeutically, they are thus encouraged to accept themselves as fallible and to challenge their self-created demands for perfection and the self-damnation that virtually always accompanies such demands (particularly when they are not met). RET emphasizes that the person is also an incredibly complex organism and one that is constantly in flux. As such, RET theory considers that humans have great potential to utilize the many opportunities they encounter to effect changes in the ways in which they think, feel, and act.

In summary, Figure 6.1 shows where rational–emotive theory stands on ten personality dimensions put forward by Corsini (1977). A unidirectional

Focus on explicit, observable behavior that can be counted and numbered	OBJECTIVE	→	SUBJECTIVE	Concern with the inner personal life of the individual – his ineffable self
Person seen as composed of parts, organs, units, elements put together to make the whole	ELEMENTARISTIC	→	HOLISTIC	The person is seen as having a certain unity and the parts as aspects of the total entity. The individual is seen as indivisible
Apersonal theories are impersonal, statistically based and consider generalities rather than individuals. They are based on group norms	APERSONAL	→	PERSONAL	Personal theories deal with the single individual. They are ideographic
Focus on the measurement of units of behavior	QUANTITATIVE	→	QUALITATIVE	Behavior is seen as too complex to be measured exactly
The individual is seen as a unit reactor, not a learner, filled with instincts and based on generalizations preestablished by heredity	STATIC	→	DYNAMIC	The individual is seen as a learner with interactions between behavior and consciousness and between consciousness and unconsciousness
The person is predominantly biologically based	ENDOGENISTIC	←	EXOGENISTIC	The person is predominantly influenced by social and environmental factors
The individual is seen as not responsible for his behavior as being the pawn of society, heredity or both	DETERMINISTIC	→	INDETERMINISTIC	The person is seen as basically under his own direction. Control is within the person and prediction is never completely possible
The individual is seen in terms of what he has inherited or learned in the past	PAST	PRESENT/FUTURE	FUTURE	The individual is seen as explained by his anticipations of future goals
The person is seen as operating on an emotional basis and with the intellect at the service of the emotions	AFFECTIVE	←	COGNITIVE	The person is seen as essentially rational with the emotions subserving the intellect
The individual is seen as rational and affected by factors within his awareness span	CONSCIOUS	←	UNCONSCIOUS	The person is seen as having considerable investment below the level of awareness

Figure 6.1. Rational-emotive therapy described on ten personality dimensions. Adapted from *Current Personality Theories* (p. 12) edited by R. J. Corsini, 1977, Itaska, IL: Peacock. Reproduced by permission of the publisher, F. E. Peacock, Publishers, Inc.

arrow (→ or ←) indicates the pole that is stressed in the theoretical underpinnings of RET. The sign ↔ indicates that the theory encompasses both poles of the dimension equally.

THE NATURE OF PSYCHOLOGICAL DISTURBANCE AND HEALTH

Rational-emotive theory posits that at the heart of psychological disturbance lies the tendency of humans to make devout, absolutistic evaluations of the perceived events in their lives. These evaluations are couched in the form of dogmatic "musts," "shoulds," "have to's," "got to's," and "oughts." Ellis (1983a) has argued that these absolutistic cognitions are at the core of a philosophy of a dogmatic religiosity that he claims to be the central feature of human emotional and behavioral disturbance. These beliefs are deemed to be irrational in RET theory in that they usually (but not invariably) impede and obstruct people in the pursuit of their basic goals and purposes. Absolute musts do not invariably lead to psychological disturbance because it is possible for a person to devoutly believe that he or she must succeed at all important projects, have confidence that he or she will be successful in these respects, and actually succeed in them and thereby not experience psychological disturbance. However, the person remains vulnerable in this respect because there is always the possibility that he or she may fail in the future. Thus, while on the grounds of probability RET theory argues that an absolutistic philosophy will frequently lead to such disturbance, it does not claim that this is absolutely so. In this way, even with respect to its view of the nature of human disturbance, RET adopts an anti-absolutistic position.

RET theory goes on to posit that if humans adhere to a philosophy of "musturbation," they will strongly tend to make a number of irrational conclusions that are deemed to be derivatives of these "musts." These derivatives are viewed as irrational because they too tend to sabotage a person's basic goals and purposes.

The first derivative is known as *awfulizing*. This occurs when an event is rated as being more than 100% bad—a truly exaggerated and magical conclusion that stems from the belief "This must not be as bad as it is."

The second derivative is known as *I-can't-stand-it-itis*. This means believing that one cannot experience virtually any happiness at all, under any conditions, if an event that must not happen actually occurs or threatens to occur.

The third derivative, known as *damnation* represents a tendency for humans to rate themselves and other people as sub-human or undeserving if the self or another does something that they "must" not do or fail to do something that they "must" do. Damnation can also be applied to the world or life conditions that are rated as being "rotten" for failing to give the person what he or she must have.

While Ellis (1984a) has argued that awfulizing, I-can't-stand-it-itis, and damnation are secondary irrational processes in that they stem from the philosophy of musts, these processes can sometimes be primary. Indeed, Wessler (1984) has argued that they are more likely to be primary and that musts are often derived from them. However, the philosophy of musts, on the one hand, and those of awfulizing, I-can't-stand-it-itis, and damnation on the other, are in all probability interdependent processes and often seem to be different sides of the same cognitive coin.

In summary, it is possible to discern two major categories of human psychological disturbance in RET theory: ego disturbance and discomfort disturbance (Ellis, 1979b, 1980a). In ego disturbance the person damns him- or herself as a result of making musturbatory demands on the self, others, and the world. In discomfort disturbance, the person again makes demands on the self, others, and the world but these demands reflect the belief that comfort and comfortable life conditions must exist.

Ellis (1984a, 1985) notes that humans also make numerous kinds of illogical assumptions when they are disturbed. In this respect RET agrees with cognitive therapists (Beck, Rush, Shaw, & Emery, 1979; Burns, 1980) that such cognitive distortions are a feature of psychological disturbance.

However, RET theory holds that such distortions almost always stem from the musts. Some of the most frequent of them are:

1. *All-or-none thinking*: "If I fail at any important task, as I *must* not, I'm a *total* failure and *completely* unlovable!"

2. *Jumping to conclusions and negative nonsequiturs*: "Since they have seen me dismally fail, as I *should* not have done, they will view me as an incompetent worm."

3. *Fortune telling*: "Because they are laughing at me for failing, they know that I *should* have succeeded, and they will despise me forever."

4. *Focusing on the negative*: "Because I *can't stand* things going wrong, as they *must* not, I can't see any good that is happening in my life."

5. *Disqualifying the positive*: "When they compliment me on the good things I have done, they are only being kind to me and forgetting the foolish things that I *should* not have done."

6. *Allness and neverness*: "Because conditions of living ought to be good and actually are so bad and so intolerable, they'll *always* be this way and I'll never have any happiness."

7. *Minimization*: "My accomplishments are the result of luck and are unimportant. But my mistakes, which I *should* never have made, are as bad as could be and are totally unforgivable."

8. *Emotional reasoning*: "Because I have performed so poorly, as I *should* not have done, I feel like a total nincompoop, and my strong feeling proves that I *am* no damned good!"

9. *Labeling and overgeneralization*: "Because I *must* not fail at important work and have done so, I am a complete loser and failure!"

10. *Personalizing*: "Since I am acting far worse than I *should* act and they are laughing, I am sure they are only laughing at me, and that is *awful!*"

11. *Phonyism*: "When I don't do as well as I *ought* to do and they still praise and accept me, I am a real phony and will soon fall on my face and show them how despicable I am!"

12. *Perfectionism*: "I realize that I did fairly well, but I *should* have done perfectly well on a task like this, and am therefore really an incompetent!"

Although RET clinicians at times discover all the illogicalities just listed—and a number of others that are less frequently found with clients—they particularly focus on the unconditional shoulds, oughts, and musts that seem to constitute the philosophic core of irrational beliefs that lead to emotional disturbance. RET clinicians hold that if they do not expose and help clients to relinquish these core beliefs, clients will most probably continue to hold them and to create new irrational derivatives from them.

RET practitioners also particularly look for awfulizing, for I-can't-stand-it-itis, and for damnation, showing clients how these almost invariably stem from their musts and can be relinquished if they give up their absolutistic demands on themselves, on other people, and on the universe. At the same time, rational-emotive therapists usually encourage their clients to have strong and persistent desires, wishes, and preferences, and to avoid feelings of detachment, withdrawal, and lack of involvement (Ellis, 1972a, 1973, 1984b, 1984c).

More importantly, RET holds that unrealistic and illogical beliefs do not *in themselves* create emotional disturbance. This is because it is quite possible for people to unrealistically believe that because they frequently fail, they always do (i.e., perceived failure), as well as it being possible for them also to believe illogically that because they have frequently failed, they always will (i.e., projected failure). But they can, in both these instances, rationally conclude, "Too bad! Even though I often fail, there is no reason why I *must* succeed. I would prefer to but I never *have to* do well. So I'll manage to be as happy as I can be even with my constantly failing." They would then rarely be emotionally disturbed.

To reiterate, the essence of human emotional disturbance, according to RET, consists of the absolutistic musts and must nots that people think *about* their failure, *about* their rejections, *about* their poor treatment by others, and *about* life's frustrations and losses. RET therefore differs from other cognitive-behavior therapists—such as those of Beck (1967, 1976), Bandura (1969, 1977), Goldfried & Davison (1976), Janis (1983), A. Lazarus (1981), R. Lazarus (1966), Mahoney (1977), Maultsby (1984), and Meichenbaum (1977)—in that it particularly stresses therapists looking for clients' dogmatic, unconditional musts, differentiating them from their preferences, and teaching them how to relinquish the former and retain the latter (Bard, 1980; Dryden, 1984a; Ellis, 1962, 1977c, 1984c, 1985a; Ellis & Becker, 1982; Ellis & Harper, 1975; Grieger & Boyd, 1980; Grieger & Grieger, 1982; Phadke, 1982; Walen, DiGiuseppe, & Wessler, 1980; Wessler & Wessler, 1980).

If the philosophy of musturbation is at the core of much psychological disturbance, then what philosophy is characteristic of psychological health? RET theory argues that a philosophy of relativism or "desiring" is a central feature of psychologically healthy humans. This philosophy acknowledges that humans have a large variety of desires, wishes, wants, preferences, and so on, but that if they refuse to escalate these nonabsolute values into grandiose dogmas and demands, they will not become psychologically disturbed. They will, however, experience appropriate negative emotions (e.g., sadness, regret, disappointment, annoyance) whenever their desires are not fulfilled. These emotions are considered to have constructive motivational properties in that they help people to both remove obstacles to goal attainment and make constructive adjustments when their desires cannot be met.

Three major derivatives of the philosophy of desiring are postulated by rational–emotive theory. They are deemed to be rational in that they tend to help people reach their goals or formulate new goals if their old ones cannot be realized.

The first derivative is known as rating or evaluating badness. Here, if a person does not get what he or she wants, he or she acknowledges that this is bad. However, because he or she does not believe "I have to get what I want," he or she holds his or her evaluation to a 0-100 continuum of badness and does not therefore rate this situation as "awful"—a rating that is placed on a nonsensical 101%-∞ (infinity) continuum. In general, when a person adheres to the desiring philosophy, the stronger his or her desire, the greater his or her rating of badness will be when he or she does not get what he or she wants.

The second derivative is known as tolerance and is the rational alternative to I-can't-stand-it-itis. Here the person (1) acknowledges that an undesirable event has happened (or may happen); (2) believes that the event should empirically occur if it does; (3) rates the event along the badness continuum; (4) attempts to change the undesired event or accepts the 'grim' reality if it cannot be modified; and (5) actively pursues other goals even though the situation cannot be altered.

The third derivative, known as acceptance is the rational alternative to damnation. Here the person accepts him- or herself and others as fallible human beings who do not have to act other than they do and as too complex and fluid to be given any legitimate or global rating. In addition, life conditions are accepted as they exist. People who have the philosophy of acceptance fully acknowledge that the world is highly complex and exists according to laws that are often outside their personal control. It is important to emphasize here that acceptance does not imply resignation. A rational philosophy of acceptance means that the person acknowledges that whatever exists empirically should exist but does not absolutely have to exist forever. This prompts the person to make active attempts to change reality. The person who is resigned to a situation usually does not attempt to modify it.

Rational-emotive theory argues that people can hold rational and irrational beliefs at the same time. Indeed, Ellis often refers to people *escalating* their desires into demands. Thus one may rationally believe "I want you to love me" and simultaneously (and irrationally) believe "Since I want you to love me, you must do so." Rational–emotive theory also makes unique distinctions between appropriate and inappropriate negative emotions. Appropriate negative emotions are deemed to be associated with rational beliefs and inappropriate negative emotions with irrational beliefs. In the following, the appropriate negative emotion is listed first:

1. *Concern versus Anxiety*. Concern is an emotion that is associated with the belief "I hope that this threat does not happen, but if it does, it

would be unfortunate." Anxiety occurs when the person believes "This threat must not happen and it would be awful if it does."

2. *Sadness versus Depression*. Sadness is deemed to occur when the person believes "It is very unfortunate that I have experienced this loss but there is no reason why it should not have happened." Depression, on the other hand, is associated with the belief "This loss should not have occurred and it is terrible that it did." In the latter case, when the person feels responsible for the loss, he or she will tend to damn themselves ("*I* am no good"), whereas if the loss is outside the person's control he or she will tend to damn the world/life conditions ("*It* is terrible"). As shown earlier, RET theory holds that it is the philosophy of musturbation implicit in such evaluations that leads people to consider that they will never get what they want—an inference that leads to feelings of hopelessness.

3. *Regret versus Guilt*. Feelings of regret or remorse occur when a person acknowledges that he or she has done something bad in public or private but accepts him- or herself as a fallible human person for doing so. The person feels badly about the act or deed but not about him- or herself because he or she holds the belief "I prefer not to act badly, but if I do, too bad!" Guilt occurs when the person damns him- or herself as bad, wicked or rotten for acting badly. Here, the person feels badly both about the act and about his or her "self" because he or she holds the belief: "I must not act badly, and if I do it's *awful* and I am a *rotten* person!"

4. *Disappointment versus Shame/Embarrassment*. Feelings of disappointment occur when a person acts "stupidly" in public and acknowledges the stupid act but accepts him- or herself in the process. The person feels disappointed about his or her action but not with him- or herself because he or she prefers but does not demand that he or she act well. Shame and embarrassment occur when the person again recognizes that he or she has acted stupidly in public and then condemns him- or herself for acting in a way that he or she should not have done. People who experience shame and embarrassment often predict that the watching audience will think badly of them, in which case they tend to agree with these perceived judgments. Thus, they often believe that they absolutely need the approval of these others. Shame can sometimes be distinguished from embarrassment in that the public "pratfall" is regarded as more serious by the person who feels ashamed than by the person who feels embarrassed. However, both emotions involve self-denigration.

5. *Annoyance versus Anger*. Annoyance occurs when another person disregards an individual's rule of living. The annoyed person does not like what the other has done but does not damn him or her for doing it. Such a person tends to believe "I wish the other person did not do that and I don't like what he or she did, but it does not follow that he or she must not break my own rule of conduct." In anger, however, the person does believe that

the other absolutely must not break this rule and thus damns the other for doing so (Ellis, 1977c).

It should be noted that rational–emotive therapists do not target appropriate negative emotions for change during therapy since they are deemed to be consequences of rational thinking.

If ego disturbance and discomfort disturbance are cornerstones of the rational–emotive view of human psychological problems, self-acceptance and a high level of discomfort tolerance are the two cornerstones of psychological health and are implicit in a philosophy of nondevout desire. Ellis (1979a) has outlined nine other criteria of positive mental health: (1) enlightened self-interest; (2) social interest; (3) self-direction; (4) acceptance of ambiguity and uncertainty; (5) scientific thinking; (6) commitment and being vitally absorbed in important projects; (7) flexibility; (8) calculated risk taking; and (9) acceptance of reality.

ACQUISITION AND PERPETUATION OF PSYCHOLOGICAL DISTURBANCE

Rational–emotive theory does not put forward an elaborate view concerning the acquisition of psychological disturbance. This partly follows from Ellis's (1976a) hypothesis that humans have a distinct biological tendency to think and act irrationally, but it also reflects the RET viewpoint that theories of acquisition do not necessarily suggest therapeutic interventions. While Ellis argues that humans' tendencies towards irrational thinking are biologically rooted, he does acknowledge that environmental variables contribute to psychological disturbance and thus encourage people to make their biologically based demands (Ellis, 1979a). Thus, Ellis (1984c) has said "parents and culture usually teach children which superstitions, taboos and prejudices to abide by, but they do not originate their basic tendency to superstitiousness, ritualism and bigotry" (p. 209).

Rational–emotive theory also posits that humans vary in their disturbability. Some people emerge relatively unscathed psychologically from being raised by uncaring or overprotective parents, while others emerge emotionally damaged from more "healthy" childrearing approaches (Werner & Smith, 1982). In this respect, Ellis (1984c) claims that "individuals with serious aberrations are more innately predisposed to have rigid and crooked thinking than those with lesser aberrations, and consequently they are likely to make lesser advances" (p. 223). Thus, the RET theory of acquisition can be summed up in the view that as humans we are not made disturbed simply by our experiences; rather we bring our ability to disturb ourselves to our experiences.

While rational–emotive theory does not put forward an elaborate view to explain the acquisition of psychological disturbance, it does deal more extensively with how such disturbance is perpetuated. First, people tend to maintain their psychological problems by their own "naive" theories concerning the nature of these problems and to what they can be attributed. They lack what Ellis (1979a) calls "RET Insight Number 1": that psychological disturbance is primarily determined by the absolutistic beliefs that people hold about negative life events (B determines C). Rather they consider that their disturbances are caused by these situations (A causes C). Since people make incorrect hypotheses about the major determinants of their problems, they consequently attempt to change A rather than B. Second, people may have Insight Number 1 but lack "RET Insight Number 2": that people remain disturbed by reindoctrinating themselves *in the present* with their absolutistic beliefs. While they may see that their problems are determined by their beliefs, they may distract themselves and thus perpetuate their problems by searching for the historical antecedents of these beliefs instead of directing themselves to change them as currently held. Third, people may have Insight Numbers 1 and 2 but still sustain their disturbance because they lack "RET Insight Number 3": only if people diligently work and practice in the present as well as in the future to think, feel, and act against their irrational beliefs are they likely to change them and make themselves significantly less disturbed. People who have all three insights clearly see that they would do better to persistently and strongly challenge their beliefs cognitively, emotively, and behaviorally to break the perpetuation of the disturbance cycle. Merely acknowledging that a belief is irrational is usually insufficient to effect change.

Ellis (1979a) has argued that the major reason why people perpetuate their psychological problems is because they adhere to a philosophy of low frustration tolerance (LFT). Such people believe that they must be comfortable, and thus do not work to effect change because such work involves experiencing discomfort. They are short-range hedonists in that they are motivated to avoid short-term discomfort, even though accepting and working against their temporary uncomfortable feelings would probably help them to reach their long-range goals. Such people rate cognitive and behavioral therapeutic tasks as "too painful," and as even more painful than the psychological disturbance for which they have achieved some measure of tolerance. They prefer to remain with their "comfortable" discomfort rather than face the change-related discomfort that they believe they must not experience. Maultsby (1975) has argued that people often back away from change because they are afraid that they will not feel right about it. He calls this the "neurotic fear of feeling a phony" and actively shows clients that these feelings of "unnaturalness" are natural concomitants of relearning. Another prevalent form of LFT is anxiety about anxiety. In this case, individuals believe that they must not be anxious and thus do not expose themselves to anxiety-provoking situations because they are anxious that they might become anxious if they did so—an experience they would rate as "awful." As such, they perpetuate their problems and overly restrict their lives to avoid experiencing anxiety.

Anxiety about anxiety constitutes an example of the clinical fact that people often make themselves disturbed about their disturbances. Having created secondary (and sometimes tertiary) disturbances about their original disturbance, they become preoccupied with these problems about problems and thus find it difficult to get back to solving the original problem. Humans are often very inventive in this respect. They can make themselves depressed about their depression, guilty about being angry, anxious about their anxiety, and so on. Consequently, people often need to tackle their disturbances about their disturbances before they can successfully solve their original problems.

RET theory endorses the Freudian view of human defensiveness in explaining how people perpetuate their psychological problems (Freud, 1937). Thus, people maintain their problems by employing various defense mechanisms (e.g., rationalization, avoidance) that are designed to help deny the existence of these problems or to minimize their severity. The RET view is that these defenses are used to ward off self-damnation tendencies and that under such circumstances, if these people were to honestly take responsibility for their problems they would severely denigrate themselves for having them. In addition, these defense mechanisms are employed to ward off discomfort anxiety, since if, again, such people admitted their problems they would rate them as "too hard to bear" or "too difficult to overcome."

Ellis (1979a) has noted that people sometimes experience a form of perceived payoff for their psychological problems other than the avoidance of discomfort. The existence of these payoffs serves to perpetuate the problems. Thus, a woman who claims to want to overcome her procrastination may avoid tackling the problem because she is afraid that should she become successful she might then be criticized by others as being "too masculine," a situation she would evaluate as "awful." Her procrastination serves to protect her (in her mind) from this "terrible" state of affairs. Dryden (1984b) has noted that "rational–emotive therapists stress the phenomenological nature of these payoffs, i.e. it is the person's view of the payoff that it is important in determining its impact, not the events delineated in the person's description" (p. 244).

Finally, the well-documented "self-fulfilling prophecy" phenomenon helps to explain why people perpetuate their psychological problems (Jones, 1977; Wachtel, 1977). Here, people act according to their evaluations and consequent predictions and thus often elicit from themselves or from others responses that they then interpret in a manner that confirms their initial hypotheses. Thus, a socially anxious man may believe that other people would not want to get to know "so worthless an individual as I truly am." He then attends a social function and acts as if he were worthless, avoiding eye contact and keeping away from others. Unsurprisingly, such social behaviour does not invite approaches from others, a lack of response that he interprets thus: "You see, I was right; other people don't want to know me. I really am no good."

In conclusion, RET theory holds that people "naturally tend to perpetuate their problems and have a strong innate tendency to cling to self-defeating, habitual patterns and thereby resist basic change. Helping clients change, then, poses quite a challenge for RET practitioners" (Dryden, 1984b, pp. 244-245).

THEORY OF THERAPEUTIC CHANGE

In the section "Image of the Person," we argued that the rational-emotive view of the person is basically an optimistic one, since although it posits that humans have a distinct biological tendency to think irrationally, it also holds that they have the capacity to choose to work towards changing this irrational thinking and its self-defeating effects.

There are various different levels of change. Rational-emotive theory holds that the most elegant and long-lasting changes that humans can effect are ones that involve the philosophical restructuring of irrational beliefs. Change at this level can be specific or general. Specific philosophical change means that individuals change their irrational absolutistic demands (musts, shoulds) about given situations to rational relative preferences. General philosophic change involves people adopting a nondevout attitude towards life events in general. Ellis has distinguished between superelegant and semielegant philosophical change at the general level. Discussing these changes Ellis has said:

By superelegant I mean that practically under all conditions for the rest of their life they would not upset themselves about anything. Very few will ever do this because it is against the human condition and people fall back to *must*urbating and thereby disturbing themselves. Some will effect a semielegant solution, meaning that in most instances they will call up a new rational-emotive philosophy that will enable them to feel sad or annoyed but not anxious, depressed, or angry when poor conditions occur. (in Weinrach, 1980, p. 156)

To effect a philosphical change at either the specific or general level, people need to do the following:

1. First, realize that they create, to a large degree, their own psychological disturbances, and that while environmental conditions can contribute to their problems, they are in general of secondary consideration in the change process.

2. Fully recognise that they do have the ability to significantly change these disturbances.

3. Understand that emotional and behavioral disturbances stem largely from irrational, absolutistic dogmatic beliefs.

4. Detect their irrational beliefs and discriminate between them and their rational alternatives.

5. Dispute these irrational beliefs using the logico-empirical methods of science.

6. Work towards the internalization of their new rational beliefs by employing cognitive, emotive, and behavioral methods of change.

7. Continue this process of challenging irrational beliefs and using multimodal methods of change for the rest of their lives.

When people effect a philosophic change at B in the ABC model, they often are able to correct spontaneously their distorted inferences of reality (overgeneralizations, faulty attributions, etc.)—which can be viewed as A cognitions (Wessler & Wessler, 1980). However, they often need to challenge these distorted inferences more directly, as RET has always emphasized (Ellis, 1962, 1971a, 1973; Ellis & Harper, 1961a, 1961b) and as Beck (Beck et al., 1979) has also stressed.

While rational–emotive theory argues that irrational beliefs are the breeding ground for the development and maintenance of inferential distortions, it is possible for people to effect inferentially based changes without making a profound philosophic change. Thus, they may regard their inferences as hunches about reality rather than facts, may generate alternative hypotheses and may seek evidence and/or carry out experiments that test out each hypothesis. They may then accept the hypothesis that represents the "best bet" of those available. Consider a man who thinks that his co-workers view him as a fool. To test this hypothesis he may first specify their negative reactions to him. These constitute the data from which he quickly draws the conclusion "They think I'm a fool." He could then realize that what he has interpreted to be negative responses to him may not be negative. If they seem to be negative, he could then carry out an experiment to test out the meaning he attributes to their responses. Thus he could enlist the help of a colleague whom he trusts to carry out a "secret ballot" of others' opinions of him. Or, he could test his hunch more explicitly by directly asking them for their view of him. As a result of these strategies, this person may conclude that his co-workers find some of his actions foolish rather than considering him to be a complete fool. His mood may lift because his inference of A (i.e., the situation) has changed, but he may still believe at B "If others think I'm a fool, they're right I am a fool—and that would be awful." Thus, he has made an inferential change but not a philosophical one. If this person were to attempt to make a philosophical change he would *first* assume that his inference were true, than address himself to his evaluations about this inference and hence challenge these if they were discovered to be irrational. Thus he might conclude, "Even if I act foolishly, that makes me a person with foolish behavior, not a foolish person. And even if they deem me a total idiot, that is simply *their* view, with which I can choose to disagree."

Rational-emotive therapists hypothesize that people are more likely to make a profound philosophical change if they first assume that their inferences are true and then challenge their irrational beliefs, rather than if they first correct their inferential distortions and then challenge their underlying irrational beliefs. However, this hypothesis awaits full empirical enquiry.

People can also make direct changes of the situation at A. Thus, in the example quoted above, the man could leave his job or distract himself from the reactions of his colleagues by taking on extra work and devoting himself to it. Or he may carry out relaxation exercises whenever he comes in contact with his co-workers and thus distract himself once again from their perceived reactions. Additionally, the man may have a word with his supervisor, who may then instruct the other workers to change their behavior towards the man.

When we use this model to consider behavioral change, it is apparent that a person can change his or her behavior to effect inferential and/or philosophical change. Thus, again using the above example, a man whose co-workers view him as a fool might change his own behavior towards them and thus elicit a different set of responses from them, which would lead him to reinterpret his previous inference, (i.e., behavior change to effect inferential change). However, if it could be determined that they did indeed consider him to be a fool, then the man could actively seek them out and show himself that he could stand the situation and that just because they think him a fool doesn't make him one, thus learning to accept himself in the face of their views while exposing himself to their negative reactions (i.e., behavior change to effect philosophical change).

While rational-emotive therapists prefer to help their clients make profound philosophical changes at B, they do not dogmatically insist that their clients make such changes. If it becomes apparent that clients are not able at any given time to change their irrational beliefs, then RET therapists would endeavor to help them either to change A directly (by avoiding the troublesome situation, or by behaving differently) or to change their distorted inferences about the situation.

DIFFERENCES WITH OTHER COGNITIVE-BEHAVIORAL THERAPIES[1] (SPECIALIZED RET VERSUS GENERAL RET)

Ellis (1980b) has distinguished between specialized RET and general RET. He argues that general RET is synonymous with broad-based cognitive-

1. We have chosen here to focus on the distinctiveness of specialized RET as compared with other cognitive-behavioral therapies. Other theorists have outlined the differences between RET and other specific schools of CBT. Thus Wessler and Wessler (1980) have outlined the differences between RET and Maultsby's Rational Behavior Therapy and Dryden (1984a) has compared and contrasted RET with Beck's Cognitive Therapy.

behavior therapy (CBT). He further argues that specialized RET differs from CBT in a number of important respects:

1. RET has a distinct philosophical emphasis that is one of its central features and that other forms of CBT appear to omit. Thus it stresses that humans appraise themselves, others, and the world in terms of (1) rational, preferential, flexible, and tolerant philosophies and in terms of (2) irrational, musturbatory, rigid, intolerant, and absolutistic philosophies.

2. RET has an existential–humanistic outlook that is intrinsic to it and that is omitted by most other CBT approaches. Thus it sees people "as holistic, goal-directed individuals who have importance in the world just because they are human and alive; it unconditionally accepts them with their limitations, and it particularly focuses upon their experiences and values, including their self-actualizing potentialities" (Ellis, 1980b, p. 327). It also shares the views of ethical humanism by encouraging people to emphasize human interest (self and social) over the interests of deities, material objects, and lower animals.

3. RET favors striving for pervasive and long-lasting (philosophically based) rather than symptomatic change.

4. It attempts to help humans eliminate all self-ratings and views self-esteem as a self-defeating concept that encourages them to make conditional evaluations of self. Instead, it teaches people *un*conditional self-acceptance (Ellis, 1972b, 1976b, 1983b).

5. It sees psychological disturbance as resulting in part from taking life too seriously and thus advocates the appropriate use of various humorous therapeutic methods (Ellis, 1977a, 1977b, 1981b).

6. RET stresses the use of antimusturbatory rather than antiempirical disputing methods. Since it considers that inferential distortions often stem from dogmatic musts, shoulds, and so on, specialized RET favors going to the philosophic core of emotional disturbance and disputing the irrational beliefs at this core rather than merely disputing antiempirical inferences which are more peripheral. Also, specialized RET favors the use of forceful logico-empirical disputing of irrational beliefs rather than only stressing the employment of rationally oriented, coping self-statements whenever possible. When feasible, RET teaches clients how to become their own scientists instead of parroting therapist-inculcated rational beliefs.

7. It employs but only mildly encourages the use of palliative cognitive methods that serve to distract people from their disturbed philosophies (e.g., relaxation methods). Specialized RET holds that such techniques may help clients better in the short-term, but do not encourage them to identify challenge and change the devout philosophies that underpin their psychological problems in the long-term. Indeed, these palliative methods may make it harder for people to engage in philosophical disputing since they may be less likely to do this when they are calm and relaxed than when they

are motivated by their emotional distress. For these reasons, RET also employs problem-solving and skill training methods, along with, but not instead of, teaching people to work at understanding and changing their irrational beliefs.

8. RET gives a more central explanatory role to the concept of discomfort anxiety in psychological disturbance than do other cognitive-behavioral therapies. Discomfort anxiety is defined as "emotional hypertension that arises when people feel (1) that their life or comfort is threatened, (2) that they must not feel uncomfortable and have to feel at ease and (3) that it is awful or catastrophic (rather than merely inconvenient or disadvantageous) when they don't get what they supposedly must" (Ellis, 1980b, p. 331). While other cognitive-behavioral therapies recognize specific instances of discomfort anxieties (e.g., "fear of fear"—Mackay, 1984), they tend not to regard discomfort disturbance to be as centrally implicated in psychological problems as does specialized RET.

9. RET emphasizes more than other approaches to CBT that humans frequently make themselves disturbed about their original disturbances. Thus in specialized RET, therapists actively look for secondary and tertiary symptoms of disturbances and encourage clients to work on overcoming these before addressing themselves to the primary disturbance.

10. RET, as this chapter shows, has clearcut theories of disturbance and its treatment, but is eclectic or multimodal in its techniques (see the section on therapeutic techniques). However, it favors some techniques (e.g., active disputing) over others (e.g., cognitive distraction) and strives for profound or elegant philosophical change where feasible.

11. It discriminates between appropriate and inappropriate negative emotions. Specialized RET considers such negative emotions as sadness, annoyance, concern, regret, and disappointment as appropriate affective responses to thwarted desires based on a nondevout philosophy of desire and it views them as healthy when they do not needlessly interfere with people's goals and purposes. However, it sees depression, anger, anxiety, guilt, shame/embarrassment, self-pity, and feelings of inadequacy usually as inappropriate emotions based on absolutistic demands about thwarted desires. RET considers these latter feelings as symptoms of disturbance because they very frequently (but not always) sabotage people's attempts to pursue constructively their goals and purposes. Other CBT approaches do not make such fine discriminations between appropriate and inappropriate negative emotions.

12. RET advocates therapists giving unconditional acceptance rather than giving warmth or approval to clients. Other cognitive-behavioral therapies tend not to make this distinction. Specialized RET holds that therapist warmth and approval have their distinct dangers in that they may unwittingly encourage clients to strengthen their dire needs for love and approval. When RET therapists unconditionally accept their clients they

also serve as good role models, in that they also help clients to accept themselves unconditionally.

13. RET stresses the importance of the use of vigor and force in counteracting irrational philosophies and behaviors (Dryden, 1984a; Ellis, 1979d). Specialized RET is alone among the cognitive-behavioral therapies in stressing that humans are, for the most part, biologically predisposed to originate and perpetuate their disturbances and thus often experience great difficulty in changing the ideological roots of these problems. Since it holds this view it urges both therapists and clients to use considerable force and vigor in interrupting clients' irrationalities.

14. RET is more selective than most other cognitive-behavioral therapies in choosing behavioral change methods. Thus, it sometimes favors the use of penalization in encouraging resistant clients to change. Often these clients won't change to obtain positive reinforcements, but may be encouraged to change to avoid stiff penalties, such as burning a hundred dollar bill when they fail to stop smoking or fail to come to work on time. Furthermore, specialized RET has reservations concerning the use of social reinforcement in therapy. It considers that humans are too reinforceable and that they often do the right thing for the wrong reason. Thus, they may change to please their socially reinforcing therapists but in doing so they have not been encouraged to think and act for their own sake. Specialized RET therapists aim to help clients become maximally nonconformist, non-dependent, and individualistic and would thus use social reinforcement techniques sparingly. Finally, specialized RET favors the use of *in vivo* desensitization and flooding methods rather than the use of gradual desensitization techniques since it argues that the former procedures best help clients to raise their level of frustration tolerance (Ellis, 1962, 1983c).

While RET therapists *prefer* to use specialized RET wherever feasible, they do not dogmatically insist that it be employed. When, on pragmatic grounds, they employ general RET, their therapeutic practice is frequently indistinguishable from that of other cognitive-behavioral therapists.

CLINICAL APPLICATIONS

In this section, we shall discuss the major clinical applications of RET. First, we shall use the therapeutic modality of individual therapy to consider (1) the therapeutic bonds that RET therapists endeavor to establish with their clients, (2) the clinical process of RET from inception to termination, and (3) the major therapeutic techniques that are employed in RET. Second, we shall outline the application of RET to a case of anxiety and a case of depression. Finally, we shall consider the other major clinical applications of RET.

INDIVIDUAL THERAPY

Therapeutic Bonds

Many psychotherapy systems regard the therapeutic relationship as the major vehicle of change in effective therapy. RET considers that the establishment of effective therapeutic bonds between clients and therapists to be an important ingredient but not a necessary component of successful therapy. Ellis (1979c) has argued that effective RET is best done in a highly active-directive manner, although he has also acknowledged that it can be successfully practiced using a more passive therapeutic style (Ellis, 1984a). Since the major goals of RET therapists are to teach clients to think more rationally and ultimately to help them to use its methods for themselves, they see themselves as educators and thus strive to establish the most appropriate learning climate for each client.

Given the major goals of RET, RET therapists strive to unconditionally accept their clients as fallible human beings who cannot be given a legitimate global rating. Therapists acknowledge that their clients often act self-defeatingly, but no matter how badly clients behave inside or outside therapy, therapists show their clients that they accept them but do not necessarily go along with their negative behaviors. In RET theory, acceptance is distinguished from warmth. Most RET therapists do not interact with their clients in a very warm fashion for two main reasons. First, undue therapist warmth may lead to the entrenchment of clients' needs for love and approval—two qualities irrationally believed to be necessary for happiness, a belief at the core of much human disturbance. Clients of warm therapists may appear to improve and certainly feel better because they come to believe that they must be worthy since their therapists like them. However, their self-acceptance is still dependent upon outside approval, and they may never have the opportunity to challenge this philosophy of conditional self-acceptance with their warm, loving therapists who may themselves have dire needs for their clients' approval. Second, undue therapist warmth may reinforce clients' philosophies of low frustration tolerance (LFT). Such warmth may certainly help clients to become more comfortable in therapy sessions, but they may get hooked on and remain in such therapy instead of taking risks in their outside lives and forcing themselves to seek out uncomfortable experiences in order to make themselves comfortable later (Ellis, 1982a). However, there may be occasions (e.g., with severely depressed clients) when therapist warmth is appropriate for a restricted period of time, and since RET therapists are not dogmatically against interacting warmly with their clients they may do so under such conditions.

Most RET therapists tend to interact in an open manner with their clients and do not hesitate to give personal information about themselves if clients ask for it, except when it is judged that clients may use such information against themselves. RET therapists often disclose to their clients the fact that they have experienced similar problems and how they solved these problems using RET. They thus serve as good role models for their clients, as well as inspiring their clients with the hope that it is possible to overcome emotional and behavioral problems.

RET therapists would agree with Carl Rogers (1957) concerning the importance of therapist empathy in helping clients. However, RET therapists would not only offer their clients affective empathy (i.e., showing their clients that they know how they feel), but also offer them philosophical empathy (i.e., showing their clients that they understand the underlying philosophies upon which their emotions are based).

RET therapists often favor an informal style of interacting with their clients. They tend to employ a good deal of humor when appropriate because, as mentioned earlier, they believe that emotional disturbance can be viewed as a result of taking things too seriously. Thus, they hypothesize that their humorous style will loosen up their clients and encourage them to stand back and laugh at their dysfunctional thinking and behavior, but not at themselves. This latter point is in keeping with the rational–emotive perspective of the self as composed of a myriad of different ever-changing aspects rather than as one rateable whole. Consequently, RET therapists direct their own humor at aspects of the client's dysfunctioning and not at the client as a person. Indeed, RET therapists often direct their humor against some of their own irrationalities and by so doing show that they do not take themselves too seriously (Ellis, 1983b).

Although RET therapists tend to favor an informal, humorous active-directive style of therapeutic participation, they are flexible in this respect and are mindful of the important question, "Which therapeutic style is most effective with which kind of client?" (Eschenroeder, 1979, p. 5). Thus, some clients learn better if their therapists assume a more formal, serious, and less self-disclosing style. In this case, RET therapists would not hesitate to emphasize these aspects of themselves for therapeutic purposes. The issue of appropriate therapeutic styles in RET warrants more formal research. Drawing upon suggestions by Beutler (1983), Dryden and Ellis (1986) have argued in this respect that:

It may be best for RET therapists to avoid (a) an overly friendly, emotionally charged style of interaction with "hysterical" clients; (b) an overly intellectual style with "obsessive-compulsive" clients; (c) an overly directive style with clients whose sense of autonomy is easily threatened; and (d) an overly active style with clients who easily retreat into passivity. This line of reasoning fits well with the notion of flexibility which rational-emotive therapists advocate as a desirable therapeutic quality. Varying one's therapeutic style in RET, however, does not mean departing from the theoretical principles on which the content of therapy is based. (p. 145)

Therapeutic Process[2]

When clients seek help from rational-emotive therapists they vary concerning how much they already know about the type of therapeutic process they are likely to encounter. Some may approach the therapist because they know he or she is a practitioner of RET, while others may know nothing about this therapeutic method. In any event, it is often beneficial to explore clients' expectations for therapy at the outset of the process. Duckro, Beal, and George (1979) have argued that it is important to distinguish between preferences and anticipations when expectations are assessed. Clients' preferences for therapy concern what kind of experience they want, while anticipations concern what service they think they will receive. Clients who have realistic anticipations for the RET therapeutic process and have a preference for this process in general require far less induction into rational-emotive therapy than clients who have unrealistic anticipations of the process and/or preferences for a different type of therapeutic experience.

Induction procedures generally involve showing clients that RET is an active-directive structured therapy oriented to discussion about clients' present and future problems, and one that requires clients to play an active role in the change process. Induction can take a number of different forms. First, therapists may develop and use a number of pre-therapy role induction procedures in which a typical course of RET is outlined and productive client behaviors demonstrated (McCaskill & McCaskill, 1983). Second, therapists may give a short lecture at the outset of therapy concerning the nature and process of rational-emotive therapy. Third, therapists may employ induction-related explanations in the initial therapy sessions, using client problem material to illustrate how these problems may be tackled in RET and to outline the respective roles of client and therapist.

The next stage of therapy concerns assessment. RET therapists in general spend little time gathering background information on their clients, although they may ask them to fill out forms designed to assess which irrational ideas they spontaneously endorse at the outset of therapy (see Figure 6.2). Rather they are likely to ask clients for a description of their major problem(s). As clients describe their problem(s), RET therapists intervene fairly early to break these down into their *ABC* components. If clients begin by describing *A* (the perceived event), then the therapists ask for *C* (their emotional and/or behavioral reactions). However, if clients begin by outlining *C*, therapists ask for a brief description of *A*.

When *A* is assessed, some rational-emotive therapists prefer to fully assess the client's inferences in search of the most relevant inference that the

2. In this section we will focus primarily on the process of specialized RET. When general RET is employed, the process of therapy is almost indistinguishable from the process of other systems of CBT covered in this handbook.

Institute for Rational - Emotive Therapy

45 East 65th Street   New York, N. Y. 10021

Personality Data Form

Instructions: Read each of the following items and circle after each one the word STRONGLY, MODERATELY or WEAKLY to indicate how much you believe in the statement described in the item. Thus, if you strongly believe that it is awful to make a mistake when people are watching, circle the word STRONGLY in item 1; and if you weakly believe that it is intolerable to be disapproved by others circle the word WEAKLY in item 2. DO NOT SKIP ANY ITEMS. Be as honest as you possibly can be.

Acceptance

1.   I believe that it is awful to make a mistake when other people are watching   STRONGLY   MODERATELY   WEAKLY
2.   I believe that it is intolerable to be disapproved of by others   STRONGLY   MODERATELY   WEAKLY
3.   I believe that it is awful for people to know certain undesirable things about one's family or one's background   STRONGLY   MODERATELY   WEAKLY
4.   I believe that it is shameful to be looked down upon by people for having less than they have   STRONGLY   MODERATELY   WEAKLY
5.   I believe that it is horrible to be the center of attention of others who may be highly critical   STRONGLY   MODERATELY   WEAKLY
6.   I believe it is terribly painful when one is criticized by a person one respects   STRONGLY   MODERATELY   WEAKLY
7.   I believe that it is awful to have people disapprove of the way one looks or dresses   STRONGLY   MODERATELY   WEAKLY
8.   I believe that it is very embarrassing if people discover what one really is like   STRONGLY   MODERATELY   WEAKLY
9.   I believe that it is awful to be alone   STRONGLY   MODERATELY   WEAKLY
10.   I believe that it is horrible if one does not have the love or approval of certain special people who are important to me   STRONGLY   MODERATELY   WEAKLY
11.   I believe that one must have others on whom one can always depend for help   STRONGLY   MODERATELY   WEAKLY

Frustration

12.   I believe that it is intolerable to have things go along slowly and not be settled quickly   STRONGLY   MODERATELY   WEAKLY
13.   I believe that it is too hard to get down to work at things it often would be better for one to do   STRONGLY   MODERATELY   WEAKLY
14.   I believe that it is terrible that life is so full of inconveniences and frustrations   STRONGLY   MODERATELY   WEAKLY
15.   I believe that people who keep one waiting frequently are pretty worthless and deserve to be boycotted   STRONGLY   MODERATELY   WEAKLY
16.   I believe that it is terrible if one lacks desirable traits that other people possess   STRONGLY   MODERATELY   WEAKLY
17.   I believe that it is intolerable when other people do not do one's bidding or give one what one wants   STRONGLY   MODERATELY   WEAKLY
18.   I believe that some people are unbearably stupid or nasty and that one must get them to change   STRONGLY   MODERATELY   WEAKLY
19.   I believe that it is too hard for one to accept serious responsibility   STRONGLY   MODERATELY   WEAKLY
20.   I believe that it is dreadful that one cannot get what one wants without making a real effort to get it   STRONGLY   MODERATELY   WEAKLY
21.   I believe that things are too rough in this world and that therefore it is legitimate for one to feel sorry for oneself   STRONGLY   MODERATELY   WEAKLY
22.   I believe that it is too hard to persist at many of the things one starts, especially when the going gets rough   STRONGLY   MODERATELY   WEAKLY
23.   I believe that it is terrible that life is so unexciting and boring   STRONGLY   MODERATELY   WEAKLY
24.   I believe that it is awful for one to have to discipline oneself   STRONGLY   MODERATELY   WEAKLY

Injustice

25.   I believe that people who do wrong things should suffer strong revenge for their acts   STRONGLY   MODERATELY   WEAKLY
26.   I believe that wrong doers and immoral people should be severely condemned   STRONGLY   MODERATELY   WEAKLY
27.   I believe that people who commit unjust acts are bastards and that they should be severely punished   STRONGLY   MODERATELY   WEAKLY

Achievement

28. I believe that it is horrible for one to perform poorly   STRONGLY   MODERATELY   WEAKLY
29. I believe that it is awful if one fails at important things   STRONGLY   MODERATELY   WEAKLY
30. I believe that it is terrible for one to make a mistake when one has to
     make important decisions   STRONGLY   MODERATELY   WEAKLY
31. I believe that it is terrifying for one to take risks or to try new things   STRONGLY   MODERATELY   WEAKLY

Worth

32. I believe that some of one's thoughts or actions are unforgivable   STRONGLY   MODERATELY   WEAKLY
33. I believe that if one keeps failing at things one is a pretty worthless person   STRONGLY   MODERATELY   WEAKLY
34. I believe that killing oneself is preferable to a miserable life of failure   STRONGLY   MODERATELY   WEAKLY
35. I believe that things are so ghastly that one cannot help feel like crying much
     of the time   STRONGLY   MODERATELY   WEAKLY
36. I believe that it is frightfully hard for one to stand up for oneself and not
     give in too easily to others   STRONGLY   MODERATELY   WEAKLY
37. I believe that when one has shown poor personality traits for a long time,
     it is hopeless for one to change   STRONGLY   MODERATELY   WEAKLY
38. I believe that if one does not usually see things clearly and act well on them
     one is hopelessly stupid   STRONGLY   MODERATELY   WEAKLY
39. I believe that it is awful to have no good meaning or purpose in life   STRONGLY   MODERATELY   WEAKLY

Control

40. I believe that one cannot enjoy himself today because of his early life   STRONGLY   MODERATELY   WEAKLY
41. I believe that if one kept failing at important things in the past, one must
     inevitably keep failing in the future   STRONGLY   MODERATELY   WEAKLY
42. I believe that once one's parents train one to act and feel in certain ways,
     there is little one can do to act or feel better   STRONGLY   MODERATELY   WEAKLY
43. I believe that strong emotions like anxiety and rage are caused by external
     conditions and events and that one has little or no control over them   STRONGLY   MODERATELY   WEAKLY

Certainty

44. I believe it would be terrible if there were no higher being or purpose on which
     to rely   STRONGLY   MODERATELY   WEAKLY
45. I believe that if one does not keep doing certain things over and over again
     something bad will happen if I stop   STRONGLY   MODERATELY   WEAKLY
46. I believe that things must be in good order for one to be comfortable   STRONGLY   MODERATELY   WEAKLY

Catastrophizing

47. I believe that it is awful if one's future is not guaranteed   STRONGLY   MODERATELY   WEAKLY
48. I believe that it is frightening that there are no guarantees that accidents and
     serious illnesses will not occur   STRONGLY   MODERATELY   WEAKLY
49. I believe that it is terrifying for one to go to new places or meet a new group
     of people   STRONGLY   MODERATELY   WEAKLY
50. I believe that it is ghastly for one to be faced with the possibility of dying   STRONGLY   MODERATELY   WEAKLY

Figure 6.2. Personality data form. Reprinted by permission of the Institute for Rational-Emotive Therapy.

client then evaluates at *B*. This is known as inference chaining (Moore, 1983). An example of this procedure is described below:

THERAPIST: So what was your major feeling here?

CLIENT: I guess I was angry.

THERAPIST: Angry about what? [Here the therapist has obtained *C* and is probing for *A*.]

CLIENT: I was angry that he did not send me a birthday card. [The client provides *A*.]

THERAPIST: And what was anger provoking about that? [Probing to see whether *A* is most relevant in the inference chain.]

CLIENT: Well . . . . he promised me he would remember. [A_2]

THERAPIST: And because he broke his promise? [Probing for relevance of A_2.]

CLIENT: I felt that he didn't care enough about me. [A_3]

THERAPIST: But let's assume that for a moment. What would be distressing about that? [Probing for relevance of A_3.]

CLIENT: Well, he might leave me? [A_4]

THERAPIST: And if he did? [Probing for relevance of A_4.]

CLIENT: I'd be left alone. [A_5]

THERAPIST: And if you were alone? [Probing for relevance of A_5.]

CLIENT: I couldn't stand that. [Irrational belief]

THERAPIST: Okay, so let's back up a minute. What would be most distressing for you, the birthday card incident, the broken promise, the fact that he didn't care, being left by your husband, or being alone? [The therapist checks to see which *A* is most relevant in a chain.]

CLIENT: Definitely being alone.

This example shows that not only are inferences linked together but that emotions are too. Here anger was linked to anxiety about being alone. While this rational–emotive therapist chose then to dispute the client's irrational belief underlying her anxiety, he still has to deal with her anger-creating belief. Other rational–emotive therapists may have chosen to take the first element in the chain (anger about the missing birthday card) and disputed the irrational belief related to anger. Skillful RET therapists do succeed in discovering the hidden issues underlying the presenting problem during the disputing process. It is important for RET therapists to assess correctly *all* relevant issues related to a presenting problem. How they do this depends upon personal style and on how particular clients react to different assessment procedures.

While *C* is assessed mainly by the client's verbal report, occasionally clients experience difficulty in accurately reporting their emotional and behavioral problems. When this occurs, RET therapists may use a number of methods to facilitate this part of the assessment process. Thus a variety of emotive (e.g., Gestalt two chair dialogue, psychodrama), imagery, and other techniques (e.g., keeping an emotion/behavior diary) can be used in this respect (Dryden, 1983).

If the assessment has revealed inappropriate negative emotions and/or dysfunctional behaviors at *C*, the therapist proceeds to help the client identify relevant irrational beliefs at *B*. An important step here is to help clients see the link between their irrational beliefs and their inappropriate affective and behavioral consequences at *C*. Some rational–emotive therapists like to give a short lecture at this point on the role of the musts in emotional disturbance and how they can be distinguished from preferences. Ellis, for example, often gives the following account:

ELLIS: Imagine that you prefer to have a minimum of $11.00 in your pocket at all times and you discover you only have $10.00. How will you feel?

CLIENT: Frustrated.

ELLIS: Right. Or you'd feel concerned or sad, but you wouldn't kill yourself. Right?

CLIENT: Right.

ELLIS: Okay. Now this time imagine that you absolutely *have to* have a minimum of $11.00 in your pocket at all times. You *must* have it, it is a *necessity*. You must, you must, you must have a minimum of $11.00 and again you look and you find you only have $10.00. How will you feel?

CLIENT: Very anxious.

ELLIS: Right, or depressed. Now remember it's the same $11.00 but a different belief. Okay, now this time you still have that same belief. You *have to* have a minimum of $11.00 at all times, you *must*. It's absolutely *essential*. But this time you look in your pocket and find that you've got $12.00. How will you feel?

CLIENT: Relieved, content.

ELLIS: Right. But with that same belief—you *have to* have a minimum of $11.00 at all times—something will soon occur to you to scare you shitless. What do you think that would be?

CLIENT: What if I lose $2.00?

ELLIS: Right. What if you lose $2.00, what if you spend $2.00, what if you get robbed? That's right. Now the moral of this model—which applies to all humans, rich or poor, black or white, male or female, young or old, in the past or in the future, assuming that humans are still human—is that people make themselves miserable if they don't get what they think they *must*, but they are also panicked when they do—because of the must. For even if they have what they think they must, they could always lose it.

CLIENT: So I have no chance to be happy when I don't have what I think I must—and little chance of remaining unanxious when I do have it?

ELLIS: Right! Your *mus*turbation will get you nowhere—except depressed or panicked!

An important goal of the assessment stage of RET is to help clients distinguish between their primary problems (e.g., depression, anxiety, withdrawal, addiction) and their secondary problems, that is, their problems about their primary problems (e.g., depression about depression, anxiety about anxiety, shame about withdrawal, or guilt about addiction). Rational–emotive therapists often assess secondary problems before primary problems because these often require prior therapeutic attention, since, for example, clients frequently find it difficult to focus on their original problem of anxiety when they are severely blaming themselves for being anxious. Secondary problems are assessed in the same manner as primary problems.

When particular problems have been adequately assessed according to the *ABC* model, and clients clearly see the link between their irrational beliefs and their dysfunctional emotional and behavioral consequences, then therapists can proceed to the disputing stage. The initial purpose of disputing is to help clients gain intellectual insight into the fact that there is no evidence in support of the existence of their absolutistic demands, or the irrational derivatives of these demands (awfulizing, I-can't-stand-it-itis, and damnation). There exists only evidence that if they stay with their nonabsolutistic preferences and if these are not fulfilled they will get unfortunate or "bad" results, while if they are fulfilled they will get desirable or "good" results. Intellectual insight in RET is defined as an acknowledgment that an irrational belief frequently leads to emotional disturbance and dysfunctional behavior, and that a rational belief almost always abets emotional health. But when people lightly and occasionally see and hold rational beliefs, they have intellectual insights that may not help them change (Ellis, 1963, 1985a, 1985b). So RET does not stop with intellectual insight but uses it as a springboard for the working through phase of RET. In this phase, clients are encouraged to use a large variety of cognitive, emotive, and behavioral techniques designed to help them achieve emotional insight. Emotional insight in RET is defined as a very strong and frequently held belief that an irrational idea is dysfunctional and that a rational idea is helpful (Ellis, 1963). When a person has achieved emotional insight he or she thinks, feels, behaves according to the rational belief.

It is mainly in the working through phase of RET that therapists frequently encounter obstacles to client progress. Three major forms of such obstacles are deemed to occur in RET: (1) relationship obstacles, (2) client obstacles, and (3) therapist obstacles.

Relationship obstacles to client progress basically take two forms. First, therapists and clients may be poorly matched and thus fail to develop productive working relationships. Early referral to a more appropriate therapist is indicated in such situations. Second, therapists and clients may get on *too* well, with the result that (1) they collude to avoid dealing with uncomfortable issues and (2) the therapists fail to encourage their clients to push themselves to change irrational beliefs in their life situation. In this case, therapy can become merely an enjoyable experience for both, with the result that client improvement would threaten the existence of this happy relationship. Here, therapists would do better to remind themselves and their clients that the major purpose of their relationship is to help the clients overcome their psychological problems and to pursue their goals *outside* of the therapeutic situation. Consequently, therapists need to strive to raise their own level of frustration tolerance and that of their clients, thus working towards this end.

Therapist obstacles to client progress also take two basic forms. First, therapists may have a number of skill deficits and therefore conduct RET in an ineffective manner. If this occurs close supervision and further training is called for. Second, therapists may bring their own dire needs for approval, success, and comfort to the therapeutic situation, interfering with client progress in the process. In this situation therapists would do better to use RET on themselves or seek personal therapy (Ellis, 1983b, 1985b).

Ellis (1983d) found that clients' own extreme level of disturbance is a significant obstacle to their own progress. He replicated a frequent finding in the psychotherapy literature that the clients who benefit most from therapy are precisely those who need it least (i.e. those who are less disturbed at the outset). Ellis (1983e, 1983f, 1984d, 1985b) has recently outlined a large variety of therapeutic strategies for use with resistant clients. First, therapists need to maintain an unusually accepting attitude towards resistant clients. Second, they should preferably strive to consistently encourage such clients to change. Third, they should persist in showing their clients the negative consequences that undoubtedly follow their refusal to work on their problems. Fourth, a good deal of therapeutic flexibility, innovation, and experimentation is called for in work with resistant clients. As Dryden and Ellis (1986) have said, "Above all, rational–emotive therapists had better be good representatives of their therapeutic system and accept themselves and tolerate the discomfort of working with difficult clients while sticking to the therapeutic task!" (p. 160).

Termination preferably takes place in RET when clients have made some significant progress and when they have become proficient in RET's self-change techniques. Thus, terminating clients should preferably be able to: (1) acknowledge that they experience inappropriate negative emotions and act dysfunctionally when they do; (2) detect the irrational beliefs that underpin these experiences; (3) discriminate between their irrational beliefs and their rational alternatives; (4) challenge these irrational beliefs; and (5) counteract them by using cognitive, emotive, and behavioral self-change methods. In addition, it is often helpful for therapists to arrange for their clients to attend a series of follow-up sessions after termination to monitor their progress and deal with any remaining obstacles to sustained improvement.

Major Therapeutic Techniques

We shall now consider the major therapeutic techniques employed in RET. Because our purpose is to highlight the unique features of RET, we shall emphasize the technical aspects of specialized RET, in which the goal is to effect profound philosophical change. When general RET is conducted, therapists employ a variety of additional techniques that are adequately covered elsewhere in this handbook. While we shall outline the most commonly employed techniques, it is important to note at the outset that RET therapists freely employ techniques derived from other schools of therapy. However, we want to stress that RET "is based on a clear-cut theory of emotional health and disturbance: The many techniques it employs are used in the light of that theory" (Ellis, 1984c, p. 234). Thus, RET therapists would be particularly mindful of both the short-term and long-term effects of particular techniques. Because they adhere to the theory's emphasis on long-range hedonism, they would rarely employ a technique that had beneficial short-range but deleterious long-range effects. While we will list techniques under "cognitive," "emotive," and "behavioral" headings, it should be noted that this is to emphasize the major modality that is tapped by the techniques. However, in keeping with the RET viewpoint that cognition, emotion, and behavior are really interdependent processes, we note that probably all of the following techniques include cognitive, emotive, and behavioral elements. "Pure" techniques (i.e., those that tap one modality without affecting others) probably do not exist.

COGNITIVE TECHNIQUES

The most commonly employed technique in RET is probably the disputing of irrational beliefs. Phadke (1982) has clearly shown that the disputing process comprises three steps. First, therapists help clients to *detect* their irrational beliefs that underpin their self-defeating emotions and behaviors. Second, they *debate* with their clients concerning the truth or falsehood of their irrational beliefs. During the process they help their clients to *discriminate* between their irrational and rational beliefs. Debating is usually conducted according to the Socratic method of asking questions such as "Where is the evidence that you must do this?" and "How does it follow that because you want this you must get it?" But skillful RET therapists use a variety of different debating styles with their clients (Dryden, 1984a; Ellis, 1985b; Wessler & Wessler, 1980; Young 1984a, 1984b, 1984c).

There are a number of cognitive written homework forms available to assist clients in disputing their irrational beliefs between sessions (e.g., see Figure 6.3).

Clients can also use audiocassettes as an aid to the disputing process. They can listen to audiotapes of therapy sessions and also dispute their own irrational beliefs on tape. Here they initiate and sustain a dialogue between the rational and irrational parts of themselves.

Clients who find the disputing process too difficult are encouraged to develop rational self-statements that they can write on small cards and repeat to themselves at various times between therapy sessions. An example of such a statement might be "I want my boyfriend's love but I don't need it."

Three cognitive methods that therapists often suggest to their clients to help them reinforce this new rational philosophy are: (1) bibliotherapy, in which clients are given self-help books and materials to read (e.g., Ellis & Becker, 1982; Ellis & Harper, 1975; Young, 1974a); (2) listening to audiocassettes of RET lectures on various themes (e.g., Ellis, 1971b, 1972a); and (3) using RET with others, in which clients use RET to help friends and relatives with their problems so that the clients can gain practice at using rational arguments.

A number of semantic methods are also employed in RET. Thus, defining techniques are sometimes employed, the purpose of which is to help clients use language in a less self-defeating manner. Thus instead of saying "I can't," clients are urged to use "I haven't yet." Referenting techniques are also employed (Danysh, 1974). Here, clients are encouraged to list both the negative and positive referents of a particular concept such as smoking. This method is employed to counteract clients' tendencies to focus on the positive aspects of a harmful habit and neglect its negative aspects.

RET therapists also employ a number of imagery techniques. Thus, rational–emotive imagery (Ellis, 1979c; Maultsby & Ellis, 1974) is often employed. Clients thereby gain practice at changing their inappropriate negative emotions to appropriate ones (C) while maintaining a vivid image of the negative event at A. Here they are in fact learning to change their self-defeating emotions by changing their underlying beliefs at B. Time projection imagery methods are also employed in RET (Lazarus, 1984). Thus, a client may say that a particular event would be "awful" if it occurred. Rather than directly challenging this irrational belief at this stage, the therapist may temporarily go along with this but help the client to picture what life might be like at regular intervals after the awful event has occurred. In this way clients are indirectly helped to change their irrational belief because they come to see that life goes on after the awful event, that they will usually recover from it, and that they can continue to pursue their original goals or develop new ones. Such realizations encourage the client to

RET SELF-HELP FORM

Institute for Rational-Emotive Therapy
45 East 65th Street, New York, N.Y. 10021
(212) 535-0822

(A) ACTIVATING EVENTS, thoughts, or feelings that happened just before I felt emotionally disturbed or acted self-defeatingly: _____

(C) CONSEQUENCE or CONDITION—disturbed feeling or self-defeating behavior—that I produced and would like to change: _____

(B) BELIEFS—Irrational BELIEFS (IBs) leading to my CONSEQUENCE (emotional disturbance or self-defeating behavior). Circle all that apply to these ACTIVATING EVENTS (A).	(D) DISPUTES for each circled IRRATIONAL BELIEF. Examples: "Why MUST I do very well?" "Where is it written that I am a BAD PERSON?" "Where is the evidence that I MUST be approved or accepted?"	(E) EFFECTIVE RATIONAL BELIEFS (RBs) to replace my IRRATIONAL BELIEFS (IBs). Examples: "I'd PREFER to do very well but I don't HAVE TO." "I am a PERSON WHO acted badly, not a BAD PERSON." "There is no evidence that I HAVE TO be approved, though I would LIKE to be."
1. I MUST do well or very well!		
2. I am a BAD OR WORTHLESS PERSON when I act weakly or stupidly.		
3. I MUST be approved or accepted by people I find important!		
4. I am a BAD, UNLOVABLE PERSON if I get rejected.		
5. People MUST treat me fairly and give me what I NEED!		
6. People who act immorally are undeserving, ROTTEN PEOPLE!		
7. People MUST live up to my expectations or it is TERRIBLE!		
8. My life MUST have few major hassles or troubles.		
9. I CAN'T STAND really bad things or very difficult people!		

10. It's AWFUL or HORRIBLE when major things don't go my way!		
11. I CAN'T STAND IT when life is really unfair!		
12. I NEED to be loved by someone who matters to me a lot!		
13. I NEED a good deal of immediate gratification and HAVE TO feel miserable when I don't get it!		
Additional Irrational Beliefs:		
14.		
15.		
16.		
17.		
18.		

(F) **FEELINGS and BEHAVIORS** I experienced after arriving at my EFFECTIVE RATIONAL BELIEFS: _____

I WILL WORK HARD TO REPEAT MY EFFECTIVE RATIONAL BELIEFS FORCEFULLY TO MYSELF ON MANY OCCASIONS SO THAT I CAN MAKE MYSELF LESS DISTURBED NOW AND ACT LESS SELF-DEFEATINGLY IN THE FUTURE.

Joyce Sichel, Ph.D. and Albert Ellis, Ph.D.
Copyright © 1984 by the Institute for Rational-Emotive Therapy.

Figure 6.3. Example of written homework form. Reprinted by permission of the Institute for Rational-Emotive Therapy.

reevaluate his or her irrational belief. Finally, a number of therapists have successfully employed RET in a hypnosis paradigm (e.g., Boutin & Tosi, 1983; Golden, 1983).

EMOTIVE TECHNIQUES

Rational–emotive therapy has often been falsely criticized for neglecting the emotive aspects of psychotherapy. However, this is far from the truth; RET therapists frequently employ a number of emotive techniques. As has already been shown, RET therapists offer their clients the emotional attitude of unconditional acceptance, using a variety of emotive techniques that are designed to help the client challenge his or her irrational beliefs but avoiding appearing to challenge the client as a person. First, a number of humorous methods are employed to encourage clients to think rationally by not taking themselves too seriously (Ellis, 1977a, 1977b). Second, RET therapists do not hesitate to model a rational philosophy through self-disclosure. They honestly admit that they have had similar problems and show that they overcame them by using RET. Thus I (WD) frequently tell clients that I used to feel ashamed of my stammer. I then relate how I accepted myself with my speech impediment and how I forced myself to tolerate the discomfort of speaking in public whenever the opportunity arose. Third, RET therapists frequently use a number of stories, mottos, parables, witticisms, poems, and aphorisms as adjuncts to cognitive disputing techniques (Wessler & Wessler, 1980). Fourth, Ellis (1977a, 1977b, 1981b) has written a number of rational humorous songs that are designed to present rational philosophies in an amusing and memorable format. The following is a rational humorous song written by Dryden to the tune of "God Save the Queen":

> God save my precious spleen
> Send me a life serene
> God save my spleen!
>
> Protect me from things odious
> Give me a life melodious
> And if things get too onerous
> I'll whine, bawl, and scream!

In an important paper, Ellis (1979d) has advocated the use of force and energy in the practice of psychotherapy. RET is unique among the cognitive-behavioral therapies in emphasizing the employment of such interventions that fully involve clients' emotions. Thus, RET therapists suggest that clients can help themselves go from intellectual to emotional insight by vigorously disputing their irrational beliefs. Vigor is often employed by clients in rational role reversal where they forcefully and dramatically adopt the role of their rational self, whose goal is to successfully dispute self-defeating beliefs as articulated by their irrational self. Force and energy also play a significant part in RET's now famous shame-attacking exercises (Ellis, 1969; Ellis & Becker, 1982). Here clients deliberately seek to act "shamefully" in public in order to accept themselves and to tolerate the ensuing discomfort. Since clients do best to harm neither themselves nor other people, minor infractions of social rules often serve as appropriate shame-attacking exercises (e.g., calling out the time in a crowded department store, wearing bizarre clothes designed to attract public attention, and going into a hardware store and asking if they sell tobacco). Risk-taking exercises come into the same category. Here clients deliberately force themselves to take calculated risks in areas where they wish to make changes. While disputing relevant irrational beliefs, I (AE) overcame my anxiety about approaching women by deliberately forcing myself to speak to 100 women in the Bronx Botanical Gardens. I (WD) pushed myself to speak on national and local radio as part of a campaign to overcome my public speaking anxiety. Both of us took these risks while showing ourselves that nothing "awful" would result from such experiences. Repeating rational self-statements in a passionate and forceful manner is also often used in conjunction with such exercises (Ellis, 1985b).

BEHAVIORAL TECHNIQUES

RET has advocated the use of behavioral techniques (particularly home-work assignments) from its inception in 1955, since it is realized that cognitive change is very often facilitated by behavioral change (Emmel-kamp, Kuipers, & Eggeraat, 1978). Since RET therapists are concerned about helping clients raise their level of frustration tolerance, they encourage them to carry out homework assignments based on *in vivo* desensitization and flooding paradigms rather than those that are based on the gradual desensitization paradigm (Ellis, 1979e; Ellis & Abrahms, 1978; Ellis & Becker, 1982; Ellis & Grieger, 1977). However, pragmatic considerations do have to be taken into account and some clients refuse to carry out such assignments. When this occurs RET therapists negotiate a compromise encouraging such clients to undertake tasks that are sufficiently challenging for them but that are not overwhelming, given their present status (Dryden, 1985).

Other behavioral methods frequently employed in RET include (1) "stay in there" activities (Grieger & Boyd, 1980) that present clients with opportunities to tolerate chronic discomfort while remaining in uncomfortable situations for a long period of time; (2) antiprocrastination exercises, in which clients are encouraged to push themselves to start tasks sooner rather than later, while again tolerating the discomfort of breaking the "mañana" habit; (3) the use of rewards and penalties that are employed to encourage clients to undertake uncomfortable assignments in the pursuit of their long-range goals (Ellis, 1979c). As mentioned earlier, stiff penalties are found to be particularly helpful with chronically resistant clients (Ellis, 1985b); (4) Kelly's fixed role therapy is sometimes employed in RET—here clients are encouraged to act as if they already think rationally, to enable them to experience the fact that change is possible.

A number of other behavioral methods are employed in both specialized and general RET (e.g., various forms of skills training methods). When these are used in specialized RET, they are done to encourage philosophical change, whereas in general RET they are employed to teach clients skills that are absent from their repertoire. When skill training is the goal in specialized RET, it is employed *along with* the disputing of irrational beliefs and *after* some measure of philosophical change has been effected.

TECHNIQUES THAT ARE AVOIDED IN RET

By now it should be clear that RET is a multimodal form of therapy that advocates the employment of techniques in the cognitive, emotive, and behavioral modalities. However, because the choice of therapeutic techniques is inspired by RET theory, the following available therapeutic techniques are avoided or used sparingly in the practice of RET (Ellis, 1979c, 1983c, 1984c).

1. Techniques that help people become more dependent (e.g., undue therapist warmth as a strong reinforcement, the creation and analysis of a transference neurosis).

2. Techniques that encourage people to become more gullible and suggestible (e.g., Pollyannish positive thinking).

3. Techniques that are long-winded and inefficient (e.g., psychoanalytic methods in general and free association in particular, encouraging clients to give lengthy descriptions of activating experiences at *A*).

4. Methods that help people feel better in the short-term rather than get better in the long-term (Ellis, 1972b; e.g., some experiential techniques like fully expressing one's feelings in a dramatic, cathartic, and abreactive manner—i.e., some Gestalt methods and primal techniques. The danger here is that such methods may encourage people to practice irrational philosophies underlying such emotions as anger).

5. Techniques that distract clients from working on their irrational philosophies (e.g., relaxation methods, Yoga and other cognitive distraction methods). These methods may be employed, however, along with cognitive disputing designed to yield some philosophic change.

6. Methods that may unwittingly reinforce clients' philosophy of low frustration tolerance (e.g., gradual desensitization).

7. Techniques that include an antiscientific philosophy (e.g., faith healing and mysticism; Ellis, 1985b).

8. Techniques that attempt to change activating events (*A*) before or without showing clients how to change their irrational beliefs (*B*) (e.g., some strategic family systems techniques).

9. Techniques that have dubious validity (e.g., neurolinguistic programming).

Finally, to reiterate, RET therapists do not absolutistically avoid using the above methods. They may on certain occasions and with certain clients utilize such techniques particularly for pragmatic purposes. For example, if faith healing is the only method that will prevent some clients from harming themselves, then RET therapists would either employ it themselves or more probably refer such clients to a faith healer (Ellis, 1985b).

CASE EXAMPLES

A Case of Anxiety

Freda was a 40-year-old divorced woman with grown-up children, both of whom lived with her. She consulted me (WD) because she suffered from severe anxiety about driving. She was involved in a car accident 18 months previously in which she was a passenger. While not seriously hurt, she had experienced anxiety when driving ever since that time. Freda's anxiety was experienced on two levels. First, she became anxious whenever a large truck approached her from the rear. Second, she became enormously anxious about her anxiety and felt intense panic. I first worked on her secondary level anxiety. Her irrational belief here was "I must not be anxious and it is horrible when I am." I disputed this belief and helped her to see that anxiety is uncomfortable, but not dangerous (Low 1952). Her primary anxiety problem was tackled next. I used "inference chaining" (Moore, 1983) to reveal that she was terrified about (1) dying "before her time" and (2) what would happen to her two sons in the event of her death. First, I helped her see that there was no law of the universe that declared that she must not die in a car crash and that she must live longer than she will live. Second, I asked her what was the worst fate she could imagine for her sons. This revealed that she was particularly anxious about her elder son, who seemed somewhat vulnerable. She was anxious that he might not be able to cope on his own and might become a vagrant, which she evaluated as "terrible." I disputed this irrational belief as well and helped her to see that if he did become a vagrant, that would be very bad or tragic but hardly terrible, since there was no law of the universe that said that he must not become a vagrant. I pointed out further that if he did become a vagrant, he might still obtain some happiness. Behaviorally, I first encouraged her to drive even though she was anxious, tolerating this experience as "bad" but not "awful." After this brought about some improvement, I urged her to seek out actively big trucks and tolerate the discomfort of being "hemmed in."

The disclosure of this theme of being hemmed in revealed further problems. She was at that same time being romantically pursued by a man in whom she felt no interest. She felt trapped because he was not discouraged by her polite requests for him to leave her alone. I asked her what would stop her from being firm and back this assertion up with a refusal to talk to him. She thought that this approach would discourage him but said that she would feel guilty if he were hurt by such a direct approach. I helped her to see that her guilt stemmed from the belief "I would be a bad person for causing him pain." First I disputed this belief and showed her that even if she did directly cause the man pain, she could accept herself as a fallible human being for acting badly. I then helped her see that she would be responsible for depriving him rather than for cruelly hurting him, since if he felt hurt or denigrated by her rejections he would create these feelings by irrationally downing himself. In the next session, she claimed success at asserting herself with the man and reported further alleviation of her driving anxiety. She spontaneously reported that feeling less hemmed in in her personal relationships helped her feel less hemmed in while driving.

In subsequent sessions, Freda discussed further problems concerning lack of assertion, guilt, and embarrassment. I helped her to see that there were links between these problems and she became increasingly proficient at detecting and disputing her irrational beliefs. Most noteworthy was the way she counteracted some of her irrational philosophies through dramatic action. I explained to her the concept of shame-attacking exercises and in the next session she reported undertaking one. For years she had been anxious about bringing men home to meet her two sons. On this occasion she met a much younger man at a dance and took him home that night. She did so to dispute her shame-inducing belief "My sons would look down on me as a cradle-snatcher and that would prove that I am a shit." She felt this was very beneficial. Her sons did make several negative comments that she did not like. She reported that she had told them that she was going to live her life her way and that she would like their approval, but that if they chose to regard her as "a desperate old woman" that was unfortunate but hardly the end of the world.

At the end of 12 weekly sessions, Freda had made significant progress in disputing her dire needs for approval and comfort. More importantly, she had learned to internalize the scientific method of disputing and saw clearly the benefits of actively working to counteract her irrational philosophies.

A 6-month follow-up revealed that she had maintained her progress. She was able to drive quite comfortably, although she still did not like having big trucks behind her. However, she was no longer anxious about encountering this situation. Interpersonally, she felt much freer about saying what she thought and acting more in her own interests even though others might view her in a negative light. She reported that her sons had changed their attitude towards her, saying, "They seem to respect the 'new me' more than the old one."

A Case of Depression

Bob, a 50-year-old man, was severely depressed after losing his job and as a result experienced sex problems. He was referred to me (WD) after his general practitioner had discovered that he was feeling suicidal. In our first session I learned that he was feeling hopeless about his future because he considered that he was "finished as a man." I very persistently showed him that he could accept himself as a man who had temporarily lost employment and erectile sufficiency, rather than damn himself as being less of a man for these two losses. His mood lifted appreciably by the end of the session, but I told him that he could telephone me between sessions if he became suicidal again.

In our second session I discovered he was also ashamed about being depressed and about seeking psychotherapeutic help. Again I helped him to dispute his irrational belief "I must be able to solve my problems on my own," and also encouraged him to counteract his shame by telling his best friend about his problems.

He reported feeling much better in our third session. He did not feel ashamed about telling his friend about his problems and had received a sympathic response from the friend who in turn confided that he had had similar problems the previous year. This actually had a profound effect on my client because it helped him to see that he could gain happiness by changing some of his priorities. He began to see that friendship was as important as achievement and that it was possible for him to redefine what it meant to be a man.

In our fourth session I disputed his anxiety-creating belief about his sexual performance, "I must get it up to be a man." Even by the fourth session it was apparent that Bob clearly understood the difference between rational and irrational beliefs. He went home and enjoyed several sexual experiences with his wife when he resolved to act on the belief that "an erection and orgasm would be nice but sex can be enjoyed without them." Additionally, Bob decided to do some voluntary work in a local hospital and enjoyed it, even though he predicted he would gain no satisfaction from doing so.

He began to show increasing interest in the area of gender identity and read several books on the pressures of being a male in today's society. He began taking a more active role doing domestic chores and by the seventh session no longer regarded it as "women's work." In the eighth session he relapsed and reported feeling depressed again. Interestingly, when this was explored, it transpired that he was condemning himself for being "an erstwhile male chauvinist." I showed him again that he was a fallible human being and that he could accept himself as such even if he had adhered to a male chauvinistic philosophy in the past and even if he still retained some of this philosophy today. We had a full discussion of the concept of unconditional self-acceptance and he resolved to act on this philosophy.

In our final two sessions we discussed several career-related issues. He decided as a result of this discussion to attend a university and study for a degree in social work. At our final session, he considered that he had changed some fundamental attitudes: "Looking back, I can realize that I had believed in the concept of the two-dimensional man. I was Okay as long as I was in a good job and my cock functioned well. Now I can see that there is much more to being a man than that. I feel you have helped me widen my horizons and I now view myself as being considerably more complex than before. I have an increased enjoyment of friendship more and sex with my wife is incredibly more enriching."

A 6-month follow-up revealed that Bob was enjoying his university course and was free from depression. At his first therapy session his Beck Depression Inventory score was in the severe range (42). At his tenth and final session of regular therapy his score had gone down to 3 and at the 6-month follow-up it was 1.

OTHER APPLICATIONS

Unlike other systems of CBT (e.g., Beck's Cognitive Therapy), which have largely been applied to and tested on restricted client problems and populations, RET from its inception has been widely applied in a variety of treatment formats to a large number of client populations experiencing a broad range of problems. Since the purpose of this section is to provide readers with an overview of the applications of RET, we decided to gain this information by surveying the first 37 issues (1966–1984) of the *Journal of Rational-Emotive Therapy* (formerly titled *Rational Living*). We shall present the findings of our survey in the three subsessions of client problems, client populations, and treatment formats. It should be noted at the outset that the articles surveyed do not clearly distinguish between specialized RET and general RET.

Client problems. RET was applied to the following clients problems: academic underachievement (Rand, 1969); anger and hostility (Ellis, 1975; Grieger, 1977; Mooney, 1980; Wessler, 1981); alcohol abuse (Brandsma, 1976; Ellis, 1982b; Sherman, 1967); anorexia nervosa (Kujoth, 1979); behavioral excesses (Watkins, 1973); blindness (Needham & Ehmer, 1980) and conversion reaction blindness (Nardi, 1980); boredom (Lehman, 1972); communication problems (Diamond & Songor, 1972); depression and suicide (Anderson, 1966; Hauck, 1971; Maultsby, 1973; Trexler, 1973);

dieting (Geis, 1970; Presby, 1979); divorce problems (Church, 1974; Ard, 1977); dog phobia (Hoellen, 1980); drug abuse and addiction (Ellis 1982b; O'Connell, Bright, & Grossman, 1978); exhibitionism (McGarry, 1984); guilt (Anderson, 1968; Ard, 1967a; Tosi & Reardon, 1976); homosexuality (Sagarin, 1970); jealousy (Hibbard, 1975); marital problems (Ellis, 1966); medical disorders (Baither & Doyle, 1981; Lefebvre & Lawlis, 1979); procrastination (Knaus, 1973); sex problems (Beher-Zimmerman, 1982; Ellis, 1971c); shame (Ellis, 1971d); speech anxiety (Straatmeyer & Watkins, 1974); test anxiety (Golden, Geller, & Hendricks, 1981; Oliver, 1975; Warren, Deffenbacher & Brading, 1976); type A behavior pattern (Weber, 1983); and unassertiveness (Howard & Tosi, 1978; Neiger & Fullerton, 1979; Wessler, 1975).

Client populations. RET was used with the following client populations: adolescents (Edwards, 1977; Grieger, 1975; Spirito & Erickson, 1979; Young, 1974b); children (Costello & Dougherty, 1977; Daly, 1971; Devoge, 1974; DiGiuseppe, 1975; Hauck, 1974; Rossi, 1977; Warren, Deffenbacher & Brading, 1976); college students (Berger, 1982; Kassinove, 1974; Smith, 1982); hospitalized in-patients (Gullo, 1966) and partly hospitalized patients (Lefkovitz & Davis, 1977); members of extreme religious cults (Lockwood, 1981); parents (Criddle, 1978); police officers (Samrock, 1978); psychotherapists (Ellis, 1983b); sportsmen and women (Ellis, 1982c; Wessler, 1980); women (Wolfe, 1976); and young adults (Ellis, 1971c; Wilson & London, 1977).

Treatment formats. RET was employed in the following treatment formats: crisis intervention (Tosi & Moleski, 1975; Wasserman & Kimmel, 1978); encounter groups (Ellis, 1969); emotive education in the classroom (DiNubile & Wessler, 1974; Knaus & Bokor, 1975; Knaus & Eyman, 1974; Wolfe *et al.*, 1969); family therapy (Ellis, 1978a, 1979f); group therapy (Ellis, 1974); marital counseling (Ard, 1967b); marital counseling in groups (McClellan & Stieper, 1973); self-help therapy (Ellis, 1978b); and sex therapy (Ellis, 1983g).

Since it would take an entire book to discuss the application of RET to the above problem areas, client populations, and treatment formats, the reader is directed to the original sources for more detailed information.

ADDITIONAL CONSIDERATIONS

In this section we shall discuss additional considerations about RET, including assessment technology and the kind of research that has been done with RET assessment; the empirical status of the RET approach, especially in regard to experimental investigation of the validity of its main treatment methods; and directions for future development in RET.

ASSESSMENT TECHNOLOGY OF RET

Assessment of the kind and degree of emotional disturbance of clients is held to be important in RET for several reasons:

1. To determine how seriously disturbed clients are, so that therapists can see how likely they are to benefit from any form of therapy—including RET—and so that they can decide which RET techniques of the many possible ones that are available may be most suitably employed and which avoided with each particular client under the conditions in which he or she can be expected to live.

2. To determine, or at least guess with a fair degree of accuracy, how difficult clients are likely to be, how they will probably take to the main RET procedures, and how long psychotherapy will take with each of them.

3. To discover which type of therapist involvement (e.g., a more or less active or a more or less passive and supportive kind) is likely to help the individual client.

4. To discover what types of skill deficiencies clients have and what kinds of training (either in the course of RET or outside of therapy) they might best undertake to remedy some of their skill deficiencies. Thus, on the basis of this assessment, certain kinds of skill training—such as assertiveness, social skills, communication, or vocational training—may be recommended for specific clients.

RET practitioners are at liberty to use all kinds of assessment procedures but generally favor the types of cognitive-behavioral interventions described in Kendall and Hollon (1980). They tend to take a dimmer view of diagnostic procedures such as the Rorschach and other projective techniques than they do of more objective personality questionnaires and behavioral tests, largely because the former often have dubious validity, incorporate questionable psychoanalytic and psychodynamic interpretations, and usually are not particularly relatable to effective treatment processes.

Ellis and many other RET practitioners take the view that although assessment interviews and some standard diagnostic tests may at times be useful in exploring clients' disturbances, perhaps the best form of assessment consists of having several RET sessions with the client. Some of the advantages of this kind of therapy-oriented assessment include:

1. In the course of such an "assessment" procedure, clients can get to work on their problems almost immediately, can gain therapeutically while being assessed, and can be helped to suffer less pain, hardship, and expense while undergoing treatment.

2. The preferable techniques to be used with different clients are often best determined mainly through experimenting with some of these techniques in the course of the therapeutic process. Where the use of standard personality tests such as the MMPI may help the therapist start off with some rather than other RET methods with a given client, only by actually

experimenting with certain specific methods is the therapist likely to see how the client reacts to them and consequently how they should be continued or discontinued.

3. Assessment procedures divorced from ongoing psychotherapy (such as giving a whole battery of tests prior to beginning therapy) may be iatrogenic for a number of clients. During this testing process, especially if the assessment procedures are longwinded and take some time to complete, clients may imagine "horrors" about themselves that lead them astray and make it more difficult for them to benefit from therapy.

4. Certain conventional assessment procedures (e.g., the Rorschach and TAT) may wrongly predict problems, symptoms, and dynamics that many clients do not really have and may help lead their therapists away from more scientifically based evaluations.

5. Clients sometimes take diagnoses obtained from complicated assessment procedures as the gospel truth, feel that they have thereby received a valid "explanation" of what ails them, and wrongly conclude that they have been helped by this "explanation." RET assessment procedures, including using therapy itself as an integral part of the assessment process, primarily focus on what clients can do to change rather than on clever diagnostic "explanations" of what ails them.

Because RET is strongly cognitive, emotive and behavioral, it assesses not only clients' irrational beliefs but also their inappropriate feelings and self-defeating behaviors. As was noted in the previous sections of this chapter, the usual RET assessment process almost always includes the following:

1. Clients are helped to acknowledge and describe their inappropriate feelings (e.g., anxiety, depression, anger, and self-hatred) and these are clearly differentiated from their negative appropriate feelings (e.g., disappointment, sadness, frustration, and displeasure).

2. They are led to acknowledge and delineate their self-defeating behaviors (e.g., compulsions, addictions, phobias, and procrastination) rather than to overemphasize idiosyncratic but nondeleterious behaviors (e.g., unusual devotion to socializing, sex, study, or work).

3. They are asked to point out specific activating events in their lives that tend to occur just prior to their experienced disturbed feelings and behaviors.

4. Their rational beliefs that accompany their activating events and that lead to undisturbed consequences are assessed and discussed.

5. Their irrational beliefs that accompany their activating events and that lead to disturbed consequences are assessed and discussed.

6. Their irrational beliefs that involve absolutistic musts and grandiose demands on themselves, others, and the universe are particularly determined.

7. Their second-level irrational beliefs that tend to be derived from their absolutistic shoulds and musts (e.g., "awfulizing," "I-can't-stand-it-

itis," "damning" of the self and others, and their unrealistic overgeneralizations) are also revealed.

8. Their irrational beliefs that lead to their disturbances about their disturbances (e.g., anxiety about anxiety and depression about being depressed) are revealed and discussed in particular.

As these specialized RET assessment and diagnostic procedures are instituted specific treatment plans are made, normally in close collaboration with the clients, in order to work first on the most important and self-sabotaging emotional and behavioral symptoms that they present and later on related and possibly less important symptoms. RET practitioners, however, always try to maintain an exceptionally open-minded, skeptical, and experimental attitude toward the clients and their problems, so that what at first seem to be their crucial and most debilitating ideas, feelings, and actions may later be seen in a different light, and emphasis may be changed to working on other equally or more pernicious irrationalities that might not be evident during the clients' early sessions.

Research on RET Tests of Irrational Beliefs

When Ellis hypothesized in his early writings on RET (Ellis, 1957a, 1957b, 1958, 1962) that emotional and behavioral disturbance stems largely from irrational beliefs, he at first outlined from ten to twelve basic irrationalities. His hypothesized irrational beliefs seemed to have such obvious face validity that they have been widely quoted in literally hundreds of articles and books on human personality and psychotherapy. But researchers soon began to check out systematically Ellis's basic disturbance-creating irrationalities and to make them the source of about 24 standardized tests. Among these RET-oriented tests, we should note those of Argabite and Nidoff (1968), Baisden (1980), Bessai (1975), Bessai and Lane (1976), Burgess & Campbell (1984), Conklin (1965), Ellis (1968), Fox (1969), Fox and Davies (1971), Hartman (1968), R. Jones (1968), Kassinove (Kassinove, Crisci, & Tiegerman, 1977), Pead (1980), Plutchik (1976), Shorkey and Sutton-Simon (1983a, 1983b), Shorkey and Whiteman (1974, 1977), Taft (1965), Wasserman (1983), and Zingle (1965).

Literally hundreds of controlled studies have been done using these irrational belief tests, and in almost all these studies the tests have been shown to distinguish reliably between various kinds of disturbed individuals and control groups. Much of the literature on these studies has been summarized by Baisden (1980), DiGiuseppe, Miller, and Trexler (1979), and Ellis (1979g).

Some of the recent studies that are not included in these summaries and that tend to support Ellis's hypothesis that irrational beliefs significantly accompany and are probably causally related to various kinds of emotional disturbance may now be cited. Evans and Picano (1983), Lohr, Bonge, and Jones (1982), Morelli, Andrews, and Morelli (1982), Shorkey and Sutton-Simon (1983b), and Smith, Boaz, and Denney (1984) found that irrational thinking is significantly correlated with general psychological maladjustment. Försterling (1983) and Tobacyk and Milford (1982) showed that there is validity to Ellis's contention that irrational beliefs are held dogmatically and musturbationally and that they lead to unrealistic inferences and attributions.

The basic irrational beliefs of RET have also been recently experimentally investigated and have been shown to be significantly correlated with the feelings and behaviors of addicts (Ward, 1983); with unusually angry individuals (Lohr, Hamberger, & Bonge, 1982); with highly anxious people (Gormally, Sipps, Raphael, Edwin, & Varvil-Weld, 1981; Himle, Thyer, & Papsdorf, 1982; Lohr, Bonge, & Jones, 1982; Witmer, Rich, Barcikowski, & Mague, 1983); with poor cognitive functioning (Prola, 1984); with psychological defensiveness (Morelli & Andrews, 1982), with severe depression (Lapointe & Crandell, 1980; Lewinsohn, Larson, & Munoz, 1982; Pead, 1980; Watkins & Rush, 1983); with political alienation (Long, 1981); with poor problem solving (Heppner, Reeder, & Larson, 1983); with lack of self-acceptance (Daly & Burton, 1983; Grabia, 1977; Smith, 1982); with psychopathy (Solomon & Ray, 1984), with unassertiveness (Lohr, Bonge, & Jones, 1982); with nurses who suffer from burnout (J. Jones, 1980); and with slow-learning high school students (Shorkey & Saski, 1981).

EMPIRICAL STATUS OF RET

The first controlled study of RET was published in 1957 and consisted of Ellis comparing the results he had obtained from using classical psychoanalysis, psychoanalytically-oriented psychotherapy, and rational–emotive therapy (Ellis, 1957b). It was hardly an unbiased study and its positive results are not to be taken too seriously.

However, starting in the 1960s, going full blast in the 1970s, and continuing apace in the 1980s, more than 200 outcome studies have been done on RET and on closely related cognitive-behavioral therapies. The great majority of these controlled studies have shown that, when compared to a control group, clients treated with RET or with a form of cognitive restructuring that is an essential part of RET fare significantly better than those who are not so treated. Outcome studies of RET have been reviewed by DiGiuseppe, Miller, and Trexler (1979), Ellis (1979g), McGovern and Silverman (1984), and Meichenbaum (1977).

Outcome studies testing the use of RET and cognitive restructuring derived from RET continue to proliferate, most of them continuing to indicate that treatment methods that consist of RET procedures help clients or subjects significantly more than control groups. Recent studies that are not included in the reviews mentioned in the previous paragraph and that show the effectiveness of RET in various treatment areas include the following: improvement in general adjustment (Leaf, Gross, Todres, Marcus, & Bradford, 1984; Rohsenow & Smith, 1982; Tucker & Newman, 1981); increased assertiveness and reduced depression (Emmelkamp & Mersch, 1982); increased performance (Bonadies & Bass, 1984); decreased addiction (Ray, Friedlander, & Solomon, 1984; Witkin & DiGiuseppe, 1984; Yates & Sambrailo, 1984); decreased anxiety (Berggren & Carlsson, 1984; Cangelosi, Gressard, & Mines, 1980; Haynes-Clements & Avery, 1984); improved parenting (Saxon, 1980); improved marital functioning (Baucom & Lester, 1983); improvement in phobias (Mavissakalian, Michelson, Greenwald, Kornblith, & Greenwald, 1983); decreased procrastination (Solomon & Rothblum, 1984); improved psychosomatic conditions (Thurman, 1984; Weber, 1983); increased self-acceptance (Daly, 1982; Daly & Burton 1983; Gardner & Oei, 1981; Wilson & Krane, 1980); improved self-actualization (Howard, 1981); improvement in erectile failure (Schlaks, 1982; Munjack *et al.*, 1984); and social skills enhancement and resolution of social anxiety (Elder, Edelstein, & Fremouw, 1981).

In addition to these empirical studies that tend to back the main therapeutic hypotheses of RET, literally hundreds of other controlled experiments have been published that tend to indicate that many of the main theoretical hypotheses of RET—especially its *ABC* theory of human disturbance—now have considerable experimental backing. Also, hundreds more research studies present evidence that many of the RET-favored therapeutic techniques such as active–directive therapy, direct disputing of irrational ideas, the use of rational or coping statements, and the employment of psychoeducational methods have distinct effectiveness. Ellis (1979g) has cited hundreds of these studies in his comprehensive review of the RET-oriented literature. If his review were brought up to date it would now include hundreds of additional studies that present empirical confirmation of many of the most important RET theories and therapeutic applications.

This is not to claim that RET has undisputed evidence of the validity of its theories or the effectiveness of its practice. Like all other major systems of psychotherapy, it is still exceptionally wanting in these respects; considerable further research needs to be done to check on its major hypotheses. Although its treatment methods have been tested many times against the methods of other kinds of psychotherapy and against nontreated control groups and they have usually been proven adequate, they have not as yet often been compared to the procedures of other popular forms of cognitive-behavior therapy, such as those created by Beck (1976), Bandura (1977), Lazarus (1981), Lazarus (1966), and Meichenbaum (1977). Considerable experimental studies could be done in this area.

DIRECTIONS FOR THE FUTURE DEVELOPMENT OF RET

The future of RET obviously cannot be predicted with complete accuracy because psychotherapy in general and rational–emotive therapy in particular may take any number of likely and unlikely turns in the next century or two. Judging by recent trends, however, we would like to make the following predictions.

RET may or may not be immensely popular under its present name in the future, but many of its most important and pioneering aspects are likely to be incorporated into almost all effective forms of therapy. Already its famous *ABC* theory of personality and emotional disturbance is more or less acknowledged and distinctly employed by most of today's professional therapists. Psychoanalysts, transactional analysts, transpersonal therapists, and even Gestalt therapists now generally accept the RET notion that activating events (*A*s) by themselves do not make people feel emotionally disturbed consequences (*C*s). Rather, their belief systems (*B*s) more directly and more importantly help to create their *C*s—their emotional and behavioral disturbances. Most therapists now pay considerable attention to their clients' unrealistic and irrational beliefs, and will probably continue to do so in years to come, though perhaps not as actively and forcefully as do RET practitioners.

Cognitive-behavior therapy, pioneered by RET, is now one of the most popular (and perhaps *the* most popular) form of psychological treatment. It and RET will probably continue to grow and eventually perhaps be the basic therapy method that includes the most effective elements of other systems.

While RET is a comprehensive system of therapy that normally uses a large number of cognitive, emotive, and behavioral methods (Dryden, 1984a; Ellis, 1984b, 1984c; Ellis & Becker, 1982; Ellis & Harper, 1975), there is good reason to believe that many more effective techniques will be invented and researched and will be added to the RET armamentarium.

RET was originally created as a one-on-one therapy and then adapted to regular group therapy (Ellis, 1962, 1982d). But, as has been stated, over the years it has been very widely used with large groups, classroom courses, workshops and seminars, intensives, and other mass applications (Ellis & Bernard, 1985; Wolfe & Brand, 1977). It is also popular in the form of RET pamphlets, books, audio cassettes, videocassettes, and programmed material (Institute for Rational-Emotive Therapy, 1985). In its mass media presentations it has already reached and affected literally millions of people, including many who are not seriously disturbed but who have used its principles to enhance and actualize their lives (Ellis, 1984e; Ellis & Bernard, 1983, 1985).

Because RET is, more than most other therapies, a psychoeducational process that involves teaching people how to look for and uproot their irrationalities, because it shows them how to keep doing rational–emotive self-help homework as a major part of the therapeutic process (Sichel & Ellis, 1984), and because it can be stated in simple, self-help terms and made available to large numbers of people (Ellis, 1978b; Ellis & Becker, 1982; Ellis & Harper, 1975; Ellis & Knaus, 1977; Young, 1974a), we believe that the future of RET is likely to reside more in its mass applications and its educational procedures than in its use for individual and group psychotherapy. We hope that its popular media applications will grow enormously over the coming years—thus fulfilling one of the fondest hopes of its originator.

RET has had many professional and lay applications and has been found useful in a number of clinical and related fields such as politics and the law, business, love, marriage and family relations, sexual fulfillment, parenting, education, communication, sports, religion, assertion training, addiction, and aging (Bernard & Joyce, 1984; Ellis, 1984e; Ellis & Bernard, 1983, 1985; Wolfe & Brand, 1977). Many additional applications of RET in these and other aspects of human life are to be confidently expected.

REFERENCES

Adler, A. (1927). *Understanding human nature.* New York: Garden City.

Adler, A. (1964). *Social interest: A challenge to mankind.* New York: Capricorn.

Anderson, C. M. (1966). Depression and suicide reassessed. *Rational Living, 1*(2), 31–36.

Anderson, C. M. (1968). Guilt-therapy techniques. *Rational Living, 3*(2), 40–41.

Ard, B. N., Jr. (1967a). Nothing's uglier than sin. *Rational Living, 2*(1), 4–6.

Ard, B. N., Jr. (1967b). The A-B-C of marriage counseling. *Rational Living, 2*(2), 10–12.

Ard, B. N., Jr. (1977). Beyond divorce: What then? *Rational Living, 12*(2), 31–34.

Argabite, A. H., & Nidorf, L. J. (1968). Fifteen questions for rating reason. *Rational Living, 3*(1), 9–11.

Baisden, H. E. (1980). *Irrational beliefs: A construct validation study.* Unpublished doctoral dissertation, University of Minnesota.

Baither, R. C., & Doyle, J. E. (1981). Inpatient compliance to psychotropic medications: An exploration of attitudes. *Rational Living, 16*(2), 35–43.

Bandura, A. (1969). *Principles of behavior modification.* New York: Holt, Rinehart & Winston.

Bandura, A. (1977). *Social learning theory.* Englewood Cliffs, NJ: Prentice-Hall.

Bard, J. (1980). *Rational–emotive therapy in practice.* Champaign, IL: Research Press.

Baucom, D. H., & Lester, G. W. (1983). The utility of cognitive restructuring as a supplement to behavioral marital therapy. *Cognitive Behaviorist, 5*(1), 2–5.

Beck, A. T. (1967). *Depression.* New York: Hoeber-Harper.

Beck, A. T. (1976). *Cognitive therapy and the emotional disorders.* New York: International Universities Press.

Beck, A. T., Rush, A. J., Shaw, B. F., & Emery, G. (1979). *Cognitive therapy of depression.* New York: Guilford.

Beher-Zimmerman, U. (1982). Treatment of a woman with fear of intercourse. *Rational Living, 17*(2), 37–39.

Berger, E. M. (1982). Self-devaluation in college students. *Rational Living, 17*(1), 23–26.

Berggren, U., & Carlsson, S. G. (1984). A psychophysiological therapy for dental fear. *Behaviour Research and Therapy, 22*, 487–492.

Bernard, M. E., & Joyce, M. R. (1984). *Rational-emotive therapy with children and adolescents: Theory, treatment strategies, preventative methods.* New York: Wiley.

Beutler, L. E. (1983). *Eclectic psychotherapy: A systematic approach.* New York: Pergamon.

Bessai, J. L. (1975). *A factorial assessment of irrational beliefs.* Unpublished master's thesis, Cleveland State University.

Bessai, J. L., & Lane, S. H. (1976). Self-rating scale for rationality: An update. *Rational Living, 11*(1), 28–29.

Bonadies, G. A., & Bass, B. A. (1984). Effects of self-verbalizations upon emotional arousal and performance: A test of rational-emotive theory. *Perceptual and Motor Skills, 59*, 939–948.

Boutin, G. E., & Tosi, D. J. (1983). Modification of irrational ideas and test anxiety through rational stage directed hypnotherapy (RSDH). *Journal of Clinical Psychology, 39*, 382–391.

Brandsma, J. M. (1976). Toward a more rational alcoholics anonymous. *Rational Living, 11*(1), 35–37.

Burgess, P., & Campbell, I. (1984). *Attitudes and belief inventory.* Melbourne: Department of Psychology, University of Melbourne.

Burns, D. D. (1980). *Feeling good: The new mood therapy.* New York: William Morrow.

Cangelosi, A., Gressard, P. P., & Mines, R. A. (1980). The effects of a rational thinking group on false concepts in adolescents. *School Counselor, 27*, 357–361.

Church, V. A. (1974). Rational therapy in divorce practice. *Rational Living, 9*(2), 34–38.

Conklin, R. C. (1965). *A psychometric instrument for the early identification of underachievers.* Unpublished master's thesis, University of Alberta.

Corsini, R. J. (Ed.). (1977). *Current personality theories.* Itasca, IL: Peacock.

Costello, R. T., & Dougherty, D. (1977). Rational behavior education in the classroom. *Rational Living, 12*(1), 13–15.

Criddle, L. (1978). Parents can enhance children's self-acceptance and confidence. *Rational Living, 13*(2), 9–14.

Daly, M. J. (1982). *An exploratory investigation of the relationships among self-esteem, irrational beliefs and dogmatism.* Doctoral dissertation, University of Missouri—Columbia.

Daly, M. J., & Burton, R. L. (1983). Self-esteem and irrational beliefs: An exploratory investigation with implications for counseling. *Journal of Counseling Psychology, 30*, 361–366.

Daly, S. (1971). Using reason with deprived pre-school children. *Rational Living, 5*(2), 12–19.

Danysh, J. (1974). *Stop without quitting.* San Francisco: International Society for General Semantics.

DeVoge, C. (1974). A behavioral approach to RET with children. *Rational Living, 9*(1), 23–26.

Diamond, L., & Songor, E. (1972). Eight rational principles of effective communication in relationships. *Rational Living, 7*(1), 36–38.

DiGiuseppe, R. (1975). The use of behavior modification to establish rational self-statements in children. *Rational Living, 10*(1), 18–20.

DiGiuseppe, R. A., Miller, N. J., & Trexler, L. D. (1979). A review of rational-emotive psychotherapy outcome studies. In A. Ellis & J. M. Whiteley (Eds.), *Theoretical and empirical foundations of rational-emotive therapy.* Monterey, CA: Brooks/Cole.

DiNubile, L., & Wessler, R. (1974). Lessons from the living school. *Rational Living, 9*(1), 29–32.

Dryden, W. (1983). Audiotape supervision by mail: A rational-emotive approach. *British Journal of Cognitive Psychotherapy, 1*(1), 57–64.

Dryden, W. (1984a). *Rational-emotive therapy: Fundamentals and innovations.* London: Croom-Helm.

Dryden, W. (1984b). Rational–emotive therapy. In W. Dryden (Ed.), *Individual therapy in Britain*. London: Harper & Row.

Dryden, W. (1985). Challenging but not overwhelming: A compromise in negotiating home-work assignments. *British Journal of Cognitive Psychotherapy, 3*(1), 77–80.

Dryden, W., & Ellis, A. (1986). Rational–emotive therapy. In W. Dryden & W. L. Golden (Eds.), *Cognitive-behavioural approaches to psychotherapy*. London: Harper & Row.

Duckro, P., Beal, D., & George, C. (1979). Research on the effects of disconfirmed role expecta-tions in psychotherapy: A critical review. *Psychological Bulletin, 86*, 260–275.

Dunlap, K. (1932). *Habits: Their making and unmaking*. New York: Liveright.

Edwards, C. (1977). RET in high school. *Rational Living, 12*(1), 10–12.

Elder, J. P., Edelstein, B. A., & Fremouw, W. J. (1981). Client by treatment interactions in response acquisition and cognitive restructuring approaches. *Cognitive Therapy and Research, 5*, 203–210.

Ellis, A. (1957a). *How to live with a "neurotic"* (rev. ed.). New York: Crown. North Hollywood, CA: Wilshire Books.

Ellis, A. (1957b). Outcome of employing three techniques of psychotherapy. *Journal of Clini-cal Psychology, 13*, 334–350.

Ellis, A. (1958). Rational psychotherapy. *Journal of General Psychology, 59*, 245–253.

Ellis, A. (1962). *Reason and emotion in psychotherapy*. Secaucus, NJ: Lyle Stuart.

Ellis, A. (1963). Toward a more precise definition of "emotional" and "intellectual" insight. *Psychological Reports, 13*, 125–126.

Ellis, A. (1966). The nature of disturbed marital interaction. *Rational Living, 1*(1), 22–26.

Ellis, A. (1968). *Personality data form*. New York: Institute for Rational–Emotive Therapy.

Ellis, A. (1969). A weekend of rational encounter. *Rational Living, 4*(2), 1–8.

Ellis, A. (1971a). *Growth through reason*. North Hollywood, CA: Wilshire Books.

Ellis, A. (1971b). *How to stubbornly refuse to be ashamed of anything* (Cassette recording). New York: Institute for Rational–Emotive Therapy.

Ellis, A. (1971c). Sexual problems of the young adult. *Rational Living, 5*(2), 2–11.

Ellis, A. (1971d). 22 ways to stop putting yourself down. *Rational Living, 6*(1), 8–15.

Ellis, A. (Speaker). (1972a). *Solving emotional problems* (Cassette recording). New York: Institute for Rational–Emotive Therapy.

Ellis, A. (1972b). Helping people get better: Rather than merely feel better. *Rational Living, 7*(2), 2–9.

Ellis, A. (1973). *Humanistic psychotherapy: The rational–emotive approach*. New York: McGraw-Hill.

Ellis, A. (1974). Rational–emotive therapy in groups. *Rational Living, 9*(1), 15–22.

Ellis, A. (1975). On the disvalue of "mature" anger. *Rational Living, 10*(1), 24–27.

Ellis, A. (1976a). The biological basis of human irrationality. *Journal of Individual Psychol-ogy, 32*, 145–168.

Ellis, A. (1976b). RET abolishes most of the human ego. *Psychotherapy: Theory, Research and Practice, 13*, 343–348.

Ellis, A. (1977a). Fun as psychotherapy. *Rational Living, 12*(1), 2–6.

Ellis, A. (Speaker). (1977b). *A garland of rational humorous songs* (Cassette recording). New York: Institute for Rational–Emotive Therapy.

Ellis, A. (1977c). *Anger—How to live with and without it*. Secaucus, NJ: Citadel Press.

Ellis, A. (1978a). A rational–emotive approach to family therapy I: Cognitive therapy. *Rational Living, 13*(2), 15–20.

Ellis, A. (1978b). Rational–emotive therapy and self-help therapy. *Rational Living, 13*(1), 3–8.

Ellis, A. (1979a). The theory of rational–emotive therapy. In A. Ellis & J. M. Whiteley (Eds.), *Theoretical and empirical foundations of rational–emotive therapy*. Monterey, CA: Brooks/Cole.

Ellis, A. (1979b). Discomfort anxiety: A new cognitive behavioral construct. Part 1. *Rational Living, 14*(2), 3-8.

Ellis, A. (1979c). The practice of rational-emotive therapy. In A. Ellis & J. M. Whiteley (Eds.), *Theoretical and empirical foundations of rational-emotive therapy.* Monterey, CA: Brooks/Cole.

Ellis, A. (1979d). The issue of force and energy in behavioral change. *Journal of Contemporary Psychotherapy, 10*(2), 83-97.

Ellis, A. (1979e). A note on the treatment of agoraphobics with cognitive modification versus prolonged exposure in vivo. *Behaviour Research and Therapy, 17,* 162-164.

Ellis, A. (1979f). A rational-emotive approach to family therapy II: Emotive and behavioral therapy. *Rational Living, 14*(1), 23-28.

Ellis, A. (1979g). Rational-emotive therapy: Research data that support the clinical and personal hypotheses of RET and other modes of cognitive-behavior therapy. In A. Ellis & J. M. Whiteley (Eds.), *Theoretical and empirical foundations of rational-emotive therapy.* Monterey, CA: Brooks/Cole.

Ellis, A. (1980a). Discomfort anxiety: A new cognitive behavioral construct. Part 2. *Rational Living, 15*(1), 25-30.

Ellis, A. (1980b). Rational-emotive therapy and cognitive behavior therapy: Similarities and differences. *Cognitive Therapy and Research, 4,* 325-340.

Ellis, A. (1981a). The place of Immanuel Kant in cognitive psychotherapy. *Rational Living, 16*(2), 13-16.

Ellis, A. (1981b). The use of rational humorous songs in psychotherapy. *Voices, 16*(4), 29-36.

Ellis, A. (1982a). Intimacy in rational-emotive therapy. In M. Fisher & G. Striker (Eds.), *Intimacy.* New York: Plenum.

Ellis, A. (1982b). The treatment of alcohol and drug abuse: A rational-emotive approach. *Rational Living, 17*(2), 15-24.

Ellis, A. (1982c). Self-direction in sport and life. *Rational Living, 17*(1), 27-34.

Ellis, A. (1982d). Rational-emotive group therapy. In G. M. Gazda (Ed.), *Basic approaches to group psychotherapy and group counseling.* Springfield, IL: Thomas.

Ellis, A. (1983a). *The case against religiosity.* New York: Institute for Rational-Emotive Therapy.

Ellis, A. (1983b). How to deal with your most difficult client: You. *Journal of Rational-Emotive Therapy, 1*(1), 3-8. Also published in: *Psychotherapy in Private Practice,* 1984, *2,* 25-36.

Ellis, A. (1983c). The philosophic implications and dangers of some popular behavior therapy techniques. In M. Rosenbaum, C. M. Franks, & Y. Jaffe (Eds.), *Perspectives in behavior therapy in the eighties.* New York: Springer.

Ellis, A. (1983d). Failures in rational-emotive therapy. In E. B. Foa & P. M. G. Emmelkamp (Eds.), *Failures in behavior therapy.* New York: Wiley.

Ellis, A. (1983e). Rational-emotive therapy (RET) approaches to overcoming resistance. I: Common forms of resistance. *British Journal of Cognitive Psychotherapy, 1*(1), 28-38.

Ellis, A. (1983f). Rational-emotive therapy (RET) approaches to overcoming resistance. II: How RET disputes clients' irrational resistance-creating beliefs. *British Journal of Cognitive Psychotherapy, 1*(2), 1-16.

Ellis, A. (1983g). Does sex therapy really have a future? *Rational Living, 18*(1), 3-6.

Ellis, A. (1984a). The essence of RET—1984. *Journal of Rational-Emotive Therapy, 2*(1), 19-25.

Ellis, A. (1984b, August). Rational-emotive therapy and transpersonal psychology. Paper presented at the 92nd Annual Convention of the American Psychological Association, Toronto.

Ellis, A. (1984c). Rational-emotive therapy. In R. J. Corsini (Ed.), *Current psychotherapies* (3rd ed.). Itasca, IL: Peacock.

Ellis, A. (1984d). Rational-emotive therapy (RET) approaches to overcoming resistance. III: Using emotive and behavioural techniques of overcoming resistance. *British Journal of Cognitive Psychotherapy, 2*(1), 11-26.

Ellis, A. (1984e). *Intellectual fascism.* New York: Institute for Rational-Emotive Therapy.

Ellis, A. (1985a). Expanding the ABCs of rational-emotive therapy. In M. J. Mahoney & A. Freeman (Eds.), *Cognition and psychotherapy.* New York: Plenum.

Ellis, A. (1985b). Rational-emotive therapy (RET) approaches to overcoming resistance. IV: Handling special kinds of clients. *British Journal of Cognitive Psychotherapy, 3*(1), 26-42.

Ellis, A., & Abrahms, E. (1978). *Brief psychotherapy in medical and health practice.* New York: Springer.

Ellis, A., & Becker, I. (1982). *A guide to personal happiness.* North Hollywood, CA: Wilshire Books.

Ellis, A., & Bernard, M. E. (Eds.). (1983). *Rational-emotive approaches to the problems of childhood.* New York: Plenum.

Ellis, A., & Bernard, M. E. (Eds.). (1985). *Clinical applications of rational-emotive therapy.* New York: Plenum.

Ellis, A., & Grieger, R. (Eds.). (1977). *Handbook of rational-emotive therapy.* New York: Springer.

Ellis, A., & Harper, R. A. (1961a). *A guide to rational living.* Englewood Cliffs, NJ: Prentice-Hall.

Ellis, A., & Harper, R. A. (1961b). *A guide to successful marriage.* North Hollywood, CA: Wilshire Books.

Ellis, A., & Harper, R. A. (1975). *A new guide to rational living.* North Hollywood, CA: Wilshire Books.

Ellis, A., & Knaus, W. (1977). *Overcoming procrastination.* New York: New American Library.

Emmelkamp, P. M. G., Kuipers, A. C. M., & Eggeraat, J. B. (1978). Cognitive modification versus prolonged exposure in vivo: A comparison with agoraphobics as subjects. *Behaviour Research and Therapy, 16,* 33-41.

Emmelkamp, P. M. G., & Mersch, P. P. (1982). Cognition and exposure in vivo in the treatment of agoraphobia: Short term and delayed effects. *Cognitive Therapy and Research, 6,* 77-88.

Eschenroeder, C. (1979). Different therapeutic styles in rational-emotive therapy. *Rational Living, 14*(1), 3-7.

Evans, R. M., & Picano, J. J. (1983). Relationships between irrational beliefs and self report indices of psychopathology. *Psychological Reports, 55,* 545-546.

Försterling, F. (1983). Interdependencies among different depressogenic cognitions. *Rational Living, 18*(1), 12-15, 22.

Fox, E. E. (1969). *A life orientation scale: Correlates of biophilia and necrophilia.* Unpublished doctoral dissertation, University of Alberta.

Fox, E. E., & Davies, R. L. (1971). Test your rationality. *Rational Living, 5*(2), 23-25.

Freud, A. (1937). *The ego and the mechanisms of defense.* London: Hogarth.

Gardner, P., & Oei, T. P. (1981). Depression and self esteem: An investigation that uses behavioral and cognitive approaches to the treatment of clinically depressed patients. *Journal of Clinical Psychology, 37,* 128-135.

Geis, H. J. (1970). The psychology of dieting. *Rational Living, 5*(1), 24-33.

Golden, W. L. (1983). Rational-emotive hypnotherapy: Principles and practice. *British Journal of Cognitive Psychotherapy, 1*(1), 47-56.

Golden, W. L., Geller, E., & Hendricks, C. (1981). A coping-skills approach to flooding therapy in the treatment of test anxiety. *Rational Living, 16*(2), 17-22.

Goldfried, M., & Davison, G. (1976). *Clinical behavior therapy.* New York: Holt, Rinehart & Winston.

Gormally, J., Sipps, G., Raphael, R., Edwin, D., & Varvil-Weld, D. (1981). The relationship between maladaptive cognitions and social anxiety. *Journal of Consulting and Clinical Psychology, 49*, 300-301.

Grabia, M. R. H. (1977). *Relationship of irrational ideas and self esteem to self disclosure, loving behavior and marital satisfaction.* Unpublished master's thesis, University of Alberta.

Grieger, R. (1975). A rational-emotive perspective on adolescent emotional problems. *Rational Living, 10*(2), 32-37.

Grieger, R. (1977). An existential component of anger. *Rational Living, 12*(2), 3-8.

Grieger, R., & Boyd, J. (1980). *Rational-emotive therapy: A skills-based approach.* New York: Van Nostrand Reinhold.

Grieger, R., & Grieger, I. (Eds.). (1982). *Cognition and emotional disturbance.* New York: Human Sciences Press.

Gullo, J. M. (1966). Counseling hospitalized patients. *Rational Living, 1*(2), 11-15.

Hartman, B. J. (1968). Sixty revealing questions for twenty minutes. *Rational Living, 3*(1), 7-8.

Hauck, P. A. (1971). A RET theory of depression. *Rational Living, 6*(2), 33-35.

Hauck, P. A. (1972). *Reason in pastoral counseling.* Philadelphia: Westminster.

Hauck, P. A. (1974). Eleven myths of child counseling. *Rational Living, 9*(1), 38-43.

Haynes-Clements, L. A., & Avery, A. W. (1984). A cognitive-behavioral approach to social skills training with shy persons. *Journal of Clinical Psychology, 40*, 710-713.

Heidegger, M. (1949). *Existence and being.* Chicago: Henry Regnery.

Heppner, P. P., Reeder, B. L., & Larson, L. M. (1983). Cognitive variables associated with personal problem-solving appraisal: Implications for counseling. *Journal of Counseling Psychology, 30*, 537-545.

Herzberg, A. (1945). *Active psychotherapy.* New York: Grune & Stratton.

Hibbard, R. W. (1975). A rational approach to treating jealousy. *Rational Living, 10*(2), 25-28.

Himle, D. P., Thyer, B. A., & Papsdorf, J. D. (1982). Relationship between rational beliefs and anxiety. *Cognitive Research and Therapy, 6*, 219-223.

Hoellen, B. (1980). Reduction of a severe dog phobia: A case study. *Rational Living, 15*(2), 21-23.

Horney, K. (1950). *Neurosis and human growth.* New York: Norton.

Howard, D. (1981). *The effects of RET in group counseling on the self actualization of seniors at Harris High School, Marikana.* Unpublished master's thesis, De La Salle University, Manila.

Howard, L., & Tosi, D. J. (1978). Effects of rational stage directed imagery and behavioral rehearsal on assertiveness. *Rational Living, 13*(2), 3-8.

Janis, I. L. (1983). *Short-term counseling.* New Haven, CT: Yale University Press.

Jones, J. W. (1980, September). *Environmental and cognitive correlates of staff burnout.* Paper presented at the First Annual Conference on Behavior Analysis, Chicago.

Jones, M. C. (1924). A laboratory study of fear: The case of Peter. *Journal of Genetic Psychology, 31*, 308-315.

Jones, R. A. (1977). *Self-fulfilling prophecies: Social, psychological and physiological effects of expectancies.* Hillsdale, NJ: Lawrence Erlbaum.

Jones, R. G. (1968). *A factored measure of Ellis' irrational belief system, with personality and maladjustment correlates.* Unpublished doctoral dissertation, Texas Technological College.

Kassinove, H. (1974). Some effects of learning RET on graduate student adjustment. *Rational Living, 9*(2), 7-8.

Kassinove, H., Crisci, R., & Tiegerman, S. (1977). Developmental trends in rational thinking: Implications for rational-emotive school mental health programs. *Journal of Community Psychology, 5*, 266-274.

Kelly, G. (1955). *The psychology of personal constructs.* New York: Norton.

Kendall, P., & Hollon, S. (1980). *Assessment strategies for cognitive-behavioral interventions.* New York: Academic Press.

Knaus, W. J. (1973). Overcoming procrastination. *Rational Living, 8*(2), 3-7.

Knaus, W. J., & Bokor, S. (1975). The effects of rational–emotive education on anxiety and self-concept in sixth grade students. *Rational Living, 10*(2), 7-10.

Knaus, W. J., & Eyman, W. (1974). Progress in rational–emotive education. *Rational Living, 9*(2), 27-29.

Korzybski, A. (1933). *Science and sanity.* San Francisco: International Society of General Semantics.

Kujoth, R. (1979). Rational thinking applied to anorexia nervosa. *Rational Living, 14*(2), 19-25.

LaPointe, K., & Crandell, C. (1980). Relationship of irrational beliefs to self-reported depression. *Cognitive Therapy and Research, 4,* 247-250.

Lazarus, A. A. (1981). *The practice of multimodal therapy.* New York: McGraw-Hill.

Lazarus, A. A. (1984). *In the mind's eye.* New York: Guilford.

Lazarus, R. (1966). *Psychological stress and the coping process.* New York: McGraw-Hill.

Leaf, R. C., Gross, P. E., Todres, A. K., Marcus, S., & Bradford, B. (1984). *Placebo-like effects of education about rational-emotive therapy.* Unpublished manuscript, Rutgers University.

Lefebvre, R. C., & Lawliss, G. F. (1979). A rational approach to medical disorders. *Rational Living, 14*(1), 17-22.

Lefkovitz, P. M., & Davis, H. J. (1977). Rational–emotive therapy in a partial hospitalization setting. *Rational Living, 12*(2), 35-38.

Lehman, P. (1972). Overcoming boredom. *Rational Living, 7*(2), 40-41.

Lewinsohn, P. M., Larson, D. W., & Munoz, R. F. (1982). The measurement of expectancies and other cognitions in depressed individuals. *Cognitive Therapy and Research, 6,* 437-446.

Lockwood, G. (1981). Rational–emotive therapy and extremist religious cults. *Rational Living, 16*(1), 13-17.

Lohr, J. M., Bonge, D., & Jones, C. (1982). Social desirability and endorsement of irrational beliefs. *Psychological Reports, 53,* 395-397.

Lohr, J. M., Hamberger, L. K., & Bonge, D. (1982, May). *Relationship of factorially validated measures of anger expression and irrational beliefs.* Paper presented at the 54th Annual Convention of the Midwest Psychological Association, Chicago.

Long, S. (1981). A psychopolitical theory of system disaffection. *Micropolitics, 1,* 395-420.

Low, A. A. (1952). *Mental health through will-training.* West Hanover, MA: Christopher.

Mackay, D. (1984). Behavioural psychotherapy. In W. Dryden (Ed.), *Individual therapy in Britain.* London: Harper & Row.

Mahoney, M. J. (1977). Personal science: A cognitive learning theory. In A. Ellis & R. Grieger (Eds.), *Handbook of rational–emotive therapy.* New York: Springer.

Maultsby, M. C., Jr. (1973). Reducing suicides from prescription drugs: A behavioral approach to irrational fears and insomnia. *Rational Living, 8*(1), 11-15.

Maultsby, M. C., Jr. (1975). *Help yourself to happiness: Through rational self-counseling.* New York: Institute for Rational–Emotive Therapy.

Maultsby, M. C., Jr. (1984). *Rational behavior therapy.* Englewood Cliffs, NJ: Prentice-Hall.

Maultsby, M. C., Jr., & Ellis, A. (1974). *Technique for using rational–emotive imagery.* New York: Institute for Rational–Emotive Therapy.

Mavissakalian, M., Michelson, L., Greenwald, D., Kornblith, S., & Greenwald, M. (1983). Cognitive-behavioral treatment of agoraphobics: Paradoxical intention vs. self-statement training. *Behaviour Research and Therapy, 21,* 75-86.

McCaskill, N. D., & McCaskill, A. (1983). Preparing patients for psychotherapy. *British Journal of Clinical and Social Psychiatry, 2,* 80-84.

McClellan, T. A., & Stieper, D. R. (1973). A structured approach to group marriage counseling. *Rational Living, 8*(2), 13-18.

McGarry, J. J. (1984). The treatment of exhibitionism by rational-emotive therapy: A case history. *Journal of Rational-Emotive Therapy, 2*(1), 32-35.

McGovern, T. E., & Silverman, M. S. (1984). A review of outcome studies of rational-emotive therapy from 1977 to 1982. *Journal of Rational-Emotive Therapy, 2*(1), 7-18.

Meichenbaum, D. (1977). *Cognitive-behavior modification.* New York: Plenum.

Mooney, W. T. (1980). Tempering of temper outbursts: A case study. *Rational Living, 15*(2), 9-12.

Moore, R. H. (1983). Inference as "A" in RET. *British Journal of Cognitive Psychotherapy, 1*(2), 17-23.

Morelli, G., & Andrews, L. (1982). Cognitive irrationality and defensiveness. *Psychological Reports, 51,* 387-393.

Morelli, G., Andrews, L., & Morelli, R. (1982). The relation involving personality variables, problem relevance, rationality and anxiousness among college women. *Cognitive Therapy and Research, 6,* 57-62.

Munjack, D. J., Schlacks, A., Sanchez, V. C., Usigli, R., Zulueta, A., & Leonard, M. (1984). Rational-emotive therapy in the treatment of erectile failure: An initial study. *Journal of Sex and Marital Therapy, 10,* 170-177.

Nardi, T. J. (1980). Conversion reaction blindness: A brief clinical study. *Rational Living, 15*(2), 33-34.

Needham, W. E., & Ehmer, M. N. (1980). RET and adjustment to blindness. *Rational Living, 15*(2), 27-32.

Neiger, S., & Fullerton, E. (1979). The art of gentle assertive behavior. *Rational Living, 14*(1), 29-34.

O'Connell, W., Bright, M., & Grossman, S. (1978). Negative nonsense and drug addiction. *Rational Living, 13*(1), 19-24.

Oliver, R. (1975). Overcoming test anxiety. *Rational Living, 10*(1), 6-12.

Pead, J. (1980). *A controlled outcome study of rational-emotive therapy for neurotic depression.* Unpublished master's thesis, University of Melbourne.

Phadke, K. M. (1982). Some innovations in RET theory and practice. *Rational Living, 17*(2), 25-30.

Plutchik, R. (1976). The self inventory: A measure of irrational attitudes and behavior. *Rational Living, 11*(1), 31-33.

Popper, K. R. (1959). *The logic of scientific discovery.* New York: Harper & Bros.

Popper, K. R. (1963). *Conjectures and refutations.* New York: Harper & Bros.

Powell, J. (1976). *Fully human, fully alive.* Niles, IL: Argus.

Presby, S. (1979). Taking the "must" out of dieting. *Rational Living, 14*(2), 29-32.

Prola, M. (1984). *Irrational beliefs and cognitive functioning.* Unpublished paper, York College, City University of New York.

Rand, M. E. (1969). Rational-emotive approaches to academic underachievement. *Rational Living, 4*(2), 16-18.

Ray, J. B., Friedlander, R. B., & Solomon, G. S. (1984). Changes in rational beliefs among treated alcoholics. *Psychological Reports, 55,* 883-886.

Reichenbach, H. (1953). *The rise of scientific philosophy.* Berkeley, CA: University of California Press.

Rogers, C. R. (1957). The necessary and sufficient conditions of therapeutic personality change. *Journal of Consulting Psychology, 21,* 95-103.

Rohsenow, D. J., & Smith, R. E. (1982). Irrational beliefs as predictors of negative affective states. *Motivation and Emotion, 2,* 299-314.

Rossi, A. S. (1977). RET with children: More than child's play. *Rational Living, 12*(2), 21-24.

Russell, B. (1930). *The conquest of happiness.* New York: New American Library.

Russell, B. (1965). *The basic writings of Bertrand Russell.* New York: Simon & Schuster.

Sagarin, E. (1970). Rational guideposts on homosexuality. *Rational Living, 5*(1), 2-7.

Samrock, W. P. (1978). RET counseling with police officers. *Rational Living, 13*(1), 13–16.

Saxon, W. (1980). *The use of rational therapy with emotionally upset parents of handicapped children.* Unpublished manuscript, School of Social Work, University of Southern Mississippi.

Schlaks, A. (1982). *Treatment of secondary erectile failure with rational-emotive therapy.* Unpublished doctoral dissertation, University of Louvain, Belgium.

Sherman, S. H. (1967). Alcoholism and group therapy. *Rational Living, 2*(2), 20–22.

Shorkey, C. T., & Saski, J. (1981). Comparison of rational beliefs of blind, deaf and non-handicapped high school students. *Perceptual and Motor Skills, 52,* 751–754.

Shorkey, C. T., & Sutton-Simon, K. (1983a). Personality Data Form: Initial reliability and validity. *Psychological Reports, 52,* 879–883.

Shorkey, C. T., & Sutton-Simon, K. (1983b). Reliability and validity of the Rational Behavior Inventory with a clinical population. *Journal of Clinical Psychology, 39,* 34–38.

Shorkey, C. T., & Whiteman, V. L. (1974). *Rational Behavior Inventory: Test booklet.* Austin, TX: Authors.

Shorkey, C. T., & Whiteman, V. L. (1977). Development of the Rational Behavior Inventory: Initial validity and reliability. *Educational and Psychological Measurement, 37,* 527–534.

Sichel, J., & Ellis, A. (1984). *RET self-help form.* New York: Institute for Rational-Emotive Therapy.

Smith, J. K. (1982). Irrational beliefs in a college population. *Rational Living, 17*(1), 35–36.

Smith, T. W., Boaz, T. L., & Denney, D. R. (1984). Endorsement of irrational beliefs as a moderator of the effects of stressful life events. *Cognitive Therapy and Research, 8,* 363–370.

Solomon, G. S., & Ray, J. B. (1984). Irrational beliefs of shoplifters. *Journal of Clinical Psychology, 40,* 1075–1077.

Solomon, L. J., & Rothblum, E. D. (1984). Academic procrastination: Frequency and cognitive-behavioral correlates. *Journal of Counseling Psychology, 31,* 503–509.

Spirito, A., & Erickson, M. T. (1979). A developmental study of the relationship among irrational beliefs, behavior problems and neuroticism in adolescent boys. *Rational Living, 14*(2), 33–38.

Straatmeyer, A. J., & Watkins, J. T. (1974). Rational-emotive therapy and the reduction of speech anxiety. *Rational Living, 9*(1), 33–37.

Taft, G. L. (1965). *A study of the relationship of anxiety and irrational ideas.* Unpublished doctoral dissertation, University of Alberta.

Thurman, C. W. (1984). *Effectiveness of cognitive-behavioral treatments in reducing type A behavior among university faculty.* Unpublished manuscript, North Texas State University.

Tillich, P. (1983). *The courage to be.* New Haven: Yale University Press.

Tobacyk, J., & Milford, G. (1982). Criterion validity for Ellis' irrational beliefs: Dogmatism and uncritical inferences. *Journal of Clinical Psychology, 38,* 605–607.

Tosi, D. J., & Moleski, R. L. (1975). Rational-emotive crises intervention therapy (RECIT). *Rational Living, 10*(1), 32–37.

Tosi, D. J., & Reardon, J. (1976). The treatment of guilt through rational stage directed therapy. *Rational Living, 11*(1), 8–11.

Trexler, L. A. (1973). The suicidal person and the restoration of hope. *Rational Living, 8*(2), 19–23.

Tucker, D. M., & Newman, J. P. (1981). Verbal versus imaginative cognitive strategies in the inhibition of emotional arousal. *Cognitive Therapy and Research, 5,* 197–203.

Wachtel, P. L. (1977). *Psychoanalysis and behavior therapy: Toward an integration.* New York: Basic Books.

Walen, S. R., DiGiuseppe, R., & Wessler, R. L. (1980). *A practitioner's guide to rational-emotive therapy.* New York: Oxford.

Ward, R. M. (1983). *An investigation of irrational belief and its implications on trait guilt: A study of male and female opiate addicts.* Unpublished doctoral dissertation, Florida Institute of Technology.

Warren, R., Deffenbacher, J. L., & Brading, P. (1976). Rational-emotive therapy and the reduction of test anxiety in elementary school students. *Rational Living, 11*(2), 26-29.

Wasserman, T. H. (1983). Development of the children's dysfunctional cognition scale. *Child and Family Behavior, 5*(4), 17-24.

Wasserman, T. H., & Kimmel, J. I. (1978). A rational-emotive crisis-intervention treatment model. *Rational Living, 13*(1), 25-30.

Watkins, J. T. (1973). RET and the treatment of behavioral excesses. *Rational Living, 8*(1), 29-31.

Watkins, J. T., & Rush, A. J. (1983). Cognitive response test. *Cognitive Therapy and Research, 7,* 425-436.

Watson, J. B., & Rayner, R. (1920). Conditioned emotional reactions. *Journal of Experimental Psychology, 3,* 1-14.

Weber, R. J. (1983). The coronary-prone personality: An analysis of the cognitive structure underlying the type A behavior pattern. *Journal of Rational-Emotive Therapy, 1*(1), 21-23.

Weinrach, S. G. (1980). Unconventional therapist: Albert Ellis. *Personnel and Guidance Journal, 59*(2), 152-160.

Werner, E. E., & Smith, R. S. (1982). *Vulnerable but invincible: A study of resilient children.* New York: McGraw-Hill.

Wessler, R. A. (1975). Self-interest and assertion. *Rational Living, 10*(2), 2-6.

Wessler, R. A. (1980). How to play golf under pressure. *Rational Living, 15*(1), 21-24.

Wessler, R. A. (1981). So you are angry: Now what's your problem. *Rational Living, 16*(1), 29-31.

Wessler, R. A., & Wessler, R. L. (1980). *The principles and practice of rational-emotive therapy.* San Francisco, CA: Jossey-Bass.

Wessler, R. L. (1984). Alternative conceptions of rational-emotive therapy: Toward a philosophically neutral psychotherapy. In M. A. Reda & M. J. Mahoney (Eds.), *Cognitive psychotherapies: Recent developments in theory, research, and practice.* Cambridge, MA: Ballinger.

Wilson, A. R., & Krane, R. V. (1980). Change in self-esteem and its effects on symptoms of depression. *Cognitive Therapy and Research, 4,* 419-421.

Wilson, S. B., & London, T. (1977). Rational behavior education with young adults. *Rational Living, 12*(1), 16-19.

Witkin, G., & DiGiuseppe, R. (1984, May). *Rational-emotive therapy, behavior modification, and imaginal rehearsal in the treatment of adult obesity.* Paper presented at the Annual Meeting of the Society of Behavioral Medicine, Philadelphia.

Witmer, J. M., Rich, C., Barcikowski, R. S., & Mague, J. C. (1983). Psychosocial characteristics mediating the stress response: An exploratory study. *Personnel and Guidance Journal, 62,* 73-77.

Wolfe, J. L. (1976). Rational-emotive therapy as an effective feminist therapy. *Rational Living, 11*(1), 2-7.

Wolfe, J. L., and the staff of the Living School. (1969). Emotional education in the classroom: The Living School. *Rational Living, 4*(2), 23-25.

Wolfe, J. L., & Brand, E. (Eds.). (1977). *Twenty years of rational therapy.* New York: Institute for Rational-Emotive Therapy.

Yates, A. J., & Sambrailo, F. (1984). Bulimia nervosa: A descriptive and therapeutic study. *Behaviour Research and Therapy, 22,* 503-517.

Young, H. S. (1974a). *A rational counseling primer.* New York: Institute for Rational-Emotive Therapy.

Young, H. S. (1974b). A framework for working with adolescents. *Rational Living, 9*(1), 3–7.

Young, H. S. (1984a). Practising RET with lower-class clients. *British Journal of Cognitive Psychotherapy, 2*(2), 33–59.

Young, H. S. (1984b). Practising RET with bible-belt christians. *British Journal of Cognitive Psychotherapy, 2*(2), 60–76.

Young, H. S. (1984c). Teaching rational self-value concepts to tough customers. *British Journal of Cognitive Psychotherapy, 2*(2), 77–97.

Zingle, H. W. (1965). *Therapy approach to counseling underachievers.* Unpublished doctoral dissertation, University of Alberta.

7

COGNITIVE THERAPY

ROBERT J. DeRUBEIS
AARON T. BECK

BASIC THEORY OF COGNITIVE THERAPY

HISTORICAL BACKGROUND

The rationale and procedures of cognitive therapy have evolved over the last two to three decades, but their initial impetus came from Beck's early interviews with depressed clients (Beck, 1963). While operating initially from a classically Freudian perspective, he found, following several systematic studies (Beck, 1961; Beck & Hurvich, 1959; Beck & Ward, 1961) that Freud's (1917/1957) formulations of the depressive syndrome (melancholia) missed the mark in several respects. Beck eschewed an anger-turned-inward model and saw that, clinically, a more satisfying formulation focused on the *content* of the depressive's negative thinking. His early descriptions emphasized the negative biases and distortions that he found common among depressed clients. These descriptions led to hypotheses about the content and processes of cognition that are relatively distinctive to depression. More importantly, he argued that these cognitive aspects are more central to depression and more verifiable than the dynamic (motivational) processes posited in work to that time. Early studies were generally supportive of this view; they have been reviewed elsewhere (see Hollon & Beck, 1979).

Beck posits that the depressive exhibits distorted information processing, which results in a consistently negative view of him- or herself, the future, and the world. These views are presumed to underlie the behavioral, affective, and motivational symptoms of depression.

BASIC THEORY

Beck's cognitive model of emotional disorders states that in order to understand the nature of an emotional episode or disturbance, one must focus on the cognitive content of one's reaction to the upsetting event or stream of thought. The heuristic and therapeutic value of the cognitive model lies in its emphasis on the relatively easily accessed (preconscious or conscious) mental events that clients can be trained to report. It does not depend on

273

"unconscious" motivations, the nature of which in psychoanalytic therapies it is the therapist's duty to ascertain.

During the treatment of depression, the beliefs reported by the client are examined as they pertain to his or her views of him- or herself, the future, and the world. This trio of domains has been labeled the "cognitive traid" (Beck, Rush, Shaw, & Emery, 1979), and is used to help the therapist and client identify areas of concern that are involved in emotional distress. The assumption is that sadness, loss of motivation, suicidal wishes, and so on are related to concerns in one (or more) of these three domains.

Similar relations between overt symptoms and beliefs are assumed to operate in other disorders as well. In anxious clients, the cognitive aspect of the anxious state is of the greatest interest. And as is the case in depression, common themes are found among clients who experience dysfunctional levels of anxiety. The anxious cognitions seem to be focused on future disaster or discomfort.

Treatment Mechanisms

Cognitive therapy focuses on beliefs of various kinds: the client's expectations, evaluations (or ascriptions), and attributions of causality or responsibility (Hollon & Kriss, 1984). Once the client has attended to the content of his or her cognitive reaction, he or she is encouraged to view it as a hypothesis (rather than as a fact), that is, as a possible but not necessarily true proposition. Framing a belief as a hypothesis has been called "distancing" to refer to the way in which one can dissociate oneself from a belief in order to allow a more objective examination of it.

Through careful scrutiny and consideration of the belief, the client can gradually arrive at a different view. If the content of this new view is not upsetting to the client, then by virtue of changing the relevant belief, change in the emotional reaction should follow. That is, with the attenuation of the cognitive basis for an emotionally upsetting reaction to an event or problem, the emotional reaction will subside.

Through repeated attempts to identify and question the content of the client's reactions to events, several things are expected to follow. First, concern over troubling events in the recent past diminishes, since the initially troubling aspects of the beliefs about them are no longer held. This has the effect of reducing the negative affect that would normally occur during ruminations about, or recollections of, these events. The result is a less negative "basal" level of emotion or mood.

Second, the "foreign," or unexplainable quality that emotional reactions hold for many clients becomes understandable, in the form of the cognitive model. This sense of control, hopefulness, and comfort that follows the adoption of the cognitive model is said to be common to many forms of psychotherapy (Frank, 1973). That is, simply by adopting a set of organizing principles or a coherent world view, the client comes to see a "light at the end of the tunnel." The simple, usable model the client learns in cognitive therapy is particularly useful in achieving this effect.

Third, as a result of experience with the successful use of the methods employed in cognitive therapy, the client begins to use them when confronted with day-to-day difficulties, large and small. When used properly, these methods should have the effect of ameliorating many of the concerns that would otherwise lead to emotional upset. Since cognitive therapy is to a great extent a skills-based therapy, it is expected that the client will eventually come to employ the approach on his or her own, tackling more and more of the problems that confront him or her. In successful cases, it is assumed that the client continues to employ the cognitive model and its auxiliary methods in the face of upsetting circumstances long after formal therapy is terminated.

Since people are often careless when they make inferences about interpersonal and self-relevant matters (cf. Nisbett & Ross, 1980), the thinking skills taught in cognitive therapy are applicable even after the depressive episode remits. Indeed, many of these skills are probably used quite often by people who never experience episodes of depression. In addition, the risk of relapse is quite high in most disorders for which cognitive therapy is used. The client who is ready to apply the thinking skills learned during therapy is assumed to be at a lower risk for subsequent relapse. Several studies have pointed to a prophylactic effect of cognitive therapy; they will be reviewed below.

Schema Work

Cognitive therapy also aims to work on another, "deeper" level. Through the analysis of many instances of emotional upset, the client and therapist come to see that the client has certain patterns of thinking, or schemata (Beck, 1964, 1972; Hollon & Kriss, 1984). Schemata are the underlying cognitive structures that organize the client's experience and that can form the basis for the individual instances of bias or distortion. These schemata are thought to represent the core of the cognitive disturbance, and can be called "core beliefs." When identified, schemata can usually be stated in the form of "if–then" propositions, and are similar in breadth to Ellis's irrational beliefs (e.g., "If I am not competent in every way, then I'm a failure"; see Ellis & Harper, 1975). Though not as readily accessible as the individual instances of thought (often called "automatic thoughts"), these schemata become apparent to the client and therapist as they identify the consistencies or themes that run through the individual instances of upset.

When these themes are identified, their utility (balance of the pros and cons of holding them) or validity (their fit with available evidence) can be examined in the same way that individual inferences are analyzed. If these inquiries help to change the client's schemata, he or she can begin to recognize situations in which these "core beliefs" are implicit in his or her reactions to potentially upsetting events; the client can then consider an alternative inference. In addition, the extent to which the client holds these core beliefs will diminish over time. This is because the beliefs and their corollaries are repeatedly challenged, and the client's commitment to them is thereby weakened. Presumably, new schemata replace the old. So, for example, the client may replace the aforementioned schema with something like, "If I've given a task the effort it's due, I can be satisfied with it."

Cognitive Errors

During the course of therapy, yet another perspective on the client's thinking is given to him or her. The client is taught that there are several "types" of thinking errors that we are all subject to, and that occur more frequently during affective episodes. These are the "cognitive errors" that Beck and others have written about (Beck *et al.*, 1979; see Table 7.1). They can be easily memorized by the motivated client, who can then look for instances of them in his or her own thinking. The labels given to these errors serve a heuristic function, reminding the client of the ways in which his or her thinking in any given instance may be in error. When the error is identified, the client can then either simply discount the inference that involved the error, or use more general analytic techniques to question the validity of the inference.

Table 7.1. Types of Cognitive Errors

---

1. *Arbitrary inference* refers to the process of drawing a specific conclusion in the absence of evidence to support the conclusion or when the evidence is contrary to the conclusion.
2. *Selective abstraction* consists of focusing on a detail taken out of context, ignoring other more salient features of the situation and conceptualizing the whole experience on the basis of this fragment.
3. *Overgeneralization* refers to the pattern of drawing a general rule or conclusion on the basis of one or more isolated incidents and applying the concept across the board to related and unrelated situations.
4. *Magnification and minimization* are reflected in errors in evaluating the significance or magnitude of an event that are so gross as to constitute a distortion.
5. *Personalization* refers to the client's proclivity to relate events to him- or herself when there is no basis for making such a connection.
6. *Dichotomous thinking* is manifested in the tendency to place experiences in one of two opposite categories; for example, flawless or defective, immaculate or filthy, saint or sinner. In describing him- or herself, the client selects the extreme negative categorization.

The Nature of the Therapeutic Interaction

Much of what distinguishes cognitive therapy from other cognitive-behavioral therapies lies in the role assumed by the therapist and the role that he or she recommends to the client. The relationship is clearly meant to be one of collaboration, in which the therapist and client assume an equal share of the responsibility for solving the client's problems. This can be distinguished from attitudes found on either side of this middle ground.

First, the client is assumed to be the expert on his or her own experience and on the meanings he or she attaches to events. That is, the cognitive therapist does not assume that he or she knows why the client reacted a certain way in a certain situation; he or she asks for the client's recollection of ongoing thoughts and images. Further, the cognitive therapist does not assume knowledge of the reason why a certain thought was upsetting; he or she asks the client. This reliance on the client's report of the meaning of his or her thoughts distinguishes cognitive therapy from Ellis's rational-emotive therapy (Ellis, 1984) on the one hand, and from a Meichenbaum-type cognitive behavior modification (CBM: Meichenbaum, 1972) on the other.

Rational-emotive therapy employs a deductive approach in which the therapist more readily infers the nature of client thinking errors on the basis of experience with other clients and knowledge of rational-emotive theory. In it can be found rules for determining the underlying or basic beliefs implied by the reactions that clients report for upsetting events. Ellis recommends that the therapist be "a step ahead" of the patient, supplying him or her with the meanings of his or her reported thoughts (see, e.g., Ellis, 1984, p. 221).

In a learning-theory-derived system such as Meichenbaum's CBM, thoughts are treated more as behaviors, so that one thought can replace another or can be differentially reinforced; there is less emphasis on the *meaning* of the thoughts involved. Though a cognitive therapist may on occasion encourage the client to view an automatic thought as a habit, and therapy may aim to eliminate the habit or replace it with a new (less distressing) one, this would not be done before the client has thoroughly explored the meanings or implications of the thought, and has decided that the meaning of the habitual thought is not true.

The assumption in cognitive therapy is that the meaning system of each client is idiosyncratic. For this reason the client must take a very active role in his or her treatment. He or she is taught to be prepared to question his or her thoughts—whatever they may be—when in the midst of emotional upset, or shortly thereafter. By contrast, in Meichenbaum's Self Instructional Training (SIT: see Meichenbaum, 1972), the therapist helps the client to prepare to make specific coping statements to him- or herself when he or she is confronted with difficulties. A simple way to refer to this difference between SIT and cognitive therapy is that in cognitive therapy, the therapist teaches the client to question his or her inferences, whereas in SIT he or she teaches the client to change them.

With the focus on questioning in cognitive therapy, it is believed by those who use this method that it is a more general approach that can be readily applied by the client to new situations or to new reactions in familiar situations. Insofar as this distinction captures a major difference between cognitive therapy and SIT, it also implies that in cognitive therapy more responsibility is placed on the shoulders of the client.

When new data are to be gathered, or experiments that address an idiosyncratic belief of the client are to be attempted, the cognitive therapist tries very hard to involve the client in planning the data collection or the experiment. His or her goal is to help the client devise tests whose results would be convincing *to the client*, rather than to the therapist, to another client, or to a logician. Thus, the client is actively involved in his or her treatment and, again, is the expert on his or her own case.

The cognitive therapist, of course, is the expert on the cognitive model and, especially at the beginning of therapy, is responsible for teaching the client the principles that underlie the therapy. He is also the expert on the analytical methods used to test the beliefs reported by the client.

As in any intense relationship, problems between therapist and client may arise. In cognitive therapy, concerns that the client has about the therapy or the therapist are actively discussed. The therapist seeks feedback, and responds to it in ways consistent with the model. That is, the therapist helps the client attend to his or her thoughts about the therapy itself and together they examine them.

CLINICAL APPLICATIONS

BEHAVIORAL METHODS

Cognitive therapy, borrowing as it does some procedures originated in other active–directive schools of therapy, often adapts behavioral methods to suit the goals of cognitive change. In the following section, the more prominent behavioral methods used in cognitive therapy will be highlighted. While at times these methods are used to increase activity or to provide experiences of pleasure or mastery, the cognitive therapist will always attend to changes in beliefs that may result from the use of these methods. Cognitive change is typically the primary goal of these methods, as will be made clear below. The cognitive therapist will often explain the assignment of behavioral tasks in this way, indicating that the client's attempts to engage in the assigned task will serve either to test a hypothesis that the client holds, or to provide a setting that will provoke the formation of new hypotheses that can subsequently be tested.

Self-Monitoring

Most clients who begin a course of cognitive therapy are asked to, for at least 1 week, keep a careful hour-by-hour record of their activities and associated moods or other pertinent phenomena. One useful variant is to have the client record his or her mood on a simple 0–100 scale, where 0 is the worst he or she has ever felt, and 100 the best. As suggested in Beck *et al.* (1979), the client can also record the degree of mastery or pleasure associated with each recorded activity.

This record can serve several functions, the most obvious of which is to acquaint the therapist with the way the client is spending his or her time. In the process, the client is often surprised by some aspect of the record, such as how much time he or she spends watching television. It can also serve as a baseline against which later records can be compared.

A number of hypotheses can be tested using self-monitoring, such as "It doesn't do any good for me to get out of bed," "I'm always miserable; it never lets up," and "My schedule is too full for me to accomplish what I must." A careful examination of the completed record is a far better basis for judging such hypotheses than is the client's memory of recent events, since his or her memory will be selective.

Another common use of the self-monitoring record is as a cue to the client's memory, so that particularly bad or particularly good events can be discussed in the session. The therapist can ask the client to recall the thoughts that occurred at the time in question.

Finally, if there are consistencies in the record, such that certain kinds of events are associated with good (or bad) moods, or with mastery or pleasure, these activities can be identified, and then sought out (or avoided). This can be implemented in the scheduling or structuring of activities.

Scheduling Activities

The purpose of scheduling activities in cognitive therapy is twofold: (1) to increase the probability that the client will engage in activities that he or she has been avoiding, and (2) to remove decision-making as an obstacle in the initiation of an activity. Since the decision has been made in the office, or in advance by the client him- or herself, the client need only carry out that which he or she has decided (or agreed) to do. This is not to suggest that clients always follow their schedules. Rather, these accounts are offered for those times when scheduling *is* successful.

When the client does not carry out the agreed upon activities, grist for the therapeutic mill is provided. This may simply be a result of the therapist being overly ambitious in assigning tasks. However, most often such "fail-ures" are quite similar in character to what has been troubling the client generally. For the cognitive therapist, then, a thorough analysis of the cognitive obstacles is indicated. For example, he or she will work through the pessimistic thoughts that prevented the client from initiating the task, pointing out that, given that the client fully believed the proposition (e.g., "I am not capable of writing this letter") at the time, it made perfect sense that he or she did not follow through on it. Then work can be done on the hypothesis itself (i.e., "I am not capable of writing this letter").

Activities that are scheduled can come from three domains: (1) those that were associated with mastery, pleasure, or good mood during self-monitoring, (2) those that had been rewarding in the past but that the client has been avoiding of late, and (3) new activities agreed upon by the client and therapist that may be rewarding or informative. When constructing the schedule, the cognitive therapist tries to help the client anticipate the obstacles—environmental or cognitive—that are likely to interfere with the scheduled activities. These obstacles can then be discussed in the session, or the schedule can be altered in order to avoid them.

A test of a hypothesis discussed in the session may be embedded in the schedule. For example, television watching can be scheduled for some evenings, reading for others, and visiting with friends for others. The client then monitors his or her mood or the degree of mastery and pleasure he or she experiences in each activity, providing a test of beliefs about the utility of these activities. An added benefit of such a suggestion is that the client is often more willing to carry out an activity if it is couched in terms of an experiment, perhaps because he or she is not committed to the activity beyond the time of the experiment.

Other Behavioral Strategies

Since tasks that are causing trouble for the client are exactly those that have been difficult to do, modifying the structure of these tasks is often appropriate. Large tasks (e.g., finding a job, giving a speech) are explicitly broken down into their smaller units (circling want-ads, outlining the main points of the speech, etc.) in order to make the task more concrete and less overwhelming. This intervention has been termed "chunking."

"Graded tasks" can also be constructed such that easier tasks or simpler aspects of larger tasks are explicitly set out as the first to be attempted. This is also referred to as "success therapy," as it is assumed that success on the earlier, easier tasks, provides an impetus to move on to the more difficult ones. Though chunking and graded task assignments may seem simplistic, it is often surprising to both the client and the therapist how these simple alterations in the structure of a task will change the client's view of the task and, subsequently, the likelihood of accomplishment.

This brief overview of common behavioral aspects of cognitive therapy was intended to show how behavioral assignments can be incorporated into cognitive therapy, and how the focus on the cognitive aspects of these assignments can produce therapeutic effects. Variations on these simple procedures, suited to the goals of a particular case, are often desirable and can provide a solid foundation for the cognitive change that is the focus of the therapy.

COGNITIVE METHODS

While the aims of the procedures that are more behavioral in nature always include, at least secondarily, an alteration in the actions of the client, many of the cognitive therapy procedures aim expressly at change in cognition, since cognitive theory considers that change in affect and behavior comes chiefly as a result of cognitive changes. Presented here will be an overview of the basic concepts employed in procedures that are explicitly aimed at cognitive change.

Daily Record of Dysfunctional Thoughts

Much of the work in cognitive therapy centers around the use of a device called the Daily Record of Dysfunctional Thoughts (DRDT: see Beck *et al.*, 1979). Though a modified version of this device or some different device may be desirable for a particular client, the DRDT will be presented here to illustrate several of the principles and options that are embedded in the cognitive therapy approach. The four most important columns in the DRDT (see Figure 7.1) correspond to the three points in the cognitive model (situation, belief, emotional consequence) plus the alternative or counter response to the beliefs (i.e., the more "rational" or functional belief). Clients are typically first taught to use the DRDT by noting those times when they experience an unpleasant or puzzling affective state. Thus, the cognitive therapist first must be certain that the client understands what he or she means by "feelings." This is the starting point of cognitive therapy. The therapist also asks the client to note the situation or stream of thoughts during which the feelings occurred. For many clients, the situation and the emotional state are the two aspects of their experience that they most readily attend to at times of emotional disturbance (e.g., "I was hurt because he didn't answer me"). It is also true that many clients view situations as directly causing emotional responses, considering in addition that there is "something" wrong with the client that results in emotional reactions that are maladaptive or upsetting. The job of the cognitive therapist is thus to teach the client to attend to his or her thoughts and images at these times. At least initially, thoughts often must be reported retrospectively in response to the in-session queries of the therapist.

Once the client is able to report situations, thoughts, and emotional reactions (preferably at the time of the event and on paper), intervention can begin. Though termed "Rational Response" on the DRDT, it is not neces-

DAILY RECORD OF DYSFUNCTIONAL THOUGHTS

DATE	SITUATION Describe: 1. Actual event leading to unpleasant emotion, or 2. Stream of thoughts, daydream, or recollection, leading to unpleasant emotion.	EMOTION(S) 1. Specify sad/ anxious/ angry, etc. 2. Rate degree of emotion, 1-100.	AUTOMATIC THOUGHT(S) 1. Write automatic thought(s) that preceded emotion(s). 2. Rate belief in automatic thought(s), 0-100%.	RATIONAL RESPONSE 1. Write rational response to automatic thought(s). 2. Rate belief in rational response, 0-100%.	OUTCOME 1. Rerate belief in automatic thought(s), 0-100%. 2. Specify and rate sub- sequent emotions, 0-100.

Explanation: When you experience an unpleasant emotion, note the situation that seemed to stimulate the emotion. (If the emotion occurred while you were thinking, daydreaming, etc., please note this.) Then note the automatic thought associated with the emotion. Record the degree to which you believe this thought: 0% = not at all; 100% = completely. In rating degree of emotion: 1 = a trace; 100 = the most intense possible.

Figure 7.1. Daily record of dysfunctional thoughts. Reprinted by permission of Aaron T. Beck.

sary to assume that clients' beliefs are always irrational, or even incorrect. To say that the work of cognitive therapy involves "coming up with rational responses" to "automatic thoughts" is a rough approximation to the actual intent of cognitive therapy. But more precisely, it involves the examination of inferences made when emotionally upset, and that may be considered the cause of the upset. Thus, whether the responses to the initial thoughts are called "rational," "adaptive," "alternative," or some other term, the intervention focuses upon helping the client to learn to question and examine his or her inferences. We shall return to the nature of the questioning involved in cognitive therapy after completing the discussion of the DRDT.

There are many useful secondary features of the DRDT that are worth mentioning. Clients can record the degree of belief in the "automatic thought," both before and after it is examined. This allows for a check on the effect of the questioning. When a high degree of belief in the automatic thought remains, it indicates that as elegant or thorough as the questioning may have seemed, it did not resolve the initial concern. Either a key meaning was missed, or the client has made a thorough and accurate characterization of the situation. In the latter case, the therapist may then help the client examine the significance or meaning of his or her characterization (see the discussion of the downward arrow technique below).

Similarly, the degree of the affective response can be recorded both before and after an analysis of the thoughts. Little or no change in affect tells the cognitive therapist that something important was missing from the analysis, such that the client still holds relevant beliefs that have not been touched upon by it. Further exploration is suggested.

Finally, there is a space where the degree of belief in the rational response can be recorded. If the response is trite (e.g., "Things will get better soon") or in any way not convincing to the client, it can be picked up here.

The DRDT can be worked on in the session, or, especially as therapy progresses, it can be used independently by the client, with the therapist checking it over during the session. Though clients eventually do the work of the DRDT without paper and pen, it is quite useful for them to save the records they have filled out since many of the concerns and responses worked through during therapy are relevant later in the therapy and after therapy has ended. When cognitive therapy has a prophylactic effect, it is assumed that, in part, it is because the client has retained the ability to attend to and question his or her thinking as was the case during therapy.

Three Questions

Though there are any number of ways to classify the questions that can be asked of inferences, one classification serves a heuristic function for clients while they learn the methods of cognitive therapy. The three kinds of questions clients are taught are: (1) "What is the evidence for and against the belief?" (2) "What are alternative interpretations of the event or situation?" and (3) "What are the real implications, if the belief is correct?" Each of the questions is stated here in a general form, and can of course be modified to suit the client's situation or style.

Downward Arrow

Oftentimes the thought reported initially by a client is in a form that would yield little if analyzed for its validity. For instance, a client may think, in response to a perceived snub by someone at a party, "She doesn't think I'm exciting enough." Though any therapist can imagine a number of reasons why this may be upsetting to the client, presumably there are some implications or meanings the client extracts from this inference that are particularly important to him or her. Thus, rather than first asking questions about how reasonable the inference is (e.g., "Did she give any other indications of her interest or disinterest?"; "Could there be other reasons why she acted that way?"), the therapist would do well to ask a question of the form, "And what would it mean (regarding you or your future) *if it were true* that she sees you as not exciting enough for her?" Though basically a variant of the third of the three questions listed above, this way of approaching a reported belief has been termed the "downward arrow" technique. "Downward arrow" refers to a series of questions that can be asked of almost any inference, where each answer begs another question. They are of the form "What if it is true that . . . ?" or "What about that bothers you?" The aim of each question is to probe for the personal meaning of the inference to the client, until an inference is brought out that will profit from the work of cognitive therapy. So, in the example, above, the downward arrow might yield "I'm basically an uninteresting person," "I'll never attract that sort of person," or some other meaning that the original inference implies for the client. It is important for the therapist to realize that the meanings are idiosyncratic and often difficult to predict, even after he or she has come to know the client well. Further, though a therapist may choose to ask the first two of the three questions immediately, there are times when it is clearly more productive first to follow the downward arrow.

Cognitive Errors

An alternative and often complementary approach to the three questions involves the therapist teaching the client to learn to recognize when his or her thinking falls into one of the categories of cognitive errors (see Table 7.1). These labels are used to remind the client that he or she, as a member of the human race, is prone to various forms of exaggeration and other biased thinking. At these times, the client can discount the improbable or illogical inference, reframe it in a less extreme form, or analyze the inference using the three questions. For example, a client may conclude that he or she has given a poor lecture, since 3 of the 40 students in the class were inattentive from time to time during the lecture. The client may then notice that he or she has "personalized," particularly if another reason can be readily given for the inattentiveness that does not involve the quality of the lecture (e.g., it was 80 degrees in the lecture hall, the students are apathetic, etc.). Alternatively, the client may decide that he or she has "overgeneralized," particularly if on reflection he or she recalls that most of the students seemed quite interested during the lecture, and that several students came to him or her after class with thoughtful questions.

Identifying Schemata

After a therapist and client have been working together for several sessions, they should notice a certain consistency to the kinds of beliefs that are involved in emotional disturbance for the client. This consistency will not be found at the "surface" level, but rather at the level of personal meaning. For example, the therapist and client may note that many of the client's entries in the DRDT include the belief "If I am not the best _____ then it is not worth pursuing, and I am worthless as a _____."

The Dysfunctional Attitudes Schedule (DAS: Weissman, 1979) is an assessment device that can be used to tap these underlying assumptions or schemata, and to track change during and following treatment. It consists of a series of attitudinal statements that the client is asked to consider. The client rates the degree to which he or she agrees with each statement. The DAS has been factor analyzed and found to contain eight interpretable factors (Riskind, Beck, & Smucker, 1983). The eight factors, along with sample items, are as follows: (1) *vulnerability* ("If a person asks for help, it is a sign of weakness"); (2) *attraction/rejection* ("I am nothing if a person I love doesn't love me"); (3) *perfectionism* ("My life is wasted unless I am a success"); (4) *imperatives* ("I should be happy all of the time"); (5) *approval* ("I do not need other people's approval in order to be happy"); (6) *dependence* ("A person cannot survive without the help of other people"); (7) *autonomous attitudes* ("My own opinions of myself are more important than others' opinions of me"); (8) and *cognitive philosophy* ("Even though a person may not be able to control what happens to him or her, he or she can control how he or she thinks"). Scores on these factors can point to the most troublesome clusters of attitudes or schemata, or the client and therapist can look for more idiosyncratic patterns.

TREATMENT PROCEDURES—DEPRESSION

As cognitive therapy has its roots in Beck's early interest in depression, more has been written about the cognitive therapy of depression than about any other disorder or clinical phenomenon. No course of treatment follows the same path, but even the flexible cognitive therapist will find striking similarities in the progression of treatment for a variety of cases of depression. The prototype course of treatment will be described below, using the concepts outlined in the previous section.

Beginning of Treatment

The cognitive therapist has several complementary goals at the beginning of treatment. They can be categorized as (1) assessment, (2) socializing the client into the cognitive model, and (3) dealing with the client's pessimism (about treatment and in general).

Assessment efforts can include administration and scoring of the self-report Beck Depression Inventory (BDI: Beck, Ward, Mendelson, Mock, & Erbaugh, 1961), which can then be used as a session-to-session measure of depression level. Though its validity as a depression severity measure has been well demonstrated (see Beck & Beamesderfer, 1974, for a review), it is as a within-client change measure that it is of most use during the course of therapy.

As discussed above, the DAS is also a useful instrument that can both point to areas of difficulty and serve as an indicator of change in dysfunctional attitudes as treatment progresses. The therapist must be careful when he or she uses the DAS as a change measure, however. Some clients learn what they are "supposed to believe," and answer in accordance with this later in treatment, even if they fail to apply these "new" beliefs in daily life. The therapist can avoid misinterpreting the results of the mid- or post-treatment DAS by asking the client what he or she meant when he or she answered the items.

It is important in the beginning of cognitive therapy that the client and therapist have a common understanding of the model that will be used during treatment. To this end, clients are asked to read the booklet *Coping with Depression* (Beck & Greenberg, 1974), or a similar description of the cognitive model of depression and its treatment. The therapist and client can discuss the client's reaction to the book, and a recent upsetting experience can be framed in the cognitive model. Though this early "socialization" of the client into the cognitive model of treatment often involves intensive didactic explanation, it serves a greater purpose than merely that of preparing the client for treatment. It has the added benefit of giving the client an account of his or her difficulties that leaves room for understanding and improvement. Thus, the client's hopelessness, a common feature of depression, is dealt with thoroughly and directly.

At the beginning of treatment, additional interventions are often directed toward the client's pessimism or hopelessness. This can take the form of working through a task that the client has not been able to tackle, and that he or she believes he or she does not have the resources to overcome. The therapist elicits and records the client's expectations for his or her performance on the task. He or she then guides the client through the anticipated obstacles to its completion. When the client is able to accomplish more than he or she expected, the success is used as a foundation upon which further attempts can be built.

The Middle Phase

Though work on cognitive coping skills has already begun in the early phase of treatment, it is in the middle phase that the therapist and client work to solidify these skills. The client works between sessions to identify the situations and thoughts that bring about negative affect. Ideally, he or she keeps a written record on the DRDT, and is beginning to question his or her thinking either at the time of or shortly following the disturbance. The therapist helps the client "fine tune" his or her responses to initial thoughts, often by using the "downward arrow" technique described above. That is, the therapist reviews the client's DRDT with him or her and helps the client to see where he or she could attempt alternative analyses of his or her automatic thoughts.

It is also during the middle phase that patterns are identified that are associated with schemata or underlying assumptions. The developmental histories of these schemata are also discussed, so as to help the client make sense of the patterns that have been identified. Without such an inquiry, the client is apt to view his or her idiosyncratic way of interpreting events in the world as coming "out of the blue." Not surprisingly, this can leave the client feeling helpless, and worse yet, believing he or she is fundamentally flawed in some way. In this respect cognitive therapy is similar to the "depth" approaches to psychotherapy, in that it aims to understand the influence of early experience upon subsequent attitudes and concerns. It differs from these approaches in that this step is not seen as a necessary one, but rather as a useful adjunct to the skills training and problem solving that take up the bulk of therapy sessions.

The Final Phase

During the final phase of therapy, gains are reviewed and therapy is focused on the prevention of relapse. The therapist and client anticipate difficult situations or problems that may arise in the future that would tax the client's coping skills. This is an important aspect of the therapy, since it is easy for clients to be unclear about the importance of the skills they have learned. Many clients attribute their recovery to changes in their environment, even if it has been through their own effort that these changes have come about. And since by this time the client is feeling better, it is vital that his or her skills be tested and demonstrated so that he or she becomes likely to call upon them when, inevitably, difficult situations arise.

It is also during this phase that the client's beliefs about his or her ability to leave therapy must be addressed. The client may believe that he or she will be fine so long as he or she remains in therapy, but that it will be impossible to handle problems on his or her own. If a collaborative working relationship has already been developed, the therapist will only need to place more responsibility for the treatment on the shoulders of the client, so that the therapist becomes more a consultant than an active therapist. This gradual shift can serve as the context for a test of the client's ability to work problems out on his or her own.

Finally, the therapist and client may agree to schedule "booster sessions" to follow up the work that has been done. Though there has been no empirical test of the effectiveness of booster sessions as preventive treatment, reports from clients and therapists alike attest to their value.

TREATMENT PROCEDURES—PANIC DISORDERS AND AGORAPHOBIA

The symptomatology in the development of a panic attack follows an almost stereotyped sequence. First, the client experiences some type of sensation that is usually unpleasant and that he or she cannot discount as nonpathological. If the client has had one or more previous panic attacks he or she may "recognize" this symptom as a prelude to such a reaction and, indeed, may anticipate that another panic attack is coming on. In any event, the progression will continue if the client ascribes some pathological significance to the particular sensation or symptom and is unable to dismiss it as not dangerous. The meaning or interpretation given by the client will "make sense" to the therapist, in that it will bear a relation to the sensation(s). Thus, a pain in the chest is likely to be interpreted as a heart attack, tightness or shortness of breath as a sign that one will stop breathing. Lightheadedness is often viewed as signalling impending loss of consciousness, numbness or tingling in the extremities as having a stroke, some mental confusion means that one is going crazy, and so on.

There are often precipitating factors of which the client is unaware that can readily explain the onset of these physiological or psychological experiences. Thus, an individual may feel faint if he or she gets up suddenly from a chair, has gone for a long time without eating, or is looking down from a high place. He or she may become generally aroused by hearing unpleasant (or even pleasant) news. Each of these sensations may be interpreted by the individual as a sign of an impending disaster.

A large proportion of clients subject to panic attacks also seem to experience hyperventilation. A person who is upset or who experiences shortness of breath, for example, may start to breathe rapidly and as a result of "blowing off" carbon dioxide may experience symptoms of alkalosis (numbness and tingling in the extremities, generalized discomfort).

A client who has had a certain amount of "cognitive strain" may have a sudden lapse of memory or difficulty in reasoning that he or she attributes to a serious mental disorder. A father experiencing a burst of emotion during a quarrel with his children may interpret the accompanying bodily feelings as a sign that he is out of control and may assault them.

As the panic attack develops, the individual's attention becomes fixed on the symptoms. He or she is now quite aware of a pounding heartbeat, faintness, dizziness, or shortness of breath. The individual then begins to focus on a catastrophic consequence of having the symptoms. This may include the fear that if the symptoms continue any longer, he or she will die. Some clients report vivid visual images such as falling down, being surrounded by people, and then being placed in an ambulance and taken to the hospital. Occasionally a client, particularly one with a high level of depression, may have an image of him- or herself lying dead in a coffin and feeling extremely lonely because he or she is isolated from other people.

One of the most striking aspects of the panic attack is the client's loss of ability during the attack to view his or her sensations objectively and to apply an appropriate label to them. Even though the client may have agreed a few minutes previously that the symptoms do not represent any serious threat to life or mental stability, he or she loses the ability to apply this information once the attack has started. It is not clear whether there is an actual suppression of the higher evaluative functions or whether the individual's attention is so focused on the symptoms and their (inappropriate) meanings that he or she does not have the cognitive capacity left to evaluate his or her interpretations. In any event, the loss of capacity to apply reason and medical knowledge to the interpretation of the symptoms seems to be a necessary component of the disorder. A client may have all the features of intense anxiety without having a panic attack if he or she retains the ability to regard his or her symptoms objectively.

The next stage in the development of the panic disorder takes the form of a vicious cycle. As the individual begins to interpret his or her symptoms (e.g., rapid heart rate, shortness of breath) as pathological, his or her sense of danger increases. This in turn produces a greater focusing on the symptoms, which itself produces an increased intensity of the symptoms. With the increased focus on the symptoms and their imagined consequences, the client becomes even less able to apply reason to his or her understanding of the symptomatology. Thus, the symptoms continue to escalate. A special feature of this progression is the client's recognition that his or her usual attempts to ward off fear, such as walking around or trying to divert his or her own attention, do not seem to quell the disturbance. The symptoms appear uncontrollable and he or she begins to believe that they will continue to escalate until a disaster occurs. In contrast to panic attacks associated with phobias of specific environmental situations (acrophobia, claustrophobia), the spontaneous "attack" represents a "phobia" (fear) of a set of internal conditions.

General Treatment Approach

Clients who have received cognitive therapy for this disorder state that they are able to cut short the panic attack by applying certain techniques as soon as they recognize the first signs. They report that they are able to "tell" themselves that the symptom is not a sign of an impending disaster. Also, they find that they can distract themselves by, for example, engaging actively in conversation. Applying relaxation or controlled breathing techniques further diminishes the sense of impending disaster. Most clients in fact are able to employ all of these methods.

The formal treatment of panic disorders consists of several steps. The client first receives a "course of instruction" regarding the nature of panic attacks and a specific re-education regarding his or her own particular set of symptoms and own interpretations of them. In this way, the client is prepared to restructure cognitively the symptoms of the attack when they occur. It is, however, important before proceeding with cognitive therapy to determine via the appropriate medical procedures that the client's symptoms are *not* indicative of some underlying organ pathology.

Clients with agoraphobia may wait until they have mastered the new information and techniques before going into the agoraphobic situation. In the case of a client with a "spontaneous panic disorder" the client needs to be prepared in advance for the unexpected occurrence of the episode.

The second step in preparing for panic attacks consists of cognitive restructuring of the symptoms of the attack. The client is provided with an alternative interpretation of his or her frightening bodily sensations. Thus, he or she learns, for example, that sudden faintness may be due to a faulty adjustment of the blood pressure mechanism following a change in posture. Similarly, the therapist indicates that hyperventilation may simply be an innocuous expression of an emotional disturbance.

In the third phase, the client learns techniques for dealing with the panic disorder itself.

1. The therapist and client must explore the specific frightening phenomena he or she experiences during the incipient and full-blown attacks. The client's specific thoughts and their meanings are elicited retrospectively (from previous attacks) and during subsequent attacks.

2. Automatic thoughts and physical symptoms are reinterpreted. Armed with the knowledge that his or her beliefs about the pathological nature of his or her experience are erroneous, the client can thus appraise the specific interpretations and images. If the client, for example, experiences tightness in the chest and then attributes this to a coronary attack or to an imminent cessation of breathing, he or she can "tell him- or herself" that this is simply a tightness of the muscles in the rib cage (if he or she can indeed demonstrate that this is the case) and that it therefore is not a sign of a serious abnormality.

3. Relaxation techniques are generally useful only in the very early stages of the panic attack. At this point, the relaxation itself may reduce the symptom, and therefore assure the client that it is not pathological. On the other hand, if the client is experiencing faintness or is already preoccupied with the notion of sudden death, attempts at relaxation may undermine his or her ability to deal effectively with the attack.

4. Another effective technique, particularly for those clients whose attacks seem to be brought on by hyperventilation, is the training of the client in certain breathing techniques. The client may be given a breathing tape to listen to and then to learn to time his or her breathing according to

the instructions on the tape. This breathing exercise ostensibly works by reducing the "blowing off of carbon dioxide" (Clark, Salkovskis, & Chalkley, 1985).

5. Related to the use of the controlled breathing technique is a method that can restore the acid–base balance by rebreathing carbon dioxide. This is accomplished by having the client breathe into a paper bag.

6. Distraction techniques constitute yet another important aspect of the treatment. There is a wide variety of techniques of varying utility, depending upon the individual and also upon the situation. If the attack begins while the client is with a group of people, for example, he or she may benefit from becoming actively engaged in conversation with other people or attempting to focus his or her attention on things in the environment. Above all, it is important that he or she becomes physically active. Some people benefit from working on a puzzle; others do well to become actively engaged in a task such as writing a description of the experience.

Induction of "Mini Panic Attacks" in the Office

The major symptoms of the panic attack can be produced in the consulting room. In this context, the therapist can better understand the client's thinking processes as the attack develops, and he or she can give the client first-hand instructions in dealing with the attack. It takes some ingenuity to instigate an attack in the office. Basically, it is important to reproduce the type of situation that can precipitate an attack. In about 60% of clients, hyperventilation itself is sufficient to start at least a "mini attack." It is generally possible to demonstrate to clients that this innocuous procedure can reproduce most of the symptoms of the attack. The client goes through the following sequence: (1) controlled breathing, which may involve (2) use of the bag for rebreathing; (3) distraction; and (4) application of reason. The client learns that he or she can "turn off" as well as "turn on" an attack. The increased sense of control reduces the client's sense of vulnerability and consequently reduces the susceptibility to full blown attacks.

For clients who are alarmed by a rapid heart rate, a mini-attack may be induced by the client's jumping up and down for a few minutes or running up a flight of stairs. The client can then be given a relaxation exercise and can be shown how to distract him- or herself and also how to reinterpret the symptoms.

If the client is agoraphobic, it is important for the therapist to work with him or her to determine those aspects of the agoraphobic situation that initially produce unpleasant sensations. These might be a sense of being crowded in a bus or subway; a feeling of strangeness in a large open place like an auditorium or a supermarket; disorientation induced by the long parallel disposition of the aisles, lanes, or corridors of public places.

It is important for the client to rehearse (in the office) his or her return to the feared environment. It is ultimately very important for him or her to learn not only to cut off the panic attack, but also to experience it—in the presence of a helper—so that he or she can consolidate a new belief that the panic attack is not a serious threat to his or her physical or mental viability. This can be accomplished through having the client image—as vividly as possible while in the office—the experience of entering the frightening place.

The induced attack, in summary, is valuable from many standpoints. First, it enables the therapist to observe first-hand the actual behavior of the client and to hear his or her description of the sensations, automatic thoughts, and images. Second, it provides an opportunity for the therapist to coach the client in the various techniques that have been developed to terminate an attack. Finally, it enables the client to practice these techniques in a controlled situation. Fortified with this understanding and the techniques for applying it, the client is prepared to meet his or her panic attacks "head on," whether they occur "spontaneously" or in the context of particular situations.

ADDITIONAL CONSIDERATIONS

EMPIRICAL STATUS OF THE APPROACH

Cognitive therapy has in recent years attracted much attention from empirically minded researchers. Beginning with reports of its effectiveness in depressed samples in the 1970s (most notably Rush, Beck, Kovacs, & Hollon, 1977), cognitive therapy has come to be seen as a therapy with demonstrated efficacy, at least with moderate forms of depression. Since the Rush *et al.* study there have been several replications and extensions of the work. Emphasis in this review of the evidence will be placed on studies that are most relevant to questions concerning clinical effectiveness. Thus, we shall review only those studies that meet the following criteria:

1. Cognitive therapy was compared (at least) with another form of active treatment or with a control group.
2. The form of cognitive therapy was individual, and derived from Beck and colleagues' theories and procedures (as articulated in Beck *et al.*, 1979).
3. Adult outpatients who met criteria for a major depressive episode comprised the treated sample, and were randomly assigned to the treatments.

Four separate research groups have conducted studies that meet these criteria. The National Institute of Mental Health is now conducting a large-scale outcome study that meets the above criteria (Elkin, Parloff, Hadley, & Autrey, 1985), but results from the study are not available at the time of this writing.

Cognitive Therapy Versus an Antidepressant Drug

The landmark study of the cognitive therapy of depressed adults was reported by Rush *et al.* (1977). It has had a profound effect on the course of depression outcome research, as it was the first published account of a randomized trial that found a psychotherapeutic approach to be superior to a pharmacological one in the treatment of depression. Using a two-group design, Rush and his colleagues found that clients treated with cognitive therapy experienced greater symptom remission by the end of the 12-week active treatment period than did those treated with imipramine (a tricyclic antidepressant). A 1-year naturalistic follow-up (Kovacs, Rush, Beck, & Hollon, 1981) revealed that by and large the clinical improvement was maintained for both groups. The group treated with cognitive therapy was lower on depression severity measures than the antidepressant medication (ADM) group at the 6- and 12-month follow-up points. However, a test of the relative rate of relapse during the follow-up period yielded no significant difference between the two groups.

This inability to find a significant differential prophylactic effect in the two groups renders problematic the hypothesis that cognitive therapy offers protection from relapse. And the problem is not unique to the Kovacs *et al.* study, as will be shown below. Two difficulties are inherent in such analyses. One, since the follow-up periods in such studies are uncontrolled (i.e., clients may enter or reenter any treatment they wish, at any time), the prophylactic effect of acute treatment is confounded with the effects of any treatments clients receive during the follow-up period. Second, since the relapse/nonrelapse distinction is dichotomous, the power of a test of between-group differences is quite low. Either very large samples or very large differences between groups are required if an effect is to reach statistical significance in a single study.

Three studies have included replications of the cognitive therapy versus tricyclic acute treatment comparison of Rush *et al.* (1977). Blackburn, Bishop, Glen, Whalley, and Christie (1981), using both a hospital outpatient and a general practice sample, found no significant differences between doctor's choice pharmacotherapy and cognitive therapy on depression outcome measures. Both treatments produced beneficial effects, though cognitive therapy produced larger (if not significantly larger) average changes than did the medication treatment.

Thus, both studies cited thus far in which cognitive therapy was directly compared with tricyclic antidepressants have yielded results that suggest that cognitive therapy is a viable alternative to standard medication treatment. Three other studies have addressed an additional outcome question: Does the combination of cognitive therapy and antidepressant medication produce effects superior to either one alone?

Beck, Hollon, Young, Bedrosian, and Budenz (1985) randomly assigned 33 unipolar depressed outpatients to either cognitive therapy alone or cognitive therapy plus amitryptiline. Both groups showed substantial improvement after the 12 weeks of treatment, and the addition of amitryptiline to cognitive therapy did not produce superior improvement. In fact, the mean end-of-treatment depression severity score of the cognitive therapy alone group was slightly (and not significantly) lower than that of the combined group. Also, an analysis of the proportion of patients who fully remitted in each group yielded a trend in favor of the cognitive therapy alone group. Since this study did not contain a condition in which only medications were given, its follow-up results cannot inform us about the relative prophylactic effects of cognitive therapy and medications.

A four-cell design was used by Murphy, Simons, Wetzel, and Lustman (1984) to test for the effectiveness of (1) cognitive therapy alone, (2) nortriptyline (NT, a tricyclic antidepressant) alone, (3) combined cognitive therapy and NT, and (4) combined cognitive therapy and a (pill) placebo. All modalities were delivered for 12 weeks. They found no differences among the treatments in their acute effects on depression symptoms; all treatments resulted in significant and substantial reductions in symptomatology. In a separate paper concerning the uncontrolled follow-up period, Simons, Murphy, Levine, and Wetzel (1986) reported that patients who received cognitive therapy during the acute treatment phase were less likely to have relapsed in the year following acute treatment. Their definition of relapse, however, included patients who returned to treatment without first evidencing symptomatic relapse.

Hollon, DeRubeis, Evans, *et al.* (1985) have also conducted a multi-cell cognitive therapy versus antidepressant medication comparison. Patients were randomly assigned to either (1) cognitive therapy alone, (2) imipramine (IMI, a tricyclic antidepressant) alone, tapered after 12 weeks, (3) IMI for 12 weeks plus a maintenance dose of IMI for 12 more months, or (4) combined cognitive therapy plus IMI, each for 12 weeks. In cells (1), (2), and (4), patients entered an uncontrolled follow-up phase after the 12-week acute treatment period. When the cognitive therapy cell was compared against the two IMI cells (pooled), there were no significant differences in acute treatment outcome, though the mean values favored cognitive therapy over IMI. The mean scores on acute outcome measures for the combined cell (cognitive therapy plus IMI) were consistently better than the means of the other cells. However, on none of the outcome measures was the mean for the cognitive therapy plus drugs group significantly better than the corresponding mean for the cognitive therapy alone cell, and only on some measures did the combined cell significantly outperform the IMI alone cells.

The results from a 2-year follow-up (Evans *et al.*, 1985) suggest, as did the Kovacs *et al.* (1981) and Simons *et al.* (1986) studies, that cognitive therapy serves a prophylactic function. Patients who had received cognitive therapy during the acute phase fared consistently better than did those who received IMI without maintenance therapy.

Several conclusions can be drawn from studies conducted thus far that have assessed the relative efficacy of cognitive therapy and pharmacotherapy in the treatment of depressed outpatients. First, cognitive therapy has been shown to be as effective as the medications against which it has been compared in the acute treatment of depressive episodes. Second, there is a consistent indication that cognitive therapy offers some protection against relapse when compared with the administration of medications over a similar treatment period, at least in the year following treatment. Given the rationale and assumptions embedded in cognitive therapy, the indications of its ability to prevent relapses are encouraging, and should lead to further efforts to understand the extent of the prophylactic effect, as well as the mechanisms that account for it.

MEASURES OF THE PROCESS OF COGNITIVE THERAPY

Over the past decade a plethora of devices has been constructed that aim to measure cognitive constructs in depression. Most have been born of an interest in theoretical questions about depression. In this section we focus on therapist and client measures that have been used specifically to address questions about cognitive therapy and its effects; they might best be categorized as "therapy process" measures. For a more general treatment of cognitive assessment, the reader can turn to one of the recent reviews in the area (e.g., Segal & Shaw, Chapter 2, this volume).

The measures and applications described below stem from an interest in such questions as: Does it matter what the therapist does in cognitive therapy (i.e., how faithful he or she is to the procedures; how high the quality of his or her work is)? That is, are there important relationships between therapist variables and client outcome? Are there certain kinds of clients who respond particularly well to cognitive therapy? Do clients change in ways that are predicted by the model of therapy in cognitive therapy? Are these changes specific to cognitive therapy, or do similar changes occur in other effective treatments? Questions such as these guide the type of thorough and particularized analysis that should be performed on any successful form of treatment (see Hollon & Kriss, 1984, for a model of change in therapy that incorporates these questions). Several measures have been developed that may help to answer some of these questions. It is to these measures and the preliminary results obtained from them that we now turn.

Therapist Measures

At least three measures of therapist in-session behavior have been developed for cognitive therapy; they are described below. Each is different from the others in its form, in the original impetus for its development, and in its optimal application. None of the measures has been thoroughly validated against therapy outcome, though there have been initial attempts to find a relation between scores on these measures and outcome.

All three are rated by third-party observers who watch or listen to entire sessions of cognitive therapy (or portions thereof). The rater then makes judgments about the therapist along several dimensions. The differences among these measurement tools in rationale, procedure, and other characteristics are emphasized below.

The Cognitive Therapy Scale (Young, 1979) was developed primarily as an evaluation tool to be used in the training and certification of cognitive therapists. The main section is comprised of 11 items, each of which is rated on a scale from zero to six. Factor analyses have yielded two factors, one called the Cognitive Techniques (CT) factor, and the other the General Therapeutic Skills (GTS) factor (Young, 1979). Items which load highly on the CT factor include those that tap: (1) agenda setting, (2) focusing on key thoughts and behaviors, (3) the therapist's strategy for change, (4) application of cognitive therapy techniques, and (5) adequacy of the assigned homework. Items which load highly on the GTS factor are those that assess: (1) use of feedback, (2) understanding or empathy, (3) interpersonal effectiveness, (4) collaboration between client and therapist, (5) pacing and efficient use of time, and (6) use of Socratic questioning. Though the two factors appear to measure different aspects of therapist behavior, the correlation between scores on these two sets of items was .70 in one study (DeRubeis, Hollon, Evans, Garvey, & Tuason, 1985). Indeed, an examination of the items that load on the GTS factor reveals that their content includes cognitive-therapy-specific behaviors. Even so, the total score yielded by the instrument (which can range from 0 to 66) can be used to rate sessions of cognitive therapy. These differentiated judgments, when summed, correspond well with overall judgments of the quality of the session made by experts (Dobson, Shaw, & Vallis, 1985; Vallis, Shaw, & Dobson, 1986). For example, a correlation between the total score of the CTS and a judgment of overall quality of the session was .95 in the DeRubeis *et al.* (1985) study.

The CTS measures both the therapist's adherence to cognitive therapy methods and the quality of the therapist's interventions. As such, it is probably best used by raters who are experts in cognitive therapy, since judgments of quality would presumably be difficult for non-experts to make. Expert raters have evidenced a reliability of .86 for the total score in one study (Hollon, Emerson, & Mandell, 1982). Whether more novice raters can be trained to achieve this level of reliability with each other and with experts remains to be seen. If not, then the CTS would be appropriate only in the hands of cognitive therapy experts.

Currently, this measure is used to track the progress of cognitive therapy trainees, and as a way to spot weaknesses in particular trainees. There are also studies underway that examine the covariation of CTS scores with measures of outcome in the treatment of depression (DeRubeis et al., 1985; ongoing studies by DeRubeis and colleagues at the University of Pennsylvania). Given the nature of this scale, it should be appropriate for the prediction of outcome, as it aims to capture both the adherence to cognitive therapy procedures and the quality of the therapy delivered. Both aspects should be important in an effective implementation of cognitive therapy. This scale also can be used to guide decisions regarding the inclusion of therapists in outcome studies; cut-off scores have been recommended for this purpose (Young, personal communication, March, 1983).

Similarly, therapy that has been conducted in outcome studies and that is preserved via audio- or video-archives can be evaluated for the adherence and quality of the therapy that was delivered. Any differences in results across outcome studies could be due to differences in the implementation of cognitive therapy; this possibility can be examined whenever tapes of sessions have been saved (see Kendall & Hollon, 1983).

The Collaborative Study Psychotherapy Rating Scale (CSPRS: Hollon, Evans, Auerbach, et al., 1985) is another therapy rating instrument that has been developed over the last several years. It has a different focus than the CTS. A primary goal of the instrument is to distinguish objectively sessions of cognitive therapy from those of other forms of therapy. Its precursor, the Minnesota Therapy Rating Scale (MTRS: DeRubeis, Hollon, Evans, & Bemis, 1981) was designed to differentiate sessions of cognitive therapy from those of Interpersonal Therapy (IPT: Klerman, Rounsaville, Chevron, Neu, & Weissman, 1979), a short-term psychoanalytically oriented treatment for depression. It did so quite well. It also yielded continuous scores on several factors, including one that measures cognitive-therapy-relevant therapist behavior and another that assesses the General Interpersonal Skills of the therapist.

The CSPRS is a newer instrument that accomplishes these same goals, but it can also be used to measure the behavior of pharmacotherapists during medication management sessions. The CSPRS is currently being applied to sessions conducted in the NIMH Collaborative Study of Depression (Elkin et al., 1985). It was designed in such a way that raters not expert in cognitive therapy are able to use the scales. To accomplish this, Hollon and his colleagues made the CSPRS items more specifically operationalized than items on the CTS, so that less is left to the judgment and knowledge of the rater. The CSPRS does not focus on the quality of the interventions per se, but rather on the extent or amount of the behavior of interest. Raters are instructed not to judge the quality of the interventions that they rate, but focus instead on the amount of time and effort spent by the therapist in a certain domain, such as helping the client attend to the thoughts experienced while in an unpleasant emotional state. Cognitive-therapy-relevant behavior is covered by 28 items, and 8 items refer to general interpersonal skills (termed "Facilitative Conditions" in this instrument). Inter-rater reliability in samples of graduate student non-expert raters has been fair to good for the composite scales (in the range of .90 for the cognitive therapy scale, and .50 for Facilitative Conditions; Hollon, Evans, Auerbach, et al., 1985).

Yet another scale that bears mention here was constructed by Luborsky, Woody, McClellan, O'Brien, and Rosenzweig (1982) for a drug addiction treatment study. The instrument measures therapists' adherence to the "core characteristics" of three different therapies: (1) cognitive-behavior therapy (CBT), (2) supportive-expressive psychotherapy (SE), and (3) drug counseling (DC). Raters listened to 15-minute segments of sessions and then rated each segment on three or four "core characteristics" of each therapy. Luborsky et al. found that the three types of therapy could be empirically distinguished using this method.

In a later report on the same drug treatment study, Luborsky, McClellan, Woody, O'Brien, and Auerbach (1985) examined the relation between the "purity" with which each type of therapy was delivered and subsequent outcome. Purity was defined as the ratio of the rating on the intended therapy (SE for supportive-expressive therapists, CBT for cognitive-behavioral therapists, DC for drug counselors) over the sum of the three sets of ratings. This ratio is a measure of the adherence or fidelity of the session to the intended form of therapy. They found that, for each of the three therapies, there was a positive correlation between "purity" and good outcome. This finding of a relation between method-specific variables (as opposed to general therapist skills) and outcome provides a kind of validation that is thus far lacking for the first two scales that were described above. The findings of this study also bode well for the further development of theory-specific therapies. Its results are at odds with the belief among many therapy process researchers that variation in method-relevant procedures has little effect on therapy outcome, and that among therapist variables, only general therapeutic skills are important for producing good outcome (see, e.g., Parloff, Waskow, & Wolfe, 1978; Strupp, 1978). Further work of this type should be pursued with all of these scales. It would help to clarify the role that different types of therapist behavior play in successful therapeutic outcomes. Findings from such studies would have direct application to therapy research and training.

Thus far, only the therapy of depressed and addicted clients has been studied with these methods. If outcome studies are to be conducted on other disorders, and if the therapy delivered in them is to be measured, these or other assessment devices will need to be adapted or developed for the purpose.

Client Measures—Prediction of Response

The effort to find predictors of response to treatment can aim toward any of several specific goals, including both theoretical and pragmatic aims. Of primarily theoretical interest would be a cognitive characteristic that would predict which clients respond best to cognitive therapy. To know which clients are unlikely to respond to cognitive therapy is of little use clinically, as it does not direct the therapist or the client to the best available treatment. The most such a predictor (termed here a "selection variable," borrowing from industrial psychology; Landy & Trumbo, 1980) would be able to do clinically is to help the therapist select which clients will get better in treatment with him or her. Whether these clients would do as well (or better or worse) in another form of treatment is not addressed by the selection question. In fact, research on prediction of outcome in depression has been almost exclusively of the selection type, in which the search has been for variables that predict good response to a *particular treatment* (Feeley, 1985).

The only differential predictor of outcome reported in the literature comes from Simons, Lustman, Wetzel, and Murphy (1985). They found that higher pretreatment scores on Rosenbaum's Self Control Scale (SCS: Rosenbaum, 1980) predicted better response in cognitive therapy, but that lower scores predicted better response in drug therapy. High scores on this measure are obtained by individuals who endorse such statements as "When I am feeling depressed I try to think about pleasant events," and "I usually plan my work when faced with a number of things to do." Simons and her colleagues interpret their findings as reflecting a "match" between the views of the world embodied in the SCS and in cognitive therapy, or, alternatively, as an indication that individuals with cognitive-therapy-relevant skills in their repertoire prior to therapy can build upon these skills in cognitive therapy. The authors caution, however, that these are preliminary data that must be replicated, especially since the finding grew out of a larger effort to find predictor variables.

Client Measures—Mechanisms of Change

Measures of cognitive characteristics have also been used to address the question regarding what changes cognitive therapy produces that reduce depressive symptoms. Answers to this question have both theoretical and pragmatic import. The theory of change in cognitive therapy can be examined by testing whether expected cognitive and behavioral changes occur during successful treatment. Pragmatically, findings that concern causal mechanisms can lead to further refinements in the therapy.

Hollon, Evans, and DeRubeis (1985) propose that there are three kinds of changes that might occur in cognitive therapy, and that could account for symptom reduction during treatment. The first two, deactivation and accommodation, refer to changes that occur in the clients' schemata. Change in a depressive schema is said to occur when the client comes to use a nondepressive schema in responding to potentially upsetting events. At the beginning of therapy, when he or she is depressed, a client's depressive schemata are said to be activated. So, for example, he or she may respond to the rejection of a manuscript with the inference, "I'll never be successful." An indication that the deactivation or accommodation of the schema has occurred would be that, upon receiving similar news following therapy, the client concludes, "I'll have to submit the manuscript to a more appropriate journal." According to this view, the difference between deactivation and accommodation is that following deactivation the depressive schema is simply suppressed, and thus liable to become active again, while following accommodation the change is in the schema itself, and is thus more enduring.

The third kind of change described by Hollon, Evans, and DeRubeis (1985) is the development of compensatory skills. Insofar as the acquisition and use of compensatory skills are responsible for change, one would expect to find that even after therapy clients are still liable to respond to potentially upsetting events by making depressive inferences immediately, but that they then apply the skills they have learned during cognitive therapy.

Each of these processes is a candidate for a mechanism that accounts for the short- and long-term change produced by cognitive therapy. Several studies have investigated these possible mechanisms of change. It has been found as a result that remission from depression leads to a return to near normalcy on a number of cognitive indices (DeRubeis et al., 1985; Dobson & Shaw, 1986; Eaves & Rush, 1984; Hamilton & Abramson, 1981; Simons, Garfield, & Murphy, 1984). The measures used could best be characterized in the Hollon, Evans, and DeRubeis (1985) proposal presented above as assessing changes in schemata (deactivation or accommodation) that result from treatment. For example, the Dysfunctional Attitudes Scale (DAS: Weissman, 1979), a measure designed to assess the operation of depressive schemata, has been found to change along with decreases in depressive symptomatology. However, similar change occurs as a result of drug therapy as well (DeRubeis et al., 1985; Simons et al., 1985). The same pattern has been found with the Automatic Thoughts Questionnaire (ATQ: Hollon & Kendall, 1980; see DeRubeis et al., 1985). Hollon, DeRubeis, and Evans (in press) have argued that the fact that a variable changes in both cognitive therapy and in drug therapy does not rule out the possibility that it is a mechanism of change in cognitive therapy. However, the clearest case can be made that a variable is a specific mechanism of change in cognitive therapy when improvement is found on that variable following cognitive therapy but not following drug therapy. To date, no measure has evidenced this pattern.

Missing from these investigations have been measures of compensatory skills. As we have argued in this chapter, it is likely that cognitive therapy exerts much of its effect through the inculcation of strategies that the client can use when confronted with potentially unpleasant situations. It may be that the acquisition and use of these strategies are specific determinants of success in cognitive therapy. It is plausible that clients treated with drug therapy, for instance, do not acquire and thus will not manifest these compensatory skills.

Perhaps the most pertinent construct that has been explored and for which measures have been developed is that of coping. To date, most measures and studies of coping strategies have grown out of interests other than cognitive therapy. Lazarus and his colleagues have developed a series of measures that assess coping from their point of view (Folkman & Lazarus, 1980; Lazarus & Folkman, 1984). Pearlin and Schooler (1979) have also developed a measure of coping. Though these measures have not been obtained from depressed clients who have gone through a course of cognitive therapy, it would be expected given the nature of cognitive therapy that clients would change their manner of coping with both major stressful events and minor annoyances or "hassles" (DeLongis, Coyne, Dakof, Folkman, & Lazarus, 1982).

Existing coping measures have one characteristic, however, that makes them poor candidates for a measure of change during cognitive therapy. Clients are asked to rate the degree to which they have used a variety of coping strategies in response to recent stressful events. Clients can fairly easily recognize those coping skills that they "should" have implemented, especially if they have been through a course of cognitive therapy. For this reason, a method is needed that would require that the client *produce*, rather than recognize, the cognitive coping skills that he or she would use in a given situation. Such measures would need to employ a free response format and a system that turns these free responses into coping categories.

FUTURE DIRECTIONS

As this chapter has revealed, cognitive therapy has thus far had its primary focus on the understanding and treatment of depression. Though there have been clinical writings addressed to other disorders and clinical problems, the majority of the empirical work, especially in the area of treatment efficacy, has concerned depression. If cognitive therapy is to broaden its impact on the therapist/scientist audience, several developments must occur. Treatments for other disorders will have to be as explicitly outlined as has the treatment for depression (cf. Beck *et al.*, 1979). There have indeed been attempts to extend the aims and principles of cognitive therapy to other disorders (e.g., Garner & Bemis, 1982, for anorexia nervosa; Beck & Emery, 1985, for anxiety disorders). Clinical trials of cognitive therapy in these disorders should then follow. If the treatment approach appears to be effective, then rigorously controlled comparisons of cognitive therapy with other treatments would be in order.

Several obstacles must be overcome if cognitive therapy is to be well tested in these other disorders. First, the measurement of treatment outcome is troublesome in the anxiety disorders, especially when compared to the precision that is achieved by the various self-report and clinician-rated measures of depression such as the BDI and the Hamilton Rating Scale for Depression (HRSD: Hamilton, 1960). For example, for panic disorders, how much weight should be given to the frequency, as opposed to the severity of the panic attacks? For generalized anxiety disorders a similar problem exists concerning frequency and severity, though the target of the measurement is not the discrete attack, but a more pervasive anxious discomfort. Measurement problems also exist for anorexia nervosa, though one major aspect of outcome—weight gain—can of course be measured well.

A second obstacle for research on these other disorders is that the standards of treatment against which they should be compared are less obvious than has been the case in the treatment of depression. Since before the Rush *et al.* (1977) study, it has been assumed that the standard of treatment against which cognitive therapy must show its efficacy is antidepressant medication. Though it can be argued that antidepressant medication is too broad a class, and that one must be more specific when referring to depression treatment, the assumption has been that these medications are more or less equivalent to one another in their overall effectiveness. Thus, it can be assumed that results from a comparison of cognitive therapy versus imipramine closely parallel what would have been found if another ADM had been used. Such research has also proceeded under the assumption that antidepressant medications in general represent the standard of treatment for outpatient, moderate-to-severe cases of depression. These kinds of assumptions are not at this time warranted in the case of anorexia nervosa or the anxiety disorders, for which there are no clearly standard treatments. Researchers in these fields will have to choose the best available treatment against which to compare cognitive therapy, knowing that other treatments will be considered by some in the field to be the more powerful "standard" treatments.

All this is not to say that research concerning the cognitive therapy of depression can now be concluded. Indeed, there are many questions which have been raised or have been left unanswered by efforts to date. A few such questions follow.

Which treatment is best for Mr. X? If cognitive therapy is a powerful treatment for depression, does that mean that anyone who is depressed will profit from it, and that it is to be preferred over other available treatments? Though we do not have the specific knowledge that would help us answer this question, a safe assumption is that in the future, we shall not consider one antidepressant treatment to be the best for everyone. Knowledge of client characteristics prior to treatment will guide the therapist to use the best available treatment for the client under consideration. Should the client be given an ADM, instead of or in addition to a course of cognitive therapy? Only the Simons et al. (1985) study described above, in which a differential predictor (Rosenbaum's SCS) was found, has so far provided information that may lead to the answers to these kinds of questions. There is clearly sufficient interest in the field to suggest that there will be further and more refined attempts to address these prediction questions.

Does cognitive therapy yield a prophylactic effect? Though several studies (Evans et al., 1985; Rush et al., 1977; Simons et al., 1985) have now pointed to an effect of cognitive therapy that lasts beyond the period of treatment, this very important characteristic must be determined more clearly. In doing this, investigators should continue to focus not only on whether symptoms return, but also on characteristics of the clients that are altered by a course of cognitive therapy, and that may account for resistance to relapse. In this we refer back to our section on attempts to measure the essential ingredients of change in cognitive therapy. These ingredients will likely include enduring changes in depressive schemata or increases in the availability and use of compensatory skills, as these are the domains that are most likely to be specifically affected by the treatment as it is now conceived (Hollon, Evans, & DeRubeis, 1985).

Along with the search for mechanisms of the prophylactic effect of cognitive therapy should come efforts to determine the optimal use of "booster sessions." Clinically, it has been observed that sessions conducted at intervals after the end of acute treatment have been beneficial to patients. Whether these booster sessions are in fact effective tools in the long-term treatment of depression remains to be empirically demonstrated. Along with an understanding of the role of booster sessions should come recommendations concerning their length and focus. Here again, efforts to assess mechanisms responsible for the prevention of the return of symptoms should be helpful. With an automobile we can examine several "subsyndromal" aspects of its functioning (oil level, carburetor adjustment, etc.) in order to prevent its breakdown. So, too, the hope is that assessments could be made of subsyndromal psychological functioning that would lead to preventive psychotherapeutic efforts.

Efforts to find both the short- and long-term active ingredients in cognitive therapy should also lead to a better understanding of what aspects of the treatment "get through" to the client. This, in turn, should help to refine the treatment, since the most powerful aspects could then be emphasized. Alternatively, methods could be developed with the aim of bolstering those aspects of the treatment that do not in the current form of cognitive therapy get through to the client.

REFERENCES

Beck, A. T. (1961). A systematic investigation of depression. *Comprehensive Psychiatry, 2*, 305–312.

Beck, A. T. (1963). Thinking and depression. *Archives of General Psychiatry, 9*, 324–333.

Beck, A. T. (1964). Thinking and depression: 2. Theory and therapy. *Archives of General Psychiatry, 10*, 561–571.

Beck, A. T. (1972). *Depression: Causes and treatment.* Philadelphia: University of Pennsylvania Press.

Beck, A. T., & Beamesderfer, A. (1974). Assessment of depression: The depression inventory. In P. Pinchot (Ed.), *Modern problems in pharmacopsychiatry* (Vol. 7). Basel, Switzerland: Harger.

Beck, A. T., & Emery, G. (1985). *Anxiety disorders and phobias.* New York: Basic Books.

Beck, A. T., & Greenberg, R. L. (1974). *Coping with depression.* New York: Institute for Rational Living.

Beck, A. T., Hollon, S. D., Young, J., Bedrosian, R., & Budenz, D. (1985). Treatment of depression with cognitive therapy and amitriptyline. *Archives of General Psychiatry, 42*, 142–148.

Beck, A. T., & Hurvich, M. (1959). Psychological correlates of depression. *Psychosomatic Medicine, 21*, 50–55.

Beck, A. T., Rush, A. J., Shaw, B. F., & Emery, G. (1979). *Cognitive therapy of depression.* New York: Guilford.

Beck, A. T., & Ward, C. H. (1961). Dreams of depressed patients: Characteristic themes in manifest content. *Archives of General Psychiatry, 5*, 462–467.

Beck, A. T., Ward, C. H., Mendelson, M., Mock, J. E., & Erbaugh, J. K. (1961). An inventory for measuring depression. *Archives of General Psychiatry, 33*, 561–571.

Blackburn, I. N., Bishop, S., Glen, A. I. M., Whalley, L. J., & Christie, J. E. (1981). The efficacy of cognitive therapy in depression: A treatment trial using cognitive therapy and pharmacotherapy, each alone and in combination. *British Journal of Psychiatry, 139*, 181–189.

Clark, D. M., Salkovskis, P. M., & Chalkley, A. J. (1985). Respiratory control as a treatment for panic attacks. *Journal of Behavior Therapy and Experimental Psychiatry, 16*, 23–30.

DeLongis, A., Coyne, J. C., Dakof, G., Folkman, S., & Lazarus, R. S. (1982). Relationship of daily hassles, uplifts, and major life events to health status. *Health Psychology, 1*, 119–136.

DeRubeis, R. J., Hollon, S. D., Evans, M. D., & Bemis, K. M. (1982). Can psychotherapies for depression be discriminated? A systematic investigation of cognitive therapy and interpersonal therapy. *Journal of Consulting and Clinical Psychology, 50*, 744–756.

DeRubeis, R. J., Hollon, S. D., Evans, M. D., Garvey, M. J., & Tuason, V. B. (1985). *Active ingredients and mechanisms in cognitive therapy and pharmacotherapy: III. Processes of change in the CPT project.* Unpublished manuscript, University of Pennsylvania, Philadelphia.

Dobson, K. S., & Shaw, B. F. (1986). Cognitive assessment of major depressive disorders. *Cognitive Therapy and Research, 10*, 13–29.

Dobson, K. S., Shaw, B. F., & Vallis, T. M. (1985). Reliability of a measure of the quality of cognitive therapy. *British Journal of Clinical Psychology, 24*, 295–300.

Eaves, G., & Rush, A. J. (1984). Cognitive patterns in symptomatic and remitted unipolar major depression. *Journal of Abnormal Psychology, 93*, 31–40.

Elkin, I., Parloff, M. B., Hadley, S. W., & Autrey, J. H. (1985). NIMH treatment of depression collaborative research program. *Archives of General Psychiatry, 42*, 305–316.

Ellis, A. (1984). Rational-emotive therapy. In R. J. Corsini (Ed.), *Current psychotherapies*. Itasca, IL: F. E. Peacock Publishers.

Ellis, A., & Harper, R. A. (1975). *A new guide to rational living*. North Hollywood, CA: Wilshire Book Company.

Evans, M. D., Hollon, S. D., DeRubeis, R. J., Piasecki, J., Tuason, V. B., & Garvey, M. J. (1985). *Relapse/recurrence following cognitive therapy and pharmacotherapy for depression: IV. Two-year follow-up of the CPT project*. Unpublished manuscript, University of Minnesota and the St. Paul-Ramsey Medical Center, Minneapolis-St. Paul, MN.

Feeley, W. M. (1985). *Selection versus placement in treatment decisions*. Unpublished manuscript, University of Pennsylvania, Philadelphia.

Folkman, S., & Lazarus, R. S. (1980). An analysis of coping in a middle-aged community sample. *Journal of Health and Social Behavior, 21*, 219–239.

Frank, J. D. (1973). *Persuasion and healing*. Baltimore: Johns Hopkins Press.

Freud, S. (1917/1957). Mourning and melancholia. In J. Strachey (Ed.), *The complete psychological works of Sigmund Freud*. London: Hogarth.

Garner, D. M., & Bemis, K. M. (1982). A cognitive-behavioral approach to anorexia nervosa. *Cognitive Therapy and Research, 6*, 123–150.

Hamilton, M. (1960). A rating scale for depression. *Journal of Neurology, Neurosurgery, and Psychiatry, 23*, 56–62.

Hamilton, E. W., & Abramson, L. Y. (1983). Cognitive patterns and major depressive disorder: A longitudinal study in a hospital setting. *Journal of Abnormal Psychology, 92*, 173–184.

Hollon, S. D., & Beck, A. T. (1979). Cognitive therapy of depression. In P. E. Kendall & S. D. Hollon (Eds.), *Cognitive-behavioral interventions: Theory, research, procedures*. New York: Academic Press.

Hollon, S. D., DeRubeis, R. J., & Evans, M. D. (in press). Causal mediation of change in treatment for depression: Discriminating between nonspecificity and noncausality. *Psychological Bulletin*.

Hollon, S. D., DeRubeis, R. J., Evans, M. D., Tuason, V. B., Wiemer, M. J., & Garvey, M. J. (1985). *Cognitive therapy and pharmacotherapy in the treatment of depression: I. Differential outcome in the CPI project*. Unpublished manuscript, University of Minnesota and the St. Paul-Ramsey Medical Center, Minneapolis-St. Paul, MN.

Hollon, S. D., Emerson, M., & Mandell, M. (1982). *Psychometric properties of the Cognitive Therapy Scale*. Unpublished manuscript, University of Minnesota and the St. Paul-Ramsey Medical Center, Minneapolis-St. Paul, MN.

Hollon, S. D., Evans, M. D., Auerbach, A., DeRubeis, R. J., Elkin, I., Lowery, A., Tuason, V. B., Kriss, M., & Piasecki, J. (1985). *Development of a system for rating therapies for depression: Differentiating cognitive therapy, interpersonal psychotherapy, and clinical management pharmacotherapy*. Unpublished manuscript, University of Minnesota and the St. Paul-Ramsey Medical Center, Minneapolis-St. Paul, MN.

Hollon, S. D., Evans, M. D., & DeRubeis, R. J. (1985). Preventing relapse following treatment for depression: The cognitive-pharmacotherapy project. In N. Schneiderman & T. Fields (Eds.), *Stress and coping* (Vol. 2), New York: Lawrence Erlbaum.

Hollon, S. D., & Kendall, P. E. (1980). Cognitive self-statements in depression: Development of an automatic thoughts questionnaire. *Cognitive Therapy and Research, 4*, 383–395.

Hollon, S. D., & Kriss, M. R. (1984). Cognitive factors in clinical research and practice. *Clinical Psychology Review, 4*, 35–76.

Kendall, P. E., & Hollon, S. D. (1983). Calibrating the quality of therapy: Collaborative archiving of tape samples from therapy outcome trials. *Cognitive Therapy and Research, 7*, 199–204.

Klerman, G. L., Rounsaville, B., Chevron, E., Neu, G., & Weissman, M. M. (1979). *Manual for *short-term interpersonal psychotherapy (IPT) of depression,* (4th Rev.). Mimeographed publication distributed by Yale University School of Medicine, New Haven, CT.

Kovacs, M., Rush, A. J., Beck, A. T., & Hollon, S. D. (1981). Depressed outpatients treated with cognitive therapy or pharmacotherapy: A one-year follow-up. *Archives of General Psychiatry, 38,* 33–39.

Landy, F. J., & Trumbo, D. A. (1980). *Psychology of work behavior.* Homewood, IL: Dorsey Press.

Lazarus, R. S., & Folkman, S. (1984). *Stress, appraisal, and coping.* New York: Springer.

Luborsky, L., McLellan, G. E., Woody, G. E., O'Brien, C. P., & Auerbach, A. (1985). Therapist success and its determinants. *Archives of General Psychiatry, 42,* 602–611.

Luborsky, L., Woody, G. E., McLellan, G. E., O'Brien, C. P., & Rosenzweig, J. (1982). Can independent judges recognize different psychotherapies? An experience with manual-guided therapies. *Journal of Consulting and Clinical Psychology, 50,* 49–62.

Meichenbaum, D. (1972). *Cognitive-behavior modification.* New York: Plenum Press.

Murphy, G. E., Simons, A. D., Wetzel, R. D., & Lustman, P. J. (1984). Cognitive therapy and pharmacotherapy: Singly and together in the treatment of depression. *Archives of General Psychiatry, 41,* 33–41.

Nisbett, R., & Ross, L. (1980). *Human inference: Strategies and shortcomings of social judgment.* Englewood Cliffs, NJ: Prentice-Hall.

Parloff, M., Waskow, I. E., & Wolfe, B. E. (1978). Research on therapist variables in relation to process and outcome. In S. L. Garfield & A. E. Bergin (Eds.), *Handbook of psychotherapy and behavior change: An empirical analysis* (2nd ed.). New York: Wiley.

Pearlin, L. I., & Schooler, C. (1979). The structure of coping. *Journal of Health and Social Behavior, 19,* 337–356.

Riskind, J. H., Beck, A. T., & Smucker, M. R. (1983, December). *Psychometric properties of the dysfunctional attitudes scale in clinical populations.* Paper presented at the World Congress on Behavior Therapy, the 17th Annual Convention of the Association for Advancement of Behavior Therapy, Washington, DC.

Rosenbaum, M. (1980). A schedule for assessing self-control behaviors: Preliminary findings. *Behavior Therapy, 11,* 109–121.

Rush, A. J., Beck, A. T., Kovacs, J. M., & Hollon, S. D. (1977). Comparative efficacy of cognitive therapy and pharmacotherapy in outpatient depressives. *Cognitive Therapy and Research, 1,* 17–37.

Simons, A. D., Garfield, S. L., & Murphy, G. E. (1984). The process of change in cognitive therapy and pharmacotherapy: Changes in mood and cognition. *Archives of General Psychiatry, 41,* 45–51.

Simons, A. D., Lustman, P. J., Wetzel, R. D., & Murphy, G. E. (1985). Predicting response to cognitive therapy of depression: The role of learned resourcefulness. *Cognitive Therapy and Research, 9,* 79–89.

Simons, A. D., Murphy, G. E., Levine, J. L., & Wetzel, R. D. (1986). Cognitive therapy and pharmacotherapy for depression: Sustained improvement over one year. *Archives of General Psychiatry, 43,* 43–48.

Strupp, H. H. (1978). Psychotherapy research and practice: An overview. In S. L. Garfield & A. E. Bergin (Eds.), *Handbook of psychotherapy and behavior change: An empirical analysis* (2nd ed.). New York: Wiley.

Vallis, T. M., Shaw, B. F., & Dobson, K. S. (1986). The Cognitive Therapy Scale: Psychometric properties. *Journal of Consulting and Clinical Psychology, 54,* 381–385

Weissman, A. N. (1979). The dysfunctional attitudes scale: A validation study. *Dissertation Abstracts International, 40,* 1389–1390B.

Young, J. (1979). *Development of an instrument for rating cognitive therapy: The Cognitive Therapy Scale.* Unpublished manuscript, University of Pennsylvania, Philadelphia.

8

A SYSTEMS, PROCESS-ORIENTED APPROACH TO COGNITIVE THERAPY

VITTORIO F. GUIDANO

In their recent overview of the latest developments in cognitive psychotherapy, Reda and Mahoney (1984) argue that it is possible to divide current cognitive approaches into two broad camps: (1) those that adopt a surface-structure associationistic model and (2) those that endorse a deep-structure constructivistic metatheory.

In the first of these approaches—where there is an attempt to broaden the associationistic-behavioristic paradigm in order to include cognitive aspects—the focus of therapy is directed towards the modification of maladaptive self-statements and behavior, supplanting them with more adaptive ones. A strategy of graduated disconfirmations via intellectual and experiential restructuring of associations and meanings is generally employed to bring about such modification. The most important representatives of this approach are Beck (1976), Ellis (1962), Goldfried (1982) and Meichenbaum (1977).

The second approach attempts to formulate a new paradigm that would enable cognitivism to be defined not so much in terms of a development of behaviorism but as a psychological trend different from either behaviorism or psychoanalysis. It emphasizes the active, generative, and intentional dimensions of personal knowing processes. In this approach assessment procedures are aimed at identifying invariant deep structures that provide the entire individual knowledge organization with coherence and stability. The strategy of therapy is therefore based upon the elaboration of alternative models of the self and the world such that the deep structures can adopt a more flexible and adaptive articulation.

The most important representative works of this latter approach are Guidano (1984), Guidano and Liotti (1983), Mahoney (1980, 1982), and Weimer (1975, 1977, 1982a, 1982b). The purpose of this chapter is to provide an overall picture of the latter of these two areas of research, outlining both a model of human behavior derived from a constructivistic systems process-oriented approach and discussing some general implications for psychotherapy.

A TENTATIVE MODEL OF HUMAN KNOWLEDGE PROCESSES

THE THEORETICAL FRAMEWORK

The discipline of evolutionary epistemology has for some time been emphasizing how evolution itself, being the expression of biological and adaptive
processes, can be considered on the same level as knowledge processes
(Campbell, 1974; Lorenz, 1973; Popper, 1972; Popper & Eccles, 1977; Weimer, 1975).

The direction of life moves toward modeling more and more of its
environment in such a way as to make possible the predicting of external
perturbations and the reducing of their effects. In recent years, evolutionary
epistemology has thus begun to include the elaboration of models allowing
for an explanation of the evolution of higher complex systems such as the
human knowing system that are capable of minimizing environmental
effects through more highly organized self-stabilizing processes.

According to Weimer (1982b), a cognitive psychology methodology
should be consonant with evolutionary epistemology. In such a manner,
cognitive psychology would be able to develop as a science in its own right,
with a specific methodology different from the one employed in the hard
sciences.

The Self-Organizing Paradigm

In the last decade, a process-oriented approach to complex systems has led to
a particular interest in concepts like organization, temporal becoming, and
dynamic equilibrium and has led to a conception of living things as autopoietic[1] systems, as systems whose distinctive characteristics are their self-
organizing abilities (Jantsch, 1981; Nicolis & Prigogine, 1977; Prigogine,
1980; Varela, 1979; Zeleny; 1981).

An autopoietic system is autonomous; it subordinates all changes to the
maintenance of its own organization, which represents the fundamental
invariant. This maintenance takes place through an ongoing and generative
process of self-renewal in order to assimilate incoming information and to
cope with perturbations arising from its exchanges with the environment.

Autonomy, defined in terms of self-reference, becomes the crucial prop-
erty underlying any self-organizing ability. As Morin (1981) put it,

the living being, from the bacterium to homo sapiens, obeys a particular logic
according to which the individual, though ephemeral, singular and marginal,
considers itself the center of the world. All others are excluded from the individual's
ontological site, including homozygous twins, congeners, fellowmen. According to a
law of exclusion that brings to mind Pauli's principles, this egocentricity, which

---

1. From "autopoiesis," a Greek word for self-production or self-renewal.

excludes from itself all other beings, this computation and ethos *for the self* furnishes the logical, organizational and existential definition of the concept of *subject*." (p. 134)

The consequent differentiation between autonomy (self-law) and allonomy ("external law") seems particularly relevant for cognitive psychology. An autopoietic system such as the human mind refers above all to a function coming from itself and is not aimed at the production of any specific output. It is concerned instead with its own self-maintenance and self-renewal. In contrast, an allopoietic system (e.g., a computer) relies on a function coming from outside—a program—in order that some specific output be produced. Given that an allopoietic system is subordinated to the production of something different from itself, it is therefore not autonomous.

Finally, an autopoietic system possesses individuality and uniqueness. In other words, it has an emerging identity that rests on an active and ongoing differentiation between self and non-self. Since its temporal becoming occurs by keeping its organization stable, an autopoietic system produces, in a certain sense, its own identity and actively maintains it in the face of environmental perturbations.

From the point of view of evolutionary epistemology, therefore, the origin of the selfhood processes corresponds to the evolutionary and systemic constraints inherent to complex systems.

Selfhood is a necessary consequence of structurally complex systems that satisfy certain constraints. That we know selves as embodied by the highest primates is, in effect, due to local factors in this region of the universe; selves could be embodied quite differently." (Weimer, 1982b, p. 352)

Motor Theories of the Mind

The human knowing system is characterized by its basic feature, namely the ability to construct models of self and the world capable of arranging and regulating reality itself.

In this perspective, the mind appears as an active, constructive system, capable of producing not only its output but also to a large extent the input it receives, including the sensations that lie at the base of its own constructions. This is why, in recent years, the need has gradually been felt to shift the conceptualization of the mind toward the so-called motor theories (Weimer, 1977) and to drop conventional sensory theories that depict the mind as a mere collector of sensations and that imply rather simplistically that the order and method with which we are acquainted actually belong to reality (Hayek, 1952; Piaget, 1970; Popper, 1972; Weimer, 1982a).

From a motor theory perspective, information processing (input) and behavior (output) are no longer considered functionally different. On the contrary, the processes underlying perception are identical to those underlying imagination, and thought processes are intertwined with motor activity in the same way. Hence we do not first know and then act, since cognitive processes are themselves actions. In this sense, as Piaget (1970) asserted, to know an object means essentially to act upon it.

Without invoking a homunculus explanation, it becomes possible to identify the inner regulatory principle with the motor self-referent organization of the mind that actively construes its identity as an individual knowing system faced with an ever-changing world. Thus the classical empiricist argument, according to which abstractions are just the result of the association of sensations, is deeply challenged since in a motor theory perspective the sensations themselves are the product of the abstract capabilities of the mind.

As Hayek (1978) pointed out with his notion of the "primacy of the abstract," the richness of the sensory world that we experience is not the starting point from which the mind derives abstractions but on the contrary is the product of a great range of abstractions that the mind must possess in order to be capable of experiencing that richness of detail. What was taken for granted in explaining the functioning of the mind—that is, that the concrete seems primary while the abstract appears to be derived from it—appears only as an "error" of our subjective experience reflecting the complex and automatic ordering ability that the human mind has acquired in the course of its evolutionary history (Hayek, 1952).

The mind is thus to be considered as a system of abstraction rules capable of bringing about a relational order of events in order to produce experience and behavior (Weimer, 1982a, p. 265). Perhaps the most remarkable consequence that this conception of mind entails is that regarding the central role played by unconscious, tacit processes (cf. Franks, 1974; Polanyi, 1966; Reber & Lewis, 1977; Shevrin & Dickman, 1980; Turvey, 1974; Weimer, 1973, 1974, 1977). From such a viewpoint the abstract, tacit processes are seen as the higher, hierarchical level. Far from being a "subconscious level" they are actually a "superconscious" one, because they govern the conscious processes without appearing in them. In Hayek's terms, products of conscious rationality are the result of human actions, but not of human design (Hayek, 1978).

Tacit and Explicit Levels of Knowing

The distinction between deep and surface cognitive structures—that is, between tacit and explicit levels of knowing—follows automatically when human cognitive processes are seen from the point of view outlined above. Indeed, a growing body of convergent evidence shows that deep–surface aspects of mental processing are the expression of a structured differentiation between two closely interconnected levels of cognitive processes. The tacit processes provide the apperceptive scaffolding that constrains the conscious, selective attention, thus allowing for the transformation of the deep ordering rules into explicit knowledge (i.e., expectations, beliefs, procedures of thought representation, etc.) (Airenti, Bara, & Colombetti, 1982a, 1982b; Tulving, 1972; Weimer, 1975). Thus, while the nature of the information of which we are conscious is, at least in part, a function of certain tacit underlying structures; on the other hand, the output of these tacit structures gets fed to the systems responsible for explicit, conscious representation (Davidson, 1980).

Finally, tacit and explicit levels of knowing are connected in a hierarchically structured relationship that possesses a specific directionality. The tacit level is the higher, organizing one since it includes the whole set of basic ordering processes constituting the system, while the explicit structural level is composed of processes that mediate one's actual relationship with the environment. The dynamic equilibrium that characterizes the temporal evolution of the tacit–explicit relationship unfolds through the discontinuous emergence of more and more highly integrated levels of thought representation (Guidano, 1984).

In other words, the forward movement in time of the tacit organizational level takes place through the ongoing elaboration of different structural models of the self and the world. In such a way, the human knowing system can undergo structural change during its temporal becoming without losing its organization (i.e., without losing its identity as an individual system).

THE ORGANIZATION OF DEVELOPMENT

From a systems, process-oriented approach, knowledge development is regarded as a progressive construction, influenced from the very beginning by the self-organizing capabilities of human mental processing. Indeed, far from being an "impersonal" construction, human knowledge is imbued with and biased by all the invariant aspects (evolutionary and cultural constraints) that define human nature and consequently determine the human way of knowing reality.

Thus the elaboration of a full sense of personal identity—and the inherent feeling of uniqueness and historical continuity—seems to be a hallmark of a human knowing system. From the earliest stages this sense is intertwined with the parallel process of cognitive growth and emotional development. Put another way, the mechanisms of identity are interwoven with the mechanisms of knowledge, and this interdependence unfolds during the development of an individual by means of the progressive construction of selfhood structures along increasingly complex and integrated levels of knowledge.

Attachment Processes and Self-Identity

The well-known theory that human beings acquire self-knowledge through interaction with other people—termed the "looking-glass self" by Cooley (1902) and later Mead (1934)—is at present supported by an increasing amount of evidence coming mainly from research on primates (Gallup, 1977; Hayes & Nissen, 1971; Linden, 1974).

Just as we learn to see ourselves in a mirror, so the child becomes conscious of himself by seeing his reflection in the mirror of other people's consciousness of himself. (Popper & Eccles, 1977, p. 110)

If valid, the looking-glass effect entails the logical consequence of assigning a crucial role to interpersonal and relational domains in the development of self-knowledge. Therefore, as Ainsworth, Blehar, Waters, and Wall (1978) remark, attachment theory (Bowlby, 1969, 1973, 1980, 1983) should be seen as a sort of explanatory theory supplying a structured framework for understanding and organizing observational and experimental data already available: a new, integrating paradigm of human development that gives us an inclusive and organized vision of all factors that contribute to the structuring of self-knowledge.

In fact, if we look at the developing child as a coherent whole, looking at his or her total functioning (Sroufe, 1979), it becomes of paramount importance to understand how the unitary development of self-knowledge comes about, rather than to focus on limited aspects of emotional or cognitive development. As soon as such a position is assumed it is immediately clear how crucial a role a primary and exclusive bond to one or two specific people may play in the whole organization (i.e., in developing a unitary representation of the self and the world). Evidence from several sources shows how difficult it is for children to form a really secure attachment to more than one person in the sense that their attachment figures are arranged in a hierarchical order with the principal figure at the top (Parkes & Stevenson-Hinde, 1982).

Uniqueness seems to be a crucial variable in attachment relationships, at least during developmental stages. One might then say that a unique relationship with an attachment figure, yielding a sort of template, provides the child with a framework within which otherwise fragmentary information about self and world can be organized into a structured whole. In other words, the uniqueness inherent to primary bonds seems to be a necessary condition for perceiving and recognizing our wholeness and may function, as it were, in a manner analogous to the principles of organization that underlie a conceptual structure of understanding (Marris, 1982).

Assuming a unitarian point of view, therefore, imitation and modeling must be considered as systemic self-reference; that is to say, as nothing other than identification processes. Therefore, internal representations of attachment figures become intertwined with representations of the self and have pervasive effects on everyday thinking and behavior (Heard & Barrett, 1982). In other words, if children extract an image of themselves using their parents as a mirror, this image does not remain mere sensorial data but instead directs and coordinates self-recognition patterns until the children become able to perceive themselves consistently with that image.

Throughout development—within the unfolding of cognitive growth and emotional differentiation—patterns of attachment shift from the lability characteristic of early infancy to the stability of adolescence and youth. Concurrently, identification processes become increasingly complex, providing the developing child with a great deal of information about the self and the world. In short, as Sroufe and Waters (1977) put it, attachment must be regarded as an organizing construct whose value lies in its integrative power.

We can now look briefly at how the interplay between emotional differentiation and cognitive growth takes shape within the unitary framework provided by attachment patterns and identification processes.

From the very earliest stages of his/her development, the child is equipped with both the primary quality of feelings and the ability to communicate them through expressive motor mechanisms (Eibl-Eibesfeldt, 1972, 1979; Ekman, 1972; Izard, 1977, 1980). However, a feeling is by nature something that is diffuse, chaotic, and not easily recognizable and controllable. It has to acquire specific connections with perceptions and actions in order to become a specific subjective emotional experience. In other words, an emotion is essentially an internal process of control expressed by the structuring of a relationship (i.e., a schema) between feelings, perceptions, and actions in memory representation (Giblin, 1981; Pribram, 1967, 1971).

Again, the identification processes inherent in attachment patterns are the unitary framework through which a whole set of crucial cues become available to children in order to shape their diffuse feelings into an ensemble of emotional schemata that give stability and continuity to their sense of self. Given the rather slow progression of cognitive abilities, self-knowledge is primarily organized around the emergence of basic patterns of emotional schemata that provide direction and focus to the unfolding perceptual/cognitive processes (Izard, 1977, 1980; Izard & Buechler, 1980). Established patterns of emotional schemata, acting as "criterion images" in the ongoing matching processes, thereby bias available cognitive abilities toward the selection of specific domains of exchange in interaction with the world and thus influence the content that self-knowledge can assume. The available content of cognitive processes can, in turn, change the intensity or quality of emotional experiences according to the nature of the decodable emotional range reached, influencing to a large extent further emotional differentiation.

The self-knowledge that emerges throughout the period of development out of the continuous interchange between emotional and cognitive processes can be seen as a rather stable configuration in mnemonic representation of basic patterns of emotional schemata, cognitions, and behavior that provide a set of abstract rules for interaction with the environment. The rules are mainly tacit and operate automatically, providing an immediate and plausible feeling of congruence in the ongoing matching process with ongoing experience.

While the developmental attachment history of the individual determines the basic patterns of emotional schemata and the set of abstract rules integrating them, only with the emergence of higher cognitive skills will the person start to reorganize his or her immediate appraisal of self on a more explicit and conscious level of self-knowledge.

Development as a Series of Progressive Steps in Self-Knowledge Reorganization

Cognitive growth achieves its highest structural levels of knowing (i.e., Piagetian formal operations) during adolescence (Bickard, 1980, Flavell, 1963). Paralleling the step-by-step attainment of higher semantic levels of information processing, the reflective dimension of consciousness is organized in progressively more complex levels, with the formation of increasingly more comprehensive and integrated selfhood structures as the person approaches adolescence (Montemayor & Eisen, 1977).

The progressive disengagement of the person's thought from the situational "here and now," as well as from the immediacy of his or her experiences, is perhaps the most outstanding feature of these slowly unfolding cognitive abilities. As a result of this metacognitive development (cf. Flavell, 1978, 1979), a distancing and decentering occurs in the relationship between the developing individual and the world, allowing a gradual shift from an immediate and absolute conception of reality to an inferred, relativistic representation of the world.

According to this perspective, developmental stages can be considered a progressive series of qualitative transformations beginning with the structuring of elementary patterns of self-recognition and ending with the emergence of a structured self-identity. In this step-by-step procedure, each emerging conception of the self depends for its structuring on the level previously reached and, in turn, determines the possible direction in which the next conception can develop. Thus, each emerging self-conception is new in form (i.e., structure), not just in content (Broughton, 1981), and is the expression of the whole structural reorganization involving the reflective dimension of consciousness and paralleling the ascension to higher structural levels of knowing.

Indeed, assuming a comprehensive view, human development appears as a process characterized by a temporal gap. On one side, the progressive scaffolding of experience that is taking place brings about an even more complex system of abstract rule; on the other side, the slow unfolding of cognitive abilities makes it possible to become partially aware of their presence only at a relatively late stage of intellectual development, usually during adolescence. At that point, the prelogical and emotional conceptions of self and world thus far structured undergo a conceptual re-elaboration, coming to form a conscious self-image able to actively direct the programming of the individual's life. The main stages in the development of self-knowledge can be sketched as follows (Guidano & Liotti, 1983):

1. *Infancy and preschool years* (until 5 years of age). The level of cognitive growth existing at this stage affords the elaboration of a primordial nucleus of self-knowledge, that is, the structuring of a basic set of deep tacit relations providing the invariant patterns of self/world recognition and biasing further self-knowledge development by selecting a specific set of meaning domains.

2. *Childhood* (roughly corresponding to from 6 to 12 years of age). The available level of cognitive growth (Piagetian concrete operations) permits an increasing representational ordering of ongoing experience, characterized by its immediate, concrete quality. In short, this stage is marked by a "realistic" understanding of reality, in which the emergence of self-conceptions essentially results in the discovery of the self as "an object" (Dickstein, 1977).

3. *Adolescence and youth* (from about 12 to 18 years of age). The available level of cognitive growth (Piagetian formal operations) affords, on the one hand, a consideration of the self as an already existing agency and, on the other hand, as something to be discovered through a process of self-reflection. In other words, adulthood starts an epistemological understanding of reality (Chandler, 1975) in which the self emerges as "a knower" (Dickstein, 1977) endowed with a full sense of personal identity and actively structuring its life planning.

THE ORGANIZATION OF SELF-KNOWLEDGE

A developed human knowing system should be regarded as including a higher, tacit, organizing level composed of basic knowledge assumptions, on which the lower level elaborates structural models of self and world, according to the data actually accessible from the upper level and afforded by actual environmental exchanges (see Figure 8.1).

Tacit Self-Knowledge

The tacit organizing level is, hierarchically speaking, the higher level of knowledge elaboration in a human knowing system (cf. Hayek's primacy of the abstract). The tacit knowledge contained at this level can be basically

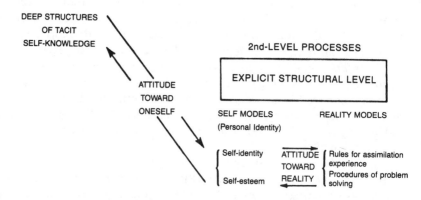

Figure 8.1. A model of the organization of self-knowledge. From *Complexity of the Self* (p. 81) by V. F. Guidano, 1987, New York: The Guilford Press. Reprinted by permission.

regarded as hierarchically arranged sets of ensembled schemata representing the apprehensional structural frame of reference that organizes the flow of ongoing information. In other words, the schemata work as sets of deep rules through which a person tacitly constructs invariant patterns of one-ness (creating self-perception) of external regularities (by which the world is perceived in the same consistent way). The functional aspects of the tacit level of knowledge organization can be briefly outlined as follows (Airenti *et al.*, 1982a, 1982b; Guidano & Liotti, 1983):

• The progressive elaboration of new frames of reference (i.e., progressively more abstract tacit rules) for their subsequent insertion and manipulation in structural models. The insertion of a set of deep rules in representational models is always a constructive process in which analytical and analogical thought procedures, biased by the tacit level, scaffold the furniture of experience in emergent representational models of self and reality. The heuristic possibilities of a specific tacit level thus depend on its organizational aspects and determine the set of worlds that are possible for that particular individual.

• The direction and coordination of most of the individual's emotional and imaginative life by the deep structures of self-knowledge that are the products of feeling tones and feeling memories (emotional schemata) processed during the course of development (Izard & Buechler, 1980; Pylyshyn, 1981). More specifically, the tacit ordering processes that regulate the progressive structuring of specific patterns for decoding one's own feelings limit the nature and range of assimilable experiences and hence define the range of all possible subjective experiences for the individual.

Structural Models of Self and Reality

The structural level consists of a set of explicit models of self and reality that stem from the tacit level and are produced by imaginal (Kieras, 1978; Pylyshyn, 1973) and verbal (Meichenbaum, 1977; Wason & Jonson-Laird, 1972) thought procedures according to ongoing experience. Compared to the more abstract tacit level of knowledge organization, representational models give a more partial and limited image of the self and world. In other words, *not all* the knowledge contained in the tacit level is used in building explicit models, nor is the knowledge content pertaining to ongoing models of self and reality represented in the stream of consciousness with all its details and at every moment.

Though represented each time in an episodic way—depending on individual needs and events—explicit knowledge generally fits the tacit knowledge level on which it depends with minimal incongruities.

PERSONAL IDENTITY

This cognitive structure is to be regarded as the emergent conceptualized polarity of the ongoing relationship between the individual levels of explicit and tacit self-knowledge. It consists, essentially, in a whole arrangement of beliefs, memories, and thought procedures about the self, producing a coherent self-image and a sense of personal singleness and continuity in time. Although personal identity is fundamentally an inferred theory of oneself, biased by one's own tacit self-knowledge, it represents the basic structure of reference and constant confrontation by which every person becomes able to monitor and evaluate him- or herself in relation to ongoing experience. A structured self-identity, in particular, provides a set of basic expectations that direct the individual's patterns of self-perception and self-evaluation in accordance with the selected self-image. The degree of congruence existing between beliefs about one's own value on the one hand, and estimates of one's own behaviors and emotions on the other, corresponds to the degree of self-acceptability and self-esteem.

Self-esteem therefore entails the "theory of emotions" to which we adhere in the relationship we establish with ourselves, as it were. This theory defines the range of emotions that we can recognize as our own, the way we label and control them, and the circumstances and ways in which we can express them. Consequently, only feelings belonging to the selected emotional range will be labeled and experienced as emotions, while feelings that are unrecognizable due to the limitations of this selected arrange are likely to be experienced as externally caused "strange" phenomena (e.g., somatic complaints, altered states of awareness, etc.). The theoretical and clinical implications of these remarks invite a host of speculations that are here left to the reader to pursue).

MODELS OF REALITY

These cognitive structures actually form representational models of the outside world. It is important to keep in mind that models of reality are the individual's only possible means of establishing a relationship with the outside world. In other words, the human knowing system cannot discriminate between external events and their inner representation (Airenti *et al.*, 1982b). From this it becomes clear that models of reality represent not only the perceived world but also any possible "imagined" world, since any imaginative procedure works on data that are consistent with deep structures.

The construction of reality models, though biased by tacit self-knowledge, is constantly regulated by personal identity structures, so as to build representational aspects of the outside world consistent with interactional attitudes toward reality defined by the self-image. This regulating activity is carried out mainly by controlling the executive procedures of the basic set of rules upon which rests the coherence and stability of reality models:

- Rules that coordinate the assimilation of experience. These determine which domains of experience are to be held as significant, as well as the patterns for integration of these experiences into preformed knowledge structures.
- Rules that coordinate problem-solving procedures. The different types of logical problem-solving procedures (Bara, 1980) employed are essential in defining both the nature of significant problems and the strategy for dealing with them, thereby influencing the very form assumed each time by experience.

The essential feature of the model expounded thus far lies in its contention that different structural levels of knowledge are organized in an overall "feedforward" relationship with complementary feedback systems of control. While tacit self-knowledge constantly biases the forward temporal movement of knowledge processes, structured personal identity appears to be the main regulator of the whole process. Indeed, as shown in Figure 8.1, any new set of deep relations can be inserted and manipulated in reality models—and therefore become an effective way of interacting with the world—only *through* personal identity structures. The level of self-awareness reached is thus an essential variable that regulates the possibilities of representing more abstract, challenging deep structures and greatly influences the quality of knowledge levels set forth by forward oscillative processes. It should be noted that the controlling function exercized by personal identity is carried out through two basic structural relationships:

Attitude toward oneself. This defines the ongoing relationship between the explicit self-image and tacit self-knowledge. Although deep structures correspond to the subject's constitutive, unavoidable way of being ("all that he or she is made of"), he or she formalizes his or her existence in a definitive way through the structuring of a specific personal identity ("all that he or she makes of him- or herself"). This formalization takes place through a dynamic relationship between the elements of the deep structures (e.g., invariant tacit rules, emotional schemata) and the emergent cognitive abilities (e.g., concept formation, decentering, and distancing).

Evidence from many sources relating to self-encoding processes suggests that in the ongoing match between tacit self-knowledge and perceived personal identity a person has virtually unlimited access to past or current available information about the self and thus sets the limits of retrieval (Bower & Gilligan, 1979; Mancuso & Ceely, 1980; Markus, 1977; Rogers, Kuiper, & Kirker, 1977). Procedures of thought representation concerned with self-image principally reflect our selective ways of processing internal information rather than the tacit self-knowledge that directly affects us. As a consequence, we cannot expect introspection to be like a window on our deep processes, but only on a biased model of them.

Attitude toward reality. This defines the ongoing structural relationship by which personal identity carries out its regulatory function in the interaction with experience, making the subject's plans and behaviors consistent with the quality of attitudes toward the self thus far structured. The structuring of an attitude toward reality is therefore hierarchically dependent on the extant structure toward the self; our way of seeing reality—and ourselves within reality—essentially depends upon how we see and conceive of ourselves. In this way, our models of the world are provided with a stability and coherence in an ever-changing world.

The tendency to maintain one's own conceptions of the world is not expressed exclusively by the widespread use of confirmatory biasing procedures in reasoning and problem solving (Mahoney & De Monbreun, 1977; Wason, 1977). Idiosyncratic problem-solving strategies also permit an active manipulation of environmental situations in order to produce events that are in keeping with the structured self-image. Swann and Read (1981), in concluding the discussion on their experimental data, cogently remark: "Through such processes, people may create—both in their own minds and in the actual social environment—a social reality that verifies, validates and sustains the very conceptions that initiate and guide these processes" (p. 371).

The Self as the Integrator of Life-Span Oscillations

Though acquiring an organized state after the period of adolescence and though possessing an internal coherence and stability, a human knowing system is not to be considered a "finished product," whose sole aim is to maintain at a more or less constant level the equilibrium it has reached with the environment.

Assuming a process-oriented approach to complex systems (Brent, 1978; Jantsch, 1981; Nicolis & Prigogine, 1977; Prigogine, 1980), human knowledge appears as an open, generative system whose ordering processes rest on a dynamic, progressive equilibrium that moves toward more and more integrated levels of organization, characterized by an increase in structural order and complexity. The principle underlying this dynamic equilibrium is called "order through fluctuations" insofar as the higher-order patterns that emerge are the result of the assimilation of disequilibriums (or fluctuations) arising from interactions with the environment. The affirmation that a human knowing system exhibits stability at any point in time implies that the system functions in its specific way with oscillations around that point. Should a fluctuation become amplified to such an extent that it goes outside the existing range of stability, the disequilibrium that emerges will help drive the system in the direction of restructuring its ordering processes (Mahoney, 1982). To put it another way, mental functioning appears to have a generative and endless directionality, not of a linear kind, but rather of a type that might be called "ongoingness" and capacity for continued ongoingness (Dell & Goolishian, 1981).

What is the nature of the fluctuations upon which the ongoingness of an individual knowing system is based? As we have seen, tacit and explicit levels of self-knowledge are connected in a structured relationship that has a specific directionality. Accessible tacit processes are converted through thought processes into representational models that constitute the only way we have of understanding reality. As a result of the ongoing tacit ordering of ongoing experience, new sets of tacit rules are intermittently emerging and subsequently being inserted into explicit models.

In cases where the tacit material fits with explicit models of the self and world with minimal incongruities, a simple recombination of available knowledge occurs and the system oscillates within its range of stability. When, on the other hand, critical life events provoke an elaboration of tacit material that exerts a challenging pressure on explicit self-models, the limits of the usual range of stability are overstepped, and the individual must reorganize his or her conscious view of him- or herself and the world.

Incidentally, it is important to note that if the mind is considered as an active system imposing its order on the environment, it becomes clear that some life events can assume a critical personal meaning only through the particular individual knowledge organization and are critical for that organization alone. In other words, it is not the "real" social world but how it is construed that plays the crucial role, and the ongoing tacit ordering of life-events into personal meanings is primary. Thus the basic process underlying the temporal evolution of any individual seems to be that of making the tacit explicit through the discontinuous emergence of more and more integrated and complex models of the self and the world (Davidson, 1980; Guidano, 1984; Welwood, 1979, 1982).

One might use the image of a series of self-transcendant leaps to describe the increase in complexity and order that characterizes the ongoingness of a human knowing system, due to the self-reference with which it is endowed. The tacit ordering of developmental events is continually re-elaborated and explicated in light of later experiences changing from peripheral and contingent causal theories to more central and integrated ones, thus increasing the subject's feelings of uniqueness and historical continuity. In this way, the range of models of the self and world that a human being can put together during his or her temporal becoming depends essentially on the heuristic power inherent in his or her tacit level, since it determines the set of worlds (either perceived, remembered, or imagined) that are possible for the individual. The structural level reached by individual knowledge during its temporal becoming can then be regarded as the emergent result of the relationship between the individual's explicit self-identity and his or her deep, tacit self-knowledge in the ongoing match with experiential data.

Again, the possibilities of reaching even more integrated and comprehensive patterns of self-awareness are strictly dependent on the individual's abilities to make explicit the emergent ordering processes of his or her tacit level of knowing.

HUMAN CHANGE PROCESSES

If the emergence of tacit oscillative processes represents the most challenging pressure upon the reorganization of conscious models of self, the outcome of these pressures depends on the integrative capacities of such models given the regulatory control that they exercise on the overall individual organization during its temporal becoming (Epstein, 1973; Greenwald, 1980; Guidano & Liotti, 1983; Mahoney, 1982). In order to allow any consistent degree of modification of self and reality, the individual must gradually elaborate an alternative self-image without experiencing interruptions in his or her structured sense of subjective continuity. Any interruption would represent a loss of the very sense of reality. Thus, maintenance and change processes rather than being viewed as opposite polarities are to be viewed as interplaying and overlapping processes that, though simultaneous, manifest themselves in different modes during the temporal becoming of knowledge: While maintenance processes are continuous, change processes are continuous only as challenges or possibilities but are discontinuous in their occurrence.

The Dynamics of Personal Change

The challenging pressures exercised by life-span oscillations on the integrative capabilities of the self differ according to their qualities and intensity. An oscillation that is appreciable but as yet contained within the range of stability will produce a reorganization of the person's attitude toward reality without any significant change in conscious self-identity: each of us is able to modify his or her own way of understanding aspects of reality without having to revise his or her self-image. These surface changes (Arnkoff, 1980; Mahoney, 1980, 1982) occur continuously and produce endless revisions of reality models according to ongoing experience. They are, above all, an expression of the level of flexibility and plasticity that an individual knowledge organization has reached.

In comparison with the surface changes, however, deep changes have quite a different importance, being in every case the expression of a modification of the conscious self-image elicited by an oscillation whose intensity and quality is such that it oversteps the existing stability range. Deep change processes—ranging from a limited restructuring of personal identity to true personal revolutions (Mahoney, 1980)—correspond to changes in patterns of attitude toward oneself as a result of the reconstruction of sets of deeper rules emerging from tacit self-knowledge. The changed attitude toward oneself will consequently produce a modification of personal identity, which will in turn entail a restructuring of the attitude to reality through which the world can be seen and dealt with in a different manner.

Since any tacit assumption has to pass through personal identity to be inserted in representational models, awareness is a facilitatory condition for converting tacit knowledge into beliefs and thought procedures (Airenti et al., 1982b). Thus the quality of self-awareness—expressed by the corresponding patterns of attitudes toward oneself—dramatically influences the oscillative procedure and the final result of a change process. The essential mechanism underlying a deep change, therefore, is the switching to a metalevel of knowledge representation elicited and regulated by the interaction of both environmental and deep pressures. A deep oscillative process—always charged with intense emotions—may have different consequences for the temporal evolution of a knowledge organization depending on whether it is of a progressive or a regressive nature.

Progressive shift. The switching to a metalevel of knowledge representation is achieved when processing possibilities determined by self-awareness patterns somehow fit with incoming deep challenges. The emergence of a more integrated personal identity renders the possibility of:

- labeling and decoding the arousal of emotions connected to the deep oscillative process with a corresponding progressive shift in self-awareness;
- manipulating even more sophisticated reality models with a corresponding progressive shift in experience assimilation.

Regressive shift. The switching to a metalevel of knowledge representation is thwarted by a pattern of self-awareness that does not allow the conversion of challenging deep pressures into beliefs and thought procedures. The failure to reach a more integrated personal identity will have relevant consequences from a clinical point of view:

- attempts to label and control the arousal of emotions related to the deep oscillatory processes by a proliferation of external, "ad hoc" theories aimed at explaining overemotionality without altering one's own self-image, constituting a regressive shift in self-awareness
- consequently, in spite of unsuccessful predictions and results, reality models become even more closely linked to stereotyped and repetitive image representations and problem-solving procedures with a corresponding regressive shift in experience assimilation.

Life-Span Development

The evolution in time of an individual knowing organization, as described above, is not a continuous linear process but rather a discontinuous, step-like one. The passage from one step to the next is, in turn, a relatively unpredictable process both in the way it occurs and in the amount of time it takes. As Dell and Goolishan (1981) put it:

One can intervene in such systems and push them to the point of instability, but one cannot control precisely when they reorganize, nor can one control in what fashion they reorganize. (p. 179)

From this point of view, progressive or regressive shifts have the same common origin. They are both traceable to the first appearance of a disequilibrium, and thus both a personal revolution (i.e., a successful deep change) and a clinical syndrome (i.e., an unsuccessful deep change) are simply the expressions of different reordering processes elicited by a deep challenging pressure.

However, the lack of determinate predictability of human behavior does not mean pure indeterminacy. As Popper (1972) put it:

We have to be indeterminists to be sure; but we also must try to understand how men, and perhaps animals, can be "influenced" or "controlled" by such things as aims, or purposes, or rules, or agreements. (p. 230)

Then, thanks to the regulatory function exerted by personal identity and attitude toward oneself, life-span development, notwithstanding its uncertainty patterns, unfolds itself according to the principle of orthogenetic change: the progression from a state of globality or lack of differentiation to a state of differentiation, integration, and hierarchic organization (Lerner & Busch-Rossnagel, 1981).

It has often been noted, in fact, that the control function carried out by personal identity tends to increase progressively with the passing of time. During juvenile and intermediate phases of life even a consistent restructuring of one's own identity is possible, while in late adulthood the possibilities of a significant identity change generally decrease. As Luckmann (1979) pointed out, personal identity tends to become a historical form of life. The terms such as "plan of life" (Popper & Eccles, 1977), or "life theme" (Csikszentmihalyi & Beattie, 1979) have been used to indicate the progressive unification that an individual's self-knowledge and actions assume in the course of his or her life.

As is evident, a systems approach to human knowledge emphasizes temporality from the very beginning as a fundamental for understanding the life-span of any living, complex system. Evidence coming mainly from the study of irreversible thermodynamics leads us to regard time not as an external—and in some way reversible—physical variable, but as an internal dimension describing the structural evolution and fluctuations of an open complex system (Prigogine, 1980). If the flow of time inherent in a human knowing system is considered as a dimension actively influencing the system's scaffolding of experience, time appears as an irreversible variable and the irreversibility itself seems to be the starting point of many processes of spontaneous organization.

Therefore, a human knowing system should be considered not only as a knowing system, but also as a historical knowing system. History essentially means an internal and irreversible transformation of physical time brought about by the system and made up of a coherent construction of sequences of events selected and arranged as a whole. In this way, when we read a biography, we usually get the impression that the individual, almost without realizing it, followed a sort of "guiding track" or, to use theater terminology, a "script."

A life theme, to conclude, is best defined as something that is progressively and dynamically constructed day by day, year by year, on the basis of events that have characterized an individual's existence, of how he or she has interpreted these events and dealt with them, and of the consequences that derived from this process. The consequences of his or her choices and actions become in turn further events that, unified in individual memory, allow him or her to build an even more uniform and comprehensive image of self and of his or her life. Using Hayek's (1978) words once more, we might say that the products of conscious rationality are the result of human actions, but not of human design.

THERAPEUTIC PRINCIPLES

A human knowing system reflects a dynamic equilibrium unfolding through successively more integrated models of the self and world. As will be elaborated below, this perspective has some remarkable consequences for the therapeutic approach. In the usual cognitive-behavioral approaches, based on the rather static conception of a circular equilibrium regulated only by feedback mechanisms, the therapy essentially aims at restoring the lost equilibrium, by increasing self-control and providing more practical problem-solving procedures.

In contrast, the basic question on which a constructivistic-cognitive therapy revolves can be formulated in this way: how can clients be aided in their personal temporal becoming by helping them assimilate the disequilibriums that have thus far thwarted their attempts to reach more integrated levels of knowledge? In the discussions that follow I shall attempt to elaborate the possible relevance of this shifting of basic questions for clinical and therapeutic pursuits.

THE "TRUTH PROBLEM" AND THE THERAPIST'S ATTITUDE TOWARD THE THERAPEUTIC RELATIONSHIP

To begin with, the cognitive analysis does not focus on the relationships between single beliefs or specimens of internal dialogue and some defined external stimulus. A systems, processed-oriented cognitive analysis should be a more comprehensive one, revolving around two basic questions: (1) what kind of developmental stages brought about this individual knowledge organization? and (2) in what way is that knowledge organization determining the very shape of moment-to-moment experience? By focusing on these questions it becomes possible to delineate the basic assumptions about the self and world upon which the individual's very sense of reality rests. This in turn affords the therapist a better understanding of some of the crucial problems that emerge in any treatment. Why are some past experiences, although present in individual memory, completely neglected? Why are new experiences during therapy so difficult to assimilate in spite of their evident logical consistency?

To put it in another way, the so-called "truth problem" is a fundamental question for both theoretical and clinical psychology. Indeed, it is a rather widely accepted notion that any epistemology presupposes—often implicitly—metaphysical assumptions about basic questions arising from human interaction with the world such as, "What is the truth?" and "How can the truth be detected?"

In the empiricist–associationistic approach the problem is solved by regarding truth as a copy of external reality that has a direct correspondence with it. Thus conceived, truth is considered singular, static, and external to humans; all other views of the world are understandable only when compared with it. Consequently, the therapist's task is to evaluate the rationality/irrationality of clients' thoughts and beliefs according to external standards taken as true. Therapies conducted from such a perspective very often become pedagogical, intentionally seeking (and even creating) any occasion useful for showing the client his or her irrationality (e.g., see some techniques of Rational–Emotive Therapy [Ellis, 1962]).

Viewing the problem from a different perspective, it is the individual's knowledge itself that, in order to make reality "real," must possess a concept of truth or, if you prefer, something that plays the same logical role. Briefly, in a systems approach truth is regarded as stemming from the core of an individual knowledge organization and therefore as something belonging uniquely to each individual. Each person, through the basic assumptions ordering his or her representations of self and world, becomes able to make a rather stable and reliable demarcation between what he or she considers real and unreal. Psychotherapy based on such a perspective does not aim at persuading clients to adopt other standards for truth but rather at helping them to recognize, understand, and better conceptualize their own personal truth—this being their only possibility for making reality real for themselves.

A systems approach has other remarkable consequences. On a theoretical level it dramatically changes our conceptualizations of rationality. Rationality, rather than being something static and absolute, like an entity, has a relativistic and interactive nature. First, it is a basic process inherent in any human knowing system. Second, this process unfolds into knowledge structures only through the scaffolding of experience that is accumulated during the individual temporal becoming. Moreover, since it stems from the core of knowledge organization, rationality is by no means to be considered only as something belonging to the domain of formal logic or deductive, analytical thinking but on the contrary includes tacit schemata and emotional aspects, which have been traditionally considered dogmatic (i.e., irrational or at least not rational). In this perspective, the whole set of tacit assumptions and explicit thought procedures that provide internal coherence and reliability to an individual's knowledge organization are considered rational for that individual, regardless of their correspondence to the classic norm of logic. At a clinical level, a therapeutic approach based on this perspective may considerably change the structure of the therapeutic relationship, as well as the strategy for facilitating a cognitive change. Rather than taking a pedagogic approach, therapy becomes an exploratory collaboration enabling the client to identify the basic assumptions underlying his or her way of experiencing reality. These are viewed as being in need of modification not because they are irrational but because they represent an outmoded solution. They are understood as having been useful when first developed, but in a changed environment they are seen to foster a world representation with little understanding power and repetitious, stereotyped problem-solving strategies. Likewise, the therapeutic intervention is not considered a strategy to persuade the client to accept more "rational" points of view, but as a strategy to modify the client's demarcation between real and not-real in order to allow him or her to assimilate (e.g., to consider now as real) neglected past memories and new available experiences.

ASSESSMENT AND THE ROLE OF DEVELOPMENTAL ANALYSIS

In a therapeutic situation, the assessment procedure is a technical way of building up explicit, conceptual models for making the underlying tacit processes evident and acting on them.

At the beginning, the therapist can catch a glimpse of the quality of the crucial tacit rules involved in the clinical picture through a careful behavioral and cognitive analysis of the client's casual theories about his or her complaints. Although these theories do not directly inform the therapist about the client's actual ongoing processes (Nisbett & Wilson, 1977), they are nevertheless influenced by the same tacit rules, and thus are useful as indirect information about them.

This assessment can be aided by providing clients with rationales and methods for self-observation. As their observational and analytic skills improve, clients acquire more distancing and decentering capabilities from certain engrained beliefs and self-images so far considered unquestionable, allowing the deeper structures underlying their conceptions of self and the world to emerge.

Moreover, in the assessment procedure, the therapist should not let the emotional level go unnoticed while focusing only on the conscious cognitive processes immediately available. On the contrary, one has to work actively on emotional aspects, being careful from the start that every explanation assimilated by the client is paralleled by a coherent emotional labeling. In other words, one has continuously to test the labeling of emotions that accompany understanding processes. In such a way a therapist can, on the one side, acquire data about the personal range of recognizable emotions of the subject and, on the other side, have the opportunity of supplying explanations about the nature and funcitons of emotions and their labeling.

By now the therapist has a draft of the client's cognitive models, which allows him or her to render a reconstruction of the tacit rules underlying the client's maladaptive behavior. However, he or she cannot afford to indulge in groundless hypothetical reconstructions, no matter how original and stimulating they may be.

As a next step, a careful developmental analysis is carried out that represents the necessary frame of reference that will allow the therapist to reconstruct the interplay between the distressing events and cognitive processing abilities that step by step have led to the maintenance of a specific self-identity and attitude toward reality. Coming back to the development of self-knowledge outlined earlier, we can see how any distortion of the patterns of family attachment will be reflected—via the looking-glass effect—in the child's developing self-identity. Hence, from a developmental viewpoint, psychotherapy should be regarded in light of attachment processes and of their relevance in building up the maladaptive conceptions of self that prevent the progression toward more integrated levels of self-knowledge and instead foster the emergence of those regressive oscillations in lifespan development that we call clinical disturbances (Bowlby, 1977a, 1979; Brown, 1982; Brown & Harris, 1978; Guidano & Liotti, 1983; Liotti, 1984; Parkes & Stevenson-Hinde, 1982).

It would be well to make clear, however, that while the therapist is reconstructing the history of a client's development, he or she should not limit him- or herself to considering the events in themselves, as it were objectively, but should consider the particular effects of a stressful event are largely dependent on the client's previous history and cognitive abilities at that stage. The eating disorders provide a clear example. It seems quite evident from clincial experience that both obesity and anorexia have their starting point in a similar stressful event: a strong disappointment coming from a loved person, usually a parent. The different effects resulting from the same event have to be attributed to the different developmental stage in which that event occurred. Thus in obese clients the disappointment was experienced in childhood, where the cognitive abilities available at that time were not capable of coping with the event, so that the subject experienced it as an overwhelming failure. In anorexic clients the disappointment occurred in adolescence where the emerging higher cognitive abilities were capable of coping with the event more or less effectively, making the subject experience it as an unbearable challenge to be striven against.

Once the developmental history has been reconstructed, the therapist is usually able to achieve three basic tasks:

- the step-by-step reconstruction of the client's cognitive models of self and reality and corresponding patterns of attitude toward themselves, (i.e., the client's cognitive organization and its actual discrepancy between the existing range of stability and the deep oscillations to be assimilated)
- the identification of the client's tacit assumptions and thought procedures that influence the scaffolding of the experiential domain in

which disequilibrium was produced, so that it becomes evident that the range of feelings that are excluded from the client's self-identity has prevented some specific events of the experiential domain involved to be assimilated in a self-referential way
  • the identification of the historical stage of the individual life-span development in which the disequilibrium occurred.

At this point, it becomes generally possible to provide clients with a better understanding of how they have organized their experience and, at the same time, to elaborate a therapeutic strategy in keeping with that understanding.

As a conclusion it is useful to bear in mind that the assessment procedure is just a reconstruction of tacit rules and by no means a one-to-one translation of them. The great epistemologist Lakatos used to say to his students that since men are not altogether rational, real history is less rational than its reconstruction.

THE SHAPING OF THE THERAPEUTIC RELATIONSHIP AND CLIENTS' RESISTANCE TO CHANGE

Knowing the basic elements of the cognitive organization that underlies the pattern of disturbed behavior and emotions, the therapist can behave from the beginning in a manner that will build a relationship that is as effective as possible for that particular client. In other words, the therapist should be able to build up a relationship that respects the client's personal identity for as long as possible and that at the same time does not confirm the basic pathogenic assumptions.

For example, in agoraphobic clients the therapist has to respect their self-images centered on the need of being in control. He or she can do this by avoiding any direct attack on their controlling attitudes and by leaving them a wide margin of control in the relationship. At the same time the therapist should avoid confirming their assumptions regarding the somatic origin of their emotional disturbances or their inborn fragility. Moreover, the therapist who can anticipate the models of self and others tacitly entertained by the client is surely better able to help the development of a collaborative working alliance than the therapist who cannot make such anticipations. As has been explicitly stated by Young and Beck (1982), the style defined as "collaborative empiricism" is one of the hallmarks of cognitive therapy. Collaborative empiricism may be seriously hindered, at the beginning of the treatment, by a therapist's attitude that, however innocent and reasonable it may appear to an outside observer, is perceived by the client as threatening because it is so encoded in his or her representational models of self and others.

Even if, shaping the therapeutic relationship according to the client's cognitive organization decreases, generally, the number and the amount of clients' resistances, they emerge all the same during a therapy being, perhaps, the expression of the same oscillative aspects that open complex systems—like human relational domain—usually exhibit in their evolving.

More specifically, in the category of resistances to change found frequently in our therapeutic practice are included phenomena such as (Liotti, 1984):

1. more or less explicit objections raised by the client to therapists' prescriptions and explanations
2. relapses following the attainment of desired changes
3. report of expected difficulties in some significant interpersonal relationship of the client (including the relationship with the therapist) as a consequence of the application of the therapeutic principles.

Instead of directly striving to overcome these resistances, a process-oriented therapist tries to make use of them in order to assess the client's "theories" that have been challenged by the use of the therapeutic strategy and, thereupon, to reconstruct those aspects of the client's developmental history that could have influenced the forming of these theories.

The topic of resistance to change has been treated with some detail in cognitive literature, however it is seldom explicitly stated that the resistances may be used as a lead to uncover specific aspects of the client's developmental history (Bugental, 1978). The discussion of these aspects may be useful in making the client accept the "novelty" implied by the foreseen change, without too strong and frightening feelings that the change will imply a radical and abrupt modification of perceived personal identity (cf. Mahoney, 1980, 1982).

SUPERFICIAL AND DEEP CHANGES

Two levels of therapeutic modification in cognitive psychotherapy can be identified; superficial change and deep change (Arnkoff, 1980; Mahoney, 1980). A superficial change coincides with the reorganization of the client's attitude toward reality without revising his or her personal identity. This level of modification in many cases allows for an improvement of the client's adaptation to the environment and a reduction of emotional distress. In a deep change, on the other hand, there is a restructuring of the client's personal identity, with the elaboration of a new attitude toward reality that involves an alternative view of the problems troubling him or her. These two types of change do not exclude one another; rather, according to clinical experience, it is often possible to reach a deep change only through a preceding superficial one.

However, the request for a deeper analysis and change has to come from clients, while the therapist should only stimulate their curiosity. There are two reasons for this. First, this deep analysis is always a process accompanied by intense emotions, often painful, so the client should not be forced to do it. Second, a "real" personal change can occur only if clients are able to produce it by themselves, so all their willingness is needed. When the client has asked for a deeper change it is useful to work again on the developmental history, requiring the client to participate as much as possible. Generally at this point the subject already knows his or her developmental history, because it was already used for obtaining a superficial change. Now it becomes possible to regard the past history from a different perspective. In simpler terms, the therapist's basic question could be the following: "Okay, as we know, you have elaborated this conception of yourself through your past history. Well, in order to understand the degree of consistancy and functionality of your self-image, we have to re-examine your history and recognize the whole set of "proofs" and "configurations" that you have considered as supporting the theories about yourself throughout development. After that we can examine the epistemological validity of such proofs and confirmations."

In some way, this becomes work on the client's memory (Bara, 1984), leading him or her to focus on the differences between episodic contingent memories and the global meanings attributed to them. In doing such work, the client is generally ready to acknowledge that the evidence upon which he or she founded his or her theories concerning personal identity are of an episodic nature, and that there is neither a logical nor a psychological reason to consider them as having an absolute meaning. In turn, this therapeutic achievement becomes a new starting point for a further restructuring of his or her self-identity.

THE STRATEGY FOR THERAPEUTIC CHANGE

Let us assume that the therapist is now directly facing the problem of guiding a client to assimilate the disequilibrium that thwarted prior attempts at reaching a more integrated level of knowledge. Such an assimilation generally becomes possible only through a revision of the cognitive models of self and reality entertained by the client.

In a personal letter Bowlby (July, 1982) suggests the following steps to achieve such a revision:

For anyone to revise a cognitive model is, as you well know, a difficult undertaking. Principal tasks of the therapist I believe to be: (a) encouraging and enabling the patient to explore his cognitive models; (b) helping the patient to recognize the cognitive models he is actually utilizing; (c) helping him trace, how he has come to have them, which I believe to have been in large measure due to his having accepted what his parents have constantly *told* him—both about themselves and about himself; (d) encouraging him to review the models in the light both of their history and also of the degree to which they correspond to his own *first-hand* experience of himself and his parents; (e) helping him recognize the sanctions his parents have used to insist that he adopts their model and not his own. Only after this process has been gone through many times are the revised models likely to be stable.

I fully subscribe to these ideas of Bowlby's and I would like to indicate some of the convergent aspects inherent in our respective clinical perspectives.

In a systems, process-oriented approach, the possibilities of reaching more integrated and comprehensive models of self and reality are strictly dependent on the individual's ability to make explicit the available sets of tacit rules. So, while proceeding along the steps proposed by Bowlby, the therapist's fundamental aim is to enable clients to consciously elaborate alternative representative models capable of better recognizing and structuring the tacit processes that are already influencing their thought procedures, albeit outside their sphere of awareness. This notion has certain consequences regarding the attitude the therapist will assume in the therapeutic situation. That is, a therapist should bear in mind that the knowledge content capable of revising the client's cognitive models is already available in some way. What is not available is the client's selective attention in recognizing it. Then the therapist should pay great respect to the client's self-knowledge. In general, it is useless and even dangerous to put new knowledge into the client's head in every possible way, since the information useful for the client comes from his or her deep structures and cannot be replaced by the therapist's conceptions about life.

A simple clinical vignette can illustrate the central role of the client's self-knowledge in being both the source of the discrepancy and the only possible integrator once the client allowed himself to elaborate alternative frames of reference.

Albert was a 35-year-old man who asked for treatment because in recent months he had been experiencing panic attacks whose content was the fear of an impending madness. Previous pharmacological treatments and relaxation techniques had been completely unsuccessful. His developmental history was characterized both by an intense attachment with an introverted, rigid mother and by a very poor economic situation that forced him to regard studying as the only possible achievement in life. He thus grew up without contacts with peers of both sexes, relying only on his mother's support, which was characterized by a low level of emotionality and strong conceptions of duty and obligation. This past experience influenced him to elaborate a self-image of a rational, logical man without emotions or anything else that could appear as "irrational" or "unpredictable." This view oriented him toward a mathematical faculty when enrolling in university. Starting to work, he felt that the only goal worth pursuing in his life was that of becoming a man composed only of abstract, logical thoughts. "I wanted to be just pure thought." At the same time, his mother died and he—accustomed to working alone with the tacit support of a female figure—married a rather old and passive woman. By the time he sought treatment their marital relationship had become a completely stagnant one. They never had affective and communicative exchanges and their sexual life, very poor from the beginning, was almost nonexistent. On weekdays he generally came home late in the evening, having spent the whole day at the research institution where he worked. His wife and children were already in bed and he usually ate his dinner in the kitchen more or less in the darkness because, he felt obliged to save energy. One day while going up to his laboratory with some colleagues the elevator suddenly jammed for 1 or 2 minutes. He did not experience any fear at the time and actually continued to converse with his captive colleagues until the elevator resumed operation. One month later he was eating alone in the kitchen at night and an image of the jammed elevator suddenly appeared in his mind. He was frightened by his discovery of a parallel, which he posed to himself as a question and an answer: "What difference is there between the jammed elevator and my home? In the final analysis, they are very similar: there is no way of getting out of them." In other words, a set of challenging deep rules regarding his affective life had become available to him. It had not, up to that moment, had the possibility of being converted into a format recognizable for him. During the intervening month there had apparently been a further tacit elaboration of the reverberating images of the jammed elevator, making them useful as cues for shaping his emergent feelings. Unfortunately the explanation available to him was that the experience represented proof for him that he, so rational and logical, was going crazy, that is, was becoming irrational and illogical, something that he has always equated with death. It is interesting to note that he had some awareness of his situation at that time, as evidenced by his connecting the "discrepant episode" with his sense of loneliness and with the unsatisfaction of his affective life. Using our terms, he was aware that the discrepancy was coming from the inside, so that half of the work was done. But it was unbearable for him to accept that the "irrational" consideration emerged from his conscious self.

The therapy was rather short-lasting in this case because Albert only needed an acceptable format for structuring and assimilating his emerging feelings and abstractions. Technically it required both a restructuring of his rigid conception about rationality and an acquiring of more integrated levels of knowledge of human relationships, so that he might be able to elaborate a conceptual format in keeping with his logical and scientific attitude.

Due to his rigid education and isolation, Albert had developed a rather poor level of skill in decoding emotions aroused in human relationships. Therefore, it became essential to help him acquire new dimensions of conceptual knowledge (e.g., what constitutes communication and intimacy, what are the rules that regulate the structuring of an affective relationship, etc.) to be able to reach more integrative capabilities for ordering and decoding his feelings. Moreover, reading technical books on human relations was in keeping with his basic attitude, according to which reality had to be analyzed and understood only by scientific, rational procedures.

Finally, in such a perspective, it might be possible to revise our conceptions concerning directiveness versus nondirectiveness. They could be seen as complementary aspects rather than opposite ones. In order to make the tacit explicit, one has to enable the client to elaborate a more integrated view of him- or herself, but in order to do this, one has to respect the client's tacit level since it represents the essential directionality to be followed. For example, it is useless and dangerous to try to convince individuals with depressive organizations that their inner view of themselves is absurd or to criticize their basic feelings about loneliness, ephemerality, and the futility of life. In some ways, these are the only possibilities they have of establishing a relationship with reality. The strategy, therefore, is to enable them to elaborate a model of themselves in which these basic feelings could also be experienced as a creative way of ordering reality and not simply as an inescapable and painful existential condition. Finally the therapist's directive way may, of course, be expressed by using classic behavioral and cognitive techniques. It is important to emphasize that generally the therapist employs these techniques for disproving client's superficial beliefs and expectations and so allowing deeper structures to emerge. In this sense a process-oriented therapist does not consider the achievement of a therapeutic goal as a matter of choosing the "right" technique, but rather, he or she always uses existing techniques (or even "invents" new techniques) that fit into the strategy of guiding the client's processes to make the tacit explicit.

CASE ILLUSTRATIONS: AGORAPHOBIA AND ANOREXIA

I shall try to exemplify the therapeutic practice that stems from the theoretical and clinical principles outlined earlier with the illustration of two clinical cases. The choice of the cases is aimed at showing how, through the adjustment of the therapist's attitude toward the client according to his or her cognitive organization, the therapeutic relationship can become an essential and flexible device for facilitating change.

While in the first case (agoraphobia) the therapeutic relationship mainly provided the client with a "secure base" from which to explore exciting and also frightening areas (Bowlby, 1977b), in the second case (anorexia nervosa) the therapeutic change was integrally connected with the very shaping of the therapeutic relationship.

AGORAPHOBIA

Preliminary Developmental Remarks

The typical agoraphobia clinical picture can be summarized in a few words (Guidano & Liotti, 1983). The situations avoided by agoraphics can be subsumed under two invariant categories:

- loneliness, marked by the absence of a trustworthy companion in the immediate environment (e.g., being alone at home, in a public place and so on);
- constriction (i.e., situations that are felt to be limiting one's freedom of movement such as traffic jams, elevators, crowded places, buses where one cannot get out at one's will, etc.).

The majority of these clients ascribe their phobic behavior to some mysterious disease, either somatic or mental. However, a close analysis of the thought procedures characterizing this "disease theory" shows an invariant aspect of agoraphobic cognition: the dreaded idea of losing control. We can confidently consider the fact of losing control in loneliness or constriction situations as the hallmark of agoraphobic organization.

Bowlby (1969, 1973, 1983) was able to identify a serious limitation of the autonomous exploration of the outside environment in children that complained in adult life of agoraphobic disturbances. As a rule, the parents of agoraphobics had not presented these obstacles to exploration and autonomy as their own wishes or demands, but, on the contrary, as a protective behavior that helped the child avoid the dangers of the external world. The indirectness of the imposed limitation has important consequences insofar as it prevents the child from perceiving the emotional distress deriving from their limitations as coming directly from a parental coercion. On the contrary, they experience their emotional distress as a part of a more complex situation and they perceive it as the effect of being lovingly protected from imaginary dangers. The anxious attachment that emerges from this context generally provides the child with a conflicting self-image that will require considerable effort on his or her part to integrate. On the one hand, the continuous contact with attention that the hyperprotective parent exhibits with the child provides him or her with a self-image as a lovable and valuable person; on the other hand, the restriction of exploratory behavior has further encouraged a weak or fragile self-image within an hostile world.

Moreover, the child must try to integrate contradictory and conflicting aspects also in structuring an image of reality. On one side, the thwarting of the inborn disposition to explore the environment is perceived as an intolerable constriction, which causes him or her to develop an intense need for freedom and independence; he or she will thus become selectively attentive to the constrictive aspects of reality. On the other side, the imagined dangers of the outside world and the presumed personal weakness contribute to the need of feeling oneself protected and reassured. In other words, the agoraphobic organization faces a dilemma of this kind: how to find an equilibrium between the need for freedom and independence that implies loneliness (and therefore danger) and the need for protection that implies dependence on others (and therefore a likely repetition of the constricting experience).

The future agoraphobic tries to find a direct solution by developing an inward overly controlling attitude toward his or her weakness and an outward overly controlling attitude toward interpersonal relationships in order to obtain protection without experiencing constriction. It is therefore not surprising that any significant alteration in the balance of affectional bonds will reflect itself in the equilibrium reached by the agoraphobic organization.

Case Illustration: Annie

Annie was a 33-year-old secondary school teacher who had been married for 1 year after a 5-year engagement. She asked for treatment because of her inability to stay alone at home or in the streets, especially in crowded places. Moreover, even with trusted companions, she could not stay in any situation where a quick escape was difficult or impossible to find (e.g., traffic jams, going on superhighways, planes, trains, buses, elevators, subways, etc.). Her symptomatology had suddenly begun 6 months earlier when she had experienced her first panic attack in a crowded street. Panic reappeared again 20 days later when she was alone in a very big square. From that moment on Annie had felt herself unable to stay alone at home or outside.

Two years earlier Annie had experienced some intense fears of tumors at a time when she and her future husband had decided to live together with another couple who were friends. These fears disappeared for a year and then reappeared again, although not as intensely as before, when her husband was working abroad 6 months after their wedding. Annie's panic attacks increased significantly when her husband returned home and they began living together, being alone for the first time in their long relationship. It was during that period that Annie experienced her first panic attack. When she came for treatment Annie didn't correlate the development of her disturbances with her contextual, interpersonal situation. She was firm in attributing her disturbances to a somatic illness not yet discovered by physicians.

Behavioral and Cognitive Aspects

With the help of the therapist's functional behavioral analysis, Annie, who was a very clever woman, soon succeeded in recognizing that "loneliness" and "constriction" were the invariant situations in which all her disturbances occurred. Annie was also able to recognize that constriction was more powerful in eliciting her feared feelings.

This allowed the therapist to shift to another level of inquiry, devoted to assessing her internal representations when imagining or staying in frightening situations. Her representations were centered on the fear of losing control. In Annie's images this took the form of both a possible fainting or an impending madness, both of which were associated with subsequent images of the shame of showing herself as weak and in need of help. These latter images were even more feared than the ones regarding losing control: "It is an unbearable situation for me. I have never needed to ask for help from anybody. I can't recognize myself; I have never behaved this way!" Her internal dialogue was focused on both the specification of the imagined danger and the instructions for controlling herself and looking for avoidance possibilities.

The therapist then began to more directly assess her causal theories about the nature of her disturbances. Annie's disease theory was rather sophisticated in comparison with those of the usual agoraphobic clients: She considered her disturbances to be due to a mental illness of a biochemical nature, in which the chemical mediators responsible were still unknown. In fact, she knew something about biochemical theories on the nature of mood oscillations and she considered them a basic proof in support of the appearance of frightening emotions outside the awareness of the individual. This "basic proof" paralleled very closely her experience of her first panic attack: "They occurred when I was perfectly calm, enjoying shopping, and without thinking of any trouble. They came on me unexpectedly like a fever attack."

When she asked why she tried to control an unpredictable attack of a somatic illness, Annie's causal theories on control began to be explicated. She regarded the problem of control as a fundamental of life: "Being in control is the only right way of facing life. It is necessary to be rational in all possible situations. Showing one's feeling and emotions is useless and even dangerous because they make you weak and dependent on everybody." By pursuing this theme it was rather easy to assess her causal theories on freedom and independence: "The goal to be pursued by a woman who is not stupid is to be free, without important engagement. Falling in love is dangerous because it makes you stupid and dependent. The only goal I can trust is intelligence because it never allows me to say "I can't.""

Developmental Aspects

Annie was an only child. Her mother was an efficient and cultured woman and Annie was strongly attached to her throughout her development, greatly admiring her self-control, her wisdom, and her ability to solve problems and to organize complex situations. Moreover, her mother was thoughtful and kind with her even if she never showed any open affection. Since her mother was a teacher she devoted herself to Annie's education. Her mother prevented her from staying with peers as well as, later, from any sort of friendly relations or social occasions, being firm in stating that home was the only place in which genuine culture could be acquired. Annie remembered very well how most of her afternoons and free time were spent at home with her mother discussing cultural and artistic topics. The mother, and thereafter Annie, considered most people unintelligent, superficial (and hence unrealiable) in most cases, and sometimes openly hostile. It is worth mentioning that toward the end of therapy Annie realized that very probably her mother had herself been agoraphobic. Indeed, Annie clearly remembered that she had never seen her mother going shopping or visiting friends alone. Each time her mother had left home she was either with Annie or with her husband.

Annie's father was hardly ever at home because of his work. He was an extroverted man, very sensitive and artisticly oriented. Moreover he was very effusive and warm with his wife and his daughter. The mother, talking with Annie, often considered her husband a wonderful adolescent; that is, as someone with a splendid and creative temperament, unfortunately embodied in an adolescent. Since her husband was so sensitive and poetical, Annie's mother always regarded him as a weak person: "He is a man that dreams away his time" was her frequent comment.

Annie loved her father very much because he was so warm and because when he was at home he used to play with her. Playing with her father constituted Annie's best memories of her infancy and childhood. Although she considered her father a marvelous companion, she did not consider him reliable in his conceptions of people and the world. Annie related that throughout her childhood she had grown up with the idea, reinforced by her mother, that women have to be very strong and efficient, self-controlled and, even more important, free, since freedom is the essential requisite for being cultured and able to use one's intelligence in a constructive, positive way.

At school Annie was a clever and capable pupil from the beginning. She remembered having always considered the boys and girls as little idiots who were continuously engaged in stupid love stories. Annie's most important goals were to be strong, intelligent, and capable. Later in school, Annie's first heterosexual friendships were always with foreign boys because "in this way it was impossible to fall in love and to have serious, limiting engagements."

After obtaining her high school certificate she spent a summer in London on holidays to learn English. On that occasion she happened to get involved in a more serious engagement with a young English boy, but as soon as she realized how important this relation could become, Annie deserted him during the night, leaving a brief note on his bedside table: "I love you very much but please pretend that I never said it." In fact, she had never said "I love you" to anyone; that was the only occasion on which she did so in her life.

After this experience Annie had a long-lasting important relationship with a man whom she considered the most intelligent of her friends. According to her he was a rational man, very self-controlled, who never showed his own emotions in communicating something to anybody. "We had a wonderfully complete intellectual relationship in which the emotional and sexual aspects were not necessary."

Later on, Annie was very disappointed when she discovered that her boyfriend was depressed because of a tormented love affair with another man whom he eventually followed to Germany. It is worth mentioning that Annie was disappointed not because he was homosexual but because he had shown himself to be so weak as to fall in love. During this period Annie met her future husband. "I don't know how and why the relationship began," she said, "because he is so different from me and from the kind of men I like. He is extroverted, very sensitive, and likes to express his emotions and feelings in almost any situation. Moreover, he is not an intellectual; on the contrary, he is always making fun of intellectuals."

Although this engagement appeared to be a long-lasting one, Annie reassured herself by firmly believing that this was a free relationship and that she didn't love him. After getting his degree, he was drafted into the army and Annie suddenly realized how much she missed him, especially from an emotional point of view. At the same time she gave up other engagements in order to stay longer with him, but never said anything about this to him. When her future husband finished the military service, they started living together with a couple of friends, and the fears of tumors that Annie began to feel made her seek more effusive and reassuring behavior from him. Finally, after their wedding and when they had started living together without friends, the fear of losing control appeared and Annie wasn't able to stay alone without her husband anymore.

Annie's Cognitive Organization

From the beginning the restriction of Annie's outside explorative behavior and contacts with peers represented the essential core around which her developmental history unfolded. Moreover, Annie acquired contradictory information about herself from the different and separate attachment patterns with her parents.

From her mother, Annie learned to perceive herself as a rational and controlled person, while from her father she learned to perceive her feelings and emotions, as well as how to let herself go with them. Annie's subsequent attempts to successfully integrate such contradictory aspects of herself led her to select her mother's model, since this was the dominant one in the family. In this way, through the tacit organization of ordering rules based on the identification of emotionality with weakness and of self-control with self-worthiness, she grew up elaborating a conscious self-image as an efficient, unemotional, controlled woman.

Moreover, her encoded feeling memories combined with her mother's advice on their potential danger led Annie to develop an overcontrolling attitude toward herself, aimed at the exclusion of the emotional and affective domains. Likewise, the limitations imposed on her exploratory behavior combined with her mother's description of the world as being populated by unreliable and stupid people led Annie to develop an attitude toward reality centered on the absolute need to be free in order to pursue the only reliable experience domains (i.e., work, career, culture, etc.). To reach such a goal Annie developed an overly controlling attitude toward any interpersonal relationship, trying to be in the "one-up" position by means of her intellectual capabilities and the exclusion of affective domains.

When Annie failed in such endeavours—as in the relationship with her English boyfriend—she quickly abandoned the situation. Moreover, the assimilation of such an experience led her to select, at first, a man who revealed himself to be a homosexual—thus avoiding from the beginning any possibility of engagement—and later her future husband, whose emotionality and lack of intellectuality seemed to give her the guarantee of controlling all aspects of the relationship.

However, after the relationship had been going on for quite a while, a set of tacit emotional schemata conveying the feeling memories of letting herself go with her father circumvented the overly controlling attitude toward herself and began to exert pressures to be assimilated and integrated into her conscious self-image. Needless to say, the husband's personality was quite similar to that of her father, to whom Annie had been very attached even though she considered him weak.

A crucial event had been the husband's departure for the military service. The subsequent feelings of missing him joined with the already activated emotional schemata and took the form, in Annie's awareness, of the need to be protected and reassured because of her fear of being affected by some tumor. Hence the phobia of tumors that appeared at that time represented Annie's attempt to assimilate her new emergent feelings without changing her conscious self-image. By adding the connotation of being ill to her self-image Annie succeeded in having a consistent explanation for her attachment behavior toward her future husband and in further excluding the information potentially available in the feelings experienced. In other words, Annie reorganized herself toward a precarious balance centered on the continuous prevention of becoming aware of her emotional life.

In this unsteady context the experience of the new kind of intimacy to which she was introduced when she started to live alone with her husband was sufficient to shift the already precarious balance toward a more critical one: The fear of tumors became the fear of reality in order to integrate the perceived dependency on her husband with her former self-image. Finally, experiencing the restrictions on her freedom that she had feared for so many years, Annie experienced unbearable feelings of constriction and selectively focused on constrictive aspects of the outside world until reaching the paradoxical aspects of a clear-cut agoraphobia.

The Therapeutic Strategy

The therapeutic strategy was carried out along the following steps:

1. The therapist shaped the therapeutic relationship in accordance with the self-image Annie had so diligently maintained. He left her a wide

margin of control in the relationship, asking Annie to regulate for herself the sequence of topics to be discussed, as well as their timing. Annie's idea on the need to be in control was thus not attacked. On the contrary, the therapist managed to use it by introducing the argument according to which problem did not lie in the idea of controlling herself, but in the way she applied that idea. It was possible within a few sessions to demonstrate to Annie that she had never really tried to control her fears, since she had been fighting to ignore or distort her painful images without reaching her stated purpose. Striving against distressing representations does not entail a controlling theme. Using Annie's tendency toward intellectual domains, little by little the therapist led her to recognize that a striking characteristic of the human species involves learning to control something by becoming able to know and to reproduce it.

2. The therapist next began to ask Annie to try to reproduce her fears through deliberate imagining of the feared situations. The therapist's aim was to modify Annie's avoiding attitude toward her fears. In a few sessions she felt herself not only capable of producing the frightening images but also of regulating their sequence. Moreover, by paying attention to such images, she was able to detect many details and feelings that had thus far appeared in her mind in a very confused and rapid way. In this manner Annie gained a better understanding of her frightening images as well as further distancing from them.

3. Annie was now ready for graduated *in vivo* exposure to the feared situations. She was instructed to face any situation without waiting passively for the appearance of the distressing representations and was told instead to try to actively reproduce them from the very beginning. As usual in these cases, no fear was felt during the exposure sessions, since Annie's attention and attitude toward the environment were changed in comparison with the past. At the beginning she was rather disappointed by her unsuccessful attempts to reproduce her fears, but she soon realized that she had discovered an effective controlling procedure. The subsequent sessions were devoted to extending Annie's new controlling procedure to all situations. She gradually increased her distance from the secure bases represented by both the therapist and her house, and little by little regained confidence in going to theatres, taking buses, and so on. While Annie was gradually reclaiming her autonomy, the therapist started discussing explicitly for the first time the causes of her disturbances, since their supposed biochemical nature was disproved by her successful controlling procedure. Instructed to use the data from her developmental history, Annie came to accept the idea of a possible connection between the disturbances and her emotional development. While exploring the consistency of such a connection Annie was ready for the next step.

4. Annie's emotional restructuring was carried out in two subsequent directions. At the beginning, the therapist aimed at making her recognize

what set of emotions were selectively neglected by her and how she could recognize these emotions only as challenges to her life when they became compelling. Many instances of her past history were examined repeatedly and in detail in order to enable Annie to recognize even the minimal aspects she excluded from her awareness. At this point it was possible to move the emotional restructuring forward into the present. Annie came to realize the connection between her perception, automatic thoughts and emotions, becoming increasingly able on the one hand to recognize even minimal labels of constrictions paralleling same aspects of her marital relation and on the other hand to recognize even minimal labels of weakness paralleling her ongoing feelings of being involved with her husband. During this step Annie developed an increasing awareness of the distinction between what she was feeling and the conscious way by which she arranged it. When Annie then asked for a better understanding of why she maintained such an emotional organization, the therapist agreed to move toward a deeper analysis.

5. As a last step, Annie went again through her developmental history, looking for any event or situation that in her memory was encoded as a proof supporting the elaboration of her enduring self-image. The process took many sessions since the reconstruction had to be complete and chronologically well ordered. As is usual in these phases, Annie modified considerably some specific memories by inserting in them feelings that had been excluded in her previous reconstructions. For example, the memories of afternoons spent with her mother were changed during reconstruction to include her formerly neglected feelings of loneliness. Her relationship with her father was also considered and Annie realized that her father's emotional schemata had become her criterion images for selecting a husband. She also reported new recollections like the one of having never seen her mother alone outside the home. In turn, this recollection clarified for her how her mother's desire to keep her away from stupid and superficial people was mixed up with her mother's own fears of staying alone at home. In this manner it became increasingly clear to Annie that her selection of a rigid, controlled self-image was the greater constriction on her life, since she was thereby prevented from matching her feelings with those of other people from the beginning.

At this point the therapy was considered essentially finished and Annie began to come to therapy every month and later every 45 days for follow-up. During the subsequent 8 months Annie continued to readjust her model of reality and her goals of life. During that time she became willingly pregnant—an undertaking that in the past had terrified her. The whole therapy lasted 12 months, with one session every week. The follow-up period lasted about 1 year, with sessions being eventually conducted every 2 months.

ANOREXIA NERVOSA

Preliminary Developmental Remarks

The basic problem underlying a complex syndrome like anorexia nervosa concerns the hindered development of a well-defined sense of personal identity. Parents of anorectics generally tend to conceal problems and difficulties, avoiding all clear and definite expressions of personal emotions and points of view. The attachment patterns emerging from such a context are thus likely to be ambiguous and indefinite. Perhaps the most specific characteristic of the "anorectigenic" family interaction is what Minuchin, Rosman, and Baker (1978) call "enmeshment"—that is, a pattern in which family members intrude on each others' thoughts and feelings. In this way the boundaries that define individual differentation are so weak that the child is deprived of a sense of authentic individuality (Bruch, 1973, 1980).

Enmeshed attachment patterns hinder the structuring of a full sense of personal identity by stifling the child's own initiative and by preventing the child from developing feelings of his or her own. From this attachment style the child extracts an ambiguous self-image in which his or her own personal worth and lovableness are vague and indefinite. This ambiguity is generally perceived by the developing child as a sense of blurred personal effectiveness, usually focused mainly on the physical and aesthetic aspects of one's self-image. There is also a heavy emphasis often placed by the family on the formal aspects of life.

The possibility of having an unacceptable body image represents the way by which anorexic clients embody their sense of personal ineffectiveness. Since being fat is the main failure to be avoided in their life, anorexics generally strive against this image of failure. In those situations in which their ineffectiveness is challenged by incoming disconfirmations, their fight becomes saliently paradoxical.

Therapeutic intervention with anorexic clients requires some strategic differences relative to other neurotic disturbances. While the general therapeutic principles sketched in the first part remain valid, their application and timing are strictly dependent on the structuring of a therapeutic relationship that is experienced by the client as reliable and safe. To put it most simply, the therapeutic relationship itself becomes the basic strategy for treating anorexics. I shall try to exemplify this point in the following case illustration.

Case Illustration: Jan

Jan was a 20-year-old woman with clear-cut anorexia nervosa. From the beginning of the syndrome 2 years previously, her weight had ranged from 80–85 pounds and she was amenorrheic.

The request for treatment came from her parents when they came to seek a therapist's advice. The parents related that the disturbance had begun when Jan was studying for her final examinations in secondary school. It had been preceeded by a brief period of compulsory overeating (bulimia). Immediately before the examinations Jan established her anorexic routine. She firmly refused any kind of food during the day and consumed only a little bread and milk during the night, when her family was asleep. Paralleling the emergence of this disturbance, Jan began to progressively withdraw from her friends, eventually reaching the point of staying at home whenever she could. The parents related that Jan was almost intractable: She often behaved in an aggressive and provocative way, blaming her parents for her abnormal behavior and, at the same time, flying into a rage followed by depression whenever the parents failed to offer her adequate protection and understanding.

Jan's behavior had become the family's tragedy for the past year, and everybody, including her 18-year-old sister, was frightened by her unpredictable behavior. From the beginning of the first session it was clear to the therapist that Jan's mother viewed herself as the director of her family's interaction rules, relegating the other members to the role of mere observers. In particular the mother showed a disguised critical attitude toward her husband, simultaneously attacking and excusing him: "Of course, doctor, my husband is not responsible for this situation. He is not capable of understanding Jan, although he has always been sympathetic toward her, but, you know, a man is a man and Jan just relies on me. She does not get along with her father and he, on the other hand, is just looking out for himself."

The therapist remained silent for the entire session, being careful to show attentiveness and interest. At the end of the session he stated that he would be willing to treat Jan, but that she would have to ask for treatment by herself. A week later Jan called for an appointment. Her first declaration was that she was there because her parents wanted her to be. In response to the therapist's questions as to what she was thinking about her parents desire, Jan's answer was a clear expression of her oscillative attributional style: "Well I don't know how any kind of treatment could be possible for me. Many times I have found myself thinking about psychotherapy. On the one hand, I would have the possibility of consulting with an experienced and competent person, but on the other hand, I believe that this consultation would eventually be useless and disappointing."

The therapist carefully avoided any explicit or implicit criticisms of her attitude, and responded by softly explaining the rationale for his therapeutic approach. He emphasized the active role played by the client in such an approach, contrasting it to the traditional and well-known psychodynamic ones. Finally, the therapist stated his confidence in the value of working with her, adding that this confidence was centered on his professional experience and not on a sense of omnipotence. He emphasized then that he needed Jan's active collaboration and insights throughout therapy. Toward the end of the session the therapist asked Jan to spend the subsequent week reflecting on whether she had any personal expectations for the therapy and, if so, to assess the kind of collaboration, if any at all, she would be willing to invest in therapy. The therapist was careful to reassure Jan that he would understand and accept her reflections and decision.

At the end of the session, the therapist telephoned Jan's mother to inform her that he had accepted Jan for treatment and to request that from this moment on family communication with him be passed through Jan.

A week later, Jan stated that, many perplexities notwithstanding, her choice was to try to collaborate in the therapy. The therapist accepted her decision and started to explain the basis for a fruitful collaborative relationship. He dispelled any implicit impression of aiming at an immediate modification that might have felt too intrusive to Jan by defining their collaboration as just a device for exploring and reconstructing her demands and troubles. Moreover, to further avoid intrusiveness, the therapist did not address the crucial topic of food, which was, incidentally, the essential upon which the mother had focused. Jan herself just skimmed over this subject during these sessions, giving the impression of testing the therapist's attitude more than a real desire to speak about it. Even on these occasions the therapist avoided responding in a manner that could confirm her fear of confronting just another variant of the same attitude toward food problems that was held by the parents.

During these sessions the therapist assumed a rather passive attitude, paying attention to Jan's arguments and limiting himself to acknowledging her evaluations and encouraging her to trust and express her feelings. When her causal theories were clearly inadequate the therapist did not refute them, but gently asked for further elucidations, clarifications, and so on. He was careful to let Jan further elaborate the former causal theories by herself. When she succeeded in reaching a more comprehensive view, the therapist rewarded her very warmly and encouraged her to continue on the same path.

During this period the therapist's essential aim was to build up a relationship in which Jan's feelings and opinions were not challenged or disconfirmed but on the contrary constituted the foundations for their subsequent exploratory task. After seven or eight sessions, Jan began to collaborate very actively and the therapist more explicitly instructed her to analyze her feelings and note all possible details. Although the subject of food still remained unexplored Jan was by now willing to speak about her difficulties in conceptualizing about her body and her uncertainty in decoding her bodily messages. The therapist's aim was to let Jan discover by herself the correlation between her uncertainty and the interfering attitude toward her feelings that her mother had always had. This emergent awareness shifted the therapist's focus onto the interactional patterns of her family. Jan and the therapist eventually planned a family session in order to assess the possibility of limiting the mother's intrusiveness. Since Jan's sister was away on winter holidays, the family session involved only Jan and her parents. The mother's behavior was characteristic from the beginning. For example, she sat between Jan and the father, discouraging any attempt at direct communication between them.

The therapist's attitude was deliberately reassuring, dispelling any fears about the possibility that someone in the family was responsible for this painful situation. He pointed out that this sort of thing generally occurred in families in which each member sincerely aimed at devoting him- or herself to the others. It is in that way, he stated that out of the members' intentions a repetitious pattern of interaction emerges in which each member feels frustrated. Since the atmosphere became silent and tense with this statement, the therapist modeled a relaxed attitude, cheerfully relating vignettes and anecdotes exemplifying self-sacrificial paradoxes and inviting them to take better care of themselves. For a while, everybody laughed and relaxed. Encouraged by such an atmosphere, Jan's parents and especially her mother discussed how well they understood this paradox and how it could be better to start again without controlling Jan at home. At this point the session reached its climax. Jan was skeptical of her mother's promises and, in response, the mother stood up and confronted her directly. "The doctor is right: We have to change. I made many mistakes in the past but I still have time to correct them. It is not important that I'm not interested in myself, I'll keep my promise no matter how it pains me. Your happiness is the essential value upon which my life rests." At this point the therapist burst out laughing and after a moment everybody began to laugh, including the mother.

After that session Jan rapidly improved and soon wanted to speak about her eating style. The therapist then began to analyze the problem of bodily appearance in our society, guiding Jan to see an explicit correlation between being thin or fat and others' judgements of lovableness. Spontaneously her interest began to shift toward her withdrawal from others and her fear of their judgement. In a couple of sessions Jan understood the entangled situations elicited by her fears of others' judgements, and she began to see her friends again.

At this point, after 5 months of therapy, Jan was doing rather well. She like being with her friends again, was more assertive in group discussions, and, above all, was relatively self-confident about her opinions and feelings. She regained most of the weight she had lost and her eating behavior was quite acceptable, even though she refused to eat with her parents. Only one essential problem remained for our work: her emotional life and relationships with men. She was, moreover, still amenorrheic. This was a very valuable point insofar as it could be a potential source of disappointments and the risk of relapse.

Jan's interests during the sessions were by now concerned mainly with people's behaviour and how to understand them, and the therapist continued his strategy of letting Jan discover new aspects by herself. She eventually fell in love with a young man, but the relationship was abruptly broken off by him after a few days. She did not want to talk about her feelings at the time but preferred to discuss general topics in human affective relations.

She immediately started to become slightly fat and complained of compulsive overeating during the night. After a week a depressive reaction emerged and continued for about a month. During this depression Jan began to criticize her eating style and described her bulimia as an automatic, repetitious behavior that was going on without her intentions or feelings. Her former anorexia also progressively appeared to her as having been a useless and ridiculous way of making her strong and independent.

After the depression had abated, Jan explicitly requested discussion and analysis of the feelings she had felt during the making and breaking of her last relationship. While discussing it Jan was impressed by her absolute expectations for an intimate relationship and wanted to work at the reconstruction of these expectations. She then started a reconstruction of her developmental history. After a brief rationale explaining the features of human development, Jan began to work very intensively and each time came back to the office with brillant examples of homework on her childhood and adolescence. In that period Jan gradually re-evaluated her relationship with her father, and began to talk more frequently with him. They sometimes met for lunch together. The reconstruction of her developmental history took 2 to 3 months. Meanwhile Jan started again to stay with people and was able to establish new relations in different social environments.

After almost 1 year of therapy Jan seemed to be quite on top of things. By now she was a smart, clever girl, self-assertive, enjoying others' company and without any apparent trouble with her eating and emotional behaviors. She had had several other romantic engagements that did not turn out well and left her feeling disappointed. However, each time she analyzed her feelings with the therapist as she had the first time, thereby acquiring even more knowledge about human relationships. It was precisely at that time that her amenorrhea disappeared. By now she was able to go on by herself, and Jan began to visit the therapist each month at first and eventually every 45 days.

During the follow-up period, which lasted 2 years, Jan did not change her active collaboration with the therapist, and at the end of that period made an important discovery by herself. She analyzed the difficulty she had been having in experiencing satisfactory sexual intercourses. She reached the conclusion that her difficulty in letting herself go was correlated with her fears of exposing herself to criticism and disconfirmations. Jan's attitude also changed impressively at home. She no longer felt resentment toward her mother and instead came to view her as a troubled woman who tried to solve all problems by seeking to be indispensable to someone. It was therefore no longer surprising or upsetting for Jan to realize that her mother would probably go on all her life being concerned about her daughter's eating behavior and romatic affairs. By now Jan was sure that this was her mother's problem, not hers, and her aims were mainly oriented toward planning her own life.

CONCLUDING REMARKS

The goal of this chapter was to outline a comprehensive model of human knowledge processes and consequently to describe a therapeutic approach consistent with this model. However, the actual limits on achieving such a goal are many and involve the research methodology of both theoretical and clinical inquiry.

From a theoretical point of view the essential problem for contemporary psychology is that of shifting to the status of a mature science. As Weimer (1982b) has clearly put it:

mature sciences are explanatory rather than descriptive. Explanation consists in rendering intelligible how and why the phenomena within a domain exhibit the properties that, descriptively, they do possess. Science explains by conjecturing theories (either tacitly or in explicit, after-the-fact construction) that tell why things must be as they are observed to be. Psychologists, in contrast, have limited their accounts to dispositional analysis of the psychological domain. Dispositional analysis is at best descriptive and cannot be considered explanatory. It is thus incumbent upon psychology to develop the sort of explanatory theory that mature sciences possess—theories that will derive surface-structure appearances lawfully from an abstract, deep-structural realm that is causally productive of those appearances. (pp. 336–337)

A change in the actual experimental methodology should thus be the prerequisite for any advance toward a more comprehensive explanatory model. Consistent with the empiricist approach that reduced the study of psychology to the description of the interaction between organism and environment, experimentation thus far has been too fragmented, too focused on the isolation of details. It has as well sometimes given the impression of being pursued as an end in itself.

In continuing to isolate and study single variables, psychologists tacitly endorse the view that there is an external ordered reality that can be discovered through a gradual and "objective" approach. Their strategy is to pose discrete and definite questions to which reality will provide clear and "factual" answers.

In contrast, if the essential problem regards an explanatory model of human behavior, we need a falsifiable hypotheses-testing approach in order to select the abstract, the basic principles according to which human knowing operates. We should not wait until reality itself gives its responses to our answers but need instead to test our responses to reality in order to ascertain what reality could resemble.

Besides a change in research methodology, our fields of inquiry should also be widened. It is obvious that a valuable way of obtaining data regarding the mental realm should come from the study of the products of the human mind. Fields like epistemology, anthropology, economics, history of religions, and so on should be considered as proper domains of inquiry for psychological research. Indeed, in these domains data could be obtained on the activity of the mind through the study of the spontaneous organizations the mind is able to produce, thereby allowing us to catch a glimpse of the invariant patterns of the human way of experiencing and structuring reality.

In this case a restructuring of attention is also needed. Such data are already available, we only have to look at them. This can be accomplished only if we change our restricted view of the laboratory and consider reality itself as the ultimate experimental chamber. Physicists have already pursued this approach. Many consequences foreseen by Einstein's theory were not liable to experimentation, for example, but all the same they were corroborated by the observations of apparently strange phenomena in the universe. The universe has demonstrated itself as a suitable laboratory for the physicist; the same may prove true for the psychologist.

From the clinical point of view the limits of our knowledge seem more evident; psychotherapy remains an ambiguous domain despite the steady production of clinical research by competing approaches. In order to have a model of therapy we first need a model of human psychopathology. Psychology has in the past addressed clinical disturbances primarily within a descriptive and dispositional framework whose main aim was to reduce the complexity of psychological disturbances by compressing them into a range of suitable terms and labels.

We therefore need a developmental, process-oriented psychopathology that can establish what the processes are and what conditions give rise to peculiar individual knowledge organizations that produce, when imbalanced, the patterns we call clinical disturbances (Bowlby, 1977a). Moreover, a developmental psychopathology may help prevent therapists from conceptualizing clients' problems in concrete, reductionistic ways, since a process-oriented approach makes it clear that, although there are similar developmental patterns in similar clients, every client is a unique natural experiment.

Finally, since the therapeutic relationship is an essential variable in all psychotherapy, we need a comprehensive model of interpersonal relations in order to understand how they can facilitate knowledge assimilation and change processes (e.g., Bowlby's approach, 1977b). At present, the therapists's ability to use relationship dynamics to facilitate change is still mainly an art rather than a science. This state of affairs makes unreliable the majority of current attempts to evaluate the effectiveness of techniques and strategies in psychotherapy. Notwithstanding the limits to our search for an explanatory model of human behavior, I believe that we should aim at such a purpose all the same, and this work might be better understood if seen as an attempt in that direction.

ACKNOWLEDGMENT

The author wishes to thank his friend and colleague Michael J. Mahoney for his comments and suggestions, which resulted in a substantial improvement in the original manuscript.

REFERENCES

Ainsworth, M. D. S., Blehar, M. C., Waters, E., & Wall, S. (1978). *Patterns of attachment.* Hillsdale, NJ: Erlbaum.

Airenti, G., Bara, B., & Colombetti, M. (1982a). Semantic network representation of conceptual and episodic knowledge. In R. Trappl (Ed.), *Advances in cybernetics and system reseach* (Vol. II). Washington, DC: Hemisphere.

Airenti, G., Bara, B., & Colombetti, M. (1982b). A two level model of knowledge and belief. In R. Trappl (Ed.), *Proceedings of 6th E.M.C.S.R.* Amsterdam: North Holland.

Arnkoff, D. B. (1980). Psychotherapy from the perspective of cognitive theory. In M. J. Mahoney (Ed.), *Psychotherapy process.* New York: Plenum.

Bara, B. G. (1980). Changing connections between knowlege representation and problem solving. In M. Borillo (Ed.), *Representation des connaissainces et raisonnement dans les sciences de l'homme et de la societé.* Le Chesnay: Editions INRIA-CNRS.

Bara, B. G. (1984). Modifications of knowledge of memory process. In M. A. Reda & M. J. Mahoney (Eds.), *Cognitive Psychotherapies.* Cambridge, MA: Ballinger.

Beck, A. T. (1976). *Cognitive therapy and the emotional disorders.* New York: International Universities Press.

Bickhard, M. H. (1980). A model of developmental and psychological processes. *Genetic Psychological Monographs, 102,* 61–116.

Bower, G. H., & Gilligan, S. G. (1979). Remembering information related to one's self. *Journal of Research in Personality, 13,* 420–432.

Bowlby, J. (1969). *Attachment and loss I: Attachment.* New York: Basic Books.

Bowlby, J. (1973). *Attachment and loss I: Separation: Anxiety and anger.* New York: Basic Books.

Bowlby, J. (1977a). The making and breaking of affectional bonds. I: Etiology and psychopathology in the light of attachment theory. *British Journal of Psychiatry, 130,* 201–210.

Bowlby, J. (1977b). The making and breaking of affectional bonds. 2: Some principles of psychotherapy. *British Journal of Psychiatry, 130,* 421–431.

Bowlby, J. (1979). On knowing what you are not supposed to know and feeling what you are not supposed to feel. *Canadian Journal of Psychiatry, 24,* 403–408.

Bowlby, J. (1980). *Loss. Sadness and depression.* London: Hogarth Press.

Bowlby, J. (1983). *Attachment and loss I: Attachment (2nd Ed.).* London: Hogarth Press.

Brent, S. B. (1978). Prigogine's model for self-organization in nonequilibrium systems: Its relevance for developmental psychology. *Human Development, 21,* 374–387.

Broughton, J. M. (1981). The divided self in adolescence. *Human Development, 24,* 13–32.

Brown, G. W. (1982). Early loss and depression. In C. M. Parkes & J. Stevenson-Hinde (Eds.), *The place of attachment in human behavior.* London: Tavistock.

Brown, G. W., & Harris, T. (1978). *Social origins of depression.* London: Tavistock.

Bruch, H. (1973). *Eating disorders: Obesity, anorexia nervosa and the person within.* New York: Basic Books.

Bruch, H. (1980). Preconditions for the development of anorexia nervosa. *American Journal of Psychoanalysis, 40,* 169–172.

Bugental, J. F. T. (1978). *Psychotherapy and process.* Boston: Addison-Wesley.

Campbell, D. T. (1974). Evolutionary epistemology. In P. A. Schilpp (Ed.), *The philosophy of Karl Popper.* La Salle, IL: The Library of Living Philosophers.

Chandler, M. J. (1975). Relativism and the problem of epistemological loneliness. *Human Development, 18,* 171–180.

Cooley, C. H. (1902). *Human nature and the social order.* New York: Scribner.

Csikszentmihalyi, M., & Beattie, O. V. (1979). Life themes: A theoretical and empirical exploration of their origins and affects. *Journal of Humanistic Psychology, 19,* 45–63.

Davidson, R. J. (1980). Consciousness and information processing: A biocognitive perspective. In J. M. Davidson & R. J. Davidson (Eds.), *The psychobiology of consciousness.* New York: Plenum.

Dell, P. F., & Goolishian, H. A. (1981). Order through fluctuations: An evolutionary epistemology for human systems. *Australian Journal of Family Therapy, 2,* 175–184.

Dickstein, E. (1977). Self and self-esteem: Theoretical foundations and their implications for research. *Human Development, 20,* 129–140.

Eibl-Eibesfeldt, I. (1972). *Love and hate. The natural history of behavior patterns.* New York: Holt, Rinehart & Winston.

Eibl-Eibesfeldt, I. (1979). Ritual and natualization from a biological perspective. In M. von Cranach, K. Foppa, W. Cepenies, & D. Ploog (Eds.), *Human Ethology.* Cambridge, England: Cambridge University Press.

Ekman, P. (1972). Universal and cultural differences in facial expression of emotion. In J. K. Cole (Ed.), *Nebraska Symposium on Motivation.* Lincoln: University of Nebraska Press.

Ellis, A. (1962). *Reason and emotion in psychotherapy.* New York: Stuart.

Epstein, S. (1973). The self-concept revisited: Or a theory of a theory. *American Psychologist, 28,* 404–416.

Flavell, J. H. (1963). *The developmental psychology of Jean Piaget.* Van Nostrand Company.

Flavell, J. H. (1978). Metacognitive development. In J. M. Scandura & C. J. Brainerd (Eds.), *Structural/process models of complex human behavior.* The Netherlands: Sijthoff & Noordhoff.

Flavell, J. H. (1979). Metacognition and cognitive monitoring. *American Psychologist, 34,* 906–911.

Franks, J. J. (1974). Toward understanding understanding. In W. B. Weimer & D. S. Palermo (Eds.), *Cognition and the symbolic processes.* Hillsdale, NJ: Erlbaum.

Gallup, G. G. (1977). Self-recognition in primates. *American Psychologist, 32,* 329–338.

Giblin, P. T. (1981). Affective development in children: An equilibrium model. *Genetic Psychology Monographs, 103,* 3–30.

Goldfried, M. R. (Ed.). (1982). *Converging themes in psychotherapy.* New York: Springer.

Greenwald, A. G. (1980). The totalitarian ego: Fabrication and revision of personal history. *American Psychologist, 35,* 603–618.

Guidano, V. F. (1984). A constructivistic outline of cognitive processes. In M. A. Reda & M. J. Mahoney (Eds.), *Cognitive Psychotherapies.* Cambridge, MA: Ballinger, 1984.

Guidano, V. F. (1987) *Complexity of the self.* New York: Guilford.

Guidano, V. F., & Liotti, G. (1983). *Cognitive processes and emotional disorders? A structural approach to psychotherapy.* New York: Guilford.

Hayek, F. A. (1952). *The sensory order.* Chicago: University of Chicago Press.

Hayek, F. A. (1978). *New studies in philosophy, politics, economics and the history of ideas.* Chicago: University of Chicago Press.

Hayes, K. J., & Nissen, C. H. (1971). Higher mental functions in a homeraised chimpanzee. In A. M. Schrier & F. Stollnitz (Eds.), *Behavioral of nonhuman primates* (Vol. 3). New York: Academic Press.

Heard, D. H., & Barrett, M. (1982). Attachment and the family relationship of children with specific reaching disability. In C. M. Parkes & J. Stevenson-Hinde (Eds.), *The place of attachment in human behavior.* London: Tavistock.

Izard, C. E. (1977). *Human emotions.* New York: Plenum.

Izard, C. E. (1980). The emergence of emotions and the development of consciousness in infancy. In J. M. Davidson & R. J. Davidson (Eds.), *The Psychobiology of consciousness.* New York: Plenum.

Izard, C. E., & Buechler, S. (1980). Aspects of consciousness and personality in terms of differential emotions theory. In R. Plutchik & H. Kellerman (Eds.), *Emotion, theory research and experience: I. Theories of emotion.* New York: Academic Press.

Jantsch, E. (1981). *The self-organizing universe.* New York: Pergamon.

Kieras, D. (1978). Beyond pictures and words: Alternative information-processing models for imagery effects in verbal memory. *Psychological Bulletin, 85,* 532–554.

Lerner, R. M., & Busch-Rossnagel, N. A. (Eds.). (1981). *Individuals as producers of their development: A life-span perspective.* New York: Academic Press.

Linden, E. (1974). *Apes, men and languagee.* New York: Penguin.

Liotti, G. (1984). Cognitive therapy, attachment theory and psychiatric nosology. In M. A. Reda & M. J. Mahoney (Eds.), *Cognitive Psychotherapies.* Cambridge, MA: Ballinger.

Lorenz, K. (1973). *Die Rückseite des spiegels.* Munich: Piper. (English translation, (1977). *Behind the mirror.* New York: Harcourt Brace Jovanovich.

Luckmann, T. (1979). Personal identity as an evolutionary and historical problem. In M. von Cranach, K. Foppa, W. Lepenies, & D. Ploog (Eds.), *Human ethology.* Cambridge, England: Cambridge University Press.

Mahoney, M. J. (1980). Psychotherapy and the structure of personal revolutions. In M. J. Mahoney (Ed.), *Psychotherapy process.* New York: Plenum.

Mahoney, M. J. (1982). Psychotherapy and human change processes. In J. H. Harvey & M. M. Parks (Eds.), *The master lecture series: I. Psychotherapy research and behavior change.* Washington, DC: American Psychological Association.

Mahoney, M. J., & De Monbreun, B. G. (1977). Psychology of the scientist: An analysis of problem-solving bias. *Cognitive Therapy & Research, 1,* 229–238.

Mancuso, J. C., & Ceely, S. G. (1980). The self as memory processing. *Cognitive Therapy & Research, 4,* 1–25.

Markus, H. (1977). Self-schemata and processing information about the self. *Journal of Personality & Social Psychology, 35,* 63–78.

Marris, P. (1982). Attachment and society. In C. M. Parkers & J. Stevenson-Hinde (Eds.), *The place of attachment in human behavior.* London: Tavistock.

Mead, G. H. (1934). *Mind, self and society.* Chicago: University of Chicago Press.

Meichenbaum, D. (1977). *Cognitive-behavior modification.* New York: Plenum.

Minuchin, S., Rosman, B. L., & Baker, L. (1978). *Psychosomatic families: Anorexia nervosa in context.* Cambridge, MA: Harvard University Press.

Montemayor, R., & Eisen, M. (1977). The development of self-conceptions from childhood to adolescence. *Developmental Psychology, 13,* 314–319.

Morin, E. (1981). Self and autos. In M. Zeleny (Ed.), *Autopoiesis: A theory of living organization.* New York: North Holland.

Nisbett, R. E., & Wilson, T. D. (1977). Telling more than we can know: Verbal reports on mental processes. *Psychological Review, 84,* 231–259.

Nicolis, G., & Prigogine, I. (1977). *Self-organization in nonequilibrium systems. From dissipative structures to order through fluctuations.* New York: Wiley.

Parkes, C. M., & Stevenson-Hinde, J. (Eds.). (1982). *The place of attachment in human behavior.* London: Tavistock.

Piaget, J. (1970). *L'épistémologie génétique.* Paris: Presses Universitaires de France.

Pribram, K. H. (1967). Emotion: Steps toward a neurophysiological theory. In D. C. Glass (Ed.), *Neurophysiology and emotion.* New York: Rockefeller University & Russel Sage Foundation.

Pribram, K. H. (1971). *Languages of the brain.* Englewood Cliffs, NJ: Prentice-Hall.

Polanyi, M. (1966). *The tacit dimension.* Garden City, NJ: Doubleday.

Popper, K. R. (1979). *Objective knowledge: An evolutionary approach* (rev. ed.). Oxford: Clarendon Press.

Popper, K. R., & Eccles, J. C. (1977). *The self and its brain.* New York: Springer.

Prigogine, I. (1980). *From time to becoming: Time and complexity in the physical sciences.* San Francisco: Freeman.

Pylyshyn, Z. (1973). What the mind's eye tells the mind's brain: A critique of mental imagery. *Psychological Bulletin, 80,* 1–22.

Pylyshyn, Z. W. (1981). The imagery debate: Analogue media versus tacit knowledge. *Psychological Review, 88,* 16–45.

Reda, M. A., & Mahoney, M. J. (Eds.). (1984). *Cognitive psychotherapies.* Cambridge, MA: Ballinger.

Reber, A. S., & Lewis, S. (1977). Implicit learning: An analysis of the form and structure of a body of tacit knowledge. *Cognition, 5,* 333–361.

Rogers, T. B., Kuiper, N. A., & Kirker, W. S. (1977). Self-reference and the encoding of personal information. *Journal of Personality and Social Psychology, 35,* 677–688.

Shevrin, H., & Dickman, S. (1980). The psychological unconscious: A necessary assumption for all psychological theory? *American Psychologist, 35,* 421–434.

Sroufe, L. A. (1979). The coherence of individual development. *American Psychologist, 34,* 834–841.

Sroufe, L. A., & Waters, E. (1977). Attachment as an organizational construct. *Child Development, 48,* 1184–1199.

Swann, W. B., & Read, S. J. (1981). Self-verification processes: How we sustain our self-conceptions. *Journal of Experimental and Social Psychology, 17,* 351–372.

Tulving, E. (1972). Episodic and semantic memory. In E. Tulving & W. Donaldson (Eds.), *Organization of memory.* New York: Academic Press.

Turvey, M. T. (1974). Constructive theory, perceptual systems and tacit knowledge. In W. B. Weimer & D. S. Palermo (Eds.), *Cognition and the symbolic processes.* Hillsdale, NJ: Erlbaum.

Varela, F. (1979). *Principles of biological autonomy.* New York: North Holland.

Wason, P. C. (1977). On the failure to eliminate hypotheses. . . . A second look. In P. N. Johnson-Laird & P. C. Wason (Eds.), *Thinking, reading in cognitive science.* Cambridge, England: Cambridge University Press.

Wason, P. C., & Johnson-Laird, P. N. (1972). *The psychology of reasoning.* Cambridge, MA: Harvard University Press.

Weimer, W. B. (1973). Psycholinguistics and Plato's paradoxes of the Meno. *American Psychologist, 28,* 15–33.

Weimer, W. B. (1974). Overview of a cognitive conspiracy: Reflections on the volume. In W. B. Weimer & D. S. Palermo (Eds.), *Cognition and the symbolic processes* (Vol. 1). Hillsdale, NJ: Erlbaum.

Weimer, W. B. (1975). The psychology of inference and expectation: Some preliminary remarks. In G. Maxwell & R. M. Anderson (Eds.), *Induction, probability and confirmation.*

Minnesota Studies in the Philosophy of Science, VI, Minneapolis: University Minnesota Press.

Weimer, W. B. (1977). A conceptual framework for cognitive psychology: Motor theories of the mind. In R. Shaw & J. D. Bransford (Eds.), *Acting, perceiving and knowing: Toward an ecological psychology.* Hillsdale, NJ: Erlbaum.

Weimer, W. B. (1982a). Hayek's approach to the problems of complex phenomena: An introduction to the theoretical psychology of the sensory order. In W. B. Weimer & D. S. Palermo (Eds.), *Cognition and the symbolic processes* (Vol. 2). Hillsdale, NJ: Erlbaum.

Weimer, W. B. (1982b). Ambiguity and the future of psychology: Meditations leibniziennes. In W. B. Weimer & D. S. Palermo (Eds.), *Cognition and the symbolic processes.* Hillsdale, NJ: Erlbaum.

Welwood, J. (1979). Self-knowledge as the basis for an integrative psychology. *Journal of Transpersonal Psychology, 11,* 23–40.

Welwood, J. (1982). The holographic paradigm and structure of experience. In K. Wilber (Ed.), *The holographic paradigm and other paradoxes.* Boulder, CO: Chambala.

Young, J. E., & Beck, A. T. (1982). Cognitive therapy: Clinical applications. In A. J. Rush (Ed.), *Short-term psychotherapies for depression.* New York: Wiley.

Zeleny, M. (Ed.). (1981). *Autopoiesis: A theory of living organization.* New York: North Holland.

PART III

OVERVIEW AND
FUTURE CONSIDERATIONS

9

THE COGNITIVE SCIENCES AND PSYCHOTHERAPY: PATTERNS IN A DEVELOPING RELATIONSHIP

MICHAEL J. MAHONEY

Cognitive theories and therapies have become a major force in contemporary approaches to psychological services. The nature and quality of the contributions made by cognitive metatheories have been debated, of course, and there are clear signs of conceptual and practical differentiation among the "cognitivists" themselves. After a brief history of "the cognitive revolution," this chapter will focus on recent developments in the cognitive and developmental sciences. The focal contrast here will be between traditional, *rationalistic* perspectives (epitomized by Ellis's rational–emotive therapy) and more recent *developmental* and *constructivistic* approaches. My remarks will address the theoretical and practical implications of these developments.

THE COGNITIVE REVOLUTION: A BRIEF HISTORY

As Weimer (1974a, 1974b) and others have aptly noted, all historical analyses necessarily involve selective reconstructions of events and developments. Rather than the simple compilation of facts, they reflect extensive interpretation and conjecture. The following brief history is no exception and, therefore, should not be read as "the way it was" or "the way it happened," but as one attempt to understand how and when the cognitive sciences came to interface so extensively with their clinical counterparts.

HISTORICAL CONTEXTS

The current "cognitive revolution," when viewed from a historical perspective, appears to be yet another expression of a long-standing dichotomy between *functionalism* and *structuralism*. Functionalism, which was forcefully expressed in the evolutionary conjectures of Lamarck and Darwin, is most apparent in current versions of *behaviorism*. The underlying assumption is that experience (here revealed in behavior) is best understood by studying its functional effects. The structuralists, on the other hand, argue that it is the organizational structure of human experience—its core ordering processes—that constrain its topography and function. This dichotomy has ostensibly been resolved by the recent developments in the study of evolutionary biology and complex phenomena that argue that structure and function are inseparable and interdependent (Guidano, 1987; Hayek, 1982; Mahoney, in press; Varela, 1979; Weimer, 1982).

Functionalism has traditionally been portrayed as reactive in emphasis. Watson, Skinner, and Wolpe have portrayed humans as primarily reactive (rather than reactive *and* proactive) by their very nature. In their analyses, behavior is a function of its environment ($B = f(E)$). Modifications of behavior therefore entail modifications of environments. As is elaborated here and elsewhere, however, cognitive theorists have challenged such extreme environmentalism and the implied linearity of causal influence (Bandura, 1978, 1985, 1986; Mahoney, 1984a). Environments are also a function of behaviors, and the relationship between an organism and its world necessarily involves a complex and dynamic reciprocity of influence. Moreover, as cognitivists are so wont to reiterate, humans do not respond "directly" to their worlds but to their ever-changing representations of those worlds.

RECENT HISTORY

Dember (1974), Mahoney (1974), Paivio (1975), Palermo (1971), and Weimer (1974c) were among the first to suggest that a scientific "paradigm revolution" involving cognition was underway in late 20th-century psychology. Above and beyond the "cognitive movement" in psychology, however, there were and are debates about the validity and even possibility of a genuine *revolution* in psychology (e.g., Briskman, 1972; Palermo, 1971; Warren, 1971; Weimer, 1974c; Weimer & Palermo, 1973, 1974, 1982). The original focus in these debates did not center on the nature of and warrant for cognitive conceptualizations, but on whether psychology—as a relatively young science—could yet claim enough stability in its development to be able to define by way of contrast a genuine ("counter*traditional*") revolution (e.g., Warren, 1971). In other words, early commentators on the palpable shift toward cognition in psychology addressed their remarks to the nature and status of the latter rather than the former. Their vehicle of conflict was (1) whether Thomas Kuhn's (1962, 1970, 1977) analysis of scientific revolutions was valid, and (2) whether Kuhn's analysis of "the structure of scientific revolutions" was applicable to psychology. Beyond the possibility that these debates were somewhat diversionary, my own views on them are closest to those expressed by Weimer (1979; in press-a, in press-b).

Future students of *psychology of science* should note that the first reactions to the cognitive revolution in 20th-century psychology were denial and diminishment (e.g., Ledwidge, 1978; Skinner, 1971, 1974; Wolpe, 1978). From the perspective of orthodox behaviorism, for example, the endorsement of *mediational* analyses of human experience was essentially blasphemous (Mahoney, 1974). Self-reports and archival records reflect that readings in cognition and "cognitive behavior modification" were explicitly prohibited by some faculty at the most conservative and orthodox enclaves of radical behaviorism (Mahoney, 1985a).

The most classic illustration of denial is rendered by a respected pioneer in clinical behavior therapy. According to Joseph Wolpe (1978), for example, there has been and could be no cognitive revolution in behavior therapy because, in his opinion, behavior therapy has *always* been cognitive. This opinion is hardly shared by all behaviorists, and the development of a Special Interest Group in cognitive-behavioral approaches led to a splintering of the Association for Advancement of Behavior Therapy. The splinter group, composed primarily of devoted conditioning theorists and therapists, is now called the Association for Behavior Analysis (formerly the Midwest Association for Behavior Analysis).

Needless to say, Skinner and Wolpe have differed diametrically in their reactions to the growing interest in cognition among their students and colleagues. Skinner openly discourages it as a retreat from behaviorism (1984), while Wolpe reframes it as anachronistic. Since his early case studies and subsequent work reflect an interest in imagery, thoughts, and the like, Wolpe does not see anything new about private events in behavior therapy. His conceptualization of those private events is, however, clearly "traditional" in the linear, associationistic metatheory that orthodox behaviorism has endorsed (Mahoney, 1974, 1984a). The "cognitive revolution" in behavior therapy is ultimately semantic if stimulus–response analyses are not differentiated from structural (three-dimensional) and developmental (four-dimensional) analyses of human learning.

CURRENT DATA

The Kuhnian technicalities aside, if, by "revolution," one means a significant and enduring shift in emphasis and conceptual scaffolding, there can be little doubt that a cognitive revolution is well underway in behavior therapy, psychology, psychiatry, and social work (Mahoney, 1985b). This shift is illustrated in Figure 9.1, which shows changes in relative preferences for various theoretical orientations among American clinical psychologists between 1960 and 1982. There are, to be sure, limitations in the representativeness of the surveys reflected in this figure (cf. Mahoney, in press-a), but the available evidence suggests an emergent and incremental interest in cognitive perspectives. Data from an 8-year longitudinal study of orthodox behaviorists and cognitivists also suggests a discernible polarization of opinions about cognitive versus conditioning models of human learning (Mahoney, 1979, 1984b; 1985b). No matter what it is labelled, a discernibly robust "shift" is underway.

The "cognitive revolution" appears to be a bonafide phenomenon of late 20th-century psychology and psychotherapy. The recent origins of this development are quite divergent and would probably include the following:

1. the shift of focus within epistemology from justifiable claims of knowledge toward viable conjectures of belief

2. the emergence and development of evolutionary epistemology and its emphasis on genotypic and phenotypic knowing processes

3. the growing relevance of the cognitive sciences for practical endeavors

4. the computer/communication 'explosions'

5. the growing interest in personal meanings and belief system influences evident in social cognition, social psychology, and experiential/phenomenological approaches to counseling

6. the practical applications of rationalism and reason as scientific/pragmatic traditions

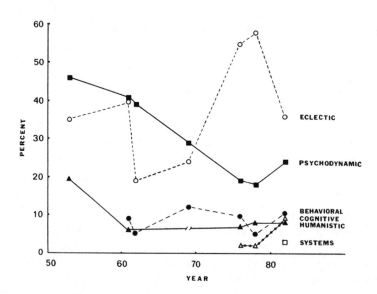

Figure 9.1. Theoretical orientations of American clinical psychologists. From *Human Change Processes* by M. J. Mahoney, in press, New York: Basic Books. Reprinted by permission.

7. recent developments in the brain and behavioral sciences that integrate central and peripheral expressions of individual knowledge organization.

Whether one makes sense of the "cognitive revolution" by denying, diminishing, or applauding it, there is an underlying message that it should or must be dealt with. I concur with aspects of this message, and what follows will be a selective commentary on what I consider to be critical and formative issues in the interface of cognitive and clinical sciences.

CURRENT COGNITIVE THERAPIES

Wilhelm Wundt and William James were prescient in anticipating the eventual differentiation of psychology along various lines of emphasis (Blumenthal, 1975, 1980, 1985; James, 1890). In commenting on the turn-of-the-century popularity of the "religion of healthy-mindedness" and what he termed the "mind cure movement," William James offered sage commentary:

The leaders in this faith have had an intuitive belief in the all-saving power of healthy-minded attitudes as such, in the conquering efficacy of courage, hope, and trust, and a correlative contempt for doubt, fear, worry, and all nervously precautionary states of mind. Their belief has in a general way been corroborated by the practical experience of their disciples; and this experience forms to-day a mass imposing in amount.

• • •

The plain fact remains that the spread of the movement has been due to practical fruits. . . . [T]he medical and clerical professions in the United States are beginning, though with much recalcitrancy and protesting, to open their eyes. It is evidently bound to develop still farther, both speculatively and practically, and its latest writers are far and away the ablest of the group. (James, 1902/1958, pp. 88–89)

The power of "positive," "right," and "rational" thinking were further affirmed by Bain (1928), Carnegie (1948), Coue (1922), DuBois (1906, 1908, 1911), Janet (1898), Maltz (1960), and Peale (1960). Explicit invitations to study and intervene upon human thought patterns were also offered by Beck (1963, 1970, 1976), Ellis (1962), and Kelly (1955).

In 1970 there were only three "cognitive therapies"—the personal construct approach developed by George Kelly (1955), Aaron T. Beck's (1963, 1970) nascent cognitive therapy, and Albert Ellis's (1962) rational–emotive therapy. These three systems are probably still most often associated with the generic term "cognitive therapy." At that time Frankl's logotherapy (1959) represented an existential-humanistic approach with cognitive emphases. As Table 9.1 shows, however, there are (as of this writing) at least 17 distinguishable cognitive therapies. Frankl (1985a, 1985b) and others have now openly acknowledged the cognitive underpinnings of various "traditional" psychotherapies (Mahoney & Freeman, 1985; Raimy, 1975, 1985). Rendered through the currently popular metaphors of cognitive psychology, Freud, Adler, Jung, Horney, Fromm, Sullivan, and others appear to have anticipated many current themes in research and theory (Breger, 1969; Goldfried, 1982).

My purpose in this chapter is neither to defend any particular taxonomy of cognitive therapies nor to dwell on its rich and diverse history at the expense of current and emerging developments. As researchers in personal knowing processes have recently documented, hindsight is often overrated and highly distorted. As we reflect on the exciting developments in the cognitive/clinical sciences, however, I think it is important that we appreciate their rich heritage.

RECENT DEVELOPMENTS IN THE COGNITIVE DEVELOPMENTAL SCIENCES

Let me now focus on what I think is happening in the broad arena of cognitive theories and therapies. As is reflected in this volume and elsewhere

Table 9.1 Current Cognitive Therapies

1. Personal Construct Therapy (Kelly, 1955)
2. Logotherapy (Frankl, 1959)
3. Rational-Emotive Therapy (Ellis, 1962)
4. Cognitive Therapy (Beck, 1970, 1976)
5. Multimodal Therapy (Lazarus, 1971, 1976)
6. Problem Solving Therapies (D'Zurilla, this volume; D'Zurilla & Goldfried, 1971; Spivack & Shure, 1974)
7. Rational Behavior Training (Goodman & Maultsby, 1974; Maultsby, 1984)
8. Rational Stage Directed Therapy (Tosi & Eshbaugh, 1980)
9. Cognitive Behavior Modification (Meichenbaum, 1977)
10. Integrated Cognitive Behavior Therapy (Wessler, 1984)
11. Motor-Evolutionary Psychotherapy (Burrell, 1983)
12. Constructivistic Cognitive Therapy (Guidano, 1984, 1987; Guidano & Liotti, 1983, 1985)
13. Cognitive Developmental Therapy (Mahoney, 1980, 1985c, in press)
14. Lay Epistemic Therapy (Kruglanski & Jaffe, 1983)
15. Neo-cognitive Psychotherapy (Suarez, 1985)
16. Piagetian Therapy (Leva, 1984; Rosen, 1985; Weiner, 1975)
17. Cognitive-Experiential Therapy (Weiner, 1985)

(Beck, Emery, & Greenberg, 1985; Ellis, 1985a; Mahoney & Freeman, 1985), there are continuing developments within the "traditional" cognitive approaches. Ellis (1985a), for example, has suggested a reformulation of his original *ABC* causal analysis, and Beck has begun to invoke ethological concepts in recent presentations of cognitive therapy (Beck et al., 1985). In addition, there are clear signs of conceptual and practical differentiations that go beyond traditional cognitive approaches. The varieties of cognitive therapy described by Guidano (1984, Chapter 8, this volume), Joyce Moniz (1985), Kruglanski and Jaffe (1983), and myself, for example, are readily distinguished from their more traditional counterparts. In this section I shall briefly overview the emerging themes of contrast within the diverse cognitive therapies.

THE REVOLUTION WITHIN THE COGNITIVE REVOLUTION

While psychology and the social sciences were struggling with the merits and implications of the cognitive revolution, substantial developments were already underway within the cognitive perspectives that were being so sweepingly endorsed by related disciplines. Future analysts of the history of ideas may well ponder the apparent association between models of human thought and the leading edges of technological development (DeMey, 1982; Dennett, 1978, 1984; Flanagan, 1984; Fodor, 1981; Gardner, 1985). When the telephone and telegraph were at the forefront of the communication revolution, the human brain was likened to a switchboard for relaying messages. With the emergence of movies, television, and computers, our models have become correspondingly more complex.

Development involves differentiation, however, and this is apparent in the recent history of the cognitive sciences. While agreeing on the overall merits of acknowledging and studying human cognition, cognitive specialists have begun to diverge on their preferred conceptualizations of cognitive processes. Although it may be oversimplifying the matter, one way of viewing these divergences is in terms of their endorsement/challenge of traditional *realism* and *rationalism*.

The fundamental contrasts among current cognitive therapies are focused on basic assumptions about (1) *ontology* (the nature of reality), (2) *epistemology* (theories of knowledge and knowing), and (3) *causality* (theories of causation). In its most extreme and naive forms, *realism presumes a singular, stable, external reality that is accurately revealed by one's senses.* This assumption is both ontological and epistemological in nature because of its dual assertions about the nature of reality and the implicit role of sense data in coming to know such a reality. Forms and facets of realism pervade Western thinking, here importantly differentiated from Eastern thinking traditions. *Rationalism presumes that thought is superior to sense and most powerful in determining experience.* Pythagoras, Plato, Epictetus, Descartes, and Kant are the patron saints of Western rationalism, while Buddha, Muhammed, and Lao-Tze occupy somewhat parallel positions in the development of Eastern rationalism (Russell, 1945; Tomlin, 1963).

One way of thinking about both realism and rationalism is to invoke the metaphor of edges or boundaries. Traditionally, realism has drawn a sharp boundary between that which is internal/external, changing/unchanging, and clear/ambiguous. As to processes in knowing, realism has endorsed a conservatively "felt/sensed" epistemology. In the extreme, this has come to be called "the doctrine of immaculate perception" (Mahoney, 1974). Rationalism, for its part, also draws a boundary. In rationalism, the primary distinction is between thought and experience, mind and body. Implicit in traditional rationalism is the belief that thought is the most powerful domain of human activity. The idea that mental representation is more powerful than actual circumstance has appealed to practitioners and clients alike for many centuries.

CONSTRUCTIVISM AND MOTOR METATHEORIES

The most powerful challenges to realism and rationalism have emanated from both historical and contemporary sources. Giambattista Vico (1744/ 1948) has been called the father of *constructivism*, a perspective that emphasizes the active and generative aspects of human cognitive processes (Von Glaserfield, 1984). In essence, *constructivism asserts that humans actively create and construe their personal and social realities.* More recent advocates of some form of constructivism would include Wilhelm Wundt, Franz Brentano, Frederick Bartlett, Jean Piaget, and George Kelly. Contemporary proponents of constructivism question whether reality is fundamentally external and stable, and whether human thought is meaningfully separable from human feeling and action (Guidano, 1984, 1987; Hayek, 1952, 1978, 1982; Joyce Moniz, 1985; Mahoney, 1985c, in press; Mancuso & Adams-Webber, 1982; Neimeyer, 1985; Varela, 1979; Von Foerster, 1984; Watzlawick, 1984; Weimer, 1977, 1982).

A fundamental aspect of modern constructivism has been its endorsement of what Weimer (1977) has termed *motor metatheories* of mind. These are families or groups of theories that portray the human mind as proactive (as well as reactive) in nature. The important contrast here is between this active, "inside-out" portrayal of cognition and the more passive, "outside-in" perspective offered by *sensory metatheories*. The latter, which have until recently dominated "information processing" approaches, portray the brain as a collector of information via the senses, and the information collected is presumed to reside in the external world:

Common to these positions is an implicit notion that cognition is to be understood "from the outside inward," that it is a matter of the structuring of sensory information by intrinsically sensory systems, and that the products of cognition must somehow subsequently be married (in a peculiar sort of shotgun wedding) to action. (Weimer, 1977, p. 270)

Where sensory metatheories highlight the role of feedback mechanisms in learning and adaptation, motor metatheories emphatically add *feedforward mechanisms* that actively constrain and influence moment-to-moment experience patterns. For the constructivist, then, the hallowed distinction between input and output must be challenged:

What the motor metatheory asserts is that there is no sharp separation between sensory and motor components of the nervous system which can be made on functional grounds and that the mental or cognitive realm is intrinsically motoric, like all the nervous system. The mind is intrinsically a motor system, and the sensory order by which we are acquainted with external objects as well as ourselves . . . is a product of what are, correctly interpreted, constructive motor skills. (Weimer, 1977, p. 272)

To be sure, these challenging reconstructions have not been popular in some traditional quarters, since much of modern psychology remains fascinated with linear models of causality and simple, "technified" strategies of intervention (Mahoney, 1986). Starting with the questionable premise that human experience can be neatly divided into cognitive, behavioral, and affective components, contemporary psychological theories have offered models of causation that hierarchically (or sequentially) rank these components. For behaviorists, behavior is the prime mover in adjustment; for the cognitivists, it is cognition. Likewise, affective theorists emphasize emotional processes as the primary crucibles for psychological development. The recent and growing interest in constructivism and convergence among the psychotherapies may portend the decline of "billiard-ball determinism" in 20th-century psychology (Arkowitz & Messer, 1984; Goldfried, 1982; Mahoney, 1984a).

THE DEVELOPMENTAL AND SYSTEMS MOVEMENTS

Constructivism and motor metatheories represented revolutions (or at least "evolutions") within the cognitive movement itself. It is important to note, however, that the generic cognitive revolution that has permeated late 20th-century psychology has not been the only trend of importance. As has been elaborated elsewhere (Mahoney, in press-a), several thematic changes in our ways of conceptualizing human experience have emerged and accelerated over the last few decades. Most pertinent to the present discussion are what might be called *the developmental movement* and *the systems movement*. The former refers not only to the growth of interest in human psychological development across the lifespan, but also to the increasing interest in fundamental *processes* of change. This process emphasis is apparent at a number of levels across specializations (Howard & Orlinsky, 1972; Mahoney, 1980, 1985c; Orlinsky & Howard, 1975; Prochaska, 1984; Rice & Greenberg, 1984).

The "systems movement" has also become increasingly visible over the last few decades. Although its origins can be traced to general systems theory and other manifestations of the cognitive revolution (Gardner, 1985), it is also clear that both systems thinking and an emphasis on general processes pervade the overall study of complex phenomena (Bateson, 1972, 1979; Brent, 1984; Cook, 1980; Hayek, 1964, 1978; Land, 1973; Laszlo, 1983; Pattee, 1973; Weimer, 1982, in press-a, in press-b). Conceptual emphasis has been shifted away from reductionism and unilinear determinism and toward an acknowledgment of complex systems, reciprocal interdependence, and co-development over time. The dynamics of interactive systems and their temporal evolution have become "hot topics" in the physical, biological, and social sciences.

Two illustrations of these trends are relevant to the present discussion. *Evolutionary epistemology* involves the study of knowing systems and their development over time. Although its historical origins are diverse, psychological interest in evolutionary epistemology is relatively recent (Campbell, 1974, 1975; Jantsch, 1980, 1981; Mahoney, in press; Reynolds, 1981). Along with increasing ratios of brain to body and neocortex to lower brain, our neurological and systemic evolution suggest punctuated "quantum leaps" in our development (Churchman, 1984; Dobzhansky, 1962; Gould, 1977, 1980; Jerison, 1973, 1976; Land, 1973; Mahoney, in press; Passingham, 1982; Washburn & Moore, 1980; Wilber, 1980; Wilson, 1980; Woodcock & Davis, 1978). With the increasing acceptance of MacLean's (1973) triune concept of the brain and work in hemispheric specialization, it is apparent that each human being possesses at least four partially independent brains with their own subsystems and processes. The hierarchical and heterarchical (quasi-horizontal) organization of the brain not only accounts for the "mystery" of desynchrony in human experience (Rachman, 1980), but it also suggests significant transformations in the meanings and processes of relapse, regression, and resistance (Mahoney, 1985c; in press; Marlatt & Gordon, 1985; Wachtel, 1982). Moreover, recent work in evolutionary epistemology dovetails nicely with constructivism and motor metatheories of cognition in emphasizing that viability is much more important than validity in mental representations of self and world.

Autopoiesis refers to self-development in complex, open systems. It has recently become a much-discussed topic in chemistry, physics, thermodynamics, and science studies following Ilya Prigogine's 1977 Nobel Prize for his reframing of Newton's Second Law of Thermodynamics (otherwise known as the "Law of Entropy"). Prigogine showed that the tendency of mass and energy to seek a totally balanced, static equilibrium is observed only in *closed* systems (e.g., the universe), but does not apply in *open*, *developing systems* (such as human life systems, nascent galaxies, and so on). As Prigogine and his colleagues have empirically and theoretically demonstrated (Prigogine, 1980; Prigogine & Stengers, 1984), self-organizing systems demonstrate a powerful *negentropic* (ordering) capacity that transforms their own basic structure when the system's dynamic equilibrium is sufficiently challenged by "perturbations." Disorder and disequilibrium are "natural" phenomena that play an integral role in the system's transformation toward a more viable, higher-order organization (Brent, 1978, 1984; Dell, 1982; Jantsch, 1980, 1981; Maturana, 1975; Maturana & Varela, 1980; Varela, 1979; Zeleny, 1980).

This principle of structural and functional transformation is called *"order through fluctuation"* and acknowledges the basic oscillatory, opponent-process nature of virtually all developmental processes (Mahoney, 1985c, in press-a). In human systems, moment-to-moment experience is integrated and assimilated via *first-* and *second-order* cognitive processes (Bateson, 1972, 1979). First-order processes involve the *assimilation* of current experience into existing structures that constrain the nature and range of phenomenological content (Piaget, 1970, 1981). *Accommodation* is a second-order process that reflects a proactive change in knowing structures (also known as *schemata*; Goldfried & Robins, 1983) that occurs when extant assimilative structures are unable to resolve and equilibrate current environmental perturbations. When an experience does not "fit" with expectations and memory structures, the latter must be modified or vindicated. Regressive development involves an entrenchment in prior knowing structures, while progressive development involves a transformational shift to higher-order contexts or metacognition (Flavell, 1979; Guidano & Liotti, 1983; Lakatos, 1970; Mahoney, 1985c).

SOCIAL LEARNING AND ATTACHMENT THEORIES

Albert Bandura's *social learning theory* represents another trend in conceptualizing and facilitating human psychological development. According to many observers, it was Bandura's (1969) book *Principles of Behavior Modification* that inspired an accelerating trend toward studying central (versus peripheral) processes in human adjustment (Mahoney & Arnkoff, 1978). His emphases on vicarious learning processes, self-regulation, cognitive representation, and causal reciprocity helped inaugurate the cognitive revolutions in both behavior therapy and psychology at large (Bandura, 1976, 1977, 1978, 1985, 1986). Likewise, his theory of self-efficacy has emphasized the central importance of beliefs about personal ability and the complexity of causal influences in human performance.

The interdependence of social relationships and personal belief/behavior systems has also been emphasized by John Bowlby (1969, 1973, 1979, 1980, 1985). Bowlby's attachment theory asserts that personal meaning systems are generated, maintained, and transformed in the context of emotional attachments. The most formative of attachment relationships, according to Bowlby, are those that develop (or fail to develop) in early life, although emotional attachments and detachments continue to influence and reflect well-being throughout the lifespan. Bowlby's work and the developmental sciences in general have come to play an increasingly visible role in recent cognitive theories and therapies (Belsky & Nezworski, 1987; Guidano, 1984, 1987; Guidano & Liotti, 1983, 1985; Liotti, 1984; Mahoney, 1980, 1981, in press). In fact, developmental and constructivistic issues have formed the primary dimensions that appear to differentiate the "old" and "new" looks in cognitive psychotherapies.

RATIONALIST VERSUS DEVELOPMENTAL COGNITIVE THERAPIES

It is clear that the cognitive therapies have been growing in visibility and popularity; there are also signs of conceptual development and diversification *within* such perspectives. The many forms of contemporary cognitive therapies (Table 9.1) suggest not only a fertile territory for theoretical development, but also an emerging differentiation among approaches to the interface of the cognitive sciences and psychological services. To date, the most salient themes of differentiation have been tacitly philosophical in nature.

In short, I suggest (here and elsewhere; Mahoney, in press) that the emergent themes reviewed in the last section—constructivism, motor metatheories, developmental and systems approaches, and the social contexts of self—that these developing interests reflect what may well be the first major differentiation within the cognitive revolution. Strictly rationalist theorists—personified by Albert Ellis and orthodox rational–emotive therapy—argue for the causal supremacy of *beliefs* about self and world. Counselors who have adopted a rationalist metatheory of helping tend to emphasize "reality contact," "realistic thinking," and "rationality" as the preferred paths toward individual psychological development. For the extreme rationalist, disorder and irrationality are synonymous. The developmentalists and constructivists, on the other hand, challenge traditional concepts of reality, knowing, and rationality, as well as disorder, disease, and development (Guidano, 1984, 1987; Hayek, 1952, 1982; Joyce Moniz, 1985; Mahoney, in press; Watzlawick, 1984; Weimer, 1977, 1979, 1982).

PHILOSOPHICAL DIFFERENCES

In brief relief, the major distinctions between rationalist and developmental perspectives can be highlighted as follows (see Table 9.2). Ontologically,

Table 9.2. Philosophical Differences between Rationalist and Developmental Cognitive Theories

Issue/Area	Rationalist View	Developmental View
1. Ontology (The nature of reality)	Realism—reality is singular, stable, and external.	Relativism—realities are individual and collective constructions of order in experience.
2. Epistemology (Theories of knowing)	Rationalism—knowledge is authorized as valid by logic or reason; reality is revealed via the senses.	Constructivism—knowing is behavioral and emotional as well as cognitive; the validity of knowledge is less important than its viability; sensation is proactive.
3. Causation (Theories of causality/change)	Associationism—learning and change are linear chains of discrete causes and effects.	Structural Differentiation—learning and development involve refinements and transformations of mental representations.

modern rationalists tend to be realists. They believe (1) in a singular, stable, and external reality whose understanding constitutes (2) the primary task and capacity of the "higher" mental processes. The developmentalists, by way of contrast, endorse relativistic and multiplistic approaches to reality. In their opinion, reality is *not* singular, stable, or neatly external. It is, instead, complex, dynamic, and both individual and collective. Rationalists tend to portray the brain as a curator of information gleaned from sense data that reliably reflect an external order. Developmentalists and constructivists, on the other hand, tend to portray the brain as an active sculptor of experience, proactively "projecting" its "expectations" onto each next millimoment of development.

Epistemologically, the rationalists and developmentalists are again at odds. The former defend a curious marriage of sense data and quasi-pure intellect. For the classical rationalist, knowledge and knowing are pure categories. Knowledge is authorized or justified via various information "sources": sense experience, empirical data, logic, science, expert authority, revelation, and so on. Inferences and judgments are deemed rational (and therefore right) when they conform to current standards for epistemic warrant. Since most contemporary rationalists and realists are also empiricists and positivists, epistemic warrant tends for them to translate as public verification (Weimer, 1979).

For the developmentalists, however, knowing is a complex process that involves active explorations toward ordering (understanding) and controlling valenced experiences. Knowledge is physical (behavioral), emotional, and representational. Knowing and learning do not entail absolute levels of objectivity and certainty. Put in other terms, we do not survive and develop because our mental representations of self–world relationships are progressively more valid, but because they are more viable. The difference is of enormous epistemic importance. Validity presumes that knowledge is correct, true, accurate, and enduring. Thus, a genuinely "valid" finding or phenomenon is considered "real." The foundational concept in ontological validity is correspondence; rationalists and realists tend to presume a potentially perfect (absolute) correspondence between mental representations and the "external" world. "Reality contact" and "rational living" are portrayed as essential themes of personal development.

The constructivists and developmentalists, however, challenge these notions and propose that individual and collective knowing processes must first be "viable" (in the literal, evolutionary sense) if the individual or collective is to survive. Viability, when applied to knowing processes, refers to such qualities as flexibility, generativity, complexity, and resilience. As cross-cultural and anthropological research have shown, technically inaccurate beliefs may still afford adaptive behavior patterns, and generously warranted beliefs may nevertheless engender maladaptive consequences. From developmental and constructivistic perspectives, all knowledge and knowing are inherently participatory (Varela, 1979).

Not surprisingly, these differences between perspectives are reflected in their epistemological preferences. With some exceptions, rationalists and realists in psychology tend to be logical positivists, operationists, and justificationists. The constructivists and developmentalists, however, are more often "critical rationalists," "ethno-phenomenologists," and vocal nonjustificationists (Laudan, 1977; Mahoney, 1976; Weimer, 1979). These differences are spelled out more extensively elsewhere, and their assumptions and differential implications are worthy of reflection. For the moment, it is important to note only that orthodox rationalists believe in authorized (guaranteed) knowledge and a stable reality that it can approximate. The constructive developmentalists, on the other hand, believe that all knowing organisms are embodied, self-developing "theories" of relationships. Acting, feeling, and knowing are inseparable expressions of adaptation and development. From this perspective, "knowing" (scientific and otherwise) is seldom technically logical, but always pervasively psychological.

Causally, the fundamental difference between traditional realists–rationalists and constructive developmentalists has to do with mechanisms of change and causal processes. Traditionally, realists and rationalists have leaned heavily toward associationism and functionalism. From these perspectives, learning involves the contiguous or contingent chaining of discrete events in the fashion first described by Aristotle. Such learning by association is said to apply not only at the stimulus–response (input–output) realm, but also between specific nerves and synapses within the nervous system. Constructive developmentalists are quick to point out, however, that associationism and what is called "billiard-ball determinism" have recently been shown to be critically flawed at both conceptual and empirical levels. Associationism has been challenged by philosophers as well as psychologists for its naively two-dimensional analysis of human learning (Bandura, 1969; Bever, Fodor, & Garrett, 1968; Brewer, 1974; Dulany, 1968; Mahoney, 1984a). In place of associationism and conditioning as the primary mechanisms of change, constructive developmentalists invoke the *structural differentiation* proposed by the likes of Hayek (1952), Piaget (1970), Werner (1948), and Wundt (1912). From this cosmological perspective, learning and change involve structural transformations in knowing. The latter entail the differentiation of previous mental representations toward more complex, higher-order cognitive classifications and organizations.

Before addressing some of the theoretical differences that reflect on these philosophical issues, two technicalities merit mention. First, constructive developmental perspectives are *not* "irrational," "antirational," or "arational" in nature. Such dichotomous thinking is unfortunately less rare than one might hope. Constructivism is admittedly "radical" in its assertions:

Radical constructivism, thus, is *radical* because it breaks with convention and develops a theory of knowledge in which knowledge does not reflect an "objective" ontological reality, but exclusively an ordering and organization of a world constituted by our experience. The radical constructivist has relinquished "metaphysical realism" once and for all and finds himself in full agreement with Piaget, who says, "Intelligence organizes the world by organizing itself." (Von Glaserfeld, 1984, p. 24)

But what is radical about constructivism is not a rejection of rationalism so much as its transformation of what it may mean to be and act rationally (Weimer, in press-a, in press-b). The tradition of rationalism and its valuation of knowledge has never been so widely adopted. What is at issue is the meanings and processes associated with the kinds of knowing we consider adaptive, viable, and valuable.

The second technicality has to do with different uses of the term "constructivism." Throughout this chapter I have been using constructivism in what may be called the "psychological sense" to denote perspectives that portray the mind as active, interactive, and representationally generative. This is essentially the same usage employed by other psychological constructivists (Guidano, 1984, 1987; Joyce Moniz, 1985; Kelly, 1955; Neimeyer, 1985; Von Foerster, 1984; Von Glaserfeld, 1984; Watzlawick, 1984).

There is another, very different meaning associated with "constructivism," however. In what could be called the "philosophical sense," constructivism refers to rationalistic interventionism. In this sense, it refers to rationalized attempts to impose order and control in complex, open systems. Diverse literatures from economics to urban planning and utopia abound with illustrations of this rationally regulatory frame of mind. Hayek (1952,

1978) and Weimer (1977, 1982, in press-a, in press-b)—who are psychological constructivists—are opposed to philosophical constructivism. Their argument, with which I concur (Mahoney, in press), is that regulatory interventions in complex, open systems tend to produce many unexpected and far-ranging results that are generally less viable than those emerging out of the natural "catallaxy" (open exchange dynamics) (Mahoney, 1985d). The practical implications of their view highlight the warrant for caution in systemic interventions and the wisdom of respecting individual differences and freedoms in development.

THEORETICAL DIFFERENCES

When there are basic philosophical differences, there will necessarily be differences in theoretical conceptualization. This is clearly the case with the rationalist-developmental distinction here emphasized. As is briefly outlined in Table 9.3, some very fundamental theoretical differences help identify these two metatheories. To begin with, their views on the basic functions of the nervous system diverge considerably. Rationalists tend to view the brain and nervous system as recipients and repositories of sensorily and logically imparted information. A healthy and functional nervous system is one that renders accurate (valid) mental representations of reality, and—what is of equal importance—translates those representations into

Table 9.3. Theoretical Differences between Rationalist and Developmental Cognitive Theories

Concept/Area	Rationalist View	Developmental View
1. Basic Functions of Human Nervous System	To *control* and direct action and feeling via *valid mental representations*	To *order* and organize experience via *viable mental representations*
2. Nature of Representation	Representations are accurate *copies* that *correspond* to the "real" world	Representations are predominantly *tacit constructions* of order that *constrain* but do not specify plans of action
3. Body–Brain Relationship	*Cerebral primacy*: the brain leads and the body follows	*Somatopsychic unity*: body and brain are inseparable and interdependent
4. Cognition–Behavior–Affect Relationship	*Rational supremacy*: "higher" intellectual processes can and should direct feelings and actions	*Holism*: thought, feeling, and action are structurally and functionally inseparable
5. Nature of Emotionality	*Emotions as problems*: negative and intense affect are to be controlled or eliminated	*Emotions as primitive, powerful knowing processes*; disorder and affective intensity are natural elements of development

effective controls on action and feeling. For the developmentalists, however, the primary task and talent of the nervous system is the idiosyncratic construction of ordered experience. From this perspective, mental representations are not to be judged by their validity (which is technically unknowable) or their power to control, but by their capacity to afford adaptation and development.

The two perspectives also view representation quite differently. Orthodox rationalists tend to view cognitive representation in terms of correspondence and storage. "Good" representations are those that involve accurate, explicit, and extensive "copies" of the external world. These copies are said to be encoded and stored in memory for accessing when expedient. In some early expressions of cognitive psychology, these copies were compared to "templates" that afforded a higher-order "match-to-sample" classification (Neisser, 1967, 1976). Constructive developmentalists, by way of contrast, reject the idea of such explicit models or templates in the mind, and suggest instead that abstract or tacit schemata are the norm in cognitive representation (cf. Goldfried & Robins, 1983). Constructivism suggests that these schemata are not explicit "blueprints" for action that reflect valid estimations of reality. Rather, they are tacit scaffoldings for experience that constrain but do not specify particulars (Hayek, 1978; Mahoney, in press).

The theoretical differences that may be most central to the distinction in question have to do with body–brain relationships and the relationships among thought, feeling, and action. Rationalists tend to believe in cerebral primacy and rational supremacy. "Cerebral primacy" refers to the belief that the brain is the primary or leading edge in human development. This is such a pervasive assumption in Western science that it is seldom acknowledged and appraised. A recent discovery in evolutionary anthropology illustrates this point. Until very recently, the dominant view in evolutionary theory was that encephalization preceded bipedalism (Gould, 1977, 1980). The sudden evolutionary leap among primates from quadruped to biped— with its transformational consequences for manual differentiation and brain structure—was thought to have been caused by a sudden increase in brain size. With the recent discovery of a small-brained *Homo erectus* ("Lucy"), however, it became clear that brain development did not precede body development (Mahoney, in press). The two were (and are) inseparable. Somewhere in that realization lies a simultaneous acknowledgement of the brain sciences *and* the integral role of behavior in neural development.

"Rational supremacy" refers to what may well be the cardinal assumption in classical rationalism—namely, that the "higher" intellectual processes should functionally dominate over the more primitive dimensions of action and feeling. This is the essence of the Stoic philosophies of Epictetus and Marcus Aurelius that begot the "positive thinking," "mind-cure," and 'rational" therapies of the late 19th and 20th centuries. "As you think, so shall you act and feel" is their explicit motto, and their message is clear. In this sense, it is the rationalistic cognitivists who occupy the cognitive apex of a thought–feeling–action triangle. The developmentalists, on the other hand, head for the center of the triangle and propose that these three categories—thought, feeling, and action—are a conceptual legacy of questionable partitions. Modern anatomical, physiological, and functional analyses suggest that traditional distinctions between sensory and motor processes, for example, are untenable, and that the quest for a "prime mover" in the triumvarate is misplaced (Mahoney, 1984c, in press; Weimer, 1977). From a developmental perspective, cognition, behavior, and affect represent interdependent expressions of holistic and systemic processes. To the extent that their conceptual differentiation is useful, they are each very important aspects of an individual's attempts to adapt and develop.

The nature of emotionality is the last issue on which I will here comment. A more elaborate rendition is offered elsewhere (Mahoney, 1985c, in press). In essence, rationalists have traditionally viewed emotions as epiphenomena and/or problems. Negative and intense emotions have been particularly denigrated, with the practical corollary that they should be controlled or eliminated. The evolution of our current concepts of feeling could easily consume a few volumes, and this would not include the history of attempts to control our own feelings. The abridged conclusion of such a survey would, I believe, suggest that we are now in the throes of an intense evolutionary struggle involving the conflict between head and heart (or gut or genitals). Intense and chronic negative affects are common among seekers of psychological services. Emotional disorders and psychopathology are veritable synonyms in modern psychology. For a variety of reasons, intensely negative emotions have come to be defined as psychological problems. From the rationalist perspective, all intense emotions (regardless of valence) have a disorganizing effect on behavior.

This disorganizing effect is generally acknowledged by developmentalists, but they hasten to add that disorganization represents a developmental phase that precedes reorganization. From a developmental perspective, feelings are primitive and powerful knowing processes that underlie their neocortical offspring (MacLean, 1973; Mahoney, in press). They represent an evolutionary leap subsequent to reptilian reflexivity and prior to higher primate reflection. Buoyed by recent work in chemistry, physics, and biology on the role of disorder and disequilibrium in systems development, several developmental theorists have begun to suggest a more positive and progressive conceptualization of affective intensity (Brent, 1978, 1984; Dell, 1982; Guidano, 1987; Mahoney, in press; Scheff, 1979). In these renditions, emotional intensity reflects a significant deviation from affective equilibrium, often (though not always) associated with an identifiable stressor. When current coping skills are inadequate to resolve this disequilibrium, the individual (as a system of systems) becomes distressed, disorganized, and—in medical models—"dis-eased." Oscillations (waves) of order and disorder ensue, and emotional intensity may increase. In *regressive* development, this pattern of disorder continues indefinitely due to the individual's inability to break out of self-perpetuating cycles. In *progressive* development, however, the disorder and disequilibrium intensify and higher-order knowing structures emerge. These cognitive transformations allow a dynamic equilibrium to be re-established and maintained until they, in turn, meet demands that initiate another phase of disorder.

PRACTICAL DIFFERENCES

Needless to say, these philosophical and theoretical differences beget still further differences in professional practice. The most salient of these are outlined in Table 9.4. When it comes down to *intervention emphases*, for example, rationalists tend to focus on current problems and their control while developmentalists focus on developmental history and current developmental processes. Likewise, there are important differences in the tacit and explicit goals of the two forms of therapy. Rationalists tend to be teleological, deriving the "direction" of preferred development and its facilitation from the designation of explicit short- and long-term goals, which usually involve the control or elimination of current "symptomatology." Developmentalists, on the other hand, tend to emphasize "teleonomic" direction (direction without a goal) that acknowledges and affirms the fundamental wisdom of self-organizing processes in systems development.

In the conceptualization of problems, rationalists are likely to equate problems with negative affect and symptoms, both of which reflect psychological deficits or dysfunctions that need to be redressed, regulated, or eradicated. This view can be contrasted with the developmental rendition of problems as discrepancies between demands on the organism and current adaptive capacities. From a developmental perspective, problems are expressions of disorder. Acute episodes of disorder reflect sudden and/or substantial shifts in ambient demands, while chronic disorders represent habitually ineffective (but self-perpetuating) cycles of crisis. When conceptualized in this way, problems become powerful opportunities for learning and current contents (instances) of higher-order patterns and processes (Mahoney, in press).

Among rationalists, the most common conceptualization of affect portrays intense and negative emotions as expressions of irrational and unrealistic beliefs. The aforementioned "as you think, so shall you feel" is the foundational assumption. Unpleasant affect (dysphoria, distress) is conceptualized as the result of "*wrong* thinking," and the latter is equated with invalid, distorted, and "unrealistic" thinking. This approach can be differentiated from the developmental view, which conceptualizes affect as a

Table 9.4. Practical Differences between Rationalist and Developmental Cognitive Therapies

Issue/Theme	Rationalist View	Developmental View
1. Intervention Emphases	a. Ahistorical b. Problem-focused c. Control-focused d. Teleological	a. Historical b. Process-focused c. Development-focused d. Teleonomic
2. Conceptualization of Problems	Problems are deficits, dysfunctions, or their emotional correlates; they should be redressed, controlled, or eliminated	Problems are current and recurrent discrepancies between challenges and capacities; they reflect limits in current affordances and should not be mistaken for their abstract ordering processes
3. Conceptualization of Affect	Affect, especially intense and negative, *is* the problem; irrational and unrealistic cognitions are its cause	Affect expresses a primitive and powerful form of knowing; emotional experience, expression, and exploration should be encouraged
4. Resistance	Resistance reflects (a) lack of motivation, (b) ambivalence, or (c) motivated avoidance. Resistance is an impediment to therapeutic change and must be "overcome"	Resistance reflects natural self-protective processes that guard systemic integrity and resist rapid or substantial "core" change; resistance should be worked *with* rather than *against*
5. Insight	Insight into irrational and unrealistic beliefs is necessary and (almost) sufficient for therapeutic change	Insight may help to transform personal meanings and scaffold change, but emotional and behavioral enactments are also very important
6. Therapeutic Relationship	The therapeutic relationship entails technical instruction and guidance	The therapeutic relationship entails a safe, caring, and intense context in and from which the client can explore and develop relationships with self and world
7. Relapse and Regression	These phenomena reflect failures in maintenance and generalization that should be avoided and minimized	These phenomena reflect limits in current capacity and/or cycles (or spirals) in psychological development; they involve important opportunities for learning

primitive and powerful form of knowing (Guidano, 1987; Mahoney, in press). Feelings somehow integrate past, present, and anticipated experiences, and—much more consistently than their neocortical counterparts— they covary with pituitary, endocrine, and lymphatic activities. It is not surprising, therefore, that developmental cognitive therapists tend to encourage emotional experience, expression, and exploration.

Practical approaches to *resistance* constitute yet another difference between these two metatheories. For orthodox rationalists, resistance represents motivational deficit, ambivalence, or avoidance. As such, it is the antithesis of change and should be minimized or avoided wherever possible, and "overcome" when necessary. Simply put, resistance is either laziness or irrational fear (Ellis, 1985b; Wachtel, 1982). From a developmental perspective, however, resistance reflects natural and healthy self-protective processes that guard against changing too much, too quickly. In this view, resistance to core structural change is fundamentally adaptive and should therefore be worked "with" rather than "against" (Bugental & Bugental, 1984; Mahoney, in press). Reluctance to change (and its complementary affect, reluctance to stop changing) reflect order- and integrity-protecting processes of a fundamental nature. Respect for these processes is more likely to facilitate progressive psychological development than their denial or attempted domination.

Insight represents a complex topic in human change processes. On some levels, it is clear that beliefs and "awareness" may facilitate or impede learning and performance (Bandura, 1969; Brewer, 1974; Mahoney, 1974; Spielberger & DeNike, 1966). The primary goal of the "insight therapies" is to produce awareness, with the assumption that insight can dramatically accelerate or improve adaptive changes. In classical psychoanalysis, insight was fostered by explicitly instructing the client to attend to his or her thoughts, dreams, feelings, and behaviors. This same basic prescription is used in rational–emotive therapy and cognitive-behavior modification. A major difference, however, is that these rationalist cognitive approaches encourage the client to translate into action and to actively "restructure" their self-talk and behavior.

Developmentalists also tend to encourage self-exploration and insight, and they include experiential exercises to help integrate the relevant cognitive, behavioral, and affective processes. From a developmental perspective, however, insight is a subtype of a family of processes that could be called *metacognitive* (Flavell, 1979; Guidano, 1987; Mahoney, 1985c, in press). In the holistic interpretation of metacognition, it is a higher-order level of knowing that appears to involve perceptual, conceptual, and experiential components. In essence, metacognition refers to knowing about knowing, but there are many fascinating subtleties to its import. For example, developmentalists do not view "awareness" and "consciousness" in the same manner, and they caution against our attributing too much power to explicit awareness. There are times when attention to and awareness of one's self may actually interfere with performance (Borkovec & O'Brien, 1977; Hayek, 1978; Jerome, 1980; Nideffer, 1976; Polanyi, 1958, 1966).

Rationalist and developmental approaches also differ in their conceptualization of the therapeutic relationship. For the former, a professional helping relationship is one that entails the service/delivery of technical instruction and guidance. What is imparted in effective rational therapy is knowledge and information, along with skills in their use. When such knowledge and information can be imparted via audiovisual and mechanical means, the relative unimportance of the human relationship in counseling becomes apparent.

Developmental therapies view the helping relationship as a critically important and unique social exchange which, when it "works," helps to establish a safe and supportive context. It is in and from this context that the client can explore and develop relationships with the self and world (Bowlby, 1979; Guidano, 1987; Guidano & Liotti, 1982, 1985; Mahoney, in press). This view is consistent with humanistic approaches in this (and several other) regard(s), and it herein aligns itself with psychoanalytic and neo-analytic thought on the therapeutic relationship (and its ongoing processes). For Freud and many others, intense emotional relationships constitute the crucibles in which psychological patterns are forged and altered. Whether it is one's relationship with a parent, sibling, friend, lover, therapist, or child, such emotionally charged attachments bear powerfully on one's experience and development. There are differences, to be sure, in how developmental and psychoanalytic writers have portrayed and pursued the helping relationship, but their mutual endorsement of its importance is worth noting.

Finally, there are differences between rationalist and developmental approaches to relapse, recidivism, and regression. For the classical rationalist, these phenomena reflect failures in generalization and maintenance, and these, in turn, suggest insufficient or inconsistent use of the knowledge and information imparted during therapy. A psychological setback signifies a probable deficit in the client's motivation or learning. Hence, such setbacks or relapses should be avoided if at all possible. From the developmental view, setbacks and the recurrence of prior (and less viable) psychological patterns are natural and virtually inevitable aspects of psychological development (Mahoney, in press; Marlatt & Gordon, 1985). Thus viewed, such phenomena represent nonlinear regressions and cycles in epistemic differentiation. A temporary relapse or regression to lower levels of functioning may reflect a quasi-catabolic process whose significance can only be appreciated when viewed in relation to its anabolic counterparts (e.g., leaps forward). This notion is borrowed from the concepts of "punctuated equilibrium" in biological evolution, "dissipative structures" in autopoiesis, and "pendulum theory" in language development (Gould, 1977, 1980; Nelson & Nelson, 1978; Prigogine, 1980). Among other interesting implications, the developmental view of relapse and regression suggests very different emphases in counseling.

CONCLUDING REMARKS

This chapter began with a brief history of the cognitive revolution and an overview of current cognitive therapies. My primary emphasis, however, has been on recent developments in the cognitive and developmental sciences. I have suggested, among other things, that a significant evolution within the cognitive revolution has involved the emergence of constructivism and motor metatheories as viewpoints competing with classical realism, rationalism, and sensory metatheories. Attachment theory, social learning theory, and the developmental and systems movements have also contributed to what I have here presented as a differentiation among current cognitive perspectives. This differentiation constituted the main focus of the second half of the chapter, in which I briefly sketched philosophical, theoretical, and practical differences between what have been called the rationalist and developmental cognitive perspectives.

The themes and issues addressed in this chapter are well represented in the present volume. Although in my discussion I have only been able to touch upon highlights of trends and differentiating issues, I hope that my remarks have offered some frameworks for understanding traditional and more recent expressions of the growing interface between cognitive and clinical sciences. More extensive commentaries and a presentation of a cognitive developmental approach are offered elsewhere (Mahoney, in press). It will be interesting to review these traditions and trends after the cognitive movement has undergone another decade of development and differentiation.

I shall, therefore, close with a reiteration of my fundamental sense that the cognitive and developmental sciences have much to offer the psychological theorist and therapist. Whether rationalist or constructivist in flavor, those perspectives that acknowledge and explore the complexities of human experience—and particularly the "inner," private, and personal aspects of that experience—clearly promise a more adequate understanding than those that deny or denigrate these dimensions. The cognitive revolution and its sequelae constitute major phenomena in late 20th-century psychology (DeMey, 1982; Flanagan, 1984; Fodor, 1981; Gardner, 1985). The importance of their direction should not be lost in our reflections on their differentiations.

REFERENCES

Arkowitz, H., & Messer, H. (Eds.). (1984). *Psychoanalytic and behavior therapy: Is integration possible?* New York: Plenum.

Bain, J. A. (1928). *Thought control in everyday life.* New York: Funk & Wagnalls.

Bandura, A. (1969). *Principles of behavior modification.* New York: Holt, Rinehart & Winston.

Bandura, A. (1976). Social learning perspective on behavior change. In A. Burton (Ed.), *What makes behavior change possible?* New York: Brunner/Mazel.

Bandura, A. (1977). Self-efficacy: Toward a unifying theory of behavioral change. *Psychological Review, 84,* 191–215.

Bandura, A. (1978). The self system in reciprocal determinism. *American Psychologist, 33,* 344–358.

Bandura, A. (1985). Model of causality in social learning theory. In M. J. Mahoney & A. Freeman (Eds.), *Cognition and psychotherapy.* New York: Plenum.

Bandura, A. (1986). *Social foundations of thought and action: A social cognitive theory.* Englewood Cliffs, NJ: Prentice-Hall.

Bateson, G. (1972). *Steps to an ecology of mind.* New York: Ballantine.

Bateson, G. (1979). *Mind and nature: A necessary unity.* New York: Bantam.

Beck, A. T. (1963). Thinking and depression, I. Idiosyncratic content and cognitive distortion. *Archives of General Psychiatry, 9,* 324–333.

Beck, A. T. (1970). Cognitive therapy: Nature and relation to behavior therapy. *Behavior Therapy, 1,* 184–200.

Beck, A. T. (1976). *Cognitive therapy and the emotional disorders.* New York: International Universities Press.

Beck, A. T., Emery, G., & Greenberg, R. L. (1985). *Anxiety disorders and phobias: A cognitive perspective.* New York: Basic Books.

Belsky, J., & Nezworski, M. T. (Eds.). (1987). *Clinical implications of attachment.* Hillsdale, NJ: Erlbaum.

Bever, T. G., Fodor, J. A., & Garrett, M. (1968). A formal limit of associationism. In T. R. Dixon & D. L. Horton (Eds.), *Verbal behavior and general behavior theory.* Englewood Cliffs, NJ: Prentice-Hall.

Blumenthal, A. L. (1975). A reappraisal of Wilhelm Wundt. *American Psychologist, 30,* 1081–1088.

Blumenthal, A. L. (1980). Wilhelm Wundt and early American psychology: A clash of cultures. In R. Rieber & K. Salzinger (Eds.), *Psychology: Theoretical-historical perspectives.* New York: Academic Press.

Blumenthal, A. L. (1985). Wilhelm Wundt: Psychology as the propaedeutic science. In C. Buxton (Ed.), *Points of view in the modern history of psychology.* New York: Academic Press.

Borkovec, T. D., & O'Brien, G. T. (1977). Relation of autonomic perception and its manipulation to the maintenance and reduction of fear. *Journal of Abnormal Psychology, 86,* 163–171.

Bowlby, J. (1969). *Attachment and loss. Vol. I: Attachment.* New York: Basic Books.

Bowlby, J. (1973). *Attachment and loss. Vol. II: Separation: Anxiety and anger.* New York: Basic Books.

Bowlby, J. (1979). *The making and breaking of affectional bonds.* London: Tavistock.

Bowlby, J. (1980). *Attachment and loss. Vol. III. Loss: Sadness and depression.* London: Hogarth Press.

Bowlby, J. (1985). The role of childhood experience in cognitive disturbance. In M. J. Mahoney & A. Freeman (Eds.), *Cognition and psychotherapy.* New York: Plenum.

Breger, L. (Ed.). (1969). *Clinical-cognitive psychology: Models and integrations.* Englewood Cliffs, NJ: Prentice-Hall.

Brent, S. B. (1978). Prigogine's model for self-organization in nonequilibrium systems: Its relevance for developmental psychology. *Human Development, 21,* 374–387.

Brent, S. B. (1984). *Psychological and social structures.* Hillsdale, NJ: Erlbaum.

Brewer, W. F. (1974). There is no convincing evidence for operant or classical conditioning in adult humans. In W. B. Weimer & D. S. Palermo (Eds.), *Cognition and the symbolic processes* (Vol. 1). Hillsdale, NJ: Erlbaum.

Bugental, J. F. T., & Bugental, E. K. (1984). A fate worse than death: The fear of changing. *Psychotherapy, 21,* 543–549.

Briskman, L. B. (1972). Is a Kuhnian analysis applicable to psychology? *Science Studies, 2,* 87–97.

Burrell, M. J. (1983). *Psychotherapy from a motor-evolutionary perspective: Implications from cognitive psychology and epistemology.* Unpublished doctoral dissertation, the Pennsylvania State University, University Park, PA.

Campbell, D. T. (1974). Evolutionary epistemology. In P. A. Schlipp (Ed.), *The philosophy of Karl Popper* (Vol. 14, I & II). LaSalle, IL: Open Court Publishing.

Campbell, D. T. (1975). On the conflicts between biological and social evolution and between psychology and moral tradition. *American Psychologist, 30,* 1103–1126.

Carnegie, D. (1948). *How to stop worrying and start living.* New York: Simon & Schuster.

Churchman, P. M. (1984). *Matter and consciousness.* Cambridge, MA: MIT Press.

Cook, N. D. (1980). *Stability and flexibility: An analysis of natural systems.* New York: Pergamon.

Coue, E. (1922). *The practice of autosuggestion.* New York: Doubleday.

Dell, P. F. (1982). Beyond Homeostasis: Toward a concept of coherence. *Family Process, 21,* 21–41.

Dember, W. N. (1974). Motivation and the cognitive revolution. *American Psychologist, 29,* 161–168.

DeMey, M. (1982). *The cognitive paradigm.* Boston: Reidel.

Dennett, D. C. (1978). *Brainstorms: Philosophical essays on mind and psychology.* Cambridge, MA: MIT Press.

Dennett, D. C. (1984). *Elbow room: The varieties of free will worth wanting.* Cambridge, MA: MIT Press.

Dobzhansky, T. (1962). *Mankind evolving: The evolution of the human species.* New Haven, CT: Yale University Press.

Dubois, P. (1906). *The influence of the mind on the body.* New York: Funk & Wagnalls.

Dubois, P. (1908). *The psychic treatment of nervous disorders.* New York: Funk & Wagnalls.

Dubois, P. (1911). *The education of self.* New York: Funk & Wagnalls.

Dulany, D. E. (1968). Awareness, rules, and propositional control: A confrontation with the S–R behavior theory. In T. R. Dixon & D. L. Horton (Eds.), *Verbal behavior and general behavior theory.* Englewood Cliffs, NJ: Prentice-Hall.

D'Zurilla, T. J., & Goldfried, M. R. (1971). Problem solving and behavior modification. *Journal of Abnormal Psychology, 78,* 107–126.

Ellis, A. (1962). *Reason and emotions in psychotherapy.* New York: Stuart.

Ellis, A. (1985a). Expanding the ABC's of rational–emotive therapy. In M. J. Mahoney & A. Freeman (Eds.), *Cognition and psychotherapy.* New York: Plenum.

Ellis, A. (1985b). *Overcoming resistance: Rational-emotive therapy with difficult clients.* New York: Springer.

Flanagan, O. J. (1984). *The science of the mind.* Cambridge, MA: MIT Press.

Flavell, J. H. (1979). Metacognition and cognitive monitoring: A new area of cognitive-developmental inquiry. *American Psychologist, 34,* 906–911.

Fodor, J. A. (1981). *Representations: Philosophical essays on the foundations of cognitive science.* Cambridge, MA: MIT Press.

Frankl, V. E. (1959). *Man's search for meaning: An introduction to logotherapy.* New York: Washington Square Press.

Frankl, V. E. (1985a). *The unheard cry for meaning: Psychotherapy and humanism.* New York: Simon & Schuster.

Frankl, V. E. (1985a). Logos, paradox, and the search for meaning. In M. J. Mahoney & A. Freeman (Eds.), *Cognition and psychotherapy.* New York: Plenum.

Gardner, H. (1985). *The mind's new science: A history of the cognitive revolution.* New York: Basic Books.

Goldfried, M. R. (Ed.). (1982). *Converging themes in psychotherapy.* New York: Springer.

Goldfried, M. R., & Robins, C. (1983). Self-schemas, cognitive bias, and the processing of learning experiences. In P. C. Kendall (Ed.), *Advances in cognitive-behavioral research and therapy* (Vol. 2). New York: Academic Press.

Goodman, D. S., & Maultsby, M. C. (1974). *Emotional well-being through rational behavior training.* Springfield, IL: Charles C Thomas.

Gould, S. J. (1977). *Ever since Darwin: Reflections in natural history.* New York: Norton.

Gould, S. J. (1980). *The panda's thumb: More reflections in natural history.* New York: Norton.

Guidano, V. F. (1984). A constructivist outline of cognitive processes. In M. A. Reda & M. J. Mahoney (Eds.), *Cognitive psychotherapies: Recent developments in theory, research, and practice.* Cambridge, MA: Ballinger.

Guidano, V. F. (1987). *Complexity of the self.* New York: Guilford.

Guidano, V F., & Liotti, G. (1983). *Cognitive processes and emotional disorders: A structural approach to psychotherapy.* New York: Guilford.

Guidano, V. F., & Liotti, G. (1985). A constructivistic foundation for cognitive therapy. In M. J. Mahoney & A. Freeman (Eds.), *Cognition and psychotherapy.* New York: Plenum.

Hayek, F. A. (1952). *The sensory order.* Chicago: University of Chicago Press.

Hayek, F. A. (1964). The theory of complex phenomena. In M. Bunge (Ed.), *The critical approach to science and philosophy: Essays in honor of K. R. Popper.* New York: Free Press.

Hayek, F. A. (1978). *New studies in philosophy, politics, economics, and the history of ideas.* Chicago: University of Chicago Press.

Hayek, F. A. (1982). The Sensory Order after 25 years. In W. B. Weimer & D. S. Palermo (Eds.), *Cognition and the symbolic processes* (Vol. 2). Hillsdale, NJ: Erlbaum.

Howard, K. L., & Orlinsky, D. E. (1972). Psychotherapeutic process. *Annual Review of Psychology, 23,* 615–668.

James, W. (1890). *Principles of psychology.* New York: Holt.

James, W. (1902/1958). *The varieties of religious experience.* New York: New American Library.

Janet, P. (1898). *Neurosis and fixed ideas.* Paris: Alcan.

Jantsch, E. (1980). *The self-organizing universe: Scientific and human implications of the emerging paradigm of evolution.* New York: Pergamon.

Jantsch, E. (Ed.). (1981). *The evolutionary vision: Toward a unifying paradigm of physical, biological, and sociocultural evolution.* Boulder, CO: Westview Press.

Jerison, H. (1973). *Evolution of the brain and intelligence.* New York: Wiley.

Jerison, H. (1976). Paleoneurology and the evolution of mind. *Scientific American, 234,* 90–101.

Jerome, J. (1980). *The sweet spot in time.* New York: Summit.

Joyce Moniz, L. (1985). Epistemological therapy and constructivism. In M. J. Mahoney & A. Freeman (Eds.), *Cognition and psychotherapy.* New York: Plenum.

Kelly, G. A. (1955). *The psychology of personal constructs.* New York: Norton.

Kruglanski, A. W., & Jaffe, Y. (1983). The lay epistemic model in cognitive therapy. In M. Rosenbaum, C. M. Franks, & Y. Jaffe (Eds.), *Perspectives on behavior therapy in the eighties.* New York: Springer.

Kuhn, T. S. (1962). *The structure of scientific revolutions.* Chicago: University of Chicago Press.

Kuhn, T. S. (1970). Logic of discovery or psychology of research? In I. Lakatos & A. Musgrave (Eds.), *Criticism and the growth of knowledge*. Cambridge, MA: Cambridge University Press.

Kuhn, T. S. (1977). *The essential tension*. Chicago: University of Chicago Press.

Lakatos, I. (1970). Falsification and the methodology of scientific research programmes. In I. Lakatos & A. Musgrave (Eds.), *Criticism and the growth of knowledge* (pp. 91–196f). Cambridge, MA: Cambridge University Press.

Land, G. T. L. (1973). *Grow or die: The unifying principle of transformation*. New York: Dell.

Laudan, L. (1977). *Progress and its problems: Towards a theory of scientific growth*. Berkeley: University of California Press.

Laszlo, E. (1983). *Systems science and world order: Selected studies*. New York: Pergamon.

Lazarus, A. A. (1971). *Behavior therapy and beyond*. New York: McGraw-Hill.

Lazarus, A. A. (1976). *Multimodal behavior therapy*. New York: Springer.

Ledwidge, B. (1978). Cognitive behavior modification: A step in the wrong direction? *Psychological Bulletin, 85*, 353–375.

Leva, L. M. (1984). Cognitive behavioral therapy in the light of Piagetian theory. In M. A. Reba & M. J. Mahoney (Eds.), *Cognitive psychotherapies: Recent developments in theory, research, and practice*. Cambridge, MA: Ballinger.

Liotti, G. (1984). Cognitive therapy, attachment theory, and psychiatric nosology: A clinical and theoretical inquiry into their interdependence. In M. A. Reba & M. J. Mahoney (Eds.), *Cognitive psychotherapies: Recent developments in theory, research, and practice*. Cambridge, MA: Ballinger.

MacLean, P. D. (1973). *A triune concept of the brain and behavior*. Toronto: University of Toronto Press.

Mahoney, M. J. (1974). *Cognition and behavior modification*. Cambridge, MA: Ballinger.

Mahoney, M. J. (1976). *Scientist as subject: The psychological imperative*. Santa Barbara, CA: Personal Empowerment Programs.

Mahoney, M. J. (1979). *Cognitive and non-cognitive views in behavior modification*. In P. O. Sjoden, S. Bates, & W. S. Dockens (Eds.), *Trends in behavior therapy*. New York: Plenum.

Mahoney, M. J. (1980). Psychotherapy and the structure of personal revolutions. In M. J. Mahoney (Ed.), *Psychotherapy process: Current issues and future directions*. New York: Plenum.

Mahoney, M. J. (1981). La importancia de los procesos evolutivos para la psicoterapia. *Analysis y modification de conducta, 7*, 155–170.

Mahoney, M. J. (1984a). Psychoanalysis and behaviorism: The yin and yang of determinism. In H. Arkowitz & S. Messer (Eds.), *Psychoanalytic and behavior therapy: Is integration possible?* New York: Plenum.

Mahoney, M. J. (1984b). Behaviorism, cognitivism, and human change processes. In M. A. Reda & M. J. Mahoney (Eds.), *Cognitive psychotherapies: Recent developments in theory, research, and practice*. Cambridge, MA: Ballinger.

Mahoney, M. J. (1984c). Integrating cognition, affect, and action: A comment. *Cognitive Therapy and Research, 8*, 585–589.

Mahoney, M. J. (1985a). Citation classic: Cognition and behavior modification. *Current Contents: Social and Behavioral Sciences, 17*, 16.

Mahoney, M. J. (1985b, November). *Reflections on the cognitive revolution*. Paper presented to the Association for Advancement of Behavior Therapy, Houston, TX.

Mahoney, M. J. (1985c). Psychotherapy and human change processes. In M. J. Mahoney & A. Freeman (Eds.), *Cognition and psychotherapy*. New York: Plenum.

Mahoney, M. J. (1985d). Open exchange and epistemic progress. *American Psychologist, 40*, 29–39.

Mahoney, M. J. (1986). The tyranny of technique. *Counseling and Values, 30*, 169–174.

Mahoney, M. J. (in press). *Human change processes: Notes on the facilitation of personal development*. New York: Basic Books.

Mahoney, M. J., & Arnkoff, D. B. (1978). Cognitive and self-control therapies. In S. L. Garfield & A. E. Bergin (Eds.), *Handbook of psychotherapy and behavior change*. New York: Wiley.

Mahoney, M. J., & Freeman, A. (Eds.). (1985). *Cognition and psychotherapy*. New York: Plenum.

Maltz, M. (1960). *Psycho-cybernetics*. Englewood Cliffs, NJ: Prentice-Hall.

Mancuso, J. C., & Adams-Webber, J. R. (Eds.). (1982). *The construing person*. New York: Praeger.

Marlatt, G. A., & Gordon, J. R. (Eds.). (1985). *Relapse prevention: Maintenance strategies in the treatment of addictive behaviors*. New York: Guilford.

Maturana, H. R. (1975). The organization of the living: A theory of the living organization. *International Journal of Man-Machine Studies, 7*, 313-332.

Maturana, H. R., & Varela, F. G. (1980). *Autopoiesis and cognition: The realization of the living*. Boston: Reidel.

Maultsby, M. C. (1984). *Rational behavior therapy*. Englewood Cliffs, NJ: Prentice-Hall.

Meichenbaum, D. (1977). *Cognitive behavior modification*. New York: Plenum.

Neimeyer, R. A. (1985). Personal constructs in clinical practice. In P. C. Kendall (Ed.), *Advances in cognitive-behavioral research and therapy* (Vol. 2). New York: Academic Press.

Neisser, U. (1967). *Cognitive psychology*. New York: Appleton-Century-Crofts.

Neisser, U. (1976). *Cognition and reality*. San Francisco: Freeman.

Nelson, K. E., & Nelson, K. (1978). Cognitive pendulums and their linguistic realization. In K. E. Nelson (Ed.), *Children's language* (Vol. I). New York: Gardner Press.

Nideffer, R. M. (1976). *The inner athlete*. New York: Crowell.

Orlinsky, D. E., & Howard, K. I. (1975). *Varieties of psychotherapeutic experience*. New York: Teachers College Press.

Passingham, R. (1982). *The human primate*. San Francisco: Freeman.

Paivio, A. (1975). Neomentalism. *Canadian Journal of Psychology, 29*, 263-291.

Palermo, D. S. (1971). Is a scientific revolution taking place in psychology? *Science Studies, 1*, 135-155.

Pattee, H. H. (Ed.). (1973). *Hierarchy theory: The challenge of complex systems*. New York: George Braziller.

Peale, N. V. (1960). *The power of positive thinking*. Englewood Cliffs, NJ: Prentice-Hall.

Piaget, J. (1970). *Psychology and epistemology: Towards a theory of knowledge*. New York: Viking.

Piaget, J. (1981). *Intelligence and affectivity: Their relationship during child development*. Palo Alto, CA: Annual Reviews.

Polanyi, M. (1958). *Personal knowledge: Towards a post-critical philosophy*. Chicago: University of Chicago Press.

Polanyi, M. (1966). *The tacit dimension*. New York: Doubleday.

Prigogine, I. (1980). *From being to becoming: Time and complexity in the physical sciences*. San Francisco: Freeman.

Prigogine, I., & Stengers, I. (1984). *Order out of chaos: Man's new dialogue with nature*. New York: Bantam.

Prochaska, J. O. (1984). *Systems of psychotherapy: A transtheoretical analysis*. Homewood, IL: Dorsey Press.

Rachman, S. J. (1980). Emotional processing. *Behaviour Research and Therapy, 18*, 51-60.

Raimy, V. (1975). *Misunderstandings of the self*. San Francisco: Jossey-Bass.

Raimy, V. (1985). Misconceptions and the cognitive therapies. In M. J. Mahoney & A. Freeman (Eds.), *Cognition and psychotherapy*. New York: Plenum.

Reynolds, P. C. (1981). *On the evolution of human behavior: The argument from animals to man.* Berkeley: University of California Press.

Rice, L. N., & Greenberg, L. S. (1984). *Patterns of change.* New York: Guilford.

Rosen, H. (1985). *Piagetian dimensions of clinical relevance.* New York: Columbia University Press.

Russell, B. (1945). *A history of Western philosophy.* New York: Simon & Schuster.

Scheff, T. J. (1979). *Catharsis in healing, ritual, and drama.* Berkeley: University of California Press.

Skinner, B. F. (1971). *Beyond freedom and dignity.* New York: Alfred A. Knopf.

Skinner, B. F. (1974). *About behaviorism.* New York: Knopf.

Skinner, B. F. (1984). The shame of American education. *American Psychologist, 39,* 947-954.

Spielberger, C. D., & DeNike, L. D. (1966). Descriptive behaviorism versus cognitive theory in verbal operant conditioning. *Psychological Review, 73,* 306-326.

Spivack, G., & Shure, M. B. (1974). *Social adjustment of young children: A cognitive approach to solving real-life problems.* San Francisco: Jossey-Bass.

Suarez, E. M. (1985). *Neo-cognitive psychotherapy.* Manuscript in preparation, Advanced Human Studies Institute, Coral Gables, FL.

Tomlin, E. W. F. (1963). *The oriental philosophers: An introduction.* New York: Harper & Row.

Tosi, D. J., & Eshbaugh, D. M. (1980). Rational stage-directed therapy and crisis intervention. In R. Herink (Ed.), *The psychotherapy handbook.* New York: New American Library.

Varela, F. J. (1979). *Principles of biological autonomy.* New York: Elsevier North Holland.

Vico, G. (1744/1948). *The new science* (T. G. Bergin & M. H. Fisch, Trans.). Ithaca, NY: Cornell University Press.

Von Foerster, H. (1984). On constructing a reality. In P. Watzlawick (Ed.), *The invented reality.* New York: Norton.

Von Glaserfeld, E. (1984). An introduction to radical constructivism. In P. Watzlawick (Ed.), *The invented reality.* New York: Norton.

Wachtel, P. L. (Ed.). (1982). *Resistance: Psychodynamic and behavioral approaches.* New York: Plenum.

Warren, N. (1971). Is a scientific revolution taking place in psychology?—Doubts and reservations. *Science Studies, 1,* 407-413.

Washburn, S. L., & Moore, R. (1980). *Ape into human: A study of human evolution.* Boston: Little, Brown.

Watzlawick, P. (Ed.). (1984). *The invented reality: Contributions to constructivism.* New York: Norton.

Weimer, W. B. (1974a). The history of psychology and its retrieval from historiography: I. The problematic nature of history. *Science Studies, 4,* 235-258.

Weimer, W. B. (1974b). The history of psychology and its retrieval from historiography: II. Some lessons for the methodology of scientific research. *Science Studies, 4,* 367-396.

Weimer, W. B. (1974c). Overview of a cognitive conspiracy: Reflections on the volume. In W. B. Weimer & D. S. Palermo (Eds.), *Cognition and the symbolic processes.* Hillsdale, NJ: Erlbaum.

Weimer, W. B. (1977). A conceptual framework for cognitive psychology: Motor theories of the mind. In R. Shaw & J. Bransford (Eds.), *Perceiving, acting, and knowing.* Hillsdale, NJ: Erlbaum.

Weimer, W. B. (1979). *Notes on the methodology of scientific research.* Hillsdale, NJ: Erlbaum.

Weimer, W. B. (1982). Hayek's approach to the problems of complex phenomena: An introduction to the theoretical psychology of The Sensory Order. In W. B. Weimer & D. S. Palermo (Eds.), *Cognition and the symbolic processes* (Vol. 2). Hillsdale, NJ: Erlbaum.

Weimer, W. B. (in press-a). Spontaneously ordered complex phenomena and the unity of the moral sciences. In G. Radnitzky (Ed.), *Unity of the sciences.* New York: Paragon House.

Weimer, W. B. (in press-b). *Rationalist constructivism, scientism, and the study of man and society.* Hillsdale, NJ: Erlbaum.

Weimer, W. B., & Palermo, D. S. (1973). Paradigms and normal science in psychology. *Science Studies, 3,* 211–244.

Weimer, W. B., & Palermo, D. S. (Eds.). (1974). *Cognition and the symbolic processes* (Vol. 1). Hillsdale, NJ: Erlbaum.

Weimer, W. B., & Palermo, D. S. (Eds.). (1982). *Cognition and the symbolic processes* (Vol. 2). Hillsdale, NJ: Erlbaum.

Weiner, M. L. (1975). *The cognitive unconscious: A Piagetian approach to psychotherapy.* Davis, CA: International Psychological Press.

Weiner, M. L. (1985). *Cognitive-experiential therapy: An integrative ego psychotherapy.* New York: Brunner/Mazel.

Werner, H. (1948). *The comparative psychology of mental development.* New York: Science Editions.

Wessler, R. L. (1984). Alternative conceptions of rational-emotive therapy: Toward a philosophically neutral psychotherapy. In M. A. Reda & M. J. Mahoney (Eds.), *The cognitive psychotherapies: Recent developments in theory, research, and practice.* Cambridge, MA: Ballinger.

Wilber, K. (1980). *The Atman project.* Wheaton, IL: Theosophical Publishing House.

Wilson, P. J. (1980). *Man: The promising primate.* New Haven, CT: Yale University Press.

Wolpe, J. (1978). Cognition and causation in human behavior and its therapy. *American Psychologist, 33,* 437–446.

Woodcock, A., & Davis, M. (1978). *Catastrophe theory.* New York: Avon.

Wundt, W. (1912). *An introduction to psychology.* New York: Macmillan.

Zeleny, M. (Ed.). (1980). *Autopoiesis, dissipative structures, and spontaneous social orders.* Washington, DC: American Association for the Advancement of Science.

10

THE PRESENT AND FUTURE OF THE COGNITIVE-BEHAVIORAL THERAPIES

KEITH S. DOBSON

Trying to examine a phenomenon while that phenomenon is in the process of change is a difficult task. This chapter, however, will attempt to identify the major issues facing the cognitive-behavioral field, even though those issues are very much in the process of flux and change. Based upon the review of the major issues facing the field, some predictions about the future directions in which cognitive-behavioral therapies will need to develop will be made.

It must be noted that in trying to encapsulate the major evolutions and developments in a field as large as cognitive-behavioral therapy, there will inevitably be some areas that are given either insufficient attention or are ignored altogether. Also, it is undoubtedly true that the biases and perspectives of the author will be involved in the identification of the emergent issues for the field. What is attempted here is thus not an exhaustive review of the present and future of cognitive-behavioral therapies but an admittedly selective review of what will likely be critical and identifiable streams of interest in the overall field.

This chapter is structured into two major sections. In the immediately following section some of the major developments and achievements of the cognitive-behavioral movement will be briefly outlined. The second section of the chapter will consist of an exercise in "crystal ball gazing": attempting to predict what will be the areas of theoretical and technique expansion that will face the field in the coming years. Within this section four major domains for future development will be identified and described. These domains relate to: (1) theoretical developments, (2) developmental aspects of psychopathology and psychotherapy, (3) cognitive assessment and change measurement, and (4) therapy expansion and evaluation.

DEVELOPMENTS IN COGNITIVE-BEHAVIORAL THERAPY

It has been repeatedly observed that a "cognitive revolution" occurred in psychology in the 1960s (Dember, 1974; Dobson & Block, Chapter 1, this volume; Mahoney, 1974, Chapter 9, this volume). This revolution evidenced itself in behavioral clinical psychology through the emergence of a number of therapeutic models and methods that incorporated the concept of cognition. The gradual inclusion of mediational concepts in behavior therapy was first seen in such areas of delay of gratification (e.g., Mischel, Ebbesen, & Zeiss, 1972), modeling of behavior (e.g., Bandura & Barab, 1971; O'Connor, 1969), and the application of behavioral principles to self-talk and "covert" behavior (e.g., Homme, 1965; Meichenbaum, & Goodman, 1971). These attempts at integrating a cognitive perspective within behavior therapy were initially resisted by some behavior therapists, but as the cognitive revolution continued other applications of mediational concepts were elaborated. In this vein, the development of self-control approaches (Kanfer, 1970, 1971; Mahoney & Thorsen, 1974) and problem-solving therapies (D'Zurilla & Goldfried, 1971; Spivack, Platt, & Shure, 1976) served to help institutionalize cognitive components to behavioral interventions. Not only were conceptual models of these therapeutic innovations developed during this period, but outcome evaluations also documented that many of the cognitive-behavioral interventions were efficacious in terms of altering the referred behavior problems.

Despite the major strides forward in the elaboration of cognitive-behavioral theory and therapy during this stage of development (roughly 1960 through 1975), it must be questioned to what extent the changes that were seen actually constituted a revolution. If a revolution is defined as a complete repudiation of a former model and practice, it is clear that what happened in the early stages of cognitive-behaviorism was not a revolution. Indeed, the earliest innovations in cognitive-behaviorism were ultimately aimed at behavior change, and so were elaborations upon a fundamentally behavioral model, rather than being a novel model altogether.

Mahoney (1974) distinguished metaphysical and methodological behaviorism, reserving the former designation for a philosophical perspective that held as a core belief "denial of the existence of 'mind'" (Mahoney, 1974, p. 11), and the latter designation for a variety of perspectives that emphasize "operationism, logical positivism, falsification, linguistic analysis, and pragmatism" (p. 16). While metaphysical behaviorism cannot accommodate cognitive and mediational concepts within its theoretical framework, methodological behaviorism may. Indeed, it is arguable that it was the behaviorists who were pragmatists and operationists that most fostered the early growth of the cognitive tradition within behavior therapy.

Perhaps the single best example of methodological behaviorism advancing mediational models of behavior change is in the area of symbolic modeling (Bandura & Barab, 1971; Bandura, Blanchard, & Ritter, 1969; Bandura & Walters, 1959; O'Connor, 1969). For example, O'Connor (1969) documented that observation of a model may lead to behavioral changes without specific attempts to reinforce the behavior under investigation. In his study a set of socially withdrawn preschool children were divided into two groups. One of the groups viewed a film that depicted a socially withdrawn child gradually overcoming his isolation by approaching and being positively received by other children. The second group of subjects watched a film that was neutral with respect to overcoming social isolation. As expected, the group that viewed the film depicting a child overcoming social isolation demonstrated a significant change in their behavior, in that they were engaged in many more social interactions than the control group. Indeed, their post-test scores were not significantly different than those for a control set of socially appropriate children.

Results such as those above, as well as a series of studies from Bandura's laboratory, have been construed as conforming to a metaphysical behavioral perspective (Aronfreed, 1969; Baer & Sherman, 1964; Gerwitz, 1971), but these explanatory attempts have been severely criticized (Mahoney, 1974). Bandura has argued (1977, 1986) that a series of four processes are necessarily involved in the phenomenon of observational learning; namely, attentional processes, retention processes (memory and mental rehearsal processes), production processes, and motivational processes (self and external reinforcement). Every one of the four constituent processes in observational learning is explicitly mediational, and has received formal research validation.

Given the inadequacies of nonmediational models to fully account for effects such as observational learning, and given also the desire of methodological behaviorists of the late 1960s to enhance the pragmatic ability of various intervention programs to effect behavioral changes, it is not surprising that mediational concepts were proposed to enhance and explain behavioral change processes. Mahoney (1974) identified three major variants on the basic mediational perspective; covert conditioning, information processing, and cognitive learning. The elaboration of these three mediational models, coupled with the empirical testing of the applicability of these models, has undoubtedly been the major contribution of the cognitive-behavioral therapy tradition. Some of the classical issues for these three mediational models are elaborated below.

MAJOR COGNITIVE-BEHAVIORAL MODELS

Covert conditioning models represent the smallest incremental theoretical step away from behaviorism towards cognitive-behaviorism. Their primary theoretical development is that they attempt to couch cognitions and other "covert behaviors" within a traditional behavioral perspective, and thereby warrant behavioral analyses of mediational processes (Homme, 1965). Early attempts to covert conditioning included forays into the domains of unwanted ruminations (Wolpe, 1969; Wolpe & Lazarus, 1966), smoking (Berecz, 1972), obesity and eating (Cautela, 1966; Foreyt & Hagen, 1973; Horan & Johnson, 1971), alcoholism (Anant, 1967; Ashem & Donner, 1968), sexual deviation (Cautela & Wisocki, 1971; Curtis & Presly, 1972; Kendrick & McCullough, 1972), and phobias (Blanchard & Draper, 1973; Flannery, 1972; Hekmat & Vanian, 1971; Lazarus, Davison, & Polefka, 1965). Within the attempts to employ covert conditioning in treatment programs a number of variations of conditioning paradigms were employed, including covert counterconditioning, thought stopping, covert control, covert modeling, covert sensitization, covert reinforcement, and covert extinction.

With the notable exception of a few covert conditioning therapies (most notably, covert sensitization in the control of socially undesirable behaviors such as alcohol consumption, sexual deviancy, overeating, and drug abuse), many of the above techniques have passed into behavioral history. Where the above techniques survive, it is highly unlikely that they would be employed in therapeutic isolation, as the only intervention used with a given client. For example, in the treatment of eating disorders, while all intervention programs ultimately aim to alter a dysfunctional behavior pattern, the awareness of the cognitive components of eating disorders (Garner & Bemis, 1982; Garfinkel & Garner, 1982; Guidano & Liotti, 1983) make assessment and intervention in the cognitive domain essential components of effective therapy. Thus, while treatment models may advocate covert conditioning components to therapy (e.g., Agras, Barlow, Chapin, Abel, & Leitenberg, 1974; Lang, 1965) few if any therapists would restrict themselves to the use of these treatment procedures.

Information processing approaches to cognitive-behavioral therapy have, relative to covert conditioning therapies, survived exceedingly well and have multiplied in number and scope. These approaches assume that individuals actively appraise their environment, and act as naive scientists as they determine how best to respond to the variety of situational and contextual demands they find themselves faced with. In addition, these models assume a linear, "rational" approach to the perception of and response to events. For example, the stress appraisal model developed by R. Lazarus (1966; Lazarus & Launier, 1978; Lazarus & Folkman, 1984) proposes that the occurrence of a notable life event will precipitate a pattern of cognitive appraisals that ultimately eventuates in a multidimensional response that includes cognitive, affective, behavioral, and physiological aspects. Embraced by this model of coping and stress is the notion that the cognitive appraisal pattern will determine (i.e., cause to begin, modify, and terminate) the subsequent responses to the initial stimulus.

The strong information processing position, that cognitions perfectly predict and control subsequent response, is embodied in a number of cognitive-behavioral models of dysfunction and therapy (D'Zurilla, in press, Chapter 3, this volume; Ellis, 1962, 1979; Lazarus & Folkman, 1984; Hamilton, 1979, 1980; Mahoney, 1974; Meichenbaum & Cameron, 1973). While there have been criticisms of the theoretical underpinnings of these approaches as being probably causally wrong (cf. Zajonc, 1980; Greenberg & Safran, 1984a) and theoretically insufficient in accounting for the development and change processes that humans display (Guidano, 1987, Chapter 8, this volume; Mahoney, 1984, Chapter 9, this volume) the jury is presently "out" on the outcome of the debate regarding the theoretical validity of information-processing models of psychopathology and psychotherapy. It is likely that the continuing discussion of this issue will constitute a major impetus for the future of cognitive-behaviorism. This point will be elaborated upon below.

There are many variations on the basic information processing paradigm that have evolved in the cognitive-behavioral field. One way to conceptualize the variations, though, is with reference to prior typologies of cognitive-behavioral approaches. Mahoney and Arnkoff (1978), in particular, have designated three types of cognitive-behavioral therapies that are of relevance to this discussion. Their typology includes coping skills therapies, problem-solving therapies, and cognitive restructuring approaches. Of these three approaches the first two are most obviously based upon an information-processing perspective. Problem-solving therapies, for example, highlight the need for objective problem perception and assessment, the generation and evaluation of alternative methods to respond to the problem, and the implementation of the putatively best alternative solution, followed by evaluation of the outcome and recycling through the problem-solving process, if necessary. This model assumes a primary role for the cognitive processes (D'Zurilla, in press, Chapter 3 this volume; Mahoney, 1974; Spivack & Shure, 1974), particularly in the problem assessment phase and the generation of potential solutions. Coping skills therapies, in contrast to the problem-solving approaches, focus upon the manners in which a client can more effectively cope with, or respond to a given problem. Stress inoculation training (Meichenbaum, 1977, 1985), for example, emphasizes the need for the client to learn to cope with a distressing event by gradually approaching the event. The techniques used to achieve this gradual inoculation include the use of increasingly distressing approximations of the final goal situation or event, and the development of internal dialogue (i.e., cognitions) that will facilitate the maximally effective response to that situation or event. Such coping skills therapies largely assume that the problem event is a veridical problem (e.g., demonstrated via social concensus) and that learning to cope with the stressor is the most effective method to minimize subjective distress and maximize personal adjustment.

Within the information-processing perspective the primary distinction between problem-solving and coping skills therapies is that the former type of therapies focus upon the appraisal aspects of the problem (e.g., How is this a problem? How bad is the problem? What coping resources do I have to bring to bear to help me with this problem?) What are the potential ways to get out of this problem?), whereas the latter types of therapies emphasize learning new and more adaptive responses for the problem that has been identified. In a very real sense, these two types of therapies complement each other, and it is perhaps not surprising that in clinical practice they are often used in tandem.

Numerous examples of problem-solving and coping skills therapies exist, as the previous chapters in this volume document (Chapters 3 and 4). These therapies have been applied to the complete range of clinical phenomena, across the age span (children, adolescents, adults, the aged), and across therapy formats (individual, marital, family and group). While there appear to be some areas where certain therapy approaches are more or less applicable, there are numerous reports of individual applications of these therapy procedures. Clinical trials, while less common, represent another emerging data source that will bear upon the future survivability of these therapy procedures.

Cognitive learning therapies constitute the third major class of cognitive-behavioral therapies identified by Mahoney (1974). These therapies were also discussed by Mahoney and Arnkoff (1978) as the cognitive restructuring therapies. The essential aspect of these therapies is that their theoretical models invoke the concepts of cognitive errors and distortions, and that the source of these errors and distortions "reside" within the afflicted person, as a cross-situational tendency. The primary exemplars of the cognitive learning/cognitive restructuring approach are Rational–Emotive Therapy (Dryden & Ellis, Chapter 6, this volume) and Cognitive Therapy (deRubeis & Beck, Chapter 7, this volume).

At a theoretical level, the cognitive learning therapies are the most distant from the traditional behavioral perspective. For example, the assumption of cross-situational cognitive patterns and processes (variously termed beliefs, assumptions, attitudes, schemas, rules for living) is quite inconsistent with the behavioral assumption of situational determinism and the critical importance of environmental contingencies. Indeed, in several respects these types of therapies are conceptually more related to various psychodynamic therapeutic formulations. Some of the commonalities in this respect include their focus on internal cognitions as causes of distress and dysfunction, the need for awareness ("insight") into cognitive patterns, the possibility of internal conflict (e.g., through competing schemata and/ or assumptions), and the need to reconcile internal beliefs and attitudes with external contingencies and realities.

The cognitive learning therapies developed on a different "track" than most of the other cognitive-behavioral therapies. whereas covert conditioning, problem-solving, and coping skills therapies were the legitimate off-

spring of their behavioral forebears, the two major cognitive learning therapies developed almost from "outside" of the behavioral field. The two
major persons to foster this type of therapy, Ellis and Beck, were both first
trained in the psychoanalytic tradition, and both repudiated aspects of their
former training while simultaneously accepting aspects of the behavioral
tradition. It is likely this former training, that exhibits itself in the form of
theorizing that conscious assumptions and beliefs are critical variables in
psychopathology and psychotherapy, that is the major point of departure
between these types of therapies and the other cognitive-behavioral therapies.

The clinical efficacy of cognitive learning approaches to therapy has
been repeatedly demonstrated in single case, uncontrolled and controlled
clinical trials (see Chapters 6 and 7, this volume). One area for further
research, however, is with respect to the range of issues that these approaches are appropriate for. Thus, while there are claims that Rational-
Emotive Therapy is applicable to a host of clinical problems (DiGuiseppe &
Miller, 1977; Dryden & Ellis, Chapter 6, this volume; Ellis, 1962, 1977) many
of the supportive data sets are not methodologically rigourous, and controlled trials are still needed in a variety of areas. Similarly, while innovative
applications of Beck's Cognitive Therapy exist (cf. Emery, Hollon, & Bedrosian, 1981), controlled clinical trials are largely confined to the problems of
depression and anxiety disorders.

A class of cognitive-behavioral therapies that has only recently
emerged, but that is conceptually distinct from the above three classes of
therapies, can be termed the "structural approaches." These approaches
have several aspects in common with cognitive learning therapies, and the
intervention techniques are largely similar. The distinction, however, lies in
the fact that these approaches assume a formal structural basis to human
cognition, emotion, and behavior (Guidano, 1984; Guidano & Liotti, 1983;
Mahoney, 1984, Chapter 9, this volume). In doing so, they assume that the
cognitive knowing of the world has a developmental basis, and that the
evolution of unique cognitive structures makes subsequent alteration to
those structures increasingly difficult. Indeed, an essential aspect of these
"developmental cognitive therapies" (Mahoney, Chapter 9, this volume) is
that the cognitive systems are autopoietic (i.e., self-organizing, able to
change and modify self, responsive to both internal and external demands,
developmental). Another major aspect of these therapies is that they assume
resistance to change, and that change itself may be sometimes disruptive,
rather than beneficial to the client.

Although the structural, developmental approach to cognitive-behavioral therapy is quite recent, there are a number of exemplars of the approach that are being enunciated (Guidano & Liotti, 1983; Mahoney, 1985;
Rosen, 1985). At a technical level, these therapies promote many of the same
intervention techniques as the cognitive learning therapies for the treatment

of daily aspects of dysfunction (see e.g., Guidano & Liotti, 1983,). However, these therapeutic approaches also emphasize aspects of functioning that are largely ignored in other cognitive-behavioral approaches. For example, these therapies are much more likely to promote historical exploration of the source of current dysfunction as a means of understanding the developmental basis for the presenting problem in therapy. Also, these therapies are much more likely to assume that cognitive mechanisms are operating of which the client has little or no awareness. These "feedforward" and automatic processing dynamics represent a significant assumption of these models, and have therapeutic implications such as the occasional need for therapist "interpretation" of clients' responses to various situations. Finally, developmental cognitive-behavioral therapies assume that "knowing" is not only intellectual, and these models tend to reject the cognitive mediational perspective that cognitions mediate between situations and the emotional/behavioral response to that event. Instead, they assume that events may be "known" only in emotional terms, and that such basic dimensions as "feels good–feels bad" form an extremely powerful basis for judgments about approach or avoidance of events, interpersonal relationships, future courses of behavior, and so on. As such, these therapies explicitly focus upon emotional processes within therapy, and rather than treat emotional resposes as disturbance, these approaches employ emotions as components to understanding the knowledge system of the client, and as reflections of changing structures over the course of therapy.

The structural models of cognitive-behaviorism are, in many respects, conceptually closer to the psychoanalytic approaches to therapy, and are conceptually the most distant from the behavioral therapies. Indeed, some psychoanalytically oriented theorists have suggested that such aspects of these models as automatic processing, cognitive processes out of awareness, historical bases of psychopathology and psychotherapy, and the potential for emotionally based dysfunction belie an implicit acknowledgment of psychoanalytic conceptions within cognitive-behaviorism (Erdelyi, 1985; Wachtel, 1977). These suggestions, accurate or not, raise some very real issues for the future development of these structural, developmental approaches, which shall be discussed below.

To conclude this section, it is worthwhile to reiterate that the cognitive-behavioral field has grown immeasurably in the recent past. Dependent upon the date employed to start counting therapies and the criteria invoked to define a cognitive approach to therapy there are variously 11 (Dobson & Block, Chapter 1, this volume) or 17 (Mahoney, Chapter 9, this volume) identifiable major cognitive-behavioral approaches to therapy. If these two previous counts are compared and nonredundant types of therapy are counted, there are 22 unique forms of therapy that are identified and labeled. This veritable explosion of therapy methods has added considerably to the theoretical and therapeutic domain of psychotherapy, and must be considered the signal achievement of the cognitive-behavioral movement.

Within the large number of therapies that have been developed, there are at least four major classes of approaches to cognition and behavior. As discussed above, these are the covert conditioning approaches, the information processing models, the cognitive learning therapies, and the structural/developmental approaches. The order of the above approaches reflects their conceptual distance from a behavioral perspective, with covert conditioning therapies endorsing many of the same principles as the behavioral approaches to therapy, and the structural/developmental approaches espousing many notions that are decidedly nonbehavioral and nonassociationistic. The order of the above approaches also more or less follows the historical growth cognitive-behaviorism, with the covert conditioning therapies being an early form of cognitive-behaviorism, and the structural/developmental perspectives being the most recent.

OTHER COGNITIVE-BEHAVIORAL DEVELOPMENTS

In addition to the development of diverse approaches to therapy, the cognitive-behavioral trend has lead to other developments that warrant mention. Included in the list of major developments are those related to theory and assessment. Within this general category of development, the notable areas include: (1) elucidation of the nature of cognition, and the role of cognition both in normal self-regulation and in psychopathology, (2) discussion of the role of affect, (3) a continuance of the behavioral emphases on testability, verifiability, and falsification of hypotheses, coupled with a continuing thrust towards empirical demonstration of theory and practice, (4) the development of a cognitive assessment technology to measure theoretically relevant concepts (cf. Merluzzi, Glass, & Genest, 1981), and (5) continued critical examination of the importance of various potential therapeutic change factors in psychotherapy, with attendant evaluation of therapy ingredients, procedural overlap between therapies, and the development of therapy manuals as a method of ensuring replicability of research findings.

The above list of major developments of cognitive-behavioral therapy also constitutes much of what will undoubtedly also be the future areas of concern and attention for the field. As such, this chapter will not attempt to chronicle the major developments in the above areas, but will discuss them in the context of what will be the enduring and/or novel areas of evolution for the field of cognitive-behaviorism.

FUTURE DEVELOPMENTS FOR
COGNITIVE-BEHAVIORAL THERAPY

Although the future of cognitive-behavioral therapies looks to be bright, and there will be many different specific developments made, what follows is an attempt to identify what will likely be the four most significant of the trends and emphases in the coming years. While these trends will continue to influence each other, as they have done in the past, they are disentangled and presented in relative isolation for the present discussion. The four major emphases will be: (1) theory growth and revision, (2) cognitive assessment, (3) therapy expansion and evaluation, and (4) exploration of developmental bases of adult disturbance. Each of these emphases is elaborated upon below.

THEORY GROWTH AND REVISION

Just as the theoretical bases of the cognitive-behavioral therapies have expanded in the past three decades, it is certain that they will continue to evidence alteration and growth in the future. These theoretical revisions will take a number of forms, and manifest themselves in a number of content areas. Generally, however, it is likely that the greatest attention will be with respect to the definition of the theoretical boundaries of the cognitive-behavioral therapies, and the extent to which cognitive-behavioral theories can be extended to incorporate phenomena previously outside of their domain. Two areas of potential development and controversy are especially germane here, and will be discussed. In turn, these are the areas of affect and cognition, and the emergence of structural, developmental perspectives.

The relationship between affect and cognition has been a topic of debate for some time in psychology. While the traditional cognitive, information processing model of cognition and affect posits that affect is the logical sequel of appraisal of the environment, and necessarily follows cognitive appraisal (Lazarus, 1982; Lazarus & Folkman, 1984), this perspective has been criticized as unnecessarily restrictive, linear, and for some psychological phenomena, wrong (Greenberg & Safran, 1984a; Leventhal, 1979; Zajonc, 1980). Indeed, it has been argued that affective responses may arise after minimal (Zajonc, 1980) or potentially no cognitive processing (Greenberg & Safran, 1984a). Greenberg and Safran (1984a), for example, cite Leventhal's emotional processing model, which posits that two semi-independent automatic processing streams are invoked when an individual encounters a given situation. One of these streams is roughly similar to the traditional information-processing, cognitive model. This stream involves stimulus perception and appraisal. The second stream, which occurs *simultaneously* with the other, is an emotional processing mechanism that is composed of a means for determining the conceptual meaning of the stimulus, the emotional meaning of the stimulus, and expressive motor mechanisms. It is based upon both stimulus appraisal and emotional processing, that a "preattentive, synthetic process" (Greenberg & Safran, 1984a, p. 566) then derives conscious perception of the situation and a felt emotional derivative.

Emotional processing models, such as the one developed by Leventhal and espoused by Greenberg and Safran, have been criticized as just as deterministic and billiard-ball-like as some of the cognitive models that were earlier criticized by the originators of the emotional processing models (Mahoney, 1984). As has been repeatedly suggested, models of cognition and affect that attempt to settle the deterministic question of whether cognition or affect precedes and causes the other are equally likely to fail in the end. Indeed, if desired, a number of competitive causal models of affect and cognition could be generated. By suggesting that certain of the processes involved were preconscious, the ability to assess the relative truth value of any of the models would be severely constrained.

It has been repeatedly opined that cognition and affect are mutually causative and interdependent. Theorists who espouse a primary role for cognition (Beck, Rush, Shaw, & Emery, 1979; Dryden & Ellis, Chapter 6 this volume; Ellis, 1962; Lazarus, 1966, 1982; Lazarus & Folkman, 1984) acknowledge that the subsequent affect influences yet still more subsequent cognitive appraisal and emotional responses. Similarly, theorists who suggest emotional supremacy also acknowledge that the awareness and knowing that follows emotional appraisal will influence subsequent emotional processing (Greenberg & Safran, 1984a, 1984b; Leventhal, 1979; Mahoney, 1984; Zajonc, 1980). Similarly, a recent review on mood and memory (Blaney, 1986) suggests that while memories may lead to changes in affect, there is also evidence that mood states may predispose certain memories.

The interdependence of affect and cognition and their mutual causality has led some to the conclusion that different theorists are in fact describing different aspects of the same phenomenon, and all are both simultaneously wrong and correct. They are wrong in the sense that their "myopic" sense of the proper causal order does not permit them to perceive contrary processes to those that they have previously theorized to be present and operative. They are correct, though, in the sense that their models and theories do indeed describe some less-than-complete part of the entire set of processes that are involved. Such apologists would favor the development of an integrated, mutually interdependent model of information and emotional processing. It is argued here, however, that such efforts have a low probability of success for two fundamental reasons.

Mutual interdependence of affect and cognition is not problematic within a closed system, in which there are no environmental inputs and no expressive, behavioral outputs. Once models have to incorporate the complex relationship of humans interacting (or "transacting," to borrow the term preferred by Lazarus, 1966, 1982; Lazarus & Folkman, 1984) with the world around them, it then becomes of consequence whether cognitive appraisal mechanisms or emotional processing systems operate, and how they do so. Consider three models that could be invoked to explain the withdrawal, sadness and apathy observed in a university woman after the breakup of a romantic relationship:

1. The first model assumes that cognitions intervene between environmental inputs and emotional-behavioral consequences. Within this model

the cognitions that occurred in response to the breakup would be predicted to be negative, sadness-inducing, and of the sort that would lead to decreased interest in doing other things (i. e., apathy). Such cognitions may or may not be reasonable in the context of the breakup, and different models of this type assume that these cognitions are in awareness, or are accessible to awareness. Excessive, maladaptive responses to the breakup, according to this model would best be reduced by assessing the negative cognitions, determining their validity, and having the woman recognize unreasonable cognitions so that she could then proceed to alter these cognitions. The dysfunctional emotions and behavior should, according to this model, more or less fall in line with the altered, less dysfunctional, thinking patterns.

2. A competing model is the emotional processing model in which emotional responses to environmental events occur simultaneously with, or even prior to, cognition about the events. Thus, in this case example the woman would have had an emotional appraisal of the breakup and may have an emotional experience of the event before she fully thinks about the event, or "cognizes" it in the sense of thinking about its consequences, the meaning of the event for her future, what the breakup means about her as a potential mate, and so on. Further, this emotional response will influence future cognitions and color them with the negative tones of the emotions. Behavior would similarly be expected to fall in line with the emotional processing of the event. Therapy within this model would focus on the emotional meaning of breakup, related emotional experiences, and the complete elaboration of the emotional patterns as a way of fully experiencing the incident and fully understanding the response of the woman. Attempts to have the woman reconceptualize the breakup or to think of it in less distressing terms would be unlikely to be fostered. Such reconceptualization would be expected to naturally occur in response to the completed emotional processing.

3. A third model would suggest that emotional and cognitive processing are inextricably intertwined processes, and that they occur simultaneously. Thus the breakup would precipitate cognitive *and* emotional patterns of appraisal likely based upon preexisting emotional and cognitive structures and schemata that predispose certain patterns of appraisal. Within this model both cognition and emotional are both causal and caused, and although these responses may be punctuated, such punctuations are necessarily artificial and will be to some extent incomplete and inaccurate. Therapy from this model would again focus on detailed investigation of the cognition–emotion connections, and in particular the development of theoretically possible schemata that could explain the observed relationships. Such theorizing is likely within this model to require historical investigation of the person in question and a longer period of therapy to be complete and accurate in the theorizing. Direct interventions with cognitive appraisals within this model would again be discouraged due to the

perceived need to fully appreciate the operative structures, and to allow the structures to naturally develop over the course of therapy.

The above three examples of competing models of cognitive–emotional links are not, of course, chosen at random. They reflect, in order (1) the cognitive determinism positions seen in such theories as those by Beck (1976; Beck et al., 1979; DeRubeis & Beck, Chapter 7, this volume) and Ellis (1962, 1977; Dryden & Ellis, Chapter 6, this volume), (2) the emotional processing models of Greenberg and Safran (1984a; 1984b) and Leventhal (1979), and (3) the structural, constructivist positions of Guidano (Guidano & Liotti, 1983, Chapter 8, this volume) and Mahoney (1984, Chapter 9, this volume). As these authors variously reflect, their models of the cognition–emotion interface has implications for how they understand the experiences of patients, and for how the process of therapy should proceed as a function of that understanding. These two factors, the understanding of patients (essentially the therapists' explanatory models of human functioning and dysfunction), and the therapeutic directives that evolve from that under-standing constitute the two areas that are likely unreconcilable differences between the various therapeutic perspectives at present. Whether future developments will enable reconciliation is difficult to anticipate. What may be needed is a novel, as yet unstated, model that elaborates the nature of cognition–emotion processes, and that allows for the possibility that in different situations (variously defined as environmental situations or inter-nal states such as mood states or states of psychopathology) the processes of cognition and emotion may be different. That is, the assumption of uni-formity that posits that either cognition always precedes emotion or that emotion always precedes cognition may not be correct, and in different circumstances and for different people different processes may predominate. Such a complex model does not yet exist, and itself may not be accurate, but it is suggested here that the above models that have been developed and argued for each have their merits and problems, and that it is likely to be some time before the disagreements regarding the determination of the "correct" or best model are resolved.

A second major thrust for future theory development in cognitive-behaviorism has already been touched upon above, but requires more clear delineation and a projection for future development. This thrust is the recent advent of constructivistic and developmental models of cognition and emotion, as exemplified in the work of Mahoney and Guidano. Mahoney (Chapter 9, this volume) has highlighted the distinctions between these approaches and the traditional rationalist cognitive-behavioral models, and has argued that rationalist cognitive-behavioral models do not, and cannot, account for a number of factors. For example, Mahoney (1983) has suggested that the automaticity of certain responses argues for "feedforward mecha-nisms" whereby certain cognitive-emotive-behavioral patterns are increased in their probability. He has further argued that these feedforward mechanisms are based in developmental events and are perpetuated by the establishment of structured mental representations of how the world operates, what can therefore be reliably expected in the world's events, and how therefore to act.

Structural models are not entirely foreign to cognitive-behaviorism, despite Mahoney's (Chapter 9, this volume) claim that past cognitive-behavioral therapies are strictly associationistic and rational in nature. Beck (Kovacs & Beck, 1977; Beck et al., 1979), for example, has discussed depressive schemas as organizing sets of knowledge about the world that have the capability of fostering depressive thinking styles. While Beck's articulation of the schema model of depression falls far short of the developmental, structural type of analysis that Mahoney, Guidano, and others are promoting, there have been past attempts to both explicate a structural model for psychopathology and to document in research settings the operate of cognitive structures such as schemata (Derry & Kuiper, 1981; Dobson & Shaw, 1986; Dobson, 1986; Kuiper, Derry, & McDonald, 1982).

The reasons why the structural and developmental perspective is likely to become a prominent issue in forthcoming years are several, although three are of primary importance. First, one of the as yet unresolved issues in cognitive-behavioral therapies is the source of the cognitive biases, problem-solving deficits, distortions, beliefs, and so on that are the basic components of the various models that have been advanced. This lack of explanation about their source has led theorists to make vague generalizations about "learning histories," to be mute on the subject, or to invoke relatively undeveloped assumptions about the operation of schemata and other cognitive structures. A fully articulated model of cognitive structures of relevance to psychopathology and psychotherapy would be a substantial advancement over our current state of knowledge about the sources of cognition. Such a model could assist in terms of research that attempts to determine populations at risk for psychopathology, and in terms of delineating populations that could receive maximal benefit from psychotherapeutic regimens. It is conceivable that complete delineation of cognitive structures may even be the basis for the matching of clients to treatments or treatment components.

A second major factor that will promote exploration of the structural and developmental models is the continuing desire amongst theorists to develop overarching models of human functioning that can be the foundation for the reconciliation of divergent models of psychopathology and psychotherapy. There has been a repeated desire to explore the similarities and points of difference among the multitude of psychotherapy approaches (cf. Wachtel, 1977, 1982), and to the extent that structural approaches hold out the promise of potentially advancing reconciliation they are likely to be discussed and developed. There are already suggestions that a rapprochment is possible between psychodynamically based therapies and structurally cognitive-behavioral therapies (Anderson, 1986; Erdelyi, 1985), and it is reasonable to suppose that such attempts at integration may be pursued in the future. Indeed, in terms of a number of ways it does appear that the structural, developmental perspective to cognitive-behavioral therapy has a number of points in common with psychodynamic models of therapy. While there is insufficient space to detail these similarities here, and that is not in any event the purpose of the current chapter, it is worthwhile noting that on a very basic dimension—namely, the extent to which a given theoretical model focuses on situational versus intrapersonal factors in the prediction of emotional states and psychopathology—it is clear that the structural, developmental models are more closely aligned to the psycho-analytically based therapies than they are to the covert conditioning thera-pies, for example. Figure 10.1 schematically represents the degree to which various therapeutic approaches emphasize external factors (i.e., are situa-tionally deterministic, focus on associationistic models of prediction, high-light observable behavioral phenomena) versus internal factors (i.e., are intrapsychically deterministic, focus on constructivistic models of predic-tion, highlight unobservable cognitive and emotional phenomena). While the absolute positions of the identified therapies on this continuum may be debated, it is clear that on this basic dimension the structural, developmen-tal perspectives are most closely aligned to psychodynamic formulations.

A third aspect of the structural developmental theories that will encour-age their continued discussion is that these are the first of the cognitive-behavioral models that include an explicit reference to developmental pro-cesses. Drawing as they do on a number of known developmental processes, these approaches offer the prospect of being able to relate childhood expe-rience to adult abnormality. Again, in this respect they are similar to the psychoanalytic therapies, although it should be noted that their approach to developmental issues and to the impact of historical events on development are distinctly different than the traditional analytic notions of trauma and repression.

In summary, there are a number of reasons why the structural, develop-mental perspectives on psychopathology and psychotherapy can and should be explored. With their potential for theoretical unification, their potential for explicating the genesis and maintenance of cognitive phenomena, and their distinctive developmental basis, these therapies are bound to receive considerable interest and development in the future.

DEVELOPMENTAL MODELS OF PSYCHOPATHOLOGY

It is predicted that within the near future there will be an increase in the desire to develop cognitive models of psychopathology in childhood groups. As has been documented (Kendall & Braswell, Chapter 5, this vol-ume) there has been a large number of cognitive-behavioral therapies devel-

---

Focus on external events, behavioral change, and associationism

---

Classical conditioning

Operant conditioning

Systematic desensitization

Covert conditioning

Self-instructional training (Meichenbaum, 1977)

Problem-solving therapy (D'Zurilla & Goldfried, 1971)

Self-control therapy
Stress inoculation training (Meichenbaum, 1977)

Personal Science (Mahoney, 1974)

Rational Behavior Therapy (Maultsby, 1984)
Rational-Emotive Therapy (Ellis, 1962)
Cognitive Therapy (Beck, 1976; Beck, Rush, Shaw, & Emery 1979)

Interpersonal Therapy (Klerman, Weissman, Rounsaville, & Chevron, 1984)
Structural Cognitive Therapy (Guidano & Liotti, 1983)

Object relations theory (psychoanalytic)

Cognitive developmental therapy (Mahoney, 1985)
Cognitive experiential therapy (Weiner, 1985)

Classical psychoanalysis

Focus on internal (cognitive/emotional) events, conceptual/epistemic change, constructivism

---

Figure 10.1 Relative position of therapeutic approaches on the internal-external continuum.

oped for children and adolescents, and it is likely that models to explain the cause of the cognitive phenomena observed in these age groups will also show signs of growth.

A prime example of where there is likely to be considerable interest in promoting developmental work is the area of depression. Within the very recent past there has been voluminous research on the diagnosis and assessment of childhood depression (Cantwell, 1985; Kazdin, Esvelot-Pawson, Sherick, & Colbus, 1985; Kazdin, Moser, Colbus, & Bell, 1985) and the ability to accurately assess these individuals will now pave the way for research that assesses cognitive phenomena in these persons. There are already signs that cognitive assessment devices for depressed children are being created and evaluated, and the tendency to push what has been established in adults to younger age groups is likely to result in better delineation of the limits of models of adult cognition and depression.

In addition to testing the limits of adult models of cognition another primary impetus for increasing developmental work will be the structural approaches to cognitive-behavioral therapy. With their developmental focus, the theoretical bases for these therapies already invokes developmental research and theory (Ainsworth, 1973; Bowlby, 1969, 1973, 1980), and it is predicted that one of the major tasks of the structural theorists will be to attempt to clearly describe, in a scientifically verifiable manner, how developmental issues and events may reveal themselves through later adult dysfunction. Already case histories are being accumulated that begin to address the nature of these very complex developmental patterns (Guidano, Chapter 8, this volume; Guidano & Liotti, 1983; Mahoney, in press), and as the field moves to formalizing these observations in the form of predictions about general development, it is likely that longitudinal research will attempt to test these predictions.

Within the efforts to describe the influence of developmental circumstances on later emotional well-being, a particular difficulty will be to articulate how it is that certain events may generate cognitive structures that later lead to proactive processing (the "feedforward" mechanisms suggested by Mahoney, Chapter 9, this volume), which in turn predisposes emotional problems and psychopathology (Sameroff, Seifer, & Zax, 1982). One intersecting issue that will require attention in the articulation of the impact of these developmental circumstances will be an explicit awareness of the normal cognitive development of children, and the explicit description of how these cognitive changes (cf. Piaget, 1954, 1969) have an impact upon the development of personal cognitive structures and processes. As most of the cognitive developmental research has focused on more or less objective tasks, it is suggested here that an increased focus on the psychology of the development of self-knowledge, self-esteem, and emotional well being (e.g., McCarthy & Hodge, 1982; Bronson, 1968) will be required before a complete description of the development of emotional dysfunction may be provided.

A second intersecting issue that will have to be addressed is the question of the "unconscious." Ever since Freud's seminal work on child trauma and its unconscious emotional scars, most descriptions of the sequelae of childhood experience have in some way invoked the notion of unconscious processes, as a way of "explaining" how these early experiences may stay cognitively active. These unconscious images, cognitions, and feelings have been thought to promote certain later interactions with others and with the world, and to proactively determine certain responses to later life events even without the awareness on the part of the person involved as to why these responses occur. This intrapsychic determinism is particularly difficult to reconcile with the cognitive-behavioral tradition of focusing on situational determinants of behavior, situational analyses of the cognition–

emotion linkages, and the verification of therapeutic value by the documentation of behavioral improvements. Further, it is very likely that in a manner similar to the way that the concept of cognition was initially rejected by behavioral theorists, criticisms will be leveled against attempts to incorporate unconscious conceptions within the cognitive-behavioral tradition.

While it is very difficult to envisage the ultimate outcome of the debate between those who promote the concept of the unconscious and those who reject it, it is more easy to imagine some of the criticisms of this integrative approach that will be advanced by those who denigrate the effort. These include the following ideas:

1. The unconscious is a theoretical heuristic only. By definition, it lies dormant until activated and even its influences can only be inferred from conscious experience and behavior. As such, the concept adds nothing to the explanatory capabilities of current cognitive-behavioral models and should be abandoned.

2. The types of unconscious constructions of early life events that have been advanced fall outside of the cognitive capabilities of children (e.g., the idea that children who experience psychological or physical abuse at an early age develop an unconscious construction of themselves as "unloveable" has been criticized as being totally beyond these children's cognitive capabilities). Attempts to revive unconscious notions therefore require so much reconceptualization and reconciliation with what is known about cognitive development that these attempts are doomed to failure.

3. The assessment of the unconscious aspects of cognition is practically impossible, and the notion should therefore not be developed. Recent attempts to develop projective cognitive assessment techniques notwithstanding (Sobell, 1981), it is debatable what these techniques are measuring. Further, it is tautological to suggest that projective devices measure unconscious phenomena, and that the results of these tests therefore validate the existence of unconscious structures or processes.

4. Even if the unconscious were accepted as a psychological fact, the impact of such an admission on therapeutic procedures would be minimal. Current cognitive-behavioral therapies achieve high levels of therapeutic outcome, and it is highly unlikely that invoking unconscious conceptions will cause demonstrable improvements in therapy results. Such efforts are therefore not worth the time and energy.

It is suggested here that developmental processes are absolutely critical to later adult psychopathology, and are likely to be important for our understanding of how therapy has the effects it does, *even if* developmental issues do not need to be directly addressed in therapy. Thus, it may be of critical importance to know that a child was emotionally abused from the ages of 5 to 7 by a stepparent, and such knowledge may help to explain certain of the person's adult interpersonal patterns, even though the therapy may never directly delve into those past events, or into the impact of those events on the child as an adult. What is necessary, however, before we can truly decide whether or not therapists will achieve better outcomes by addressing these childhood issues is considerable research examining such developmental issues as whether or not early experience reveals itself in later dysfunction, the impact of parental and other upbringing experiences on childhood and adult functioning, the cognitive processes that children are capable of and how these capabilities may interact with experiences at different developmental stages, and the prospective, longitudinal assessment of self- and other-knowledge and how such knowledge relates to psychological adjustment or maladjustment. There is a vast amount that is not known about developmental issues and how these issues relate to later adult dysfunction, and the exploration of these issues may lead to major breakthroughs in our understanding and treatment of both child and adult dysfunction.

COGNITIVE ASSESSMENT

As various models of cognition and cognitive–emotional linkage are developed, it will be necessary to simultaneously devise and validate methods to assess these models. One particularly crucial aspect of this validation process that has been recognized for some time (Meichenbaum & Cameron, 1981; Mischel, 1981) is the need to develop reliable and valid cognitive assessment techniques. As has been previously documented, there has been much effort to devise various procedures to assess cognitions. A partial list of the cognitive assessment methods that have been researched includes: projective techniques, imaginal assessment procedures, personal construct tests, think-aloud methods, assessment of memories, rating techniques, computer-assisted measures of cognitive processes and outcomes, thought listing, and the tried and true paper-and-pencil questionnaire method. Additionally, these various techniques have been adopted in a wide number of content areas, and with a great diversity of subject populations (Merluzzi et al., 1981; Segal & Shaw, Chapter 2, this volume).

The impetus for cognitive assessment arises from a number of sources. For one, in order to validate cognitive models of dysfunction it is necessary to have a technology to measure the important constructs in the model, and the cognitive assessment measures attempt to fulfill this function. Second, cognitive assessment techniques permit investigations of cognition–emotion linkages and cognition–behavior linkages that were previously not possible. The existence of a technology, in other words, permits experimentation with various combinations and permutations of that technology, and the consequent pushing back of the frontier of knowledge vis-à-vis the role of cognition in human functioning. Third, as the cognitive-behavioral models suggest that cognitive modification is an essential component of psychotherapy, it has been suggested (e.g., Shaw & Dobson, 1981) that valid and sensitive cognitive assessment measures are required to be able to document the shifts in cognition that accompany therapeutic change, and also to begin to assess the temporal sequencing of cognitive versus behavioral versus emotional change over the course of therapy. In short, cognitive assessment devices are critical to the validation of the models that guide theoretical development and therapeutic intervention. Without such devices the scientific community is no more likely to accept the conjectures of cognitive-behavioral theorists than early astronomers were to believe that the earth revolved about the sun.

It is predicted that two continuing thrusts in the field will be the attempts to develop and validate a wide variety of cognitive assessment devices, with particular applications to specific types of dysfunction and to specific populations. Additionally, it is suggested that an issue that will gather importance in the cognitive assessment literature will be the differential assessment of cognitive structures, as opposed to cognitive processes. This assessment distinction is a reflection of the theoretical developments that will be spurred by the structural, developmental approaches to cognitive-behaviorism. As such, it is expected that future assessment devices will be categorized as measures of structure or process. Within the former category a variety of methods have been, and will continue to be, developed that will attempt to assess relatively broad and temporally stable cognitive structures. Such cognitive structures have been variously labelled as schemas, beliefs, assumptions, cognitive constructs, and rules for living, and various instruments have been developed to measure these aspects of functioning (see Segal & Shaw, Chapter 2, this volume, for a review). Measures of cognitive process are much more difficult to characterize, as they are by definition much more specific. In general, though, these assessment procedures and devices examine temporally brief, situationally specific, and individually sensitive aspects of cognition. An excellent example of this type of assessment is the self-efficacy predictions made by phobics during their treatment (cf. Bandura, 1986).

Although it is possible to distinguish cognitive structure and cognitive process assessment methodologies, there of course must be a relationship between the two assessment methods. It is suggested that mapping out the relationship between certain cognitive structures and cognitive processes will also be a developing interest in the cognitive assessment literature. Already there are studies that correlate cognitive structure and cognitive process measures (e.g., Dobson & Shaw, 1986), and this trend is bound to continue and expand in the future.

THERAPY EXPANSION AND EVALUATION

The signal achievement of the cognitive-behavioral tradition, as has already been suggested, is the creation and development of a veritable armamentarium of intervention techniques and therapies. It is by far the safest prediction of this chapter that the past efforts in this vein will continue into the future. Thus, it is highly likely that new therapy techniques will emerge, as theoretical developments spawn creative solutions to therapeutic necessities. These developments are most likely to occur where theory is under maximal review and expansion. Thus, it is predicted that a major area of therapy development will be in the treatment of children (Kendall & Braswell, Chapter 5, this volume). Another emerging area for new therapeutic innovation is in the area of marital and family therapy (Dobson, Jacobson, & Victor, in press; Jacobson, 1983, 1984). Both of these areas and others besides will spawn novel ideas as the practitioners strive to apply to them what is known about cognitive processes and therapies.

In addition to novel techniques, it is also almost certain that existing interventions will be pushed to the limits of their applicability via clinicians who attempt to apply these methods with different client problems or populations. As an example, although cognitive therapy was largely developed to address the treatment needs in the area of depression (Beck *et al.*, 1979), the approach has since been expanded to such diverse client problems as agoraphobia (Coleman, 1981), sexual dysfunction (Fox & Emery, 1981), anxiety (Beck & Emery, 1985; Hollon, 1981) and anorexia nervosa (Garner & Bemis, 1982). Such creative diversification of therapy techniques has also occurred with other specific forms of therapy (Ellis, 1977; Bandura, 1986). Associated with the expansion of existing therapies is the continual need for research that documents the appropriateness of such expansions. It is quite conceivable that a given therapy developed for one problem or client group may not be equally beneficial to another problem or group, and so continuing evaluation of such expansion is critical. Such research is likely to continue to be a major focus of the cognitive-behavioral field.

Yet another area where there is likely to be continuing evaluation of cognitive-behavioral therapies is in their comparative efficacy related to other forms of therapeutic intervention. One of the first areas where comparative research was conducted was in contrasting cognitive-behavioral therapies with behavioral therapies. While recent meta-analyses have all concluded that cognitive-behavioral therapies are superior to no-treatment or placebo controls, the conclusions regarding comparative studies with behavioral treatments are less clear-cut. While Shapiro and Shapiro (1982) suggested cognitive-behavioral therapies were superior to behavioral therapy, other studies (Berman, Miller, & Massman, 1985; Dobson, 1986; Miller & Berman, 1983) have failed to support an unequivocal therapeutic advantage for cognitive-behavioral therapy. It is therefore likely that continuing efforts in this area will be seen.

Beyond the comparison of cognitive-behavioral interventions and behavioral therapies, it is likely that there will be increasing attempts to document the relative efficacy of cognitive-behavioral versus other treatment paradigms and methods. For example, a recent meta-analysis (Steinbruck, Maxwell, & Howard, 1983) suggested that psychotherapy had average effect sizes larger than pharmacotherapy in the treatment of depression. While that study did not isolate the relative effects of cognitive-behavioral therapies, such contrasts (e. g., Dobson, 1986) will help to establish the relative utility of various treatment approaches in the treatment of specific problems and groups. Studies such as that conducted by the National Institute of Mental Health (Elkin, Parloff, Hadley, & Autry, 1985) will help to document the relative efficacy of diverse therapy models and techniques, and will be important in a number of ways to future investigators and clinicians.

It is of note that contrasts like those of the NIMH may also establish that treatments lead to comparable outcomes. Such results should not be taken necessarily as failures to have successful therapies. It is highly plausible that there are many therapeutic roads to recovery. Such results may then lead to other research questions such as: What are the mechanisms of change that are specific to the different therapies?; What are the common ingredients across therapeutic regimens?; Are there client or problem characteristics that are related to better outcome with one or another of the available treatments for the individual coming for therapy? There are already research attempts at divining what are the shared and unique aspects of different therapeutic modalities (DeRubeis, Hollon, Evans, & Bemis, 1982), and such efforts to document the nature of different therapies may then lead to subsequent research that investigates the outcomes associated with the different therapy procedures that have been identified.

Finally, it is predicted that an emerging area of research with respect to therapy will be the empirical investigation of change processes in cognitive-behavioral therapies. The models of change that have been advanced require examination, and one of the natural "laboratories" within which such investigations may occur are the patients who undergo therapy. It is precisely because the cognitive-behavioral therapies make specific predictions about the nature of change that investigations can try to document if the changes that actually occur over the course of therapy coincide with the theoretical predictions. Additionally, as the structural models become more developed, and the cognitive assessment technology is improved, it may become possible to not only assess when a given client is "cured" (i. e., is no longer experiencing significant current distress or disorder) but to make predictions about whether the patient is likely to suffer from recurrent problems in the future. But otherwise, as our understanding of cognitive predispositions for disorder become more articulated and measureable, we may begin to have truly causal models of disorder that will allow us to make such improved estimates of when a client is at lower risk for future difficulties. If and when such developments occur we can also proceed to determine the risk of persons who are not currently in distress and who perhaps have preventive interventions to lower the likelihood of their having to experience prolonged or seriously debilitating problems. It is predicted that there will be continuing efforts to determine cognitive risk factors for various forms of psychopathology and interpersonal difficulty, and in the context of therapy, continued investigations of the long-term effects of therapy, such that risk factors may be identified.

CONCLUDING REFLECTIONS

This chapter has attempted to briefly encapsulate the major trends in the cognitive-behavioral field, and to identify the most likely areas for future expansion of the field. The chapter has been necessarily terse in its discussion of the various areas that have been developed, but has suggested that four broad areas are likely to receive the most attention and energy in the coming several years. These areas were theory development, increased recognition of the importance of childhood and developmental issues in psychopathology, cognitive assessment issues and technology, and therapy expansion and evaluation. Within each of these four broad areas a number of more specific issues have been identified, and what are thought to be some of the directions the field will grow in have been suggested. What the future will actually hold for the field of cognitive-behavioral therapy is, of course, open to wide conjecture, and only the passage of time will reveal the truth in this regard. It is to be hoped that the identification of major issues and tasks will help to consolidate the field into some form of identifiable unit, and to place new developments into a framework that will permit theoretically meaningful work, and that will, in turn, be of practical use.

REFERENCES

Agras, S., Barlow, D. H., Chapin, H. N., Abel, G., & Leitenberg, H. (1974). Behavior modification of anorexia nervosa. *Archives of General Psychiatry, 30,* 279–286.

Ainsworth, M. D. S. (1973). The development of infant–mother attachment. In B. M. Caldwell & H. N. Ricciuti (Eds.), *Review of child development research* (Vol. 3). Chicago: University of Chicago Press.

Anant, S. (1967). A note on the treatment of alcoholics by a verbal aversion technique. *Canadian Psychologist, 8,* 19–22.

Anderson, D. D. (1986, May). *Cognitive behavior therapy, cognitive intervening variables and some classic therapeutic concerns.* Paper presented at the Annual Meeting of the Western Psychological Association, Seattle, WA.

Aronfreed, J. (1969). The problem of imitation. In L. Lipsitt of H. W. Reese (Eds.), *Advances in child development and behavior* (Vol. 4). New York: Academic Press.

Ashem, B., & Donner, L. (1968). Covert sensitization with alcoholics: A controlled replication. *Behaviour Research and Therapy, 6,* 7–12.

Baer, D. M., & Sherman, J. A. (1964). Reinforcement control of generalized initiation in young children. *Journal of Experimental Child Psychology, 1,* 37–49.

Bandura, A. (1977). *Social learning theory.* Englewood Cliffs, NJ: Prentice-Hall.

Bandura, A. (1986). *Social foundations of thought and action: A social cognitive theory.* Englewood Cliffs, NJ: Prentice-Hall.

Bandura, A., & Barab, P. G. (1971). Conditions governing nonreinforced imitation. *Developmental Psychology, 5,* 244–255.

Bandura, A., Blanchard, E. B., & Ritter, B. (1969). Relative efficacy of desensitization and modeling approaches for inducing behavioral, affective, and attitudinal changes. *Journal of Personality and Social Psychology, 13,* 173–199.

Bandura, A., & Walters, R. H. (1959). *Adolescent aggression.* New York: Ronald Press.

Beck, A. T. (1976). *Cognitive therapy and the emotional disorders.* New York: International Universities Press.

Beck, A. T., & Emery, G. (1985). *Anxiety disorders and phobias: A cognitive perspective.* New York: Basic Books.

Beck, A. T., Rush, A. J., Shaw, B. F., & Emery, G. (1979). *Cognitive therapy of depression.* New York: Guilford.

Berecz, J. (1972). Modification of smoking behavior through self-administered punishment of imagined behavior: A new approach to aversion therapy. *Journal of Consulting and Clinical Psychology, 38,* 244–250.

Berman, J. S., Miller, R., C., & Massman, P. J. (1985). Cognitive therapy vs. systematic desensitization: Is one treatment superior? *Psychological Bulletin, 97,* 951–461.

Blaney, P. H. (1986). Affect and memory: A review. *Psychological Bulletin, 99,* 229–246.

Blanchard, E., & Draper, D. O. (1973). Treatment of a rodent phobia by covert reinforcement: A single subject experiment. *Behavior Therapy, 4,* 559–564.

Bowlby, J. (1969). *Attachment and loss I: Attachment.* New York: Basic Books.

Bowlby, J. (1973). *Attachment and loss II: Separation.* New York: Basic Books.

Bowlby, J. (1980). *Attachment and loss III: Loss.* New York: Basic Books.

Bronson, G. (1968). The development of fear. *Child Development, 39,* 409–432.

Cantwell, D. P. (1985). Depression in childhood: Clinical picture and diagnostic criteria. In D. P. Cantwell & G. A. Carlson (Eds.), *Affective disorders in childhood and adolescence: An update.* Jamaica, NY: Spectrum.

Cautela, J. R. (1966). Treatment of compulsive behavior by covert sensitization. *Psychological Record, 16,* 33–41.

Cautela, J. R., & Wisocki, P. A. (1971). Covert sensitizaiton for the treatment of sexual deviations. *Psychological Records, 21,* 37–48.

Coleman, R. E. (1981). Cognitive-behavioral treatment of agoraphobia. In G. Emery, S. D. Hollon, & R. C. Bedrosian (Eds.), *New directions in cognitive therapy: A casebook.* New York: Guilford.

Curtis, R. H., & Presly, A. S. (1972). The extinction of homosexual behavior by covert sensitization: A case study. *Behaviour Research and Therapy, 10,* 81–83.

Dember, W. N. (1974). Motivation and the cognitive revolution. *American Psychologist, 29,* 161–168.

Derry, P. A., & Kuiper, N. A. (1981). Schematic processing and self-reference in clinical depression. *Journal of Abnormal Psychology, 90,* 286–297.

DeRubeis, R. J., Hollon, S. D., Evans, M. D., & Bemis, K. M. (1982). Can psychotherapies for depression be discriminated? A systematic investigation of cognitive therapy and interpersonal therapy. *Journal of Consulting and Clinical Psychology, 50,* 744–756.

DiGiuseppe, R. A., & Miller, N. J. (1977). A review of outcome studies of rational–emotive therapy. In A. Ellis & R. Greiger (Eds.), *Handbook of Rational-emotive therapy.* New York: Springer Books.

Dobson, K. S. (1986, June). *A meta-analysis of cognitive therapy of depression.* Paper presented at the Canadian Psychological Association, Toronto, Ontario.

Dobson, K. S. (1986). The self-schema in depression. In L. M. Hartman & K. R. Blankstein (Eds.), *Perception of self in emotional disorder and psychotherapy.* New York: Plenum.

Dobson, K. S., Jacobson, N. S., & Victor, J. (in press). Towards an integration of cognitive therapy and behavioral marital therapy for depression. In J. F. Clarkin, G. Haas, & I. Glick (Eds.), *Affective disorders and the family: Assessment and treatment*. New York: Guilford.

Dobson, K. S., & Shaw, B. F. (1986). Cognitive assessment with major depressive disorders. *Cognitive Therapy and Research, 10*, 13–29.

D'Zurilla, T. J. (in press). *Problem-solving therapy: A social competence approach to clinical intervention*. New York: Springer.

D'Zurilla, T. J., & Goldfried, M. R. (1971). Problem-solving and behavior modification. *Journal of Abnormal Psychology, 78*, 107–126.

Elkin, I., Parloff, M. B., Hadley, S. W., & Autry, J. H. (1985). NIMH treatment of depression collaborative research program. *Archives of General Psychiatry, 42*, 305–316.

Ellis, A. (1962). *Reason and emotion in psychotherapy*. New York: Lyle, Stuart.

Ellis, A. (1977). The basic clinical theory of rational-emotive therapy. In A. Ellis & R. Greiger (Eds.), *Handbook of rational-emotive therapy*. New York: Springer.

Ellis, A. (1979). The theory of rational-emotive therapy. In A. Ellis & J. Whiteley (Eds.), *Theoretical and empirical foundations of rational-emotive therapy*. Monterey, CA: Brooks/Cole.

Emery, G., Hollon, S. D., & Bedrosian, R. C. (Eds.). (1981). *New directions in cognitive therapy*. New York: Guilford.

Erdelyi, M. H. (1985). *Psychoanalysis: Freud's cognitive psychology*. New York: Freeman.

Flannery, R. B. (1972). A laboratory analogue of two covert reinforcement procedures. *Journal of Behavior Therapy and Experimental Psychiatry, 3*, 171–177.

Foreyt, J. P., & Hagen, R. L. (1973). Covert sensitization: Conditioning or suggestion? *Journal of Abnormal Psychology, 82*, 17–23.

Fox, S., & Emery, G. (1981). Cognitive therapy of sexual dysfunctions: A case study. In G. Emery, S. D. Hollon, & R. C. Bedrosian (Eds.), *New directions in cognitive therapy*. New York: Guilford.

Garfinkel, P. E., & Garner, D. M. (1982). *Anorexia nervosa: A multidimensional perspective*. New York: Brunner/Mazel.

Garner, D. M., & Bemis, K. M. (1982). A cognitive-behavioral approach to anorexia nervosa. *Cognitive Therapy and Research, 6*, 123–150.

Gerwitz, J. L. (1971). The roles of overt responding and extrinsic reinforcement in "self-" and "vicarious-reinforcement" and in "observational learning" and imitation. In R. Glaser (Ed.), *The nature of reinforcement*. New York: Academic Press.

Greenberg, L. S., & Safran, J. D. (1984a). Integrating affect and cognition: A perspective on the process of therapeutic change. *Cognitive Therapy and Research, 8*, 559–578.

Greenberg, L. S., & Safran, J. D. (1984b). Hot cognition—Emotion coming in from the cold: A reply to Rachman and Mahoney. *Cognitive Therapy and Research, 8*, 591–598.

Guidano, V. F. (1984). A constructivist outline of cognitive processes. In M. A. Reda, & M. J. Mahoney (Eds.), *Cognitive psychotherapies: Recent developments in theory, research and practice*. Cambridge, MA: Ballinger.

Guidano, V. F. (1987). *Complexity of the self*. New York: Guilford.

Guidano, V. F., & Liotti, G. (1983). *Cognitive processes and emotional disorders: A structural approach to psychotherapy*. New York: Guilford.

Hamilton, V. (1979). An information processing approach to neurotic anxiety and the schizophrenias. In V. Hamilton & D. M. Warburton (Eds.), *Human stress and cognition: An information processing approach*. New York: Wiley.

Hamilton, V. (1980). An information processing analysis of environmental stress and life crises. In J. G. Sarason & C. D. Spielberger (Eds.), *Stress and anxiety* (Vol. 7). Washington: DC: Hemisphere.

Hekmat, H., & Vanian, D. (1971). Behavior modification through covert semantic desensitization. *Journal of Consulting and Clinical Psychology, 36*, 248–251.

Hollon, S. D. (1981). Cognitive-behavioral treatment of drug-induced pansituational anxiety states. In G. Emery, S. D. Hollon, & R. C. Bedrosian (Eds.), *New directions in cognitive therapy*. New York: Guilford.

Homme, L. E. (1965). Perspectives in psychology: XXIV. Control of coverants, the operants of the mind. *Psychological Record, 15*, 501–511.

Horan, J. J., & Johnson, R. G. (1971). Covert conditioning through a self-management application of the Premack principle: Its effect on weight reduction. *Journal of Behavior Therapy and Experimental Psychiatry, 2*, 243–249.

Jacobson, N. S. (1983). Clinical innovations in behavioral marital therapy. In K. D. Craig & R. J. McMahon (Eds.), *Advances in clinical behavior therapy*. New York: Brunner/Mazel.

Jacobson, N. S. (1984). The modification of cognitive processes in behavioral marital therapy: Integrating cognitive and behavioral intervention strategies. In K. Hahlweg & N. S. Jacobson (Eds.), *Marital interaction: Analysis and modification*. New York: Guilford.

Kanfer, F. H. (1970). Self-regulation: Research, issues, and speculation . In C. Neuringer & J. L. Michael (Eds.), *Behavior modification in clinical psychology*. New York: Appleton-Century-Crofts.

Kanfer, F. H. (1971). The maintenance of behavior by self-generated stimuli and reinforcement. In A. Jacobs & L. B. Sachs (Eds.), *The psychology of private events: Perspectives on covert response systems*. New York: Academic Press.

Kazdin, A. E., Esvelot-Pawson, K., Sherick, R. B., & Colbus, D. (1985). Assessment of overt behavior and childhood depression among psychiatrically disturbed children. *Journal of Consulting and Clinical Psychology, 53*, 201–210.

Kazdin, A. E., Moser, J., Colbus, D., & Bell, R. (1985). Depressive symptoms among physically abused and psychiatrically disturbed children. *Journal of Abnormal Psychology, 94*, 298–307.

Kendrick, S. R., & McCullough, J. P. (1972). Sequential phases of covert reinforcement and covert sensitization in the treatment of homosexuality. *Journal of Behavior Therapy and Experimental Psychiatry, 3*, 229–231.

Kleiman, G. L., Weissman, M. M., Rounsoville, B., & Chevron, E. (1984). *Interpersonal psychotherapy of depression*. New York: Basic Books.

Kovacs, M., & Beck, A. T. (1977). Cognitive-affective processes in depression. In C. E. Izard (Ed.), *Emotions and psychopathology*. New York: Plenum.

Kuiper, N. A., Derry, P. A., & MacDonald, M. R. (1982). Self-reference and person perception in depression: A social cognition perspective. In G. Weary & H. Mirels (Eds.), *Integration of Clinical and Social Psychology*. New York: Oxford University Press.

Lang, P. J. (1965). Behavior therapy with a case of anorexia nervosa. In L. P. Ullman & L. Krasner (Eds.), *Case studies in behavior modification*. New York: Holt, Rinehart & Winston.

Lazarus, A. A., Davison, G. C., & Polefka, D. A. (1965). Classical and operant factors in the treatment of a school phobia. *Journal of Abnormal Psychology, 70*, 225–229.

Lazarus, R. S. (1966). *Psychological stress and the coping process*. New York: McGraw-Hill.

Lazarus, R. S. (1982). Thoughts on the relations between emotion and cognition. *American Psychologist, 37*, 1019–1024.

Lazarus, R. S., & Folkman, S. (1984). *Stress, appraisal and coping*. New York: Springer.

Lazarus, R. S., & Launier, R. (1978). Stress-related transactions between person and environment. In L. A. Pervin & M. Lewis (Eds.), *Internal and external determinants of behavior*. New York: Plenum.

Leventhal, H. (1979). A perceptual motor processing model of emotion. In P. Pliner, K. Blankstein, & I. Spigel (Eds.), *Advances in the study of communication and affect*. New York: Plenum.

Mahoney, M. J. (1974). *Cognition and behavior modification.* Cambridge, MA: Ballinger.

Mahoney, M. J. (1980). Psychotherapy and the structure of personal revolutions. In M. Mahoney (Ed.), *Psychotherapy process: Current issues and future directions.* New York: Plenum.

Mahoney, M. J. (1983). Cognition, consciousness, process of personal change. In K. D. Craig & R. J. McMahon (Eds.), *Advances in clinical behavior therapy.* New York: Bunner/Mazel.

Mahoney, M. J. (1984). Behaviorism, cognitivism, and human change processes. In M A. Reda & M. J. Mahoney (Eds.), *Cognitive psychotherapies: Recent developments in theory, research and practice.* Cambridge, MA: Ballinger.

Mahoney, M. J. (1985). Psychotherapy and human change processes. In M. J. Mahoney & A. Freeman (Eds.), *Cognition and psychotherapy.* New York: Plenum.

Mahoney, M. J. (in press). *Human change processes: Notes on the facilitation of personal development.* New York: Basic Books.

Mahoney, M. J., & Arnkoff, D. (1978). cognitive and self control therapies. In S. Garfield & A. E. Bergin (Eds.), *Handbook of psychotherapy and behavior change.* New York: Wiley.

Mahoney, M., & Thoresen, G. (1974). Self-control applications: Behavioral programming. In M. Mahoney & C. Thoresen (Eds.), *Self control: Power to the person.*

Maultsby, M. C. (1984). *Rational behavior therpay.* Englewood cliffs, NJ: Prentice-Hall.

McCarthy, J. D., & Hodge, D. R. (1982). Analysis of age effects in longitudinal studies of adolescent self-esteem. *Developmental Psychology, 18,* 372-379.

Meichenbaum, D. (1977). *Cognitive-behavior modification.* New York: Plenum.

Meichenbaum, D. (1985). *Stress inoculation training.* New York: Pergamon.

Meichebaum, D., & Cameron, R. (1973). Training schizophrenics to talk to themselves: A means of developing attentional controls. *Behavior Therapy, 4,* 515-534.

Meichenbaum, D., & Goodman, J. (1971). Training impulsive children to talk to themselves: A means of developing self-control. *Journal of Abnormal Psychology, 77,* 115-126.

Merluzzi, T. V., Glass, C. R., & Genest, M. (Eds.). (1981). *Cognitive assessment.* New York: Guilford.

Miller, R. C., & Berman, J. S. (1983). The efficacy of cognitive behavior therapies: A quantitative review of the research evidence. *Psychological Bulletin, 94,* 39-53.

Mischel, W. (1981). A cognitive social learning approach to assessment. In T. V. Merluzzi, C. R. Glass, & M. Genest (Eds.), *Cognitive assessment.* New York: Guilford.

Mischel, W., Ebbesen, E. B., & Zeiss, A. M. (1972). Determinants of selective memory about the self. *Journal of Consulting and Clinical Psychology, 44,* 92-103.

O'Connor, R. D. (1969). Modification of social withdrawal through symbolic modeling. *Journal of Applied Behavior Analysis, 2,* 15-22.

Piaget, J. (1954). *The construction of reality in the child.* New York: Ballantine Books.

Piaget, J. (1969). *The child's conception of the world.* Totowa, NJ: Littlefield, Adams.

Rosen, H. (1985). *Piagetian dimensions of clinical relevance.* New York: Columbia University Press.

Sameroff, A. J., Seifer, R., & Zax, M. (1982). Early development of children at risk for emotional disorder. *Monographs of the Society for Research in Development, 47* (Serial #199).

Shapiro, D. A., & Shapiro, D. (1982). Meta-analysis of comparative therapy outcome studies: A replication and refinement. *Psychological Bulletin, 92,* 581-604.

Shaw, B. F., & Dobson, K. S. (1981). The cognitive assessment of depression. In T. Merluzzi, C. Glass, & M. Genest (Eds.), *Cognitive assessment.* New York: Guilford.

Sobell, H. J. (1981). Projective methods of cognitive analysis. In T. V. Merluzzi, C. R. Glass, & M. Genest (Eds.), *Cognitive assessment.* New York: Guilford.

Spivack, G., Platt, J., & Shure, M. (1976). *The problem-solving approach to adjustment.* San Francisco, CA: Jossey-Bass.

Spivack, G., & Shure, M. (1974). *Social adjustment of young children: A cognitive aproach to solving real-life problems.* San Francisco: Jossey-Bass.

Steinbrueck, S. M., Maxwell, S. E., & Howard, G. S. (1983). A meta-analysis of psychotherapy and drug therapy in the treatment of unipolar depression with adults. *Journal of consulting and Clinical Psychology, 51*, 856–863.

Wachtel, P. (1977). *Psychoanalysis and behavior therapy: Toward an integration.* New York: Basic Books.

Wachtel, P. (Ed.). (1982). *Resistance: Psychodynamic and behavioral approaches.* New York: Plenum.

Weiner, M. L. (1985). *Cognitive-experiential therapy: An integrative ego psychotherapy.* New York: Brunner/Mazel.

Wolpe, J. (1969). *The practice of behavior therapy.* New York: Pergamon.

Wolpe, J., & Lazarus, A. A. (1966). *Behavior therapy techniques.* New York: Pergamon.

Zajonc, R. B. (1980). Feeling and thinking: Preferences need no inferences. *American Psychologist, 35*, 151–175.

INDEX